TOYOTA

TERCEL
1984-94 REPAIR MANUAL

Senior Vice President	Ronald A. Hoxter
Publisher and Editor-In-Chief	Kerry A. Freeman, S.A.E.
Executive Editors	Dean F. Morgantini, S.A.E., W. Calvin Settle, Jr., S.A.E.
Managing Editor	Nick D'Andrea
Special Products Manager	Ken Grabowski, A.S.E., S.A.E.
Senior Editors	Jacques Gordon, Michael L. Grady, Debra McCall, Kevin M. G. Maher, Richard J. Rivele, S.A.E., Richard T. Smith, Jim Taylor, Ron Webb
Project Managers	Martin J. Gunther, Will Kessler, A.S.E., Richard Schwartz
Production Manager	Andrea Steiger
Product Systems Manager	Robert Maxey
Director of Manufacturing	Mike D'Imperio
Editor	Will Kessler

Manufactured in USA
© 1995 Chilton Book Company
Chilton Way, Radnor, PA 19089
ISBN 0-8019-8595-1
Library of Congress Catalog Card No. 93-074296
3456789012 5432109876

Contents

Contents

DRIVE TRAIN 7

SUSPENSION AND STEERING 8

BRAKES 9

BODY AND TRIM 10

GLOSSARY

MASTER INDEX

SAFETY NOTICE

Proper service and repair procedures are vital to the safe, reliable operation of all motor vehicles, as well as the personal safety of those performing repairs. This manual outlines procedures for servicing and repairing vehicles using safe, effective methods. The procedures contain many NOTES, CAUTIONS, and WARNINGS which should be followed along with standard procedures to eliminate the possibility of personal injury or improper service which could damage the vehicle or compromise its safety.

It is important to note that the repair procedures and techniques, tools and parts for servicing motor vehicles, as well as the skill and experience of the individual performing the work vary widely. It is not possible to anticipate all of the conceivable ways or conditions under which vehicles may be serviced, or to provide cautions as to all of the possible hazards that may result. Standard and accepted safety precautions and equipment should be used when handling toxic or flammable fluids, and safety goggles or other protection should be used during cutting, grinding, chiseling, prying,or any other process that can cause material removal or projectiles.

Some procedures require the use of tools specially designed for a specific purpose. Before substituting another tool or procedure, you must be completely satisfied that neither your personal safety, nor the performance of the vehicle will be endangered.

Although information in this manual is based on industry sources and is complete as possible at the time of publication, the possibility exists that some car manufacturers made later changes which could not be included here. While striving for total accuracy, Chilton Book Company cannot assume responsibility for any errors, changes or omissions that may occur in the compilation of this data.

PART NUMBERS

Part numbers listed in this reference are not recommendation by Chilton for any product by brand name. They are references that can be used with interchange manuals and aftermarket supplier catalogs to locate each brand supplier's discrete part number.

SPECIAL TOOLS

Special tools are recommended by the vehicle manufacturer to perform their specific job. Use has been kept to a minimum, but where absolutely necessary, they are referred to in the text by the part number of the tool manufacturer. These tools can be purchased, under the appropriate part number, from your local dealer or regional distributor, or an equivalent tool can be purchased locally from a tool supplier or parts outlet. Before substituting any tool for the one recommended, read the SAFETY NOTICE at the top of this page.

ACKNOWLEDGMENTS

The Chilton Book Company expresses appreciation to Toyota Motor Corp. for their generous assistance.

No part of this publication may be reproduced, transmitted or stored in any form or by any means, electronic or mechanical, including photocopy, recording, or by information storage or retrieval system without prior written permission from the publisher.

1

ROUTINE
MAINTENANCE

HOW TO USE THIS BOOK

Chilton's Total Car Care Manual for the Toyota Tercel is intended to teach you more about the inner workings of your automobile and save you money on its upkeep. Sections 1 and 2 will probably be the most frequently used in the book. The first section contains information that may be required at a moment's notice. Aside from giving the location of various serial numbers and the proper towing instructions, it also contains all the information on basic day-to-day maintenance that you will need to ensure good performance and long vehicle component life. Section 2 contains the necessary tune-up procedures to assist you not only in keeping the engine running properly and at peak performance levels, but also in restoring some of the more delicate vehicle components to operating condition in the event of a failure. Sections 3 through 10 cover repairs (rather than maintenance) for various portions of your car.

When using the Table of Contents, refer to the bold listings for the subject of the section and the smaller listings (or the index) for information on a particular component.

In general, there are some qualities of a proficient mechanic which must be kept in mind when a non-professional does work on his/her car.

1. A sound knowledge of the construction of the parts you are working with; their order of assembly, etc.

2. A knowledge of potentially hazardous situations; particularly how to prevent them.

3. Manual dexterity and common sense.

This book provides step-by-step instructions and illustrations whenever possible. Use them carefully and wisely — don't just jump headlong into disassembly, review the complete service procedure first. When there is doubt about being able to readily reassemble something, make a careful drawing (mark vacuum hoses etc. or matchmark components such as a driveshaft to the rear flange) of the component before disassembling it. Installation always looks simple when everything is still assembled.

Always replace cotter pins, gaskets, O-rings and oil seals etc. with new ones. Non-reusable parts are indicated in the component illustrations by a diamond symbol.

CAUTIONS, WARNINGS, AND NOTES will be provided where appropriate to help prevent you from injuring yourself or damaging your car. Consequently, you should always read through the entire procedure before beginning the work so as to familiarize yourself with any special problems which may occur during the given procedure. Since no number of warnings could cover every possible situation, you should work slowly and try to envision what is going to happen in each operation ahead of time.

When it comes to tightening fasteners, there is generally a slim area between too loose to properly seal or resist vibration and so tight as to risk damage or warping. When dealing with major engine parts, or with any aluminum component, it pays to buy a torque wrench and go by the recommended figures.

When reference is made in this book to the right side or the left side of the car, it should be understood that the positions are always to be viewed from the front seat. This means that the LEFT SIDE of the car is the DRIVER'S SIDE and RIGHT SIDE is the PASSENGER'S SIDE. This will hold true throughout the book, regardless of how you might be looking at the car at the time.

Always be conscious of the need for safety in your work. Never get under a car unless it is firmly supported by jackstands or ramps. Never smoke around, or allow flame near the battery or the fuel system. Keep your clothing, hands and hair clear of the fan and pulleys when working near the engine if it is running. Most importantly, try to be patient; even in the midst of an argument with a stubborn bolt, reaching for the largest hammer in the garage is usually a cause for later regret and more extensive repair. As you gain confidence and experience, working on your car may become a source of pride and satisfaction.

TOOLS AND EQUIPMENT

▶ **See Figures 1, 2, 3, 4, 5, 6, 7, 8, 9, 10, 11 and 12**

➡**Special tools are occasionally necessary to perform a specific job or are recommended to make a job easier. Their use has been kept to a minimum. When a special tool is indicated, it will be referred to by the manufacturer's designation. Toyota designates these as SST (Special Shop Tools), followed by the part number. Where possible, an illustration will be provided. Some special tools are unique to the vehicle, others are the manufacturer's version of common repair tools. These tools can usually be purchased from your local Toyota dealer or from an automotive parts store.**

The service procedures in this book pre-suppose a familiarity with hand tools and their proper use. However, since it is possible that you may have a limited amount of experience with the sort of equipment needed to work on an automobile, this section is designed to help you assemble a basic set of

tools. The tools listed here should handle most of the jobs you may undertake.

In addition to the normal assortment of screwdrivers and pliers, automotive service work requires an investment in wrenches, sockets (along with the handles needed to drive them), and various measuring tools such as a torque wrench and feeler gauges.

You will find that virtually every nut and bolt on your Toyota is metric. Therefore, despite a few close size similarities, standard inch size tools will not fit and MUST NOT be used. You will need a set of metric wrenches as your most basic tool kit, ranging from about 6mm to 17mm in size. High quality forged wrenches are available in three styles: open end, box end, and combination open/box end. The combination tools are generally the most desirable as a starter set; the wrenches shown in the accompanying illustration are of the combination type. If you plan to do any work on hydraulic fittings, a set of line wrenches (sometimes called flare nut wrenches) is highly recommended.

The other set of tools inevitably required is a ratchet handle and socket set. This set should have the same size range as your wrench set. The ratchet, extension, and flex drives for the sockets are available in many sizes; it is advisable to choose a ⅜ in. drive set initially. One break in the inch/metric sizing war is that metric sized sockets sold in the U.S. have inch sized drive (¼ in., ⅜ in., ½ in., etc.). Thus, if you already have an inch sized socket set, you need only buy new metric sockets in the sizes needed. Sockets are available in 6 and 12-point versions; 6-point types are stronger and are a good choice for a first set. The choice of a drive handle for the sockets should be made with some care.

If this is your first set, take the plunge and invest in a flex-head ratchet; it will get into many places otherwise accessible only through a long chain of universal joints, extensions, and adapters. An alternative is a flex handle, which lacks the ratcheting feature but has a head which pivots 180 degrees. In addition to the range of sockets mentioned, a rubber lined spark plug socket should be purchased with the set. Since spark plug size varies, you should know (or ask) which size is appropriate for your car.

The most important thing to consider when purchasing hand tools is quality. Don't be misled by the low cost of "bargain tools". Forged wrenches, tempered screwdriver blades, and fine tooth ratchets are much better investments than their less expensive counterparts. The skinned knuckles and frustration inflicted by poor quality tools make any job an unhappy chore. Another consideration is that quality hand tools come with an unbeatable replacement guarantee: if the tool breaks, you get a new one, no questions asked.

Most jobs can be accomplished using the tools on the accompanying lists. There will be an occasional need for a special tool, such as snapring pliers; such a need will be mentioned in the text. It would not be wise to buy a large assortment of tools on the theory that someday they may be needed. Instead, the tools should be acquired one or two at a time, each for a specific job. This will avoid unnecessary expense and help insure that you have the right tool for the job at hand.

The tools needed for basic maintenance jobs, in addition to the wrenches and sockets mentioned, include:
- A floor jack, with a lifting capacity at least equal to the weight of the car. Capacity of 1½ times the weight is better.
- Jackstands, for support.
- Oil filter wrench.
- Oil filler spout or funnel.
- Grease gun.
- Battery post and clamp cleaner.
- Container for draining oil.
- Many rags for the inevitable spills.
- Oil absorbent gravel or cat box filler gravel, for absorbing spilled fluids. Keep a broom handy.

In addition to these items there are several others which are not absolutely necessary, but handy to have around. These include a transmission funnel and filler tube, a drop (trouble) light on a long cord, an adjustable (crescent) wrench, and slip joint pliers. After performing a few projects on the car, you'll be amazed at the other tools and non-tools which are handy for your workbench. Some useful household items to have around are: a large turkey baster or siphon, empty coffee cans and ice trays (for storing parts), ball of twine, assorted tape, markers and pens, whisk broom, tweezers, golf tees (for plugging vacuum lines), metal coat hangers or a roll of mechanics's wire (to hold components out of the way), dental pick or similar long, pointed probe, a strong magnet, a small mirror (for seeing into recesses and under manifolds) and various small pieces of lumber.

A hydraulic floor jack is one of the best investments you can make if you are serious about repairing and maintaining your own car. The small jack that comes with the car is simply NOT SAFE to use for anything more than changing a flat. The hydraulic floor jack (1½ ton is fine for the Toyota) will pay for itself quickly in convenience, utility and much greater safety. Watch the ads for your local department or automotive store. A good jack is often on sale somewhere.

A more advanced list of tools, suitable for tune-up work, can be drawn up easily. While the tools are slightly more sophisticated, they need not be outrageously expensive. The key to these purchases is to make them with an eye towards adaptability and wide range. A basic list of tune-up tools could include:
- Tachometer/dwell meter.
- Spark plug gauge and gapping tool.
- Feeler gauges for valve adjustment.
- Timing light.

You will need both wire type and flat type feeler gauges, the former for the spark plugs and the latter for the valves. The choice of a timing light should be made carefully. A light which works on the DC current supplied by the car battery is the best choice; it should have a xenon tube for brightness. Since many of the newer cars have electronic ignition, and since nearly all cars will have it in the future, the light should have an inductive pickup which clamps around the number one spark plug cable (the timing light illustrated has one of these pickups).

In addition to these basic tools, there are several other tools and gauges which you may find useful. These include:
- A compression gauge. The screw-in type is slower to use, but eliminates the possibility of a faulty reading due to escaping pressure.
- A manifold vacuum gauge.
- A test light.
- A combination volt/ohmmeter.

Finally, you will find a torque wrench necessary for all but the most basic work. The beam-type models are perfectly adequate. The click-type (breakaway) torque wrenches are more accurate, but are much more expensive.

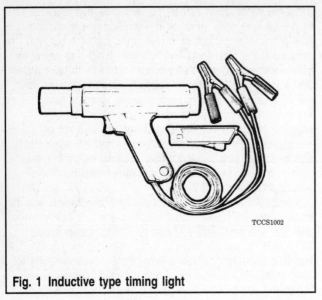

Fig. 1 Inductive type timing light

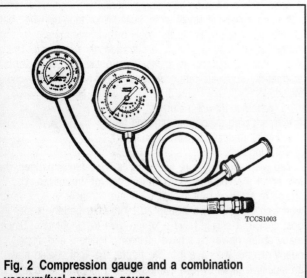

Fig. 2 Compression gauge and a combination vacuum/fuel pressure gauge

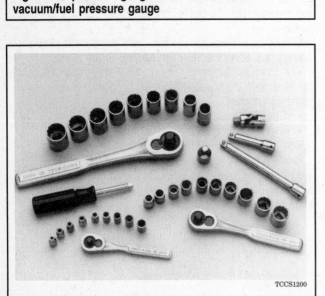

Fig. 3 All but the most basic procedures will require an assortment of ratchets and sockets

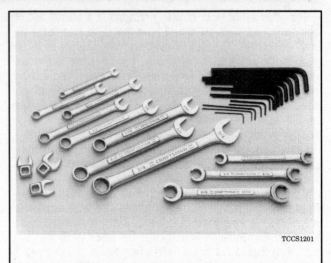

Fig. 4 In addition to ratchets, a good set of wrenches and hex keys will be necessary

Fig. 5 A hydraulic floor jack and a set of jackstands are essential for lifting and supporting the vehicle

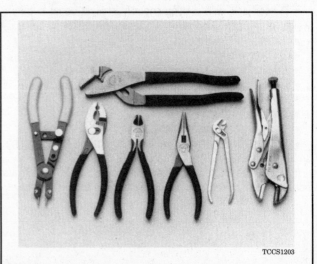

Fig. 6 An assortment of pliers will be handy, especially for old rusted parts and stripped bolt heads

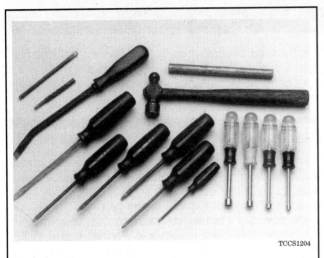

Fig. 7 Various screwdrivers, a hammer, chisels and prybars are necessary to have in your toolbox

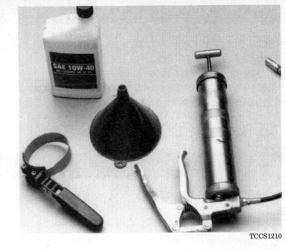

Fig. 10 A few inexpensive lubrication tools will make regular service easier

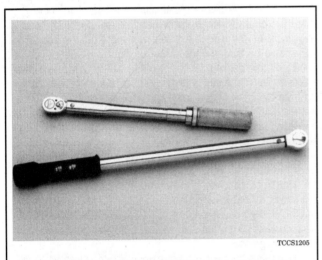

Fig. 8 Many repairs will require the use of a torque wrench to assure the components are properly fastened

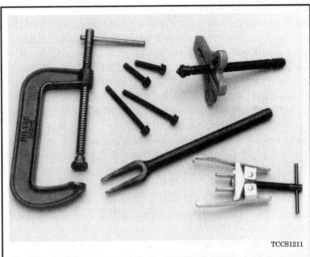

Fig. 11 Various pullers, clamps and separator tools are needed for the repair of many components

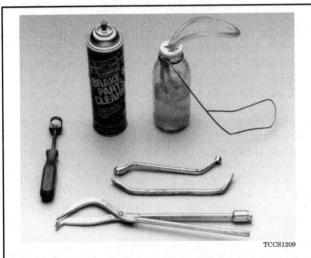

Fig. 9 Although not always necessary, specialized brake tools will save time

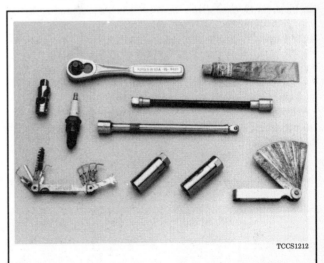

Fig. 12 A variety of tools and gauges are needed for spark plug service

SERVICING YOUR CAR SAFELY

It is virtually impossible to anticipate all of the hazards involved with automotive maintenance and service, but care and common sense will prevent most accidents.

The rules of safety for mechanics range from "don't smoke around gasoline", to "use the proper tool for the job". The trick to avoiding injuries is to develop safe work habits and take every possible precaution.

Dos

• Do keep a fire extinguisher and first aid kit within easy reach.

• Do wear safety glasses or goggles when cutting, drilling, grinding or prying, even if you have 20-20 vision. If you wear glasses for the sake of vision, they should be made of hardened glass that can serve also as safety glasses, or wear safety goggles over your regular glasses.

• Do shield your eyes whenever you work around the battery. Batteries contain sulfuric acid. In case of contact with the eyes or skin, flush the area with water or a mixture of water and baking soda and get medical attention immediately.

• Do use safety stands for any undercar service. Jacks are for raising vehicles; safety stands are for making sure the vehicle stays raised until you want it to come down. Whenever the car is raised, block the wheels remaining on the ground and set the parking brake.

• Do use adequate ventilation when working with any chemicals or hazardous materials. Like carbon monoxide, the asbestos dust resulting from brake lining wear can be poisonous in sufficient quantities.

• Do disconnect the negative battery cable when working on the electrical system. The secondary ignition system can induce up to 40,000 volts.

• Do follow manufacturer's directions whenever working with potentially hazardous materials. Both brake fluid and antifreeze are poisonous if taken internally.

• Do properly maintain your tools. Loose hammerheads, mushroomed punches and chisels, frayed or poorly grounded electrical cords, excessively worn screwdrivers, spread wrenches (open end), cracked sockets, slipping ratchets, or faulty droplight sockets can cause accidents.

• Do use the proper size and type of tool for the job at hand.

• Do when possible, pull on a wrench handle rather than push on it, and adjust your stance to prevent a fall.

• Do be sure that adjustable wrenches are tightly closed on the nut or bolt and pulled so that the face is on the side of the fixed jaw.

• Do select a wrench or socket that fits the nut or bolt. The wrench or socket should be straight, not cocked.

• Do set the parking brake and block the drive wheels if the work requires the engine running.

Don'ts

• Don't run an engine in a garage or anywhere else without proper ventilation — EVER! Carbon monoxide is poisonous; it takes a long time to leave the human body and you can build up a deadly supply of it in your system by simply breathing in a little every day. You may not realize you are slowly poisoning yourself. Always use power vents, windows, fans or open the garage doors.

• Don't work around moving parts while wearing a necktie or other loose clothing. Short sleeves are much safer than long, loose sleeves; hard-toed shoes with neoprene soles protect your toes and give a better grip on slippery surfaces. Jewelry such as watches, fancy belt buckles, beads or body adornment of any kind is not safe working around a car. Long hair should be hidden under a hat or cap.

• Don't use pockets for toolboxes. A fall or bump can drive a screwdriver deep into your body. Even a wiping cloth hanging from the back pocket can wrap around a spinning shaft or fan.

• Don't smoke when working around gasoline, cleaning solvent or other flammable material.

• Don't smoke when working around the battery. When the battery is being charged, it gives off explosive hydrogen gas.

• Don't use gasoline to wash your hands; there are excellent soaps available. Gasoline may contain additives which may enter the body through a cut. Gasoline also removes all the natural oils from the skin so that bone dry hands will suck up oil and grease.

• Don't service the air conditioning system unless you are equipped with the necessary tools and training. The refrigerant, R-12, is extremely cold when compressed, and will instantly freeze any surface it contacts, including your eyes. Although the refrigerant is normally non-toxic; R-12 becomes a deadly poisonous gas in the presence of an open flame. One good whiff of the vapors from burning refrigerant can be fatal.

• Don't use screwdrivers for anything other than turning screws! A screwdriver used as a prying tool or chisel can snap when least expected, causing bodily harm. Besides, you may ruin a good tool when it is used for purposes other than those intended.

• Don't use a bumper jack, scissors or pantograph jack that comes with the car for anything other than changing a flat tire! If you are serious about repairing and maintaining your own car, then one of the best investments you can make is in a hydraulic floor jack of at least 1½ ton capacity.

SERIAL NUMBER IDENTIFICATION

Vehicle

▶ See Figures 13, 14, 15 and 16

The serial number on all models consists of a 17 digit format. All models have the Vehicle Identification Number (VIN) stamped on a plate which is attached to the left side of the instrument panel or dashboard (the 17 digit VIN is displayed in three separate locations on each vehicle). This plate is visible through the windshield.

The VIN is also stamped on a name plate in the engine compartment which is usually located on the firewall.

The certification plate on the left door or door post is also stamped with the VIN.

Engine and Transaxle

▶ See Figure 17

The engine serial number consists of an engine series identification number, followed by a 7 digit production number. The serial number is stamped on the rear left side of the engine.

The manual and automatic transaxle identification numbers are stamped on the housing or on an identification tag which is attached to the unit.

Fig. 14 Overall view of an engine compartment, note that the identification plate can be found on the firewall

Fig. 15 Another plate containing the VIN is normally found on the engine compartment firewall

Fig. 13 The VIN plate is located on the left side of the instrument panel and is visible through the windshield

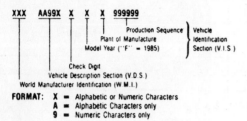

The sections of the V.I.N. have been separated for description purposes; however, the actual V.I.N. on the vehicles will not have any spaces between the sections.

The 17 digit V.I.N. is displayed in three separate locations on each vehicle.

- Name plate within engine compartment.
- V.I.N. plate on top left dashboard.
- Certification plate on left door or door post.

The section of the V.I.N. used to translate to the Series Prefix/ Japan Model Code is the vehicle description section identified under the column heading V.D.S.

85991016

Fig. 16 The 17 digit VIN used on all models

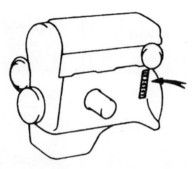

85991017

Fig. 17 A common engine serial number location

ENGINE IDENTIFICATION

Year	Engine Displacement Liters (cc)	Engine Series (ID/VIN)	Fuel System	No. of Cylinders	Engine Type
1984	1.4 (1452)	3A, 3A-C	Carb.	4	SOHC
1985	1.4 (1452)	3A, 3A-C	Carb.	4	SOHC
1986	1.4 (1452)	3A, 3A-C	Carb.	4	SOHC
1987	1.4 (1452)	3A, 3A-C	Carb.	4	SOHC
	1.5 (1456)	3E	Carb.	4	SOHC
1988	1.4 (1452)	3A, 3A-C	Carb.	4	SOHC
	1.5 (1456)	3E	Carb.	4	SOHC
1989	1.5 (1456)	3E	Carb.	4	SOHC
1990	1.5 (1456)	3E	Carb.	4	SOHC
	1.5 (1456)	3E-E	EFI	4	SOHC
1991	1.5 (1456)	3E-E	EFI	4	SOHC
1992	1.5 (1456)	3E-E	EFI	4	SOHC
1993	1.5 (1456)	3E-E	EFI	4	SOHC
1994	1.5 (1456)	3E-E	EFI	4	SOHC

85991c01

MANUAL TRANSAXLE APPLICATION CHART

Year	Model		Transaxle Identification	Transaxle Type
1984	Tercel	FWD	Z-44	4-speed
		FWD	Z-52	5-speed
		4WD	Z-52F	5-speed
1985	Tercel	FWD	Z-45	4-speed
		FWD	Z-46	4-speed
		FWD	Z-53	5-speed
		4WD	Z-54F	5-speed
1986	Tercel	FWD	Z-45	4-speed
		FWD	Z-46	4-speed
		FWD	Z-53	5-speed
		4WD	Z-54F	5-speed
1987	Tercel Sedan	FWD	C-140	4-speed
		FWD	C-141	4-speed
		FWD	C-150	5-speed
	Tercel Wagon	FWD	Z-53	5-speed
		4WD	Z-54F	5-speed
1988	Tercel Sedan	FWD	C-140	4-speed
		FWD	C-141	4-speed
		FWD	C-150	5-speed
	Tercel Wagon	4WD	Z-54F	5-speed
1989	Tercel	FWD	C-140	4-speed
		FWD	C-141	4-speed
		FWD	C-150	5-speed
1990	Tercel	FWD	C-140	4-speed
		FWD	C-141	4-speed
		FWD	C-150	5-speed
1991	Tercel	FWD	C-141	4-speed
		FWD	C-150	5-speed
1992	Tercel	FWD	C-141	4-speed
		FWD	C-150	5-speed
1993	Tercel	FWD	C-141	4-speed
		FWD	C-150	5-speed
1994	Tercel	FWD	C-141	4-speed
		FWD	C-150	5-speed

FWD—Front Wheel Drive
4WD—Four Wheel Drive

85991c02

AUTOMATIC TRANSAXLE APPLICATION CHART

Year	Model		Transaxle Identification
1984	Tercel	FWD	A55
1984½	Tercel	4WD	A55F
1985	Tercel	FWD	A55
		4WD	A55F
1986	Tercel	FWD	A55
		4WD	A55F
1987	Tercel Sedan	FWD	A132L
	Tercel Wagon	FWD	A55
		4WD	A55F
1988	Tercel Sedan	FWD	A132L
	Tercel Wagon	4WD	A55F
1989	Tercel	FWD	A132L
1990	Tercel	FWD	A132L
1991	Tercel	FWD	A132L
1992	Tercel	FWD	A132L
1993	Tercel	FWD	A132L
1994	Tercel	FWD	A132L

FWD—Front Wheel Drive
4WD—Four Wheel Drive

85991c03

ROUTINE MAINTENANCE

Air Cleaner

All of the dirt and dust present in the air is kept out of the engine by means of the air cleaner filter element. Proper maintenance is vital, as a clogged element not only restricts the air flow and thus the power, but can also cause premature engine wear.

The filter element should be cleaned and inspected periodically. Remove the filter element and using low pressure compressed air, blow the dirt out.

➡ **The filter element used on Toyota vehicles is of the dry, disposable type. It should never be washed, soaked or oiled.**

The filter element must be replaced at the proper intervals. Be sure to use the correct one; all Toyota elements are of the same type but they come in a variety of sizes.

REMOVAL & INSTALLATION

▶ **See Figures 18, 19, 20, 21, 22 and 23**

1. Unfasten the wing nut and/or clips that retain the air filter element cover. Remove the cover and air filter element.
2. Clean out the filter case (air cleaner) with a rag. Fit the filter element into the air cleaner. Make certain it is not upside down (the filter usually marked for correct installation). Double check that the element is properly seated; if it is crooked, the cover won't seat and air leaks will admit unfiltered air into the motor.
3. Installation is the reverse of the removal procedures.

Fig. 19 To replace the air cleaner element on carbureted engines, first remove the wing nut

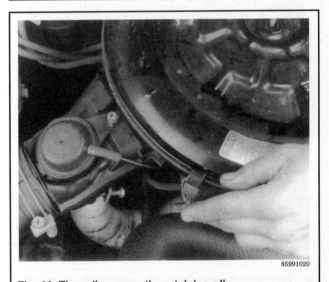

Fig. 20 Then disengage the retaining clip

Fuel Filter

The replaceable fuel filter is located in the fuel line, either mounted on the firewall under the hood or located at the rear of the car near the tank.

The filter should be inspected for external damage and/or leakage at least once a year; it should be changed at the proper intervals or more often under dry, dusty conditions.

Removal and installation procedures differ slightly for each year and application.

✳✳CAUTION

Do not smoke or have open flame near the car when working on the fuel system.

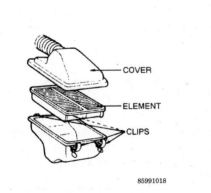

Fig. 18 Exploded view of the air cleaner assembly on fuel injected engines

Fig. 21 The cover can now be removed and the element replaced

Fig. 22 When replacing the element, be sure it is the proper size and type

Fig. 23 Align the arrows when installing the cover

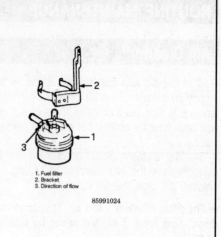

1. Fuel filter
2. Bracket
3. Direction of flow

Fig. 24 Fuel filter and mounting bracket on carbureted engines

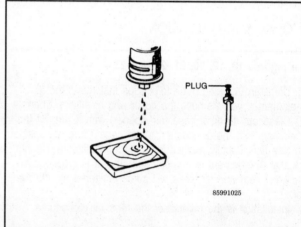

PLUG

Fig. 25 Place a pan under the fuel filter to catch the dripping fuel, remember loosen the bolt or fitting slowly to relieve pressure

REMOVAL & INSTALLATION

◗ See Figures 24, 25, 26 and 27

Carbureted Engines

✳✳CAUTION

Safety is very important when preforming fuel system maintenance. Always perform this service operation on a COLD engine. Failure to conduct fuel system maintenance and repairs in a safe manner may result in serious personal injury.

1. Disconnect the negative battery cable.
2. Remove the gas hose clamps from the inlet and outlet hoses.
3. Work the hoses off (contain spillage) of the fuel filter necks.

4. Snap the filter out of its bracket and replace it with a new one. Replace the gas line hose or clamps as necessary.

➡The arrow on the fuel filter MUST always point toward the carburetor.

5. Installation of the remaining components is in the reverse order of removal. Run the engine for a few minutes and check the fuel filter for any leaks.

Fuel Injected Engines

❊❊CAUTION

Safety is very important when preforming fuel system maintenance. Always perform this service operation on a COLD engine. The fuel system is under pressure — fuel pressure must be released before removing the fuel filter. Failure to conduct fuel system maintenance and repairs in a safe manner may result in serious personal injury.

1. Disconnect the negative battery cable. Unbolt the retaining screws and remove the protective shield for the fuel filter (if so equipped).
2. Place a pan under the delivery pipe (large connection) to catch the dripping fuel and SLOWLY loosen the union bolt to bleed off the fuel pressure.
3. Remove the union bolt and drain the remaining fuel.
4. Disconnect and plug the inlet line.
5. Unbolt and remove the fuel filter.

To install:

➡When tightening the fuel line union bolts to the fuel filter, you must use a torque wrench. Use a crow's foot wrench attachment when tightening the fittings. The tightening torque is very important, as under or over tightening may cause fuel leakage. Insure that there is no fuel line interference and that there is sufficient clearance between it and any other parts.

6. Lightly coat the flare nut, union nut and bolt threads with engine oil.
7. hand-tighten the inlet line to the fuel filter.

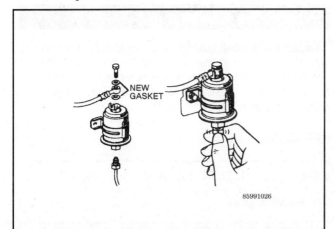

Fig. 26 Exploded view of the fuel filter components on fuel injected engines, be sure to hand-tighten the inlet line before using a wrench

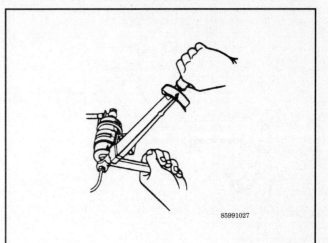

85991027

Fig. 27 A crow's foot attachment must be used with a torque wrench when tightening fuel lines using a torque wrench

8. Install the fuel filter and then tighten the inlet bolt to 22 ft. lbs. (30 Nm).
9. Reconnect the delivery pipe using new gaskets and then tighten the union bolt to 22 ft. lbs. (30 Nm).
10. Run the engine for a few minutes and check for any fuel leaks.
11. Install the protective shield (if so equipped).

PCV Valve

The PCV valve regulates crankcase ventilation during various engine operating conditions. At high vacuum (idle speed and partial load range) it will open slightly and at low vacuum (full throttle) it will open fully. This causes vapor to be removed from the crankcase by the engine vacuum and then sucked into the combustion chamber where it is burned.

REMOVAL & INSTALLATION

▶ **See Figures 28, 29, 30 and 31**

1. Check the ventilation hoses for leaks or clogging. Clean or replace as necessary.
2. Locate the PCV valve in the cylinder head cover or in the manifold-to-crankcase line. Pull the valve out from the cover, then remove it from the hose.
3. Blow into the cylinder head side of the valve. There should be a free passage of air through the valve.
4. Blow into the intake manifold end of the valve. There should be little or no passage of air through the valve.
5. If the PCV valve failed either of the preceding two checks, it will require replacement.
6. Installation is in the reverse order of removal procedure.

➡On some models with fuel injection there is no PCV valve. The vapor passage in the ventilation lines is controlled by two orifices. To check the PCV system on these models, inspect the hoses for cracks, leaks or other damage. Blow through the orifices to make sure they are not blocked. Replace all components as necessary.

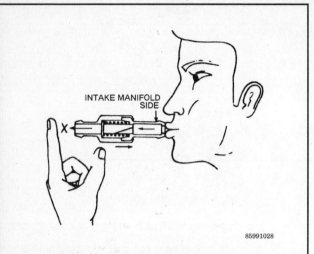

Fig. 28 Air should not flow through the PCV valve when blowing through the intake manifold side

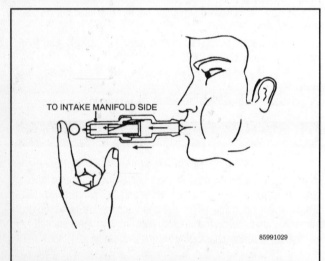

Fig. 29 Air should pass through the PCV valve when blowing through the cylinder head side

Fig. 30 Removing the PCV valve from the valve cover

Fig. 31 Be sure to insert the correct end of the PCV valve into the hose

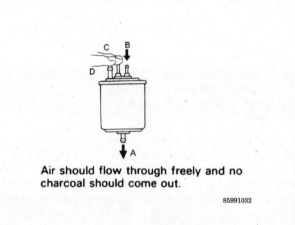

Air should flow through freely and no charcoal should come out.

Fig. 32 Testing the evaporative canister on 3A-C engines

Evaporative Canister

Inspect the charcoal canister assembly at the correct intervals (refer to the maintenance schedule charts). Check the fuel and vapor lines and the vacuum hoses for proper connections and correct routing, as well as condition. Replace clogged, damaged or deteriorated parts as necessary.

SERVICING

▶ See Figures 32, 33, 34, 35 and 36

Carbureted Engines

1. Disconnect the hoses to the canister. Label hoses for correct installation.
2. Plug pipes A and B (C and D on 3A-C engines) with your fingers and blow compressed air through pipe C (B on 3A-C engines).

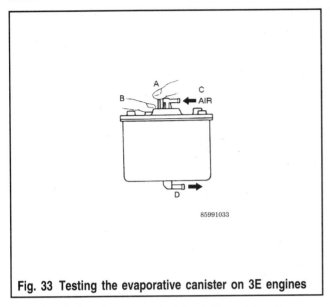

Fig. 33 Testing the evaporative canister on 3E engines

3. Check that air comes out of the bottom of the pipe without resistance. No charcoal should blow out.
4. Replace the canister, if necessary.
5. Reconnect the hoses.

Fuel Injected Engines

1. Using LOW pressure compressed air (0.68 psi or 4.71 kpa), blow into port A and check that air flows without resistance from the other pipes. Blow the same pressure air into port B and check that air does not flow from the other pipes.
2. Clean the filter by blowing compressed air (43 psi or 294 kpa) into port A while holding port B closed. No charcoal should come out.
3. Replace the canister, if necessary.

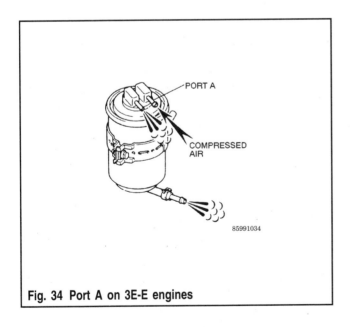

Fig. 34 Port A on 3E-E engines

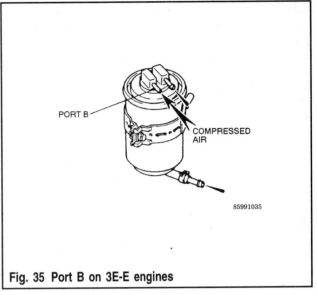

Fig. 35 Port B on 3E-E engines

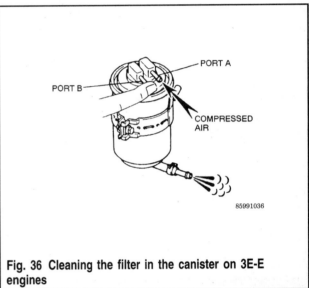

Fig. 36 Cleaning the filter in the canister on 3E-E engines

Battery

GENERAL MAINTENANCE

All batteries, regardless of type, should be kept clean on the outside and should be kept tightly secured by a battery hold-down device. If this is not done, battery acid can leak out, making it discharge faster and leaking corrosive acid can eat away components under the hood. A battery that is not maintenance free must be checked periodically for electrolyte level. You cannot add water to a maintenance free battery, but it must also be checked for proper electrolyte level as indicated by the color of the "eye".

FLUID LEVEL

▶ **See Figures 37 and 38**

Check the battery electrolyte level at least once a month, or more often in hot weather or during periods of extended car operation. On non-maintenance free batteries, the level can be checked through the case on translucent batteries; the cell caps must be removed on other models. The electrolyte level in each cell should be kept filled to the split ring inside, or the line marked on the outside of the case.

If the level is low, add only distilled water through the opening until the level is correct. Each cell is completely separate from the others, so each must be checked and filled individually.

If water is added in freezing weather, the car should be driven several miles to allow the water to mix with the electrolyte. Otherwise, the battery could freeze.

The electrolyte level on maintenance-free batteries is indicated by the color of the "eye", usually found on top of the battery. If this indicator appears to be clear or pale yellow in color, the battery should be replaced.

CABLES

▶ **See Figures 39, 40, 41 and 42**

Once a year (or as necessary), the battery terminals and the cable clamps should be cleaned. Loosen the clamps and remove the cables, negative cable first. On batteries with posts on top, the use of a puller specially made for the purpose is recommended. These are inexpensive, and available in auto parts stores. Side terminal battery cables are secured with a bolt.

Clean the cable clamps and the battery terminal with a wire brush, until all corrosion, grease, etc., is removed and the metal is shiny. It is especially important to clean the inside of the clamp (an old knife is useful here) thoroughly, since a small deposit of foreign material or oxidation there will prevent a sound electrical connection and inhibit either starting or charging. Special tools are available for cleaning these parts,

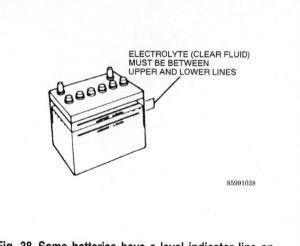

Fig. 38 Some batteries have a level indicator line on the side of the case

one type for conventional batteries and another type for side terminal batteries.

Before installing the cables, loosen the battery hold-down clamp or strap, remove the battery and check the battery tray. Clear it of any debris, and check it for soundness (battery tray can be cleaned with baking soda and water solution). Rust should be wire brushed away, and the metal given a couple coats of anti-rust paint. Replace the battery and tighten the hold-down clamp or strap securely, but be careful not to overtighten, which will crack the battery case.

After the clamps and terminals are clean, reinstall the cables, negative cable last; DO NOT hammer on the clamps to install. Tighten the clamps securely, but do not distort them. Give the clamps and terminals a thin external coat of grease after installation, to retard corrosion.

Check the cables at the same time that the terminals are cleaned. If the cable insulation is cracked or broken, or if the ends are frayed, the cable should be replaced with a new cable of the same length and gauge.

✳✳CAUTION

Keep flame or sparks away from the battery; it gives off explosive hydrogen gas. Battery electrolyte contains sulfuric acid. If you should splash any on your skin or in your eyes, flush the affected area with plenty of clear water; if it lands in your eyes, get medical help immediately.

TESTING

▶ **See Figure 43**

Specific Gravity Test

At least once a year, check the specific gravity of the battery. It should be between 1.20 and 1.26 in. Hg at room temperature. This test cannot be performed on maintenance free batteries in the usual way, instead the built-in indicator must be used.

The specific gravity of non-sealed (maintenance free) batteries can be checked with the use of a hydrometer, an inexpen-

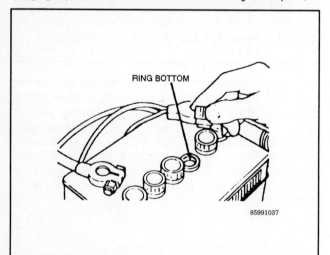

Fig. 37 Fill each battery cell to the bottom of the split ring with water

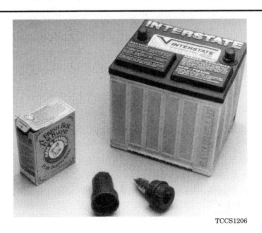

Fig. 39 Battery maintenance may be accomplished with household items (such as baking soda to neutralize spilled acid) or with special tools such as this post and terminal cleaner

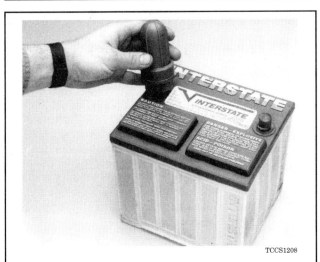

Fig. 40 Place the tool over the terminals and twist to clean the post

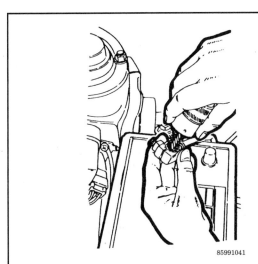

Fig. 41 Clean the inside of the clamps with a wire brush, or special tool

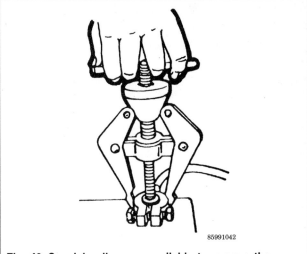

Fig. 42 Special pullers are available to remove the clamps

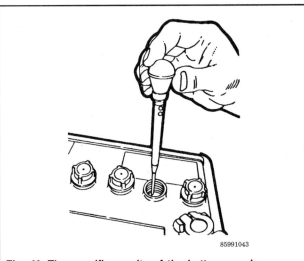

Fig. 43 The specific gravity of the battery can be checked with a simple hydrometer

sive instrument available from many sources, including auto parts stores. The hydrometer has squeeze bulb at one end and a nozzle at the other. Battery electrolyte is sucked into the hydrometer until the float is lifted from its seat. The specific gravity is then read by noting the position of the float. Generally, if after charging, the specific gravity between any two cells varies more than 50 points (0.050), the battery is bad and should be replaced.

It is not possible to check the specific gravity in this manner on sealed (maintenance free) batteries. Instead, the indicator built into the top of the case must be relied on to display any signs of battery deterioration. If the indicator is dark, the battery can be assumed to be OK. If the indicator is light, the specific gravity is low, and the battery should be charged or replaced.

Load Test

A true test of a battery's condition is the load test. It requires the use of a special carbon pile to simulate an electrical load on the battery. Normally, a battery is tested at half it's cold cranking amps rating or a three times the amp-hour rating for 15 seconds.

Generally, if after 15 seconds the battery voltage is not at 9.6 volts or more, the battery either needs to be recharged or replaced.

❋❋CAUTION

Never load test a battery unless the electrolyte level is sufficiently full, otherwise it may explode causing personal injury.

CHARGING

A battery should be charged at a slow rate to keep the plates inside from getting too hot. However if some maintenance free batteries are allowed to discharge until they are almost "dead", they may have to be charged at a high rate to bring them back to "life". Always follow the battery charger manufacturer's instructions on charging the battery.

REPLACEMENT

When it becomes necessary to replace the battery, select a battery with a rating equal to or greater than the battery originally installed. Deterioration and just plain aging of the battery cables, starter motor, and associated wires makes the battery's job harder in successive years. The slow increase in electrical resistance over time makes it prudent to install a new battery with a greater capacity than the old. Details on battery removal and installation are covered in Section 3.

Belts

INSPECTION

▶ **See Figures 44, 45, 46 and 47**

Check the condition of the drive belts and check/adjust the belt tension every 10,000-15,000 miles (16,000-24,000 km) or 1 year.

1. Inspect the belts for signs of glazing or cracking. A glazed belt will be perfectly smooth from slippage, while a good belt will have a slight texture of fabric visible. Cracks will usually start at the inner edge of the belt and run outward. Replace the belt at the first sign of cracking or if the glazing is severe.

2. By placing your thumb midway between the two pulleys, it should be possible to depress the belt about ¼-½ inch (6-13mm). It is best to use a drive belt tension gauge to check belt tension. If any of the belts can be depressed more than this, or cannot be depressed this much, adjust the tension. Inadequate tension will result in slippage and wear, while excessive tension will damage bearings and cause belts to fray or crack.

3. All drive belts should be replaced every 60,000 miles (96,500 km) or as necessary. Drive belts should be replaced

for preventive maintenance. It is always best to replace all drive belts at one time during this service operation.

ADJUSTING

Alternator

To adjust the tension of the alternator drive belt on older models, loosen the pivot and mounting bolts on the alternator. Using a wooden hammer handle, a broomstick or your hand, move the alternator one way or the other until the proper tension is achieved. Do not use a screwdriver or any other metal device such as a pry bar, as a lever. Newer models use a tension adjusting bolt. Loosen the pivot bolt and the locking bolt, then turn the tension adjusting bolt until proper tension is achieved. Tighten the bolts securely, run the engine about minute, stop the engine then recheck the belt tension.

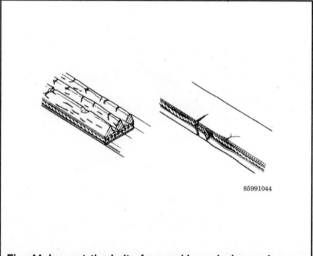

Fig. 44 Inspect the belts for cracking, glazing and separation of the core

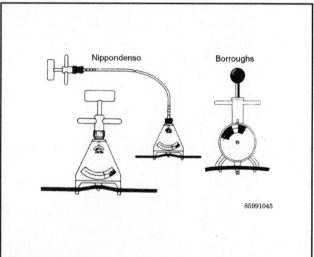

Fig. 45 A belt tension gauge should be used when checking the belt

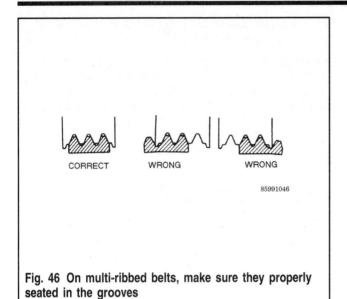

Fig. 46 On multi-ribbed belts, make sure they properly seated in the grooves

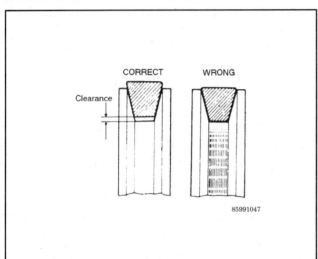

Fig. 47 On conventional belts, check that the bottom of the belt does not touch the pulley groove

Air Conditioning Compressor

A/C compressor (always use caution when working near the A/C compressor to avoid damaging the refrigerant lines) belt tension can be adjusted by turning the tension adjusting bolt which is located on the compressor tensioner bracket. Turn the bolt clockwise to tighten the belt and counterclockwise to loosen it.

Air Pump

To adjust the tension of the air pump drive belt, loosen the adjusting lever bolt and the pivot bolt. Move the pump in or out until the desired tension is reached.

➡**The tension should be checked between the air pump and the crankshaft pulley on cars without air conditioning. On cars with A/C the tension should be checked between the compressor and the crankshaft pulley.**

Power Steering Pump

Tension on the power steering belt is adjusted by means of an idler pulley (some models may use just a lower adjusting bracket setup, similar to the alternator adjustment service procedure). Loosen the lock bolt and turn the adjusting bolt on the idler pulley until the desired tension is felt, then tighten the lock bolt.

REMOVAL & INSTALLATION

If a belt must be replaced, the driven unit must be loosened and moved to its extreme loosest position (usually by moving it toward the center of the motor). After removing the old belt, check the pulleys for dirt or built-up material which could affect belt contact. Carefully install the new belt, it may appear to be just a little too small to fit over the pulley flanges. Fit the belt over the largest pulley (usually the crankshaft pulley at the bottom center of the motor) first, then work on the smaller one(s). Gentle pressure in the direction of rotation is helpful. Some belts run around a third or idler pulley, which acts as an additional pivot in the belt's path. It may be possible to loosen the idler pulley as well as the main component, making your job much easier. Depending on which belt(s) you are changing, it may be necessary to loosen or remove other interfering belts to get at the one(s) you want.

When buying replacement belts, remember that the fit is critical according to the length of the belt, the width of the belt, the depth of the belt and the angle or profile of the V shape (always match up old belt with new belt if possible). The belt shape should exactly match the shape of the pulley; belts that are not an exact match can cause noise, slippage and premature failure.

After the new belt is installed, draw tension on it by moving the driven unit away from the motor and tighten its mounting bolts. This is sometimes a three or four-handed job; you may find an assistant helpful. Make sure that all the bolts you loosened are retightened and that any other loosened belts also have the correct tension. A new belt can be expected to stretch a bit after installation so be prepared to re-adjust your new belt.

➡**After installing a new belt, run the engine for about 5 minutes and then recheck the belt tension.**

Hoses

The upper and lower radiator hoses along with all heater hoses should be checked for deterioration, leaks (hoses sometime swell up before breaking) and loose hose clamps every 15,000 miles (24,000 km) or 1 year. Replace the hose clamps when replacing the radiator or heater hose.

REMOVAL & INSTALLATION

▶ See Figure 48

❋❋CAUTION

When draining the coolant, keep in mind that cats and dogs are attracted by ethylene glycol antifreeze, and are quite likely to drink any that is left in an uncovered container or in puddles on the ground. This will prove fatal in sufficient quantity. Always drain the coolant into a sealable container. Coolant should be reused unless it is contaminated or several years old.

1. Drain the cooling system. This is always done with the engine COLD. Follow this service procedure:
   a. Remove the radiator cap.
   b. Position a pan under the drain cock on the bottom of the radiator. Additionally, some engines have a drain plug on the side of the engine block, near the oil filter. This may be opened to aid in draining the cooling system. If for some reason the radiator drain cock can't be used, you can loosen and remove the lower radiator hose at its joint to the radiator.
   c. If the lower hose is to be used as the drain, loosen the clamp on the hose and slide it back so it's out of the way. Gently break the grip of the hose on its fitting by twisting. Do not exert too much force or you will damage the radiator fitting. As the hose loosens, you can expect a gush of fluid to come out — be ready!
   d. Remove the hose end from the radiator and direct the hose into the drain pan. You now have fluid running from both the hose and the radiator.
   e. When the system stops draining, proceed with replacement of the damaged hose.
2. Loosen the hose clamps at each end of the hose to be removed.
3. Working the hose back and forth, slide it off its connection remove the old hose. Install the new hose as needed. A

small amount of light grease or coolant on the inside of the hose end will ease installation.

➡Radiator and heater hoses should be routed with no kinks and, when installed, should be in the same position as the original. If other than specified hose is used, make sure it does not rub against either the engine or the frame while the engine is running, as this may wear a hole in the hose. Contact points may be insulated with a piece of sponge or foam; plastic wire ties are particularly handy for this job.

4. Position the new hose clamps at least ¼ in. (6mm) or more from the end of the hose and tighten them. Make sure that the hose clamps are beyond the raised bead of the tube and placed in the center of the clamping surface before tightening them.
5. Fill the system with coolant. Toyota strongly recommends the coolant mixture be a 50-50 mix of antifreeze and water. This mixture gives best combination of antifreeze and anti-boil characteristics for year-round driving.
6. Install and tighten the radiator cap. Start the engine and check visually for leaks. Allow the engine to warm up fully and continue to check your work for signs of leakage. A very small leak may not be noticed until the system develops internal pressure. Leaks at hose ends are generally clamp related and can be cured by snugging the clamp slightly. Larger leaks may require removing the hose, and again to do this, YOU MUST WAIT UNTIL THE ENGINE HAS COOLED DOWN. NEVER UNCAP A HOT RADIATOR! After all leaks are cured, check the coolant level in the radiator (with the engine cold) and fill the coolant level as necessary.

Air Conditioning System

❋❋CAUTION

The refrigerant used in A/C systems is an extremely cold substance. When exposed to air, it will instantly freeze any surface it comes in contact with, including your eyes. It is imperative to use eye and skin protection when working on A/C systems.

SAFETY PRECAUTIONS

➡R-12 refrigerant is a chlorofluorocarbon which, when released into the atmosphere, contributes to the depletion of the ozone layer. Ozone filters out harmful radiation from the sun. Consult the laws in your area before servicing the air conditioning system. In some states it is illegal to perform repairs involving refrigerant unless the work is done by a certified technician. It is also likely that you will not be able to purchase R-12 without proof that you are properly trained and certified to work on A/C systems.

• The refrigerant used in A/C systems is an extremely cold substance. When exposed to air, it will instantly freeze any surface it comes in contact with, including your eyes.
• Although normally non-toxic, refrigerant gas becomes highly poisonous in the presence of an open flame. One good whiff of the vapor formed by refrigerant can be fatal. Keep all

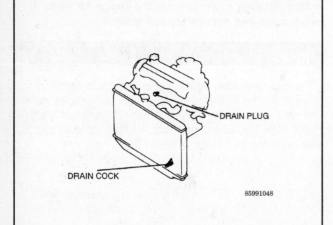

Fig. 48 Common draincock and plug locations. Remember, never drain hot coolant

DRAIN PLUG

DRAIN COCK

85991048

forms of fire (including cigarettes) well clear of the air conditioning system.

• It has been established that the chemicals in R-12 (used on 1984-1993 models) contribute to the damage occurring in the upper atmosphere. 1994 models use ozone-friendly R-134a refrigerant.

• Under no circumstances should R-12 be allowed to enter an R-134a system, or vice versa. Never mix parts between the systems as they are not compatible. This includes O-rings and refrigerant oil.

• Servicing (recovery, evacuation and charging) of the A/C system, should be left to a professional certified mechanic with the proper equipment and related training.

SYSTEM INSPECTION

A lot of A/C problems can be avoided by running the air conditioner at least once a week, regardless of the season. Simply let the system run for at least 5 minutes a week (even in the winter), and you'll keep the internal parts lubricated as well as preventing the hoses from hardening.

Checking For A/C Oil Leaks

Refrigerant leaks show up only as oily areas on the various components because the compressor oil is transported around the entire system along with the refrigerant. Look for oily spots on all the hoses and lines (especially on the hose and tube connections). If there are oily deposits, the system may have a leak, and you should have it checked by a qualified mechanic.

Check the A/C Compressor Belt

The compressor drive belt should be checked frequently for tension and condition. Refer to the information in this section on "Belts".

Keep the A/C Condenser Clear

The condenser is mounted in front of the radiator (and is often mistaken for the radiator). It serves to remove heat from the air conditioning system and to cool the refrigerant. Proper air flow through the condenser is critical to the operation of the system.

Periodically inspect the front of the condenser for bent fins or foreign material (dirt, bugs, leaves, etc.). If any cooling fins are bent, straighten them carefully with needle nose pliers. You can remove any debris with a stiff bristle brush or hose.

REFRIGERANT LEVEL CHECKS

▶ See Figures 49 and 50

Factory installed Toyota air conditioners have a sight glass for checking the refrigerant charge. The sight glass is on top of the receiver/drier which is located in the front of the engine compartment, on the right or left side of the condenser assem-

bly (some models are in front of the condenser/some are located on side of engine compartment).

➡**If your car is equipped with an aftermarket air conditioner, the following system check may not apply. Contact the manufacturer of the unit for instructions on system checks.**

1. With the engine and the air conditioning system running, look for the flow of refrigerant through the sight glass. If the air conditioner is working properly, you'll be able to see a continuous flow of clear refrigerant through the sight glass, with perhaps an occasional bubble at very high temperatures.

2. Cycle the air conditioner ON and OFF to make sure what you are seeing is refrigerant. Since the refrigerant is clear, it is possible to mistake a completely discharged system for one that is fully charged. Turn the system OFF and watch the sight glass. If there is refrigerant in the system, you'll see bubbles during the OFF cycle. If you observe no bubbles when the system is running and the air flow from the unit in the car is delivering cold air, everything is OK.

3. If you observe bubbles in the sight glass while the system is operating, the system is low on refrigerant.

4. Oil streaks in the sight glass are an indication of trouble. Most of the time, if you see oil in the sight glass, it will appear as series of streaks, although occasionally it may be a solid stream of oil. In either case, it means that part of the charge has been lost. This is almost always accompanied by a reduction in cold air output within the car.

GAUGE SETS

▶ See Figure 51

Generally described, this tool is a set of two gauges, a manifold and three hoses. By connecting the proper hoses to the car's system, the gauges can be used to "see" the air conditioning system at work. Do not use the gauge set as a means for discharging the system.

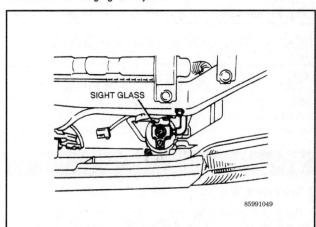

SIGHT GLASS

85991049

Fig. 49 A common location for the receiver-drier unit and sight glass. It may also be located next to the front right shock tower

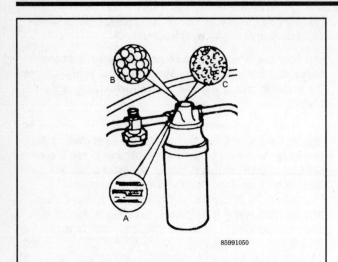

Fig. 50 Oil streaks (A), constant bubbles (B), or foam (C) are indicators that the system is low on refrigerant

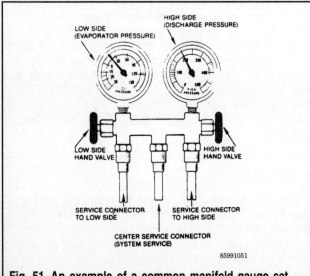

Fig. 51 An example of a common manifold gauge set

DISCHARGING, EVACUATING AND CHARGING

Discharging, evacuating and charging the air conditioning system must be performed by a properly trained and certified mechanic in a facility equipped with refrigerant recovery/recycling equipment that meets SAE standards.

Windshield Wipers

▶ See Figure 52

For maximum effectiveness and longest element life, the windshield and wiper blades should be kept clean. Dirt, tree sap, road tar and so on will cause streaking, smearing and blade deterioration if left on the glass. It is advisable to wash the windshield carefully with a commercial glass cleaner at least once a month. Wipe off the rubber blades with the wet

rag afterwards. Do not attempt to move the wipers back and forth across the windshield by hand; damage to the motor and drive mechanism will result.

If the blades are found to be cracked, broken or torn, they should be replaced immediately. Replacement intervals will vary with usage, although deterioration usually limits blade life to about one year. If the wiper pattern is smeared or streaked, or if the blade chatters across the glass, the blades should be replaced. It is easiest and most sensible to replace them in pairs.

There are basically three different types of wiper blade refills, which differ in their method of replacement. One type has two release buttons, approximately 1/3 of the way up from the ends of the blade frame. Pushing the buttons down releases a lock and allows the rubber blade to be removed from the frame. The new blade slides back into the frame and locks into place.

The second type of refill has two metal tabs which are unlocked by squeezing them together. The rubber blade can then be withdrawn from the frame jaws. A new one is installed by inserting it into the front frame jaws and sliding it rearward to engage the remaining frame jaws. There are usually four jaws; when installing, be certain that the refill is engaged in all of them. At the end of its travel, the tabs will lock into place on the front jaws of the wiper blade frame.

The third type is a refill made from polycarbonate. The refill has a simple locking device at one end which flexes downward out of the groove into which the jaws of the holder fit, allowing easy release. By sliding the new refill through all the jaws and pushing through the slight resistance when it reaches the end of its travel, the refill will lock into position.

Regardless of the type of refill used, make sure that all of the frame jaws are engaged as the refill is pushed into place and locked. The metal blade holder and frame will scratch the glass if allowed to touch it.

Tires and Wheels

▶ See Figures 53 and 54

Common sense and good driving habits will afford maximum tire life. Fast starts, sudden stops and hard cornering are hard on tires and will shorten their useful life span. If you avoid full throttle starts, allow yourself sufficient time to stop, and take corners at a reasonable speed, the life of your tires will increase greatly. Also make sure that you don't overload your vehicle or run with incorrect pressure in the tires. Both of these practices increase tread wear.

Inspect your tires frequently. Be especially careful to watch for bubbles in the tread or side wall, deep cuts, or underinflation. Remove any tires with bubbles. If the cuts are so deep that they penetrate to the cords, discard the tire. Any cut in the sidewall of a radial tire renders it unsafe. Also look for uneven tread wear patterns that indicate that the front end is out of alignment or that the tires are out of balance.

Store the tires at the proper inflation pressure if they are mounted on wheels. Keep them is a cool dry place, laid on their sides. If the tires are stored in the garage or basement, do not let them stand on a concrete floor; set them on strips of wood.

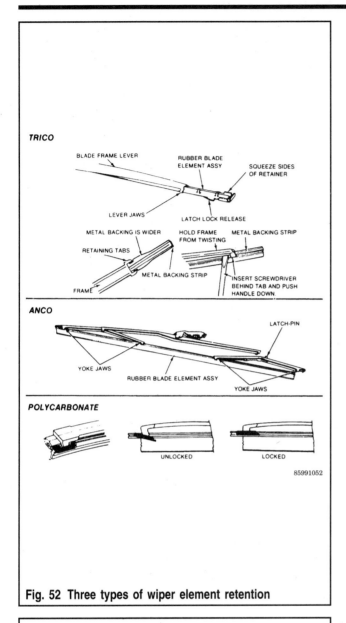

Fig. 52 Three types of wiper element retention

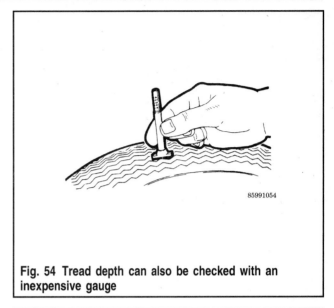

Fig. 54 Tread depth can also be checked with an inexpensive gauge

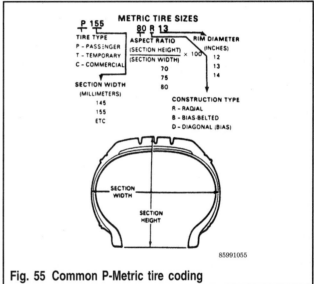

Fig. 55 Common P-Metric tire coding

TIRE ROTATION

So that the tires wear more uniformly, it is recommended that the tires be rotated — NEVER A USE COMPACT SPARE TIRE OTHER THAN FOR TEMPORARY USE! Proper rotation can only be done when all four tires are of the same size and load rating capacity. Any abnormal wear should be investigated and the cause corrected.

Studded snow tires may lose their studs if their direction of rotation is reversed. Mark the wheel position or direction of rotation on studded snow tires before removal.

➡**Avoid overtightening the lug nuts otherwise the brake disc or drum may become permanently distorted. Alloy wheels can be cracked by overtightening. Always tighten the lug nuts in a criss-cross pattern.**

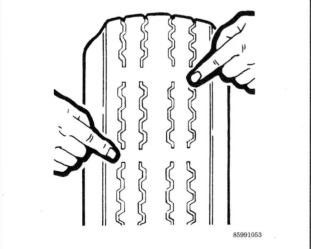

Fig. 53 Tread wear indicators will appear when the tire is worn out

TIRE DESIGN

▶ **See Figure 55**

When buying new tires, you should keep the following points in mind, especially if you are switching to larger tires or a different.profile series (50, 60, 70):

1. All four tires should be of the same construction type. Radial, bias or bias-belted tires must NOT be mixed. Radial tires are highly recommended for their excellent handling and fuel mileage characteristics.

2. The wheels must be the correct width for the tire. Tire dealers have charts of tire and wheel compatibility. A mismatch can cause sloppy handling and rapid tread wear. The tread width should match the rim width (inside bead to inside bead) within 1 in. (25mm). For radial tires the rim width should be 80 percent or less of the tire (not tread) width.

3. The height (mounted diameter) of the new tires can change speedometer accuracy, engine speed per given road speed, fuel mileage, acceleration, and ground clearance.

4. Most models use a space-saving spare tire mounted on a special wheel. This wheel and tire is for EMERGENCY USE ONLY. Never try to mount a regular tire on a special spare wheel.

5. There shouldn't be any body interference when the car is loaded, on bumps or in turning through maximum range.

TIRE INFLATION

▶ **See Figures 56 and 57**

The importance of proper tire inflation cannot be overemphasized. A tire employs air under pressure as part of its structure. It is designed around the supporting strength of air at a specified pressure. For this reason, improper inflation drastically reduces the tire's ability to perform as it was intended. A tire will lose some air in daily use; having to add a few pounds of air periodically is not necessarily a sign of a leaking tire.

Tire pressures should be checked regularly with a reliable pressure gauge. Too often the gauge on the end of the air hose at your corner garage or service station is not accurate enough because it suffers too much abuse. Always check tire pressure when the tires are cold, as pressure increases with temperature. If you must move the vehicle to check the tire inflation, do not drive more than 1 mile (1.6 km) before checking. A cold tire is one that has not been driven on for a long period of time.

Never exceed the maximum tire pressure embossed on the tire! This maximum pressure is rarely the correct pressure for everyday driving. Consult your owner's manual for the proper tire pressures for your vehicle.

CARE OF SPECIAL WHEELS

If you have invested money in magnesium, aluminum alloy or sport wheels, special precautions should be taken to make sure your investment is not wasted and that your special wheels look good for the lifetime of the car.

Special wheels are easily scratched and/or damaged. Occasionally check the rims for cracking, impact damage or air leaks. If any of these are found, replace the wheel. In order to prevent this type of damage, and the costly replacement of a special wheel, observe the following precautions:

• Use extra care not to damage the wheels during removal, installation, balancing, etc. After removal of the wheels from the car, place them on a mat or other protective surface. If they are to be stored for any length of time, support them on strips of wood. Never store tires upright — the tread will develop flat spots.

• While driving, watch for sharp obstacles.

• When washing, use a mild detergent and water. Avoid cleansers with abrasives or the use of hard brushes. There are many cleaners and polishes for special wheels. Use them.

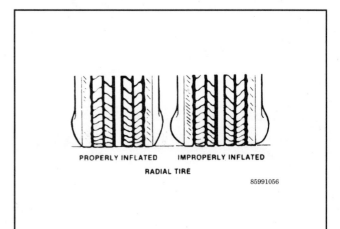

Fig. 56 Radial tires have a characteristic sidewall bulge; don't try to measure the air pressure by looking at the tire, use a pressure gauge

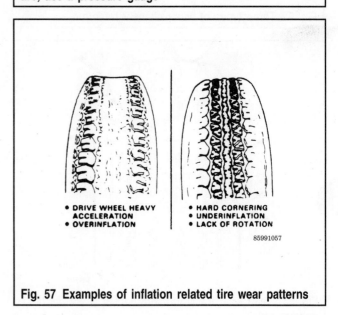

Fig. 57 Examples of inflation related tire wear patterns

• If possible, remove your special wheels from the car during the winter months. Salt and sand used for snow removal can severely damage the finish.

• Make sure that the recommended lug nut torque is never exceeded or the wheel may crack. Never use snow chains on special wheels; severe scratching will occur.

FLUIDS AND LUBRICANTS

Fluid Disposal

Used fluids such as engine oil, transmission fluid, antifreeze and brake fluid are hazardous wastes and must be disposed of properly. Before draining any fluids, consult with local authorities; in many cases, waste oil, etc., is accepted in recycling programs. A number of service stations and auto parts stores are also accepting waste fluids for recycling.

Be sure of the recycling center's policies before draining the fluids, as many will not accept mixed fluids such as oil and antifreeze.

Fuel and Engine Oil Recommendations

▶ **See Figures 58, 59 and 60**

OIL

The Society of Automotive Engineers (SAE) grade number indicates the viscosity of the engine oil and thus its ability to lubricate at a given temperature. The lower the SAE grade number, the lighter the oil; the lower the viscosity, the easier it is to crank the engine in cold weather.

Oil viscosities should be chosen from those oils recommended for the lowest anticipated temperatures during the oil change interval.

Multi-viscosity oils (10W-30, 20W-50, etc.) offer the important advantage of being adaptable to temperature extremes. They allow easy starting at low temperatures, yet they give good protection at high speeds and engine temperatures. This is a decided advantage in changeable climates or in long distance touring.

The American Petroleum Institute (API) designation indicates the classification of engine oil used under certain given operating conditions. Only oils designated for use "Service SG" or better should be used. Oils of the SG type perform a variety of functions inside the engine in addition to their basic functions inside the engine in addition to their basic function as a lubricant. Through a balanced system of metallic detergents and polymeric dispersions, the oil prevents the formation of high and low temperature deposits and also keeps sludge and particles of dirt in suspension. Acids, particularly sulfuric acid, as well as other by-products of combustion, are neutralized. Both the SAE grade number and the API designation can be found on the label of the oil bottle.

For recommended oil viscosities, refer to the chart.

➡**Non-detergent or straight mineral oils should not be used in your car.**

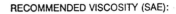
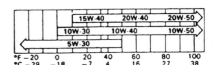

RECOMMENDED VISCOSITY (SAE):

TEMPERATURE RANGE ANTICIPATED BEFORE NEXT OIL CHANGE

85991058

Fig. 58 Oil viscosity chart for 1984-1989 models

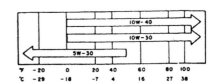

RECOMMENDED VISCOSITY (SAE):

TEMPERATURE RANGE ANTICIPATED BEFORE NEXT OIL CHANGE

85991059

Fig. 59 Oil viscosity chart for 1990-1991 models

SYNTHETIC OIL

There are many excellent synthetic and fuel-efficient oils currently available that can provide better gas mileage, longer service life, and in some cases better engine protection. These benefits do not come without a few hitches, however, the main one being the price of synthetic oils, which can be three or four times the price per quart of conventional oil.

Synthetic oil is not for every car and ever type of driving, so you should consider your engine's condition and your type of

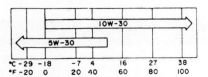

RECOMMENDED VISCOSITY (SAE):

TEMPERATURE RANGE ANTICIPATED
BEFORE NEXT OIL CHANGE

85991060

Fig. 60 Oil viscosity chart for 1992-1994 models

driving. Also, check your car's warranty conditions regarding the use of synthetic oils.

Both brand new engines and older, high mileage engines may be the wrong candidates for synthetic oil. The synthetic oils are so slippery that they may prevent proper break-in of new engines; most manufacturer's recommend that you wait until the engine is properly broken in — 5,000 miles (8,046 km) — before using synthetic oil. Older engines with wear have a different problem with synthetics. Slippery synthetic oils get past worn parts easily. If your car is leaking oil past old seals you'll have a much greater leak problem with synthetics.

Consider your type of driving. If most of your accumulated mileage is high speed, highway type driving, the more expensive synthetic oils may be of benefit. Extended highway driving gives the engine chance to warm up, accumulating less acids in the oil and putting less stress on the engine over the long run. Under these conditions, the oil change interval can be extended (as long as your oil filter can last the extended life of the oil) up to the advertised mileage claims of the synthetics. Cars with synthetic oils may show increased fuel economy in highway driving, due to less internal friction. However, many automotive experts agree that 50,000 miles (80,465 km) is far too long to keep any oil in your engine.

Cars used under harder circumstances, such as stop and go, city type driving, short trips, or extended idling, should be serviced more frequently. For the engines in these cars, the much greater cost of synthetic oils may not be worth the investment. Internal wear increases much quicker on these cars, causing greater oil consumption and leakage.

FUEL

All Tercels covered in this manual are designed to run on unleaded fuel. The use of leaded fuel in a car requiring un- leaded fuel will plug the catalytic converter (NEVER USE LEADED FUEL IN AN UNLEADED VEHICLE), rendering it in- operative and will increase exhaust back-pressure to the point where engine output will be severely reduced. In all cases, the minimum octane rating of the fuel used must be at least Re- search Octane No. 91 (pump octane rating 87) or higher.

The use of a fuel too low in octane (a measurement of anti- knock quality) will result in spark knock. Since many factors affect operating efficiency, such as altitude, terrain, air temper- ature and humidity, knocking may result even though the rec- ommended fuel is being used. If persistent knocking occurs, it may be necessary to switch to a higher grade of fuel. Continu- ous or heavy knocking may result in engine damage.

➡**Your engine's fuel requirement can change with time, mainly due to carbon buildup, which changes the com- pression ratio. If your engine pings, knocks or runs on, switch to a higher grade of fuel. Sometimes just changing brands will cure the problem. If it becomes necessary to retard the timing from specifications, don't change it more than a few degrees. Retarded timing will reduce power output and fuel mileage, it will also increase the engine temperature.**

Engine

OIL LEVEL CHECK

▶ See Figures 61 and 62

✳✳CAUTION

Prolonged and repeated skin contact with used engine oil, with no effort to remove the oil, may be harmful. Always follow these simple precautions when handling used motor oil:

- Avoid prolonged skin contact with used motor oil.
- Remove oil from your skin by washing thoroughly with soap and water or waterless hand cleaner. Do not use gaso- line, thinners or other solvents.
- Avoid prolonged skin contact with oil-soaked clothing.

Every time you stop for fuel, check the engine oil as follows:

1. Park the car on level ground.
2. When checking the oil level it is best for the engine to be at operating temperature, although checking the oil immedi-

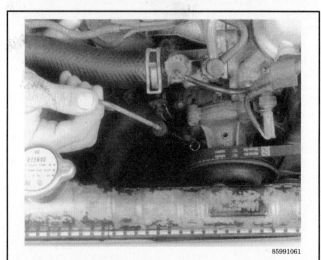

85991061

Fig. 61 The oil level dipstick is often found at the front of the engine

ately after stopping will lead to a false reading. Wait a few minutes after turning off the engine to allow the oil to drain back into the crankcase.

3. Open the hood and locate the dipstick. Pull the dipstick from its tube, wipe it clean and reinsert it.

4. Pull the dipstick out again and, holding it horizontally, read the oil level. The oil should be between the **F** and **L** or high and low marks on the dipstick. If the oil is below the **L** or low mark, add oil of the proper viscosity through the capped opening on the top of the cylinder head cover. See the Oil and Fuel Recommendations chart in this section for the proper viscosity and rating of oil.

5. Replace the dipstick and check the oil level again after adding any oil. Be careful not to overfill the crankcase. Approximately 1 quart (0.9L) of oil will raise the level from the **L** or low mark to the **F** or high mark. Excess oil will generally be consumed at an accelerated rate and could cause engine damage.

OIL AND FILTER CHANGE

▶ See Figures 63, 64, 65, 66, 67 and 68

➡**It is recommended that all vehicles should have the oil changed every 3,750 miles (6,000 km) or 6 months. Always replace the oil filter when changing the engine oil in the vehicle. These mileage figures are the Toyota recommended intervals assuming severe driving conditions (trips less than 5 miles, extensive idling/heavy traffic, dusty conditions, etc.). If your driving habits do not meet these conditions and consists chiefly of extended highway driving, the interval is every 7,500 miles (12,000 km) or 1 year.**

The oil drain plug is located on the bottom, rear of the oil pan (bottom of the engine, underneath the car — some models are on the side of oil pan).

Always drain the oil after the engine has been running long enough to bring it to normal operating temperature. Hot oil will flow easier and more contaminants will be removed along with the oil than if it were drained cold. To change the oil and filter:

1. Run the engine until it reaches normal operating temperature, then shut the engine **OFF**.

2. Jack up the front of the car and support on safety stands.

3. Slide a drain pan of at least 6 quart (5.7L) capacity under the oil pan.

4. Loosen the drain plug. Turn the plug out by hand. By keeping an inward pressure on the plug as you unscrew it, oil won't escape past the threads and you can remove it without being burned by hot oil. The engine oil will be hot. Keep your arms, face and hands away from the oil as it drains out.

5. Allow the oil to drain completely and then install the drain plug. Don't overtighten the plug, or you'll be buying a new pan or a replacement plug for stripped threads.

6. Using a strap wrench, remove the oil filter. Keep in mind that it's holding about 1 quart (0.9L) of dirty, hot oil.

7. Empty the old filter into the drain pan and dispose of the filter.

➡**Please dispose of used motor oil properly. Do not throw it in the trash or pour it on the ground. Take it to your dealer or local service station for recycling.**

Fig. 63 Most oil drain plugs are located on the bottom of the oil pan, however, some may also be on the side

Fig. 62 When adding oil, pour through the oil filler hole in the valve cover

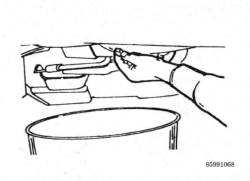

Fig. 64 Keep an inward pressure on the drain plug as you unscrew it to prevent the oil from spilling over your hands

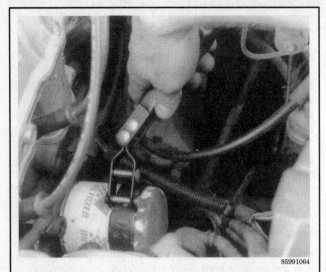

Fig. 65 Use a strap wrench to REMOVE the oil filter

Fig. 66 Before installing a new oil filter, coat the gasket with clean oil

Fig. 67 Add the proper amount of oil through the filler hole in the valve cover

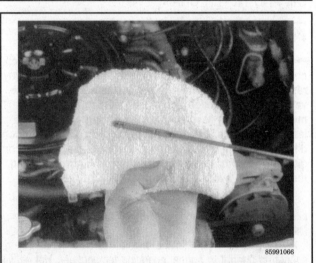

Fig. 68 Check the oil and be sure it is at the proper level

8. Using a clean rag, wipe off the filter adaptor on the engine block. Be sure that the rag doesn't leave any lint which could clog an oil passage.

9. Coat the rubber gasket on the filter with fresh oil. Spin it onto the engine by hand; when the gasket touches the adaptor surface give it another ½-¾ turn. No more, or you'll squash the gasket and it may leak (some oil filters have installation directions about how tight to make the oil filter — follow the directions as necessary).

10. Refill the engine with the correct amount of fresh oil. See the Capacities Chart.

11. Check the oil level on the dipstick. It is normal for the level to be a bit above the full mark. Start the engine and allow it to idle for a few minutes.

➡**Do not run the engine above idle speed until it has built up oil pressure, indicated when the oil light goes out.**

12. Shut off the engine, allow the oil to drain for a minute, and check the oil level. Check around the filter and drain plug for any leaks, and correct as necessary.

Manual Transaxle

FLUID RECOMMENDATIONS

All manual transaxles use API GL-4 or GL-5 (oil grade), 75W-90 or 80W-90 (viscosity) gear oil.

LEVEL CHECK

▶ **See Figure 69**

The oil in the manual transaxle should be checked at least every 15,000 miles (24,000 km) and replaced every 25,000-30,000 miles (40,200-48,200 km) if necessary.

1. With the car parked on a level surface, remove the filler plug from the side of the transaxle housing.

2. If the lubricant begins to trickle out of the hole, there is enough. Otherwise, carefully insert your finger (watch out for sharp threads) and check to see if the oil is up to the edge of the hole.

3. If not, add oil through the hole until the level is at the edge of the hole. Most gear lubricants come in a plastic squeeze bottle with a nozzle, making additions simple. You can also use a common everyday kitchen baster.

4. Install the filler plug.

DRAIN AND REFILL

▶ See Figures 70, 71, 72, 73, 74, 75 and 76

All Wagons Including 4WD Models and 1984-1986 Sedans

1. Raise and safely support the vehicle as necessary. The oil must be hot before it is drained. If the car is driven until the engine is at normal operating temperature, the oil should be hot enough.

2. Remove the filler plugs to provide a vent. 4WD models have three plugs, 2WD models have two plugs.

3. Remove the three drain plugs on the bottom of the transaxle. Place large container underneath the transmission to catch the fluid.

4. Allow the oil to drain completely. Clean off the drain plugs, then install them. Tighten the front two plugs until just snug, leave the extension housing drain plug loose about 8 turns.

5. Fill the transaxle with the appropriate gear oil. This usually comes in a plastic squeeze bulb or use a kitchen baster to squirt the oil in. On 4WD models, always fill from the transfer adaptor filler plug. Refer to the Capacities Chart for the proper amount of oil to put in.

6. The oil level should come up to the top of the filler hole.

7. Install the filler plugs, then tighten the extension housing plug, drive the car for a few minutes, stop, and check for any leaks.

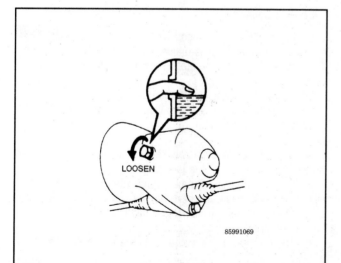

Fig. 69 Checking the oil level on manual transaxles

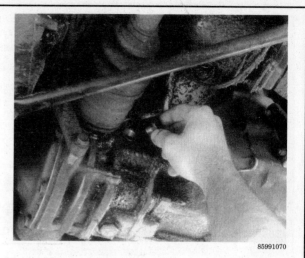

Fig. 70 Remove all the filler plugs to provide a vent, front differential plug shown

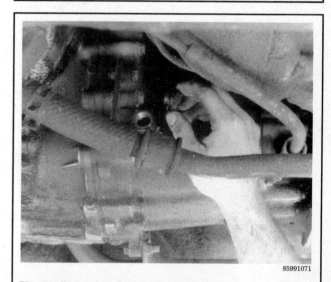

Fig. 71 Removing the transaxle fill plug

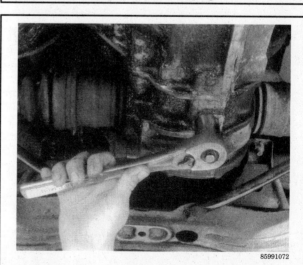

Fig. 72 All three drain plugs should be removed as well — front differential shown

Fig. 73 Removing the transaxle drain plug

Fig. 74 Removing the extension housing drain plug

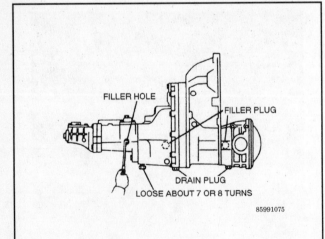

Fig. 75 On 4WD models, always fill from the transfer adapter fill plug

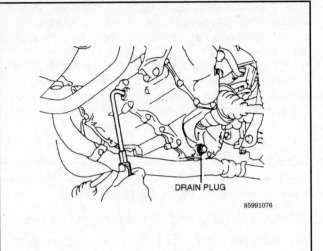

Fig. 76 Fill and drain plug locations on 1987-1994 sedans

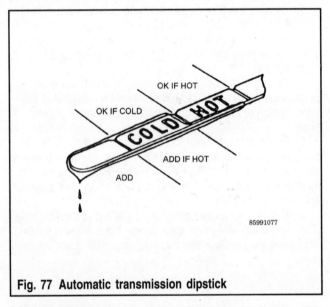

Fig. 77 Automatic transmission dipstick

1987-1994 Sedans

1. Raise and safely support the vehicle as necessary. The oil must be hot before it is drained. If the car is driven until the engine is at normal operating temperature, the oil should be hot enough.

2. Remove the filler plug to provide a vent.

3. The drain plug is on the bottom of the transaxle. Place a large container underneath the transmission and remove the plug.

4. Allow the oil to drain completely. Clean off the plug, then install it. Tighten it until it is just snug.

5. Fill the transaxle with the appropriate gear oil. This usually comes in a plastic squeeze bulb or use a kitchen baster to squirt the oil in. Refer to the Capacities Chart for the proper amount of oil to put in.

6. The oil level should come up to the top of the filler hole.

7. Replace the filler plug, drive the car for a few minutes, stop, and check for any leaks.

➡ **Please dispose of used oil properly. Do not throw it in the trash or pour it on the ground. Take it to your dealer or local service station for recycling.**

Automatic Transaxle

FLUID RECOMMENDATIONS

All automatic transaxles use ATF type Dexron®II automatic transmission fluid.

LEVEL CHECK

◆ **See Figures 77 and 78**

Check the automatic transaxle fluid level at least every 15,000 miles (24,000 km) (more often if possible — checking once a month is smart). The dipstick is in the rear of the engine compartment.

The fluid level should be checked only when HOT (normal operating temperature).

1. Park the car on a level surface with the engine idling. Shift the transaxle into **N** or **P** and set the parking brake.

2. Remove the dipstick, wipe it clean and reinsert it firmly. Be sure that it has been pushed all the way in. Remove the dipstick and check the fluid level while holding it horizontally. With the engine running, the fluid level should be between the second and third notches on the dipstick.

3. If the fluid level is below the second notch, add the required type of transmission fluid until the proper level is reached. This is easily done with the aid of a funnel. Check the level often as you are filling the transaxle. Be extremely careful not to overfill it. Overfilling will cause slippage, seal damage and overheating. Approximately one pint (0.47L) of transmission fluid will raise the level from one notch to the other.

The fluid on the dipstick should always be a bright red color. If it is discolored (brown or black), or smells burnt, serious transmission troubles (probably due to overheating) should be suspected. The transmission should be inspected by a qualified service (ASE certified) technician to locate the cause of the burnt fluid.

DRAIN AND REFILL

◆ **See Figure 79**

The automatic transaxle fluid should be changed at least every 25,000-30,000 miles (40,200-48,200 km). If the car is normally used in severe service, such as stop-and-go driving, trailer towing or the like, the interval should be halved. The fluid should be hot before it is drained; a 20 minute drive will accomplish this.

85991078

Fig. 78 When necessary, add automatic transmission fluid through the transmission dipstick tube

Toyota automatic transaxles usually have a drain plug in them so you can remove the plug, drain the fluid, replace the plug and then refill.

1. Raise and safely support the vehicle as necessary. Remove the plug and drain the fluid into a large pan.

2. Install the drain plug.

3. It is a good idea to measure the amount of fluid drained from the transaxle to determine the correct amount of fresh fluid to add. This is because some parts of the transmission may not drain completely and using the dry refill amount specified in the Capacities Chart could lead to overfilling. Fluid is added only through the dipstick tube. Always use the proper type automatic transmission fluid.

4. Add ATF type Dexron®II automatic transmission fluid (vehicle must be on a level surface when refilling) to the correct level.

5. Replace the dipstick after filling. Start the engine and allow it to idle. DO NOT race the engine.

6. After the engine has idled for a few minutes, shift the transmission slowly through the gears (always hold your foot on the brake pedal) and then return it to Park. With the engine still idling, check the fluid level on the dipstick. If necessary, add more fluid to raise the level to specification.

7. Check the drain plug for transmission fluid leakage. Dispose of used transmission oil properly. Do not throw it in the trash or pour it on the ground. Take it to your dealer or local service station for recycling.

PAN AND FILTER SERVICE

◆ **See Figures 80, 81 and 82**

Always replace the transaxle pan gasket when the oil pan is removed. Note the location of all transaxle oil filter (strainer) retaining bolts. Always torque all transaxle oil pan retaining bolts in progressive steps.

➡ **This service operation should be performed with the engine and transaxle COLD.**

1. Raise and safely support the vehicle as necessary. Remove the plug and drain the fluid. When the fluid stops flowing

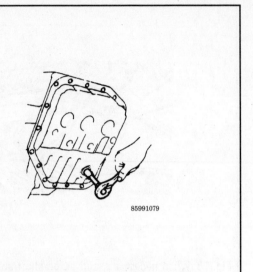

Fig. 79 Drain plug location on automatic transaxles

out of the drain hole, loosen the pan retaining screws until the pan can be pulled down at one corner. If the pan is stuck, tap the edges lightly with a plastic mallet to loosen it; DON'T pry it or wedge a screwdriver into the seam. Lower the corner of the pan and allow the remaining fluid to drain out.

2. After the pan has drained completely, remove the pan retaining screws, then remove the pan and gasket.

3. Clean the pan thoroughly and allow it to air dry. If you wipe it out with a rag you run the risk of leaving bits of lint in the pan which could clog the tiny hydraulic passages in the transaxle.

4. With the pan removed, the transaxle filter is visible. Remove the 3 bolts holding the filter and remove the filter and gasket if so equipped.

➡**On some models filter retaining bolts are different lengths and MUST BE reinstalled in their correct locations. Take great care not to interchange them.**

5. Clean the mating surfaces for the oil pan and the filter; make sure all traces of the old gasket material is removed.

6. Install the new filter assembly (some models use a gasket under the oil filter). Install the 3 retaining bolts in their correct locations and tighten only to 7 ft. lbs. (10 Nm).

7. Install the pan (magnets in the correct location in oil pan) using a new gasket and torque retaining bolts in progressive steps to about 60 inch lbs. (7 Nm).

8. Install the drain plug.

9. It is a good idea to measure the amount of fluid drained from the transaxle to determine the correct amount of fresh fluid to the be added. This is because some parts of the transaxle may not drain completely. Do not overfill the transaxle assembly.

10. With the engine **OFF**, add fresh Dexron® II fluid through the dipstick tube to the correct level. Refer to the Capacities Chart as necessary.

11. Start the engine (always hold your foot on the brake) and shift the gear selector into all positions from P through L, allowing each gear to engage momentarily. Shift into P. DO NOT race the engine!

12. With the engine idling, check the fluid level. Add fluid up to correct level on the dipstick.

13. Check the transmission/transaxle oil pan and drain plug for oil leakage. Dispose of used oil properly. Do not throw it in the trash or pour it on the ground. Take it to your dealer or local service station for recycling.

Front Drive Axle

➡**This procedure applies to vehicles equipped with automatic transaxles only.**

FLUID RECOMMENDATIONS

Wagons 1984-1986 sedans use API GL-5 (oil grade), SAE 90 (viscosity) gear oil. 1987-1994 sedans use Dexron® II automatic transmission fluid.

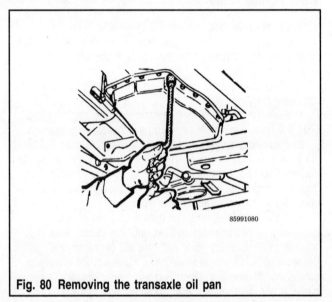

Fig. 80 Removing the transaxle oil pan

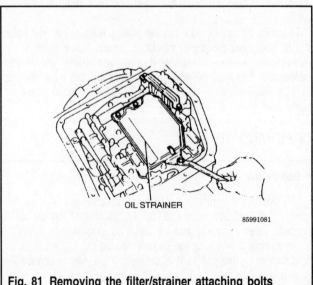

OIL STRAINER

Fig. 81 Removing the filter/strainer attaching bolts

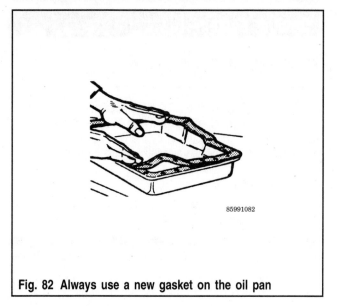

Fig. 82 Always use a new gasket on the oil pan

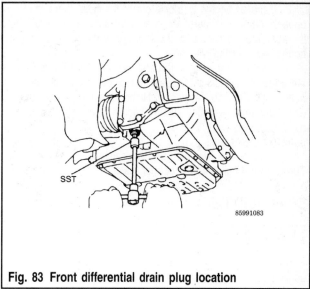

Fig. 83 Front differential drain plug location

LEVEL CHECK

The oil in the differential should be checked at least every 15,000 miles (24,000 km) and replaced every 25,000-30,000 miles (40,200-48,200 km).

1. With the car parked on a level surface, remove the filler plug from the differential assembly. The plug on the bottom of the differential assembly is the drain plug.

2. If the oil begins to trickle out of the hole, there is enough. Otherwise, carefully insert your finger (watch for sharp threads) into the hole and check to see if the oil is up to the bottom edge of the filler hole.

3. If necessary, add the appropriate fluid through the opening until the level is at the edge of the hole. Most gear oils come in a plastic squeeze bottle with a nozzle, making additions simple. You can also use a common everyday kitchen baster.

4. Replace the filler plug and run the engine for a while. Turn off the engine and check for leaks.

DRAIN AND REFILL

▶ **See Figures 83 and 84**

The fluid in the differential should be changed at least every 25,000-30,000 miles (40,200-48,200 km). To drain and fill the differential, proceed as follows:

1. Park the vehicle on a level surface. Set the parking brake.

2. Remove the filler (upper) plug. Place a container which is large enough to catch all of the differential oil, under the drain plug.

3. Remove the drain (lower) plug and gasket, if so equipped. Allow all of the oil to drain into the container.

4. Install the drain plug. Tighten it so that it will not leak, but do not overtighten.

5. Refill with the proper lubricant. Be sure that the level reaches the bottom of the filler plug.

6. Install the filler plug and check for leakage.

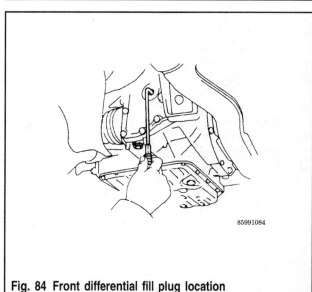

Fig. 84 Front differential fill plug location

Rear Drive Axle

FLUID RECOMMENDATIONS

The rear differential on four wheel drive Tercels uses API GL-5 hypoid type gear oil, SAE 90 or 80W-90.

LEVEL CHECK

▶ **See Figure 85**

The oil in the differential should be checked at least every 15,000 miles (24,000 km) and replaced every 25,000-30,000 miles (40,200-48,200 km).

1. With the car parked on a level surface, remove the filler plug from the back of the differential assembly. The plug on the bottom of the differential assembly is the drain plug.

2. If the oil begins to trickle out of the hole, there is enough. Otherwise, carefully insert your finger (watch for sharp threads) into the hole and check to see if the oil is up to the bottom edge of the filler hole.

3. If necessary, add oil through the hole until the level is at the edge of the hole. Most gear oils come in a plastic squeeze bottle with a nozzle, making additions simple. You can also use a common everyday kitchen baster. Use standard GL-5 hypoid type gear oil, SAE 90 or SAE 80W-90, if you live in a particularly cold area.

4. Replace the filler plug and run the engine for a while. Turn off the engine and check for leaks.

DRAIN AND REFILL

▶ **See Figure 86**

The gear oil in the differential should be changed at least every 25,000-30,000 miles (40,200-48,200 km).

To drain and fill the differential, proceed as follows:

1. Park the vehicle on a level surface. Set the parking brake.

2. Remove the filler (upper) plug. Place a container which is large enough to catch all of the differential oil, under the drain plug.

3. Remove the drain (lower) plug and gasket, if so equipped. Allow all of the oil to drain into the container.

4. Install the drain plug. Tighten it so that it will not leak, but do not overtighten.

5. Refill with the proper grade and viscosity of axle lubricant. Be sure that the level reaches the bottom of the filler plug.

6. Install the filler plug and check for leakage.

Cooling System

FLUID RECOMMENDATIONS

The correct coolant for the Tercel is any permanent, high quality ethylene glycol antifreeze mixed in a 50-50 concentration with water. This mixture gives the best combination of antifreeze and anti-boil characteristics within the engine.

LEVEL CHECK

▶ **See Figures 87 and 88**

✳✳CAUTION

Always allow the car to sit and cool for an hour or so (longer is better) before removing the radiator cap. To avoid injury when working on a warm engine, cover the radiator cap with a thick cloth and turn it slowly counter-clockwise until the pressure begins to escape. After the pressure has completely escaped, remove the cap. Never remove the cap until the pressure is released.

It's best to check the coolant level when the engine is COLD. The radiator coolant level should be between the LOW and the FULL lines on the expansion tank when the engine is cold. If low, check for leakage and add coolant up to the FULL line but do not overfill it.

➡**Check the freeze protection rating of the antifreeze at least once a year or as necessary with a suitable antifreeze tester.**

DRAIN AND REFILL

▶ **See Figures 89, 90 and 91**

The engine coolant should be changed every 30,000 miles (48,200 km) or 2 years, whichever comes first. Replacing the

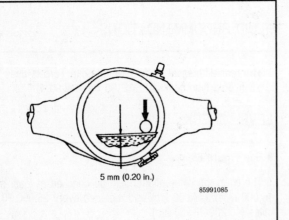

5 mm (0.20 in.)

85991085

Fig. 85 Fluid level in the rear differential on four wheel drive models

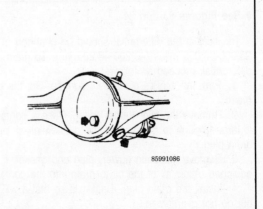

85991086

Fig. 86 Fill and drain plug locations on four wheel drive models

Fig. 87 A common expansion tank location

Fig. 88 Adding coolant to the expansion tank

coolant is necessary to remove the scale, rust and chemical by-products which build up in the system.

1. Draining the cooling system is always done with the motor **COLD**.
2. Remove the radiator cap.
3. Position the drain pan under the drain cock on the bottom of the radiator. Additionally, some engines have a drain cock on the side of the engine block, near the oil filter. This should be opened to aid in draining the cooling system completely. If for some reason the radiator drain cock can't be used, you can loosen and remove the lower radiator hose at its joint to the radiator.

✳✳CAUTION

When draining the coolant, keep in mind that cats and dogs are attracted by ethylene glycol antifreeze, and are quite likely to drink any that is left in an uncovered container or in puddles on the ground. This will prove

fatal in sufficient quantity. Always drain the coolant into a sealable container. Coolant should be reused unless it is contaminated or several years old.

4. If the lower hose is to be used as the drain, loosen the clamp on the hose and slide it back so it's out of the way. Gently break the grip of the hose on its fitting by twisting or prying with a suitable tool. Do not exert too much force or you will damage the radiator fitting. Remove the hose end from the radiator and direct the hose into the drain pan. You now have fluid running from both the hose and the radiator.
5. When the system stops draining, close both draincocks as necessary.
6. Using a funnel if necessary, fill the radiator with a 50-50 solution of antifreeze and water. Allow time for the fluid to run through the hoses and into the engine.
7. Fill the radiator to just below the neck. With the radiator cap off, start the engine and let it idle; this will circulate the coolant and begin to eliminate air in the system. Top up the radiator as the level drops.
8. When the level is reasonably stable, shut the engine **OFF**, then replace the radiator cap. Fill the expansion tank to a level halfway between the LOW and FULL lines, then cap the expansion tank.
9. Drive the car for 10 or 15 minutes; the temperature gauge should be fully within the normal operating range. It is helpful to set the heater to its hottest setting while driving — this circulates the coolant throughout the entire system and helps eliminate air bubbles.
10. After the engine has cooled (2-3 hours), check the level in the radiator and the expansion tank adding coolant as necessary.

FLUSHING AND CLEANING THE SYSTEM

Proceed with draining the system as outlined earlier. When the system has drained, reconnect any hoses and close the radiator draincock. Move the temperature control for the heater to its hottest position; this allows the heater core to be flushed as well. Using a garden hose or bucket, fill the radiator and

Fig. 89 Place a container under the radiator draincock to catch the coolant

Fig. 90 Most engines have a coolant drain plug located in the engine block as well

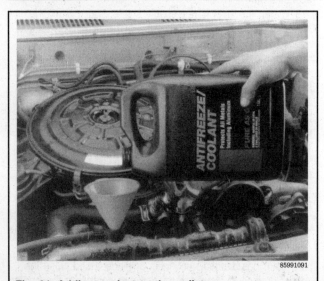

Fig. 91 Adding coolant to the radiator

allow the water to run out the engine drain cock. Continue until the water runs clear. Be sure to clean the expansion tank as well.

If the system is badly contaminated with rust or scale, you can use a commercial flushing solution to clean it out. Follow the manufacturer's instructions. Some causes of rust are air in the system, failure to change the coolant regularly, use of excessively hard or soft water, and/or failure to use the correct mix of antifreeze and water.

After the system has been flushed, continue with the refill procedures outlined earlier. Check the condition of the radiator cap and its gasket, replacing the radiator cap as necessary.

Brake and Clutch Master Cylinders

FLUID RECOMMENDATIONS

All Tercels use DOT 3 or SAE J1703 brake fluid. The brake and clutch master cylinders use the same type of brake fluid.

LEVEL CHECK

▶ **See Figures 92, 93, 94 and 95**

The brake and clutch master cylinders are located under the hood, in the left rear section of the engine compartment. They are made of translucent plastic so that the levels may be checked without removing the tops. The fluid level in both reservoirs should be checked at least every 15,000 miles (24,000 km) or 1 year. The fluid level should be maintained at the upper most mark on the side of the reservoir. Any sudden decrease in the level indicates a possible leaks in the system and should be checked immediately.

When making additions of brake fluid, use only fresh, uncontaminated brake fluid meeting or exceeding DOT 3 standards. Be careful not to spill any fluid on painted surfaces, as it eats the paint. Do not allow the fluid container or the master cylinder reservoir to remain open any longer than necessary; brake fluid absorbs moisture from the air, reducing its effectiveness and causing corrosion in the lines.

Power Steering Pump

FLUID RECOMMENDATIONS

All Tercels use ATF Dexron®II transmission fluid.

Fig. 92 The fluid level should be between the MAX and MIN lines on master cylinder reservoirs

Fig. 93 Clean the top of the master cylinder filler cap before removing it to prevent dirt from entering the system

Fig. 94 Adding brake fluid to the master cylinder reservoir

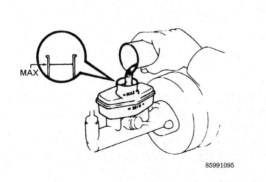

Fig. 95 Fill the master cylinder slowly to prevent the creation of air bubbles in the system

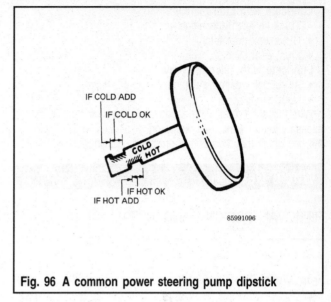

Fig. 96 A common power steering pump dipstick

LEVEL CHECK

▶ **See Figure 96**

The fluid level in the power steering reservoir should be checked at least every 15,000 miles (24,000 km) or 1 year. The vehicle should be parked on level ground, with the engine warm and running at normal idle. Remove the filler cap and check the level on the dipstick; it should be in between the edges of the cross-hatched area on older models or within the **HOT** area of the dipstick on newer models. If the level is low, add Dexron®II type ATF until the proper level is achieved.

Chassis Greasing

Chassis lubrication is limited to greasing the ball joint assemblies on some models every 25,000-30,000 miles (40,200-48,200 km) or 1 year.
1. Remove the screw plug from the ball joint. Install a grease nipple.
2. Using a hand operated grease gun, lubricate the ball joint with NLGI #1 or NLGI #2 molybdenum disulfide lithium based grease.
3. Remove the nipple and reinstall the screw plug.
4. Repeat for the other ball joint(s).

Body Lubrication

There is no set period recommended by Toyota for body lubrication. However, it is a good idea to lubricate the following body points at least once a year, especially in the fall before cold weather.
Lubricate with engine oil:
- Door lock latches
- Door lock rollers
- Door, hood and hinge pivots

Lubricate with Lubriplate:
- Trunk lid latch and hinge
- Glove box door latch
- Front seat slides

Lubricate with silicone spray:
- All rubber weather stripping
- Hood stops

When finished lubricating a body part, be sure that all the excess lubricant has been wiped off, especially in the areas of the car which may come in contact with clothing.

Wheel Bearings

REMOVAL, PACKING AND INSTALLATION

▶ **See Figures 97, 98, 99, 101, 100, 102, 103 and 104**

Front Wheel Drive Models

The rear wheel bearings (inner and outer bearings) should be inspected and serviced frequently in areas of heavy road salt use or extremely rainy areas. To inspect and clean the rear wheel bearings follow this procedure:

1. Raise and safely support the vehicle. Remove the rear tire/wheel assembly.

2. Remove the grease cap (don't distort it) the cotter pin, lock cap and nut.

3. Hold the outside of the hub/drum with your fingers and place the thumbs lightly against the inner edge of the hub/drum. Pull outward gently; the whole assembly will slide off and your thumbs will keep the outer wheel bearing from falling to the ground. The inner bearing (on the other side of the hub/drum) is held in by the grease seal.

4. Place the hub/drum assembly on the work bench. Remove the outer bearing and flat washer. Turn the assembly over and use a seal remover or similar suitable tool to pry out the inner grease seal. A small prytool and a hammer handle (to use as a fulcrum) may be used to carefully pry out the seal. Remove the inner bearing.

➡ **Since this is a maintenance procedure, DO NOT attempt to remove the bearing races from the inside of the hub/drum. The races should be removed only in the event of bearing replacement, refer to Section 8 as necessary.**

5. Clean all the components thoroughly, including the inside of the hub/drum, both bearings and the stub axle on which everything mounts. All traces of the old grease must be removed.

➡ **Use only proper commercial parts cleaners. Do not use gasoline or similar products for cleaning parts. A stiff-bristled parts cleaning brush or even an old, clean paint brush is very handy for cleaning bearings.**

6. After cleaning, allow all the parts to air dry. Never blow bearings dry with compressed air, as bearing damage could occur.

7. Inspect all the parts. Look carefully for any signs of imperfect surfaces, cracking, bluing or looseness. Check the matching surface on which the bearings run; the races should be virtually perfect and free of damage.

To install:

8. Repack the wheel bearings using high quality multi-purpose (MP) grease. Each bearing must be fully packed. The use of a bearing packer is highly recommended but the job can be done by hand.

9. To repack the rear wheel bearings follow this procedure:

a. Place a golf ball-sized lump of MP grease in the palm of your hand.

b. Hold the bearing in your other hand and force the wide side of the bearing into the grease. Use a pushing and scraping motion to force the grease up into the rollers. Continue this until grease oozes out the small side of the bearing.

c. Change the position by which you hold the bearing and repeat the procedure, forcing grease into an untreated area of the bearing.

d. Continue around the bearing until all the rollers are packed solid with grease.

e. Place the bearing on a clean, lint-free rag or towel while greasing other components.

10. Coat the inside of the hub/drum with a liberal layer of grease. Remember that the stub axle comes through here; don't pack it solid.

11. Fill the grease cup about ½ full of MP grease.

12. Install the inner bearing into the hub/drum. Use a new grease seal and install it with a seal installer or equivalent. Do not attempt to use a hammer or drift; the seal may be damaged. Coat the lip of the seal lightly with a bit of MP grease.

13. Fit the outer bearing loosely into place and put the large flat washer over it. Again holding the washer and bearing in place with your thumbs, fit the hub/drum assembly onto the stub axle. Make sure the small tooth on the inside of the bearing washer aligns with the groove in the stub axle.

14. Install the outer bearing and thrust washer.

15. Adjust the preload as follows:

a. Install the adjusting nut onto the axle. Use the torque wrench and set the adjusting nut to 22 ft. lbs. (30 Nm).

b. Turn the hub/drum right and left two or three times each way; this will allow the bearings to seat in the correct position.

c. Loosen the adjusting nut until it can be turned by hand. Confirm that there is absolutely no brake drag.

d. Using a spring scale, measure and make note of the rotation frictional force of the oil seal.

e. Tighten the adjusting nut until the preload is within specification. The preload specification is 0.9-2.2 lbs. in addition to rotation friction force of the oil seal. Insure that the hub rotates smoothly.

16. Install the lock cap, a new cotter pin (always!) and the grease cap. If the cotter pin hole does not line up, first try turning the lock cap to a different position. If this is ineffective, tighten the nut by the smallest possible amount.

17. Check rear brake shoe adjustment. Install the tire/wheel assembly.

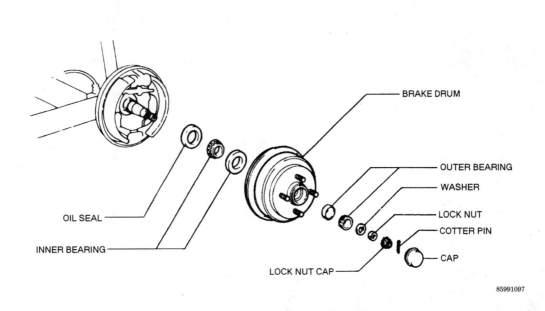

BRAKE DRUM

OUTER BEARING

WASHER

LOCK NUT

COTTER PIN

CAP

OIL SEAL

INNER BEARING

LOCK NUT CAP

85991097

Fig. 97 Exploded view of the rear wheel bearing assembly

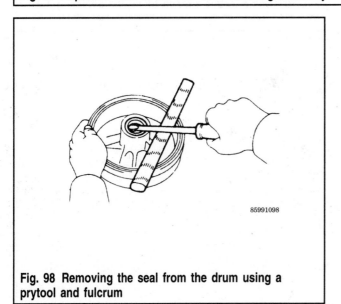

85991098

Fig. 98 Removing the seal from the drum using a prytool and fulcrum

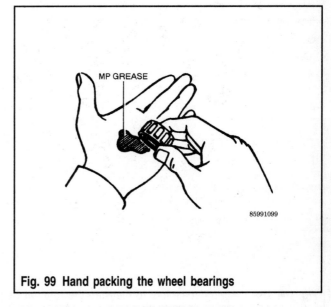

MP GREASE

85991099

Fig. 99 Hand packing the wheel bearings

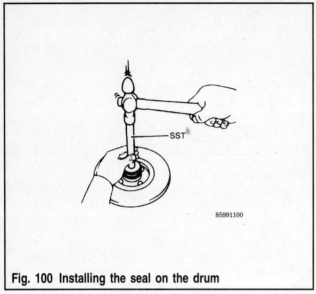

Fig. 100 Installing the seal on the drum

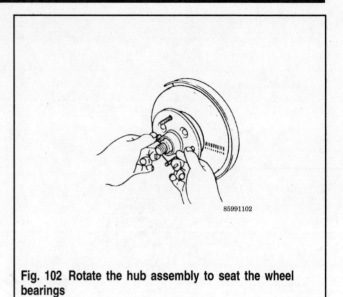

Fig. 102 Rotate the hub assembly to seat the wheel bearings

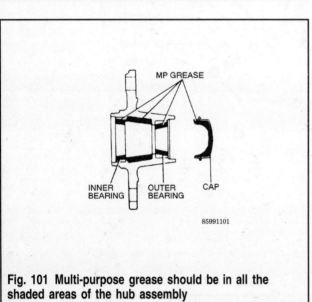

Fig. 101 Multi-purpose grease should be in all the shaded areas of the hub assembly

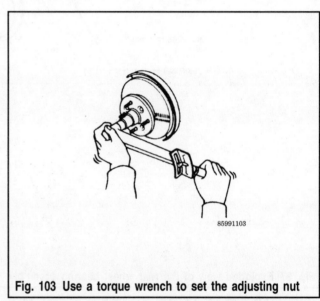

Fig. 103 Use a torque wrench to set the adjusting nut

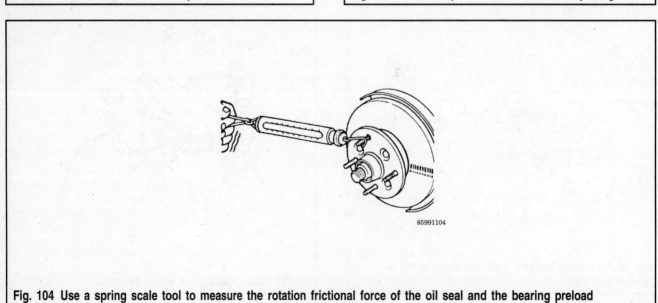

Fig. 104 Use a spring scale tool to measure the rotation frictional force of the oil seal and the bearing preload

JUMP STARTING A DEAD BATTERY

▶ **See Figure 105**

Whenever a vehicle must be jump started, precautions must be followed in order to prevent the possibility of personal injury. Remember that batteries contain a small amount of explosive hydrogen gas which is a byproduct of battery charging. Sparks should always be avoided when working around batteries, especially when attaching jumper cables. To minimize the possibility of accidental sparks, follow the procedure carefully.

❄❄CAUTION

NEVER hook the batteries up in a series circuit or the entire electrical system will go up in smoke, especially the starter!

Jump Starting Precautions

1. Be sure that both batteries are of the same voltage. Most vehicles covered by this manual and most vehicles on the road today utilize a 12 volt charging system.
2. Be sure that both batteries are of the same polarity (have the same terminal, in most cases NEGATIVE grounded).
3. Be sure that the vehicles are not touching or a short could occur.
4. On serviceable batteries, be sure the vent cap holes are not obstructed.
5. Do not smoke or allow sparks anywhere near the batteries.
6. In cold weather, make sure the battery electrolyte is not frozen. This can occur more readily in a battery that has been in a state of discharge.
7. Do not allow electrolyte to contact your skin or clothing.

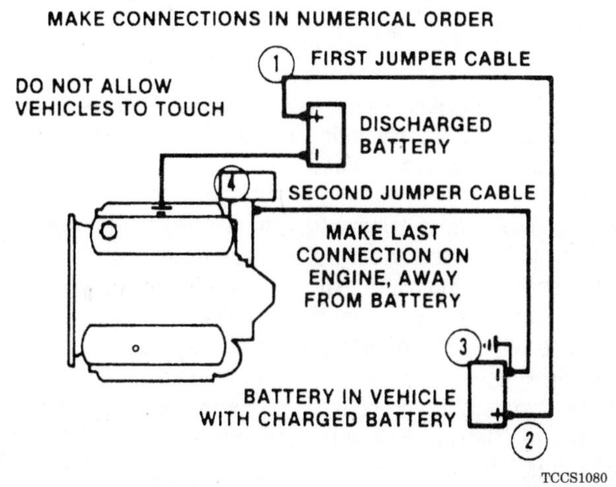

MAKE CONNECTIONS IN NUMERICAL ORDER

DO NOT ALLOW VEHICLES TO TOUCH

① FIRST JUMPER CABLE

DISCHARGED BATTERY

SECOND JUMPER CABLE

MAKE LAST CONNECTION ON ENGINE, AWAY FROM BATTERY

BATTERY IN VEHICLE WITH CHARGED BATTERY

TCCS1080

Fig. 105 Connect the jumper cables to the batteries and engine in the order shown

Jump Starting Procedure

1. Make sure that the voltages of the 2 batteries are the same. Most batteries and charging systems are of the 12 volt variety.
2. Pull the jumping vehicle (with the good battery) into a position so the jumper cables can reach the dead battery and that vehicle's engine. Make sure that the vehicles do NOT touch.
3. Place the transmissions of both vehicles in **NEUTRAL** or **PARK**, as applicable, then firmly set their parking brakes.

➡**If necessary for safety reasons, both vehicle's hazard lights may be operated throughout the entire procedure without significantly increasing the difficulty of jumping the dead battery.**

4. Turn all lights and accessories off on both vehicles. Make sure the ignition switches on both vehicles are turned to the **OFF** position.
5. Cover the battery cell caps with a rag, but do not cover the terminals.
6. Make sure the terminals on both batteries are clean and free of corrosion or proper electrical connection will be impeded. If necessary, clean the battery terminals before proceeding.
7. Identify the positive (+) and negative (-) terminals on both battery posts.
8. Connect the first jumper cable to the positive (+) terminal of the dead battery, then connect the other end of that cable to the positive (+) terminal of the booster (good) battery.
9. Connect one end of the other jumper cable to the negative (-) terminal of the booster battery and the other cable clamp to an engine bolt head, alternator bracket or other solid, metallic point on the dead battery's engine. Try to pick a ground on the engine that is positioned away from the battery in order to minimize the possibility of the 2 clamps touching should one loosen during the procedure. DO NOT connect this clamp to the negative (-) terminal of the bad battery.

❄❄CAUTION

Be very careful to keep the jumper cables away from moving parts (cooling fan, belts, etc.) on both engines.

10. Check to make sure that the cables are routed away from any moving parts, then start the donor vehicle's engine. Run the engine at moderate speed for several minutes to allow the dead battery a chance to receive some initial charge.
11. With the donor vehicle's engine still running slightly above idle, try to start the vehicle with the dead battery. Crank the engine for no more than 10 seconds at a time and let the starter cool for at least 20 seconds between tries. If the vehicle does not start in 3 tries, it is likely that something else is also wrong.
12. Once the vehicle is started, allow it to run at idle for a few seconds to make sure that it is operating properly.
13. Turn on the headlights, heater blower and, if equipped, the rear defroster of both vehicles in order to reduce the se-

verity of voltage spikes and subsequent risk of damage to the vehicles' electrical systems when the cables are disconnected.

14. Carefully disconnect the cables in the reverse order of connection. Start with the negative cable that is attached to the engine ground, then the negative cable on the donor bat-tery. Disconnect the positive cable from the donor battery and finally, disconnect the positive cable from the formerly dead battery. Be careful when disconnecting the cables from the positive terminals not to allow the alligator clips to touch any metal on either vehicle or a short and sparks will occur.

TRAILER TOWING

→Always consult with your Toyota dealer about trailer weight and special equipment. Some vehicles are not recommended to tow a trailer; some vehicles have different weight limits between manual and automatic transaxle types. Please consult your local Toyota dealer for specific advice regarding hitch assembly. Towing a trailer qualifies as severe duty for the tow vehicle. Maintenance must be performed more frequently.

General Recommendations

♦ See Figures 106 and 107

Your vehicle was primarily designed to carry passengers and cargo. It is important to remember that towing a trailer will place additional loads on your vehicle's engine, drive train, steering, braking and other systems. However, if you find it necessary to tow a trailer, using the proper equipment is a must.

Local laws may require specific equipment such as trailer brakes or fender mounted mirrors. Check with your local authorities.

The trailer hitch assembly should conform to all applicable laws and be sufficient for the maximum trailer load.

Almost all trailers now come equipped with rear and side lighting. A wiring harness must be installed to connect the automotive lighting and brake light systems to the trailer. Any reputable hitch installer can perform this installation. You can also install the harnesses, but great care must be paid to matching the correct wires during the installation. Each circuit must be wired individually for taillights, brake lights, right and left turn signals and in many cases, reverse lights. If the trailer is equipped with electric brakes, the wiring for this circuit should be installed at the same time as the lighting harness. Remember that the additional lighting may exceed the present fuse rating in the car's fusebox; an upgrade may be necessary.

Cooling System

One of the most common, if not the most common, problems associated with trailer towing is engine overheating.

The cooling system should be checked frequently and main-tained in top notch condition. If the engine temperature gauge indicates overheating, particularly on long grades, immediately turn off the air conditioner (if in use), pull off the road and stop in a safe location. Do not attempt to "limp in" with a hot motor — you may cause severe damage.

Transmission

The increased load of a trailer causes an increase in the temperature of the automatic transmission fluid. Heat is the

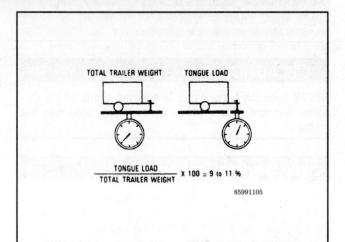

Fig. 106 The trailer cargo load should be distributed so that the tongue load is 9-11 percent of the total trailer weight, not exceeding the maximum of 150 lbs.

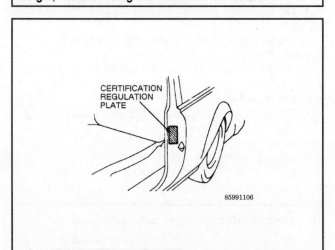

Fig. 107 The gross vehicle weight rating (GVWR) must not be exceeded. This rating can be found on the certification regulation plate

worst enemy of an automatic transmission. As the temperature of the fluid increases, the life of the fluid decreases.

It is essential, therefore, that you install an automatic trans-mission cooler or supplement the one already present.

The cooler, which consists of a multi-tube, finned heat ex-changer, is usually installed in front of the radiator or air condi-tioning compressor, and hooked inline with the transmission cooler tank inlet line. Follow the cooler manufacturer's installa-tion instructions.

Select a cooler of at least adequate capacity, based upon the combined gross weights of the car and trailer.

Cooler manufacturers recommend that you use an aftermarket cooler in addition to the present cooling tank in your radiator.

➡**A transmission cooler can sometimes cause slow or harsh shifting in the transmission during cold weather, until the fluid has a chance to come up to normal operating temperature. Some coolers can be purchased with or retrofitted with a temperature bypass valve which will allow fluid flow through the cooler only when the fluid has reached operating temperature or above.**

Handling A Trailer

Towing a trailer with ease and safety requires a certain amount of skill that can only be gained through experience. Many trailer accidents occur because the driver forgot some of the basics.

- When loading the trailer, keep about 60 percent of the weight forward of the axle. This will prevent the trailer from trying to pass the car during cornering.
- Always perform a walk-around check of all the lighting before pulling out.
- Check the tire pressure and condition on both the car and trailer frequently. Underinflated and overinflated tires are a hazard.
- After connecting the trailer, observe the car for any extreme nose-up or nose-down attitudes. If the car is not approximately level with the trailer connected, rebalance the load in the trailer.

- Stopping distances are increased dramatically. Allow plenty of room and anticipate stops. Sudden braking may jackknife the trailer or throw the car into a skid.
- Accelerate slowly and smoothly. Jerky driving will cause increased wear on the drive line.
- Avoid sharp turns. The trailer will always turn "inside" the car; allow plenty of room.
- Crosswinds and rough roads decrease stability. Know when you're about to be passed by a large vehicle and prepare for it.
- If swaying begins, grip the steering wheel firmly and hold the vehicle straight ahead. Reduce speed gradually without using the brake. If you make NO extreme corrections in brakes, throttle or steering, the car and trailer will stabilize quickly.
- Passing requires much greater distances for acceleration. Plan ahead. Remember to allow for the length of the trailer when pulling back in.
- Use a lower gear to descend long grades. Slow down before downshifting.
- Avoid riding the brake. This will overheat the brakes and reduce their efficiency.
- When parking the combination, always apply the parking brake and place blocks under the trailer wheels. A heavy trailer may literally drag the car down a grade. Don't forget to remove the chocks before leaving.
- Backing up with a trailer is a skill to be practiced before it is needed. Find a large open area (get permission if necessary) and spend at least an hour learning how to do it.

TOWING THE VEHICLE

▶ **See Figures 108, 109 and 110**

The absolute best way to have the car towed or transported is on a flat-bed or rollback transporter. These units are becoming more common and are very useful for moving disabled vehicles quickly. Most vehicles have lower bodywork and undertrays which can be easily damaged by the sling of a conventional tow truck; an operator unfamiliar with your particular model can cause severe damage to the suspension or drive line by hooking up chains and J-hooks incorrectly. If a flatbed is not available (you should specifically request one), the car may be towed by a hoist or conventional tow vehicle.

Front wheel drive cars with automatic transaxles must be towed with the drive wheels off the ground. FWD cars with a manual transaxles can be towed with either end up in the air or with all four wheels on the ground. You need only remember that the transaxle must be in Neutral, the parking brake must be off and the ignition switch must be in the **ACC** position. The steering column lock is not strong enough to hold the front wheels straight under towing.

On 4WD vehicles with manual transaxles, tow the vehicle with the rear wheels on the ground. (If the vehicle is lifted

from the rear use a towing dolly under the front wheels) Release the parking brake and put the transaxle in Neutral. The rear drive control lever must be in FWD.

On 4WD vehicles with automatic transaxles, tow with the rear wheels on the ground. Release the parking brake and put the transmission into Neutral. Never tow a vehicle with a automatic transaxle from the rear or with the front wheels (drive wheels) on ground.

Most vehicles have conveniently located tie-down hooks at the front of the vehicle. These make ideal locations to secure a rope or chain for towing the car or extracting it from an off-road excursion. The vehicle may only be towed on hard surfaced roads and only in a normal or forward direction.

If the vehicle is being pulled with all four wheels on the ground, the driver must be in the vehicle to control it. Before towing, the parking brake must be released and the transmission put in neutral. DO NOT flat tow the vehicle if the brakes, steering, axles, suspension or drive line is damaged. If the engine is not running, the power assists for the steering and brakes will not be operating. Steering and braking will require more time and much more effort without the assist.

TIE DOWN TABS

85991107

Fig. 108 Tie down locations on the Tercel

85991108

Fig. 109 FWD towing procedure, note the last method cannot be used for automatic transaxle vehicles

PRECAUTIONS WHEN TOWING FULL-TIME 4WD VEHICLES

1. Use one of the methods shown below to tow the vehicle.
2. When there is trouble with the chassis and drivetrain, use method ① (flat bed truck) or method ② (sling type toe truck with dollies)
3. Recommended Methods: No. ① , ② or ③
   Emergency Method: No. ④

Type of Transaxle / Towing Method	Manual Transaxle			Automatic Transaxle			
	Parking Brake	T/M Shift Lever Position	Center Diff.	Parking Brake	T/M Shift Lever Position	Center Diff. Control Switch	Mode Select Lever on Transaxle
① Flat Bed Truck	Applied	1st Gear	Free or Lock (Center Differential Control Switch "ON" or "OFF")	Applied	"P" range	"AUTO" or "OFF"	Free (Normal Driving) No Special Operation Necessary
② Sling-Type Tow Truck with Dollies							
③ Sling-Type Two Truck (Front wheels must be able to rotate freely)	Released	Neutral	Free (Center Differential Control Switch "OFF")	Release	"N" range	"OFF"	↑
④ Towing with a Rope	Released	Neutral	Free (Center Differential Control Switch "OFF")	Released	"N" range	"OFF"	↑

NOTE: Do not tow the vehicle at a speed faster than 18 mph (30 km/h) or a distance greater than 50 miles (80 km).

NOTE: Do not use any towing methods other than those shown above.
For example, the towing method shown below is dangerous, so do not use it.

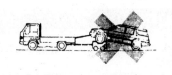

During towing with this towing method, there is a danger of the drivetrain heating up and causing breakdown, or of the front wheels flying off the dolly.

85991109

Fig. 110 Four wheel drive towing procedures

JACKING

▶ See Figures 111 and 112

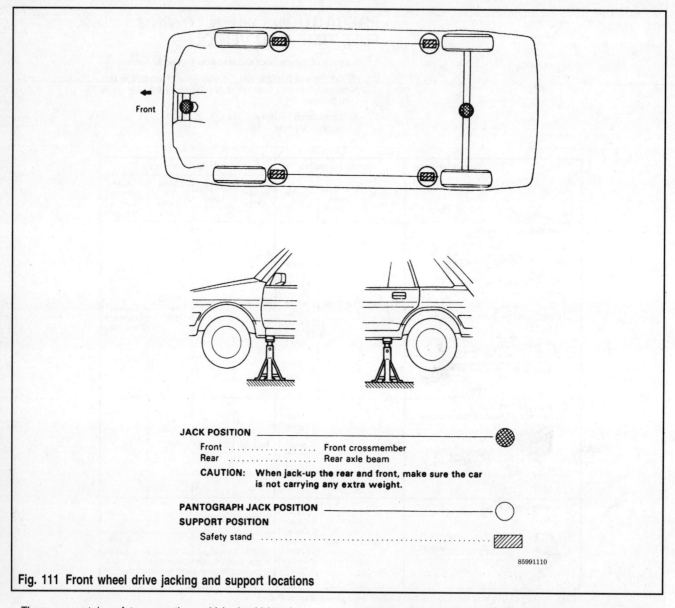

JACK POSITION
Front .... Front crossmember
Rear .... Rear axle beam
CAUTION: When jack-up the rear and front, make sure the car
is not carrying any extra weight.

PANTOGRAPH JACK POSITION
SUPPORT POSITION
Safety stand ....

85991110

Fig. 111 Front wheel drive jacking and support locations

There are certain safety precautions which should be observed when jacking the vehicle. They are as follows:

1. Always jack the car on a level surface.

2. Set the parking brake, and block the wheels which aren't being raised. This will keep the car from rolling off the jack.

3. During emergency tire changes, at least block the wheel diagonally opposite the one which is being raised.

➡**The tool kit which is supplied with most Toyota passenger cars includes a wheel block.**

4. If the vehicle is being raised in order to work underneath it, support it with jackstands. Do not place the jackstands

against the sheet metal panels beneath the car, as the panels could become distorted.

❊❊CAUTION

Do not work beneath a vehicle supported only by a tire changing jack.

5. Do not use a bumper jack to raise the vehicle; the bumpers are not designed for this purpose.

6. Do not use cinder blocks to support a vehicle. They could crumble with little or no warning, dropping the vehicle and possibly causing serious injury.

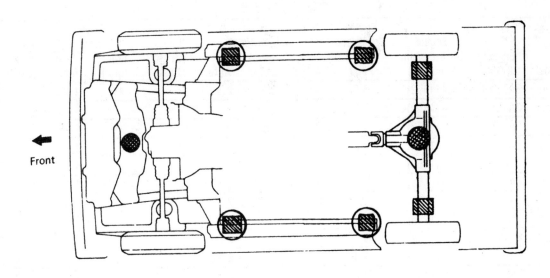

JACK POSITION —————————————————⬤

      Front .... Center of crossmember

      Rear .... Center of rear axle housing

PANTOGRAPH JACK POSITION ———————————○

SUPPORT POSITION

      Safety stand .... ▨

85991111

Fig. 112 Four wheel drive jacking and support locations

CAPACITIES

Year	Model	Engine ID/VIN	Engine Displacement Liters (cc)	Engine Crankcase with Filter	Transmission (pts.)			Transfer Case	Drive Axle		Fuel Tank (gal.)	Cooling System (qts.)
					4-Spd	5-Spd	Auto.		Front (qts.)	Rear (qts.)		
1984	Tercel	3A, 3A-C	1.4 (1452)	3.5	3.5	3.5①	2.3②	—	1③	1.1④	13.2	5.6
1985	Tercel	3A, 3A-C	1.4 (1452)	3.5	3.5	3.5①	2.3②	—	1③	1.1④	13.2	5.6
1986	Tercel	3A, 3A-C	1.4 (1452)	3.5	3.5	3.5①	2.3②	—	1③	1.1④	13.2	5.6
1987	Tercel	3A, 3A-C	1.4 (1452)	3.5	2.5⑦	2.5⑦	2.6⑤	—	1.5③⑥	1.1④	13.2	5.6
		3E	1.5 (1456)	3.4	2.5⑦	2.5⑦	2.6⑤	—	1.5③⑥	1.1④	11.9	5.3
1988	Tercel	3A, 3A-C	1.4 (1452)	3.5	2.5⑦	2.5⑦	2.6⑤	—	1.5③⑥	1.1④	13.2	5.6
		3E	1.5 (1456)	3.4	2.5⑦	2.5⑦	2.6⑤	—	1.5③⑥	1.1④	11.9	5.3
1989	Tercel	3E	1.5 (1456)	3.4	2.5	2.5	2.6	—	1.5③	—	11.9	5.5
1990	Tercel	3E	1.5 (1456)	3.4	2.5	2.5	2.6	—	1.5③	—	11.9	5.5
		3E-E	1.5 (1456)	3.4	2.5	2.5	2.6	—	1.5③	—	11.9	5.9
1991	Tercel	3E-E	1.5 (1456)	3.4	2.5	2.5	2.6	—	1.5③	—	11.9	5.5
1992	Tercel	3E-E	1.5 (1456)	3.4	2.5	2.5	2.6	—	1.5③	—	11.9	5.5
1993	Tercel	3E-E	1.5 (1456)	3.4	2.5	2.5	2.6	—	1.5③	—	11.9	5.5
1994	Tercel	3E-E	1.5 (1456)	3.4	2.5	2.5	2.6	—	1.5③	—	11.9	5.5

① Four Wheel Drive—4.1, includes transfer case
② Four Wheel Drive—4.4
③ Automatic Transaxle only
④ Four Wheel Drive only
⑤ 2.3 on FWD Wagon, 4.4 on 4WD Wagon
⑥ 1 on Automatic Transaxle Wagon
⑦ 3.5 on FWD Wagon, 4.1 on 4WD Wagon

85991c04

MAINTENANCE SCHEDULES

MAINTENANCE SCHEDULE
(3A-C Engine)

Maintenance operations: A = Check and/or adjust if necessary;
R = Replace, change or lubricate;
I = Inspect and correct or replace if necessary

NORMAL CONDITION SCHEDULE

System	Service interval (Odometer reading or months, whichever comes first) / Maintenance items	Maintenance services beyond 60,000 miles (96,000 km) should be performed at the same intervals shown in each maintenance schedule.					
	Miles x 1,000	10	20	30	40	50	60
	Km x 1,000	16	32	48	64	80	96
	Months	12	24	36	48	60	72
ENGINE	Valve clearance ★ *			A			A
	Drive belts(1)			I			I
	Engine oil and oil filter ★ *	R	R	R	R	R	R
	Engine coolant(2)						R
	Exhaust pipes and mountings			I			I
FUEL	Idle speed and fast idle speed *(3)			A			
	Throttle positioner system (3)			A			
	Air filter ★ *			R			R
	Fuel line and connections			I			I
	Fuel filler cap gasket						R
IGNITION	Spark plugs ★ *			R			R
EVAP	Charcoal canister						I
BRAKES	Brake lining and drums		I		I		I
	Brake pads and discs		I		I		I
	Brake line pipes and hoses		I		I		I
CHASSIS	Steering linkage		I		I		I
	Drive shaft boots		I		I		I
	Ball joints and dust covers		I		I		I
	Automatic transmission, manual transmission, differential and steering gear housing oil (5)		I		I		I
	Rear wheel bearing grease (ex. wagon) (4)				R		
	Bolts and nuts on chassis and body		I		I		I

Maintenance services indicated by a star (★) or asterisk (*) are required under the terms of the Emission Control Systems Warranty. See Owner's Guide for complete warranty information.

★   For vehicles sold in California
*   For vehicles sold outside California

NOTE:
(1)   After 60,000 miles (96,000 km) or 72 months, inspect every 10,000 miles (16,000 km) or 12 months.
(2)   After 60,000 miles (96,000 km) or 72 months, replace every 30,000 miles (48,000 km) or 36 months.
(3)   After 30,000 miles (48,000 km) or 36 months, adjustment is not necessary.
(4)   Change every 40,000 miles (64,000 km) or 48 months.
(5)   Inspect the steering gear housing for oil leakage only.

85991112

Fig. 113 Normal condition maintenance schedule on 3A-C engines

Follow the severe condition schedule if vehicle is operated mainly under one or more of the following severe conditions:

- Towing a trailer, using a camper or car top carrier.
- Repeat short trips less than 5 miles (8 km) and outside temperatures remain below freezing.
- Extensive idling such as police, taxi or door-to-door delivery use.
- Operating on dusty, rough, muddy or salt spread roads.

SEVERE CONDITION SCHEDULE

Service interval (Odometer reading or months, whichever comes first)

Maintenance services beyond 60,000 miles (96,000 km) should be performed at the same intervals shown in each maintenance schedule.

System	Maintenance items	5	10	15	20	25	30	35	40	45	50	55	60
(Miles x 1,000)		5	10	15	20	25	30	35	40	45	50	55	60
(Km x 1,000)		8	16	24	32	40	48	56	64	72	80	88	96
(Months)		6	12	18	24	30	36	42	48	54	60	66	72
ENGINE	Timing belt												(1)R
	Valve clearance ★ *						A						A
	Drive belts (2)						I						I
	Engine oil and oil filter ★ *	R	R	R	R	R	R	R	R	R	R	R	R
	Engine coolant (3)												R
	Exhaust pipes and mountings		I				I			I			I
FUEL	Idle speed and fast idle speed * (4)						A						
	Throttle positioner system						A						
	Air filter ★ * (6)	I	I	I	I	I	R	I	I	I	I	I	R
	Fuel line and connections						I						I
	Fuel filler cap gasket												R
IGNITION	Spark plugs ★ *						R						R
EVAP	Charcoal canister												I
BRAKES	Brake lining and drums		I		I		I		I		I		I
	Brake pads and discs		I		I		I		I		I		I
	Brake line pipes and hoses				I				I				I
CHASSIS	Steering linkage		I		I		I		I		I		I
	Drive shaft boots		I		I		I		I		I		I
	Ball joints and dust covers		I		I		I		I		I		I
	Automatic transmission, manual transmission, differential and steering gear housing oil (8)				R				R				R
	Rear wheel bearing grease (ex. wagon) (5)									R			
	Bolts and nuts on chassis and body (7)		I				I			I			I

Maintenance services indicated by a star (★) or asterisk (*) are required under the terms of the Emission Control Systems Warranty. See Owner's Guide for complete warranty information.

- ★ For vehicles sold in California
- * For vehicles sold outside California

NOTE:
(1) For the vehicles frequently idled for extensive periods and/or driven for long distance at low speeds such as taxi, police and door-to-door delivery, it is recommended to change at 60,000 miles (96,000 km).
(2) After 60,000 miles (96,000 km) or 72 months, inspect every 10,000 miles (16,000 km) or 12 months.
(3) After 60,000 miles (96,000 km) or 72 months, replace every 30,000 miles (48,000 km) or 36 months.
(4) After 30,000 miles (48,000 km) or 36 months, adjustment is not necessary.
(5) Change every 45,000 miles (72,000 km) or 54 months.
(6) Applicable when operating mainly on dusty roads. If not, follow the normal condition schedule.
(7) Applicable when operating mainly on rough and/or muddy roads. If not, follow the normal condition schedule.
(8) Inspect the steering gear housing for oil leakage only.

85991113

Fig. 114 Severe condition maintenance schedule on 3A-C engines

MAINTENANCE SCHEDULE

Maintenance operations: A = Check and adjust if necessary;
R = Replace, change or lubricate;
I = Inspect and correct or replace if necessary

SCHEDULE A

CONDITION

- Towing a trailer, using a camper or car top carrier.
- Repeat short trips less than 5 miles (8 km) and outside temperatures remain below freezing.
- Extensive idling and/or low speed driving for a long distance such as police, taxi or door-to-door delivery use.
- Operating on dusty, rough, muddy or salt spread roads.

System	Service interval (Odometer reading or months, whichever comes first) / Maintenance items	Maintenance services beyond 60,000 miles (96,000 km) should be performed at the same intervals shown in each maintenance schedule.											
	Miles x 1,000	5	10	15	20	25	30	35	40	45	50	55	60
	Km x 1,000	8	16	24	32	40	48	56	64	72	80	88	96
	Months	6	12	18	24	30	36	42	48	54	60	66	72
ENGINE	Timing belt						R(1)						
	Valve clearance ★						A						A
	Drive belts (2)												I
	Engine oil and oil filter ★	R	R	R	R	R	R	R	R	R	R	R	R
	Engine coolant (3)												R
	Exhaust pipes and mountings			I			I			I			I
FUEL	Idle speed and fast idle speed (4)						A						
	Throttle positioner system (4)						A						
	Air filter ★ (6)	I	I	I	I	I	R	I	I	I	I	I	R
	Fuel lines and connections						I						I
	Fuel tank cap gasket												R
IGNITION	Spark plugs ★ *						R						R
EVAP	Charcoal canister												I
BRAKES	Brake linings and drums		I		I		I		I		I		I
	Brake pads and discs		I		I		I		I		I		I
	Brake line pipes and hoses				I				I				I
CHASSIS	Steering linkage (7)		I		I		I		I		I		I
	Drive shaft boots		I		I		I		I		I		I
	Ball joints and dust covers		I		I		I		I		I		I
	Automatic transaxle, manual transaxle, differential and steering gear housing oil (8)				R				R				R
	Rear wheel bearings (5)								R				
	Bolts and nuts on chassis and body (7)		I		I		I		I		I		I

Maintenance services indicated by a star (★) or asterisk (*) are required under the terms of the Emission Control Systems Warranty. See Owner's Guide or Warranty Booklet for complete warranty information.

★ For vehicles sold in California
* For vehicles sold outside California

NOTE:
(1) For vehicles frequently idled for extensive periods and/or driven for long distance at low speeds such as taxi, police and door-to-door delivery, it is recommended to change at 60,000 miles (96,000 km).
(2) After 60,000 miles (96,000 km) or 72 months, inspect every 10,000 miles (16,000 km) or 12 months.
(3) After 60,000 miles (96,000 km) or 72 months, change every 30,000 miles (48,000 km) or 36 months.
(4) After 30,000 miles (48,000 km) or 36 months, adjustment is not necessary.
(5) Change every 40,000 miles (64,000 km) or 48 months.
(6) Applicable when operating mainly on dusty roads. If not, follow the SCHEDULE B.
(7) Applicable when operating mainly on rough and/or muddy roads. If not, follow the SCHEDULE B.
(8) For the steering gear housing, inspect for oil leakage only.

85991114

Fig. 115 Severe condition maintenance schedule on 3E engines

SCHEDULE B
CONDITION

Conditions other than those listed for SCHEDULE A

System	Service interval (Odometer reading or months, whichever comes first) / Maintenance items	Maintenance services beyond 60,000 miles (96,000 km) should be performed at the same intervals shown in each maintenance schedule.					
		Miles x 1,000	10	20	30	40	50	60
		Km x 1,000	16	32	48	64	80	96
		Months	12	24	36	48	60	72
ENGINE	Valve clearance ★				A			A
	Drive belts(1)							I
	Engine oil and oil filter ★		R	R	R	R	R	R
	Engine coolant(2)							R
	Exhaust pipes and mountings				I			I
FUEL	Idle speed and fast idle speed (3)				A			
	Throttle positioner system (3)				A			
	Air filter ★				R			R
	Fuel lines and connections				I			I
	Fuel tank cap gasket							R
IGNITION	Spark plugs ★ *				R			R
EVAP	Charcoal canister							I
BRAKES	Brake linings and drums			I		I		I
	Brake pads and discs			I		I		I
	Brake line pipes and hoses			I		I		I
CHASSIS	Steering linkage			I		I		I
	Drive shaft boots			I		I		I
	Ball joints and dust covers			I		I		I
	Automatic transaxle, manual transaxle, differential and steering gear housing oil			I		I		I
	Rear wheel bearing grease (4)					R		
	Bolts and nuts on chassis and body			I		I		I

Maintenance services indicated by a star (★) or asterisk (*) are required under the terms of the Emission Control Systems Warranty. See Owner's Guide or Warranty Booklet for complete warranty information.

 ★ For vehicles sold in California
 * For vehicles sold outside California

NOTE:
(1) After 60,000 miles (96,000 km) or 72 months, inspect every 10,000 miles (16,000 km) or 12 months.
(2) After 60,000 miles (96,000 km) or 72 months, change every 30,000 miles (48,000 km) or 36 months.
(3) After 30,000 miles (48,000 km) or 36 months, adjustment is not necessary.
(4) Change every 40,000 miles (64,000 km) or 48 months.

85991115

Fig. 116 Normal condition maintenance schedule on 3E engines

MAINTENANCE SCHEDULE

SCHEDULE A

CONDITIONS:

Maintenance operation: A = Check and adjust if necessary;
R = Replace, change or lubricate;
I = Inspect and correct or replace if necessary

- Towing a trailer, using a camper or car top carrier.
- Repeated short trips of less than 5 miles (8 km) and outside temperature remains below freezing.
- Extensive idling and/or low speed driving for long distances such as police, taxi or door-to-door delivery use.
- Operating on dusty, rough, muddy or salt spread roads.

Maintenance services beyond 60,000 miles (96,000 km) should continue to be performed as the same intervals shown in each maintenance schedule.

Service interval (Odometer reading or months, whichever comes first)

Miles × 1,000 → 3.75 | 7.5 | 11.25 | 15 | 18.75 | 22.5 | 26.25 | 30 | 33.75 | 37.5 | 41.25 | 45 | 48.75 | 52.5 | 56.25 | 60
km × 1,000 → 6 | 12 | 18 | 24 | 30 | 36 | 42 | 48 | 54 | 60 | 66 | 72 | 78 | 84 | 90 | 96

System	Maintenance items	3.75	7.5	11.25	15	18.75	22.5	26.25	30	33.75	37.5	41.25	45	48.75	52.5	56.25	60	Months
ENGINE	Timing belt (1)																R	–
	Valve clearance★								A								A	A: Every 36 months
	Drive belts	I: First period, 60,000 miles (96,000 km) or 72 months																I: After that, every 7,500 miles (12,000 km) or 12 months
	Engine oil and oil filter★	R	R	R	R	R	R	R	R	R	R	R	R	R	R	R	R	R: Every 6 months
	Engine coolant	R: First period, 45,000 miles (72,000 km) or 36 months																R: After that, every 30,000 miles (48,000 km) or 24 months
	Exhaust pipes and mountings			I			I				I				I			I: Every 24 months
FUEL	Idle speed	A: First period, 7,500 miles (12,000 km) or 12 months, and 15,000 miles (24,000 km) or 24 months																A: After that, every 15,000 miles (24,000 km) or 24 months
	Air filter★ (2)	I	I	I	I	I	I	I	R	I	I	I	I	I	I	I	R	I: Every 6 months / R: Every 36 months
	Fuel lines and connections (3)								I								I	I: Every 36 months
	Fuel tank cap gasket																R	R: Every 72 months
IGNITION	Spark plugs★•								R								R	R: Every 36 months
EVAP	Charcoal canister																I	I: Every 72 months

Maintenance services beyond 60,000 miles (96,000 km) should continue to be performed as the same intervals shown in each maintenance schedule.

Service interval (Odometer reading or months, whichever comes first)

Miles × 1,000 → 3.75 | 7.5 | 11.25 | 15 | 18.75 | 22.5 | 26.25 | 30 | 33.75 | 37.5 | 41.25 | 45 | 48.75 | 52.5 | 56.25 | 60
km × 1,000 → 6 | 12 | 18 | 24 | 30 | 36 | 42 | 48 | 54 | 60 | 66 | 72 | 78 | 84 | 90 | 96

System	Maintenance items	3.75	7.5	11.25	15	18.75	22.5	26.25	30	33.75	37.5	41.25	45	48.75	52.5	56.25	60	Months
BRAKES	Brake linings and drums		I		I		I		I		I		I		I		I	I: Every 12 months
	Brake pads and discs		I		I		I		I		I		I		I		I	I: Every 12 months
	Brake line pipes and hoses				I				I				I				I	I: Every 24 months
CHASSIS	Steering linkage		I		I		I		I		I		I		I		I	I: Every 12 months
	Ball joints and dust covers		I		I		I		I		I		I		I		I	I: Every 12 months
	Drive shaft boots		I		I		I		I		I		I		I		I	I: Every 12 months
	Automatic transmission, manual transmission and differential oil				R				R				R				R	R: Every 24 months
	Steering gear housing oil (4)				I				I				I				I	I: Every 24 months
	Rear wheel bearing								R								R	R: Every 48 months
	Bolts on body (5)		I		I		I		I		I		I		I		I	I: Every 12 months

★ or * mark indicates maintenance which is part of the Emission Control System. The warranty period is in accordance with the owner's guide or the warranty booklet.

  ★ : California specification vehicles.

  * : Vehicles other than California specification vehicles.

NOTE:

(1) Applicable to vehicle operated under conditions of extensive idling and/or low speed driving for long distances such as police, taxi or door-to-door delivery use.

(2) Applicable when operating mainly on dusty roads.

(3) Includes inspection of vapor vent system.

(4) Check for oil leaks from steering gear box.

(5) Applicable only when operating mainly on rough, muddy roads. The applicable parts are listed below. For other usage conditions, refer to SCHEDULE B.

  - Bolts for sheet installation.

85991116

Fig. 117 Severe condition maintenance schedule on 3E-E engines

SCHEDULE B
CONDITIONS:

Conditions other than those listed for SCHEDULE A.

System	Maintenance items	Service interval (Use odometer reading or months, whichever comes first)									Months
		Maintenance services beyond 60,000 miles (96,000 km) should continue to be performed as the same intervals shown for each maintenance schedule.									
		Miles x 1,000	7.5	15	22.5	30	37.5	45	52.5	60	
		km x 1,000	12	24	36	48	60	72	84	96	
ENGINE	Valve clearance★					A				A	A: Every 36 months
	Drive belts	I: First period, 60,000 miles (96,000 km) or 72 months I: After that, every 7,500 miles (12,000 km) or 12 months									
	Engine oil and oil filter★		R	R	R	R	R	R	R	R	R: Every 12 months
	Engine coolant	R: First period, 45,000 miles (72,000 km) or 36 months R: After that, every 30,000 miles (48,000 km) or 24 months									
	Exhaust pipes and mountings					I				I	I: Every 36 months
FUEL	Idle speed	A: First period, 7,500 miles (12,000 km) or 12 months, and 15,000 miles (24,000 km) or 24 months A: After that, every 15,000 miles (24,000 km) or 24 months									
	Air filter★					R				R	R: Every 36 months
	Fuel lines and connections (1)					I				I	I: Every 36 months
	Fuel tank cap gasket									R	R: Every 72 months
IGNITION	Spark plugs★*					R				R	R: Every 36 months
EVAP	Charcoal canister									I	I: Every 72 months

System	Maintenance items	Service interval (Use odometer reading or months, whichever comes first)									Months
		Maintenance services beyond 60,000 miles (96,000 km) should continue to be performed as the same intervals shown for each maintenance schedule.									
		Miles x 1,000	7.5	15	22.5	30	37.5	45	52.5	60	
		km x 1,000	12	24	36	48	60	72	84	96	
BRAKES	Brake linings and drums			I		I		I		I	I: Every 24 months
	Brake pads and discs			I		I		I		I	I: Every 24 months
	Brake line pipes and hoses			I		I		I		I	I: Every 24 months
CHASSIS	Steering linkage			I		I		I		I	I: Every 24 months
	Ball joints and dust covers			I		I		I		I	I: Every 24 months
	Drive shaft boots			I		I		I		I	I: Every 24 months
	Automatic transmission, manual transmission and differential oil (2)			I		I		I		I	I: Every 24 months
	Steering gear housing oil (3)			I		I		I		I	I: Every 24 months
	Rear wheel bearing					R				R	R: Every 48 months
	Bolts on body (4)			I		I		I		I	I: Every 24 months

★ or * mark indicates maintenance which is part of the warranty conditions for the Emission Control System. The warranty period is in accordance with the owner's guide or the warranty booklet.

   ★ : California specification vehicles.

   * : Vehicles other than California specification vehicles.

NOTE:

(1) Includes inspection of vapor vent system.

(2) Check for oil leaks.

(3) Check for oil leaks from steering gear box.

(4) The applicable parts are listed below.

   ● Bolts for sheet installation.

85991117

Fig. 118 Normal condition maintenance schedule on 3E-E engines

2

ENGINE PERFORMANCE AND TUNE-UP

FIRING ORDER

♦ See Figure 1

➡ To avoid confusion, spark plug wires should be replaced one at a time. The firing order for all 4-cylinder engines is 1-3-4-2. The No. 1 spark plug is always located closest to the front of the engine (water pump or timing belt assembly). The distributor tower terminal cap usually is marked for the No. 1 location.

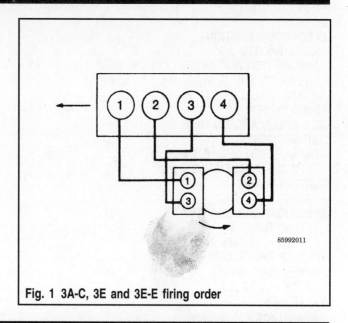

Fig. 1 3A-C, 3E and 3E-E firing order

TUNE-UP PROCEDURES

Spark Plug Wires

REMOVAL & INSTALLATION

♦ See Figures 2 and 3

When installing new spark plug wires (cables), replace them ONE AT A TIME to avoid mix-ups. Start by replacing the longest one first. Remove the wire from the end of the spark plug by grasping the wire by the rubber boot. If the boot sticks to the plug, remove it by twisting and pulling at the same time. Do not pull the wire itself or you will damage the core. Install the boot firmly over the spark plug. Route the wire over the same path as the original. Insert the nipple firmly into the tower on the cap or the coil.

TESTING

♦ See Figure 4

At every tune-up, visually inspect the spark plug cables for burns, cuts, or breaks in the insulation. Check the boots and the nipples on the distributor cap and coil. Replace any damaged wiring.

Every 30,000 miles or so, the resistance of the wires may be checked with an ohmmeter. Wires with excessive resistance will cause misfiring, and may make the engine difficult to start in damp weather. Generally the useful life of the cables is 30,000-50,000 miles.

To check resistance, remove the distributor cap, leaving the wires attached. Connect one lead of an ohmmeter to an electrode within the cap; connect the other lead to the corresponding spark plug terminal (remove it from the plug for this test). Replace any wire which shows a resistance over $25,000\Omega$.

Test the high tension lead from the coil by connecting the ohmmeter between the center contact in the distributor cap and either of the primary terminals of the coil. If resistance is more than $25,000\Omega$, remove the cable from the coil and check the resistance of the cable alone. Anything over $15,000\Omega$ is cause for replacement. It should be remembered that resistance is also a function of length; the longer the cable, the greater the resistance. Thus, if the cables on your car are longer than the factory originals, resistance will be higher, quite possibly outside these limits.

Spark Plugs

♦ See Figure 5

Spark plugs ignite the air and fuel mixture in the cylinder as the piston reaches the top of the compression stroke. The controlled explosion that results forces the piston down, turning the crankshaft and the rest of the drive train.

The average life of a normal, spark plug (platinum plugs 60,000 mile change interval) is about 15,000-20,000 miles, although manufacturers are now claiming spark plug lives of up to 30,000 miles or more. This is, however, dependent on a number of factors: the mechanical condition of the engine, the type of fuel, the driving conditions and the driver.

Manufacturers are now required to certify that the spark plugs in their engines will meet emission specifications for 30,000 miles if all maintenance is performed properly. Certain types of plugs can be certified even beyond this point.

When you remove the spark plugs, check their condition. They are a good indicator of the condition of the engine. When a regular spark plug is functioning normally or, more accurately, when the plug is installed in an engine that is functioning properly, the plugs can be taken out, cleaned, gapped, and reinstalled without doing the engine any harm. When, and if, a spark plug fouls and being to misfire, you will have to investi-

GASOLINE ENGINE TUNE-UP SPECIFICATIONS

Year	Engine ID/VIN	Engine Displacement Liters (cc)	Spark Plugs Gap (in.)	Ignition Timing (deg.) MT	AT	Fuel Pump (psi)	Idle Speed (rpm) MT	AT	Valve Clearance In.	Ex.
1984	3A, 3A-C	1.4 (1452)	0.043②	5B	5B	2.6–3.5	①	①	0.008	0.012
1985	3A, 3A-C	1.4 (1452)	0.043②	5B	5B	2.6–3.5	①	①	0.008	0.012
1986	3A, 3A-C	1.4 (1452)	0.043②	5B	5B	2.6–3.5	①	①	0.008	0.012
1987	3A, 3A-C	1.4 (1452)	0.043②	5B	5B	2.6–3.5	①	①	0.008	0.012
	3E	1.5 (1456)	0.043	3B	3B	2.6–3.5	①	①	0.008	0.008
1988	3A, 3A-C	1.4 (1452)	0.043②	5B	5B	2.6–3.5	①	①	0.008	0.012
	3E	1.5 (1456)	0.043	3B	3B	2.6–3.5	①	①	0.008	0.008
1989	3E	1.5 (1456)	0.043	3B	3B	2.6–3.5	700	900	0.008	0.008
1990	3E	1.5 (1456)	0.043	3B	3B	2.6–3.5	700	900	0.008	0.008
	3E-E	1.5 (1456)	0.043	10B	10B	38–44	800	800	0.008	0.008
1991	3E-E	1.5 (1456)	0.043	10B	10B	33–37	750	800	0.008	0.008
1992	3E-E	1.5 (1456)	0.043	10B	10B	33–37	750	800	0.008	0.008
1993	3E-E	1.5 (1456)	0.043	10B	10B	33–37	750	800	0.008	0.008
1994	3E-E	1.5 (1456)	0.043	10B	10B	33–37	750	800	0.008	0.008

NOTE: The lowest cylinder pressure should be within 75% of the highest cylinder pressure reading. For example, if the highest cylinder is 134 psi, the lowest should be 101. Engine should be at normal operating temperature with throttle valve in the wide open position.
The underhood specifications sticker often reflects tune-up specification changes in production. Sticker figures must be used if they disagree with those in this chart.
① See underhood emission label
② 3A—0.031

85992c01

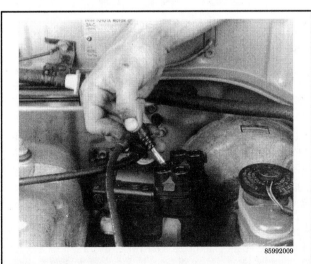

Fig. 2 Remove the spark plug wire from the coil by pulling straight up

Fig. 3 Be sure to reinstall the spark plug wire holddown clips

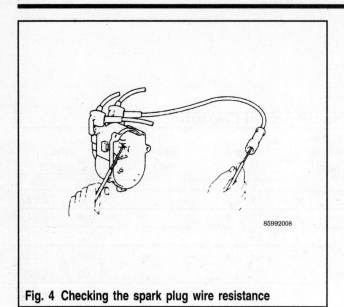

Fig. 4 Checking the spark plug wire resistance

gate, correct the cause of the fouling, and either clean or replace the plug. There are several reasons why a spark plug will foul and you can learn which is at fault by just looking at the plug.

Spark plugs suitable for use in your Toyota's engine are offered in a number of different heat ranges. The amount of heat which the plug absorbs is determined by the length of the lower insulator. The longer the insulator, the hotter the plug will operate; the shorter the insulator, the cooler it will operate. A spark plug that absorbs (or retains) little heat and remains too cool will accumulate deposits of lead, oil, and carbon, because it is not hot enough to burn them off. This leads to fouling and consequent misfiring. A spark plug that absorbs too much heat will have no deposits, but the electrodes will burn away quickly and, in some cases, pre-ignition may result. Pre-ignition occurs when the spark plug tips get so hot that they ignite the fuel/air mixture before the actual spark fires. This premature ignition will usually cause a pinging sound under conditions of low speed and heavy load. In severe cases, the heat may become high enough to start the fuel/air mixture

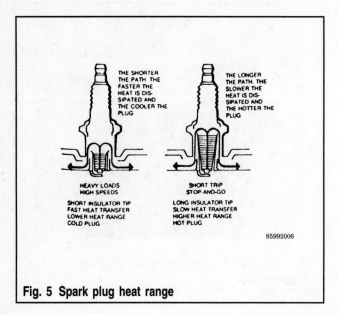

Fig. 5 Spark plug heat range

burning throughout the combustion chamber rather than just to the front of the plug. In this case, the resultant explosion will be strong enough to damage pistons, rings, and valves.

In most cases the factory recommended heat range is correct; it is chosen to perform well under a wide range of operating conditions. However, if most of your driving is long distance, high speed travel, you may want to install a spark plug one step colder than standard. If most of your driving is of the short trip variety, when the engine may not always reach operating temperature, a hotter plug may help burn off the deposits normally accumulated under those conditions.

REMOVAL & INSTALLATION

◗ **See Figures 6, 7, 8, 9, 10 and 11**

1. Number the spark plug wires (mark at the end of plug wire or boot) so that you won't cross them when you replace them.
2. Remove the wire from the end of the spark plug by grasping the wire by the rubber boot. If the boot sticks to the plug, remove it by twisting and pulling at the same time. Do not pull the wire itself or you will damage the core.

Fig. 6 Twist and pull the spark plug wire by its boot, not the wire

3. Use the correct size spark plug socket (spark plug sockets come in two sizes ⅝ and ¹³⁄₁₆ in. — use the correct size socket for the spark plug) to loosen all of the plugs about two turns.

➡**On most engines the cylinder head is cast from aluminum. Remove the spark plugs when the engine is cold to prevent damage to the threads.**

If removal of the plugs is difficult, apply a few drops of penetrating oil or silicone spray to the area around the base of the plug, and allow it a few minutes to work.

4. If compressed air is available, apply it to the area around the spark plug holes. Otherwise, use a rag or a brush to clean the area. Be careful not to allow any foreign material to drop into the spark plug holes.
5. Remove the plugs by unscrewing them the rest of the way from the engine.

Fig. 7 Removing the spark plug

Check the spark plugs for deposits and wear. If they are not going to be replaced, clean the plugs thoroughly (never clean platinum plugs — just replace the platinum plugs). Remember that any kind of deposit will decrease the efficiency of the plug. Regular spark plugs can be cleaned on a spark plug cleaning machine, which can sometimes be found in service stations, or you can do an acceptable job of cleaning with a stiff brush. If the plugs are cleaned, the electrodes must be filed flat. Use an ignition point file, not an emery board or the like, which will leave deposits. The electrodes must be filed perfectly flat with sharp edges; rounded edges reduce the spark plug voltage by as much as 50% .

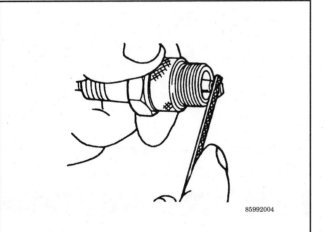

Fig. 8 Regular spark plugs in good condition can be filed and reused

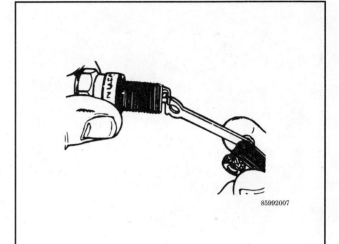

Fig. 9 Adjust the spark plug gap by bending the side electrode

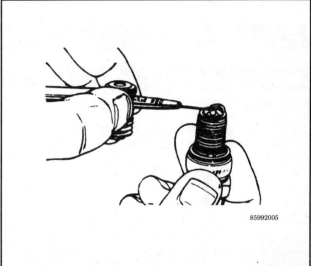

Fig. 10 Always use a wire gauge to check the plug gap

Check spark plug gap before installation. The ground electrode (the L-shaped one connected to the body of the plug) must be parallel to the center electrode and the specified size wire gauge (see Tune-Up Specifications) should pass through the gap with a slight drag.

Fig. 11 Be careful not to cross-thread when installing the spark plug

Always check the gap on new regular spark plugs, too; they are not always set correctly at the factory. Do not use a flat feeler gauge when measuring the gap, because the reading will be inaccurate. Wire gapping tools usually have a bending tool attached, use that to adjust the side electrode until the proper distance is obtained. Absolutely never bend the center electrode. Also, be careful not to bend the side electrode too far or too often; it may weaken and break off within the engine, causing serious damage.

To install:

6. Lubricate the threads of the spark plugs with a drop of oil. Install the plugs and tighten them hand tight (a long piece of vacuum hose attached to the top of the spark plug will help you start the spark plug by hand). Take care not to cross-thread them.

7. Tighten the spark plugs with the correct size spark plug socket. Do not apply the same amount of force you would use for a bolt; just snug them in. If a torque wrench is available, tighten to 13-15 ft. lbs. (18-20 Nm).

8. Install the spark plug wires on their respective spark plugs. Make sure the spark plug wires are firmly connected. You will be able to feel them click into place.

ELECTRONIC IGNITION

Description and Operation

▶ See Figure 12

Electronic ignition systems offer many advances over the conventional breaker point ignition system. By eliminating the points, maintenance requirements are greatly reduced. An electronic ignition system is capable of producing much higher voltage, which in turn aids in starting, reduces spark fouling and provides better emission control.

➡ **This book contains simple testing procedures for your Tercel electronic ignition system. More comprehensive testing on this system and other electronic control systems on your car can be found in CHILTON'S ELECTRONIC ENGINE CONTROLS MANUAL, available at your local retailer.**

The electronic ignition system consists of a distributor with a signal generator, an ignition coil and an electronic igniter. The signal generator is used to activate the electronic components of the ignition. It is located in the distributor and consists of three main components; the signal rotor, the pick-up coil and the permanent magnet. The signal rotor (not to be confused with the normal rotor) revolves with the distributor shaft, while the pickup coil and the permanent magnet are stationary. As the signal rotor spins, the teeth on it pass a projection leading from the pickup coil. As they pass, voltage is allowed to flow through the system, firing the spark plugs. There is no physical contact and no electrical arcing, hence no need to replace burnt or worn parts.

Service consists of inspection of the distributor cap, rotor and the ignition wires, replacing them as necessary. In addition, the air gap between the signal rotor and the projection on the pickup coil should be checked periodically.

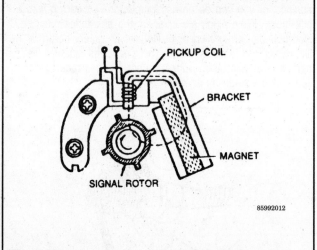

Fig. 12 Components of an electronic ignition signal generator

Diagnosis and Testing

▶ See Figures 13, 14, 15, 16, 17, 18, 19, 20 and 21

To check that spark is occurring at the spark plugs, perform this spark test.

1. Disconnect the spark plug wire from a spark plug.
2. Remove the spark plug.
3. Reconnect spark plug wire and ground the spark plug.
4. Check for spark while cranking the engine. Do not crank the engine for than 1 or 2 seconds to prevent the engine from starting. If it does start, turn it off immediately.

If no spark occurs, continue the test as follows:

5. Check the connections of the ignition coil, ignitor and distributor connectors.
6. Check the resistance of the spark plug wires.

7. Check the power supply to the ignition coil. Turn the ignition ON and check for battery voltage at the positive terminal of the ignition coil.

8. Check the ignition coil primary resistance (cold).

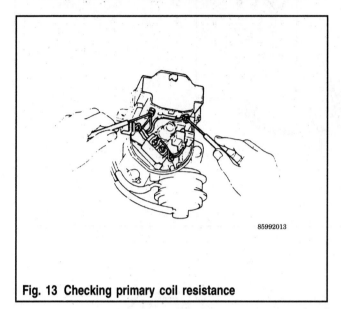

Fig. 13 Checking primary coil resistance

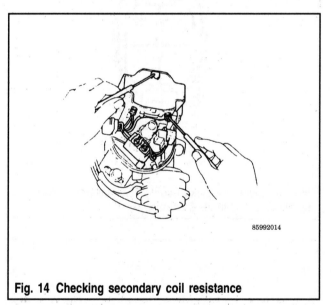

Fig. 14 Checking secondary coil resistance

   a. 0.4-0.5Ω on all except Canada and wagon
   b. 1.2-1.5Ω on Canada and wagon

9. Check the ignition coil secondary resistance (cold).

   a. 7.7-10.4kΩ on all Canada, wagons and on 1984-1986 sedans
   b. 10.2-13.8kΩ on 1987-1994 U.S sedans

10. Check the air gap between the pick-up coil and the signal rotor teeth as follows:

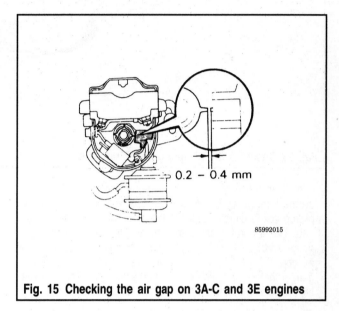

0.2 – 0.4 mm

Fig. 15 Checking the air gap on 3A-C and 3E engines

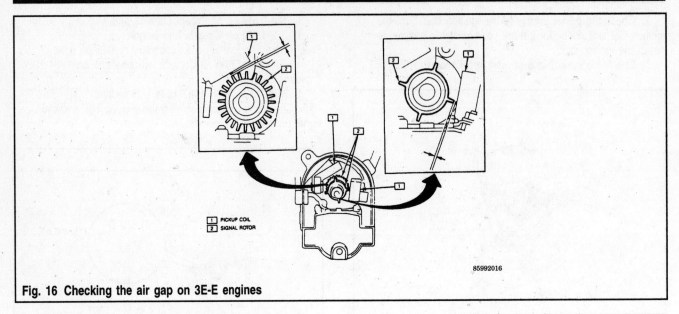

Fig. 16 Checking the air gap on 3E-E engines

a. Turn the engine over (you may use a socket wrench on the front pulley bolt to do this) until the projection on the pickup coil is directly opposite the signal rotor tooth.

b. Get a non-ferrous (paper, brass, or plastic) feeler gauge of 0.3mm (0.012 in.), and insert it into the pick-up coil air gap. DO NOT use an ordinary metal feeler gauge! The gauge should just touch either side of the gap. The permissible range is 0.2-0.4mm (0.008-0.016 in.).

➡The air gap is not adjustable. If the gap is not within specifications, the pick-up coil assembly must be replaced.

11. Check the pick-up coil resistance (cold).

Fig. 18 Check the pickup coil resistance from these terminals on 1990 3E-E engines

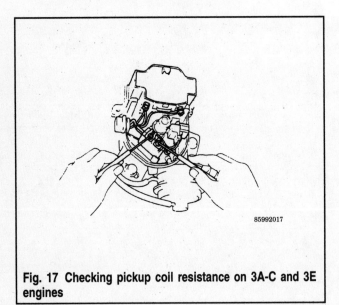

Fig. 17 Checking pickup coil resistance on 3A-C and 3E engines

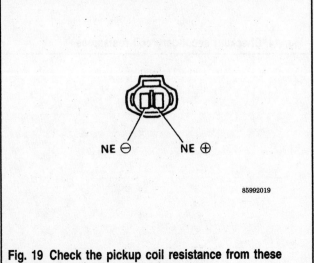

Fig. 19 Check the pickup coil resistance from these terminals on 1991 to 1994 3E-E engines

a. 1984-1990 3A-C and 3E — 140-180Ω

b. 1990 3E-E — G and NE pick-up coil resistance 140-180Ω

c. 1991 3E-E — NE pick-up coil resistance 410-510Ω

d. 1992-1994 3E-E — NE pick-up coil resistance 370-530Ω

12. If the ignition system still fails to produce a spark, replace the ignitor.

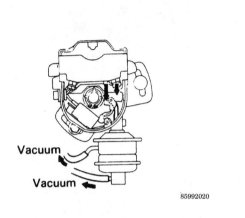

Fig. 20 On 3A-C and 3E engines, apply vacuum to these hoses and check for vacuum advance movement

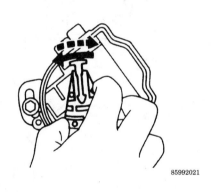

Fig. 21 On 3A-C and 3E engines, check for proper governor advance movement by turning the rotor counterclockwise, then release it and check that the rotor returns clockwise quickly

Adjustments

There are no adjustments possible inside the distributor. If the air gap between the signal rotor and the pick-up coil is not within specifications, the distributor must be replaced.

Parts Replacement

The two most commonly replaced parts in the distributor (aside from the cap and rotor as maintenance) will be the

signal generator and the igniter. Replacement of any internal piece usually requires removal of the distributor from the engine.

➡The distributor on some engines contain no replaceable parts except the ignition coil. Any other failed item in the distributor requires replacement of the complete unit.

REMOVAL & INSTALLATION

▶ See Figures 22, 23 and 24

Distributor

✳✳WARNING

Once the distributor is removed, the engine should not be turned or moved out of position. Should this occur, please refer to the Distributor procedures of Section 3.

Fig. 22 Disconnect all of the distributor electrical connections

Fig. 23 Mark the distributor position before removing it

1. Label and disconnect the coil and spark plug wiring at the distributor cap.

2. Disconnect the distributor wire at its connector.

3. Remove the distributor hold down bolts. Before moving or disturbing the distributor, mark the position of the distributor relative to the engine. Use a marker or tape so the mark doesn't rub off during the handling of the case.

Fig. 24 Once the holddown bolt has been removed, the distributor can be removed from the engine

4. Remove the distributor from the engine.

To install:

5. If the engine has not been moved out of position, align the rotor with the mark you made earlier and reinstall the distributor. Position it carefully and make sure the drive gear engages properly within the engine. Complete the installation by following the steps above in reverse order. For complete reinstallation instructions, refer to the Distributor procedures in Section 3.

Ignition Coil, Igniter and Pickup Coil Assembly

▶ **See Figures 25, 26, 27, 28 and 29**

➡**Review the complete service procedure before this repair. Note position and routing of all internal distributor assembly wiring.**

1. Remove the distributor as outlined above. Make certain the negative battery cable is disconnected before beginning the work.

2. Remove the distributor cap and rotor.

3. Remove the dust cover over the distributor components and remove the dust cover over the ignition coil.

4. Remove the nuts and disconnect the wiring from the ignition coil.

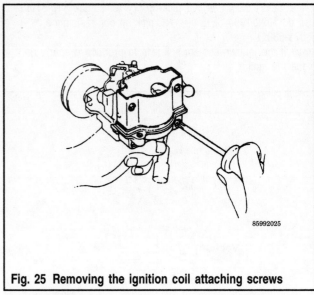

Fig. 25 Removing the ignition coil attaching screws

5. Remove the four screws and remove the ignition coil from the distributor.

6. At the igniter terminals, disconnect the wiring from the connecting points.

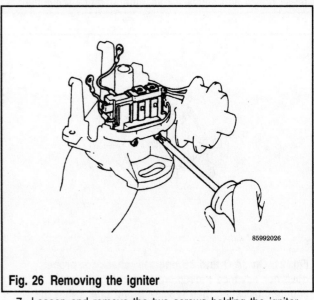

Fig. 26 Removing the igniter

7. Loosen and remove the two screws holding the igniter and remove it from the distributor.

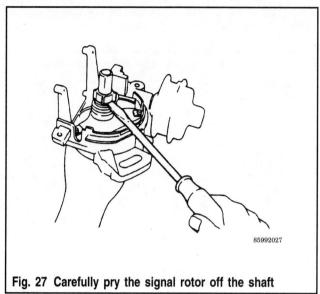

Fig. 27 Carefully pry the signal rotor off the shaft

8. If the signal rotor is to be replaced, use a screwdriver and CAREFULLY pry the rotor and spring up and off the shaft. When replacing the rotor, use a small bearing driver or long socket to fit over the shaft on top of the signal rotor. Tap gently; the force will be equally distributed and the rotor will slide evenly into place.

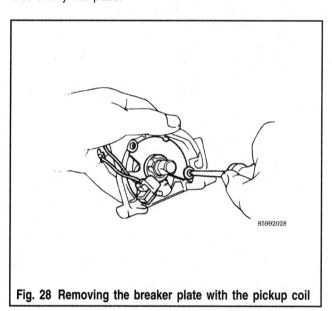

Fig. 28 Removing the breaker plate with the pickup coil

➡At this point of the service procedure, the breaker plate with the signal generator (pick-up coil) can be removed from the distributor housing by removing the retaining screws.

To install:

9. Install the igniter and connect its wiring. Pay particular attention to the correct routing of the wiring within the housing. There is one correct position only; any other wiring placements risk damage.

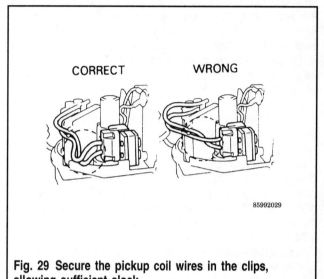

Fig. 29 Secure the pickup coil wires in the clips, allowing sufficient slack

10. Install the ignition coil and secure its wiring. Again, watch the wiring positions.
11. Reinstall the dust covers, the packing and distributor rotor.
12. Reinstall the distributor and set the engine timing.

IGNITION TIMING

Timing

▶ See Figures 30 and 31

Ignition timing is the measurement (in degrees) of crankshaft position at the instant the spark plug fires. Ignition timing is adjusted by loosening the distributor locking device and turning the distributor in the engine.

It takes a fraction of a second for the plug to completely ignite the mixture in the cylinder. Because of this, the spark plug must fire before the piston reaches TDC (top dead center, the highest point in its travel), if the mixture is to be com-pletely ignited as the piston passes TDC. This measurement is given in degrees (of crankshaft rotation) before the piston reaches top dead center (BTDC). If the ignition timing setting for your engine is 7 degrees BTDC, this means that the spark plug must fire at a time when the piston for that cylinder is 7 degrees before top dead center of its compression stroke. However, this only holds true while your engine is at idle speed.

As you accelerate from idle, the speed of your engine (rpm) increases. The increase in rpm means that the pistons are now traveling up and down much faster. Because of this, the spark plugs will have to fire even sooner if the mixture is to be completely ignited as the piston passes TDC. To accomplish this, the distributor incorporates means to advance the timing of the spark as the engine speed increases.

The distributor in your carbureted vehicle has two means of advancing the ignition timing. One is called centrifugal or governor advance and is actuated by weights in the distributor. The other is called vacuum advance and is controlled by the large circular housing on the side of the distributor.

In addition, some distributors have a vacuum-retard mechanism which is contained in the same housing on the side of the distributor as the vacuum advance. The function of this mechanism is to retard the timing of the ignition spark under certain engine conditions. The causes more complete burning of the air/fuel mixture in the cylinder and consequently lowers exhaust emissions. Because these mechanisms change ignition timing, it is necessary to disconnect and plug the vacuum lines from the distributor when setting the base ignition timing.

The fuel injected vehicles have neither a centrifugal advance nor a vacuum unit. All the timing changes are controlled electronically by the ECM. This solid state 'brain" receives data from many sensors (including the distributor), and commands changes in spark timing (and other functions) based on immediate driving conditions. This instant response allows the engine to be kept at peak performance and economy throughout the driving cycle. Basic timing can still be checked and adjusted on these motors.

If the ignition timing is set too far advanced (BTDC), the ignition and expansion of the air/fuel mixture in the cylinder will try to force the piston down while it is still traveling upward. This causes engine ping, a sound which resembles marbles being dropped into an empty tin can. If the ignition timing is too far retarded (after, or ATDC), the piston will have already started down on the power stroke when the air/fuel mixture ignites and expands. This will cause the piston to be forced down only a portion of its travel. This results in poor engine performance and lack of power.

Ignition timing adjustment is checked with a timing light. This instrument is connected to the number one (No. 1) spark plug of the engine. The timing light flashes every time an electrical current is sent from the distributor through the No. 1 spark plug wire to the spark plug. The crankshaft pulley and the front cover of the engine are marked with a timing pointer and a timing scale.

When the timing pointer is aligned with the 0 mark on the timing scale, the piston in the No. 1 cylinder is at TDC of it compression stroke. With the engine running, and the timing light aimed at the timing pointer and timing scale, the stroboscopic (periodic) flashes from the timing light will allow you to check the ignition timing setting of the engine. The timing light flashes every time the spark plug in the No. 1 cylinder of the engine fires. Since the flash from the timing light makes the crankshaft pulley seem to stand still for a moment, you will be able to read the exact position of the piston in the No. 1 cylinder on the timing scale on the front of the engine.

If you're buying a timing light, make sure the unit you select is rated for electronic or solid-state ignitions. Generally, these lights have two wires which connect to the battery with alligator clips and a third wire which connects to No. 1 plug wire. The best lights have an inductive pick-up on the third wire; this allows you to simply clip the small box over the wire. Older lights may require the removal of the plug wire and the instal-

lation of an in-line adapter. Buy quality the first time and the tool will give lasting results and ease of use.

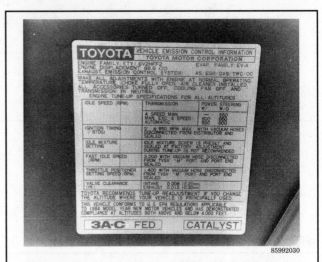

Fig. 30 Always follow the procedures and specifications on the emissions label for all engine adjustments

Fig. 31 A high quality timing light will provide ease of use and good results

INSPECTION AND ADJUSTMENT

◆ See Figures 32 and 33

Carbureted Engines

These engines requires a special tachometer hook-up to the service connector coming out of the distributor. As many tachometers are not compatible with this hook-up, we recommend that you consult with the manufacturer or salesman before purchasing a certain type.

➡**NEVER allow the ignition coil terminal to become grounded; severe and expensive damage can occur to the coil and/or igniter.**

1. Warm the engine to normal operating temperature. Do not attempt to check timing or idle speed on a cold motor —

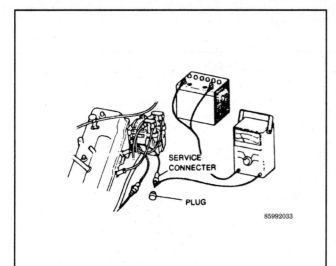

Fig. 32 Tachometer hook up on carbureted engines

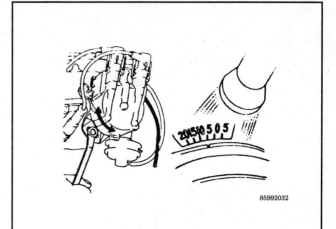

Fig. 33 Timing marks on carbureted engines. Be sure to disconnect and plug the vacuum hoses at the distributor

all the readings will be different. Connect a tachometer and check the engine idle speed to be sure it is within the specification given in the Tune-Up Specifications chart or underhood emission sticker. Adjust the idle if needed and shut the engine off.

2. If the timing marks are difficult to see, use a dab of paint or chalk to make them more visible.

3. Connect a timing light according to the manufacturer's instructions.

4. Label and disconnect the vacuum line(s) from the distributor vacuum unit. Plug it (them) with a pencil or golf tee(s).

5. Be sure that the timing light wires are clear of the fan and start the engine.

6. Allow the engine to run at the specified idle speed with the gearshift in correct position. Refer to the underhood emission sticker as necessary.

✴✴CAUTION

Be sure that the parking brake is set and the wheels are blocked to prevent the car from rolling in either direction.

7. Point the timing light at the marks on the tab alongside the crank pulley. With the engine at idle, timing should be at the specification given on the Tune-Up Specification Chart in this section or refer to the underhood emission sticker as necessary.

8. If the timing is not at the specification, loosen the bolts at the base of the distributor just enough so that the distributor can be turned. Turn the distributor to advance or retard the timing as required. Once the proper marks are seen to align with the timing light, timing is correct.

9. Stop the engine and tighten the bolts. Connect the vacuum line(s) to the distributor vacuum unit.

Fuel Injected Engines

▶ See Figures 34, 35 and 36

➡This is a general service procedure for setting base ignition timing. Refer to underhood emission sticker for any additional service procedures steps.

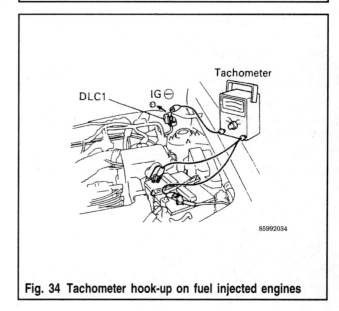

Fig. 34 Tachometer hook-up on fuel injected engines

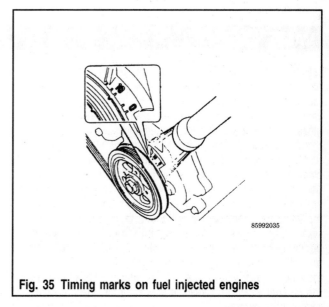

Fig. 35 Timing marks on fuel injected engines

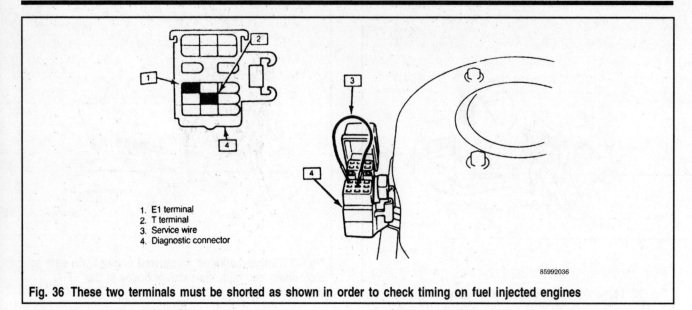

1. E1 terminal
2. T terminal
3. Service wire
4. Diagnostic connector

85992036

Fig. 36 These two terminals must be shorted as shown in order to check timing on fuel injected engines

These engines require a special tachometer hook-up to the service connector in the diagnostic connector. As many tachometers are not compatible with this hook-up, we recommend that you consult with the manufacturer or salesman before purchasing a certain type.

➡**NEVER allow the ignition coil terminal (tachometer terminal) to become grounded; severe and expensive damage can occur to the coil and/or igniter.**

1. Warm the engine to normal operating temperature. Turn off all electrical accessories. Do not attempt to check timing specification or idle speed on a cold motor — all the readings will be different.

2. Connect a tachometer and check the engine idle speed to be sure it is within the specification given in the Tune-Up Specifications chart or underhood emission sticker.

3. Using a small jumper wire, short both terminals of the Check Engine connector located near the wiper motor. On some engines remove the cap on the diagnostic connector.

Using a small jumper wire, short terminals E1 and T together. Adjust idle speed as necessary.

4. If the timing marks are difficult to see, shut engine off use a dab of paint or chalk to make them more visible.

5. Connect a timing light according to the manufacturer's instructions.

6. Start the engine and use the timing light to observe the timing marks. With the jumper wire in the connector the timing should be to specifications (refer to underhood emission sticker as necessary) with the engine fully warmed up (at correct idle speed) and the transmission in correct position. If the timing is not correct, loosen the bolts at the distributor just enough so that the distributor can be turned. Turn the distributor to advance or retard the timing as required. Once the proper marks are seen to align with the timing light, timing is correct.

7. Without changing the position of the distributor, tighten the distributor bolt(s) and double check the timing with the light (check idle speed as necessary).

8. Disconnect the jumper wire at the Check Engine connector or Diagnostic connector.

9. Shut the engine off and disconnect all test equipment.

VALVE LASH

Refer to the owner's manual for vehicle maintenance schedule (usually 30,000 miles/48 months or 60, 000 miles/72 months — some 1984 vehicles 15,000 miles/12 months) for valve clearance adjustment (lash) as all years and model engines have different mile and time intervals.

Valve lash is one factor which determines how far the intake and exhaust valves will open into the cylinder. If the valve clearance is too large, part of the lift of the camshaft will be used up in removing the excessive clearance, thus the valves will not be opened far enough. This condition has two effects, the valve train components will emit a tapping noise as they take up the excessive clearance, and the engine will perform poorly, since the less the intake valve opens, the smaller the amount of air/fuel mixture admitted to the cylinders will be. The less the exhaust valves open, the greater the back-pressure in the cylinder which prevents the proper air/fuel mixture from entering the cylinder.

If the valve clearance is too small, the intake and exhaust valves will not fully seat on the cylinder head when they close. When a valve seats on the cylinder head it does two things, it seals the combustion chamber so none of the gases in the cylinder can escape and it cools itself by transferring some of the heat it absorbed from the combustion process through the cylinder head and into the engine cooling system. Therefore, if the valve clearance is too small, the engine will run poorly (due to gases escaping from the combustion chamber), and the valves will overheat and warp (since they cannot transfer heat unless they are touching the seat in the cylinder head).

➡**While all valve adjustments must be as accurate as possible, it is better to have the valve adjustment slightly loose than slightly tight, as burnt valves may result form overly tight adjustments.**

Adjustment

♦ **See Figures 37, 40, 38, 39, 41 and 42**

1. Start the engine and run it until it reaches normal operating temperature.

2. Stop the engine. Remove the air cleaner assembly. Remove the valve cover.

✳✳CAUTION

Be careful when removing components; the engine will be hot.

3. Turn the crankshaft until the pointer or notch on the pulley aligns with the **0** or the **T** mark on the timing scale. This will ensure that the engine is at TDC. Turning the engine (with a wrench on the crankshaft bolt) is much easier if the spark plugs are removed.

➡Check that the rocker arms on the No. 1 cylinder are loose and those on the No. 4-cylinder are tight. If not, turn the crankshaft one complete revolution (360 degrees).

Fig. 37 Checking and adjusting valve lash

4. Using a feeler gauge, check the clearance between the bottom of the rocker arm and the top of the valve stem. This measurement should correspond to the one given in the Tune-Up Specifications Chart in this section. Check only the first set of valves shown in the accompanying illustrations for your engine.

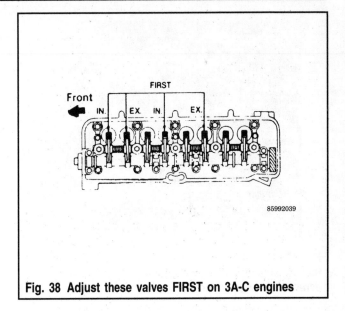

Fig. 38 Adjust these valves FIRST on 3A-C engines

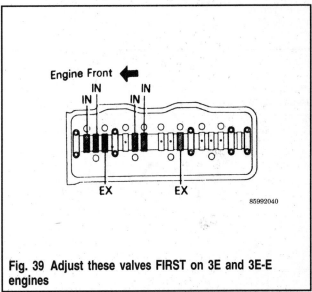

Fig. 39 Adjust these valves FIRST on 3E and 3E-E engines

5. If the clearance is not within specifications, the valves will require adjustment. Loosen the locknut on the rocker arm and, still holding the nut with an open end wrench, turn the adjustment screw to achieve the correct clearance. This is a detail oriented job; work for exact clearance.

6. Once the correct clearance is achieved, keep the adjustment screw from turning with your screwdriver and then tighten the locknut. Recheck the valve clearance.

Fig. 40 Once the correct clearance is achieved, keep the adjustment screw from turning with your screwdriver and tighten the locknut

7. After the correct set of valves have been adjusted, turn the engine one complete revolution (360 degrees) and adjust the second set of valves shown in the illustration.

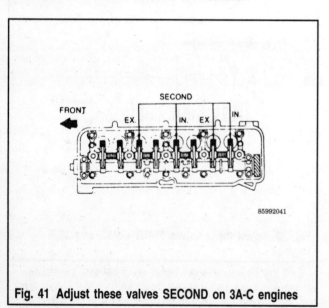

Fig. 41 Adjust these valves SECOND on 3A-C engines

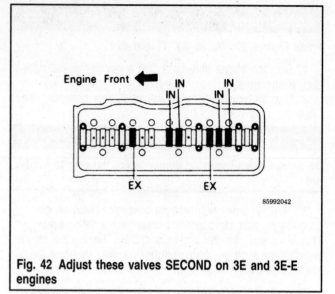

Fig. 42 Adjust these valves SECOND on 3E and 3E-E engines

8. Use a new gasket and then install the valve cover. Install any other components which were removed for access to the cover.

9. Start the engine. Listen for any excessive tapping (indicating a loosened rocker) and check the valve cover for any signs of oil leaks.

IDLE SPEED AND MIXTURE ADJUSTMENT

Carbureted Engines

This section contains only adjustments as they normally apply to engine tune-up. Descriptions of the carburetor and fuel systems and complete adjustment procedures can be found in Section 5.

When the engine in your Toyota is running, the amount of air/fuel mixture that enters the engine is controlled by the throttle plates in the bottom of the carburetor. When the engine is not running, the throttle plates are closed, completely blocking off the bottom of the carburetor from the inside of the engine.

The throttle plates are connected, through the throttle linkage, to the gas pedal inside the car. What you actually are doing when you depress the gas pedal is opening the throttle plate in the carburetor to admit more air/fuel mixture to the engine. The further you open the throttle plates in the carburetor, the higher the engine speed becomes.

To keep the engine idling, it is necessary to open the throttle plates slightly. To prevent having to keep your foot on the gas pedal when the engine is idling, an idle speed adjusting screw is included on the carburetor. This screw has the same effect as keeping your foot on the gas pedal — it holds the throttle plate open just a bit. When the screw is turned in, it opens the throttle, raising the idle speed of the engine. This screw is called the curb idle adjusting screw, and the procedures in this section will tell you how to adjust it.

When you first start the car after an overnight period, the cold motor requires a different air-fuel mixture to run properly.

Because of the different mixture, the idle speed must be higher during cold engine operation. This High Idle (sometimes called cold idle or fast idle) speed is also adjustable and should be checked periodically. If the high idle is too low, the car will bog and stall until it warms up. If the high idle is set too high, the engine is wasting fuel and suffering increased and premature wear.

Before performing any carburetor adjustments, ALL of the following conditions must be met:

- All accessories are switched off
- Ignition timing is set correctly and all vacuum lines are connected
- Transaxle in Neutral and engine warmed up to normal operating temperature
- Choke opened fully
- Fuel level in carburetor sight glass at the correct level. If the level is too high or low, adjust the float level as explained in Section 5.

IDLE SPEED ADJUSTMENT

▶ **See Figures 43, 44 and 45**

Once all the above conditions are met, the curb idle can be adjusted by turning the adjusting screw or knob at the rear of the carburetor. Turn it clockwise to raise the idle and counterclockwise to lower it. Keep a close eye on the tachometer while turning the screw; sometimes a small change in the adjustor causes a big change in the idle speed. Adjust the idle speed to the rpm shown in the Tune-Up Specifications chart.

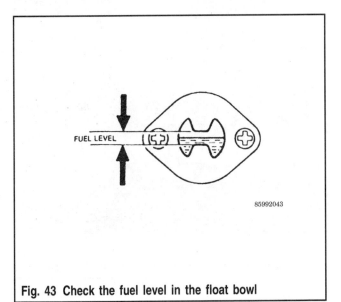

Fig. 43 Check the fuel level in the float bowl

Fig. 44 Idle speed adjustment screw on 3A-C carbureted engines

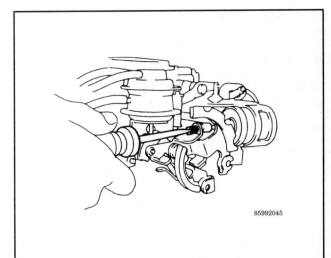

Fig. 45 Idle speed adjustment screw on 3E carbureted engines

HIGH IDLE ADJUSTMENT

▶ **See Figures 46, 47, 48, 49 and 50**

1. Stop the engine and remove the air cleaner and its housing.
2. Plug the hot idle compensator hose. It's the hose that runs from the lower front part of the carburetor body to a small valve on the air cleaner housing. If not plugged, it will create a vacuum leak causing either a rough idle or stalling.

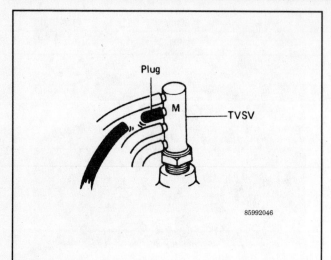

Fig. 46 Plugging the M port on the TVSV valve, 3A-C models

3. On 3A-C models, find the vacuum valve with five hoses connected to it between the block and the firewall. One hose will be in a separate position and four will be in line. This is the Thermostatic Vacuum Switching Valve (TVSV). Of the four hoses in line, one will be tabled **M**; it's usually the second one from the upper or outer end of the valve. Give the hose on the **M** port ½ turn and remove it from the port. Plug the port (not the hose) with an airtight plug to prevent vacuum leaks.

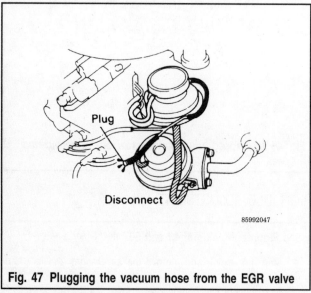

Fig. 47 Plugging the vacuum hose from the EGR valve

4. On 3E models, disconnect and plug the Exhaust Gas Recirculation (EGR) valve hose.

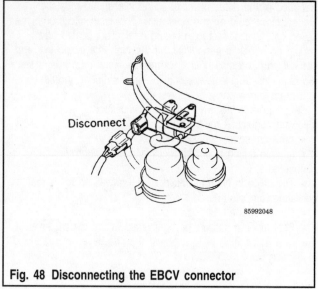

Fig. 48 Disconnecting the EBCV connector

5. Disconnect the Electronic Air Bleed Control Valve (EBCV) connector.

6. Hold the throttle plate open slightly (you can move the linkage with your fingers or pull gently on the accelerator cable) and move the choke plate to its fully closed position. Hold the choke closed as you release the throttle cable.

7. Start the engine but DO NOT move the gas pedal or the accelerator cable. The engine has been fooled into thinking it's cold — the choke is set and the high idle is engaged.

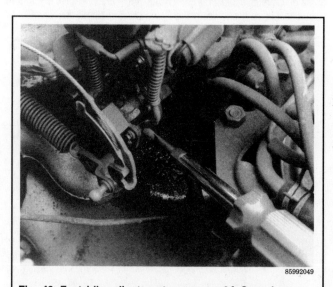

Fig. 49 Fast idle adjustment screw on 3A-C engines

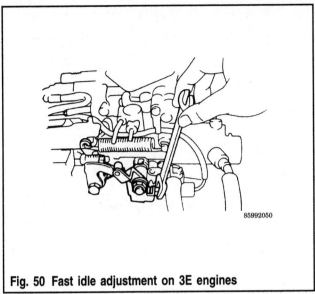

Fig. 50 Fast idle adjustment on 3E engines

8. Adjust the high idle by turning the fast idle adjusting screw. Set the fast idle between 2,800 and 3,000 rpm.

❊❊CAUTION

The engine is running at high speed. Beware of moving parts and hot surfaces.

9. When the fast idle is set correctly, shut the engine off. Reconnect all hoses and electrical connections. Remove the plug from the hot idle compensator hose.

10. Reinstall the air cleaner housing and the filter; connect the hose.

IDLE MIXTURE ADJUSTMENT

▶ **See Figures 51, 52, 53, 54, 55, 56, 57 and 58**

To conform with Federal regulations, the idle mixture adjusting screw is adjusted at the factory and plugged with a steel plug by the manufacturer. Under normal conditions there should be no need to remove this plug.

When troubleshooting rough idle, check all other possible causes before attempting to adjust the idle mixture. Only if no other factors are found to be at fault should the idle mixture be adjusted. Since this repair involves removal of the carburetor, it is recommended that the car be thoroughly checked on an exhaust emissions analyzer as part of the diagnostic procedure before committing to the repair. If you perform this repair incorrectly or if the idle mixture is not the cause of your problem, you may cause the car to become uncertifiable under Federal and State or Provincial emission laws.

1. Following the procedures given in Section 5, remove the carburetor.

2. Using the following procedure remove the Mixture Adjusting Screw plug (MAS plug):

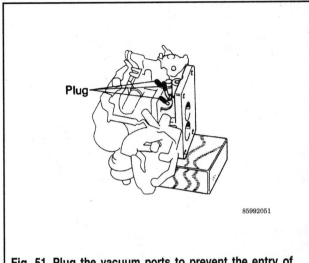

Fig. 51 Plug the vacuum ports to prevent the entry of steel particles when drilling

a. Plug all of the carburetor ports to prevent the entry of steel particles when drilling.

b. Mark the center of the plug with a punch.

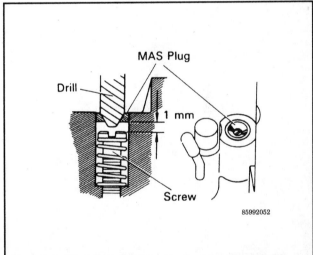

Fig. 52 Drilling the mixture adjustment screw (MAS) plug

c. Drill a 6mm hole in the center of the plug. As there is only 1mm clearance between the plug and the screw below it, drill carefully and slowly to avoid drilling onto the screw. The drill may force the plug off at any time.

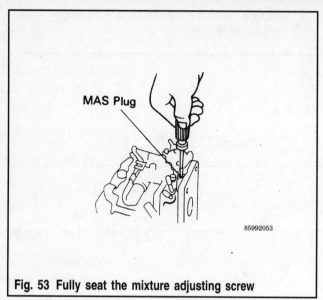

Fig. 53 Fully seat the mixture adjusting screw

d. Through the hole in the plug, fully screw in the mixture adjusting screw with a screwdriver.

➡**Be careful not to damage the screw tip by tightening the screw too tightly.**

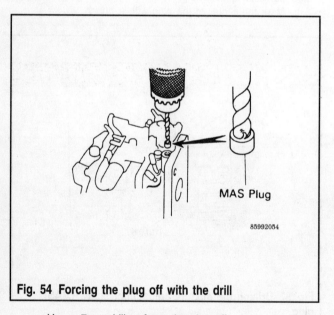

Fig. 54 Forcing the plug off with the drill

e. Use a 7mm drill to force the plug off.

3. Remove the mixture adjusting screw.

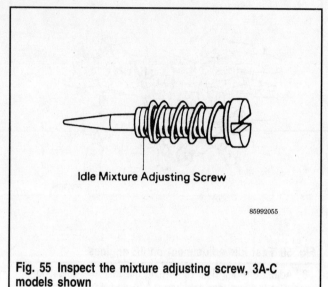

Fig. 55 Inspect the mixture adjusting screw, 3A-C models shown

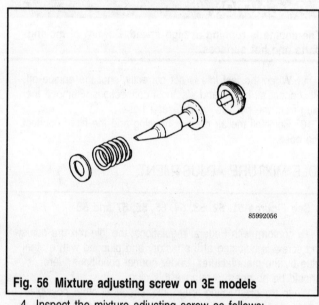

Fig. 56 Mixture adjusting screw on 3E models

4. Inspect the mixture adjusting screw as follows:
a. Blow off any steel particles with compressed air.
b. If the drill has gnawed into the screw top or if the tapered portion is damaged, replace the screw.

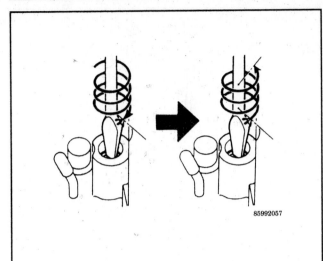

Fig. 57 On 3A-C models, fully seat the adjusting screw, then back out the specified number of turns

5. Reinstall the mixture adjusting screw. On 3A-C models, fully seat the idle mixture adjusting screw and then back it out 3¼ turns (except Canada, 2½ turns). On 3E models, screw in until the head is 0.138 in. (3.5mm) below the lower surface of the carburetor.

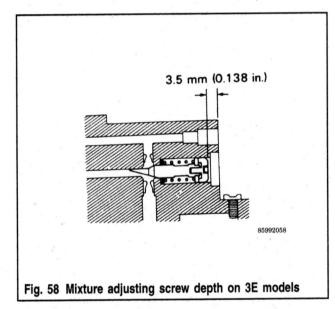

3.5 mm (0.138 in.)

Fig. 58 Mixture adjusting screw depth on 3E models

➡ **Be careful not to damage the screw tip by tightening the screw too tight.**

6. Reinstall the carburetor on the engine. Reconnect the vacuum hoses to their proper locations.
7. Reinstall the air cleaner.
8. Adjust the idle speed and mixture as follows:
   a. Check the following initial conditions:
   - The air cleaner is installed
   - The engine is at normal operating temperature
   - The choke is fully open
   - All accessories are switch off
   - All vacuum lines are connected
   - The ignition timing is correct
   - The transaxle is in neutral (N)
   - The float level is correct
   - The front wheels are pointed straight ahead (power steering equipped vehicles)
   b. Start the engine
   c. Turn the mixture adjustment screw slowly until the maximum idle speed is obtained. The preliminary adjustment of should be fairly close.
   d. Set the idle speed by turning the idle speed adjusting screw. The idle mixture speed should be as shown on either the underhood Emissions Label or the Tune-Up Specifications chart.
   e. Before moving to the next step, repeat adjustments until the maximum speed will not raise any further no matter how much the idle mixture adjusting screw is adjusted.
   f. Final adjust to 650 rpm on 3A-C models and to 700 (M/T) or 900 (A/T) rpm on 3E models by turning the mixture adjusting screw.
   g. Final adjust the idle speed to specification by turning the idle adjusting screw.
9. Reinstall the mixture adjusting screw plugs. Remove the air cleaner and the EGR vacuum modulator bracket. With the tapered end of the plug facing inward, tap in the plug until it is even with the carburetor surface.
10. Reinstall the EGR vacuum modulator bracket and the air cleaner.

Fuel Injected Engines

IDLE SPEED ADJUSTMENT

▶ **See Figure 59**

One of the merits of electronic fuel injection is that it requires so little adjustment. The computer (ECM) does most of the work in compensating for changes in climate, engine temperature, electrical load and driving conditions. The curb idle on the fuel injected engines should be checked periodically but not adjusted unless off specifications by more than 50 rpm.

The idle speed adjusting screw is located on the side of the throttle body. You can find the the throttle body by following the accelerator cable to its end. The adjusting screw may have a cap over it. If so, pop the cap off with a small screwdriver.

With the engine fully warmed up, properly connect a tachometer. Make sure that all the electrical accessories (cooling fan off) on the car are turned off and disconnect the idle up Vacuum Switching Valve (VSV) connector. Start the engine (race the engine at 2,500 rpm for about 2 minutes). The idle speed should be as shown on the underhood Emissions Label or in the Tune-Up Specifications chart, adjust a necessary.

If for any reason the idle cannot be brought into specification by this adjustment, return the screw to its original setting. Diagnostic procedures should be performed by a qualified technician to find the real cause of the problem. Do not try to cure other problems with this adjustment.

MIXTURE ADJUSTMENT

The air/fuel ratio burned within the engine is controlled by the ECM, based on information delivered by the various sensors on the engine. It is not adjustable as a routine maintenance item. The easiest way to check the air/fuel mixture is to put the car through a tail pipe emissions test. Whether or not this is required in your area, it's a good way of putting numbers on the combustion efficiency of the engine. The engine can only burn so much fuel; if too much is being delivered, it will show up on the test as unburned hydrocarbons (HC).

Putting the car through this test once a year from the time it is newly acquired can provide an excellent baseline for diagnosing future problems.

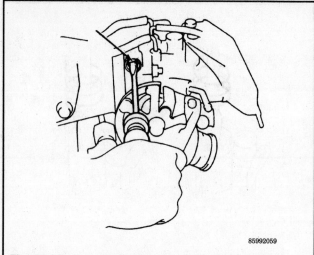

Fig. 59 Idle speed adjusting screw on fuel injected engines

85992059

3

ENGINE
AND
ENGINE
REBUILDING

BASIC ELECTRICITY

Understanding Basic Electricity

For any electrical system to operate, it must make a complete circuit. This simply means that the power flow from the battery must make a full circle. When an electrical component is operating, power flows from the battery to the components, passes through the component (load) causing it to function, and returns to the battery through the ground path of the circuit. This ground may be either another wire or the actual metal part of the car depending upon how the component is designed.

Perhaps the easiest way to visualize this is to think of connecting a light bulb with two wires attached to it to the battery. If one of the two wires was attached to the negative (-) post of the battery and the other wire to the positive (+) post, the light bulb would light and the circuit would be complete. Electricity could follow a path from the battery to the bulb and back to the battery. Its not hard to see that with longer wires on our light bulb, it could be mounted anywhere on the car. Further, one wire could be fitted with a switch so that the light could be turned on and off at will. Various other items could be added to our primitive circuit to make the light flash, become brighter or dimmer under certain conditions or advise the user that it's burned out.

Some automotive components are grounded through their mounting points. The electrical current runs through the chassis of the vehicle and returns to the battery through the ground (-) cable; if you look, you'll see that the battery ground cable connects between the battery and the body of the car.

Every complete circuit must include a "load"(something to use the electricity coming from the source). If you were to connect a wire between the two terminals of the battery (DON'T do this) without the light bulb, the battery would attempt to deliver its entire power supply from one pole to another almost instantly. This is a short circuit. The electricity is taking a short cut to get to ground and is not being used by any load in the circuit. This sudden and uncontrolled electrical flow can cause great damage to other components in the circuit and can develop a tremendous amount of heat. A short in an automotive wiring harness can develop sufficient heat to melt the insulation on all the surrounding wires and reduce a multiple wire cable to one sad lump of plastic and copper. Two common causes of shorts are broken insulation (thereby exposing the wire to contact with surrounding metal surfaces or other wires) or a failed switch (the pins inside the switch come out of place and touch each other).

Some electrical components which require a large amount of current to operate also have a relay in their circuit. Since these circuits carry a large amount of current (amperage or amps), the thickness of the wire in the circuit (wire gauge) is also greater. If this large wire were connected from the load to the control switch on the dash, the switch would have to carry the high amperage load and the dash would be twice as large to accommodate wiring harnesses as thick as your wrist. To prevent these problems, a relay is used. The large wires in the circuit are connected from the battery to one side of the relay and from the opposite side of the relay to the load. The relay is normally open, preventing current from passing through the circuit. An additional, smaller wire is connected from the relay to the control switch for the circuit. When the control switch is turned on, it grounds the smaller wire to the relay and completes its circuit. The main switch inside the relay closes, sending power to the component without routing the main power through the inside of the car. Some common circuits which may use relays are the horn, headlights, starter and rear window defogger systems.

It is possible for larger surges of current to pass through the electrical system of your car. If this surge of current were to reach the load in the circuit, it could burn it out or severely damage it. To prevent this, fuses, circuit breakers and/or fusible links are connected into the supply wires of the electrical system. These items are nothing more than a built-in weak spot in the system. It's much easier to go to a known location (the fusebox) to see why a circuit is inoperative than to dissect 15 feet of wiring under the dashboard, looking for what happened.

When an electrical current of excessive power passes through the fuse, the fuse blows and breaks the circuit, preventing the passage of current and protecting the components.

A circuit breaker is basically a self repairing fuse. It will open the circuit in the same fashion as a fuse, but when either the short is removed or the surge subsides, the circuit breaker resets itself and does not need replacement.

A fuse link (fusible link or main link) is a wire that acts as a fuse. One of these is normally connected between the starter relay and the main wiring harness under the hood. Since the starter is the highest electrical draw on the car, an internal short during starting could direct about 130 amps into the wrong places. Consider the damage potential of introducing this current into a system whose wiring is rated at 15 amps and you'll understand the need for protection. Since this link is very early in the electrical path, it's the first place to look if nothing on the car works but the battery seems to be charged and is properly connected.

Electrical problems generally fall into one of three areas:
• The component that is not functioning is not receiving current.
• The component is receiving power but not using it or using it incorrectly (component failure).
• The component is improperly grounded.

The circuit can be can be checked with a test light and a jumper wire. The test light is a device that looks like a pointed screwdriver with a wire on one end and a bulb in its handle. A jumper wire is simply a piece of wire with alligator clips on each end. If a component is not working, you must follow a systematic plan to determine which of the three causes is the villain.

1. Turn on the switch that controls the item not working.

➡**Some items only work when the ignition switch is turned ON.**

2. Disconnect the the power supply wire from the component.

3. Attach the ground wire on the test light to a good metal ground.

4. Touch the end probe of the test light to the power wire; if there is current in the wire, the light in the test light will come on. You have now established that current is getting to the component.

5. Turn the ignition or dash switch off and reconnect the wire to the component.

If the test light did not go on, then the problem is between the battery and the component. This includes all the switches, fuses, relays and the battery itself. The next place to look is the fusebox; check carefully either by eye or by using the test light across the fuse clips. The easiest way to check is to simply replace the fuse. If the fuse is blown, and upon replacement, immediately blows again, there is a short between the fuse and the component. This is generally (not always) a sign of an internal short in the component. Disconnect the power wire at the component again and replace the fuse; if the fuse holds, the component is the problem.

If all the fuses are good and the component is not receiving power, find the switch for the circuit. Bypass the switch with the jumper wire. This is done by connecting one end of the jumper to the power wire coming into the switch and the other end to the wire leaving the switch. If the component comes to life, the switch has failed.

✳✳WARNING

Never substitute the jumper for the component. The circuit needs the electrical load of the component. If you bypass it, you will cause a short circuit.

Checking the ground for any circuit can mean tracing wires to the body, cleaning connections or tightening mounting bolts for the component itself. If the jumper wire can be connected to the case of the component or the ground connector, you can ground the other end to a piece of clean, solid metal on the car. Again, if the component starts working, you've found the problem.

A systematic search through the fuse, connectors, switches and the component itself will almost always yield an answer. Loose and/or corroded connectors, particularly in ground circuits, are becoming a larger problem in modern cars. The computers and on-board electronic (solid state) systems are highly sensitive to improper grounds and will change their function drastically if one occurs.

Remember that for any electrical circuit to work, ALL the connections must be clean and tight.

Battery, Starting and Charging Systems

BASIC OPERATING PRINCIPLES

Battery

The battery is the first link in the chain of mechanisms which work together to provide cranking of the automobile engine. In most modern cars, the battery is a lead/acid electrochemical device consisting of six 2v subsections (cells) connected in series so the unit is capable of producing approximately 12v of electrical pressure. Each subsection consists of a series of

positive and negative plates held a short distance apart in a solution of sulfuric acid and water.

The two types of plates are of dissimilar metals. This causes a chemical reaction to be set up, and it is this reaction which produces current flow from the battery when its positive and negative terminals are connected to an electrical appliance such as a lamp or motor. The continued transfer of electrons would eventually convert the sulfuric acid to water, and make the two plates identical in chemical composition. As electrical energy is removed from the battery, its voltage output tends to drop. Thus, measuring battery voltage and battery electrolyte composition are two ways of checking the ability of the unit to supply power. During the starting of the engine, electrical energy is removed from the battery. However, if the charging circuit is in good condition and the operating conditions are normal, the power removed from the battery will be replaced by the alternator which will force electrons back through the battery, reversing the normal flow, and restoring the battery to its original chemical state.

Starting System

The battery and starting motor are linked by very heavy electrical cables designed to minimize resistance to the flow of current. Generally, the major power supply cable that leaves the battery goes directly to the starter, while other electrical system needs are supplied by a smaller cable. During starter operation, power flows from the battery to the starter and is grounded through the car's frame and the battery's negative ground strap.

The starting motor is a specially designed, direct current electric motor capable of producing a great amount of power for its size. One thing that allows the motor to produce a great deal of power is its tremendous rotating speed. It drives the engine through a tiny pinion gear (attached to the starter's armature), which drives the very large flywheel ring gear at a greatly reduced speed. Another factor allowing it to produce so much power is that only intermittent operation is required of it. Thus, little allowance for air circulation is required, and the windings can be built into a very small space.

The starter solenoid is a magnetic device which employs the small current supplied by the start circuit of the ignition switch. This magnetic action moves a plunger which mechanically engages the starter and closes the heavy switch connecting it to the battery. The starting switch circuit consists of the starting switch contained within the ignition switch, a transmission neutral safety switch or clutch pedal switch, and the wiring necessary to connect these in series with the starter solenoid or relay.

The pinion, a small gear, is mounted to a one way drive clutch. This clutch is splined to the starter armature shaft. When the ignition switch is moved to the **START** position, the solenoid plunger slides the pinion toward the flywheel ring gear via a collar and spring. If the teeth on the pinion and flywheel match properly, the pinion will engage the flywheel immediately. If the gear teeth butt one another, the spring will be compressed and will force the gears to mesh as soon as the starter turns far enough to allow them to do so. As the solenoid plunger reaches the end of its travel, it closes the contacts that connect the battery and starter and then the engine is cranked.

As soon as the engine starts, the flywheel ring gear begins turning fast enough to drive the pinion at an extremely high rate of speed. At this point, the one-way clutch begins allowing the pinion to spin faster than the starter shaft so that the starter will not operate at excessive speed. When the ignition switch is released from the starter position, the solenoid is de-energized, and a spring pulls the gear out of mesh interrupting the current flow to the starter.

Some starters employ a separate relay, mounted away from the starter, to switch the motor and solenoid current on and off. The relay replaces the solenoid electrical switch, but does not eliminate the need for a solenoid mounted on the starter used to mechanically engage the starter drive gears. The relay is used to reduce the amount of current the starting switch must carry.

Charging System

The automobile charging system provides electrical power for operation of the vehicle's ignition system, starting system and all the electrical accessories. The battery serves as an electrical surge or storage tank, storing (in chemical form) the energy originally produced by the engine driven generator. The system also provides a means of regulating output to protect the battery from being overcharged and to avoid excessive voltage to the accessories.

The storage battery is a chemical device incorporating parallel lead plates in a tank containing a sulfuric acid/water solution. Adjacent plates are slightly dissimilar, and the chemical reaction of the two dissimilar plates produces electrical energy when the battery is connected to a load such as the starter motor. The chemical reaction is reversible, so that when the generator is producing a voltage (electrical pressure) greater than that produced by the battery, electricity is forced into the battery, and the battery is returned to its fully charged state.

Newer automobiles use alternating current generators or alternators, because they are more efficient, can be rotated at higher speeds, and have fewer brush problems. In an alternator, the field rotates while all the current produced passes only through the stator winding. The brushes bear against continuous slip rings. This causes the current produced to periodically reverse the direction of its flow. Diodes (electrical one way valves) block the flow of current from traveling in the wrong direction. A series of diodes is wired together to permit the alternating flow of the stator to be rectified back to 12 volts DC for use by the vehicles's electrical system.

The voltage regulating function is performed by a regulator. The regulator is often built in to the alternator; this system is termed an integrated or internal regulator.

ENGINE ELECTRICAL

Ignition Coil

TESTING

▶ See Figures 1 and 2

➡This test requires the use of an ohmmeter. When using this tool, make sure the scale is set properly for the range of resistance you expect to encounter during the test. Always perform these tests with the ignition OFF.

Primary Resistance

In order to check the coil primary resistance, you must first disconnect all wires from the ignition coil terminals. Using an ohmmeter, check the resistance between the positive and the negative terminals on the coil. The resistance should be:
- 0.4-0.5 Ω on all except Canada and wagons
- 1.2-1.5 Ω on Canada and wagons

If the resistance is not within these tolerances (range), the ignition coil must be replaced.

Secondary Resistance

In order to check the coil secondary resistance, you must first disconnect all wires from the ignition coil terminals. Using an ohmmeter, check the resistance between the positive terminal and the coil wire terminal. The resistance should be:
- 7.7-10.4 kΩ on all Canada, wagons and 1984-1986 sedans
- 10.2-13.8 kΩ on 1987-1994 U.S sedans

If the resistance is not within these tolerances (range), the coil must be replaced.

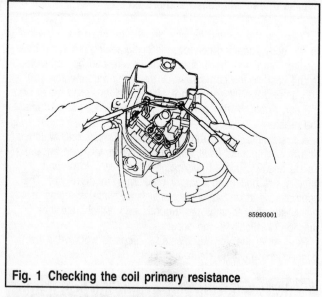

85993001

Fig. 1 Checking the coil primary resistance

REMOVAL & INSTALLATION

▶ See Figures 3, 4, 5, 6, 7 and 8

Although it is easier to access the internal coil with the distributor removed, it can be changed without removing the distributor. A selection of various short screwdrivers will be required for access to the screws.
1. Disconnect the negative battery cable.
2. Remove the distributor cap with the wires attached and set it aside.
3. Remove the rotor and the dust cover(s).

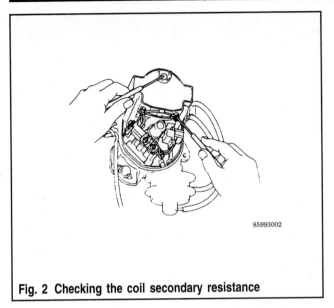

Fig. 2 Checking the coil secondary resistance

4. Remove the nuts and disconnect the wires from the terminals on the coil.

5. Remove the four retaining screws and remove the coil. Note the gasket below the coil — remove it carefully to avoid damage.

To install:

6. Install the coil, paying close attention to the gasket and its placement.

7. Connect the wiring to the coil and be careful of the routing of the wires.

8. Install the dust cover(s), the rotor and the cap.

9. Reconnect the battery.

Igniter (Ignition Module)

REMOVAL & INSTALLATION

1. Remove the distributor. Make certain the negative battery cable is disconnected before beginning this procedure.

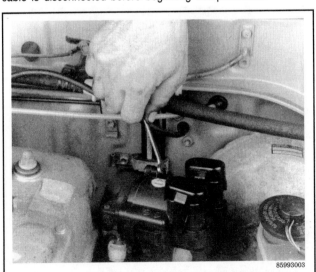

Fig. 3 The distributor cap is retained by small bolts

Fig. 4 Once the retaining bolts have been removed, the cap can be lifted out from the distributor. Be careful not to damage any components in the process

Fig. 5 The rotor can be pulled straight out from the distributor shaft. If the metal contact on the end of the rotor is bent, it must be replaced, not straightened

Fig. 6 The ignition coil dust cover is retained by two small tangs on the coil. Use care when removing it to prevent breaking the clips

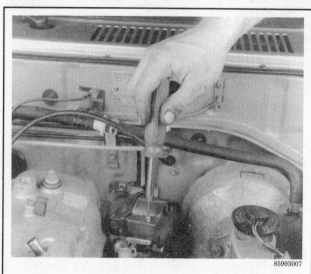

Fig. 7 Removing the ignition coil attaching screws

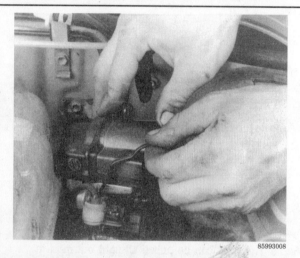

Fig. 8 Always be sure that the gasket is in place before installing the distributor cap

2. Remove the distributor cap and rotor.

3. Remove the dust cover from the distributor components, then remove the dust cover from the ignition coil.

4. Remove the nuts and disconnect the wiring from the ignition coil.

5. Remove the four screws and remove the ignition coil from the distributor.

6. At the igniter terminals, disconnect the wiring from the connecting points.

7. Loosen and remove the two screws holding the igniter and remove it from the distributor.

To install:

8. Install the igniter and connect its wiring. Pay particular attention to the correct routing of the wiring within the housing. There is one correct position only; any other wiring placements risk damage.

9. Install the ignition coil and secure its wiring. Again, watch the wiring positions.

10. Reinstall the dust covers, rotor and distributor cap.

11. Reinstall the distributor and set the engine timing.

Distributor

REMOVAL

▶ See Figure 9

❋❋WARNING

Once the distributor is removed, the engine should NOT be turned or moved out of position. Should this occur, please refer to the correct procedure in order to set initial timing.

1. Disconnect the negative battery cable.

2. Disconnect the distributor wire(s) at its connector.

3. Label and disconnect the vacuum hose(s) running to the vacuum advance unit on the side of the distributor, if so equipped.

4. Remove the distributor cap (leave the spark plug wires connected) and swing it out of the way. If necessary, label and disconnect the coil and spark plug wiring at the distributor cap.

5. Carefully note the position of the distributor rotor relative to the distributor housing (also note position of distributor to the engine assembly); a mark made on the casing/housing will be necessary during reassembly. Use a marker or tape so the mark doesn't rub off during handling of the case/housing.

6. Remove the distributor hold-down bolt.

7. Carefully pull the distributor from the engine assembly. Remove the O-ring from the distributor shaft if so equipped.

INSTALLATION

Engine not disturbed

1. If the engine has not been moved out of position, align the rotor with the mark you made earlier and reinstall the distributor. Position it carefully and make sure the drive gear engages properly within the engine. Install the hold-down bolt.

Fig. 9 Distributor hold-down bolt location

2. Install the distributor cap and connect the vacuum lines to their correct ports, if so equipped.

3. Connect the wiring to the distributor and the battery cable.

4. Check and adjust the timing as necessary.

Engine disturbed

If the engine has been cranked, dismantled or the timing otherwise lost while the distributor was out, proceed as follows.

1. Remove the No. 1 spark plug.

2. Place your finger over the spark plug hole and rotate the crankshaft clockwise to Top Dead Center (TDC). Watch the timing mark on the pulley; as it approaches the **0** point, you should feel pressure (compression) on your finger. If not, turn the crankshaft another full rotation and line up the timing mark to the **0**. This time you should feel compression.

3. Temporarily install the rotor in the distributor without the dust cover. Turn the distributor shaft so that the rotor is pointing toward the No. 1 terminal in the distributor cap.

4. Align the matchmarks on the distributor body and the block which were made during the removal. Install the distributor in the block by rotating it slightly (no more than one gear tooth in either direction) until the driven gear (lubricate the drive gear with clean engine oil) meshes with the drive.

5. If necessary, rotate the distributor once it is installed, so that the projection on the pickup coil is almost opposite the signal rotor tooth. Temporarily tighten the hold-down bolt.

6. Remove the rotor and install the dust cover. Replace the rotor and the distributor cap.

7. Install the primary wire and the vacuum line(s) if so equipped.

8. Install the No. 1 spark plug. Connect the cables to the spark plugs in the proper order by using the marks made during removal. Install the high tension lead if it was removed.

9. Start the engine. Adjust the ignition timing as necessary.

Alternator

ALTERNATOR PRECAUTIONS

Several precautions must be observed with alternator to avoid damaging the unit:

• If the battery is removed or disconnected for any reason, make sure that it is reconnected with the correct polarity. Reversing the battery connections will result in serious damage.

• When utilizing a booster battery as a starting aid, always connect it as follows: positive-to-positive, and negative (booster battery) to a good ground on the engine of the car being started.

• Never use a fast charger as a booster to start a car with an alternator.

• When servicing the battery with a fast charger, always disconnect the car battery cables.

• Never attempt to polarize an alternator.

• Never apply more than 12 volts when attempting to jump start the vehicle.

• Do not use test lamps of more than 12 volts (V) for checking diode continuity.

• Do not short across or ground any of the terminals on the alternator.

• Never disconnect the alternator or the battery with the engine running.

• Always disconnect the battery terminals when performing any service on the electrical system.

• Disconnect the battery ground cable if arc welding (such as body repair) is to be done on any part of the car.

Noise from an alternator may be caused by a loose drive pulley, a loose belt, loose mounting bolts, worn or dirty bearings or worn internal parts. A high frequency whine that is heard at high engine speed or full alternator output is acceptable and should not be considered a sign of alternator failure.

TESTING

▶ **See Figures 10, 11 and 12**

There are several tests that can be done with inexpensive equipment. The first thing to do is to see if the discharge warning lamp on the dashboard illuminates when the ignition switch is turned **ON**. If it does not, check for blown fuses, a burned out bulb, or bad connections.

If the warning lamp does light with the ignition switch **ON**, but stays on with the engine running, check for the following:

• Proper electrolyte level (specific gravity) in the battery
• Loose or missing alternator belt
• Loose or corroded battery cable
• A blown fuse or fusible link
• A shorted or open wire

If everything checks out OK, but the charge lamp is still on, the alternator itself is probably to blame. This does not mean the entire alternator needs to be replaced. Many times the voltage regulator may be faulty and cause a no charge condition. Check the alternator and regulator operation by performing the following tests.

➡**If a battery/alternator tester is available, connect the tester to the charging circuit as per manufacturer's instructions.**

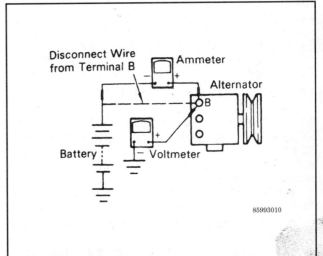

Fig. 10 Connect a voltmeter and ammeter to the charging circuit as shown

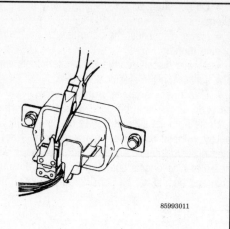

85993011

Fig. 11 The voltage regulator on models without the IC regulator is adjustable

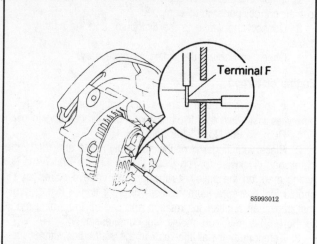

Terminal F

85993012

Fig. 12 Grounding Terminal F on models with the IC regulator

1. Connect a voltmeter and ammeter to the charging circuit as follows:

   a. Disconnect the wire from terminal B of the alternator and connect it to the negative probe of the ammeter.

   b. Connect the test probe from the positive (+) terminal of the ammeter to terminal B of the alternator.

   c. Connect the positive (+) probe of the voltmeter to terminal B of the alternator.

   d. Ground the negative (-) probe of the voltmeter.

✳✳CAUTION

Keep all wires, tools, etc., away from moving engine parts. Serious personal injury and damage to the car will result otherwise.

2. With the engine running from idle to 2,000 rpm, check the reading on the ammeter and voltmeter. Note that the following readings are taken at an ambient temperature of 77° F (25°C). Voltage will decrease slightly as temperature increases.
Amperage:
• Less than 10 amps on all models and years
Voltage:
• 13.8-14.8 V on 1984-1986 models without IC regulator
• 13.8-14.4 V on 1984 models with IC regulator
• 13.5-15.1 V on 1985-1987 models with IC regulator
• 13.9-15.1 V on 1988-1994 models with IC regulator

3. On models without the IC regulator, if the voltage reading is not within specifications, adjust or replace the regulator. The regulator can be adjusted by bending the regulator adjusting arm.

4. If the voltage reading is less than specified on models with the IC regulator, proceed as follows:

   a. With terminal F grounded, start the engine and check the voltage reading of terminal B.

   b. If the voltage is greater than specified, replace the IC regulator.

   c. If the voltage is less than specified, the alternator is probably at fault.

5. Remove the ground from terminal F, if applicable.

6. To check the charging system under a load:

   a. With the engine running at 2,000 rpm, turn on the high beams and place the heater fan control switch on HI.

   b. Check the amperage reading on the ammeter. It should read 30 amps or more.

   c. If the reading is less than 30 amps, the alternator is faulty.

➡With the battery fully charged, the reading may sometimes be less than 30 amps.

REMOVAL & INSTALLATION

◗ See Figures 13, 14, 15 and 16

✳✳CAUTION

On models equipped with a Supplemental Restraint System (SRS) or "air bag," work must NOT be started until at least 90 seconds have passed from the time that both the ignition switch is turned to the LOCK position and the negative cable is disconnected from the battery.

1. Disconnect the negative battery cable.

➡Failure to disconnect the battery can cause personal injury and damage to the car. If a tool is accidentally shorted at the alternator, it will become hot enough to cause a serious burn. On some models, the alternator is mounted very low on the engine. It may be necessary to remove the gravel shield and work from underneath the car in order to gain access to the alternator retaining bolts.

2. Unplug the large connector from the alternator.
3. Remove the nut(s) and the single wire(s) from the alternator.
4. Loosen the adjusting lock bolt and pivot bolt. Remove the drive belt. It may be necessary to remove other belts for access.
5. Remove the lower bolt first, support the alternator and remove the upper bolt. Remove the alternator from the car.

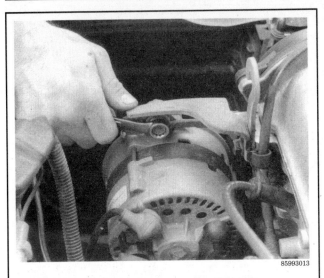

Fig. 13 Removing the alternator adjusting bolt

Fig. 14 Be careful not to break the retaining clip when unplugging the electrical connector

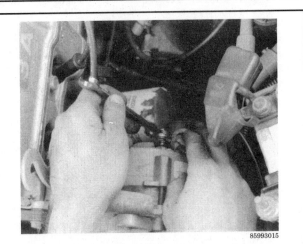

Fig. 15 The battery must be disconnected before disengaging any electrical connections from the alternator

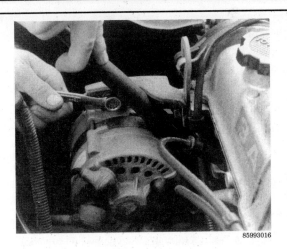

Fig. 16 When adjusting the belt tension, always pry on the center of the alternator, not the aluminum end frames

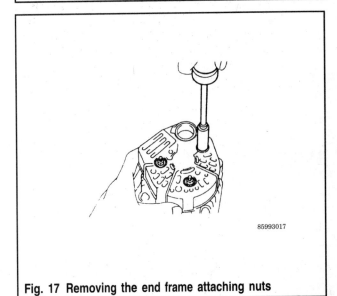

Fig. 17 Removing the end frame attaching nuts

To install:

6. Install the alternator onto the bracket. Leave the bolts finger-tight so that the belt may be adjusted to the correct tension.

7. Adjust the drive belt tension.

8. Connect the wires and plug the connector into the alternator. Make sure that the electrical plugs and connections are properly seated and secured.

9. Connect the negative battery cable and check for proper alternator operation.

Regulator

REMOVAL & INSTALLATION

♦ **See Figures 17, 18, 19, 20 and 21**

Except IC Regulator

Some 1984-1986 models are equipped with a voltage regulator that is not integral with the alternator. It is located on the left fender apron of the engine compartment. If you are uncertain as to which regulator is in your car, a label on the alternator will specify if it has an internal (IC) regulator.

1. Unplug the electrical connector.
2. Remove the regulator attaching screws and remove it from the vehicle.
3. Installation is the reverse of removal.

IC Regulator

The voltage regulator is contained within the alternator. It is called an Integrated Circuit (IC) type. The alternator must be removed to replace the regulator.

1. Disconnect the negative battery cable.
2. Remove the alternator following the procedures and cautions located earlier in this section.
3. Support the alternator on a workbench, pulley end down, but do not let it rest on the pulley itself.
4. On the side of the alternator, remove the plastic terminal insulator or dust cover, if applicable.
5. Remove the three nuts and remove the end cover.
6. Remove the five screws and carefully remove the brush holder and then the IC regulator. Be careful to keep track of various small parts (washers, etc) — they will be needed during reassembly.

To install:

7. Place the cover over the brush holder. Install the regulator and the brush holder onto the alternator and secure them with the five screws. Make sure the brush holder's cover doesn't slip to one side during installation.
8. Before reinstalling the rear cover, check that the gap between the bush holder and the regulator is approximately 0.04 in. (1mm). After confirming this gap, install the rear alternator cover and its three nuts.
9. Install the terminal insulator or dust cover. Hold the alternator horizontally and spin the pulley by hand. Make sure everything turns smoothly and there is no sign of noise or binding.

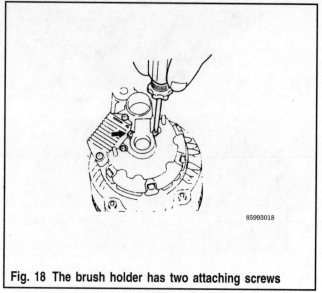

85993018

Fig. 18 The brush holder has two attaching screws

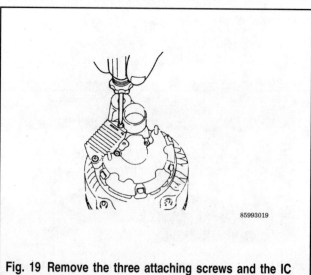

85993019

Fig. 19 Remove the three attaching screws and the IC regulator

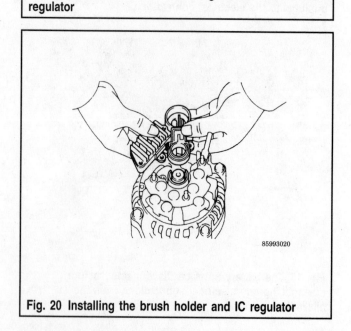

85993020

Fig. 20 Installing the brush holder and IC regulator

Battery

REMOVAL & INSTALLATION

▶ See Figure 22

1. Disconnect the negative battery cable (special pullers are available to remove the clamps on post terminals).

✲✲CAUTION

Spilled acid can be neutralized with a baking soda and water solution. If you get acid in your eyes, flush it out with lots of clean water and get to a doctor as quickly as possible.

2. Disconnect the positive battery cable.

3. Remove the bolts holding the battery retainer and remove the retainer.
4. Remove the battery. The battery is a fairly heavy item, use care in lifting it out of the car.

To install:

5. Clean the battery posts thoroughly before reinstalling or when installing a new one.
6. Clean the cable clamps, using the special tools or a wire brush, both inside and out.
7. Install the battery in the car.
8. Make certain that the retainer is correctly placed and its bolts are tight. Connect the positive cable first, then the negative cable. On post terminals, do not hammer the connector into place. The terminals should be coated with dielectric grease to prevent corrosion.

➡Removing the battery may require resetting various digital equipment such as radio memory and the clock.

ALTERNATOR SPECIFICATIONS

		Alternator		
Year	Engine (cc)	Field Current @ 12V (amps)	Output (amps)	Regulated Volts @ 75°F
1984	All	10	30	13.8–14.4①
1985	All	10	30	13.5–15.1①
1986	All	10	30	13.5–15.1①
1987	All	10	30	13.5–15.1
1988	All	10	30	13.9–15.1
1989	All	10	60	13.9–15.1
1990	All	10	60	13.9–15.1
1991	All	10	60	13.9–15.1
1992	All	10	60	13.9–15.1
1993	All	10	60	13.9–15.1
1994	All	10	60	13.9–15.1

① 13.8–14.8 on models without IC Regulator

85993300

Starter

TESTING

▶ See Figures 23 and 24

➡These tests must not be performed longer than 3-5 seconds to avoid burning out the coil.

Reduction Type

1. Remove the starter from the vehicle.
2. Secure the starter solidly in an appropriate holding fixture.
3. Connect an ammeter in series with the positive (+) lead of a battery and terminal numbers 30 and 50 of the starter.

✲✲CAUTION

DO NOT ground the positive leads against the starter or holding fixture! Starter damage and serious injury could result.

4. Connect the negative (-) lead of a battery to the starter housing.
5. Check that the starter rotates smoothly and steadily with the pinion gear moving out. Check that the ammeter shows 90 amps or less of current.

Conventional Type

1. Remove the starter from the vehicle.
2. Secure the starter solidly in an appropriate holding fixture.
3. Connect an ammeter in series with the positive (+) lead of a battery and both terminals at the starter.

✲✲CAUTION

DO NOT ground the positive leads against the starter or holding fixture! Starter damage and serious injury could result.

4. Connect the negative (-) lead of a battery to the starter housing.

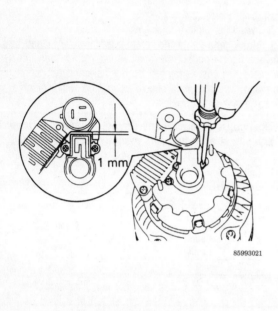

Fig. 21 Make sure the gap between the brush holder connector is as specified

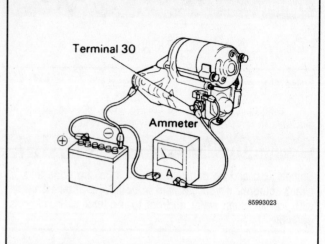

Fig. 23 Connect the ammeter as shown on reduction type starters

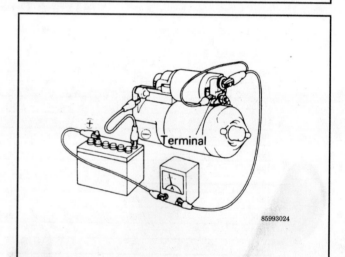

Fig. 24 On conventional type starters, connect the ammeter as shown

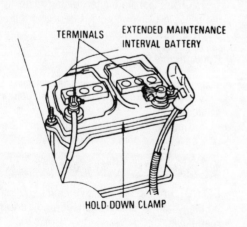
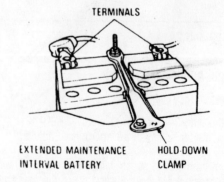

Fig. 22 Two types of battery hold-down clamps

5. Check that the starter rotates smoothly and steadily with the pinion gear moving out. Check that the ammeter shows 50 amps or less of current.

REMOVAL & INSTALLATION

▶ See Figure 25

❊❊CAUTION

On models equipped with a Supplemental Restraint System (SRS) or "air bag," work must NOT be started until at least 90 seconds have passed from the time that both the ignition switch is turned to the LOCK position and the negative cable is disconnected from the battery.

1. Disconnect the negative battery cable.
2. Disconnect all the wiring from the starter terminals. On some models, it may be necessary to remove the transaxle cable and bracket from the transaxle.
3. Remove the heat insulator, if equipped, and the starter mounting bolts.
4. Remove the starter.
5. Installation is the reverse of the removal procedure.

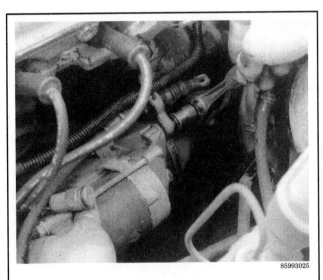

85993025

Fig. 25 Removing the starter from the vehicle

SOLENOID REPLACEMENT

▶ See Figures 26, 27 and 28

The starter solenoid (magnetic switch) is an integral part of the reduction type starter. It cannot be replaced without partial disassembly of the starter. On the conventional type starter, the solenoid (magnetic switch) can be replaced without disassembly.

Reduction Type

1. Remove the starter following the cautions and procedures described earlier.
2. Remove the nut connecting the lead wire from the magnetic switch terminal.
3. Remove the two through-bolts. Pull out the field frame assembly together with the armature from the magnetic switch.
4. Remove the two screws attaching the starter housing to the magnetic switch assembly.
5. Separate the starter housing together with the idler gear and clutch assembly from the magnetic switch.

To install:

6. Install the starter housing together with the idler gear and clutch assembly onto the magnetic switch.
7. Align the protrusion of the field frame with the groove of the magnetic switch.
8. Install the field frame assembly onto the magnetic switch. Secure the assembly with the two through-bolts.
9. Connect the lead wire to the magnetic switch terminal and install the nut.
10. Test the starter for proper operation.
11. Install the starter.

Conventional Type

1. Remove the starter following the cautions and procedures described earlier.
2. Remove the nut connecting the lead wire from the magnetic switch terminal.
3. Loosen the two nuts holding the magnetic switch to the drive housing.
4. Lift the magnetic switch up and out to unhook the plunger from the drive lever.

To install:

5. Hook the plunger underneath the drive lever.
6. Install the two attaching nuts.
7. Install the magnetic switch lead wire and nut.
8. Test the starter for proper operation.
9. Install the starter.

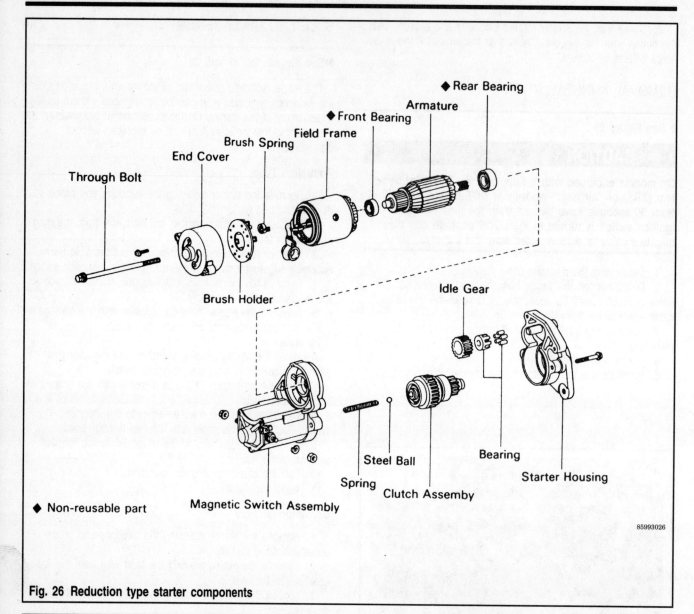

Rear Bearing

Armature

Front Bearing

Field Frame

Brush Spring

End Cover

Through Bolt

Brush Holder

Idle Gear

Starter Housing

Bearing

Steel Ball

Spring

Clutch Assemby

Magnetic Switch Assembly

◆ Non-reusable part

85993026

Fig. 26 Reduction type starter components

85993028

Fig. 27 When installing the magnetic switch, make sure to engage the plunger stud underneath the drive lever

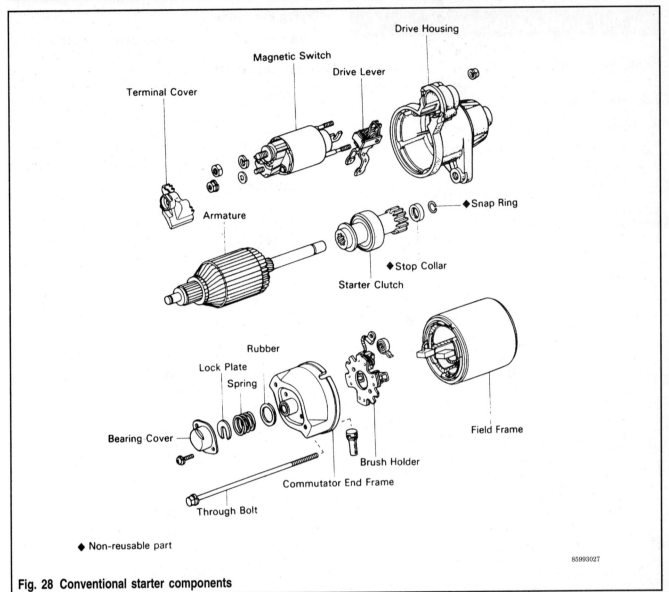

Fig. 28 Conventional starter components

STARTER SPECIFICATIONS

| Year | Load Test | | No-Load Test | | |
	Amps	Volts	Amps	Volts	RPM
1984 ①	Not Recommended		90	11.5	3,500 +
1985 ①	Not Recommended		90	11.5	3,500 +
1986 ①	Not Recommended		90	11.5	3,500 +
1987 ①	Not Recommended		90	11.5	3,500 +
1988 ①	Not Recommended		90	11.5	3,500 +
1989 ①	Not Recommended		90	11.5	5,800 +
1990 ①	Not Recommended		90	11.5	5,800 +
1991 ①	Not Recommended		90	11.5	5,800 +
1992 ①	Not Recommended		90	11.5	5,800 +
1993 ①	Not Recommended		90	11.5	5,800 +
1994 ①	Not Recommended		90	11.5	5,800 +

① Conventional type starter—50 amps, 11 volts,
   5.000 rpm

Sending Units and Sensors

REMOVAL & INSTALLATION

▶ See Figures 29, 30 and 31

Water Temperature Senders and Sensors

1. Disconnect the negative battery cable.
2. Drain the cooling system.
3. Unplug the electrical connector.
4. Remove the sensor using a suitable tool.
5. Installation is the reverse of removal. Fill the cooling system and check for leaks.

Cooling Fan Switch

The cooling fan switch is also known as the water temperature switch. Follow the procedures for Water Temperature Senders and Sensors.

Oil Pressure Sender

1. Disconnect the negative battery cable.
2. Unplug the electrical connector.
3. Remove the sensor using a suitable tool.
4. Installation is the reverse of removal. Check for leaks.

Fuel Level Sender

The fuel level sending unit removal and installation procedure is covered in Section 5.

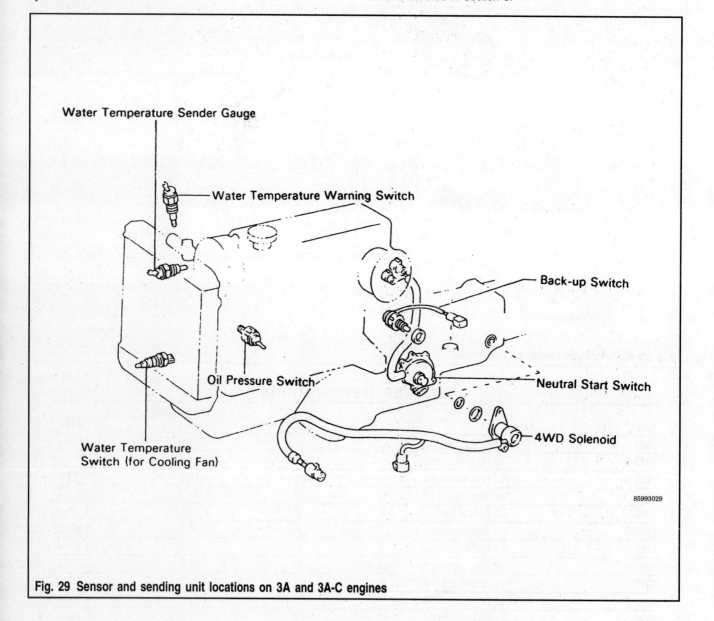

Fig. 29 Sensor and sending unit locations on 3A and 3A-C engines

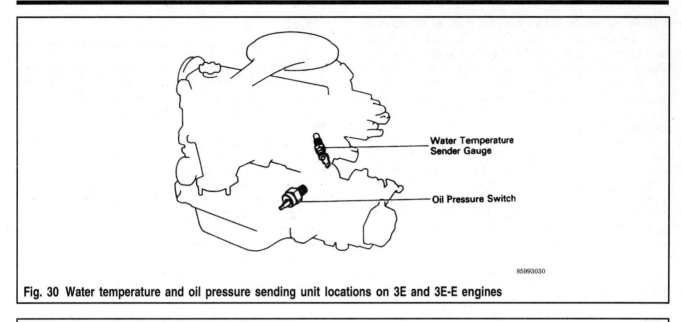

Fig. 30 Water temperature and oil pressure sending unit locations on 3E and 3E-E engines

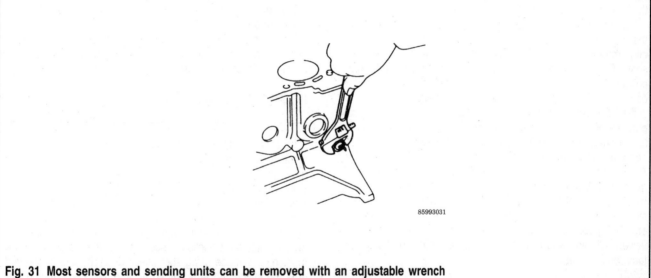

Fig. 31 Most sensors and sending units can be removed with an adjustable wrench

ENGINE MECHANICAL

Understanding the Engine

The engine is basically a metal block containing a series of round chambers or cylinders. The upper part of the engine block is usually an iron or aluminum alloy casting. The casting forms outer walls around the cylinders with hollow areas in between, through which coolant circulates. The lower block provides a number of rigid mounting points for the crankshaft and its bearings. The lower block is referred to as the crankcase.

The crankshaft is a long, steel shaft mounted at the bottom of the engine and free to turn in its mounts. The mounting points (generally four to seven) and the bearings for the crankshaft are called main bearings. The crankshaft is the shaft which is made to turn through the function of the engine; this motion is then passed into the transaxle and on to the drive wheels.

Attached to the crankshaft are the connecting rods which run up to the pistons within the cylinders. As the air/fuel mixture explodes within the tightly sealed cylinder, the piston is forced downward. This motion is transferred through the connecting rod to the crankshaft and turns the shaft. As one piston finishes its power stroke, its next upward journey forces the burnt gasses out of the cylinder through the now-open exhaust valve. By the top of the stroke, the exhaust valve has closed and the intake valve has begun to open, allowing the fresh air/fuel charge to be sucked into the cylinder by the downward stroke of the piston. The intake valve closes, then the piston once again comes back up and compresses the charge in the closed cylinder. Near the top of this stroke the spark plug fires, the charge explodes and another power stroke takes place. If you count the piston motions in between power strokes, you'll see why most automotive engines are called four-stroke or four-cycle engines.

While one cylinder is performing this cycle, all the others are also contributing; but in different timing. Obviously, all the cylinders cannot fire at once or the power flow would not be steady. As any one cylinder is on its power stroke, another is on its exhaust stroke, another on intake and another on compression. These constant power pulses keep the crank turning; a large round flywheel attached to the end of the crankshaft provides a stable mass to smooth out the rotation.

At the top of the engine, the cylinder head provides tight covers for the cylinders. They contain machined chambers into which the fuel charge is forced as the piston reaches the top of its travel. These combustion chambers contain at least one intake and one exhaust valve which are opened and closed through the action of the camshaft. The spark plugs are screwed into the cylinder head so that the tips of the plugs protrude into the chamber.

Since the timing of the valve action (opening and closing) is critical to the combustion process, the camshaft is driven by the crankshaft via a belt or chain. The valves are operated either by pushrods (called overhead valves — the valves are above the cam) or by the direct action of the cam pushing on the valves (overhead cam).

Lubricating oil is stored in a pan or sump at the bottom of the engine. It is force fed to all the parts of the engine by the oil pump which may be driven off either the crank or the cam shaft. The oil lubricates the entire engine by travelling through passages in the block and head. Additionally, circulation of the oil provides 25-40 percent of the engine cooling.

If all this seems very complicated, keep in mind that the sole purpose of any motor — gas, diesel, electric, solar, etc — is to turn a shaft. The motion of the shaft is then harnessed to perform a task such as pumping water, moving the car, etc. Accomplishing this shaft turning in an automotive engine requires many supporting systems such as fuel delivery, exhaust handling, lubrication, cooling, starting, etc. Operation of these systems involve principles of mechanics, vacuum, electronics, etc. Being able to identify a problem by what system is involved will allow you to begin accurate diagnosis of the symptoms and causes.

Engine Overhaul Tips

Most engine overhaul procedures are fairly standard. In addition to specific parts replacement procedures and specifications for your individual engine, this section also is a guide to accepted rebuilding procedures. Examples of standard rebuilding practice are shown and should be used along with specific details concerning your particular engine.

Competent and accurate machine shop services will ensure maximum performance, reliability and engine life. In most instances it is more profitable for the do-it-yourself mechanic to remove, clean and inspect the component, buy the necessary parts and deliver these to a shop for actual machine work.

On the other hand, much of the rebuilding work (crankshaft, block, bearings, piston rods, and other components) is well within the scope of the do-it-yourself mechanic. Patience, proper tools, and common sense coupled a basic understanding of the motor can yield satisfying and economical results.

TOOLS

The tools required for an engine overhaul or parts replacement will depend on the depth of your involvement. With a few exceptions, they will be the tools found in a mechanic's tool kit (see Section 1). More in depth work will require any or all of the following:
- A dial indicator (reading in thousandths) mounted on a universal base
- Micrometers and telescope gauges
- Jaw and screw type pullers
- Gasket scrapers
- Valve spring compressor
- Ring groove cleaner
- Piston ring expander and compressor
- Ridge reamer
- Cylinder hone or glaze breaker
- Plastigage®
- Engine stand

The use of most of these tools is illustrated in this section. Many can be rented for a one time use from a local parts jobber or tool supply house specializing in automotive work.

Occasionally, the use of special tools is called for. See the information on Special Tools and the Safety Notice in the front of this book before substituting another tool.

INSPECTION TECHNIQUES

Procedures and specifications are given in this section for inspecting, cleaning and assessing the wear limits of most major components. Other procedures such as Magnaflux® and Zyglo® can be used to locate material flaws and stress cracks. Magnaflux® is a magnetic process applicable only to ferrous (iron and steel) materials. The Zyglo® process coats the material with a fluorescent dye penetrant and can be used on any material. Checks for suspected surface cracks can be more readily made using spot check dye. The dye is sprayed onto the suspected area, wiped off and the area sprayed with a developer. Cracks will show up brightly.

OVERHAUL TIPS

Aluminum has become extremely popular for use in engines, due to its low weight. Observe the following precautions when handling aluminum parts:
- Never hot tank aluminum parts (the caustic hot tank solution will eat the aluminum.)
- Remove all aluminum parts (identification tag, etc.) from engine parts prior to tanking.
- Always coat threads lightly with engine oil or anti-seize compounds before installation to prevent seizure.
- Never overtighten bolts or spark plugs especially in aluminum threads.

Stripped threads in any component can be repaired using any of several commercial repair kits (Heli-Coil®, Microdot®, Keenserts®, etc.).

When assembling the engine, any parts that will be in frictional contact must be prelubed to provide lubrication at initial start-up. Any product specifically formulated for this purpose can be used, but engine oil is not recommended as a prelube.

When semi-permanent (locked, but removable) installation of bolts or nuts is desired, threads should be cleaned and coated with Loctite® or other similar, commercial non-hardening sealant.

REPAIRING DAMAGED THREADS

▶ **See Figures 32, 33, 34, 35 and 36**

Several methods of repairing damaged threads are available. Heli-Coil® (shown here), Keenserts® and Microdot® are among the most widely used. All involve basically the same principle — drilling out stripped threads, tapping the hole and installing a prewound insert — making welding, plugging and oversize fasteners unnecessary.

Two types of thread repair inserts are usually supplied: a standard type for most inch coarse, inch fine, metric course and metric fine thread sizes and a spark lug type to fit most

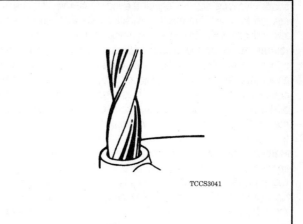

Fig. 34 Drill out the damaged threads with the specified drill. Be sure to drill completely through the hole or to the bottom of a blind hole

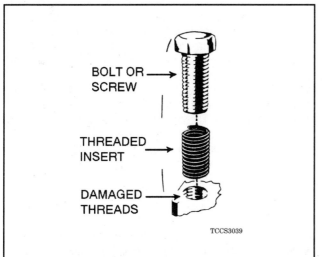

Fig. 32 Damaged bolt hole threads can be replaced with thread repair inserts

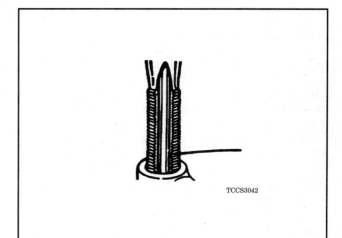

Fig. 35 Using the kit, tap the hole in order to receive the thread insert. Keep the tap well oiled and back it out frequently to avoid clogging the threads.

Fig. 33 Standard thread repair insert (left), and spark plug thread insert

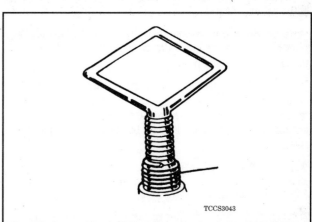

Fig. 36 Screw the threaded insert onto the installer tool until the tang engages the slot. Thread the insert into the hole until it is ¼ or ½ turn below the top surface, then remove the tool and break off the tang using a punch.

spark plug port sizes. Consult the individual manufacturer's catalog to determine exact applications. Typical thread repair kits will contain a selection of prewound threaded inserts, a tap (corresponding to the outside diameter threads of the insert) and an installation tool. Spark plug inserts usually differ because they require a tap equipped with pilot threads and a combined reamer/tap section. Most manufacturers also supply blister-packed thread repair inserts separately in addition to a master kit containing a variety of taps and inserts plus installation tools.

Before attempting to repair a threaded hole, remove any snapped, broken or damaged bolts or studs. Penetrating oil can be used to free frozen threads. The offending item can be removed with locking pliers or using a screw/stud extractor. After the hole is clear, the thread can be repaired, as shown in the series of accompanying illustrations and in the kit manufacturer's instructions.

Checking Engine Compression

▶ See Figure 37

A noticeable lack of engine power, excessive oil consumption and/or poor fuel mileage measured over an extended period are all indicators of internal engine wear. Worn piston rings, scored or worn cylinder bores, leaking head gaskets, sticking or burnt valves and worn valve seats are all possible culprits here. A check of each cylinder's compression will help you locate the problems.

As mentioned in Section 1, a screw in type compression gauge is more accurate than the type you simply hold against the spark plug hole. Although it takes slightly longer to use, it's worth the time to obtain a more accurate reading. Follow the procedures below.

1. Warm up the engine to normal operating temperature.
2. Remove all the spark plugs.
3. Disconnect the high tension lead from the ignition coil.
4. Fully open the throttle either by operating the carburetor throttle linkage by hand or by having an assistant floor the accelerator pedal.
5. Screw the compression gauge into the No. 1 spark plug hole until the fitting is snug.

➡**Be careful not to crossthread the plug hole. On aluminum cylinder heads use extra care, as the threads in these heads are easily ruined.**

6. Ask an assistant to depress the accelerator pedal fully on both carbureted and fuel injected vehicles. Then, while you read the compression gauge, ask the assistant to crank the engine two or three times in short bursts using the ignition switch.

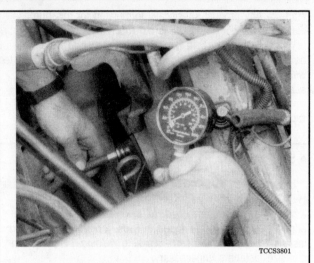

Fig. 37 A screw-in type compression gauge is more accurate and easier to use

7. Read the compression gauge at the end of each series of cranks, and record the highest of these readings. Repeat this procedure for each of the engine's cylinders.

As a general rule, new motors will have compression of about 150-170 Pounds per Square Inch (psi). This number will decrease with age and wear. The number of pounds of pressure that your test shows is not as important as the evenness between all the cylinders. Many cars run very well with all cylinders at 105 psi. The lower number simply shows a general deterioration internally. This car probably burns a little oil and may be a bit harder to start, but based on these numbers doesn't warrant an engine tear-down yet.

Compare the highest reading of all the cylinders. Any variation of more than 10 percent should be considered a sign of potential trouble. For example, if your compression readings for cylinders 1 through 4 were: 135 psi, 125 psi, 90 psi and 125 psi, it would be fair to say that cylinder number three is not working efficiently and is almost certainly the cause of your oil burning, rough idle or poor fuel mileage.

8. If a cylinder is unusually low, pour a tablespoon of clean engine oil into the cylinder through the spark plug hole and repeat the compression test. If the compression comes up after adding the oil, it appears that the cylinder's piston rings or bore are damaged or worn. If the pressure remains low, the valves may not be seating properly (a valve job is needed), or the head gasket may be blown near that cylinder. If compression in any two adjacent cylinders is low, and if the addition of oil doesn't help the compression, there is leakage past the head gasket. Oil and coolant in the combustion chamber can result from this problem. There may be evidence of water droplets on the engine dipstick when a head gasket has blown.

GENERAL ENGINE SPECIFICATIONS

Model	Year	Engine Type	Engine Displacement Cu. In. (cc)	System Type	Horsepower (@ rpm)	Torque @ rpm (ft. lbs.)	Bore × Stroke (in.)	Compression Ratio
Tercel	1984	3A, 3A-C	88.6 (1452)	Carb.	62 @ 5,200	75 @ 2,800	3.05 × 3.03	9.0:1
	1985	3A, 3A-C	88.6 (1452)	Carb.	62 @ 5,200	75 @ 2,800	3.05 × 3.03	9.0:1
	1986	3A, 3A-C	88.6 (1452)	Carb.	62 @ 5,200	75 @ 2,800	3.05 × 3.03	9.0:1
	1987	3A, 3A-C	88.6 (1452)	Carb.	62 @ 5,200	75 @ 2,800	3.05 × 3.03	9.0:1
		3E	88.9 (1456)	Carb.	78 @ 6,000	87 @ 4,000	2.87 × 3.54	9.3:1
	1988	3A, 3A-C	88.6 (1452)	Carb.	62 @ 5,200	75 @ 2,800	3.05 × 3.03	9.0:1
		3E	88.9 (1456)	Carb.	78 @ 6,000	87 @ 4,000	2.87 × 3.54	9.3:1
	1989	3E	88.9 (1456)	Carb.	78 @ 6,000	87 @ 4,000	2.87 × 3.54	9.3:1
	1990	3E	88.9 (1452)	Carb.	78 @ 6,000	87 @ 4,000	2.87 × 3.54	9.3:1
		3E-E	88.9 (1456)	EFI	82 @ 5,200	89 @ 4,400	2.87 × 3.54	9.3:1
	1991	3E-E	88.9 (1456)	EFI	82 @ 5,200	89 @ 4,400	2.87 × 3.54	9.3:1
	1992	3E-E	88.9 (1456)	EFI	82 @ 5,200	89 @ 4,400	2.87 × 3.54	9.3:1
	1993	3E-E	88.9 (1456)	EFI	82 @ 5,200	89 @ 4,400	2.87 × 3.54	9.3:1
	1994	3E-E	88.9 (1456)	EFI	82 @ 5,200	89 @ 4,400	2.87 × 3.54	9.3:1

85993302

VALVE SPECIFICATIONS

Year	Engine ID/VIN	Engine Displacement Liters (cc)	Seat Angle (deg.)	Face Angle (deg.)	Spring Test Pressure (lbs.)	Spring Installed Height (in.)	Stem-to-Guide Clearance (in.)		Stem Diameter (in.)	
							Intake	Exhaust	Intake	Exhaust
1984	3A, 3A-C	1.4 (1452)	45	44.5	52	1.520	0.0010–0.0024	0.0012–0.0026	0.2744–0.2750	0.2742–0.2748
1985	3A, 3A-C	1.4 (1452)	45	44.5	52	1.520	0.0010–0.0024	0.0012–0.0026	0.2744–0.2750	0.2742–0.2748
1986	3A, 3A-C	1.4 (1452)	45	44.5	52	1.520	0.0010–0.0024	0.0012–0.0026	0.2744–0.2750	0.2742–0.2748
1987	3A, 3A-C	1.4 (1452)	45	44.5	52	1.520	0.0010–0.0024	0.0012–0.0026	0.2744–0.2750	0.2742–0.2748
	3E	1.5 (1456)	45	44.5	35	1.384	0.0010–0.0024 ①	0.0012–0.0026	0.2350–0.2356 ①	0.2348–0.2354
1988	3A, 3A-C	1.4 (1452)	45	44.5	52	1.520	0.0010–0.0024	0.0012–0.0026	0.2744–0.2750	0.2742–0.2748
	3E	1.5 (1456)	45	44.5	35	1.384	0.0010–0.0024 ①	0.0012–0.0026	0.2350–0.2356 ①	0.2348–0.2354
1989	3E	1.5 (1456)	45	44.5	35	1.384	0.0010–0.0024 ①	0.0012–0.0026	0.2350–0.2356 ①	0.2348–0.2354
1990	3E, 3E-E	1.5 (1456)	45	44.5	35	1.384	0.0010–0.0024 ①	0.0012–0.0026	0.2350–0.2356 ①	0.2348–0.2354
1991	3E-E	1.5 (1456)	45	44.5	35	1.384	0.0010–0.0024 ①	0.0012–0.0026	0.2350–0.2356 ①	0.2348–0.2354
1992	3E-E	1.5 (1456)	45	44.5	35	1.384	0.0010–0.0024 ①	0.0012–0.0026	0.2350–0.2356 ①	0.2348–0.2354
1993	3E-E	1.5 (1456)	45	44.5	35	1.384	0.0010–0.0024 ①	0.0012–0.0026	0.2350–0.2356 ①	0.2348–0.2354
1994	3E-E	1.5 (1456)	45	44.5	35	1.384	0.0010–0.0024 ①	0.0012–0.0026	0.2350–0.2356 ①	0.2348–0.2354

① Includes Sub-Intake Valve

85993303

CAMSHAFT SPECIFICATIONS

All measurements given in inches.

Year	Engine ID/VIN	Engine Displacement Liters (cc)	Journal Diameter				Elevation		Bearing Clearance	Camshaft End Play
			1	2	3	4	In.	Ex.		
1984	3A, 3A-C	1.4 (1452)	1.1015–1.1022	1.1015–1.1022	1.1015–1.1022	1.1015–1.1022	1.5528–1.5531 ①	1.5528–1.5531 ①	0.0015–0.0029	0.0031–0.0071
1985	3A, 3A-C	1.4 (1452)	1.1015–1.1022	1.1015–1.1022	1.1015–1.1022	1.1015–1.1022	1.5528–1.5531 ①	1.5528–1.5531 ①	0.0015–0.0029	0.0031–0.0071
1986	3A, 3A-C	1.4 (1452)	1.1015–1.1022	1.1015–1.1022	1.1015–1.1022	1.1015–1.1022	1.5528–1.5531 ①	1.5528–1.5531 ①	0.0015–0.0029	0.0031–0.0071
1987	3A, 3A-C	1.4 (1452)	1.1015–1.1022	1.1015–1.1022	1.1015–1.1022	1.1015–1.1022	1.5528–1.5531	1.5528–1.5531	0.0015–0.0029	0.0031–0.0071
	3E	1.5 (1456)	1.0622–1.0628	1.0622–1.0628	1.0622–1.0628	1.0622–1.0628	1.3917–1.3957 ②	1.4106–1.4116	0.0015–0.0029	0.0031–0.0071
1988	3A, 3A-C	1.4 (1452)	1.1015–1.1022	1.1015–1.1022	1.1015–1.1022	1.1015–1.1022	1.5528–1.5531	1.5528–1.5531	0.0015–0.0029	0.0031–0.0071
	3E	1.5 (1456)	1.0622–1.0628	1.0622–1.0628	1.0622–1.0628	1.0622–1.0628	1.3917–1.3957 ②	1.4106–1.4116	0.0015–0.0029	0.0031–0.0071
1989	3E	1.5 (1456)	1.0622–1.0628	1.0622–1.0628	1.0622–1.0628	1.0622–1.0628	1.3917–1.3957 ②	1.4106–1.4116	0.0015–0.0029	0.0031–0.0071
1990	3E, 3E-E	1.5 (1456)	1.0622–1.0628	1.0622–1.0628	1.0622–1.0628	1.0622–1.0628	1.3917–1.3957 ②	1.4106–1.4116	0.0015–0.0029	0.0031–0.0071
1991	3E-E	1.5 (1456)	1.0622–1.0628	1.0622–1.0628	1.0622–1.0628	1.0622–1.0628	1.3917–1.3957 ②	1.4106–1.4116	0.0015–0.0029	0.0031–0.0071
1992	3E-E	1.5 (1456)	1.0622–1.0628	1.0622–1.0628	1.0622–1.0628	1.0622–1.0628	1.3917–1.3957 ②	1.4106–1.4116	0.0015–0.0029	0.0031–0.0071
1993	3E-E	1.5 (1456)	1.0622–1.0628	1.0622–1.0628	1.0622–1.0628	1.0622–1.0628	1.3917–1.3957 ②	1.4106–1.4116	0.0015–0.0029	0.0031–0.0071
1994	3E-E	1.5 (1456)	1.0622–1.0628	1.0622–1.0628	1.0622–1.0628	1.0622–1.0628	1.3917–1.3957 ②	1.4106–1.4116	0.0015–0.0029	0.0031–0.0071

① 1984 to 1986 3A-C 4-speed M/T: 1.5366–1.5370 Intake and Exhaust
② Sub-Intake Valve: 1.3744–1.3783

85993304

CRANKSHAFT AND CONNECTING ROD SPECIFICATIONS

All measurements are given in inches.

Year	Engine ID/VIN	Engine Displacement Liters (cc)	Crankshaft				Connecting Rod		
			Main Brg. Journal Dia.	Main Brg. Oil Clearance	Shaft End-play	Thrust on No.	Journal Diameter	Oil Clearance	Side Clearance
1984	3A, 3A-C	1.4 (1452)	1.8892–1.8898	0.0012–0.0026	0.0008–0.0073	3	1.5742–1.5748	0.0008–0.0020	0.0059–0.0098
1985	3A, 3A-C	1.4 (1452)	1.8892–1.8898	0.0012–0.0026	0.0008–0.0073	3	1.5742–1.5748	0.0008–0.0020	0.0059–0.0098
1986	3A, 3A-C	1.4 (1452)	1.8892–1.8898	0.0012–0.0026	0.0008–0.0073	3	1.5742–1.5748	0.0008–0.0020	0.0059–0.0098
1987	3A, 3A-C	1.4 (1452)	1.8892–1.8898	0.0012–0.0026	0.0008–0.0073	3	1.5742–1.5748	0.0008–0.0020	0.0059–0.0098
	3E	1.5 (1456)	1.9683–1.9685	0.0006–0.0014	0.0008–0.0087	3	1.8110–1.8113	0.0006–0.0019	0.0059–0.0138
1988	3A, 3A-C	1.4 (1452)	1.8892–1.8898	0.0012–0.0026	0.0008–0.0073	3	1.5742–1.5748	0.0008–0.0020	0.0059–0.0098
	3E	1.5 (1456)	1.9683–1.9685	0.0006–0.0014	0.0008–0.0087	3	1.8110–1.8113	0.0006–0.0019	0.0059–0.0138
1989	3E	1.5 (1456)	1.9683–1.9685	0.0006–0.0014	0.0008–0.0087	3	1.8110–1.8113	0.0006–0.0019	0.0059–0.0138
1990	3E, 3E-E	1.5 (1456)	1.9683–1.9685	0.0006–0.0014	0.0008–0.0087	3	1.8110–1.8113	0.0006–0.0019	0.0059–0.0138
1991	3E-E	1.5 (1456)	1.9683–1.9685	0.0006–0.0014	0.0008–0.0087	3	1.8110–1.8113	0.0006–0.0019	0.0059–0.0138
1992	3E-E	1.5 (1456)	1.9683–1.9685	0.0006–0.0014	0.0008–0.0087	3	1.8110–1.8113	0.0006–0.0019	0.0059–0.0138
1993	3E-E	1.5 (1456)	1.9683–1.9685	0.0006–0.0014	0.0008–0.0087	3	1.8110–1.8113	0.0006–0.0019	0.0059–0.0138
1994	3E-E	1.5 (1456)	1.9683–1.9685	0.0006–0.0014	0.0008–0.0087	3	1.8110–1.8113	0.0006–0.0019	0.0059–0.0138

85993305

PISTON AND RING SPECIFICATIONS

All measurements are given in inches.

Year	Engine ID/VIN	Engine Displacement Liters (cc)	Piston Clearance	Ring Gap			Ring Side Clearance		
				Top Compression	Bottom Compression	Oil Control	Top Compression	Bottom Compression	Oil Control
1984	3A, 3A-C	1.4 (1452)	0.0039–0.0047	0.0079–0.0157	0.0059–0.0138	0.0039–0.0236	0.0016–0.0031	0.0012–0.0028	Snug
1985	3A, 3A-C	1.4 (1452)	0.0039–0.0047	0.0079–0.0157	0.0059–0.0138	0.0039–0.0236	0.0016–0.0031	0.0012–0.0028	Snug
1986	3A, 3A-C	1.4 (1452)	0.0039–0.0047	0.0079–0.0157	0.0059–0.0138	0.0039–0.0236	0.0016–0.0031	0.0012–0.0028	Snug
1987	3A, 3A-C	1.4 (1452)	0.0039–0.0047	0.0079–0.0157	0.0059–0.0138	0.0039–0.0236	0.0016–0.0031	0.0012–0.0028	Snug
	3E	1.5 (1456)	0.0028–0.0035	0.0102–0.0143	0.0118–0.0177	0.0059–0.0157	0.0016–0.0031	0.0012–0.0028	Snug Snug
1988	3A, 3A-C	1.4 (1452)	0.0039–0.0047	0.0079–0.0157	0.0059–0.0138	0.0039–0.0236	0.0016–0.0031	0.0012–0.0028	Snug
	3E	1.5 (1456)	0.0028–0.0035	0.0102–0.0143	0.0118–0.0177	0.0059–0.0157	0.0016–0.0031	0.0012–0.0028	Snug Snug
1989	3E	1.5 (1456)	0.0028–0.0035	0.0102–0.0143	0.0118–0.0177	0.0059–0.0157	0.0016–0.0031	0.0012–0.0028	Snug Snug
1990	3E	1.5 (1456)	0.0028–0.0035	0.0102–0.0143	0.0118–0.0177	0.0059–0.0157	0.0016–0.0031	0.0012–0.0028	Snug Snug
	3E-E	1.5 (1456)	0.0028–0.0035	0.0102–0.0143	0.0118–0.0224	0.0059–0.0205	0.0016–0.0031	0.0012–0.0028	Snug Snug
1991	3E-E	1.5 (1456)	0.0028–0.0035	0.0102–0.0143	0.0118–0.0224	0.0059–0.0205	0.0016–0.0031	0.0012–0.0028	Snug Snug
1992	3E-E	1.5 (1456)	0.0028–0.0035	0.0102–0.0143	0.0118–0.0224	0.0059–0.0205	0.0016–0.0031	0.0012–0.0028	Snug Snug
1993	3E-E	1.5 (1456)	0.0028–0.0035	0.0102–0.0143	0.0118–0.0224	0.0059–0.0205	0.0016–0.0031	0.0012–0.0028	Snug Snug
1994	3E-E	1.5 (1456)	0.0028–0.0035	0.0102–0.0143	0.0118–0.0224	0.0059–0.0205	0.0016–0.0031	0.0012–0.0028	Snug Snug

85993306

TORQUE SPECIFICATIONS
All readings in ft. lbs.

Year	Engine ID/VIN	Engine Displacement Liters (cc)	Cylinder Head Bolts	Main Bearing Bolts	Rod Bearing Bolts	Crankshaft Damper Bolts	Flywheel Bolts	Manifold	
								Intake	Exhaust
1984	3A, 3A-C	1.4 (1452)	43	43	36	87	58	18	18
1985	3A, 3A-C	1.4 (1452)	43	43	36	87	58	18	18
1986	3A, 3A-C	1.4 (1452)	43	43	36	87	58	18	18
1987	3A, 3A-C	1.4 (1452)	43	43	36	87	58	18	18
	3E	1.5 (1456)	See Text	42	29	112	65	14	38
1988	3A, 3A-C	1.4 (1452)	43	43	36	87	58	18	18
	3E	1.5 (1456)	See Text	42	29	112	65	14	38
1989	3E	1.5 (1456)	See Text	42	29	112	65	14	38
1990	3E	1.5 (1456)	See Text	42	29	112	65	14	38
	3E-E	1.5 (1456)	See Text	42	29	112	65	14	38
1991	3E-E	1.5 (1456)	See Text	42	29	112	65	14	38
1992	3E-E	1.5 (1456)	See Text	42	29	112	65	14	38
1993	3E-E	1.5 (1456)	See Text	42	29	112	65	14	38
1994	3E-E	1.5 (1456)	See Text	42	29	112	65	14	38

NOTE: On all engine torque procedures refer to necessary text for any additional service procedure or specification change.

85993307

Engine

REMOVAL & INSTALLATION

▶ See Figures 38, 39, 40, 41, 42, 43, 44, 45, 46, 47, 48, 49, 50, 51, 52, 53, 54, 55, 56, 57, 58, 59 and 60

➡All wires, hoses and necessary components should be marked before removal for correct installation. Review the complete service procedure before continuing.

1984-1986 Sedans and All Wagons

1. Disconnect the negative battery cable.
2. With the help of an assistant, remove the hood (mark hood hinges for correct installation) from the car. Be careful not to damage the paint finish.

3. Drain the engine coolant.

❋❋CAUTION

When draining the coolant, keep in mind that cats and dogs are attracted by ethylene glycol antifreeze, and are quite likely to drink any that is left in an uncovered container or in puddles on the ground. This will prove fatal in sufficient quantity. Always drain the coolant into a sealable container. Coolant should be reused unless it is contaminated or several years old.

4. Drain the engine oil and transmission fluids.

❋❋CAUTION

Used motor oil may cause skin cancer if repeatedly left in contact with the skin for prolonged periods. Although this is unlikely unless you handle oil on a daily basis, it is wise to thoroughly wash your hands with soap and water immediately after handling used motor oil.

5. Remove the battery and the battery carrier.

6. Remove the air cleaner assembly.

7. Remove the radiator.

8. On air conditioned vehicles, remove the A/C condenser fan.

9. If so equipped, remove the power steering pump from its mounts and lay it aside. Leave the hoses attached. The pump may be hung on a piece of stiff wire to be kept out of the way.

10. Remove the air conditioning compressor, if applicable, from its mounts and position out of the way. DO NOT loosen any hoses or fittings — simply move the compressor out of the way. It may be hung from a piece of stiff wire.

11. Label and remove all wiring running to the motor. Be careful when unhooking wiring connectors; many have locking devices which must be released.

12. Disconnect the accelerator cable.

13. Disconnect the throttle linkage on Automatic Transaxle (A/T) cars.

14. Label and disconnect vacuum hoses. Make sure your labels contain accurate information for reconnecting both ends of the hose. Make sure the labels will stay on the hoses.

15. Disconnect the fuel lines.

➡ **Release pressure slowly and contain spillage. Observe no smoking/no open flame precautions. Have a Class B-C (dry powder) fire extinguisher within arm's reach at all times.**

16. Remove the the Air Suction (AS) filter from the engine block.

17. Remove the transaxle upper mount bolts.

18. Raise the vehicle. Be sure that the vehicle is supported securely.

19. Remove the exhaust front pipe.

20. On A/T equipped cars, remove the cooler lines.

21. On Manual Transaxle (M/T) cars, disconnect the clutch release cable.

22. Remove the stiffener plates.

23. Remove the engine mounting absorber.

24. Remove the two bolts holding the engine mounting insulator to the crossmember.

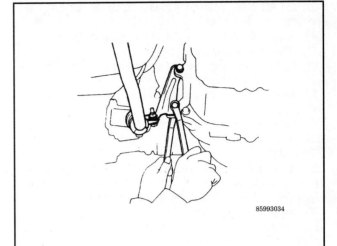

Fig. 39 Removing the engine stiffener plate; 3A and 3A-C engines

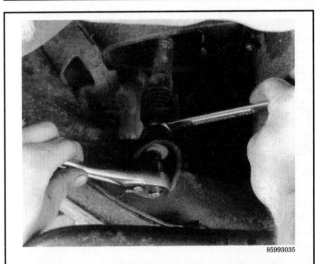

Fig. 40 Disconnecting the engine mounting absorber from the crossmember; 3A and 3A-C engines

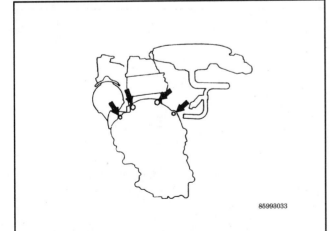

Fig. 38 Transaxle upper mounting bolt locations; 3A and 3A-C engines

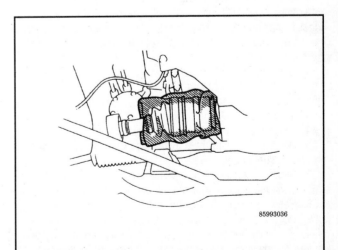

Fig. 41 Its a good idea to wrap both drive shaft boots with shop towels before removing the engine; 3A and 3A-C engines

25. On A/T cars, remove the torque converter cover and the converter mounting bolts.

26. Wrap both driveshaft boots with a shop towel.

27. Place a jack under the transaxle.

28. Remove the transaxle lower mounting bolts. Hold the starter during this procedure.

29. Attach a engine hoist chain to the lift brackets of the engine.

30. Remove the engine from the vehicle slowly and carefully. Make sure the engine is clear of all wiring and hoses.

To install:

31. Apply multi-purpose grease to the input shaft and the front of the release bearing on M/T cars. On A/T cars, apply multi-purpose grease to the center hub of the torque converter.

32. Install a guide pin on A/T cars.

33. Lower the engine into the engine compartment. On A/T models, align the guide pin with one of the drive plate holes. Connect the engine to the transaxle.

34. Install the starter and the transaxle lower mounting bolts. Remove the chain hoist.

35. Remove the guide pin and install the torque converter mounting bolts on A/T models.

36. Take the jack out from under the transaxle.

37. Install the engine mounting bolts.

38. Install the mounting absorber.

39. Install the stiffener plates.

40. On M/T models, connect the clutch release cable. On A/T models, install the cooler pipes.

41. Install the exhaust front pipe.

42. Lower the vehicle.

43. Install the transaxle upper mounting bolts.

44. Install the AS filter to the engine block.

45. Paying close attention to proper routing and labeling, connect the wiring and vacuum hoses to the engine.

46. Connect the throttle and accelerator cables to the engine.

47. Depending on equipment, reinstall the power steering pump and/or the air conditioning compressor. Tighten the mounting bolts enough to hold the unit in place but no more; the belts will be installed later.

48. Connect the heater hoses.

49. Install the drive belts (alternator, power steering and air conditioning) and make sure the belts are properly seated on the pulleys. Adjust the belts to the correct tension and tighten the bolts.

50. Connect the fuel hoses. Use new clamps if necessary.

51. Install the radiator and fan.

52. Remove the shop towels on the driveshaft boots.

53. Install the air cleaner assembly onto the carburetor.

54. Install the washer and radiator reserve tanks.

55. Have an assistant help install the hood. Make sure its is properly adjusted and secure.

56. Refill the transmission with the proper fluid.

57. Refill the engine oil to the proper level.

58. Refill the engine coolant with the proper amount of fluid.

59. Double check all installation items, paying particular attention to loose hoses or hanging wires, untightened nuts, poor routing of hoses and wires (too tight or rubbing) and tools left in the engine area.

60. Check all fluid levels. Bleed systems as necessary. Make all necessary adjustments. Start the engine. Check for any fluid leaks, road test the vehicle for proper operation.

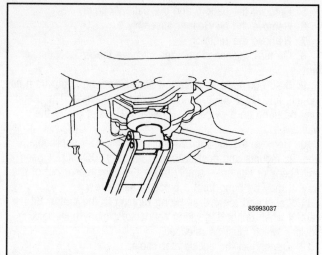

Fig. 42 Support the transaxle with a floor jack; 3A and 3A-C engines

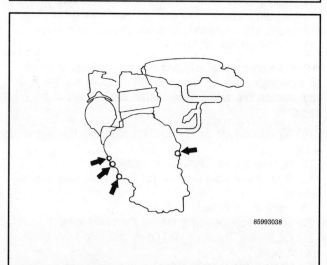

Fig. 43 Transaxle lower mounting bolt locations; 3A and 3A-C engines

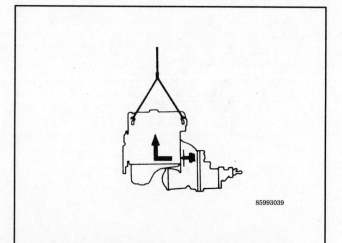

Fig. 44 Lift the engine out of the vehicle slowly and carefully. Protect the fenders from damage by placing fender covers over them; 3A and 3A-C engines

1987-1994 Sedans

✳✳CAUTION

On models equipped with a Supplemental Restraint System (SRS) or "air bag," work must NOT be started until at least 90 seconds have passed from the time that both the ignition switch is turned to the LOCK position and the negative cable is disconnected from the battery.

1. Remove the battery.
2. Drain the cooling system and save the coolant for reuse.
3. Remove the washer and radiator reserve tanks.
4. Drain the engine oil and the transmission fluids.
5. With the help of an assistant, remove the hood (mark hood hinges for correct installation) from the car. Be careful not to damage the paint finish.
6. Remove the air cleaner assembly from the engine.
7. Remove the engine under covers.
8. Remove the radiator.
9. Disconnect the upper radiator hose from the engine and remove the overflow hose.
10. Remove the coolant hose at the cylinder head rear coolant pipe and remove the coolant hose at the thermostat housing.
11. Remove all heater hoses.
12. Remove the cruise control actuator, if equipped.
13. Disconnect the accelerator and throttle cables.
14. Remove the fuel hoses.

➡On 3E-E engines, the fuel system is under pressure. Release pressure slowly and contain spillage. Observe no smoking/no open flame precautions. Have a Class B-C (dry powder) fire extinguisher within arm's reach at all times.

15. Remove the charcoal canister.
16. Loosen the adjustor(s) and remove the alternator belt, the power steering and/or air conditioning drive belts depending on equipment.
17. Label and remove all wiring running to the motor. Be careful when unhooking wiring connectors; many have locking devices which must be released.
18. Label and disconnect vacuum hoses. Make sure your labels contain accurate information for reconnecting both ends of the hose. Make sure the labels will stay on the hoses.
19. Disconnect the wiring at the transaxle.
20. Disconnect the speedometer cable at the transaxle.
21. Disconnect the transaxle control cables.
22. Remove the clutch release cylinder and selecting bell crank on manual transaxle cars.
23. Remove the intake manifold stay, if equipped.
24. Remove the Vacuum Switching Valve (VSV).
25. If so equipped, remove the power steering pump from its mounts and lay it aside. Leave the hoses attached. The pump may be hung on a piece of stiff wire to be kept out of the way.
26. Remove the air conditioning compressor, if applicable, from its mounts and position out of the way. DO NOT loosen any hoses or fittings — simply move the compressor out of the way. It may be hung from a piece of stiff wire.
27. Disconnect the exhaust pipe from the manifold. Be ready to deal with rusty hardware.

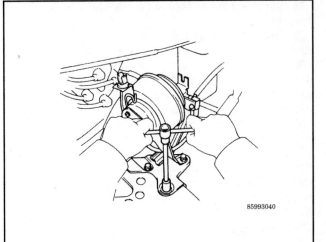

Fig. 45 Removing the cruise control actuator on 3E and 3E-E engines

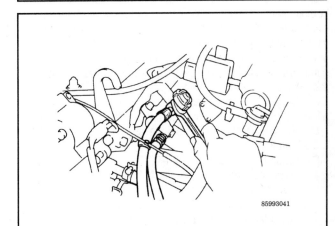

Fig. 46 When disconnecting fuel lines on 3E-E engines, keep in mind that a small amount of fuel pressure may be left even after following the pressure relief procedure. Loosen the fuel lines slowly

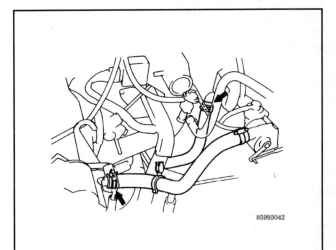

Fig. 47 Disconnect the heater hoses at these points; 3E and 3E-E engines

28. Disconnect the air hose at the converter pipe, if so equipped.

29. Disconnect the steering knuckles at the lower control arms.

30. Have an assistant step on the brake pedal while you loosen the nuts and bolts holding the driveshafts to the transaxle.

31. Remove the driveshafts.

32. Install the engine hoist to the lifting brackets on the engine. Keep the wiring harness in front of the chain. Draw tension on the hoist enough to support the engine but no more. Double check the hoist attachments before proceeding.

33. Disconnect the front and rear mounts at the crossmember by first removing the two bolt covers and removing the two bolts at each mount. Remove the center crossmember under the engine.

34. Remove the through-bolt to the right side engine mount.

35. Remove the left side transaxle mount bolt and remove the mount.

36. Lift the engine and transaxle assembly out of the engine compartment, proceeding slowly and watching for any interference. Clear the battery carrier support while lowering the transaxle. Pay particular attention to not damaging the right side engine mount, the power steering housing and the neutral safety switch. Make sure wiring, hoses and cables are clear of the engine.

37. Support the engine assembly on a suitable stand; do not allow it to remain on the hoist for any length of time.

38. Remove the transaxle from the engine.

To install:

39. Install the transaxle to the engine.

40. Lower the engine and transaxle into the car, paying attention to clearance and proper position. Raise and lower the vehicle as necessary to perform each service operation.

41. Install the left side transaxle mount and its bolt(s).

42. Install and tighten the right side through-bolt for the motor mount.

43. Connect the front and rear mountings for the crossmember and reinstall the bolt covers.

44. When the engine is securely mounted within the car, the lifting devices may be removed.

45. Connect the driveshafts to the transaxle. Install the driveshaft assembly to the rear differential on four wheel drive vehicles.

46. Reconnect the steering knuckles to the lower control arms.

47. Connect the exhaust pipe.

48. Depending on equipment, reinstall the power steering pump and/or the air conditioning compressor. Tighten the mounting bolts enough to hold the unit in place but no more; the belts will be installed later.

49. Install the Vacuum Switching Valve (VSV).

50. Install the intake manifold stay.

51. Install the selecting bell crank and clutch release cylinder on manual transaxle cars.

52. Connect the transaxle control cables.

53. Reconnect the speedometer cable at the transaxle.

54. Paying close attention to proper routing and labeling, connect the wiring and vacuum hoses to the engine.

55. Connect the heater hoses.

56. Install the drive belts (alternator, power steering and air conditioning) and make sure the belts are properly seated on the pulleys. Adjust the belts to the correct tension and tighten the bolts.

57. Install the charcoal canister.

58. Connect the fuel hoses. Use new clamps if necessary.

59. Connect the accelerator and throttle cables.

60. Install the cruise control actuator.

61. Install the radiator.

62. Attach the coolant hoses: at the thermostat housing, at the cylinder head rear pipe, at the overflow, and at the outlet for the upper hose. Insure that the hoses are firmly over the ports; use new clamps wherever needed.

63. Install the air cleaner assembly.

64. Install the washer and radiator reserve tanks.

65. Have an assistant help install the hood. Make sure its is properly adjusted and secure.

66. Refill the transmission with the proper fluid.

67. Refill the engine oil to the proper level.

68. Refill the engine coolant with the proper amount of fluid.

69. Install the engine under covers.

70. Double check all installation items, paying particular attention to loose hoses or hanging wires, untightened nuts, poor routing of hoses and wires (too tight or rubbing) and tools left in the engine area.

71. Check all fluid levels. Bleed systems as necessary. Make all necessary adjustments. Start the engine. Check for any fluid leaks, road test the vehicle for proper operation.

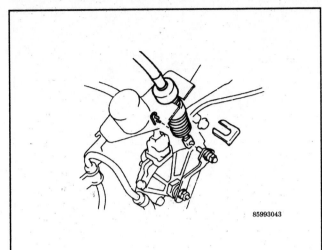

Fig. 48 The transmission control cables are retained with clips; 3E and 3E-E engines

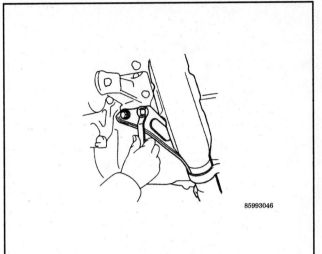

Fig. 51 On 3E and 3E-E engines, the exhaust pipe stay must be disconnected from the engine block

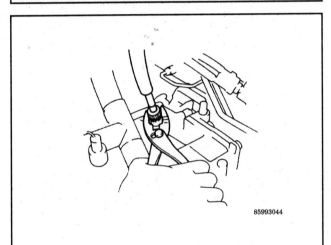

Fig. 49 The speedometer cable can be loosened from the transaxle with a pair of slip-joint pliers; 3E and 3E-E engines

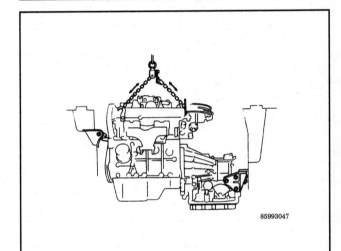

Fig. 52 The hoist should be securely attached to the engine hangers

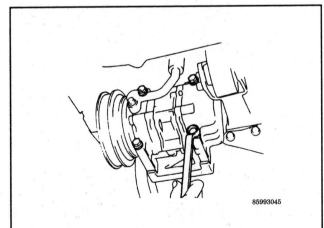

Fig. 50 It is not necessary to remove the air conditioning compressor when removing the engine. Simply hang it aside with a piece of stiff wire

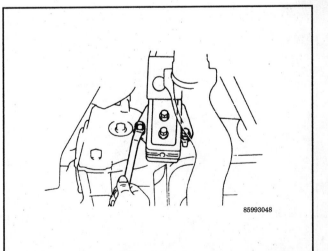

Fig. 53 Removing the two bolts from the rear mounting insulator; 3E and 3E-E engines

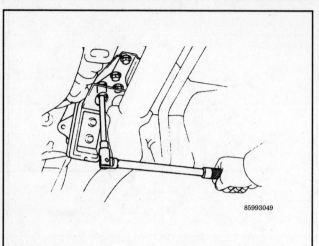

Fig. 54 The rear mounting insulator can be removed after these four bolts have been removed; 3E and 3E-E engines

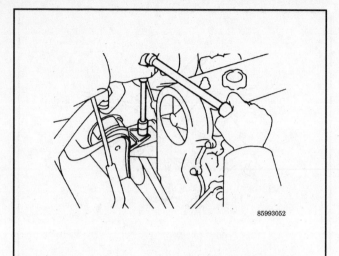

Fig. 57 Remove the remaining right hand insulator attaching bolts and insulator; 3E and 3E-E engines

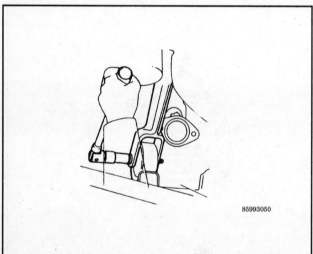

Fig. 55 Removing the front mounting insulator through-bolt; 3E and 3E-E engines

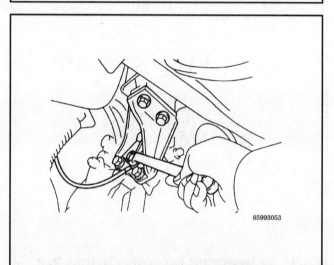

Fig. 58 Be sure remove the ground strap from the left hand mounting bracket; 3E and 3E-E engines

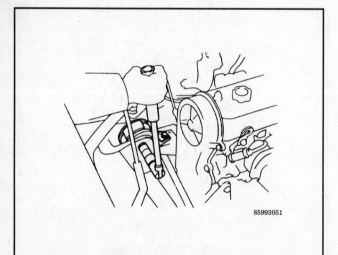

Fig. 56 Removing the right hand mounting insulator through-bolt; 3E and 3E-E engines

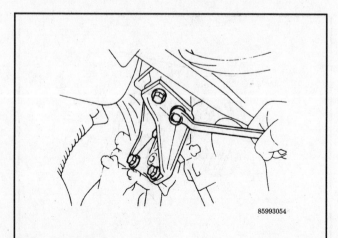

Fig. 59 Remove the remaining bolts from the left hand mounting bracket, then remove it from the engine; 3E and 3E-E engines

Fig. 60 Lift the engine out of the vehicle slowly and carefully. Protect the fenders by placing fender covers over them

Rocker Arm (Valve) Cover

REMOVAL & INSTALLATION

▶ See Figures 61, 62, 63 and 64

✳✳CAUTION

On models equipped with a Supplemental Restraint System (SRS) or "air bag," work must NOT be started until at least 90 seconds have passed from the time that both the ignition switch is turned to the LOCK position and the negative cable is disconnected from the battery.

1. Disconnect the negative battery cable. Remove the air cleaner and its assorted hoses and lines.
2. Tag and disconnect any wires, hoses or lines which might interfere with the cylinder head cover removal.
3. Unthread the retaining screws/bolts and then lift off the cylinder head cover. Be careful not to lose the washers.

➡If the cylinder head cover is stuck, tap it lightly with a rubber mallet to loosen it. DO NOT attempt to pry it off.

To install:
4. Using a new gasket and silicone sealant, install the cylinder head cover.

Fig. 61 On some engines, it will be necessary to remove these two upper timing belt cover bolts

5. Tighten the bolts down evenly, working from the center to the ends, until they are snug. Do not overtighten, as this may distort the gasket and cause oil leaks.

Installation of the remaining components is in the reverse order of removal.

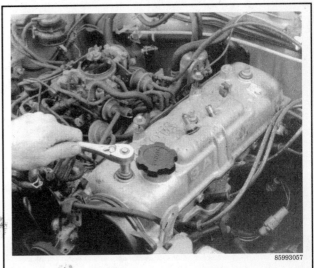

Fig. 62 Removing the valve cover attaching nuts

Fig. 63 Be careful not to lose the sealing grommets

Fig. 65 The rocker arm assembly may be accessed once the valve cover is removed — 3A and 3A-C engines

Fig. 64 Always replace the valve cover gasket to ensure a leak-free installation

Fig. 66 The rocker arm assembly bolts must be loosened and tightened in sequence on 3A and 3A-C engines

Rocker Arms

REMOVAL & INSTALLATION

3A and 3A-C Engines

▶ See Figures 65, 66, 67, 68, 69 and 70

1. Remove the valve cover as described previously.
2. Loosen the rocker support bolts, in three steps, using the proper sequence.
3. Remove the bolts and remove the rocker assembly from the head. Inspect the valve contacting surfaces for wear. Inspect the rocker-to-shaft clearance by wiggling the rocker on the shaft. There should be virtually no play; any noticeable motion requires replacement of the rocker arms and/or the shaft.
4. Disassemble the rockers from the shaft. Check the contact surfaces for signs of visible wear or scoring.

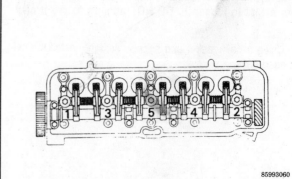

Fig. 67 On 3A and 3A-C engines, the rocker arm assembly bolts must be loosened using this sequence

5. Using either an inside micrometer or a dial indicator, measure the inside diameter of the rocker arm. Using a regular micrometer, measure the diameter of the shaft. Maximum allowable difference (oil clearance) between the two measurements is 0.0024 in. (0.06mm).

To install:

6. After replacing any needed parts, loosen the adjusting screw lock nuts.

7. The rocker shaft has oil holes in it. When assembling the rockers onto the shaft, make sure the holes point (when viewed from the end of the shaft) at the 3, 6 and 9 o'clock positions.

➡**Failure to observe this positioning will starve the rockers for oil, causing expensive and premature wear.**

8. Loosen the valve adjusting screw lock nuts then install the rocker assembly on the head. Tighten the retaining bolts in three steps using the correct sequence. Torque the bolts to 18 ft. lbs. (25 Nm) on the third pass.

9. Adjust the valves using the procedures in Section 2.

3E and 3E-E Engines

▸ **See Figures 71, 72, 73, 74, 75, 76, 77, 78 and 79**

1. Remove the valve cover following the procedures and cautions described earlier.

2. Loosen the camshaft bearing cap bolts, a little at a time, using the proper sequence.

➡**Do not remove the distributor bearing cap.**

3. Remove the camshaft.
4. Arrange the bearing caps in order, do not mix them!
5. Loosen the rocker arm adjusting screw locknuts.
6. While lifting the top of the spring, pry off the spring with a small prytool.
7. Remove the rocker arms and arrange them in order. Check the contact surface for any signs of pitting or wear.

To install:

8. Check that the adjusting screw is positioned as shown and install a new spring to the rocker arm.

Fig. 68 Removing the rocker arm assembly on 3A and 3A-C engines

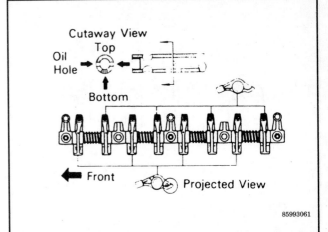

Fig. 69 When assembling the rockers on 3A and 3A-C engines, the oil holes must be positioned as shown. Failure to do so will result in rapid valve train wear

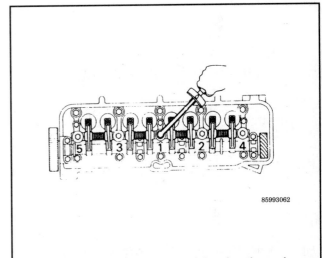

Fig. 70 Use this sequence when tightening the rocker assembly on 3A and 3A-C engines

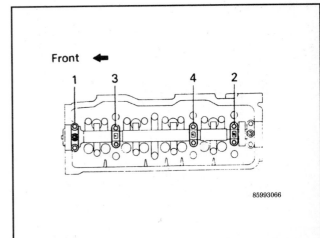

Fig. 71 The camshaft bearing bolts on 3E and 3E-E engines must be loosened in several passes using the sequence shown

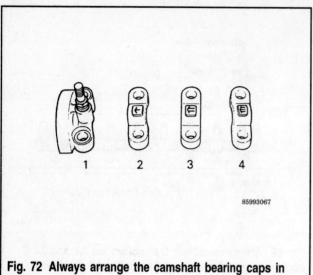

Fig. 72 Always arrange the camshaft bearing caps in the correct order

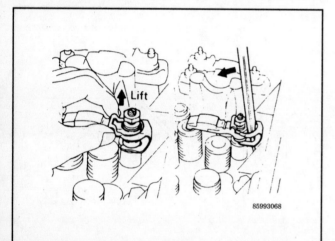

Fig. 73 While lifting the top of the rocker arm spring, pry the spring off with a small prytool — 3E and 3E-E engines

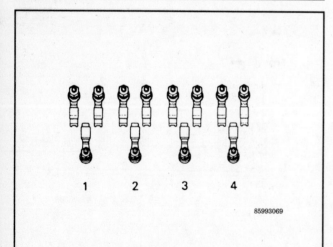

Fig. 74 Arrange the rocker arms in the correct order — 3E and 3E-E engines shown

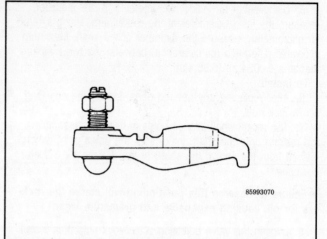

Fig. 75 On 3E and 3E-E engines, the rocker arm adjusting screw should be positioned as shown before installation

Fig. 76 Press the bottom lip of the rocker arm spring with a small prytool until it fits into the groove on the rocker arm pivot — 3E and 3E-E engines

9. Using a small prytool, press the bottom lip of the spring until it fits into the groove on the rocker arm pivot.

➡**Make sure the valve adjusting screw is in the rocker arm pivot.**

10. Pry the rocker spring clip onto the pivot. Pull the rocker arm up and down to check that there is spring tension and that the rocker does not rattle.

11. Install the camshaft. Refer to the procedures later in this section.

12. Adjust the valves as described in Section 2.

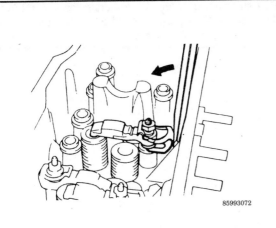

Fig. 77 Prying the rocker arm spring onto the rocker arm pivot

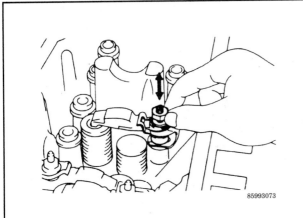

Fig. 78 Check that there is spring tension on the rocker arm by pulling it up and down, it should not rattle — 3E and 3E-E engines

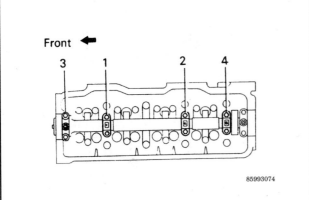

Fig. 79 On 3E and 3E-E engines, always uniformly tighten the bearing cap bolts in several passes using this sequence

Fig. 80 Always observe the positioning of the thermostat in the housing before removing it

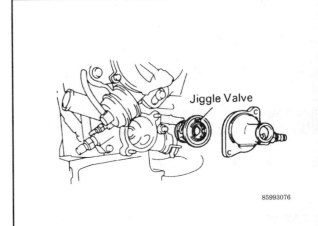

Fig. 81 The thermostat should be installed with the jiggle valve upwards

Thermostat

REMOVAL & INSTALLATION

▶ See Figures 80 and 81

The thermostat's purpose is to control the flow into the engine from the radiator. During warm up, the thermostat remains closed so that the coolant within the engine heats quickly and aids the warming up process.

As the coolant temperature increases, the thermostat gradually opens, allowing a supply of lower temperature coolant (from the radiator) to enter the water pump and circulate through the engine.

➡A thermostat should never be removed as a counter-measure to overheating problems. This will only decrease the cooling system efficiency and add to the problem. The vehicle cooling system should be serviced with necessary components replaced.

1. Drain the cooling system and save the coolant for reuse.
2. Remove the water inlet housing (disconnect any electrical connections on the housing) and remove the thermostat. Carefully observe the positioning of the thermostat within the housing before removal.
3. Install the new thermostat in the housing, making sure it is in correctly. It is possible to install it backwards. Additionally, make certain that the air bleed valve aligns with the protrusion on the water inlet housing. Failure to observe this placement can result in poor air bleeding and possible overheating.
4. Install the water inlet housing cover with a new gasket. Install the two hold-down bolts and torque to 43 inch lbs. (4.9 Nm). Do not overtighten these bolts!
5. Refill the cooling system with coolant.
6. Start the engine. During the warm up period, observe the temperature gauge for normal behavior. Also during this period, check the water inlet housing area for any sign of leakage. Remember to check for leaks under both cold and hot conditions.

Intake Manifold

REMOVAL & INSTALLATION

▶ See Figures 82, 83, 84 and 85

✳✳CAUTION

On models equipped with a Supplemental Restraint System (SRS) or "air bag," work must NOT be started until at least 90 seconds have passed from the time that both the ignition switch is turned to the LOCK position and the negative cable is disconnected from the battery.

3A and 3A-C Engines

Please refer to the Combination Manifold procedure in this section.

3E and 3E-E Engines

1. Disconnect the negative battery cable. On 3E-E engines, relieve the fuel pressure.
2. Drain the cooling system. Remove the air cleaner assembly.

✳✳CAUTION

When draining the coolant, keep in mind that cats and dogs are attracted by ethylene glycol antifreeze, and are quite likely to drink any that is left in an uncovered container or in puddles on the ground. This will prove

fatal in sufficient quantity. Always drain the coolant into a sealable container. Coolant should be reused unless it is contaminated or several years old.

3. Tag and disconnect all wires, hoses or cables that interfere with intake manifold removal.
4. Remove any other components necessary in order to gain access to the intake manifold attaching nuts and bolts.
5. Remove the intake manifold stay.
6. If necessary, remove the carburetor.
7. Disconnect the intake manifold water hoses.
8. Remove the five intake manifold retaining bolts and two nuts. Remove the gasket and intake manifold from the vehicle.
9. Using a precision straight edge and thickness gauge, check the surface contacting the cylinder head for warpage. It should not exceed 0.0020 in. (0.05mm) on 3E-E engines or 0.0079 in. (0.20mm) on 3E engines. If the warpage exceeds these specifications, replace the manifold.

To install:
10. Install a new intake manifold gasket to the cylinder head.

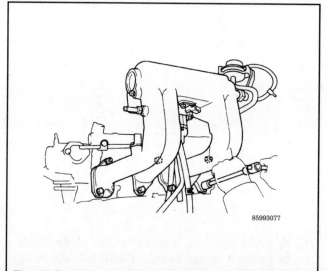

Fig. 82 Removing the intake manifold on 3E-E engines

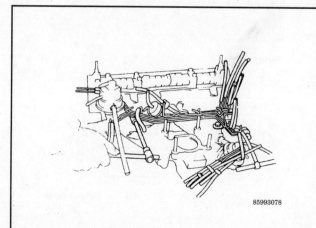

Fig. 83 On 3E engines, removing the air pipes will ease intake manifold removal. Be sure to label all hoses and wires before disconnecting them

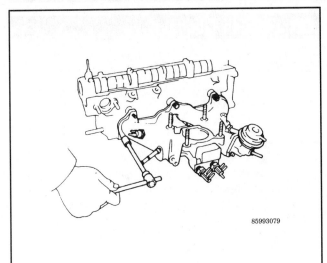

Fig. 84 Removing the intake manifold on 3E engines

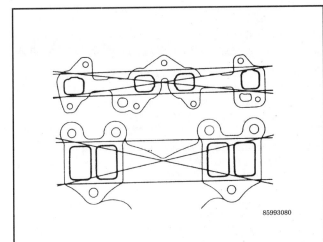

Fig. 85 Both the intake and the exhaust manifolds should be checked for warpage at these angles

11. Install the intake manifold then torque the nuts and bolts to specification. Work from the center to the ends in steps.

12. Connect all hoses, wires or cables which were removed earlier.

13. Install the carburetor, if applicable.

14. Install the manifold stay and the air cleaner assembly.

15. Fill the cooling system.

16. Start the engine, check for leaks and roadtest for proper operation.

Exhaust Manifold

REMOVAL & INSTALLATION

▶ **See Figures 86, 87 and 88**

3A and 3A-C Engines

Please refer to the Combination Manifold procedure in this section.

3E and 3E-E Engines

❋❋CAUTION

On models equipped with a Supplemental Restraint System (SRS) or "air bag," work must NOT be started until at least 90 seconds have passed from the time that both the ignition switch is turned to the LOCK position and the negative cable is disconnected from the battery.

1. Disconnect the negative battery cable.

2. Remove any components necessary to gain access to the exhaust manifold retaining bolts.

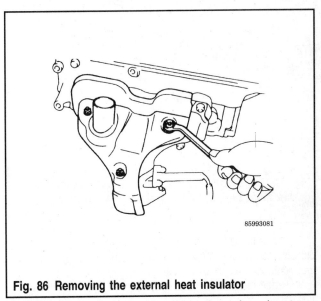

Fig. 86 Removing the external heat insulator

3. Disconnect the exhaust manifold bolts at the exhaust pipe. Disconnect the oxygen sensor electrical wire. It may be necessary to raise and support the vehicle safely before removing these bolts.

4. Remove the three external heat insulator attaching bolts.

5. Remove the six exhaust manifold retaining nuts. Remove the exhaust manifold, internal heat insulator and gaskets from the vehicle.

6. Using a precision straight edge and thickness gauge, check the surface contacting the cylinder head for warpage. It should not exceed 0.0118 in. (0.30mm). If the warpage exceeds these specifications, replace the manifold.

To install:

7. Install a new exhaust manifold gasket, the **E** mark on the gasket must face outward.

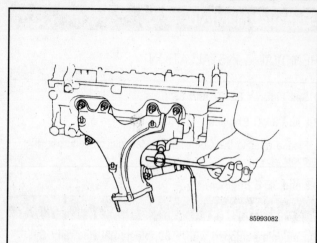

85993082

Fig. 87 Removing the internal heat insulator and the exhaust manifold

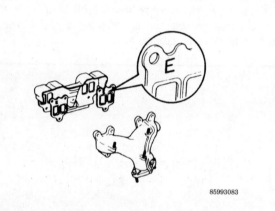

85993083

Fig. 88 On 3E and 3E-E engines, the exhaust manifold gasket must be installed with the E mark facing outward

8. Assemble the internal heat insulator and exhaust manifold onto the engine. Tighten the nuts, refer to the torque specifications chart in this section.

9. Install the external heat insulator and tighten the bolts until snug.

10. Connect the exhaust pipe to the manifold.

11. Install or connect any other components removed earlier.

12. Start the engine and check for exhaust leaks. Road test for proper operation.

Combination Manifold

REMOVAL & INSTALLATION

◆ **See Figures 89 and 90**

The intake and exhaust manifolds on 3A and 3A-C engines are a one-piece or combination design. They can not be separated from each other or serviced individually.

1. Disconnect the negative battery cable.

2. Remove the air cleaner assembly.

3. Label and disconnect all vacuum hoses at the carburetor.

4. Disconnect the accelerator cable and, for automatic transmissions, the throttle cable.

5. Label and disconnect the electrical connections at the carburetor.

6. Disconnect the fuel line at the fuel pump.

7. Carefully loosen and remove the carburetor mounting bolts and remove the carburetor.

✳✳CAUTION

The carburetor bowls contain gasoline which may spill or leak during removal. Observe no smoking/no open flame precautions. Have a Class B-C (dry powder) fire extinguisher within arm's reach at all times.

➡ **Keep the carburetor level (do not tilt) during removal and handling. As soon as it is off the car, wrap or cover it with a clean towel to keep dirt out.**

8. Remove the Early Fuel Evaporation (EFE) gasket.

9. Remove the vacuum line and dashpot bracket.

10. Carefully remove the heat shields on the manifold; don't break the bolts.

11. Safely elevate and support the vehicle on jackstands.

12. Disconnect the exhaust pipe at the manifold and exhaust bracket at the engine.

13. Remove the hose at the converter pipe, if equipped.

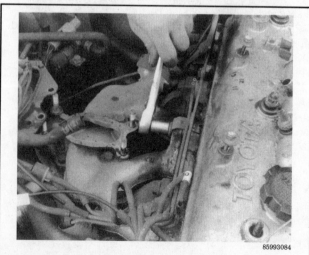

85993084

Fig. 89 Removing the combination manifold, note that the hoses and their connections are labeled

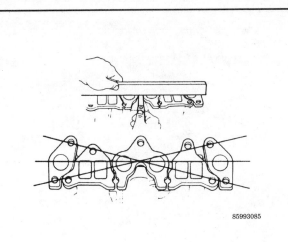

Fig. 90 Check the combination manifold for warpage at these angles

14. Lower the car to the ground and remove or disconnect the vacuum hose to the brake booster.

15. Remove the bracket for the accelerator and throttle cables.

16. Evenly loosen and then remove the bolts and nuts holding the manifold to the engine. Remove the manifold and its gaskets.

17. Using a precision straight edge and a feeler gauge, check the mating surfaces of the manifold for warpage. If the warpage is greater than 0.008 in. (0.2mm) Intake — 0.012 in. (0.3mm) Exhaust, replace the manifold.

To install:

18. When reinstalling, always use new gaskets and make sure they are properly positioned. Place the manifold in position and loosely install the nuts/bolts until all are just snug. Double check the placement of the manifold and in two passes torque the retaining nuts/bolts to specification.

19. Reinstall the bracket for the accelerator and throttle cables, then connect the vacuum hose to the brake vacuum booster.

20. Elevate and safely support the car on jackstands.

21. Reconnect the hose at the converter pipe. Install the exhaust bracket at the engine and, using new gaskets, connect the exhaust pipe to the manifold.

22. Lower the vehicle to the ground. Install the heat shield onto the manifold.

23. Reinstall the vacuum line and the dashpot bracket.

24. Install the EFE gasket.

25. Reinstall the carburetor using the procedures outlined in Section 5. Engage the electrical connectors to the carburetor.

26. Connect and secure the fuel line to the fuel pump.

27. Attach the accelerator cable and throttle valve cable (automatic trans.).

28. Observing the labels made earlier, install the vacuum lines. Be careful of the routing and make sure that each line fits snugly on its port. Double check each line for crimps or twists.

29. Install the air cleaner assembly and connect the negative battery cable.

30. Fill the cooling system.

31. Start the engine, check for leaks and roadtest for proper operation.

Radiator

REMOVAL & INSTALLATION

▶ **See Figures 91, 92, 93, 94, 95, 96, 97, 98 and 99**

✳✳CAUTION

On models equipped with a Supplemental Restraint System (SRS) or "air bag," work must NOT be started until at least 90 seconds have passed from the time that both the ignition switch is turned to the LOCK position and the negative cable is disconnected from the battery.

1. Disconnect the negative battery cable.

2. Remove the engine under covers, if applicable.

3. Drain the cooling system.

4. On fuel injected engines, it will be necessary to remove the air intake duct assembly.

5. Disconnect the coolant reservoir hose.

6. Unfasten the clamps, then remove the radiator upper and lower hoses.

7. If equipped with an automatic transmission, remove the oil cooler lines using a line wrench. Place a container under the fittings to catch the fluid. Immediately plug the hose to prevent oil from escaping.

8. Disconnect the electric cooling fan connector.

9. Unbolt and remove the radiator supports and the radiator. Use care not to damage the radiator fins.

10. Remove the cooling fan from the radiator, if applicable.

To install:

11. If removed earlier, install the cooling fan onto the radiator.

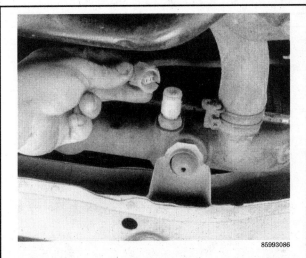

Fig. 91 Unplug any electrical connections on/near the radiator

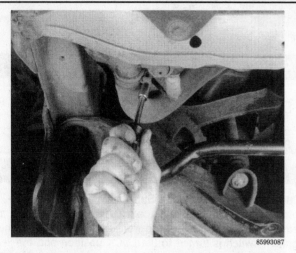

Fig. 92 Removing the lower radiator hose. On automatic transaxle cars, disconnect the oil cooler lines also

Fig. 93 The overflow tank hose can be removed by pressing the retaining tangs together, then by twisting and pulling the hose from it's connection

Fig. 94 Hose clamps like the one shown can be removed with a pair of slip joint pliers

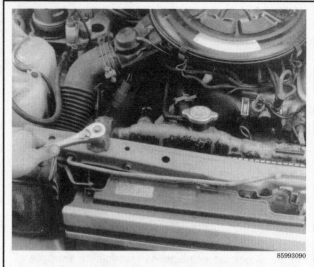

Fig. 95 Removing the upper radiator support brackets

Fig. 96 Use care when removing the radiator to prevent damaging the fins

12. Place the radiator into position and install the two upper supports.

➥After installation, check that the rubber cushions of the supports are not compressed.

13. Reconnect all electrical and hose connections which were removed earlier.

14. Assemble the air intake duct assembly on fuel injected vehicles.

15. Install the engine under covers, if applicable.

16. Connect the negative battery cable.

17. Remember to check the transmission fluid level on cars with automatic transmissions. Fill the radiator to the specified level.

18. Start the engine and check for leaks.

Fig. 97 Check that the rubber cushion on the underside of the bracket is still intact and in good condition

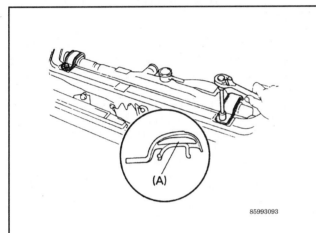

Fig. 98 After the support brackets have been installed, confirm that the rubber cushion is not compressed

Fig. 99 Be sure you are adding coolant to the coolant overflow tank, not the washer reservoir

Fig. 100 On some models, the cooling fan is located behind the front grille

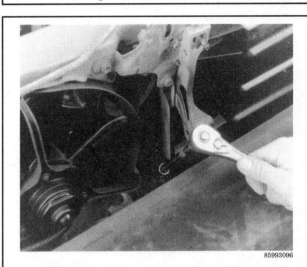

Fig. 101 An extension is useful when removing the lower attaching bolt

Engine Fan

REMOVAL & INSTALLATION

▶ See Figures 100, 101, 102 and 103

1984-1986 Sedans and All Wagons

1. Disconnect the negative battery cable.
2. Unplug the fan electrical connection.
3. Remove the front grille.
4. Remove the fan attaching bolts and remove the fan.
5. Installation is the reverse of removal. Test for proper operation.

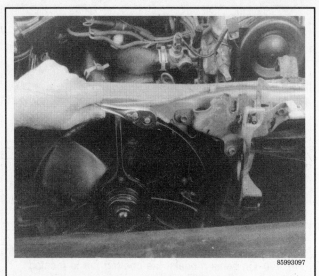

Fig. 102 Removing the upper attaching bolt

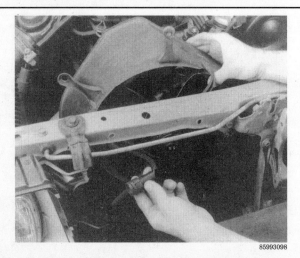

Fig. 103 Make sure the electrical connection is unplugged when removing the cooling fan

1987-1994 Sedans

❋❋CAUTION

On models equipped with an Supplemental Restraint System (SRS) or "air bag," work must NOT be started until at least 90 seconds have passed from the time that both the ignition switch is turned to the LOCK position and the negative cable is disconnected from the battery.

1. Disconnect the negative battery cable and unplug the fan electrical connection.
2. On fuel injected engines, remove the air intake duct.
3. If necessary, drain the coolant to an appropriate level and remove the upper radiator hose.
4. Remove the fan attaching bolts and remove the fan.
5. Installation is the reverse of removal. Refill the cooling system and check for leaks. Test the fan motor for proper operation.

TESTING

▶ See Figures 104, 105, 106 and 107

Cooling Fan Operation

❋❋CAUTION

Keep your hands and any other objects away from the fan and rotating engine parts at all times. Serious personal injury could result otherwise.

LOW TEMPERATURE TEST

1. The engine coolant temperature must be below the following:
    a. On 1984-1986 Sedans and all Wagons — 181°F (83°C)
    b. On 1987-1990 Sedans with carbureted engines — 172°F (78°C)
    c. On 1990-1994 Sedans with fuel injected engines — 181°F (83°C)
2. Turn the ignition **ON**, the cooling fan should not be running. If it does run, check the cooling fan relay and temperature switch for proper operation. Also check for a separated connector or severed wire between the relay and temperature switch.
3. Unplug the temperature switch connector, the cooling fan should now run. If it does not, check for a defective fan relay or motor. Also, check for a short circuit between the fan relay and temperature switch.
4. Reconnect the temperature switch wire.

HIGH TEMPERATURE TEST

1. Start the engine and raise the coolant temperature to above the following:
    a. On 1984-1986 Sedans and all Wagons — 194°F (90°C)
    b. On 1987-1988 Sedans with carbureted engines — 190°F (88°C)
    c. On 1989-1990 Sedans with carbureted engines — 192°F (89°C)
    d. On 1990-1994 Sedans with fuel injected engines — 201°F (94°C)
2. Check that the cooling fan turns on at the specified temperature. If it does not, replace the temperature switch.

CURRENT DRAW TEST

1. Connect an ammeter in series with a battery and the fan motor connector.
2. Look for smooth fan rotation and check the current draw reading on the ammeter. **DO NOT** touch the fan!
3. Compare the reading with the specifications listed on the Cooling Fan specifications chart.
4. Replace the motor if it is out of specification.

Temperature Switch

1. Remove the water temperature switch using the procedures outlined earlier in this section.
2. Submerge the sensing area of the switch in a water bath.

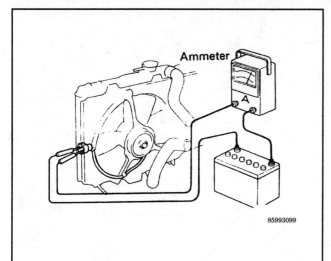

Fig. 104 The ammeter should be connected as shown for the current draw test

3. Using an ohmmeter, check that there is continuity between the two terminals (or between the single terminal and the switch body) when the water temperature is below the following:

    a. On 1984-1986 Sedans and all Wagons — 181°F (83°C)

    b. On 1987-1990 Sedans with carbureted engines — 172°F (78°C)

    c. On 1990-1994 Sedans with fuel injected engines — 181°F (83°C)

4. Using an ohmmeter, check that there is no continuity between the two terminals (or between the single terminal and the switch body) when the water temperature is above the following:

    a. On 1984-1986 Sedans and all Wagons — 194°F (90°C)

    b. On 1987-1988 Sedans with carbureted engines — 190°F (88°C)

    c. On 1989-1990 Sedans with carbureted engines — 192°F (89°C)

    d. On 1990-1994 Sedans with fuel injected engines — 201°F (94°C)

5. If the switch does not perform as specified, replace it.

Cooling Fan Relay

CONTINUITY TEST

1. Check for continuity between terminals 1 and 2.
2. Check for continuity between terminals 3 and 4.

3. If continuity between the terminals is not as specified, replace the relay.

OPERATION TEST

1. Apply battery voltage to terminals 1 and 2.
2. There should be no continuity between terminals 3 and 4.
3. If there is continuity between terminals 3 and 4, replace the relay.

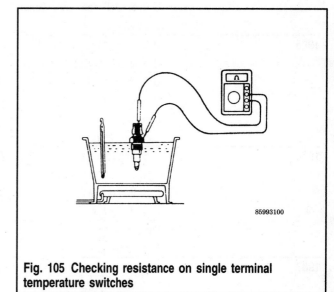

Fig. 105 Checking resistance on single terminal temperature switches

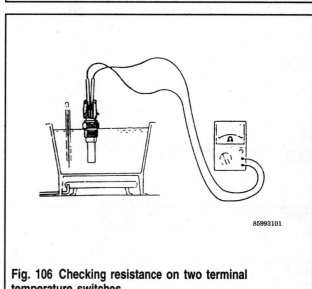

Fig. 106 Checking resistance on two terminal temperature switches

COOLING FAN SPECIFICATIONS

Year	Application	Current Draw (amps)
1984	U.S. M/T and all Canada (Except Canada 2WD Wagon A/T)	4.2–5.4
	U.S. A/T (Except 2WD Wagon A/T)	5.8–7.4
	2WD Wagon A/T	8.8–10.8
1985	U.S. and Canada Sedan, M/T	4.2–5.2
	U.S. and Canada Sedan, A/T	5.8–7.4
	U.S. Wagon, M/T	5.8–7.4
	U.S. Wagon, A/T	8.8–10.8
	Canada Wagon, M/T	4.2–5.4
	Canada Wagon, A/T	5.8–7.4
1986	U.S. and Canada Sedan, M/T	4.2–5.2
	U.S. and Canada Sedan, A/T	5.8–7.4
	U.S. Wagon, M/T	5.8–7.4
	U.S. Wagon, A/T	8.8–10.8
	Canada Wagon, M/T	4.2–5.4
	Canada Wagon, A/T	5.8–7.4
1987	All Sedans	3.2–4.4
	U.S. Wagon, M/T	5.8–7.4
	U.S. Wagon, A/T	9.7–9.9
	Canada Wagon, M/T	4.2–5.4
	Canada Wagon, A/T	5.8–7.4
1988	All Sedans	3.2–4.4
	U.S. Wagon, M/T	5.8–7.4
	U.S. Wagon, A/T	9.7–9.9
	Canada Wagon, M/T	4.2–5.2
	Canada Wagon, A/T	5.8–7.4
1989	M/T	5.7–7.7
	A/T	8.6–11.6
	Tercel EZ	3.1–4.3
1990	M/T	6.0–7.4
	A/T	8.8–10.8
	Tercel EZ	3.2–4.4
1991	U.S. A/T	8.8–10.8
	All others	6.0–7.4
1992	U.S. A/T	8.8–10.8
	All others	6.0–7.4
1993	U.S. A/T	8.8–10.8
	All others	6.0–7.4
1994	A/T	5.7–7.7
	M/T	8.6–11.6

85993308

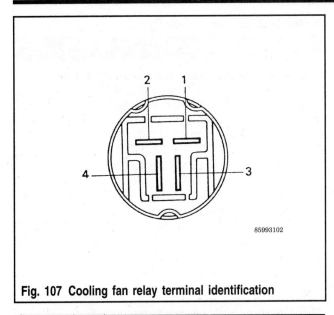

Fig. 107 Cooling fan relay terminal identification

Condenser Fan

REMOVAL & INSTALLATION

▶ See Figures 108 and 109

> **✳✳CAUTION**
>
> On models equipped with a Supplemental Restraint System (SRS) or "air bag," work must NOT be started until at least 90 seconds have passed from the time the ignition switch is turned to the LOCK position and the negative cable is disconnected from the battery.

This fan is found on air conditioned vehicles. It is located next to the radiator in the engine compartment on 1984-1986 sedans and all wagons. On 1987-1994 sedans, it is located in front of the radiator (behind the front grille).

1. Disconnect the negative battery cable.
2. If necessary for clearance, partially or completely remove the radiator.
3. Remove the fan attaching bolts and unplug the electrical connector.
4. Remove the fan from the vehicle.
5. Installation is the reverse of removal.

Water Pump

REMOVAL & INSTALLATION

▶ See Figures 110, 111, 112, 113 and 114

> **✳✳CAUTION**
>
> When draining the coolant, keep in mind that cats and dogs are attracted by ethylene glycol antifreeze, and are quite likely to drink any that is left in an uncovered container or in puddles on the ground. This will prove

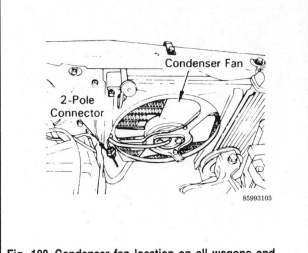

Fig. 108 Condenser fan location on all wagons and 1984-1986 sedans

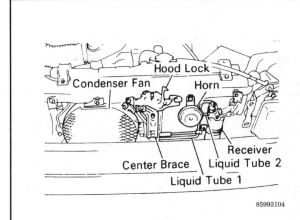

Fig. 109 The condenser fan is located behind the front grille on 1987-1994 sedans

fatal in sufficient quantity. Always drain the coolant into a sealable container. Coolant should be reused unless it is contaminated or several years old.

3A and 3A-C Engines

1. Disconnect the negative battery cable.
2. Drain and remove the radiator, see the caution.
3. Remove the water pump pulley and the drive belt.
4. Remove the water outlet housing and bypass pipe.
5. Remove the water inlet housing and thermostat.
6. Remove the upper front timing belt cover.
7. Disconnect the heater outlet hose from the outlet pipe and then remove the outlet pipe mounting bolt.
8. Remove the oil level dipstick tube retaining bolt, then remove the dipstick and tube. Be sure to plug the hole in the oil pump body.
9. Remove the three water pump attaching bolts and remove the pump.

Fig. 110 The water pump pulley can be removed after removing the three attaching bolts

Fig. 111 Be careful not to get any coolant on the timing belt when removing the water pump

10. Remove the two nuts attaching the heater outlet pipe to the pump.

To install:

11. Install the water pump and oil level dipstick tube. Torque the bolts to 11 ft. lbs. (15 Nm).

12. Install the outlet hose and pipe.

13. Install the front timing belt cover and thermostat housing.

14. Install the water outlet housing and bypass pipe.

15. Remove the water pump pulley and drive belt.

16. Adjust the drive belt. Refill engine coolant. Start the engine and check for coolant leaks.

3E and 3E-E Engines

❈❈CAUTION

On models equipped with a Supplemental Restraint System (SRS) or "air bag," work must NOT be started until at least 90 seconds have passed from the time the ignition switch is turned to the LOCK position and the negative cable is disconnected from the battery.

1. Disconnect the negative battery cable.

2. Drain the radiator, see the caution.

3. Remove the engine undercover. On 3E engines remove the High Altitude Compensation (HAC) valve from the bracket.

4. Remove the oil dipstick, drive belt and intake manifold stay. Remove the Air Suction (AS) valve and ground strap, if equipped.

5. On 3E engines, disconnect the No. 1 water by-pass hose from the carburetor.

6. Remove the oil dipstick tube. Remove the alternator and adjusting bar.

7. On the 3E engines, disconnect the intake manifold water hose from the intake manifold.

8. Remove the water pump pulley.

9. Remove the water inlet pipe mounting bolt from the cylinder block.

10. Remove the water pump retaining bolts and nuts. Remove the water pump.

To install:

11. Apply sealer to the water pump and install a new O-ring to the water inlet pipe.

12. Install the water pump. Torque the attaching bolts and nuts to specification.

13. Connect the water inlet pipe to the cylinder block.

14. On 3E engines, connect the intake manifold water hose to the intake manifold.

15. Install the alternator and adjusting bar.

16. Install the oil dipstick tube.

17. On 3E engines, connect the No. 1 water by-pass hose to the carburetor.

18. Install the intake manifold stay. Remember to attach the ground strap and Air Suction (AS) valve, if equipped.

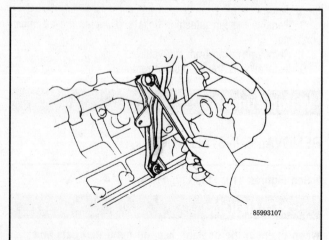

Fig. 112 Removing the intake manifold stay on 3E and 3E-E engines

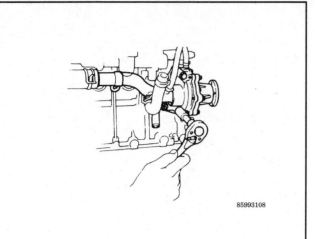

Fig. 113 Removing the water pump on 3E and 3E-E engines

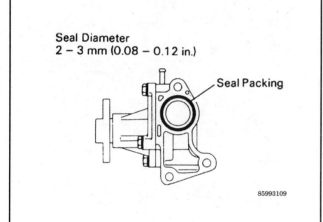

Seal Diameter
2 – 3 mm (0.08 – 0.12 in.)

Seal Packing

Fig. 114 Sealer should be applied to this area on 3E and 3E-E engines

19. Install the drive belt and tighten the pulley bolts.
20. Install the oil level dipstick and the HAC valve on 3E engines.
21. Install the RH engine under cover.
22. Adjust the drive belt. Refill engine coolant. Start the engine and check for coolant leaks.

Cylinder Head

REMOVAL & INSTALLATION

3A and 3A-C Engines

▶ See Figures 115, 116, 117, 118, 119, 120, 121 and 122

➡All wires and hoses should be labelled at the time of removal. Review the complete service procedure before starting this repair. Refer to to the Torque Specification Chart when tightening all attaching bolts and nuts. Always change the oil and oil filter after this repair is finished.

1. Disconnect the negative battery cable.
2. Drain the cooling system.
3. Remove the air cleaner assembly.
4. Elevate and safely support the vehicle on jackstands.
5. Drain the engine oil.
6. Disconnect the exhaust pipe from the exhaust manifold and the exhaust bracket from the engine.
7. Disconnect the hose at the converter pipe, if equipped.
8. If equipped with power steering, loosen the pivot bolt at the power steering pump.
9. Lower the vehicle to the ground.
10. Disconnect the accelerator and throttle control cables at the carburetor and bracket.
11. Label and disconnect the wiring at the cowl, the oxygen sensor and the distributor.
12. Label and disconnect all vacuum hoses.
13. Disconnect the fuel hoses at the fuel pump.
14. Remove the upper radiator hose from the engine.
15. Remove the water outlet assembly from the head. Remove the heater hose.
16. If equipped with power steering, remove the adjusting bracket.
17. Label and disconnect the vacuum hoses and spark plug wires at the distributor. Remove the distributor.
18. Remove the PCV valve from the valve cover.
19. Reposition or disconnect the wiring harness running along the head.

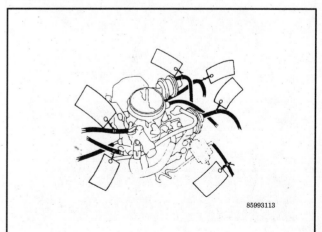

Fig. 115 Before disconnecting vacuum and electrical connections, use tags to identify how they should be reconnected

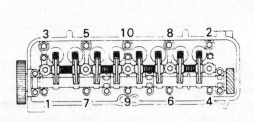

Fig. 116 The cylinder head bolts must be loosened gradually, in several passes, using the correct sequence — 3A and 3A-C engines shown

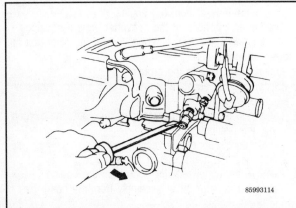

Fig. 117 If the cylinder head is difficult to lift off, use a small prybar between the cylinder head and block partitions. Be careful not to damage any cylinder head or block surfaces

Fig. 118 Have an assistant help you lift the cylinder head from the engine block

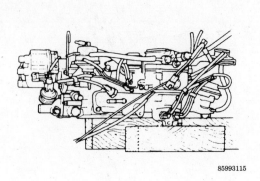

Fig. 119 Place the cylinder head on wooden blocks to prevent damage to the surfaces

Fig. 120 When installing the head, always torque the bolts to specification using several passes of the correct sequence

20. Remove the upper timing belt cover bolts.
21. Remove the valve cover and its gasket.
22. Remove the water pump pulley bolts and the pulley.
23. Remove the alternator belt.
24. Matchmark the camshaft pulley and the cylinder head so that the marks can be realigned during reinstallation. With chalk or crayon, mark the timing belt with an arrow showing the direction of rotation and mark the belt-to-pulley alignment as well.
25. Loosen the bolt holding the timing belt idler pulley; move the idler to release tension on the belt and snug the bolt to hold the idler in the loosened position.
26. Carefully pull or slide the timing belt off the cam pulley. Do not crimp the belt and do not force it off the pulley with tools.

27. Loosen and remove the head bolts gradually, in three passes and in the order shown in the illustration.

❄❄WARNING

Head warpage or cracking can occur if the correct removal procedure is not followed.

28. Remove the cylinder head with the manifolds and carburetor attached. If the head is difficult to lift off, gently pry it up with a suitable tool placed between the head and the projection on the block. If prying is needed, be careful not to score or gouge the mating surfaces of the head and/or the block.

29. Keeping the head upright, place it on wooden blocks on the workbench. If the head is to receive further work, the various external components will need to be removed. If the head is not to be worked on, the mating surface must be cleaned of all gasket and sealant material before reinstallation.

To install:

30. Clean the engine block mating surface of all gasket and sealant material. Use plastic or wooden scrapers to prevent damage to the surfaces. Remove all traces of liquids from the surface and clean out the bolt holes.

31. Install the new head gasket on the block with the sealer facing upwards.

32. Place the head in position and make sure it is properly seated and aligned.

33. Install the cylinder head bolts. Tighten them gradually, in three passes, in the order shown. On the first pass, tighten all the bolts to 14 ft. lbs. (19 Nm). On the second pass the bolts are tightened to 30 ft. lbs. (41 Nm) and on the last pass the bolts are tightened to their final setting of 43 ft. lbs. (58 Nm).

❄❄WARNING

Failure to follow this procedure exactly may cause either premature gasket failure or head damage.

34. Align the camshaft pulley mark(s) made during disassembly with the marks on the head and or block.

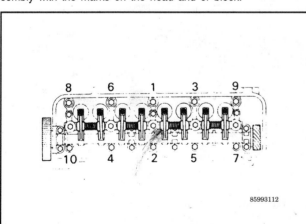

85993112

Fig. 121 Cylinder head bolt torque sequence — 3A and 3A-C engines. Note that this sequence is different than the removal sequence

35. Install the timing belt onto the cam pulley, being careful not to allow the belt to become mispositioned on the lower (crank) pulley. Handle the belt carefully and avoid getting fluids or lubricants on the belt.

36. Loosen the holding bolt for the timing belt idler pulley and allow it to tension the belt.

37. Turn the crankshaft clockwise through at least two full revolutions; finish the rotation by aligning the timing marks at TDC. Double check that the small triangular mark on the cam pulley is at the top and pointing up.

38. Tighten the bolt for the timing belt idler pulley to 27 ft. lbs. (37 Nm).

39. Check the timing belt tension. Refer to the Timing Belt procedure in this section for details.

40. If the head was disassembled during the repair, adjust the valves at this time. If the head was not disassembled, the valves need not be adjusted.

41. Install the valve cover and the upper timing cover.

42. Install the water pump pulley and bolts; install the alternator belt and adjust it to the correct tension.

43. Correctly position or reconnect the wiring harness running along the head.

44. Install the PCV valve in the valve cover.

45. Correctly install the distributor and connect the wiring, vacuum lines and spark plug wires.

46. Install the power steering adjusting bracket if so equipped.

47. Install the heater hose, the water outlet at the head and connect the upper radiator hose to the engine.

48. Connect the fuel lines to the fuel pump.

49. Observing the labels made earlier, connect the vacuum hoses to their ports. Make sure the hoses fit securely on the fittings and are not crimped or twisted.

50. Connect the wiring at the cowl, the oxygen sensor and the distributor.

51. Connect the accelerator and throttle control cables at the bracket and at the carburetor.

52. Safely raise and support the vehicle on jackstands.

53. If equipped with power steering, tighten the pivot bolt for the pump.

54. Connect the hose at the converter pipe.

55. Connect the exhaust bracket to the engine and connect the exhaust pipe to the manifold.

56. Lower the vehicle to the ground.

57. Install the air cleaner assembly.

58. Change the oil and oil filter.

59. Confirm that the radiator and engine draincocks are closed, then fill the cooling system with the correct amount of coolant. Install the radiator cap.

60. Double check all installation items, paying particular attention to loose hoses or hanging wires, untightened nuts, poor routing of hoses and wires (too tight or rubbing) and tools left in the engine area.

61. Connect the negative battery cable.

62. Start the engine; during the warm up period, check carefully for any signs of fluid leaks or engine overheating.

63. When the engine has reached normal operating temperature, check the ignition timing and adjust the idle speed as necessary. Road test the vehicle for proper operation.

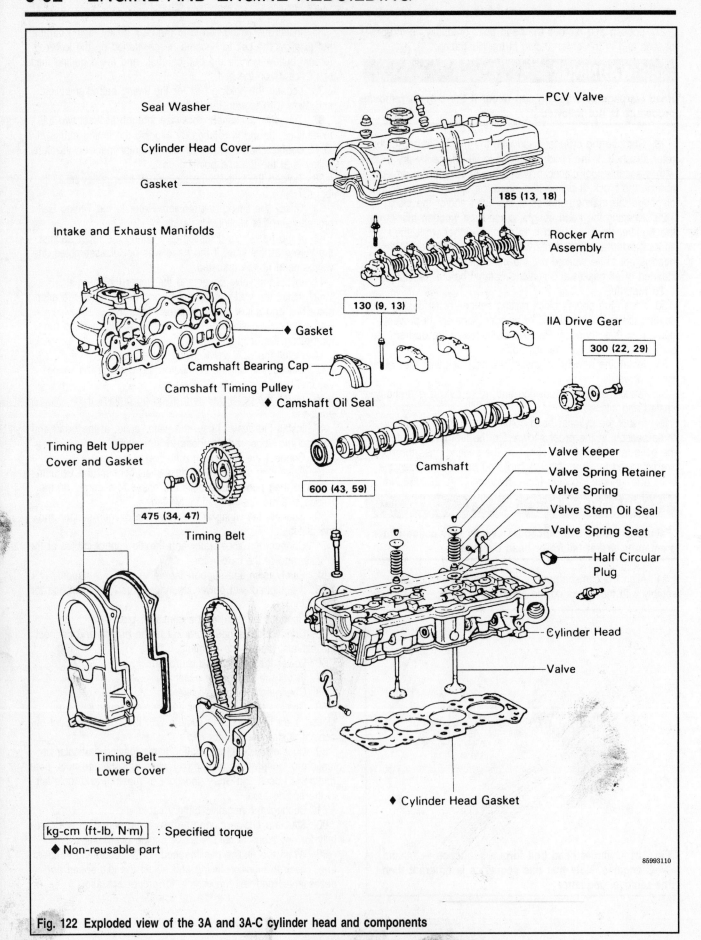

Seal Washer

Cylinder Head Cover

Gasket

Intake and Exhaust Manifolds

PCV Valve

185 (13, 18)

Rocker Arm Assembly

130 (9, 13)

◆ Gasket

Camshaft Bearing Cap

Camshaft Timing Pulley

◆ Camshaft Oil Seal

IIA Drive Gear

300 (22, 29)

Camshaft

Timing Belt Upper Cover and Gasket

475 (34, 47)

Timing Belt

600 (43, 59)

Valve Keeper

Valve Spring Retainer

Valve Spring

Valve Stem Oil Seal

Valve Spring Seat

Half Circular Plug

Cylinder Head

Valve

Timing Belt Lower Cover

◆ Cylinder Head Gasket

kg-cm (ft-lb, N·m) : Specified torque

◆ Non-reusable part

85993110

Fig. 122 Exploded view of the 3A and 3A-C cylinder head and components

3E and 3E-E Engines

▶ See Figures 115, 117, 118, 119, 120, 123, 124, 125, 126, 127 and 128

➡All wires and hoses should be labelled or marked at the time of removal. Review the complete service procedure before starting this repair. Refer to the Torque Specifications Chart when tightening all attaching bolts and nuts. Always change the oil and oil filter after this repair is finished.

✳✳CAUTION

On models equipped with a Supplemental Restraint System (SRS) or "air bag," work must NOT be started until at least 90 seconds have passed from the time the ignition switch is turned to the LOCK position and the negative cable is disconnected from the battery.

1. Disconnect the negative battery cable. Remove the right side under engine splash shield. Relieve the fuel pressure on the 3E-E engine.
2. Drain the engine coolant from the radiator.
3. Remove the power steering pump and bracket (if equipped).
4. On models with A/C and without power steering, remove the idler pulley/bracket.
5. Disconnect the radiator hoses. Disconnect the accelerator and throttle valve cables.
6. Disconnect the heater inlet hose. Disconnect and plug the fuel lines. On the 3E-E engines, remove the pulsation damper, then disconnect the fuel inlet and return hoses.
7. Disconnect the power brake booster vacuum line from the intake manifold.
8. Disconnect the water inlet hose. Disconnect the intake manifold water hose from the intake manifold.
9. Tag (for identification) all vacuum lines, hoses and wires or harnesses to the intake manifold and cylinder head and disconnect them.
10. Remove the evaporative and cold enrichment Vacuum Switching Valves (VSV), if so equipped.

11. Disconnect the water by-pass hoses from the carburetor.
12. Disconnect the exhaust pipe from the exhaust manifold.
13. Remove the intake manifold stay bracket and ground strap. Remove the engine wire harness bracket clamp from the intake manifold.
14. Remove the cylinder head cover.
15. Remove the timing belt and camshaft timing pulley.
16. Loosen and remove the head mounting bolts gradually in three passes working from the ends of the cylinder head inward.
17. Lift the head straight up from the engine block.
18. Clean all gasket surfaces.

To install:
19. Service the head as necessary.
20. Install a new cylinder head gasket. Torque the cylinder head mounting bolts in three progressive steps. Torque to 22 ft. lbs. (30 Nm) in the first pass, 36 ft. lbs. (49 Nm) in the second pass and finally for the third pass, tighten the head bolts an additional 90 degrees from the second pass. Tighten the bolts in sequence from the center of the head outwards (refer to the torque sequence illustration).
21. Adjust the valve clearance if any work was performed on the head.
22. Install the cylinder head cover.
23. Install the intake manifold stay bracket and ground strap.
24. Connect the exhaust pipe to the exhaust manifold. Use two new nuts and torque to specification.
25. Connect the water bypass hose to the carburetor.
26. Install the evaporative and cold enrichment breaker VSVs.
27. Connect all vacuum hoses and wires.
28. Connect all heater hoses.
29. Connect the fuel hoses, use new clamps and gaskets as necessary.
30. Attach the accelerator and throttle cables.
31. Connect the radiator hoses.
32. Install the idler pulley bracket, power steering pump bracket and the power steering pump.
33. Install the engine under cover.
34. Fill the radiator with coolant and connect the negative battery cable.

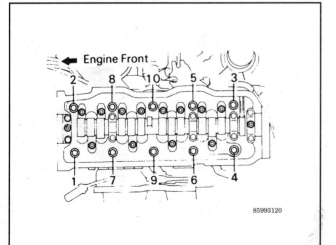

Fig. 123 Cylinder head bolt removal sequence for 3E and 3E-E engines

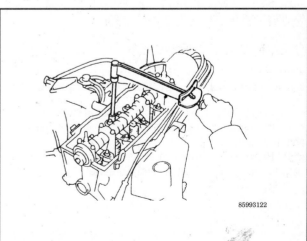

Fig. 124 The cylinder head bolts should always be tightened gradually in several passes using the correct sequence

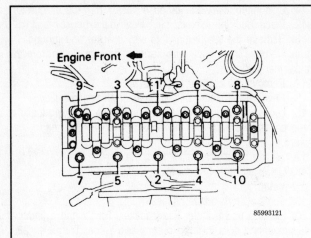

Fig. 125 Cylinder head bolt tightening sequence for 3E and 3E-E engines

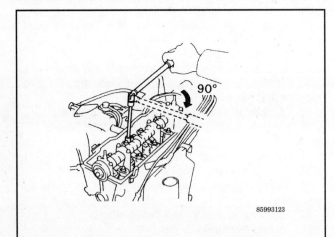

Fig. 126 Tightening the cylinder head bolts an additional 90 degrees on 3E and 3E-E engines. This is commonly called the angle torquing method

35. Start the engine, then check ignition timing and carburetor adjustments. Roadtest for proper operation.

CLEANING AND INSPECTION

▶ **See Figures 129, 130, 131, 132, 133, 134 and 135**

1. With the head removed from the car, remove the carburetor, the fuel pump and the intake and exhaust or combination manifolds.

2. Remove the rocker arm assembly (keep all parts in order), following the procedures outlined earlier.

3. Remove and inspect the camshaft and valves, following the procedures outlined later in this Section.

4. Using a wire brush chucked into an electric drill, remove all the carbon from the combustion chambers in the head. Be careful not to scratch the head.

5. Use a gasket scraper and remove all material from the manifold and head surfaces, again being careful not to scratch the surface.

6. Use a valve guide brush or a fine-bristled rifle bore brush with solvent to clean the valve guides.

7. Use a clean cloth and a stiff bristle brush with solvent to thoroughly clean the head assembly. Make sure that no material is washed into the bolt holes or passages. If possible, dry the head with compressed air to remove fluid and solid matter from all the passages.

➡ **Do not clean the head in a hot tank or chemical bath.**

8. With the head clean and dry, use a precision straight-edge and a feeler gauge to measure the head for warpage. It should not exceed 0.0020 in. (0.05mm). Also measure the warpage on the manifold faces. On 3A and 3A-C engines it should not be greater than 0.0039 in. (0.10mm). On 3E and 3E-E engines it should not exceed 0.0020 in. (0.05mm). Any warpage in excess of the maximum requires replacement of the head.

9. If all is well with the head to this point, it is highly recommended that it be taken to a professional facility such as a machine shop for sophisticated crack testing. The various procedures are much more reliable than simple examination by eye. The cost is reasonable and the peace of mind is well worth the cost. If any cracks are found, the head must be replaced.

10. While the head is being checked, carefully scrape the carbon from the tops of the pistons. Don't scratch the metal of the piston tops and don't damage the cylinder walls. Remove all the carbon and fluid from the cylinder.

11. If repairs are needed to the valves, camshaft or other components, follow the appropriate procedures outlined in this Section.

CYLINDER HEAD RESURFACING

The Toyota cylinder heads for all engines may be resurfaced by a reputable machine shop. Resurfacing is recommended if the engine suffered a massive overheating, such as from a failed head gasket.

The heads are manufactured to be as light as possible; consequently, there is not much excess metal on the face. Any machining must be minimal. If too much metal is removed, the head becomes unusable. A head which exceeds the maximum warpage specification CANNOT be resurfaced. The machine shop will have a list of minimum head thicknesses; at no time may this minimum be exceeded.

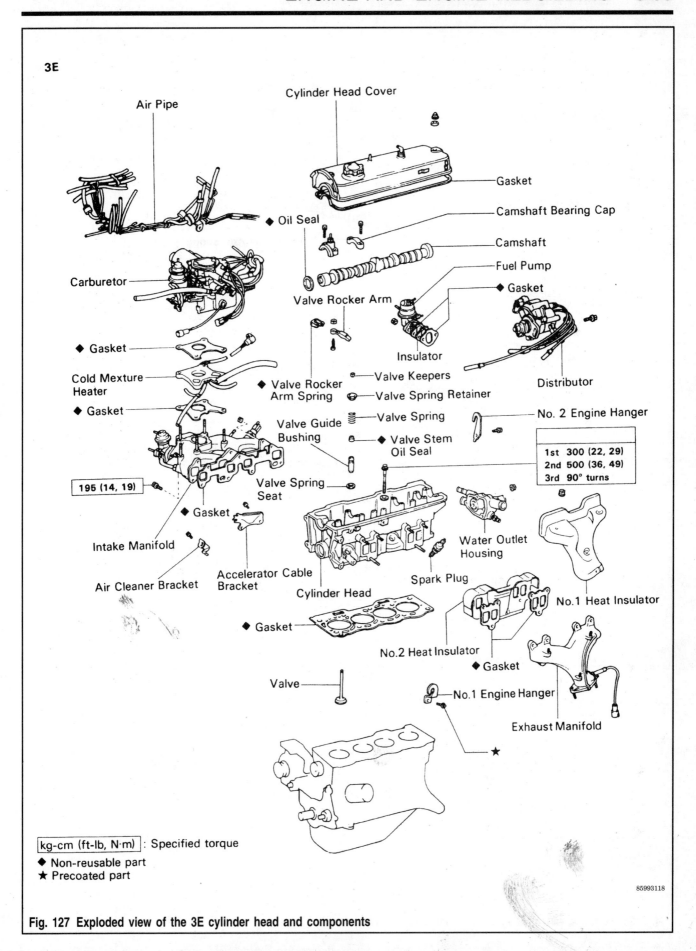

3E

Air Pipe

Cylinder Head Cover

Gasket

Camshaft Bearing Cap

◆ Oil Seal

Camshaft

Fuel Pump

◆ Gasket

Carburetor

Valve Rocker Arm

Insulator

Distributor

◆ Gasket

Valve Keepers

Cold Mexture Heater

◆ Valve Rocker Arm Spring

Valve Spring Retainer

◆ Gasket

Valve Spring

No. 2 Engine Hanger

Valve Guide Bushing

◆ Valve Stem Oil Seal

1st	300 (22, 29)
2nd	500 (36, 49)
3rd	90° turns

195 (14, 19)

Valve Spring Seat

◆ Gasket

Intake Manifold

Accelerator Cable Bracket

Water Outlet Housing

No.1 Heat Insulator

Air Cleaner Bracket

Spark Plug

Cylinder Head

No.2 Heat Insulator

◆ Gasket

◆ Gasket

No.1 Engine Hanger

Valve

Exhaust Manifold

★

kg-cm (ft-lb, N·m) : Specified torque

◆ Non-reusable part

★ Precoated part

85993118

Fig. 127 Exploded view of the 3E cylinder head and components

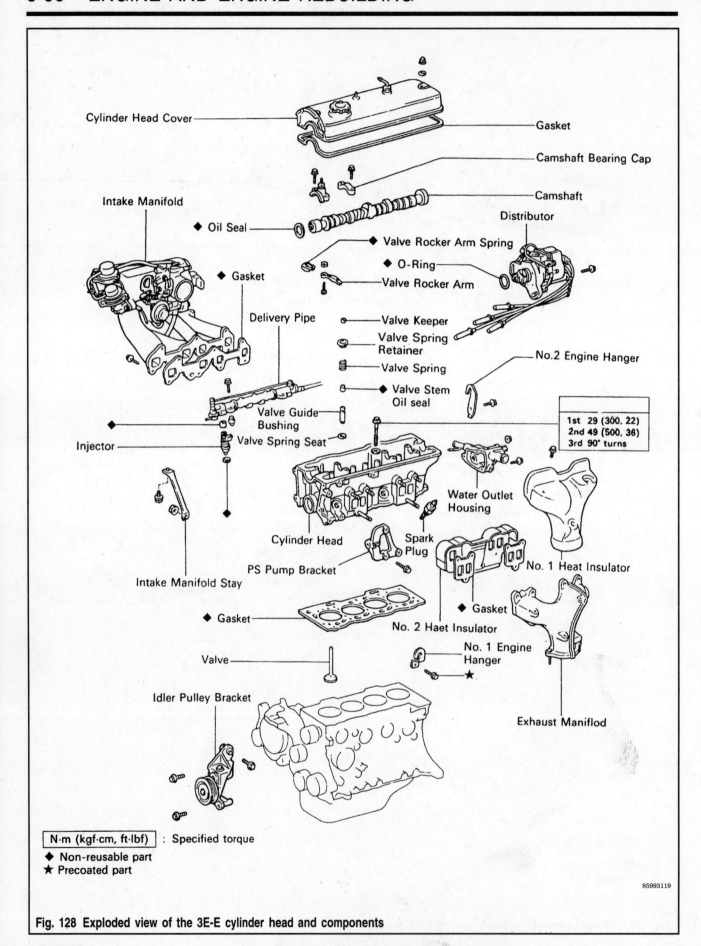

Fig. 128 Exploded view of the 3E-E cylinder head and components

Fig. 129 It's a good idea to clean the tops of the pistons while the head is removed

Fig. 130 A wire wheel may be used to clean the combustion chambers of carbon deposits

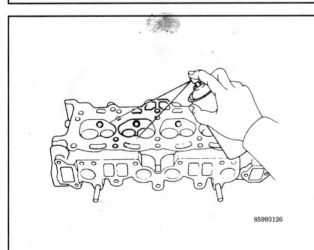

Fig. 131 The cylinder head can be checked for cracks using a dye penetrant

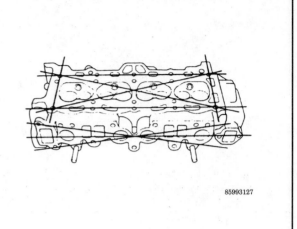

Fig. 132 Check the cylinder head for warpage on all sides and diagonally; 3A and 3A-C engines shown

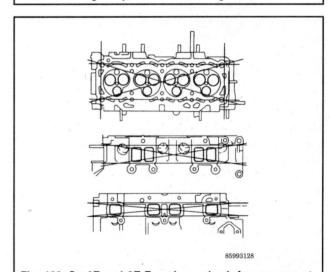

Fig. 133 On 3E and 3E-E engines, check for warpage at these angles

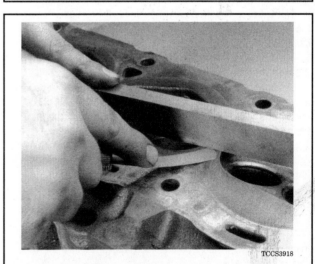

Fig. 134 Checking the cylinder head warpage across the head surface at an angle

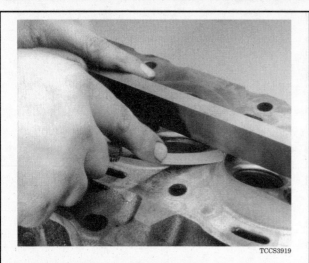

Fig. 135 Checking for cylinder head warpage straight across the head surface

Valves

REMOVAL & INSTALLATION

▶ See Figures 136, 137, 138 and 139

➡This procedure requires the use of a valve stem compressor. This common tool is available at most auto supply stores. It may also be possible to rent one from a tool supplier. It is absolutely essential that all components be kept in order after removal. Old ice trays make excellent holders for small parts. The containers should be labeled so that the parts may be reinstalled in their original location. Keep the valves in numbered order in a holder such as an egg carton or an inverted box with holes punched in it. Label the container so that each valve may be replaced in its exact position. (Example: Exhaust No. 1, No. 2 etc.)

1. Following the procedures outlined in this section, remove the head from the engine then remove the rocker arms and camshaft.
2. Compress the valve spring (using a valve spring compressor) and remove the keepers at the top of the valve.
3. Slowly release the tension on the compressor and remove it. Remove the spring retainer (upper cap), the valve spring, the valve stem oil seal and the lower spring seat. On 3E and 3E-E engines, use pliers to pull out the oil seal.
4. The valve is then removed from the bottom of the head.
5. Repeat for each valve in the head, keeping them labeled and in order.
6. Thoroughly clean and decarbon each valve. Inspect each valve and spring as outlined later in this section.

To install:
7. Lubricate the the valve stem and guide with engine oil. Install the valve in the cylinder head and position the lower spring seat.
8. Lubricate the new valve stem seal with engine oil and install it onto the valve stem over the lower seat.

9. Install the valve spring and the upper seat, compress the spring and install the two keepers. Relax tension on the compressor and make sure everything is properly placed. Tap on the installed valve stem with a plastic mallet to ensure proper locking of the retainers.
10. Complete the reassembly of the head by installing the camshafts and the manifolds. Refer to the procedures in this Section.

INSPECTION AND LAPPING

▶ See Figures 140, 141, 142, 143, 144, 145, 146, 147, 148, 149 and 150

➡Accurate measuring equipment capable of reading to 0.0001 (ten thousandths) inch is necessary for this work. A micrometer and a hole (bore) gauge will be needed.

Inspect the valve faces and seats for pits, burned spots, and other evidence of poor seating. The valve can be refaced to

Fig. 136 A valve spring compressor must be used to remove the valves

Fig. 137 A small magnetic probe makes valve keeper extraction easier

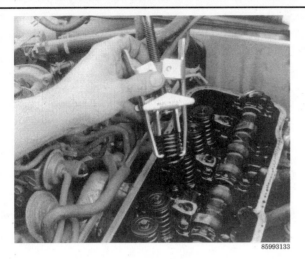

Fig. 138 The valve springs should be inspected and tested before reinstallation

Fig. 139 The valve spring seat must be in place before installing the valve spring

remove pits and carbon. If the valve is in such poor shape that refacing it will reduce the margin thickness out of specification, discard the valve. Never try to straighten and reuse a bent valve. It is recommended that any seat resurfacing or valve refacing be done by a reputable machine shop.

Check the valve stem for scoring and/or burned spots. If the stem and head are in acceptable condition, clean the valve thoroughly with solvent to remove all gum and varnish.

Use the micrometer to measure the diameter of the valve stem. Use the hole gauge to measure the inside diameter of the valve guide for that valve. Subtract the stem diameter from the guide diameter and compare the difference to the Valve Specifications Chart. If not within specification, determine the cause (worn valve or worn guide) and replace the worn part(s).

The valve head margin thickness should be checked both before and after refacing. If at any time it is below the mini-

mum thickness specification, it must be replaced. The specifications are as follows:

3A and 3A-C Engines
- Intake — 0.020 in. (0.5mm)
- Exhaust — 0.039 in. (1.0mm)

3E and 3E-E Engines
- Intake, Sub-Intake and Exhaust — 0.031 in. (0.8mm)

Check the top of each valve stem for pitting and unusual wear. The stem tip can be ground flat if worn, but the minimum valve length or longer MUST be maintained. If valve length is less than specified, it must be replaced. Minimum valve length specifications are as follows:

3A and 3A-C Engines
- Intake — 4.1879 in. (106.38mm)
- Exhaust — 4.1839 in. (106.28mm)

3E and 3E-E Engines
- Intake — 3.6126 in. (91.76mm)
- Sub-Intake — 3.5945 in. (91.30mm)
- Exhaust — 3.6126 in. (91.76mm)

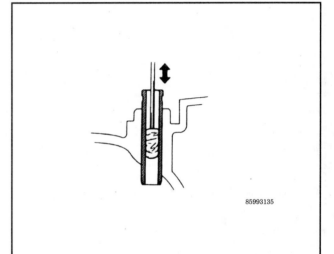

Fig. 140 Use a valve guide brush and solvent to clean the valve guide bushings

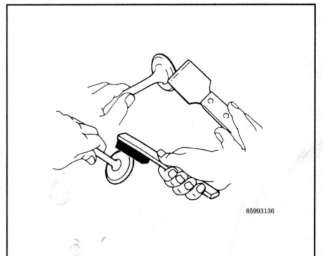

Fig. 141 When cleaning the valves, be careful not to damage the seat valve surface

The valves should also be checked for proper seat contact.

1. Apply a thin coat of prussian blue (or white lead) to the valve face and place the valve in the head.

2. Apply light pressure to the valve, but do not rotate it.

3. Carefully remove the valve from the head then check the valve and seat. If blue appears 360 degrees around the valve seat, the seat and valve are are concentric.

4. Check that the seat contact is in the middle of the valve face. It should be 0.047-0.063 in. (1.2-1.6mm) in width.

5. If the valve and seat are not concentric or the seat width is out of specification, you should consult a reputable machine shop for proper refacing.

6. After machine work has been performed on valves/seats, it may be necessary to lap the valves to assure proper con-

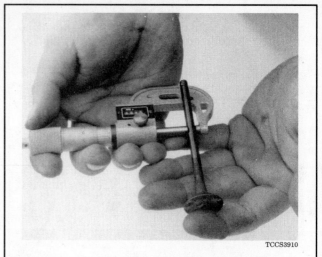

Fig. 144 Use a micrometer to check the valve stem diameter

tact. For this, you should first consult your machine shop to determine if lapping is necessary. Some machine shops will perform this for you as part of the service, but the precision machining which is available today often makes lapping unnecessary. Additionally, the hardened valves/seats used in modern automobiles may make lapping difficult or impossible. If your machine shop recommends that you lap the valves proceed as follows:

a. Coat the valve face and seat with a light coat of valve grinding compound. Attach the suction cup end of the valve grinding tool to the head of the valve (it helps to moisten it first).

b. Rotate the tool between the palms, changing position and and lifting the tool often to prevent grooving. Lap in the valve until a smooth, evenly polished surface is evident on both the seat and face.

c. Remove the valve from the head. Wipe away all traces of grinding compound from the surfaces. Clean out the valve guide with a solvent-soaked rag. Make sure there are NO traces of compound in or on the head.

d. Proceed through the remaining valves, lapping them one at a time to their seats. Clean the area after each valve is done.

e. When all the valves have been lapped, thoroughly clean or wash the head with solvent. There must be NO trace of grinding compound present.

REFACING

▶ See Figure 151

Due to the skill involved and the high cost of purchasing the proper equipment, it is recommended that valve refacing be handled by a reputable machine shop.

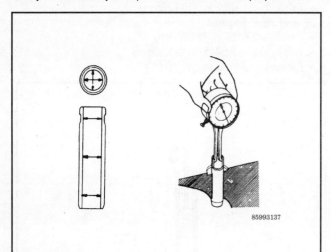

Fig. 142 Measure the inside diameter of the valve guide at these points

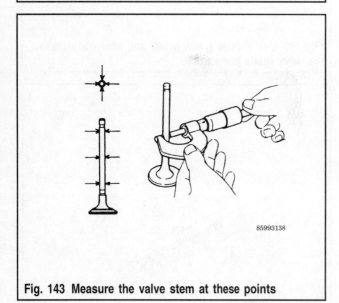

Fig. 143 Measure the valve stem at these points

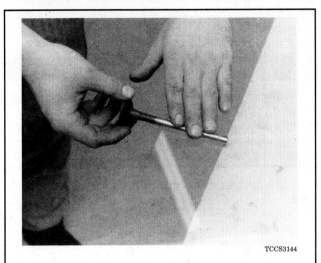

Fig. 145 Valve stems may be rolled on a flat surface to check for bends

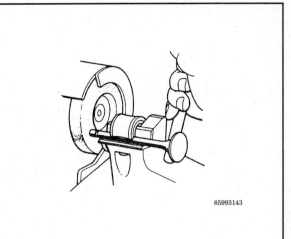

Fig. 148 If the valve stem tip is worn, it can be refinished. Do not grind more than the minimum overall length allows

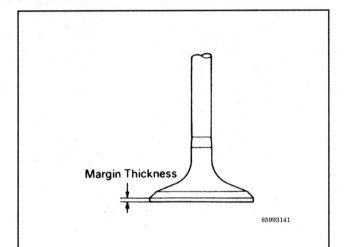

Fig. 146 If the valve head margin thickness is less than the minimum specification, replace the valve

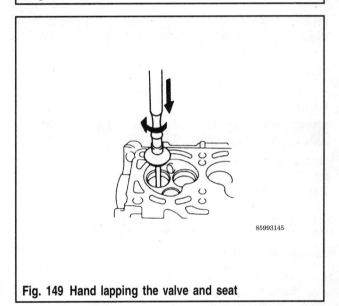

Fig. 149 Hand lapping the valve and seat

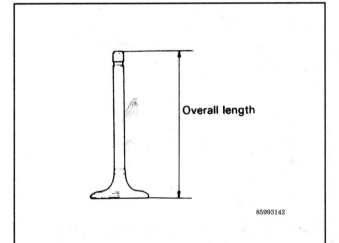

Fig. 147 The overall length of the valve must be checked as well

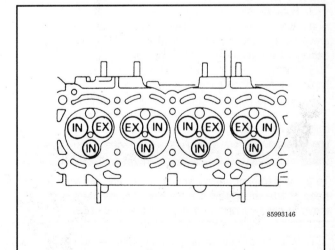

Fig. 150 On 3E and 3E-E engines, be sure that the valves are installed in the correct order

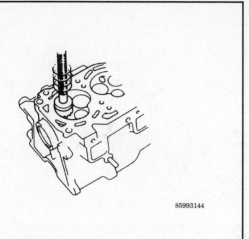

Fig. 151 Resurfacing of the valve seats should be performed by a reputable machine shop

Valve Stem Seals

REPLACEMENT

▶ See Figures 152, 153 and 154

✳✳CAUTION

On models equipped with a Supplemental Restraint System (SRS) or "air bag," work must NOT be started until at least 90 seconds have passed from the time the ignition switch is turned to the LOCK position and the negative cable is disconnected from the battery.

Cylinder Head Installed

1. Disconnect the negative battery cable.
2. Remove the valve cover, camshaft and rockers using the procedures outlined in this section.
3. Remove the spark plugs.
4. Attach a fixture at the flywheel or front of the engine to prevent the engine from rotating. Make sure the fixture will not damage any components in case of movement.
5. Thread an adaptor into the spark plug holes that can be hooked up to a shop compressor air hose.
6. Apply 90 psi of compressed air to the adaptor hose. This is done to keep the valves from dropping down into the cylinder when the valve springs are removed.

✳✳CAUTION

To avoid personal injury, wear eye and ear protection. Keep hands and clothing away from engine parts that move in case air pressure does cause rotation.

7. With the cylinder under pressure, remove the valve spring retainer and the spring using a spring compressor tool.

Hitting the spring retainer lightly with a soft hammer may help loosen the valve keepers if the retainer will not move downwards exposing the keepers.

✳✳WARNING

DO NOT push the valve downwards into the cylinder when the spring is removed. Doing so will only introduce the potential of the valve dropping into the cylinder, possibly causing valve, piston, and cylinder wall damage. Head removal would be required to retrieve it.

8. With the valve spring and retainer removed, remove the oil seal. On 3E and 3E-E engines, remove the seal using a pair of pliers.
   To install:
9. Install a new seal. Rotate the oil seal to check that it is firmly installed.
10. Install the valve spring, retainer and keepers. Follow procedures described earlier.
11. Release the air pressure from the cylinder.
12. Install the rockers, camshaft, and valve cover as described in this section. Adjust the valves as necessary.
13. Install the spark plugs.
14. Connect the negative battery cable. Start the engine and check for proper operation.

Cylinder Head Removed

1. Remove the cylinder head. Use the procedures outlined earlier in this section.
2. Remove the camshaft, rockers, valve springs and retainers using the appropriate procedures.
3. Remove the oil seal. On 3E and 3E-E engines, remove the seal using a pair of pliers.
4. Installation is the reverse of removal. Refer to the appropriate procedures in this section to assure proper installation.
5. Connect the negative battery cable. Start the engine and check for proper operation.

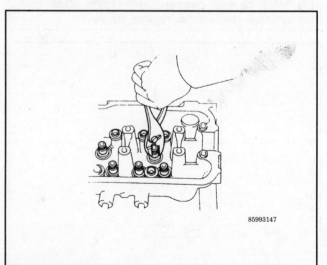

Fig. 152 Use pliers to pull out the oil seal on 3E and 3E-E engines

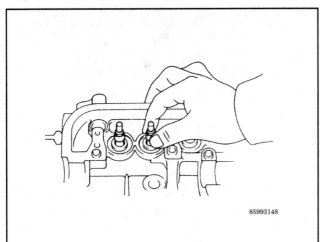

Fig. 153 Installing the valve seals on 3A and 3A-C engines

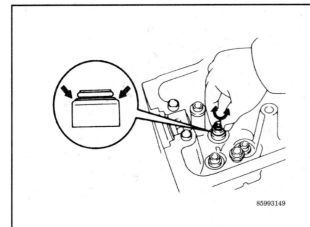

Fig. 154 When installing the valve seals on 3E and 3E-E engines, push down on the points shown. Rotate the oil seal to check that it is firmly seated

Valve Springs

REMOVAL & INSTALLATION

Valve spring removal and installation is part of the Valves removal and installation procedure covered earlier in this section.

INSPECTION

▶ **See Figures 155, 156 and 157**

Valve spring squareness, free length and tension should be checked while the valve train is disassembled. Place each valve spring on a flat surface next to a steel square. Rotate it against the edge of the square to check for distortion. If the squareness is not within 0.079 in. (2mm), replace the spring.

Check the free length of the spring with a pair of vernier calipers. It should be 1.756 in. (44.6mm) on 3A and 3A-C engines and 1.6346 in. (41.52mm) on 3E and 3E-E engines. If the free length of the spring is not within specification, replace the spring. Using a spring tester, measure the tension of the valve spring at the specified installed length. Compare the readings with the Valve Specifications Chart. If it is not within specification, replace the spring.

Valve Seats

REMOVAL & INSTALLATION

The valve seats for all Toyota engines are not replaceable. A failed seat (which cannot be recut) requires replacement of the head. Seat recutting is a precise procedure and should be performed by a machine shop. Seat concentricity should also be checked by a professional facility.

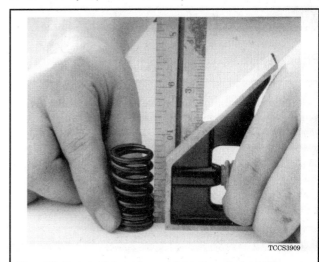

Fig. 155 Rotate the spring against the edge of the square to check for distortion

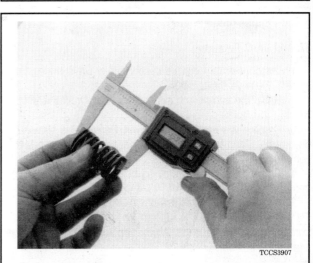

Fig. 156 Use a caliper gauge to check valve spring free length

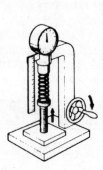

Fig. 157 The valve spring must be tested for correct tension at it's installed length

Valve Guides

REMOVAL & INSTALLATION

Replacing the valve guides involves heating the head to high temperatures and driving the old guide out with the use of special tools. The head may have to be machined for an oversize guide if the bushing bore dimension is over the standard specifications. The new guide is then reamed for the proper valve stem-to-guide clearance. This repair requires a high level of mechanical skill and should only be performed by a reputable machine shop.

Oil Pan

REMOVAL & INSTALLATION

▶ See Figures 158 and 159

3A and 3A-C Engines

1. Disconnect the negative battery cable. Drain the cooling system. Remove the radiator.
2. Raise the vehicle and support it safely. Drain the engine oil.
3. Remove the engine under cover. Remove the stabilizer bracket bolts and lower the stabilizer assembly. Remove the right and left stiffener plates.
4. Remove the oil pan retaining bolts. Remove the oil pan from the vehicle.
5. Installation is the reverse of the removal procedure. Tighten the oil pan bolts to 48 inch lbs. (5.4 Nm), working from the center to the ends. Always replace the oil pan gasket and refill with clean engine oil. Start engine check for leaks.

Fig. 158 Loosening the oil pan attaching bolts

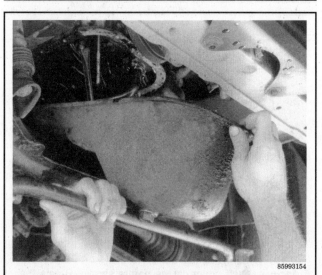

Fig. 159 Removing the oil pan from the vehicle

3E and 3E-E Engines

✳✳CAUTION

On models equipped with a Supplemental Restraint System (SRS) or "air bag," work must NOT be started until at least 90 seconds have passed from the time the ignition switch is turned to the LOCK position and the negative cable is disconnected from the battery.

1. Disconnect the negative battery terminal. Raise the vehicle and support it safely. Drain the oil.
2. Remove the right hand engine under cover. Remove the sway bar and any other necessary steering linkage parts.
3. Disconnect the exhaust pipe from the manifold. Raise the engine enough to take the weight off of it.
4. Remove the timing belt. Refer to the necessary service procedure in this section.
5. Continue to raise the engine enough to remove the oil pan. Remove the oil pan retaining bolts. Remove the oil pan.

6. Installation is the reverse of the removal procedure. Tighten the oil pan bolts to specification (working from the center to the ends). Always replace the oil pan gasket and refill with clean engine oil. Start engine check for leaks.

Oil Pump

REMOVAL

♦ See Figures 160, 161 and 162

3A and 3A-C Engines

1. Disconnect the negative battery cable.
2. Raise the front of the vehicle and support it on safety stands.
3. Drain the engine oil. Drain the coolant and then remove the radiator.

✳✳CAUTION

When draining the coolant, keep in mind that cats and dogs are attracted by ethylene glycol antifreeze, and are quite likely to drink any that is left in an uncovered container or in puddles on the ground. This will prove fatal in sufficient quantity. Always drain the coolant into a sealable container. Coolant should be reused unless it is contaminated or several years old.

4. Remove the oil pan and the oil strainer.
5. Remove the crankshaft pulley and the timing belt as detailed in this section.
6. Remove the oil level dipstick and tube.
7. Remove the pump body mounting bolts and then use a rubber mallet to carefully tap the oil pump body from the cylinder block.

3E and 3E-E Engines

✳✳CAUTION

On models equipped with a Supplemental Restraint System (SRS) or "air bag," work must NOT be started until at least 90 seconds have passed from the time the ignition switch is turned to the LOCK position and the negative cable is disconnected from the battery.

1. Disconnect the negative battery cable.
2. Remove the right hand engine splash shield and disconnect the exhaust pipe from the manifold.
3. Remove the timing belt, refer to the appropriate procedure in this section.
4. Drain the engine oil. Remove the oil pan, the oil strainer and the dipstick. Follow the necessary service procedures in this Section.

✳✳CAUTION

The EPA warns that prolonged contact with used engine oil may cause a number of skin disorders, including cancer! You should make every effort to minimize your exposure to used engine oil. Protective gloves should be worn

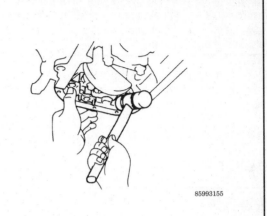
Fig. 160 Carefully tap the oil pump body with a plastic faced hammer to remove it

Fig. 161 Removing the oil pump from the engine

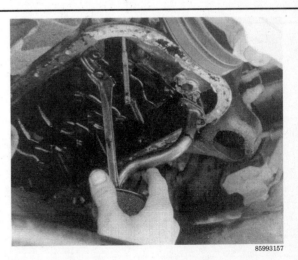
Fig. 162 The oil strainer should be removed and cleaned as well

when changing the oil. Wash your hands and any other exposed skin areas as soon as possible after exposure to used engine oil. Soap and water, or waterless hand cleaner should be used.

5. Remove the pressure regulator valve assembly.
6. Remove the nine oil pump mounting bolts and the tensioner spring bracket.
7. Using a plastic faced hammer, carefully tap off the oil pump. Service as necessary.

INSPECTION

▶ See Figures 163, 164, 165, 166, 167, 168, 169 and 170

3A and 3A-C Engines

GEAR TYPE

1. Using a feeler gauge, measure the clearance between the driven gear and body.
2. Clearance should not exceed 0.0079 in. (0.20mm). If the clearance is greater than specified, replace the gear and/or body.
3. Measure the clearance between both the gear tips and the crescent with a feeler gauge.
4. The maximum clearance allowed is 0.0138 in. (0.35mm). If it is greater than specified, replace the gears and/or body.
5. Using a feeler gauge and flat block, measure the side clearance.
6. Clearance should not be greater than 0.004 in. (0.1mm). If it exceeds the amount specified, replace the gears and/or body.

ROTOR TYPE

1. Using a feeler gauge, measure the clearance between the driven rotor and body.
2. Clearance should not exceed 0.0079 in. (0.20mm). If the clearance is greater than specified, replace the rotor set and/or body.
3. Measure the clearance between both rotor tips with a feeler gauge.

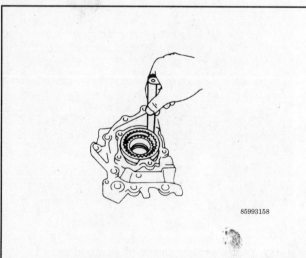

Fig. 163 Measuring the body clearance — oil pump on the 3A and 3A-C engines

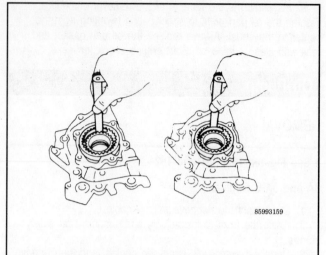

Fig. 164 Measuring the tip clearance — oil pump on the 3A and 3A-C engines

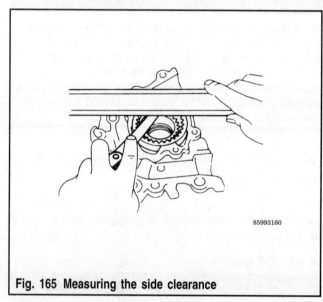

Fig. 165 Measuring the side clearance

4. The maximum clearance allowed is 0.0138 in. (0.35mm). If it is greater than specified, replace the rotor set.
5. Using a feeler gauge and flat block, measure the side clearance.
6. Clearance should not greater than 0.004 in. (0.1mm). If it exceeds the amount specified, replace the rotor and/or body.

3E and 3E-E Engines

PRESSURE REGULATOR

1. Using snapring pliers, remove the snapring.
2. Remove the retainer, spring and piston.
3. Coat the valve piston with engine oil and check that it falls smoothly into the valve hole by it's own weight. If necessary, replace the valve.
4. Assemble the valve in reverse order of removal.

PUMP

1. Using a feeler gauge, measure the clearance between the driven rotor and body.

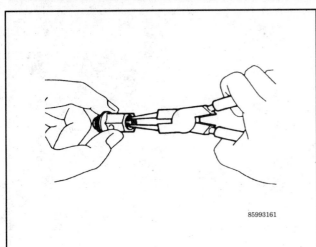

Fig. 166 Remove the snapring with a pair of snapring pliers

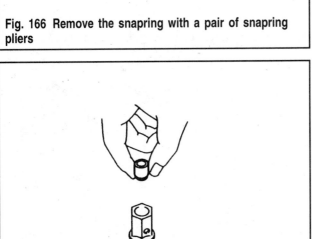

Fig. 167 The valve should fall smoothly into the valve hole under it's own weight

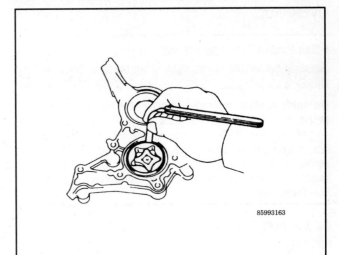

Fig. 168 Inspecting the body clearance — oil pump on 3E and 3E-E engines

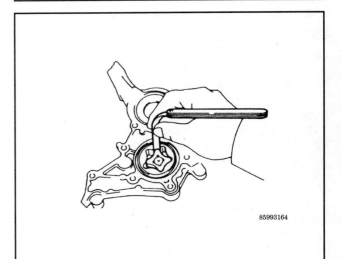

Fig. 169 Inspecting the tip clearance — oil pump on 3E and 3E-E engines

2. Clearance should not exceed 0.0079 in. (0.20mm). If the clearance is greater than specified, replace the rotor set and/or body.

3. Measure the clearance between both rotor tips with a feeler gauge.

4. The maximum clearance allowed is 0.0079 in. (0.20mm). If it is greater than specified, replace the rotor set.

5. Using a feeler gauge and flat block, measure the side clearance.

6. Clearance should not be greater than 0.0039 in. (0.10mm). If it exceeds the amount specified, replace the rotor and/or body.

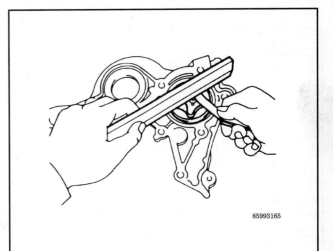

Fig. 170 Side clearance inspection — oil pump on 3E and 3E-E engines

OVERHAUL

♦ See Figures 171, 172, 173 and 174

✳✳WARNING

On some models, the gears/rotors in the oil pump are timed. Failure to install them correctly will result in major engine damage. BEFORE removal, matchmark the drive and driven gears/rotors to the oil pump body with a marker that will not smudge or rub off. It is imperative that the gears/rotors be installed in the correct position on these models.

3A and 3A-C Engines

1. Using snapring pliers, remove snapring retaining the relief valve assembly.
2. Remove the retainer, spring and relief valve piston.
3. Remove the five bolts retaining the oil pump cover.
4. Measure the body, tip and side clearances, as described earlier. Replace any components necessary.
5. Before removing the gears/rotors, matchmark the drive and driven gears/rotors to the oil pump body with a marker that will not smudge or rub off.
6. Lift the gears/rotors out as a set.
7. Pry out the oil seal from the pump body with a small prytool, using a wooden hammer handle as a fulcrum.
8. Install a new oil seal, driving it in with a seal driver tool. Be careful not to install the new oil seal slantwise.
9. Coat the oil seal lightly with multi-purpose grease.
10. Install the gear/rotor set in the body. Be sure that the matchmarks made earlier are aligned.
11. Turn the drive gear several rotations. Make sure they both rotate and do not lock up or require excessive force to turn at any time.
12. Install the oil pump cover with the five screws. Torque to 8 ft. lbs. (10.3 Nm).
13. Insert the relief valve piston, spring and retainer into the pump body. Using snapring pliers, install the snapring.

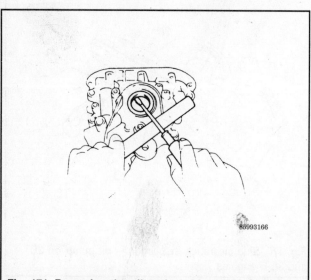

Fig. 171 Removing the oil seal on 3A and 3A-C engines

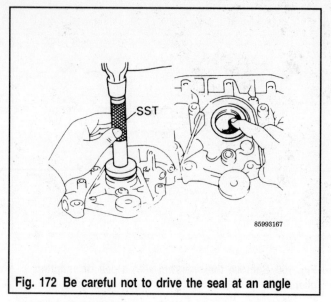

Fig. 172 Be careful not to drive the seal at an angle

3E and 3E-E Engines

1. Measure the body, tip and side clearances, as described earlier. Replace any components necessary.
2. Before removing the rotors, matchmark the drive and driven rotors to the oil pump body with a marker that will not smudge or rub off.
3. Lift the rotors out as a set.
4. Pry out the oil seal from the pump body with a small prytool.
5. Install a new oil seal, driving it in with a seal driver tool. Be careful not to install the new oil seal cocked to one side or at an angle. The seal should be driven to a depth of approximately 0.04 in. (1mm) from the oil pump body edge.
6. Coat the oil seal lightly with multi-purpose grease.
7. Install the rotor set in the body. Be sure that the matchmarks made earlier are aligned.
8. Turn the drive rotor several rotations. Make sure both rotors rotate and do not lock up or require excessive force to turn at any time.

INSTALLATION

♦ See Figures 175 and 176

3A and 3A-C Engines

To install:
1. Position a new gasket on the cylinder block.
2. Position the oil pump on the block so that the teeth on the pump drive gear are engaged with the teeth of the crankshaft gear.
3. Install the oil pump retaining bolts and torque to 16 ft. lbs. (22 Nm).
4. Install the oil level dipstick and guide.
5. Install the oil strainer. Torque the bolts/nuts to 82 inch lbs. (9.3 Nm).
6. Install the oil pan. Refer to the procedure in this section.
7. Lower the vehicle and install the timing belt.
8. Refill with engine oil.
9. Install and fill the radiator. Start the engine and check for leaks.

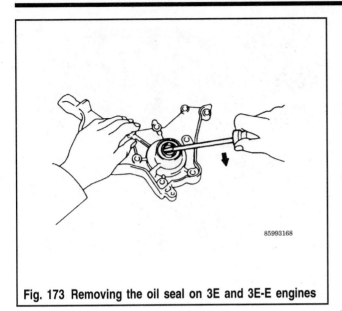

Fig. 173 Removing the oil seal on 3E and 3E-E engines

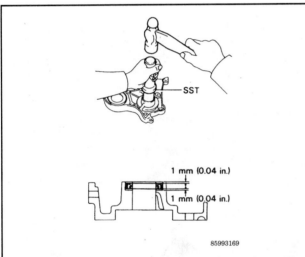

Fig. 174 Drive the seal to the appropriate depth on 3E and 3E-E engines

10. Recheck the fluid levels.

3E and 3E-E Engines

1. Make sure the pump surface is clean, then apply a sealant to the pump body.

2. Place a new O-ring into the groove.

3. Install the oil pump and the tension spring bracket with the nine bolts. Torque to 65 inch lbs. (7.4 Nm).

4. Install the pressure regulator valve and torque to 22 ft. lbs. (29 Nm).

5. Install the oil strainer and torque the attaching bolts to 65 inch lbs. (7.4 Nm).

6. Install the oil pan and oil dipstick.

7. Install the timing belt.

8. Connect the exhaust pipe and install the right hand engine under cover.

9. Refill with engine oil. Start the engine and check for leaks.

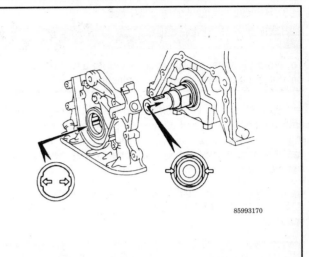

Fig. 175 Installing the oil pump on 3A and 3A-C engines

10. Recheck the oil level.

Crankshaft Damper

REMOVAL & INSTALLATION

▶ See Figures 177 and 178

✳✳CAUTION

On models equipped with a Supplemental Restraint System (SRS) or "air bag," work must NOT be started until at least 90 seconds have passed from the time the ignition switch is turned to the LOCK position and the negative cable is disconnected from the battery.

1. Disconnect the negative battery cable.
2. Remove the accessory belts.

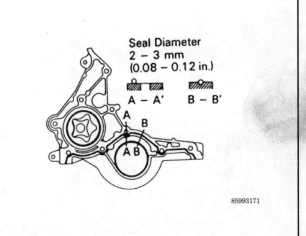

Fig. 176 Apply sealant to the points shown — 3E and 3E-E engines

3. Remove the crankshaft pulley bolt.

✳✳CAUTION

To avoid personal injury, wear gloves to avoid getting cut on the radiator fins. Wear eye protection.

➡This bolt can be very difficult to get off. Spray the bolt with penetrating oil and allow it to soak in overnight. Using air powered tools may make the job easier, but the radiator and possibly other components may have to be removed for clearance.

4. Using a suitable puller, remove the pulley and set key.
5. Installation is the reverse of removal. Torque the bolt to specification.

Timing Belt Cover

REMOVAL & INSTALLATION

◆ See Figures 179 and 180

3A and 3A-C Engines

1. Disconnect the negative battery terminal.
2. Remove all the drive belts.
3. Bring the engine to the top dead center timing position.
4. Remove the crankshaft pulley with a suitable puller.
5. Remove the water pump pulley.
6. Remove the upper and lower timing case covers.
7. Installation is the reverse of removal. Torque the crankshaft pulley bolt to 87 ft. lbs. (118 Nm).

Fig. 178 If the damper does not come off easily, a special puller must be used

Fig. 180 Removing the timing belt cover

Fig. 177 Removing the crankshaft pulley bolt

Fig. 179 Removing the timing belt cover attaching bolts

3E and 3E-E Engines

✳✳CAUTION

On models equipped with a Supplemental Restraint System (SRS) or "air bag," work must NOT be started until at least 90 seconds have passed from the time the ignition switch is turned to the LOCK position and the negative cable is disconnected from the battery.

1. Disconnect the negative battery cable. Remove the air cleaner assembly. Remove all drive belts.

2. If the vehicle is equipped with cruise control, remove the actuator and bracket assembly.

3. Raise and support the vehicle safely. Remove the right side front tire and wheel. Remove the right side engine splash shield. Remove the right side mount insulator.

4. Remove the valve cover. Remove the crankshaft pulley and remove the timing cover mounting bolts and cover.

5. Install in the reverse order procedure. Tighten all bolts to specification, as found on the component torque specifications chart in this section.

Timing Belt and Camshaft Sprocket

REMOVAL & INSTALLATION

▶ **See Figures 181, 182, 183, 184, 185, 186, 187, 188, 189, 190, 191, 192, 193, 194, 195, 196, 197, 198, 199, 200 and 201**

On vehicles frequently idled for extensive periods and/or driven for long distances at low speeds, it is recommended to change the timing belt at 60,000 mile (96,000km) intervals.

➡ **Timing belts must always be handled carefully and kept completely free of dirt, grease, fluids and lubricants. This includes any accidental contact from spillage. These same precautions apply to the pulleys and contact surfaces on which the belt rides. The belt must never be crimped, twisted or bent. Never use tools to pry or wedge the belt into place. Such actions will damage the structure of the belt and possibly cause breakage.**

3A and 3A-C Engines

1. Disconnect the negative battery cable.
2. Remove the radiator.
3. Remove the air cleaner assembly and the drive belts.
4. Remove the rocker arm (valve) cover.
5. Rotate the crankshaft clockwise to the TDC position on the compression stroke for No. 1 cylinder. Insure that the crankshaft marks align at zero and that the rocker arms on No. 1 cylinder are loose.
6. Remove the timing belt covers using the procedures described earlier in this section.
7. Remove the timing belt guide.
8. If reusing the belt, make matchmarks on the belt and both pulleys showing the exact placement of the belt. Mark an arrow on the belt showing its direction of rotation.

9. Loosen the timing belt idler pulley mount bolt, push it as far left as it will go and temporarily tighten the bolt. This will relieve tension from the belt.

10. Carefully slip the timing belt off the pulleys.

11. Remove the idler pulley mount bolt, pulley and return spring.

➡ **Do not disturb the position of the camshaft or the crankshaft during removal.**

12. Use an adjustable wrench mounted on the flats of the camshaft to hold the cam from moving. Loosen the center bolt in the camshaft sprocket and remove the sprocket.

13. Check the timing belt carefully for any signs of cracking or deterioration. Pay particular attention to the area where each tooth or cog attaches to the backing of the belt. If the belt shows signs of damage, check the contact faces of the pulleys for possible burrs or scratches.

14. Check the idler pulley by holding it in your hand and spinning it. It should rotate freely and quietly. Any sign of grinding or abnormal noise indicates a need to replace the pulley.

15. Check the free length of the tension spring. Correct length is 1.512 in. (38.4mm) measured at the inside faces of the hooks. A spring which has stretched during use will not apply the correct tension to the pulley; replace the spring.

16. Test the tension of the spring. It should have 8 lbs. (3.83 kg) of tension at 1.976 in. (50.2mm) of length. If in doubt, replace the spring.

To install:

17. Align the pin of the camshaft with the hole in the sprocket, then install the camshaft timing belt sprocket. Tighten the center bolt to specification.

18. Before reinstalling the belt, double check that the crank and camshafts are exactly in their correct positions. The alignment mark on the end of the camshaft bearing cap should show through the small hole in the camshaft pulley and the small mark on the crankshaft timing belt pulley should align with the mark on the oil pump.

19. Reinstall the timing belt idler pulley and the tension spring. Pry the pulley to the left as far as it will go and temporarily tighten the retaining bolt. This will hold the pulley in its loosest position.

20. Install the timing belt, observing the matchmarks made earlier. Make sure the belt is fully and squarely seated on the upper and lower pulleys.

21. Loosen the retaining bolt for the timing belt idler pulley and allow it to tension the belt.

22. Temporarily install the crankshaft pulley bolt and turn the crank clockwise two full revolutions from TDC to TDC. Insure that each timing mark realigns exactly.

➡ **Always turn the crankshaft clockwise!**

23. Tighten the timing belt idler pulley retaining bolt to 27 ft. lbs. (37 Nm).

24. Measure the timing belt deflection, look for 0.24-0.28 in. (6-7mm) of deflection at 4.4 pounds (2 kg) of pressure. If the deflection is not correct, readjust the idler pulley.

25. Remove the bolt from the end of the crankshaft.

26. Install the valve cover.

27. Install the timing belt guide onto the crankshaft and install the timing belt covers.

28. Install air cleaner assembly and the accessory belts.

29. Adjust the accessory belts and install the radiator.
30. Refill the radiator. Start the engine and check for leaks.

3E and 3E-E Engines

❊❊CAUTION

On models equipped with a Supplemental Restraint System (SRS) or "air bag," work must NOT be started until at least 90 seconds have passed from the time the ignition switch is turned to the LOCK position and the negative cable is disconnected from the battery.

1. Disconnect the negative battery cable. Remove the right side engine under cover. On 3E-E engines, disconnect the accelerator and throttle cables.
2. Disconnect the PCV hoses.
3. Remove the drive belts. Remove the air cleaner, air intake collector assemblies and the spark plugs.
4. Remove the ground strap and vacuum transmitting valves from the right hand engine mounting insulator.

5. Slightly raise the engine and remove the right side engine mounting insulator assembly.
6. Remove the valve cover. Set the engine to TDC on the compression stroke. Remove the crankshaft pulley using the procedures described earlier.
7. Remove both timing belt covers and the timing belt guide.
8. If using the old belt, matchmark it in the direction of engine rotation and the position on the pulleys.
9. Remove the tension spring. Loosen the timing belt idler pulley mount bolt, push it as far left as it will go and temporarily tighten it.
10. Carefully slip the timing belt off the pulleys.
11. Remove the idler pulley mount bolt and pulley.

➡**Do not disturb the position of the camshaft or the crankshaft during removal.**

12. Use an adjustable wrench mounted on the flats of the camshaft to hold the cam from moving. Loosen the center bolt in the camshaft sprocket and remove the sprocket.

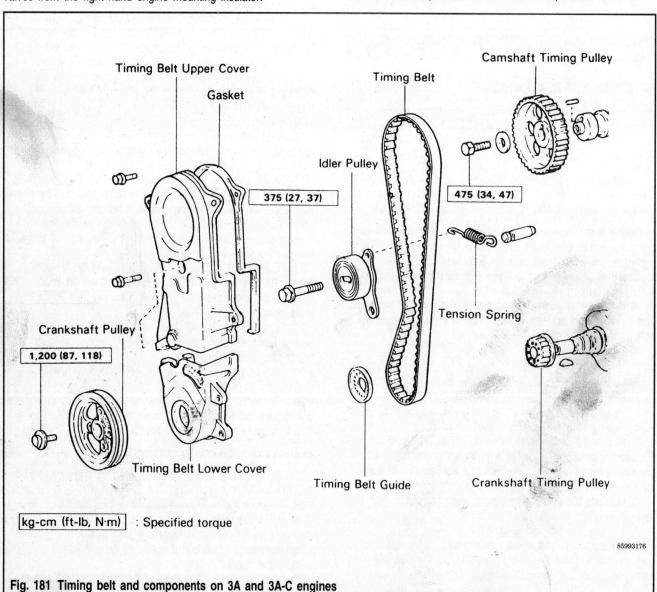

kg-cm (ft-lb, N·m) : Specified torque

85993176

Fig. 181 Timing belt and components on 3A and 3A-C engines

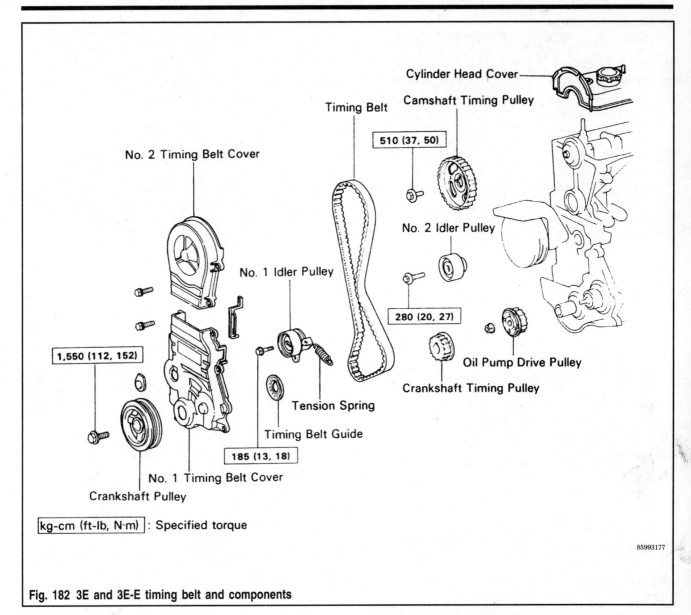

Cylinder Head Cover

Timing Belt   Camshaft Timing Pulley

510 (37, 50)

No. 2 Timing Belt Cover

No. 2 Idler Pulley

No. 1 Idler Pulley

280 (20, 27)

1,550 (112, 152)

Oil Pump Drive Pulley

Tension Spring

Crankshaft Timing Pulley

Timing Belt Guide

185 (13, 18)

No. 1 Timing Belt Cover

Crankshaft Pulley

kg-cm (ft-lb, N·m) : Specified torque

85993177

Fig. 182 3E and 3E-E timing belt and components

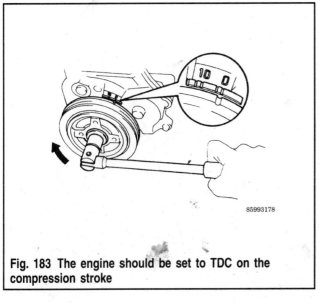

85993178

Fig. 183 The engine should be set to TDC on the compression stroke

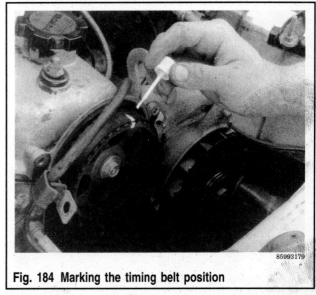

85993179

Fig. 184 Marking the timing belt position

Fig. 185 Because belt tension is determined by the idler pulley position, the center mounting bolt must be loosened when removing the belt

Fig. 188 Removing the timing belt lower cover on 3A and 3A-C engines

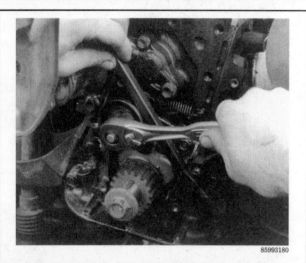

Fig. 186 Tension is removed from the belt when the idler pulley is at the full left position

Fig. 189 Removing the timing belt guide

Fig. 187 Removing the tension spring

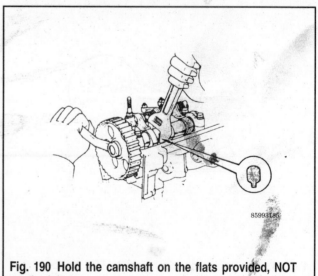

Fig. 190 Hold the camshaft on the flats provided, NOT on the lobes

13. Check the timing belt carefully for any signs of cracking or deterioration. Pay particular attention to the area where each tooth or cog attaches to the backing of the belt. If the belt shows signs of damage, check the contact faces of the pulleys for possible burrs or scratches.

14. Check the idler pulley by holding it in your hand and spinning it. It should rotate freely and quietly. Any sign of grinding or abnormal noise indicates a need to replace the pulley.

15. Check the free length of the tension spring. Correct length is 1.512 in. (38.4mm) measured at the inside faces of the hooks. A spring which has stretched during use will not apply the correct tension to the pulley; replace the spring.

16. Test the tension of the spring. It should have 11.3 lbs. (5.11 kg) of tension at 2.028 in. (51.5mm) of length. If in doubt, replace the spring.

To install:

17. To install the camshaft timing sprocket, align the camshaft pin with the No. 1 camshaft bearing cap mark. Align the pin hole under the 3E mark with the camshaft pin and install it on the camshaft. Torque the retaining bolt to 37 ft. lbs. (50 Nm).

18. Align the TDC marks on the oil pump body and the crankshaft timing pulley. Install the idler pulley and pry the pulley toward the left as far as it will go, then temporarily tighten the retaining bolt.

19. Install the timing belt. If reusing the old belt, align it with the marks made during the removal procedure.

20. Inspect the valve timing and the belt tension. Install the tension spring and loosen the idler pulley set bolt. Temporarily install the crankshaft pulley bolt and turn the crankshaft 2 complete revolutions. Always turn the crankshaft in the clockwise direction.

21. Check that each pulley aligns with the proper markings. Torque the idler pulley bolt to 13 ft. lbs. (18 Nm).

22. Check for proper belt tension. The belt should have tension between the oil pump pulley and the No. 2 idler pulley (this is the idler pulley without the tension spring attached to it). Install the belt guide.

23. Install the timing belt covers. Align and install the crankshaft pulley. Torque the pulley bolt to 112 ft. lbs. (152 Nm).

24. Installation of the remaining components is the reverse of the removal procedure. Service components as required. Make all necessary engine adjustments and roadtest for proper operation.

Fig. 192 The timing belt should not come in contact with oil, water or steam. Never bend or twist the timing belt

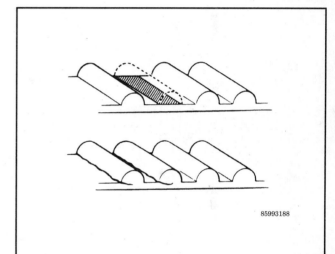

Fig. 193 The timing belt should be inspected for cracks and missing teeth

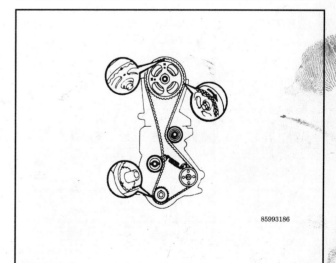

Fig. 191 Correct timing mark placement on 3E and 3E-E engines

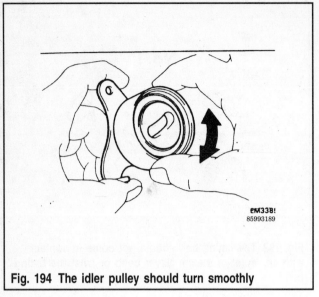

Fig. 194 The idler pulley should turn smoothly

Fig. 197 Aligning the marks on the crankshaft for 3A and 3A-C engines

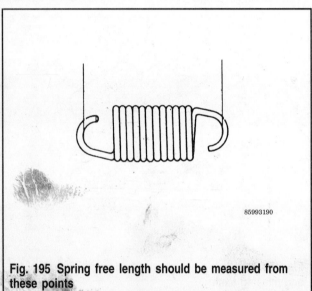

Fig. 195 Spring free length should be measured from these points

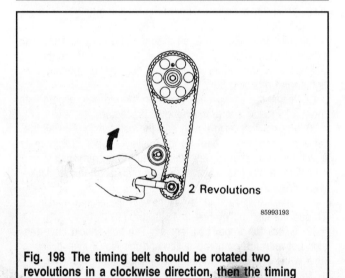

Fig. 198 The timing belt should be rotated two revolutions in a clockwise direction, then the timing marks should be rechecked for correct placement

Fig. 196 Correct camshaft timing mark placement on 3A and 3A-C engines

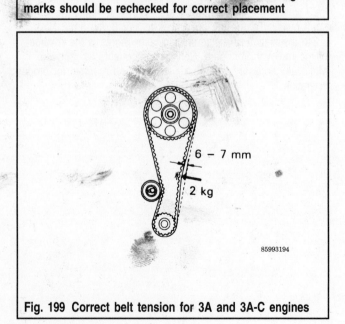

Fig. 199 Correct belt tension for 3A and 3A-C engines

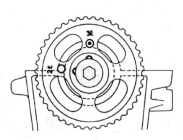

Fig. 200 When installing the camshaft sprocket on 3E and 3E-E engines, the 3E mark must align with the camshaft knock pin hole as shown

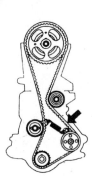

Fig. 201 On 3E and 3E-E engines, check that there is tension on the belt at this point

Camshaft and Bearings

REMOVAL & INSTALLATION

▶ See Figures 202, 203, 204, 205, 206, 207, 208, 209, 210 and 211

➡Camshaft end-play (thrust clearance) must be checked before the cam is removed. Please refer to the Inspection section for details.

❋❋CAUTION

On models equipped with a Supplemental Restraint System (SRS) or "air bag," work must NOT be started until at least 90 seconds have passed from the time the ignition switch is turned to the LOCK position and the negative cable is disconnected from the battery.

1. Remove the valve cover.
2. Drain the cooling system.

❋❋CAUTION

When draining the coolant, keep in mind that cats and dogs are attracted by ethylene glycol antifreeze, and are quite likely to drink any that is left in an uncovered container or in puddles on the ground. This will prove fatal in sufficient quantity. Always drain the coolant into a sealable container. Coolant should be reused unless it is contaminated or several years old.

3. Loosen the water pump pulley bolts.
4. Remove the alternator belt.
5. Raise the vehicle and safely support it on jackstands.
6. Remove the power steering pivot bolt, if so equipped.
7. Remove the bolt which goes through both the upper and lower timing belt covers.
8. Lower the vehicle to the ground. Remove the power steering pump belt, if so equipped.

Fig. 202 The camshaft bearing caps must always be loosened gradually using the proper sequence

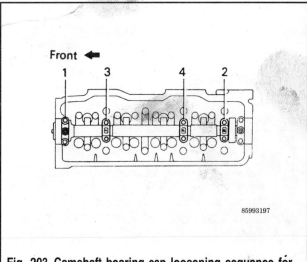

Fig. 203 Camshaft bearing cap loosening sequence for 3E and 3E-E engines

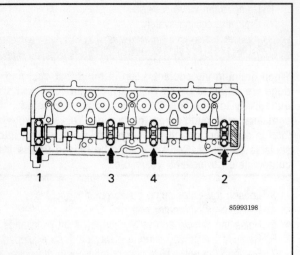

Fig. 204 3A and 3A-C camshaft bearing cap loosening sequence

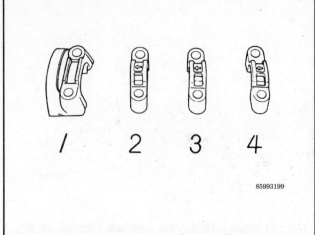

Fig. 206 The camshaft bearing caps should always be placed in order

9. Remove the water pump pulley.

10. Disconnect the upper radiator hose at the engine water outlet.

11. Label and disconnect vacuum hoses.

12. Remove the upper timing belt cover and its gasket.

13. At the distributor, label and disconnect the spark plug wires, the vacuum hoses and the electrical connections. Remove the distributor.

14. Disconnect the hoses at the fuel pump and remove the fuel pump.

15. Remove the distributor gear bolt.

16. Remove the rocker arm assembly on 3A and 3A-C engines.

17. Rotate the crankshaft clockwise and set the engine to TDC on the compression stroke for the No. 1 cylinder. Make sure the rockers for cylinder No. 1 are loose. If not, rotate the crankshaft one full turn.

18. Matchmark and remove the timing belt from the camshaft pulley. Support the belt so that it doesn't change position on the crankshaft pulley.

19. Loosen the camshaft bearing cap bolts a little at a time and in the correct sequence. After removal, label each cap.

20. Remove the camshaft oil seal (at the pulley end) and then remove the camshaft by lifting it straight out of its bearings.

➡Although reasonable in weight, the cam is brittle in nature. Handle it gently and do not allow it to fall or hit objects. It may break into pieces.

To install:

21. When reinstalling, coat all the bearing journals with engine oil and place the camshaft in the cylinder head.

22. Place the bearing caps on each journal with the arrows pointing towards the front of the engine.

23. Apply multi-purpose grease to the inside of the oil seal. and apply liquid sealer on the outer circumference of the oil seal.

24. Install the seal in position, being very careful to get it straight. Do not allow the seal to cock or move out of place during installation.

Fig. 205 Removing the camshaft bearing cap

Fig. 207 Be careful not to damage the camshaft or any other components when removing it

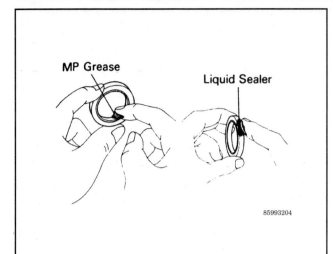

Fig. 208 Applying liquid sealer and grease to the oil seal

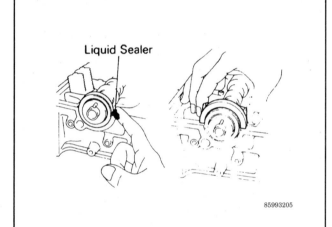

Fig. 209 Apply liquid sealer here before installing the No. 1 bearing cap

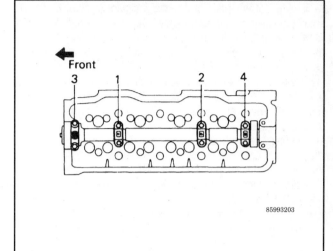

Fig. 210 Camshaft bearing cap tightening sequence on 3E and 3E-E engines

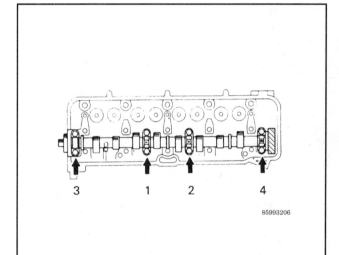

Fig. 211 Camshaft bearing cap tightening sequence on 3A and 3A-C engines

25. Install the bearing cap for bearing No. 1 and apply silicone sealant to the lower ends of the of the seal.

26. Tighten each bearing cap little at a time and in the correct sequence. Tighten the bolts to the figure listed in the component torque specifications chart in this section.

27. Hold the camshaft with an adjustable wrench, then tighten the drive gear bolt to the figure listed in the component torque specifications chart in this section..

28. Install the timing belt as previously outlined.

29. Install the rocker arm assembly.

30. Install the fuel pump with a new gasket and connect the hoses.

31. Install the distributor and connect its vacuum hoses, electrical connections and the spark plug wires.

32. Install the upper timing belt cover but don't install the bolt which holds both the upper and the lower covers yet.

33. Connect the vacuum hoses.

34. Connect the upper radiator hose to the water outlet.

35. Install the water pump pulley.

36. Install the power steering drive belt if so equipped.

37. Elevate the vehicle and safely support it on jackstands.

38. Install the bolt which connects the upper and lower timing belt covers.

39. Install the power steering pump pivot bolt and the belt; adjust the belt tension.

40. Lower the vehicle. Install the alternator belt and adjust it to the correct tension.

41. Install the rocker arm (valve) cover with a new gasket.

42. Refill the cooling system.

INSPECTION

▶ **See Figures 212, 213, 214, 215 and 216**

The end-play or thrust clearance of the camshaft must be measured with the camshaft installed in the head. It must be checked before removal and after reinstallation. To check the end-play, mount a dial indicator accurate to 0.0001 (ten thousandths) of an inch on the end of the block, so that the tip bears on the end of the camshaft (the timing belt must be removed). Set the scale on the dial indicator to zero. Using a small prybar or similar tool, gently lever the camshaft back and forth in its mounts. Record the amount of deflection shown on the gauge and compare this number to the Camshaft Specifications Chart in this section.

Excessive end-play may indicate either a worn camshaft or a worn head; the worn cam is most likely and much cheaper to replace. Chances are good that if the cam is worn in this dimension (axial), substantial wear will show up in other measurements. A worn head must be replaced.

Mount the cam in V-blocks and set the dial indicator up on the round center journal. Zero the dial and rotate the camshaft. The circular runout should not exceed the following:

- 0.0024 in. (0.06mm) on 1984-1985 3A and 3A-C engines
- 0.0079 in. (0.20mm) on 1986-1988 3A and 3A-C engines
- 0.0016 in. (0.04mm) on 1987-1994 3E and 3E-E engines

The cam must be replaced if runout is excessive.

Using a micrometer or caliper, measure the diameter of all the journals and the height of all the lobes. Record the readings and compare them to the Camshaft Specifications Chart

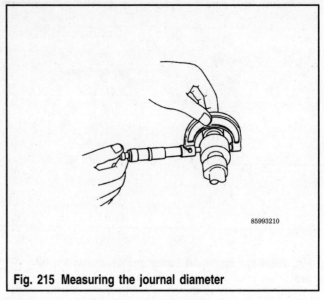

Fig. 215 **Measuring the journal diameter**

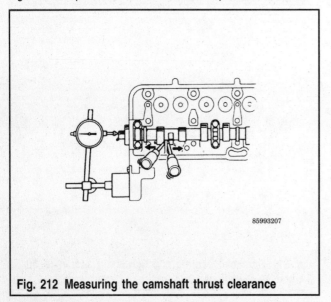

Fig. 212 **Measuring the camshaft thrust clearance**

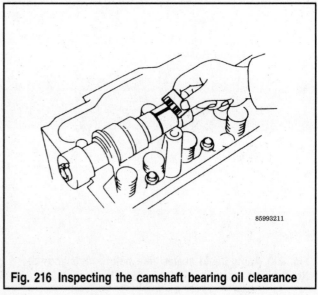

Fig. 216 **Inspecting the camshaft bearing oil clearance**

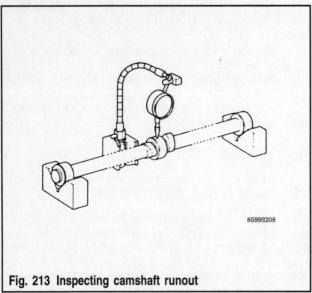

Fig. 213 **Inspecting camshaft runout**

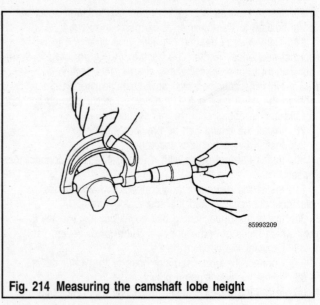

Fig. 214 **Measuring the camshaft lobe height**

in the beginning of this section. Any measurement beyond the stated limits indicates wear and the camshaft must be replaced.

Lobe wear is generally accompanied by scoring or visible metal damage on the lobes. Overhead camshaft engines are very sensitive to proper lubrication with clean, fresh oil. A worn cam may be your report card for poor maintenance intervals and late oil changes. If a new cam is required, order new rockers to accompany it so that there are two new surfaces in contact.

The clearance between the camshaft and its journals (bearings) must also be measured. Clean the camshaft, the journals and the bearing caps of any remaining oil and place the camshaft in position on the head. Lay a piece of compressible gauging material (Plastigage® or similar) on top of each journal on the cam.

Install the bearing caps in their correct order with the arrows pointing towards the front (pulley end) of the motor. Install the bearing cap bolts, then tighten them in three passes to the figure listed in the component torque specifications chart in this section.

➡**Do not turn the camshaft with the gauging material installed.**

Remove the bearing caps (in the correct order) and measure the gauging material at its widest point by comparing it to the scale provided with the package. Compare these measurements to the Camshaft Specifications Chart in this section. Any measurement beyond specifications indicates excessive wear. If you have already measured the cam (or replaced it) and determined it to be usable, excess bearing clearance indicates the need for a new head due to wear of the journals.

Remove the camshaft from the head and remove all traces of the gauging material. Check carefully for any small pieces clinging to contact faces.

Pistons and Connecting Rods

REMOVAL

▶ **See Figures 217, 218, 219, 220 and 221**

➡**These procedures may be performed with the engine in the car. If additional overhaul work is to be performed, it will be easier if the engine is removed and mounted on an engine stand. Most stands allow the block to be rotated, giving easy access to both the top and bottom. These procedures require certain hand tools which may not be in your tool box. A cylinder ridge reamer, a numbered punch set, piston ring expander, snapring tools and piston installation tool (ring compressor) are all necessary for correct**

piston and rod repair. These tools are commonly available from retail tool suppliers; you may be able to rent them from larger automotive supply houses.

❊❊CAUTION

On models equipped with a Supplemental Restraint System (SRS) or "air bag," work must NOT be started until at least 90 seconds have passed from the time the ignition switch is turned to the LOCK position and the negative cable is disconnected from the battery.

1. Remove the cylinder head.
2. Elevate and safely support the vehicle on jackstands.
3. Drain the engine oil.
4. Remove any splash shield or rock guards which are in the way and remove the oil pan.
5. Using a numbered punch set, mark the cylinder number on each piston rod and bearing cap. Do this BEFORE loosening any bolts.
6. Loosen and remove the rod cap nuts and the rod caps. It will probably be necessary to tap the caps loose; do so with a small plastic mallet or other soft-faced tool. Keep the bearing insert with the cap when it is removed.
7. Use short pieces of hose to cover the bolt threads; this protects the bolt, the crankshaft and the cylinder walls during removal.
8. One piston will be at the lowest point in its cylinder. Cover the top of this piston with a rag. Examine the top area of the cylinder with your fingers, looking for a noticeable ridge around the cylinder. If any ridge is felt, it must be carefully removed by using the ridge reamer. Work with extreme care to avoid cutting too deeply.   When the ridge is removed, carefully remove the rag and ALL the shavings from the cylinder. No metal cuttings may remain in the cylinder or the wall will be damaged when the piston is removed. A small magnet or an oil soaked rag can be helpful in removing the fine shavings.
9. After the cylinder is de-ridged, squirt a liberal coating of engine oil onto the cylinder walls until evenly coated. Carefully push the piston and rod assembly upwards from the bottom by using a wooden hammer handle on the bottom of the connecting rod.
10. The next lowest piston should be gently pushed downwards from above. This will cause the crankshaft to turn and relocate the other pistons as well. When the piston is in its lowest position, repeat the steps used for the first piston. Repeat the procedure for each of the remaining pistons.
11. When all the pistons are removed, clean the block and cylinder walls thoroughly with solvent.

CLEANING AND INSPECTION

▶ **See Figures 222, 223, 224, 225 and 226**

Pistons

With the pistons removed from the engine, use a ring removing tool (ring expander) to remove the rings. Keep the rings labeled and stored by piston number. Clearly label the pistons by number so that they do not get interchanged.

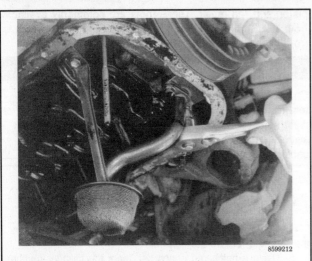

Fig. 217 The oil strainer must be removed in order to access all the connecting rods

Fig. 220 Place lengths of rubber hose over the connecting rod studs in order to protect the crankshaft and cylinders from damage

Fig. 218 Always mark the bearing cap before removing it

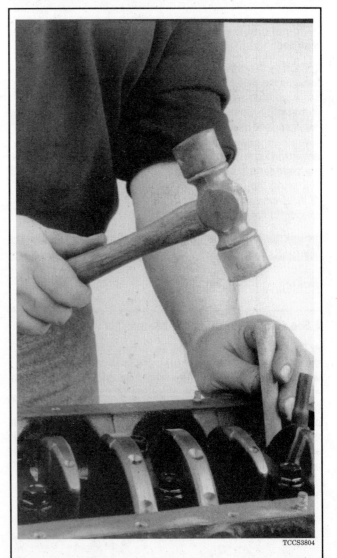

Fig. 221 Carefully tap the piston out of the bore using a wooden dowel

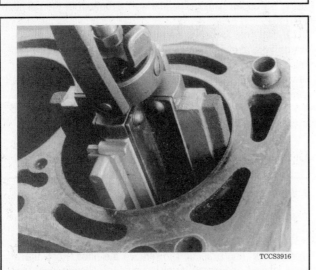

Fig. 219 Removing the ridge from the cylinder bore using a ridge cutter

Clean the carbon from the piston top and sides with a stiff bristle brush and cleaning solvent. Do not use a wire brush for cleaning.

✷✷CAUTION

Wear goggles during this cleaning; the solvent is very strong and can cause eye damage.

Clean the ring grooves (lands) either with a specially designed tool or with a piece of a broken piston ring. Remove all the carbon from the grooves and make sure that the groove shape (profile) is square all the way around the piston. When all the lands have been cleaned, again bathe the piston in solvent and clean the lands with the bristle brush.

Before any measurements are begun, visually examine the piston (a magnifying glass can be handy) for any signs of cracks — particularly in the skirt area — or scratches in the metal. Anything other than light surface scoring disqualifies the piston from further use. The metal will become unevenly heated and the piston may break apart during use.

Hold the piston and rod upright and attempt to move the piston back and forth along the piston pin (wrist pin). There should be NO motion in this axis. If there is, replace the piston and wrist pin.

Accurately measure the cylinder bore diameter in two dimensions (thrust and axial, or if you prefer, left-right and fore-aft) and in three locations (upper, middle and bottom) within the cylinder. That's six measurements in each bore; record them in order.

Having recorded the bore measurements, now measure the piston diameter. Do this with a micrometer at right angles to the piston pin. The location at which the piston is measured varies by engine type:
- 3A and 3A-C: Measure at a point 5mm from lower edge of the oil ring groove
- 3E and 3E-E: Measure at a right angle to the piston pin center line, 0.91 in. (23mm) from the piston head

The piston-to-cylinder wall clearance (sometimes called oil clearance) is determined by subtracting the piston diameter from the measured diameter of its respective cylinder. The difference will be in thousandths or ten-thousandths of an inch. Compare this number to the Piston and Ring Specifications Chart in this section. Excess clearance may indicate the need for either new pistons or block reboring.

Connecting Rods

The connecting rods must be free from wear, cracking and bending. Visually examine the rod, particularly at its upper and lower ends. Look for any sign of metal stretching or wear. The piston pin should fit cleanly and tightly through the upper end, allowing no side-play or wobble. The bottom end should also be an exact ½ circle, with no deformity of shape. The bolts must be firmly mounted and parallel.

The rods may be taken to a machine shop for exact measurement of twist or bend. This is easier and cheaper than purchasing a seldom used rod-alignment tool.

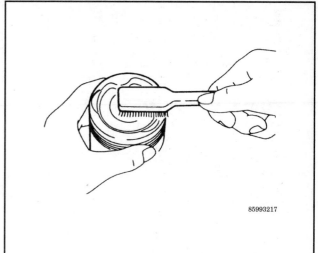

Fig. 222 Use a soft brush and solvent to clean the piston tops

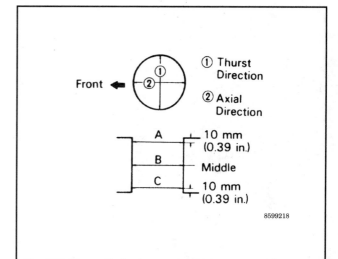

Fig. 223 The cylinder bores should be measured at these positions

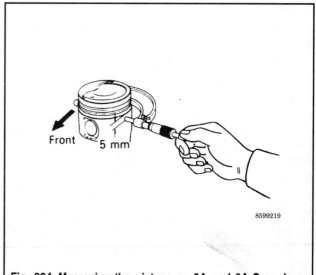

Fig. 224 Measuring the pistons on 3A and 3A-C engines

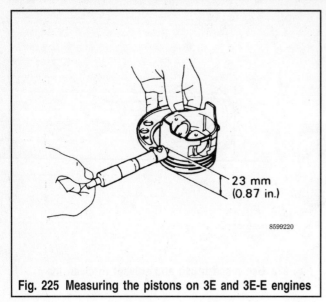

Fig. 225 Measuring the pistons on 3E and 3E-E engines

23 mm
(0.87 in.)

8599220

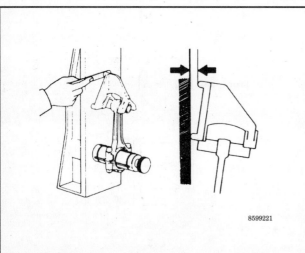

8599221

Fig. 226 A machine shop can check the connecting rods for bends or twists

HONING

▶ See Figure 227

Most inspection and service work on the cylinder block should be handled by a machinist or professional engine rebuilding shop. Included in this work are bearing alignment checks, line boring, deck resurfacing, hot-tanking and cylinder block boring. Any or all of this work requires that the block be completely stripped of all components and transported to the shop. A block that has been checked and properly serviced will last much longer than one whose owner cut corners during a repair.

Cylinder de-glazing (honing) can be performed by the owner/mechanic who is careful and takes time to be accurate. The cylinder bores become glazed during normal operation of the engine as the rings ride up and down constantly. This shiny glaze must be removed in order for a new set of piston rings to seat properly.

Cylinder hones are available at most auto tool stores and parts jobbers. Install the hone into the chuck of a variable speed drill (preferred in place of a constant speed drill). With the piston, rod and crankshaft assemblies removed from the block, insert the hone into the cylinder. If the crankshaft is not being removed from the block, cover it completely with oil soaked rags to prevent grit from collecting on it.

➡**Make sure the drill and hone are kept square to the cylinder bore during the entire honing procedure.**

Start the drill and move the hone up and down in the cylinder at a rate which will produce approximately a 60 degree crosshatch pattern. DO NOT extend the hone below the bottom of the cylinder bore. After the crosshatched pattern is established, remove the hone.

Wash the cylinder with a solution of detergent and water to remove the honing and cylinder grit. Wipe the bores out several times with a clean rag soaked in fresh engine oil. If applicable, carefully remove the rags from the crankshaft and check closely to see that NO grit has found its way onto the crankshaft.

PISTON PIN REPLACEMENT

➡**The piston and pin are a matched set and must be kept together. Label everything and store parts in identified containers.**

1. Remove the pistons from the engine and remove the rings from the pistons.
2. Support the piston and rod on its side in a press. Make certain the piston is square to the motion of the press and that the rod is completely supported with blocks. Leave open space below the piston for the pin to emerge.
3. Line up the press and insert a brass rod of a slightly smaller diameter as the piston pin. It is important that the rod press evenly on the entire face of the pin, but not on the piston itself.
4. Using smooth and controlled motion, press the pin free of the piston. Do not use sudden or jerky motions; the piston may crack.

TCCS3913

Fig. 227 Using a ball type hone for the cylinder bore

5. When reassembling, identify the front of the piston by its small dot or cavity on the top. Identify the front of the piston rod by the small mark cast into one face of the rod. Make sure the marks on the piston and rod are both facing the same direction. Also insure that the correct piston pin is to be reinstalled — they are not interchangeable.

6. Insert the piston under the press. Position the rod and support it. Coat the piston pin with clean oil and press it into place, using the same press set-up as removal.

PISTON RING REPLACEMENT

◆ **See Figures 228, 229, 230, 231 and 232**

➡**Although a piston ring can be reused if in good condition and carefully removed, it is recommended that the rings be replaced with new ones any time they are removed from the pistons.**

A piston ring expander is necessary for removing piston rings without damaging them; any other method (screwdriver blades, pliers, etc.) usually results in the rings becoming bent, scratched or broken. When the rings are removed, clean the grooves thoroughly with a bristle brush and solvent. Make sure that all traces of carbon and varnish are removed.

❈❈WARNING

Wear goggles during this cleaning; the solvent is very strong and can cause eye damage. Do not use a wire brush or a caustic solvent on the pistons.

Check the piston condition and diameter following procedures outlined earlier in this section. Piston ring end-gap should be checked when the rings are removed from the pistons. Incorrect end-gap indicates that the wrong size rings are being used; ring breakage could occur.

Squirt some clean oil into the cylinder so that the top 50-75mm (2-3 in.) of the wall is covered. Gently compress one of the rings to be used and insert it into the cylinder. Use an upside-down piston and push the ring down a little beyond the bottom of piston ring travel. Using the piston to push the ring keeps the ring square in the cylinder; if it is crooked, the next measurement may be inaccurate.

Using a feeler gauge, measure the end-gap in the ring and compare it to the Piston and Ring Specifications chart in this section. If the gap is excessive, either the ring is incorrect or the cylinder walls are worn beyond acceptable limits. If the measurement is too tight, the ends of the ring may be filed to enlarge the gap after the ring is removed form the cylinder. If filing is needed, make certain that the ends are kept square and that a fine file is used.

Check the pistons to see that the ring grooves and oil return holes have been properly cleaned. Slide each piston ring into its groove and check the side clearance with a feeler gauge. Make sure you insert the feeler gauge between the ring and its lower edge; any wear that develops forms a step at the inner portion of the lower land. If the piston grooves have worn to the extent that fairly high steps exist on the lower land, the piston must be replaced. Rings are not sold in oversize thicknesses to compensate for ring groove wear.

Using the ring expander, install the rings on the piston, *lowest ring first.* There is a high risk of ring breakage or piston damage if the rings are installed by hand or without the expander. The correct spacing of the ring end-gaps is critical to oil control. No two gaps should align, they should be evenly spaced around the piston. Once the rings are installed, the pistons must be handled carefully and protected from dirt and impact.

ROD BEARING REPLACEMENT

◆ **See Figures 233, 234 and 235**

Connecting rod bearings on all engines consist of two halves or shells which are not interchangeable in the rod and cap. When the shells are in position, the ends extend slightly beyond the rod and cap surfaces so that when the bolts are tightened, the shells will be clamped tightly in place. This in-

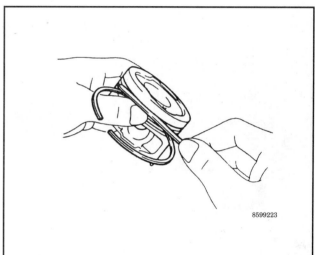

Fig. 228 Measuring the clearance between the piston ring and groove

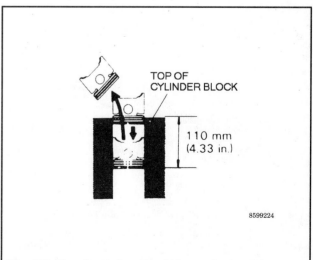

Fig. 229 The piston ring should be pushed to this depth

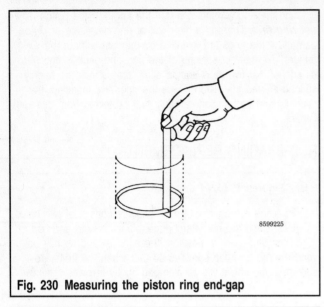

Fig. 230 Measuring the piston ring end-gap

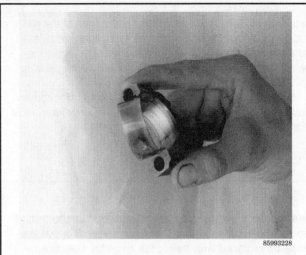

Fig. 233 Align the tang on the bearing with the groove in the cap

Fig. 231 Use a ring expander tool to remove the piston rings

Fig. 232 Clean the piston grooves using a ring groove cleaner

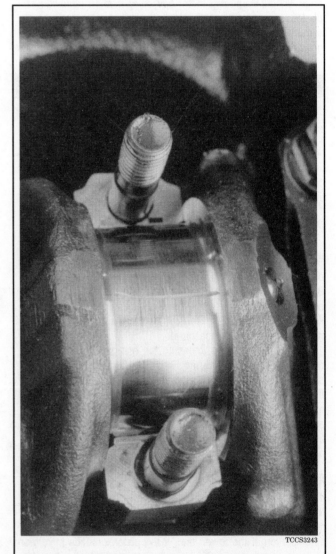

Fig. 234 Apply a strip of gauging material to the bearing journal, then install and torque the cap

sures a positive seating and prevents turning. A small tang holds the shells in place within the cap and rod housings.

➡**The ends of the bearing shells must never be filed flush with the mating surface of the rod or cap.**

If a rod becomes noisy or is worn so that its clearance on the crankshaft is out of specification, a new bearing of the correct undersize must be selected and installed. There is no provision for adjustment. Under no circumstances should the rod end or cap be filed to compensate for wear, nor should shims of any type be used.

Inspect the rod bearings while the rods are out of the engine. If the shells are scored or show flaking they should be replaced. ANY scoring or ridge on the crankshaft means the crankshaft must be replaced. Because of the metallurgy in the crankshaft, welding and regrinding the crankshaft is not recommended. The bearing faces of the crank may not be restored to their original condition or attempts may cause premature bearing wear and possible failure.

Replacement bearings are available in three standard sizes marked either 1, 2 or 3 on the bearing shell and possibly on the rod cap. Do not confuse the mark on the bearing cap with the cylinder number. It is quite possible that No. 3 piston rod contains a number 1 size bearing. The rod cap may have a 1 marked on it. (You should have stamped a 3 or other identifying code on both halves of the rod before disassembly.)

Measuring the clearance between the connecting rod bearings and the crankshaft (oil clearance) is done with a plastic measuring material such as Plastigage® or similar product.

1. Remove the rod cap with the bearing shell. Completely clean the cap, bearing shells and the journal on the crankshaft. Blow any oil from the oil hole in the crank. The plastic measuring material is soluble in oil and will begin to dissolve if the area is not totally free of oil.

2. Place a piece of the measuring material lengthwise along the bottom center of the lower bearing shell. Install the cap and shell, then tighten the bolts in three passes to specifications.

➡**Do not turn the crankshaft with the measuring material installed.**

3. Remove the bearing cap with the shell. The flattened plastic material will be found sticking to either the bearing shell or the crank journal. DO NOT remove it yet.

4. Use the scale printed on the packaging for the measuring material to measure the flattened plastic at its widest point. The number within the scale which is closest to the width of the plastic indicates the bearing clearance in thousandths of an inch.

5. Check the specifications chart for the proper clearance. If there is any measurement approaching the maximum acceptable value, replace the bearing.

6. When the correct bearing is determined, clean off the gauging material, oil the bearing thoroughly on its working face and install it in the cap. Install the other half of the bearing into the rod end and attach the cap to the rod. Tighten the nuts evenly, in three passes to specifications.

7. With the proper bearing installed and the nuts properly tightened, it should be possible to move the connecting rod back and forth a bit on the crankshaft. If the rod cannot be moved, either the bearing is too small or the rod is misaligned.

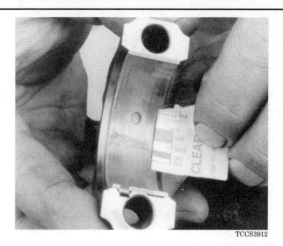

TCCS3912

Fig. 235 After the bearing cap has been removed, use the gauge supplied with the material to check bearing clearances

INSTALLATION

▸ **See Figures 236, 237 and 238**

1. When ready for reassembly, remember that all the pistons, rods and caps must be reinstalled in the correct cylinder. Make certain that all labels and stamped numbers are present and legible. Double check the piston rings; make certain that the ring gaps DO NOT line up, but are evenly spaced around the piston at about 120 degree intervals. Double check the bearing insert at the bottom of the rod for proper mounting. Reinstall the protective rubber hose pieces on the bolts.

2. Liberally coat the cylinder walls and the crankshaft journals with clean, fresh engine oil. Also apply oil to the bearing surfaces on the connecting rod and the cap.

3. Identify the "Front" mark on each piston and rod and position the piston loosely in its cylinder with the marks facing the front (pulley end) of the motor.

✳✳WARNING

Failure to observe the marking and its correct placement can lead to sudden engine failure.

4. Install the ring compressor (piston installation tool) around one piston and tighten it gently until the rings are compressed almost completely.

5. Gently push down on the piston top with a wooden hammer handle or similar soft-faced tool and drive the piston into the cylinder bore. Once all three rings are within the bore, the piston will move with some ease.

➡**If any resistance or binding is encountered during the installation, DO NOT apply force. Tighten or adjust the ring compressor and/or reposition the piston. Brute force will break the ring(s) or damage the piston.**

6. From underneath, pull the connecting rod into place on the crankshaft. Remove the rubber hoses from the bolts. Check the rod cap to confirm that the bearing is present and correctly mounted, then install the rod cap (observing the correct number and position) and its nuts. Leaving the nuts finger-

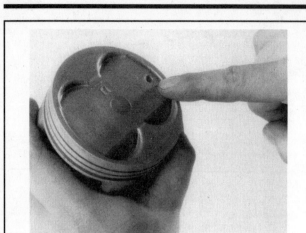

Fig. 236 Most pistons are marked to indicate positioning in the engine. The mark usually faces the front of the engine

Fig. 237 Installing the piston into the block using a ring compressor and the handle of a hammer

Fig. 238 Thread the nuts by hand, then torque the caps to specification

Fig. 239 Removing the rear end plate

Fig. 240 Loosening the rear main seal attaching bolts

tight will make installation of the remaining pistons and rods easier.

7. Assemble the remaining pistons in the same fashion.

8. With all the pistons installed and the bearing caps secured finger-tight, the retaining nuts may be tightened to their final setting. For each pair of nuts, make three passes alternating between the two nuts on any given rod cap. The intent is to draw each cap up to the crank straight and under even pressure at the nuts.

9. Turn the crankshaft through several clockwise rotations, making sure everything moves smoothly and there is no binding. With the piston rods connected, the crank may be stiff to turn — try to turn it in a smooth continuous motion so that any binding or stiff spots may be felt.

10. Reinstall the oil pan. Even if the engine is to remain apart for other repairs, install the oil pan to protect the bottom end and tighten the bolts to the correct specification — this eliminates one easily overlooked mistake during future reassembly.

11. If the engine is to remain apart for other repairs, pack the cylinders with crumpled newspaper or clean rags (to keep out dust and grit) and cover the top of the motor with a large rag. If the engine is on a stand, the whole block can be protected with a large plastic trash bag.

12. If no further work is to be performed, continue reassembly by installing the head, timing belt, etc.

13. When the engine is restarted after reassembly, the exhaust will be very smoky as the oil within the cylinders burns off. This is normal; the smoke should clear quickly during warm up. Depending on the condition of the spark plugs, it may be wise to check for any oil fouling after the engine is shut off.

Rear Main Seal

REMOVAL & INSTALLATION

▸ See Figures 239, 240 and 241

✳✳CAUTION

On models equipped with a Supplemental Restraint System (SRS) or "air bag," work must NOT be started until at least 90 seconds have passed from the time the ignition switch is turned to the LOCK position and the negative cable is disconnected from the battery.

1. Remove the transaxle from the vehicle. Follow procedures outlined in Section 7.

2. If equipped with a manual transaxle, perform the following procedures:
   a. Matchmark the pressure plate and flywheel.
   b. Remove the pressure plate-to-flywheel bolts and the clutch assembly from the vehicle.
   c. Remove the flywheel-to-crankshaft bolts and the flywheel. The flywheel is a moderately heavy component. Handle it carefully and protect it on the workbench.

Fig. 241 Removing the rear main seal

3. If equipped with an automatic transaxle, perform the following procedures:
   a. Matchmark the flywheel (flexplate or driveplate) and crankshaft.
   b. Remove the torque converter drive plate-to-crankshaft bolts and the torque converter drive plate.

4. Remove the bolts holding the rear end plate to the engine, then remove the rear end plate.

5. Remove the rear oil seal retainer-to-engine bolts, rear oil seal retainer-to-oil pan bolts and the rear oil seal retainer.

6. Using a small pry bar, pry the rear oil seal retainer from the mating surfaces.

7. Using a drive punch or a hammer and a small prytool, drive the oil seal from the rear bearing retainer.

➡When removing the rear oil seal, be careful not to damage the seal mounting surface.

8. Using a putty knife, clean the gasket mounting surfaces. Make certain that the contact surfaces are completely free of oil and foreign matter.

To install:
9. Clean the oil seal mounting surface.

10. Using multi-purpose grease, lubricate the new seal lips.

11. Using a seal installation tool or a smooth, round driver, tap the seal straight into the bore of the retainer.

12. Position a new gasket on the retainer and coat it lightly with gasket sealer. Fit the seal retainer into place on the motor; be careful when installing the oil seal over the crankshaft.

13. Install the oil seal retainer bolts. Tighten them 82 inch lbs. (9.3 Nm) on 3A and 3A-C engines and 65 inch lbs. (7.4 Nm) on 3E and 3E-E engines.

14. Install the rear end plate. Tighten it's bolts until snug.

15. Reinstall either the flexplate (automatic) or the flywheel (manual), carefully observing the matchmarks made earlier. Tighten the flexplate bolts or the flywheel bolts to the figure listed in the component torque specifications chart.

16. Install the torque converter (automatic) or the clutch disc and pressure plate (manual).

17. Reinstall the transaxle, following procedures outlined in Section 7.

Crankshaft and Main Bearings

REMOVAL & INSTALLATION

▸ See Figures 242, 243, 244 and 245

1. Remove the engine assembly from the car, following procedures outlined earlier in this section. Mount the engine securely on a stand which allows it to be rotated.

2. Remove the timing belt and tensioner assemblies.

3. Turn the engine upside down on the stand. Remove the oil pan and the oil strainer.

4. Remove the oil pump.

5. Remove the clutch and pressure plate (M/T).

6. Remove either the flywheel (manual) or the drive plate (automatic).

7. Remove the rear end plate.

8. Remove the rear oil seal retainer.

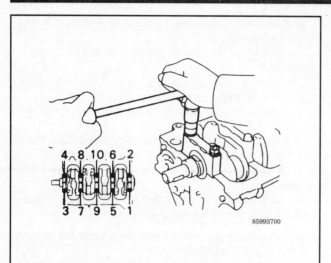

Fig. 242 On 3E and 3E-E engines, loosen the main bearing cap bolts using this sequence

Fig. 243 The caps should be marked as to their cylinder number and direction before removal

removed. Note and/or label the thrust washers as to their placement and position. If they are to be reused, they must be reinstalled precisely in their original positions.

14. Remove the remaining caps. Keep the caps in order and keep the bearing shells with their respective caps.

15. Lift the crankshaft out of the block. Be careful, the crankshaft is a moderately heavy component.

16. Remove the upper bearing shells from the block and place them in order with the corresponding bearing caps.

17. Check and measure the crankshaft and bearings according to the procedures found under Cleaning and Inspection later in this section.

To install:

18. When reassembling, clean the bearing caps and journals in the block thoroughly. Coat the bearings with a liberal application of clean motor oil.

19. Fit the upper bearings halves into the block and position the lower bearing halves in the bearing caps.

20. Place the crankshaft into the engine block, making sure it fits exactly into its mounts.

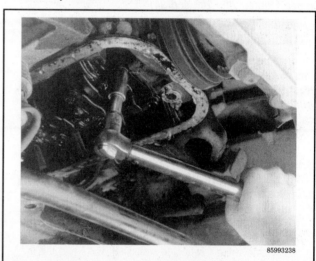

Fig. 244 Always torque the bearing caps to specification

9. Using a numbered punch set, mark each connecting rod cap with its correct cylinder number. Remove the rod caps and their bearings; keep the bearings with their respective caps.

10. Measure the crankshaft end-play (thrust clearance) before removing the crank. Attach a dial indicator to the end of the block and set the tip to bear on the front end of the crankshaft. With a small prytool, gently move the crankshaft back and forth and record the reading shown on the dial.

11. Maximum allowable end-play is 0.0118 in (0.30mm) on 3A and 3A-C engines and 0.012 in. (0.3mm) on 3E and 3E-E engines.

If the end-play is excessive, the thrust washers will need to be replaced as a set.

12. Gradually loosen and remove the main bearing cap bolts in three passes. On 3E and 3E-E engines, loosen the bolts using the correct sequence. Remove just the bolts, leaving the caps in place.

13. When all the bolts are removed, use two bolts placed in the No. 3 bearing cap to wiggle the cap back and forth. This will loosen the cap and allow it (with the thrust washers) to be

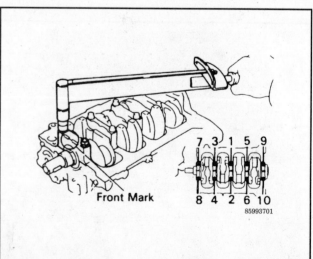

Fig. 245 Main bearing cap bolt tightening sequence on 3E and 3E-E engines

21. Install the upper thrust washers on the center main bearing with the oil grooves facing outward.

22. Install the main bearing caps and the lower thrust washers in the proper sequence. Make sure the arrows on the caps point towards the front (pulley end) of the motor.

23. Tighten the cap bolts to specification in three passes. On 3E and 3E-E engines, use the correct sequence.

24. Double check the end-play of the crankshaft by repeating the procedure described earlier.

25. Turn the crankshaft through one or two full clockwise rotations, making sure that it turns smoothly and evenly with no binding.

26. Attach the piston rods, following procedures given earlier in this section. Remember that the rod caps must be reinstalled in their original positions.

27. Install a new rear main oil seal into the retainer and install the retainer onto the block. Tighten the bolts to specification.

28. Install the rear end plate on the engine.

29. Install either the driveplate (automatic) or the flywheel (manual), observing the matchmarks made during removal.

30. If equipped with a manual transaxle, reinstall the clutch disc and pressure plate.

31. Install the oil pump.

32. Install the oil strainer and oil pan, using new gaskets.

33. Rotate the engine into its upright position and continue reassembly of the timing belt, idler pulley and covers.

34. Reinstall the engine in the car, following procedures outlined earlier in this section.

CLEANING AND INSPECTION

▶ See Figures 246, 247 and 248

With the crankshaft removed from the engine, clean the crank, bearings and block areas thoroughly. Visually inspect each crankshaft section for any sign of wear or damage, paying close attention to the main bearing journals. ANY scoring or ridge on the crankshaft means the crankshaft must be replaced. Because of the crankshaft metallurgy, welding and/or regrinding the crankshaft is not recommended. The bearing faces of the crank may not be restored to their original condition which would cause the risk of premature bearing wear and possible failure.

Using a micrometer, measure the diameter of each journal on the crankshaft and record the measurements. The acceptable specifications for both connecting rod and main journals are found in the Crankshaft and Connecting Rod specifications chart in this section. If ANY journal is beyond the acceptable range, the crank must be replaced.

Additionally, each journal must be measured at both outer edges. When one measurement is subtracted from the other, the difference is the measurement of journal taper. Any taper beyond 0.0031 in. (0.08mm) is a sign of excess wear on the journal; the crankshaft must be replaced.

Fig. 248 A dial gauge may also be used to check crankshaft runout

Fig. 246 A dial gauge may be used to check crankshaft end-play

Fig. 247 Carefully pry the shaft back and forth while reading the dial indicator

BEARING REPLACEMENT

▶ **See Figures 249 and 250**

1. With the engine out of the car and inverted on a stand, remove the main bearing caps following the procedures given earlier in this section.

2. Once the bearing caps are removed, the lower bearing shell may be inspected. Check closely for scoring or abrasion of the bearing surface. If this lower bearing is worn or damaged, both the upper and lower half should be replaced.

➡ **Always replace bearing shells in complete pairs.**

3. If the lower bearing half is in good condition, the upper shell may also be considered usable.

4. The bearing shells, the crank throws and the flat surface of the engine block (on the oil pan face) are stamped with numbers (1 through 5) indicating the standard bearing size. This size is determined during the initial manufacturing and assembly process; replacement bearings must be of the same code (thickness) if the correct clearances are to be maintained. If the code on the bearing shell is unreadable, use the number on the block and/or the number on the crank throw to determine the bearing code. For 3E and 3E-E engines, refer to the selection chart to find the correct bearing for that position.

5. Lift the crankshaft from the engine block and remove the upper bearing shells. Clean the area thoroughly (including the crankshaft journals) and allow the surfaces to air dry.

6. Install the upper bearing shells, then carefully place the crankshaft in position. Install the lower bearing shells into clean, dry caps. Do not oil the upper/lower bearing shells or the crankshaft journals at this time.

7. Place a piece of plastic gauging material (such as Plastigage® or similar) lengthwise (fore-and-aft) across the full width of each of the five crankshaft main bearing journals. Remember that the measuring material is dissolved by oil. Keep the crankshaft and bearings clean and dry.

8. Install the bearing caps with their bearing shells in their correct location and with the arrows pointing towards the front of the motor.

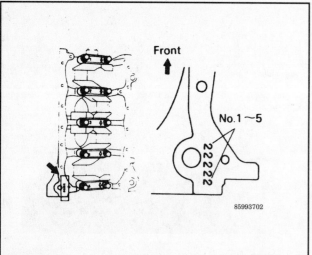

Fig. 249 Main bearing identification on 3A and 3A-C engines

9. Install the bearing cap bolts and tighten them in three passes (and in the correct sequence, if applicable) to specification. Follow the procedures outlined in this section.

➡ **Do not rotate the crankshaft with the measuring plastic installed.**

10. Observing the correct removal sequence, gradually loosen and remove the bearing cap bolts. Carefully remove the bearing caps; the gauging material will be stuck to either the inside of the bearing shell or the face of the crankshaft.

11. Using the scale provided with the package of the gauging material, measure the material at its widest point. This measurement represents the main bearing oil clearance and should be checked against the Crankshaft and Connecting Rod Specifications chart in this section.

12. Remove every piece of the plastic gauging material from the crank and bearing caps. Remove the crankshaft, then coat the journals and bearings with clean motor oil.

13. Install the main bearing caps and the lower thrust washers. Make sure the arrows on the caps point towards the front (pulley end) of the motor.

14. Tighten the cap bolts in three passes (and in the correct sequence, if applicable) to specification. Follow the procedures outlined in this section.

15. Double check the end-play of the crankshaft. Turn the crankshaft through one or two full clockwise rotations, making sure that it turns smoothly and evenly with no binding.

Flywheel and Ring Gear

REMOVAL & INSTALLATION

▶ **See Figures 251, 252 and 253**

➡ **This procedure may performed with the engine in the car, however, access will be cramped.**

1. Remove the transaxle, following the procedures outlined in Section 7.

2. For cars equipped with automatic transaxles:

   a. Matchmark the torque converter and the driveplate. Correct positioning will be required during reassembly.

   b. Remove the bolts holding the torque converter to the driveplate and remove the torque converter. DON'T drop it.

   c. Matchmark the driveplate and the crankshaft.

   d. Loosen the retaining bolts a little at a time in a criss-cross pattern. Support the driveplate as the last bolts are removed and then lift the driveplate away from the engine.

3. For manual transaxle cars:

   a. Matchmark the pressure plate assembly and the flywheel.

   b. Loosen the pressure plate retaining bolts a little at a time and in a criss-cross pattern. Support the pressure plate and clutch assembly as the last bolt is removed and lift them away from the flywheel.

   c. Matchmark the flywheel and crankshaft. Loosen the retaining bolts evenly in a criss-cross pattern. Support the flywheel during removal of the last bolts and remove the flywheel.

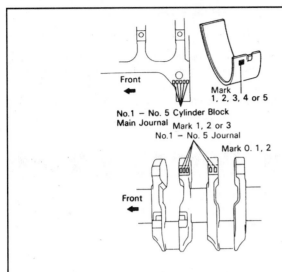

Cylinder Block	No.	1	2	3	1	2	3	1	2	3
Crankshaft	No.	0	0	0	1	1	1	2	2	2
Bearing	No.	1	2	3	2	3	4	3	4	5

Fig. 250 Main bearing identification and selection chart on 3E and 3E-E engines

Fig. 251 The flywheel should be matchmarked before removal

Fig. 252 The flywheel is heavy, be careful when removing it

Fig. 253 Torque the flywheel bolts to specification

4. Carefully inspect the teeth on the flywheel or driveplate for any signs of wearing or chipping. If anything beyond minimal contact wear is found, replace the unit.

➡Since the flywheel is driven by the starter gear, you would be wise to inspect the starter drive should any wear be found on the flywheel teeth. A worn starter can cause damage to the flywheel.

To install:

5. When reassembling, place the flywheel or driveplate in position on the crankshaft and make sure the matchmarks align. Install the retaining bolts finger-tight.

6. Tighten the bolts using three passes of a diagonal pattern. Tighten the flywheel bolts (manual transmission) or the driveplate bolts (automatic transmission) to the figure found in the component torque specifications chart.

7. Install either the clutch and pressure plate assembly or the torque converter. Refer to the appropriate procedures in this manual.

➡**If the clutch appears worn or cracked in any way, replace it with a new disc, pressure plate and release bearing. The slight extra cost of the parts will prevent having to remove the transaxle again later.**

8. Reinstall the transaxle assembly.

EXHAUST SYSTEM

Safety Precautions

For a number of reasons, exhaust system work can be among the most dangerous types of work you can do on your car. Always observe the following precautions:

• Support the car extra securely. Not only will you often be working directly under it, but you'll frequently be using a lot of force, say, heavy hammer blows, to dislodge rusted parts. This can cause a car that's improperly supported to shift and possibly fall.

• Wear goggles. Exhaust system parts are almost always rusty. Metal chips can be dislodged, even when you're only turning rusted bolts. Attempting to pry pipes apart with a chisel makes the chips fly even more frequently.

• If you're using a cutting torch, keep it a GREAT distance from either the fuel tank or lines. Stop what you're doing and feel the temperature of the fuel lines and the tank frequently. Even slight heat can expand and/or vaporize fuel, resulting in accumulated vapor, or even a liquid leak, near your torch.

• Watch where your hammer blows fall and make sure you hit squarely. You could easily tap a brake or fuel line when you hit an exhaust system part with a glancing blow. Inspect all lines and hoses in the area where you've been working.

✳✳CAUTION

Be very careful when working on or near the catalytic converter. External temperatures can reach 1,500°F (816°C) and more, exposing you to the danger of severe burns. Removal or installation should be performed only on a cold exhaust system.

A number of special exhaust system tools can be rented from auto supply houses or local stores that rent special equipment. A common one is a tail pipe expander, designed to enable you to join pipes of identical diameter.

It may also be quite helpful to use solvents designed to loosen rusted bolts or flanges. Soaking rusted parts the night before you do the job can speed the work of freeing rusted parts considerably. Remember that these solvents are often flammable. Apply only to parts after they are cool.

The exhaust system of most engines consists of four pieces. At the front of the car, the first section of pipe connects the exhaust manifold to the catalytic converter. On some models, this pipe contains a section of flexible, braided pipe. The catalytic converter is a sealed, non-serviceable unit which can be easily unbolted from the system and replaced if necessary.

An intermediate or center pipe containing a built-in resonator (pre-muffler) runs from the catalytic converter to the muffler at

RING GEAR REPLACEMENT

If the ring gear teeth on the driveplate or flywheel are damaged, the assembly must be replaced. The ring gear cannot be separated or reinstalled individually.

If a flywheel is replaced on a manual transmission car, the installation of a new clutch disc, pressure plate and release bearing is highly recommended.

the rear of the car. Should the resonator fail, the entire pipe must be replaced. The muffler and tailpipe at the rear should always be replaced as a unit.

The exhaust system is attached to the body by several welded hooks and flexible rubber hangers; these hangers absorb exhaust vibrations and isolate the system from the body of the car. A series of metal heat shields runs along the exhaust piping, protecting the underbody from excess heat.

When inspecting or replacing exhaust system parts, make sure there is adequate clearance from all points on the body to avoid possible overheating of the floorpan. Check the complete system for broken damaged, missing or poorly positioned parts. Rattles and vibrations in the exhaust system are usually caused by misalignment of parts. When aligning the system, leave all the nuts and bolts loose until everything is in its proper place, then tighten the hardware working from the front to the rear. Remember that what appears to be proper clearance during repair may change as the car moves down the road. The motion of the engine, body and suspension must be considered when replacing parts.

REMOVAL & INSTALLATION

▶ **See Figures 254 and 255**

✳✳CAUTION

DO NOT perform exhaust repairs with the engine or exhaust hot. Allow the system to cool completely before attempting any work. Exhaust systems are notorious for sharp edges, flaking metal and rusted bolts, gloves and eye protection are required.

➡**ALWAYS use a new gasket at each pipe joint whenever the joint is disassembled. Use new nuts and bolts to hold the joint properly. These two low-cost items will serve to prevent future leaks as the system ages.**

Front Pipe

1. Elevate and safely support the vehicle on jackstands.
2. Disconnect the oxygen sensor.
3. Remove the two bolts holding the pipe to the exhaust manifold.
4. Remove the two bolts holding the pipe to the catalytic converter.
5. Remove the bolts from the crossmember bracket and remove the pipe from under the car.

Fig. 254 A deep socket is usually necessary to loosen the exhaust system nuts

To install:

6. Attach the new pipe to the crossmember bracket. Install the bolts at both the manifold and the catalyst ends, leaving them finger-tight until the pipe is correctly positioned. Make certain the gaskets are in place and straight.

7. Tighten the pipe-to-manifold bolts.

8. Tighten the bolts at the converter.

9. Reconnect the oxygen sensor.

10. Lower the vehicle to the ground, start the system and check for leaks. Small exhaust leaks will be most easily heard when the system is cold.

Catalytic Converter

With the car safely supported on jackstands, the converter is removed simply by removing the two bolts at either end. Some models have an air suction pipe attached to the converter which must be disconnected (2 bolts) before removal. When reinstalling the converter, install it with new gaskets and tighten the end bolts to specification (refer to the illustration). Reconnect the air suction pipe and lower the car to the ground.

Intermediate Pipe (Resonator Pipe)

1. Elevate and safely support the vehicle on jackstands.

2. Remove the two bolts holding the pipe to the catalytic converter.

3. Remove the bolts holding the intermediate pipe to the muffler inlet pipe.

4. Disconnect the rubber hangers and remove the pipe.

To install:

5. Install the new pipe by suspending it in place on the rubber hangers. Install the gaskets at each end and install the bolts finger-tight.

6. Double check the placement of the pipe and insure proper clearance to all body and suspension components.

7. Tighten the bolts holding the pipe to the catalytic converter, then tighten the bolts to the muffler inlet pipe.

8. Lower the car to the ground. Start the engine and check for leaks.

Muffler and Tailpipe Assembly

1. Elevate and safely support the vehicle on jackstands.

2. Remove the two bolts holding the muffler inlet pipe to the intermediate pipe.

3. Disconnect the forward bracket on the muffler.

4. Disconnect the rear muffler bracket (three bolts) and remove the muffler from under the car.

To install:

5. When reinstalling, suspend the muffler from its front and rear hangers and check it for correct positioning under the body. If the old muffler had been rattling or hitting the body it is possible that the hangers and brackets have become bent from a light impact.

6. Attach the inlet pipe to the intermediate pipe and tighten.

7. Lower the vehicle to the ground, start the engine and check for leaks.

Complete System

If the entire exhaust system is to be replaced, it is much easier to remove the system as a unit than remove each individual piece. Disconnect the first pipe at the manifold joint and work towards the rear removing brackets and hangers as you go. Don't forget to disconnect the air suction pipe on the catalytic converter on some models. Remove the rear muffler bracket and slide the entire exhaust system out form under the car.

When installing the new assembly, suspend it from the flexible hangers first, then attach the fixed (solid) brackets. Check the clearance to the body and suspension, then install the manifold joint bolts.

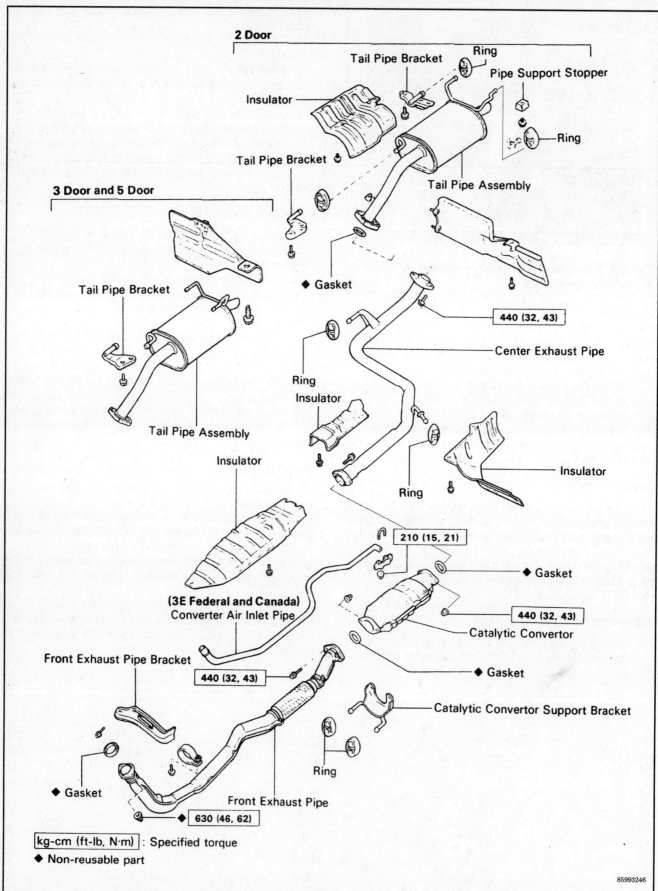

2 Door
Tail Pipe Bracket
Ring
Pipe Support Stopper
Insulator
Ring
Tail Pipe Bracket
Tail Pipe Assembly

3 Door and 5 Door
Tail Pipe Bracket
Gasket
440 (32, 43)
Center Exhaust Pipe
Ring
Insulator
Tail Pipe Assembly
Insulator
Ring
Insulator
210 (15, 21)
Gasket
(3E Federal and Canada)
Converter Air Inlet Pipe
440 (32, 43)
Catalytic Convertor
Front Exhaust Pipe Bracket
440 (32, 43)
Gasket
Catalytic Convertor Support Bracket
Gasket
Ring
Front Exhaust Pipe
630 (46, 62)

kg-cm (ft-lb, N·m) : Specified torque
◆ Non-reusable part

85993246

Fig. 255 Exploded view of a common Tercel exhaust system

Part tightened	kg-cm	ft-lb	N·m
Camshaft timing pulley x Camshaft	475	34	47
Timing belt idler pulley x Cylinder block	375	27	37
Crankshaft pulley x Crankshaft	1,200	87	118
Camshaft bearing cap x Cylinder head	130	9	13
IIA drive gear x Camshaft	300	22	29
Rocker arm support x Cylinder head	250	18	25
Manifold x Cylinder head	250	18	25
Cylinder head x Cylinder block	600	43	59
Valve clearance adjusting screw lock nut	185	13	18
Main bearing cap x Cylinder block	600	43	59
Connecting rod cap x Connecting rod	500	36	49
Rear oil seal retainer x Cylinder block	95	82 in.-lb	9.3
Flywheel x Crankshaft	800	58	78
Drive plate x Crankshaft	650	47	64
Engine mounting insulator x Crossmember	450	33	44
Stiffener plate x Cylinder block	400	29	39
Stiffener plate x Transaxle case	400	29	39
Exhaust front pipe x Exhaust manifold	630	46	62
Water pump x Cylinder block	150	11	15
Oil pump x Cylinder block	220	16	22
Oil strainer x Cylinder block (Oil pump)	95	82 in.-lb	9.3
Oil pan x Cylinder block (Oil pump, Rear oil seal retainer)	55	48 in.-lb	5.4
Fuel pipe x Carbureter	250	18	25
Spark plug x Cylinder block	180	13	18
Engine oil drain plug x Oil pan	250	18	25

85993250

Fig. 256 Component torque specifications chart for 3A and 3A-C engines

Part tightened		kg-cm	ft-lb	N·m
Cylinder head bolt	First	300	22	29
	Second	500	36	49
	Third	Tighten the bolt an additional 90° after achieving specified torque		
Cylinder head x Camshaft bearing cap		140	10	14
Cylinder head x Spark plug		180	13	18
Cylinder head x Intake manifold		195	14	19
Cylinder head x Exhaust manifold		520	38	51
Cylinder head x No. 1 engine hanger		210	15	21
Cylinder head x No. 2 engine hanger		590	43	58
Cylinder block x RH engine mounting bracket		440	32	43
Cylinder block x Oil pump		75	65 in.-lb	7.4
Cylinder block x Crankshaft bearing cap		580	42	57
Cylinder block x Water pump		175	13	17
Cylinder block x No. 1 idler pulley		185	13	18
Cylinder block x No. 2 idler pulley		280	20	27
Cylinder block x Oil strainer		75	65 in.-lb	7.4
Cylinder block x Oil regulator		300	22	29
Cylinder block x Drain plug		250	18	25
Camshaft x Camshaft timing pulley		510	37	50
Valve clearance adjusting nut x Rocker arm		120	9	12
Crankshaft x Crankshaft pulley		1,550	112	152
Crankshaft x Flywheel		900	65	88
Connecting rod x Connecting rod cap		400	29	39
Oil pan x Drain plug		250	18	25
RH engine mounting bracket x Insulator		650	47	64
RH engine mounting insulator x RH member		490	35	48
LH engine mounting bracket x Transaxle case		490	35	48
LH engine mounting bracket x Insulator		740	54	73
Rear engine mounting bracket x Transaxle case (A/T)		590	43	58
Rear engine mounting bracket x Insulator (M/T)		650	47	64
Rear engine mounting insulator x Body		740	54	73

85993251

Fig. 257 Component torque specifications chart for 3E and 3E-E engines

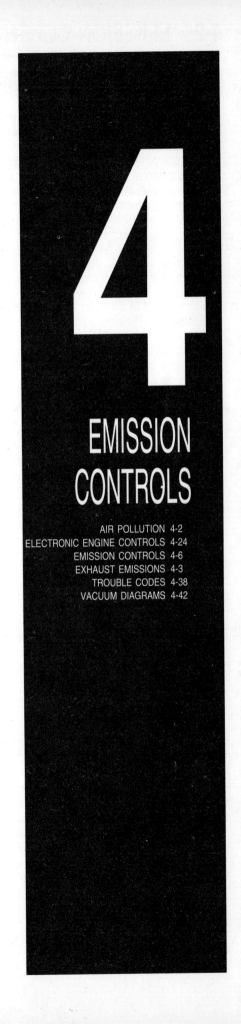

4

EMISSION CONTROLS

AIR POLLUTION

The earth's atmosphere, at or near sea level, consists approximately of 78 percent nitrogen, 21 percent oxygen and 1 percent other gases. If it were possible to remain in this state, 100 percent clean air would result. However, many varied causes allow other gases and particulates to mix with the clean air, causing the air to become unclean or polluted.

Certain of these pollutants are visible while others are invisible, with each having the capability of causing distress to the eyes, ears, throat, skin and respiratory system. Should these pollutants become concentrated in a specific area and under certain conditions, death could result due to the displacement or chemical change of the oxygen content in the air. These pollutants can also cause great damage to the environment and to the many man made objects that are exposed to the elements.

To better understand the causes of air pollution, the pollutants can be categorized into 3 separate types, natural, industrial and automotive.

Natural Pollutants

Natural pollution has been present on earth since before man appeared and continues to be a factor when discussing air pollution, although it causes only a small percentage of the overall pollution problem existing in our country today. It is the direct result of decaying organic matter, wind born smoke and particulates from such natural events as plain and forest fires (ignited by heat or lightning), volcanic ash, sand and dust which can spread over a large area of the countryside.

Such a phenomenon of natural pollution has been recently seen in the form of volcanic eruptions, with the resulting plume of smoke, steam and volcanic ash blotting out the sun's rays as it spreads and rises higher into the atmosphere. As it travels into the atmosphere the upper air currents catch and carry the smoke and ash, while condensing the steam back into water vapor. As the water vapor, smoke and ash traveled on their journey, the smoke dissipates into the atmosphere while the ash and moisture settle back to earth in a trail hundred of miles long. In some cases, lives are lost and millions of dollars of property damage result. Ironically, man can only stand by and watch it happen.

Industrial Pollution

Industrial pollution is caused primarily by industrial processes, the burning of coal, oil and natural gas, which in turn produce smoke and fumes. Because the burning fuels contain large amounts of sulfur, the principal ingredients of smoke and fumes are sulfur dioxide and particulate matter. This type of pollutant occurs most severely during still, damp and cool weather, such as at night. Even in its less severe form, this pollutant is not confined to just cities. Because of air movements, the pollutants move for miles over the surrounding countryside, leaving in its path a barren and unhealthy environment for all living things.

Working with Federal, State and Local mandated regulations and by carefully monitoring the emissions, big business has greatly reduced the amount of pollutant emitted from its industrial sources, striving to obtain an acceptable level. Because of the mandated industrial emission clean up, many land areas and streams in and around the cities that were formerly barren of vegetation and life, have now begun to move back in the direction of nature's intended balance.

Automotive Pollutants

The third major source of air pollution is automotive emissions. The emissions from the internal combustion engine were not an appreciable problem years ago because of the small number of registered vehicles and the nation's small highway system. However, during the early 1950's, the trend of the American people was to move from the cities to the surrounding suburbs. This caused an immediate problem in transportation because the majority of suburbs were not afforded mass transit conveniences. This lack of transportation created an attractive market for the automobile manufacturers, which resulted in a dramatic increase in the number of vehicles produced and sold, along with a marked increase in highway construction between cities and the suburbs. Multi-vehicle families emerged with a growing emphasis placed on an individual vehicle per family member. As the increase in vehicle ownership and usage occurred, so did pollutant levels in and around the cities, as suburbanites drove daily to their businesses and employment, returning at the end of the day to their homes in the suburbs.

It was noted that a fog and smoke type haze was being formed and at times, remained in suspension over the cities, taking time to dissipate. At first this 'smog", derived from the words 'smoke" and 'fog", was thought to result from industrial pollution but it was determined that automobile emissions shared the blame. It was discovered that when normal automobile emissions were exposed to sunlight for a period of time, complex chemical reactions would take place.

It is now known that smog is a photo chemical layer which develops when certain oxides of nitrogen (NOx) and unburned hydrocarbons (HC) from automobile emissions are exposed to sunlight. Pollution was more severe when smog would become stagnant over an area in which a warm layer of air settled over the top of the cooler air mass, trapping and holding the cooler mass at ground level. The trapped cooler air would keep the emissions from being dispersed and diluted through normal air flows. This type of air stagnation was given the name 'Temperature Inversion".

Temperature Inversion

In normal weather situations, the surface air is warmed by heat radiating from the earth's surface and the sun's rays and will rise upward, into the atmosphere. Upon rising it will cool through a convection type heat exchange with the cooler upper air. As warm air rises, the surface pollutants are carried upward and dissipated into the atmosphere.

When a temperature inversion occurs, we find the higher air is no longer cooler but warmer than the surface air, causing the cooler surface air to become trapped. This warm air blanket can extend from above ground level to a few hundred or even a few thousand feet into the air. As the surface air is trapped, so are the pollutants, causing a severe smog condition. Should this stagnant air mass extend to a few thousand feet high, enough air movement with the inversion takes place to allow the smog layer to rise above ground level but the pollutants still cannot dissipate. This inversion can remain for days over an area, with the smog level only rising or lowering from ground level to a few hundred feet high. Meanwhile, the pollutant levels increase, causing eye irritation, respiratory problems, reduced visibility, plant damage and in some cases, disease.

This inversion phenomenon was first noted in the Los Angeles, California area. The city lies terrain resembling a basin and with certain weather conditions, a cold air mass is held in the basin while a warmer air mass covers it like a lid.

Because this type of condition was first documented as prevalent in the Los Angeles area, this type of trapped pollution was named Los Angeles Smog, although it occurs in other areas where a large concentration of automobiles are used and the air remains stagnant for any length of time.

Internal Combustion Engine Pollutants

Consider the internal combustion engine as a machine in which raw materials must be placed so a finished product comes out. As in any machine operation, a certain amount of wasted material is formed. When we relate this to the internal combustion engine, we find that through the input of air and fuel, we obtain power during the combustion process to drive the vehicle. The by-product or waste of this power is, in part, heat and exhaust gases with which we must dispose.

EXHAUST EMISSIONS

Composition Of The Exhaust Gases

The exhaust gases emitted into the atmosphere are a combination of burned and unburned fuel. To understand the exhaust emission and its composition, we must review some basic chemistry.

When the air/fuel mixture is introduced into the engine, we are mixing air, composed of nitrogen (78 percent), oxygen (21 percent) and other gases (1 percent) with the fuel, which is 100 percent hydrocarbons (HC), in a semi-controlled ratio. As the combustion process is accomplished, power is produced to move the vehicle while the heat of combustion is transferred to the cooling system. The exhaust gases are then composed of nitrogen, a diatomic gas (N_2), the same as was introduced in the engine, carbon dioxide (CO_2), the same gas that is used in beverage carbonation and water vapor (H_2O). The nitrogen (N_2), for the most part passes through the engine unchanged, while the oxygen (O_2) reacts (burns) with the hydrocarbons (HC) and produces the carbon dioxide (CO_2) and the water vapors (H_2O). If this chemical process would be the only process to take place, the exhaust emissions would be harmless. However, during the combustion process, other compounds are formed which are considered dangerous. These pollutants are carbon monoxide (CO), hydrocarbons (HC), oxides of nitrogen (NOx) oxides of sulfur (SOx) and engine particulates.

Heat Transfer

The heat from the combustion process can rise to over 4,000°F (2,204°C). The dissipation of this heat is controlled by a ram air effect, the use of cooling fans to cause air flow and having a liquid coolant solution surrounding the combustion area to transfer the heat of combustion through the cylinder walls and into the coolant. The coolant is then directed to a thin-finned, multi-tubed radiator, from which the excess heat is transferred to the atmosphere by 1 of the 3 heat transfer methods, conduction, convection or radiation.

The cooling of the combustion area is an important part in the control of exhaust emissions. To understand the behavior of the combustion and transfer of its heat, consider the air/fuel charge. It is ignited and the flame front burns progressively across the combustion chamber until the burning charge reaches the cylinder walls. Some of the fuel in contact with the walls is not hot enough to burn, thereby snuffing out or quenching the combustion process. This leaves unburned fuel in the combustion chamber. This unburned fuel is then forced out of the cylinder and into the exhaust system, along with the exhaust gases.

Many attempts have been made to minimize the amount of unburned fuel in the combustion chambers due to the snuffing out or quenching, by increasing the coolant temperature and lessening the contact area of the coolant around the combustion area. Design limitations within the combustion chambers prevent the complete burning of the air/fuel charge, so a certain amount of the unburned fuel is still expelled into the exhaust system, regardless of modifications to the engine.

HYDROCARBONS

Hydrocarbons (HC) are essentially fuel which was not burned during the combustion process or which has escaped into the atmosphere through fuel evaporation. The main sources of incomplete combustion are rich air/fuel mixtures, low engine temperatures and improper spark timing. The main sources of hydrocarbon emission through fuel evaporation on most cars used to be the vehicle's fuel tank and carburetor bowl.

To reduce combustion hydrocarbon emission, engine modifications were made to minimize dead space and surface area in the combustion chamber. In addition the air/fuel mixture was made more lean through the improved control which feedback carburetion and fuel injection offers and by the addition of external controls to aid in further combustion of the hydrocarbons outside the engine. Two such methods were the addition of an air injection system, to inject fresh air into the exhaust manifolds and the installation of a catalytic converter, a unit that is able to burn traces of hydrocarbons without affecting the internal combustion process or fuel economy. The vehicles covered in this manual may utilize either, both or none of these methods, depending on the year and model.

To control hydrocarbon emissions through fuel evaporation, modifications were made to the fuel tank to allow storage of the fuel vapors during periods of engine shut-down.

Modifications were also made to the air intake system so that at specific times during engine operation, these vapors may be purged and burned by blending them with the air/fuel mixture.

CARBON MONOXIDE

Carbon monoxide is formed when not enough oxygen is present during the combustion process to convert carbon (C) to carbon dioxide (CO_2). An increase in the carbon monoxide (CO) emission is normally accompanied by an increase in the hydrocarbon (HC) emission because of the lack of oxygen to completely burn all of the fuel mixture.

Carbon monoxide (CO) also increases the rate at which the photo chemical smog is formed by speeding up the conversion of nitric oxide (NO) to nitrogen dioxide (NO_2). To accomplish this, carbon monoxide (CO) combines with oxygen (O_2) and nitric oxide (NO) to produce carbon dioxide (CO_2) and nitrogen dioxide (NO_2). ($CO + O_2 + NO = CO_2 + NO_2$).

The dangers of carbon monoxide, which is an odorless and colorless toxic gas are many. When carbon monoxide is inhaled into the lungs and passed into the blood stream, oxygen is replaced by the carbon monoxide in the red blood cells, causing a reduction in the amount of oxygen being supplied to the many parts of the body. This lack of oxygen causes headaches, lack of coordination, reduced mental alertness and should the carbon monoxide concentration be high enough, death could result.

NITROGEN

Normally, nitrogen is an inert gas. When heated to approximately 2,500°F (1,371°C) through the combustion process, this gas becomes active and causes an increase in the nitric oxide (NOx) emission.

Oxides of nitrogen (NOx) are composed of approximately 97-98 percent nitric oxide (NO). Nitric oxide is a colorless gas but when it is passed into the atmosphere, it combines with oxygen and forms nitrogen dioxide (NO_2). The nitrogen dioxide then combines with chemically active hydrocarbons (HC) and when in the presence of sunlight, causes the formation of photo chemical smog.

OZONE

To further complicate matters, some of the nitrogen dioxide (NO_2) is broken apart by the sunlight to form nitric oxide and oxygen. (NO_2 + sunlight = NO + O). This single atom of oxygen then combines with diatomic (meaning 2 atoms) oxygen (O_2) to form ozone (O_3). Ozone is one of the smells associated with smog. It has a pungent and offensive odor, irritates the eyes and lung tissues, affects the growth of plant life and causes rapid deterioration of rubber products. Ozone can be formed by sunlight as well as electrical discharge into the air.

The most common discharge area on the automobile engine is the secondary ignition electrical system, especially when inferior quality spark plug cables are used. As the surge of high voltage is routed through the secondary cable, the circuit

builds up an electrical field around the wire, acting upon the oxygen in the surrounding air to form the ozone. The faint glow along the cable with the engine running that may be visible on a dark night, is called the 'corona discharge." It is the result of the electrical field passing from a high along the cable, to a low in the surrounding air, which forms the ozone gas. The combination of corona and ozone has been a major cause of cable deterioration. Recently, different and better quality insulating materials have lengthened the life of the electrical cables.

Although ozone at ground level can be harmful, ozone is beneficial to the earth's inhabitants. By having a concentrated ozone layer called the 'ozonosphere", between 10 and 20 miles (16-32km) up in the atmosphere, much of the ultra violet radiation from the sun's rays are absorbed and screened. If this ozone layer were not present, much of the earth's surface would be burned, dried and unfit for human life.

There is much discussion concerning the ozone layer and its density. A feeling exists that this protective layer of ozone is slowly diminishing and corrective action must be directed to this problem. Much experimentation is presently being conducted to determine if a problem exists and if so, the short and long term effects of the problem and how it can be remedied.

OXIDES OF SULFUR

Oxides of sulfur (SOx) were initially ignored in the exhaust system emissions, since the sulfur content of gasoline as a fuel is less than $1/10$ of 1 percent. Because of this small amount, it was felt that it contributed very little to the overall pollution problem. However, because of the difficulty in solving the sulfur emissions in industrial pollutions and the introduction of catalytic converter to the automobile exhaust systems, a change was mandated. The automobile exhaust system, when equipped with a catalytic converter, changes the sulfur dioxide (SO_2) into the sulfur trioxide (SO_3).

When this combines with water vapors (H_2O), a sulfuric acid mist (H_2SO_4) is formed and is a very difficult pollutant to handle since it is extremely corrosive. This sulfuric acid mist that is formed, is the same mist that rises from the vents of an automobile battery when an active chemical reaction takes place within the battery cells.

When a large concentration of vehicles equipped with catalytic converters are operating in an area, this acid mist will rise and be distributed over a large ground area causing land, plant, crop, paints and building damage.

PARTICULATE MATTER

A certain amount of particulate matter is present in the burning of any fuel, with carbon constituting the largest percentage of the particulates. In gasoline, the remaining particulates are the burned remains of the various other compounds used in its manufacture. When a gasoline engine is in good internal condition, the particulate emissions are low but as the engine wears internally, the particulate emissions increase. By visually inspecting the tail pipe emissions, a determination can be made as to where an engine defect may exist. An engine with light gray or blue smoke emitting from the tail pipe normally indicates an increase in the oil consumption through burning due to internal engine wear. Black smoke would indicate a defective fuel delivery system, causing the engine to operate in a rich mode. Regardless of the color of the smoke, the internal part of the engine or the fuel delivery system should be repaired to prevent excess particulate emissions.

Diesel and turbine engines emit a darkened plume of smoke from the exhaust system because of the type of fuel used. Emission control regulations are mandated for this type of emission and more stringent measures are being used to prevent excess emission of the particulate matter. Electronic components are being introduced to control the injection of the fuel at precisely the proper time of piston travel, to achieve the optimum in fuel ignition and fuel usage. Other particulate after-burning components are being tested to achieve a cleaner emission.

Good grades of engine lubricating oils should be used, which meet the manufacturers specification. Cut-rate oils can contribute to the particulate emission problem because of their low flash or ignition temperature point. Such oils burn prematurely during the combustion process causing emissions of particulate matter.

The cooling system is an important factor in the reduction of particulate matter. With the cooling system operating at a temperature specified by the manufacturer, the optimum of combustion will occur. The cooling system must be maintained in the same manner as the engine oiling system, as each system is required to perform properly in order for the engine to operate efficiently for a long time.

Other Automobile Emission Sources

Before emission controls were mandated on the internal combustion engines, other sources of engine pollutants were discovered, along with the exhaust emission. It was determined the engine combustion exhaust produced 60 percent of the total emission pollutants, fuel evaporation from the fuel tank and carburetor vents produced 20 percent, with another 20 percent being produced through the crankcase as a by-product of the combustion process.

CRANKCASE EMISSIONS

Crankcase emissions are made up of water, acids, unburned fuel, oil fumes and particulates. The emissions are classified as hydrocarbons (HC) and are formed by the small amount of unburned, compressed air/fuel mixture entering the crankcase from the combustion area during the compression and power strokes, between the cylinder walls and piston rings. The head of the compression and combustion help to form the remaining crankcase emissions.

Since the first engines, crankcase emissions were allowed into the atmosphere through a road draft tube, mounted on the lower side of the engine block. Fresh air came in through an open oil filler cap or breather. The air passed through the crankcase mixing with blow-by gases. The motion of the vehicle and the air blowing past the open end of the road draft tube caused a low pressure area at the end of the tube.

Crankcase emissions were simply drawn out of the road draft tube into the air.

To control the crankcase emission, the road draft tube was deleted. A hose and/or tubing was routed from the crankcase to the intake manifold so the blow-by emission could be burned with the air/fuel mixture. However, it was found that intake manifold vacuum, used to draw the crankcase emissions into the manifold, would vary in strength at the wrong time and not allow the proper emission flow. A regulating type valve was needed to control the flow of air through the crankcase.

Testing, showed the removal of the blow-by gases from the crankcase as quickly as possible, was most important to the longevity of the engine. Should large accumulations of blow-by gases remain and condense, dilution of the engine oil would occur to form water, soots, resins, acids and lead salts, resulting in the formation of sludge and varnishes. This condensation of the blow-by gases occur more frequently on vehicles used in numerous starting and stopping conditions, excessive idling and when the engine is not allowed to attain normal operating temperature through short runs.

FUEL EVAPORATIVE EMISSIONS

Gasoline fuel is a major source of pollution, before and after it is burned in the automobile engine. From the time the fuel is refined, stored, pumped and transported, again stored until it is pumped into the fuel tank of the vehicle, the gasoline gives off unburned hydrocarbons (HC) into the atmosphere. Through redesigning of the storage areas and venting systems, the pollution factor was diminished, but not eliminated, from the refinery standpoint. However, the automobile still remained the primary source of vaporized, unburned hydrocarbon (HC) emissions.

Fuel pumped from an underground storage tank is cool but when exposed to a warmer ambient temperature, will expand. Before controls were mandated, an owner would fill the fuel tank with fuel from an underground storage tank and park the vehicle for some time in warm area, such as a parking lot. As the fuel would warm, it would expand and should no provisions or area be provided for the expansion, the fuel would spill out the filler neck and onto the ground, causing hydrocarbon (HC) pollution and creating a severe fire hazard. To correct this condition, the vehicle manufacturers added overflow plumbing and/or gasoline tanks with built in expansion areas or domes.

However, this did not control the fuel vapor emission from the fuel tank. It was determined that most of the fuel evaporation occurred when the vehicle was stationary and the engine not operating. Most vehicles carry 5-25 gallons (19-95 liters) of gasoline. Should a large concentration of vehicles be parked in one area, such as a large parking lot, excessive fuel vapor emissions would take place, increasing as the temperature increases.

To prevent the vapor emission from escaping into the atmosphere, the fuel system is designed to trap the fuel vapors while the vehicle is stationary, by sealing the fuel system from the atmosphere. A storage system is used to collect and hold the fuel vapors from the carburetor and the fuel tank when the engine is not operating. When the engine is started, the storage system is then purged of the fuel vapors, which are drawn into the engine and burned with the air/fuel mixture.

EMISSION CONTROLS

Due to varying state, federal, and provincial regulations, specific emission control equipment may vary by area of sale. The U.S. emission equipment is divided into two categories: California and Federal. In this section, the term 'California' applies only to cars originally built to be sold in California. Some California emissions equipment are not shared with equipment installed on cars built to be sold in the other states. Models built to be sold in Canada also have specific emissions equipment, although in many cases the Federal and Canadian equipment are the same.

Both carbureted and fuel injected cars require an assortment of systems and devices to control emissions. Newer cars rely more heavily on computer (ECM) management of many of the engine controls. This eliminates many of the vacuum hoses and linkages around the engine. Remember that not every component is found on every car.

Crankcase Ventilation System

OPERATION

▶ See Figures 1, 2 and 3

➡Used on all engines.

A closed positive crankcase ventilation (PCV) system is used on all Toyota models. This system cycles incompletely burned fuel which works its way past the piston rings back into the intake manifold for reburning with the fuel/air mixture. The oil filler cap is sealed and the air is drawn from the top of the crankcase into the intake manifold through a valve with a variable orifice.

This valve (commonly known as the PCV valve) regulates the flow of air into the manifold according to the amount of manifold vacuum. When the throttle plates are open fairly wide, the valve is fully open. However, at idle speed, when the manifold vacuum is at maximum, the PCV valve reduces the flow.

A plugged valve or hose may cause a rough idle, stalling or low idle speed, oil leaks in the engine and/or sludging and oil deposits within the engine and air cleaner. A leaking valve or hose could cause an erratic idle or stalling.

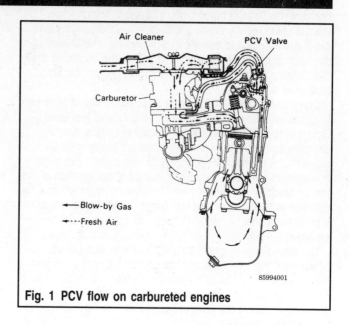

Fig. 1 PCV flow on carbureted engines

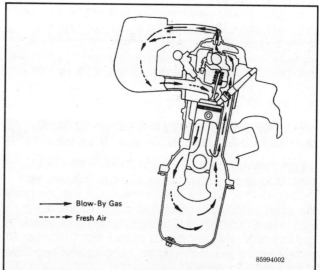

Fig. 2 PCV flow on fuel injected engines

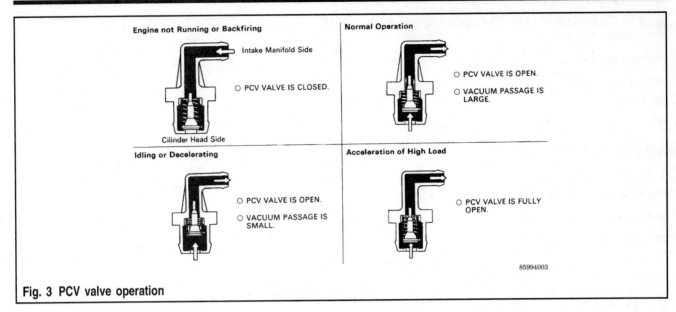

Engine not Running or Backfiring

Intake Manifold Side

○ PCV VALVE IS CLOSED.

Cilinder Head Side

Normal Operation

○ PCV VALVE IS OPEN.

○ VACUUM PASSAGE IS LARGE.

Idling or Decelerating

○ PCV VALVE IS OPEN.

○ VACUUM PASSAGE IS SMALL.

Acceleration of High Load

○ PCV VALVE IS FULLY OPEN.

85994003

Fig. 3 PCV valve operation

TESTING

The PCV valve is easily checked with the engine running at normal idle speed (warmed up). Remove the PCV valve from the valve cover or intake manifold, but leave it connected to its hose. Place your thumb over the end of the valve to check for vacuum. If there is no vacuum, check for plugged hoses or ports. If these are open, the valve is faulty. With the engine off, remove the PCV valve completely. Shake it end to end, listening for the rattle of the needle inside the valve. If no rattle is heard, the needle is jammed (probably with oil sludge) and the valve should be replaced.

An engine which is operated without crankcase ventilation can be damaged very quickly. It is important to check and change the PCV valve at regular maintenance intervals.

REMOVAL & INSTALLATION

Remove the PCV valve from the cylinder head cover or intake manifold. Remove the hose from the valve. Take note of which end of the valve was in the manifold. This one-way valve must be reinstalled correctly or it will not function. While the valve is removed, the hoses should be checked for splits, kinks and blockages. Check the vacuum port (that the hoses connect to) for any clogging.

Remember that the correct function of the PCV system is based on a sealed engine. An air leak at the oil filler cap and/or around the oil pan can defeat the design of the system.

Evaporative Emission Controls

OPERATION

➡**Used on all engines.**

This system reduces hydrocarbon emissions by storing and routing evaporated fuel from the fuel tank and the carburetor's float chamber (carbureted engines only) through the charcoal canister to the intake manifold for combustion in the cylinders at the proper time.

When the ignition is OFF, hydrocarbons from the carburetor float chamber pass through the control valve into the canister. Fuel vapors from the fuel tank pass into the charcoal canister through a check valve located on the canister.

When the ignition is switch ON, but the engine is NOT running, the control valve is energized blocking the movement of fuel vapor from the carburetor's float chamber. Vapors from the fuel tank can still flow and be stored in the charcoal canister.

With the engine running above 1,500 rpm, the fuel vapors are purged from the canister into the intake manifold. If deceleration occurs, the throttle position switch opens (disconnects) and the ECM detects the change. The control valve is de-energized and the purging of vapor is stopped. This eliminates the delivery of excess fuel vapor during periods of poor or reduced combustion.

When there is pressure in the fuel tank (such as from summer heat or long periods of driving) the canister valve opens, allowing vapor to enter the canister and be stored for future delivery to the engine.

TESTING

Before embarking on component removal or extensive diagnosis, perform a complete visual check of the system. Every vacuum line and vapor line (including the lines running to the tank) should be inspected for cracking, loose clamps, kinks and obstructions. Additionally, check the tank for any signs of deformation or crushing. Each vacuum port on the engine or manifold should be checked for restriction by dirt or sludge.

The evaporative control system is generally not prone to component failure in normal circumstances; most problems can be tracked to the causes listed above.

Fuel Filler Cap

Check that the filler cap seals effectively. Remove the filler cap and pull the safety valve outward to check for smooth operation. Replace the filler cap if the seal is defective or if it is not operating properly.

Charcoal Canister

Check the canister using the procedures described in Section 1.

➡ **Do not attempt to wash the charcoal canister. Also be sure that no activated carbon comes out of the canister during the cleaning process.**

Outer Vent Control Valve

▸ **See Figures 4, 5, 6 and 7**

➡ **Used on 3A-C and 3E engines.**

3A-C ENGINES

1. Label and disconnect the hoses from the control valve but leave the wiring for the valve connected.
2. Check that the valve is open by blowing air through it when the ignition switch is in the OFF position.
3. Check that the valve is closed when the ignition switch is in the ON position.
4. Reconnect the hoses to the proper locations. If the valve doesn't operate correctly, double check the fuse and wiring before replacing the valve.

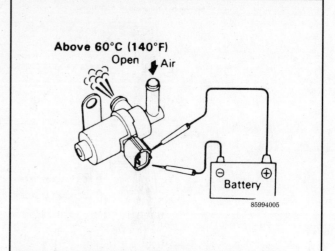

Fig. 5 The outer vent control valve should be open under these conditions on 3E engines

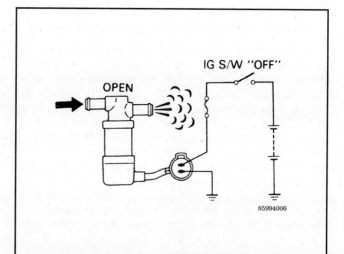

Fig. 6 On 3A-C engines, the outer vent control valve should be open with the ignition switch off

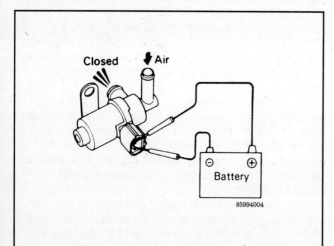

Fig. 4 On 3E engines, there should be no airflow with battery voltage applied to the terminals of the outer vent control valve

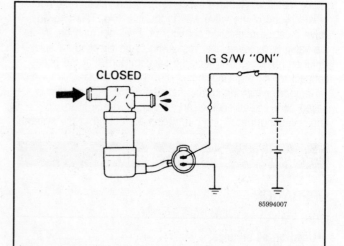

Fig. 7 With the ignition switch on, the valve should be closed

3E ENGINES

1. Label and disconnect the wires and hoses from the control valve.

2. Apply battery voltage to the terminals and check that the valve is closed by blowing air through it.

3. Check that the valve is closed below 115°F(46°C) or open above 140°F(60°C) without voltage applied to the terminals.

4. Reconnect the hoses to the proper locations. If the valve doesn't operate correctly, double check the wiring before replacing the valve.

Water Temperature Switch

▶ **See Figures 8 and 9**

➡**Used on 3A-C and 3E engines.**

1. Drain the coolant from the radiator into a clean container.

❈❈CAUTION

When draining the coolant, keep in mind that cats and dogs are attracted by the ethylene glycol antifreeze, and are quite likely to drink any that is left in an uncovered container or in puddles on the ground. This will prove fatal in sufficient quantity. Always drain the coolant into a sealable container. Coolant should be reused unless it is contaminated or several years old.

2. Remove the thermoswitch.

3. Cool the switch off until the temperature is below 109°F (43°C) on 3A-C engines or 118°F (48°C) on 3E engines. Check that there is continuity through the switch by the use of an ohmmeter.

4. Using hot water, bring the temperature of the switch to above 131°F (55°C) on 3A-C engines or 140°F (60°C) on 3E engines. Check that there is no continuity when the switch is above this temperature.

5. Apply sealer to the threads of the switch and reinstall it.

6. Refill the radiator with coolant.

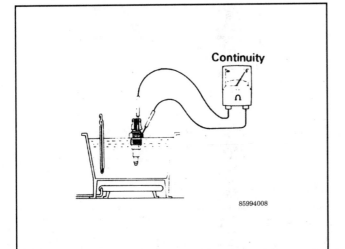

Fig. 8 The water temperature switch should have continuity when below its calibrated temperature

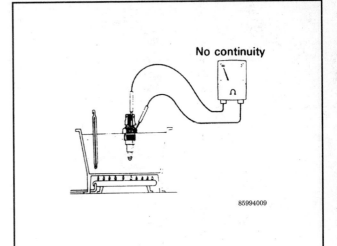

Fig. 9 When above its calibrated temperature, the switch should not have continuity

Vacuum Switching Valve

▶ **See Figures 10, 11, 12 and 13**

➡**Used on 3A-C and 3E engines.**

1. Connect battery voltage to the terminals of the EVAP vacuum switching valve (VSV).

2. Blow air into the pipe and check that it is open.

3. Remove the voltage source from the terminals and check that the valve is closed.

4. Using an ohmmeter, check that there is no continuity between the positive terminal and the VSV body. If there is continuity, replace the valve.

5. Using an ohmmeter, measure the resistance between the two terminals. It should be between 38-44Ω at 68°F (20°C). If not, replace the valve.

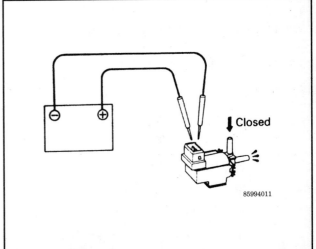

Fig. 11 Without battery voltage applied to the terminals, the VSV should be closed

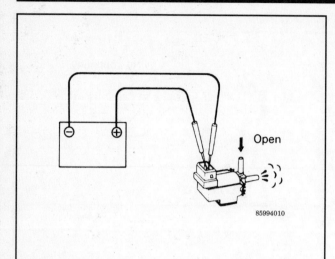

Fig. 10 The VSV should be open with battery voltage applied to the terminals

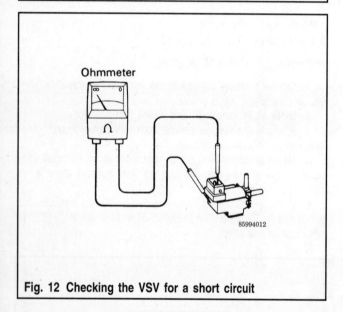

Fig. 12 Checking the VSV for a short circuit

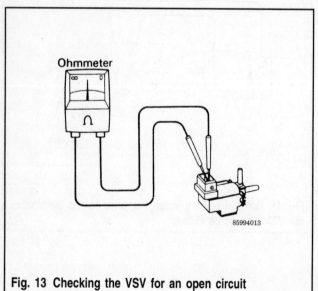

Fig. 13 Checking the VSV for an open circuit

Vacuum Switch (A)
▶ See Figures 14 and 15

➡**Used on 3A-C engines.**

1. Using an ohmmeter, check for continuity between the switch terminal and body with the engine off and cold.
2. Start the engine and warm it to normal operating temperature.
3. Check that there is no continuity between the switch terminal and body.

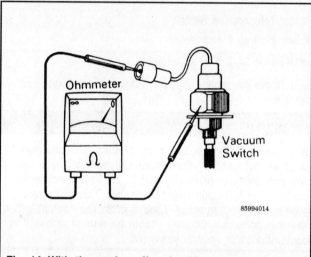

Fig. 14 With the engine off and cold, vacuum switch (A) should have continuity

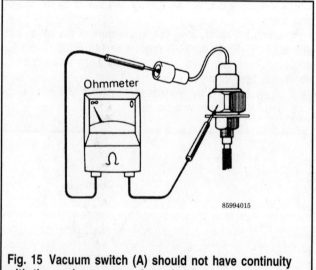

Fig. 15 Vacuum switch (A) should not have continuity with the engine warm and running

REMOVAL & INSTALLATION

▶ See Figure 16

Removal and installation of the various evaporative emission control system components consists of labeling or marking and unfastening hoses, loosening retaining screws, and removing the part which is to be replaced from its mounting point.

➡**When replacing any EVAP system hoses, always use hoses that are fuel-resistant or are marked EVAP. Use of hose which is not fuel-resistant will lead to premature hose failure.**

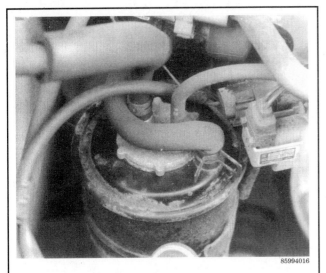

Fig. 16 A common evaporative canister

Exhaust Gas Recirculation

OPERATION

➡**Used on 3A-C, 3E and 3E-E engines.**

The EGR system reduces oxides of nitrogen. This is accomplished by recirculating some of the exhaust gases through the EGR valve to the intake manifold, lowering peak combustion temperatures.

The EGR vacuum modulator controls the EGR valve by modulating the vacuum signal with an atmospheric bleed. This bleed is controlled by the amount of exhaust pressure acting on the bottom of the EGR vacuum modulator (diaphragm).

Since recirculation of exhaust gas is undesirable at low rpm or idle, the system limits itself by sensing the exhaust flow. Under low load conditions, such as low speed driving, the exhaust pressure is low. In this state, the diaphragm in the modulator is pushed down by spring force and the modulator valve opens to allow outside air into the vacuum passage. The vacuum in the line is reduced, the EGR valve does not open as far, and the amount of recirculation is reduced.

Under high load conditions or high rpm driving, the exhaust pressure is increased. This pushes the modulator diaphragm upwards and closes the bleed valve. A full vacuum signal is transmitted to the EGR valve; it opens completely and allows full recirculation. The slight reduction in combustion tempera-

ture (and therefore power) is not noticed at highway speeds or under hard acceleration.

Some vehicles also control the EGR with a vacuum switching valve (VSV). This device allows the ECM to further control the EGR under certain conditions. The ECM will electrically close the VSV if the engine is not warmed up, the throttle valve is in the idle position or if the engine is under very hard acceleration. Aside from these conditions, this EGR system (late models) operates in accordance with the normal vacuum modulator function.

SERVICING

EGR Valve

▶ **See Figure 17**

1. Remove the EGR valve.
2. Check the valve for sticking and heavy carbon deposits. If a problem is found, clean or replace the valve.
3. Reinstall the EGR valve with a new gasket.

Fig. 17 The EGR valve should be cleaned of carbon deposits

Vacuum Modulator

3A-C ENGINES

▶ **See Figures 18 and 19**

1. Label and disconnect the two vacuum hoses from their ports.
2. Plug one port with your finger.
3. Blow air into the other port. Check that the air passes freely through the air filter side of the modulator.
4. Start the engine, maintain it at 3,000 rpm.
5. Repeat the steps above. Check that there is a strong resistance to air flow.
6. Reconnect the vacuum hoses to the proper locations.

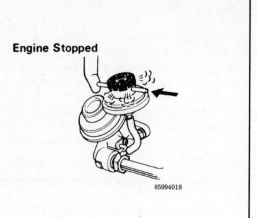

Fig. 18 Modulator air flow with the engine stopped; 3A-C engines

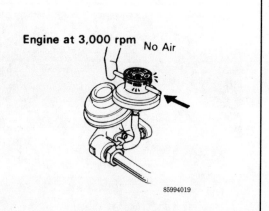

Fig. 19 Modulator air flow with the engine running at speed; 3A-C engines

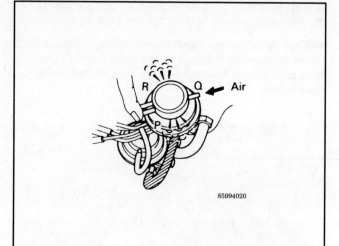

Fig. 20 Modulator air flow with the engine stopped; 3E and 3E-E engines

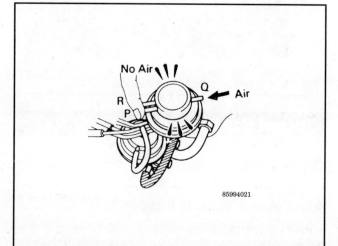

Fig. 21 Modulator air flow with the engine at speed; 3E and 3E-E engines

3E AND 3E-E ENGINES

▶ See Figures 20 and 21

1. Label and disconnect the vacuum hoses from ports **P**, **Q**, and **R** of the EGR vacuum modulator.
2. Plug the **P** and **R** ports with your fingers.
3. Blow air into port **Q**. Check that the air passes freely through the air filter side of the modulator.
4. Start the engine, maintain it at 3,000 rpm for 3E engines or 2,500 rpm for 3E-E engines.
5. Repeat the steps above. Check that there is a strong resistance to air flow.
6. Reconnect the vacuum hoses to the proper locations.

Vacuum Switching Valve

▶ See Figures 22, 23, 24 and 25

➡Used on 3E-E engines.

1. The vacuum switching circuit is checked by blowing air into the pipe under the following conditions:
   a. Connect the vacuum switching valve terminals to battery voltage.
   b. Blow into the tube and check that the VSV switch is open.
   c. Remove battery voltage from the terminals.
   d. Blow into the tube and check that the VSV switch is closed (no flow).
2. Check for a short circuit within the valve. Using an ohmmeter, check that there is no continuity between the positive terminal and the VSV body. If there is continuity, replace the VSV.
3. Check for an open circuit. Using an ohmmeter, measure the resistance (ohms) between the two terminals of the valve.

The resistance should be 38-44Ω at 68°F (20°C). If the resistance is not within specifications, replace the VSV.

➡The resistance will vary slightly with temperature. It will decrease in cooler temperatures and increase with heat, slight variations due to temperature range are not necessarily a sign of a failed valve.

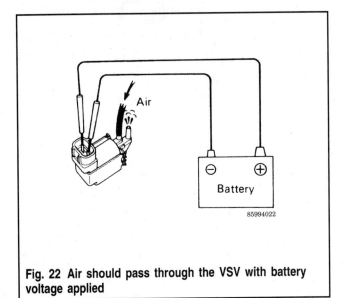

Fig. 22 Air should pass through the VSV with battery voltage applied

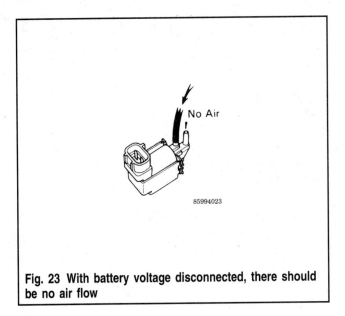

Fig. 23 With battery voltage disconnected, there should be no air flow

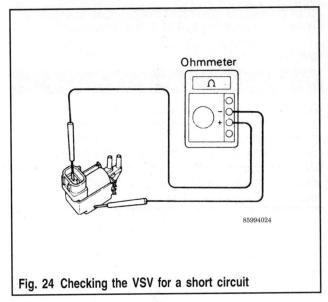

Fig. 24 Checking the VSV for a short circuit

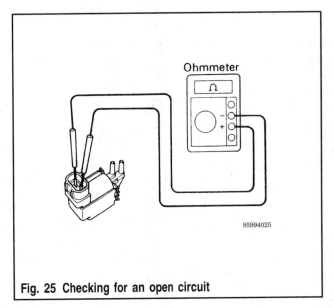

Fig. 25 Checking for an open circuit

Bi-metal Vacuum Switching Valve
▶ See Figures 26, 27, 28 and 29

➡Used on 3E engines.

Despite the impressive name, the BVSV valve does nothing more than allow vacuum to flow through the system depending on engine coolant temperature. The bi-metallic element within the switch reacts to temperature changes, opening or closing the valve at a pre-determined level. To test the valve:

1. Drain the coolant from the radiator into a suitable container.

✳✳CAUTION

When draining the coolant, keep in mind that cats and dogs are attracted by the ethylene glycol antifreeze, and are quite likely to drink any that is left in an uncovered container or in puddles on the ground. This will prove fatal in sufficient quantity. Always drain the coolant into a sealable container. Coolant should be reused unless it is contaminated or several years old.

2. Label and disconnect the hoses from the BVSV.

3. Remove the valve.

4. Using cool water, cool the threaded part of the valve to below 104°F (40°C).

   a. M/T — check that air flows from port M to ports L and N.

   b. A/T — check that air flows through the ports

5. Using warm water, heat the threaded part of the valve to above 129°F (54°C)and blow into the ports again. The valve should not allow air to flow.

6. Apply liquid sealer to the threads of the BVSV and reinstall it. Connect the vacuum lines.

7. Refill the radiator with coolant.

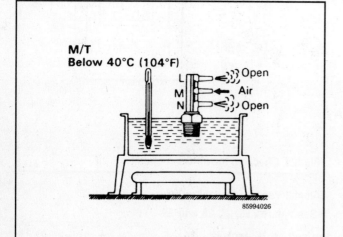

Fig. 26 BVSV air flow when below its calibrated temperature; 3E engines with manual transaxle

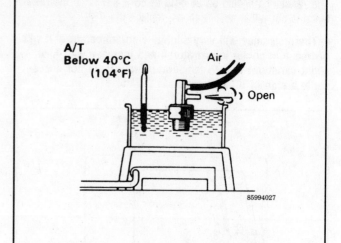

Fig. 27 BVSV air flow when below its calibrated temperature; 3E engines with automatic transaxle

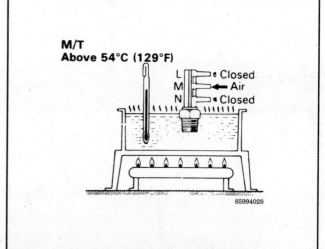

Fig. 28 BVSV air flow when above its calibrated temperature; 3E engines with manual transaxle

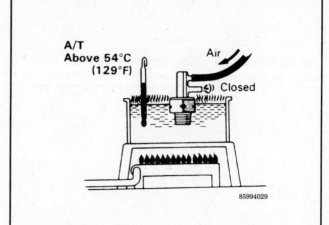

Fig. 29 BVSV air flow when above its calibrated temperature; 3E engines with automatic transaxle

Thermostatic Vacuum Switching Valve

▶ See Figures 30, 31 and 32

➡Used on 3A-C engines.

1. Drain the cooling system.

❄❄CAUTION

When draining the coolant, keep in mind that cats and dogs are attracted by the ethylene glycol antifreeze, and are quite likely to drink any that is left in an uncovered container or in puddles on the ground. This will prove fatal in sufficient quantity. Always drain the coolant into a sealable container. Coolant should be reused unless it is contaminated or several years old.

2. Remove the thermostatic vacuum switching valve (TVSV).
3. Cool the thermostatic vacuum switching valve to below 45°F (7°C).
4. Check that air flows from pipe **J** to pipes **M** and **L**, and flows from pipe **K** to pipe **N**.
5. Heat the thermostatic vacuum switching valve to 63-122°F (17-50°C), generally room temperature.
6. Check that air flows from pipe **K** to pipes **N** and **L** and flows from pipe **J** to pipe **M**.
7. Heat the TVSV to above 154°F (68°C).
8. Check that air flows from the pipe **K** to pipes **M** and **L**, and does **NOT** flow from pipe **J** to any other pipes.
9. Apply liquid sealer to the threads of the TVSV and reinstall.
10. Refill the cooling system.
11. If a problem is found with any of the above procedures, replace the valve

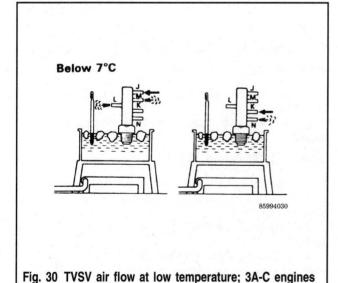

Fig. 30 TVSV air flow at low temperature; 3A-C engines

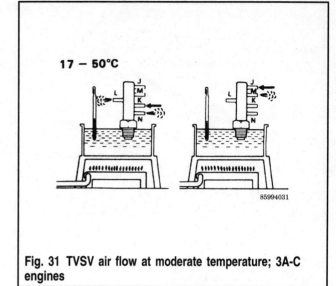

Fig. 31 TVSV air flow at moderate temperature; 3A-C engines

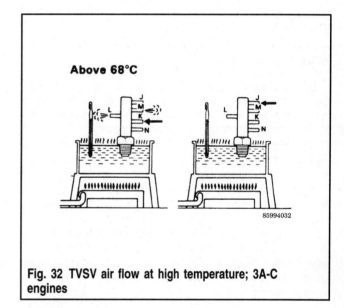

Fig. 32 TVSV air flow at high temperature; 3A-C engines

Check Valve

▶ See Figure 33

Inspect the check valve (one-way valve) by gently blowing air into each end of the valve or hose. Air should flow from the orange pipe to the black pipe but SHOULD NOT flow from the black pipe to the orange pipe.

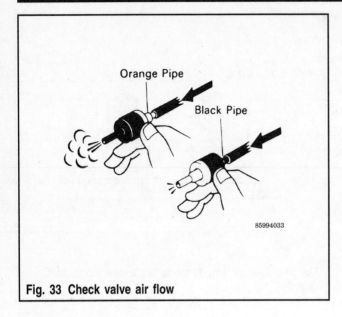

Fig. 33 Check valve air flow

REMOVAL & INSTALLATION

▶ **See Figures 34 and 35**

EGR equipment is generally simple to work on and easy to get to on the engine. The air cleaner assembly will need to be removed. Always label each vacuum hose before removing it — they must be replaced in the correct position.

Most of the valves and solenoids are made of plastic. Be very careful during removal not to break or crack the ports; you have NO chance of gluing a broken fitting. Remember that the plastic has been in a hostile environment (heat and vibration); the fittings become brittle and less resistant to abuse or accidental impact.

EGR valves are generally held in place by two bolts. The bolts can be difficult to remove due to corrosion. Once the EGR valve is off the engine, clean the bolts and the bolt holes of any rust or debris. Always replace the gasket any time the valve is removed.

Fig. 34 On some engines, it may be necessary to remove the exhaust gas crossover pipe before removing the EGR valve

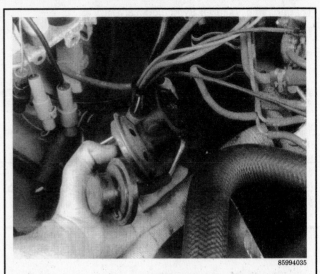

Fig. 35 EGR valves are usually secured with two bolts

Air Suction

OPERATION

➡ **Used on 3A-C and 3E engines.**

The air suction (AS) system brings fresh, filtered air into the exhaust ports to reduce HC and CO emissions. On some applications, it also supplies the air necessary for the oxidizing reaction in the catalytic converter.

TESTING

Air Suction Valve

▶ **See Figures 36, 37, 38, 39 and 40**

WITHOUT VACUUM DIAPHRAGM

1. Blow hard through the outlet side of the AS valve, there should be no air flow.
2. There should be flow through the outlet pipe when sucked.

WITH VACUUM DIAPHRAGM

1. Apply vacuum to the AS valve diaphragm.
2. Blow hard through the outlet side of the AS valve, there should be no air flow.
3. There should be flow through the outlet pipe when sucked.
4. Release the vacuum. Check that very little air flows when the outlet pipe is sucked.

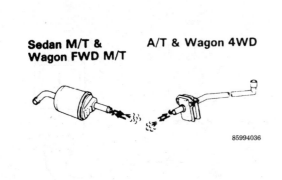

Fig. 36 Air suction valves found on 3A-C federal engines

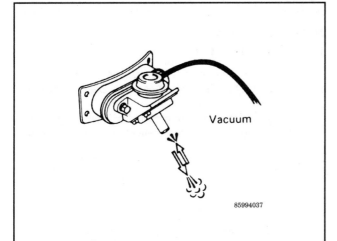

Fig. 37 Air suction valve found on 3A-C California and most 3A-C Canada engines

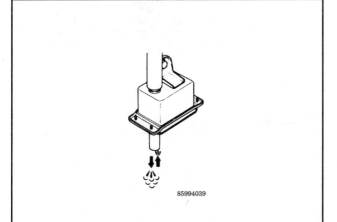

Fig. 39 Air suction valve found on 3E federal and Canada engines

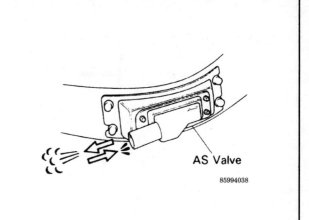

Fig. 38 Air suction valve found on most manual transaxle wagons with 3A-C Canada engines

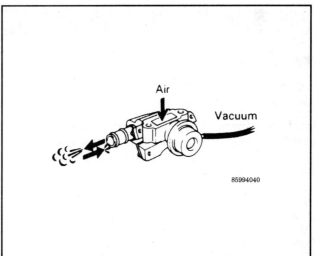

Fig. 40 Air suction valve found on 3E California engines

Vacuum Transmitting Valve

▶ See Figure 41

1. Check that air flows without resistance from **B** to **A**.
2. Check that air flows with difficulty from **A** to **B**.
3. If a problem is found, replace the vacuum delay valve.

➡If replacing the vacuum transmitting valve, side A should face towards the AS valve.

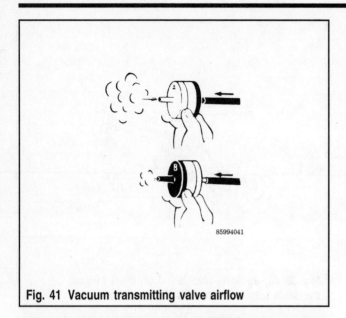

Fig. 41 Vacuum transmitting valve airflow

Cold Mixture Heater

OPERATION

➡Used on 3A-C and 3E engines.

The cold-mixture heater (CMH) system reduces cold engine emissions and improves driveability during engine warm-up. The intake manifold is heated during cold engine warm-up to accelerate vaporization of the fuel.

If the engine is running and the coolant temperature is below a predetermined limit, the computer energizes the cold mixture heater relay. This in turn allows battery voltage to be applied to the cold mixture heater. The CMH is a multi-element heater ring that is mounted between the carburetor base and the intake manifold. Once the coolant temperature exceeds a certain limit, the CMH relay is de-energized and the heater elements turn off.

TESTING

Mixture Heater Element
▶ See Figure 42

1. Unplug the wiring connector.
2. Using an ohmmeter, check the resistance between the heater terminals. The resistance should be 0.5-2.2Ω. Readings outside this range require replacement of the heater element.

3. Replug the wiring connector.

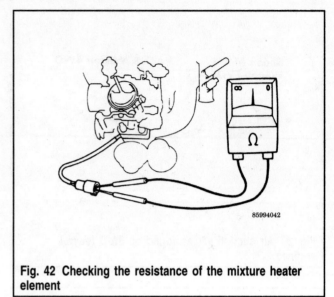

Fig. 42 Checking the resistance of the mixture heater element

Mixture Heater Relay
▶ See Figures 43 and 44

1. Check that there is continuity between the No. 1 and 2 terminals. Check that there is NO continuity between the No. 3 and 4 terminals.
2. Apply battery voltage to terminal No. 1 and 2. Use the ohmmeter to check for continuity between terminals 3 and 4.

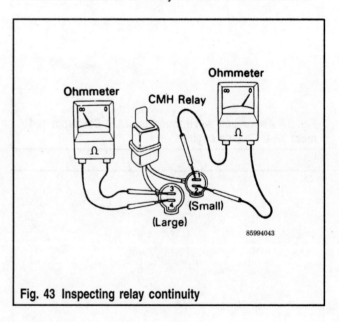

Fig. 43 Inspecting relay continuity

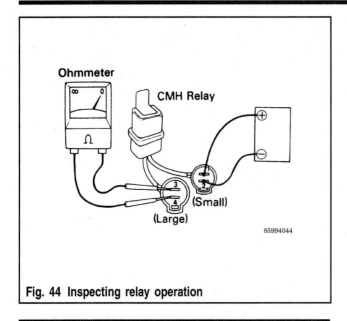

Fig. 44 Inspecting relay operation

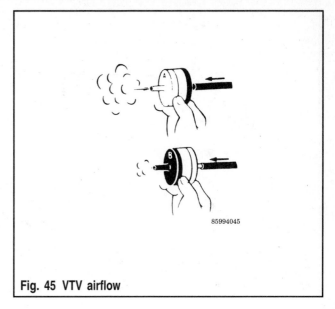

Fig. 45 VTV airflow

Throttle Positioner

OPERATION

➡Used on 3A-C and 3E engines.

To reduce HC and CO emissions, the throttle positioner (TP) opens the throttle valve to slightly more than the idle position when decelerating. This keeps the air/fuel ratio from becoming excessively rich when the throttle valve is quickly closed. In addition, the TP is used to increase idle rpm when power steering fluid pressure exceeds a calibrated value and/or when a large electrical load is placed on the electrical system (headlights, rear defogger etc).

TESTING

Vacuum Transmitting Valve
♦ See Figure 45

1. Check that air flows without resistance from **B** to **A**.
2. Check that air flows with difficulty from **A** to **B**.
3. If a problem is found, replace the vacuum delay valve.

➡**When replacing the vacuum transmitting valve, side A should face the throttle positioner.**

Vacuum Switching Valve
♦ See Figures 46, 47, 48 and 49

➡Used on 3E engines.

1. The vacuum switching circuit is checked by blowing air into the pipe under the following conditions:
   a. Connect the vacuum switching valve terminals to battery voltage.
   b. Blow into the tube and check that the VSV switch is open.
   c. Remove battery voltage from the terminals.
   d. Blow into the tube and check that the VSV switch is closed (no flow).
2. Check for a short circuit within the valve. Using an ohmmeter, check that there is no continuity between the positive terminal and the VSV body. If there is continuity, replace the VSV.
3. Check for an open circuit. Using an ohmmeter, measure the resistance (ohms) between the two terminals of the valve. The resistance should be 38-44Ω at 68°F (20°C). If the resistance is not within specifications, replace the VSV.

➡**The resistance will vary slightly with temperature. It will decrease in cooler temperatures and increase with heat, slight variations due to temperature range are not necessarily a sign of a failed valve.**

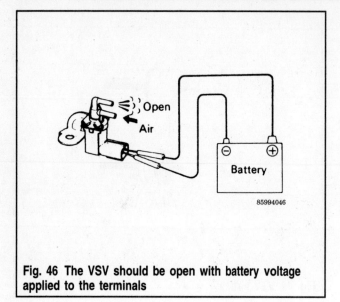

Fig. 46 The VSV should be open with battery voltage applied to the terminals

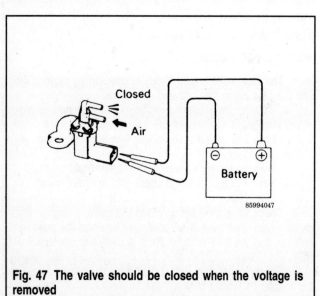

Fig. 47 The valve should be closed when the voltage is removed

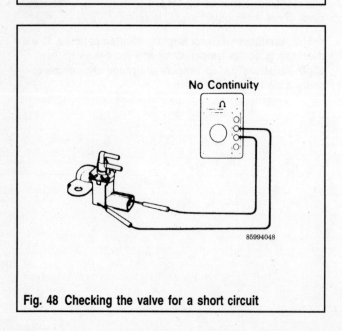

Fig. 48 Checking the valve for a short circuit

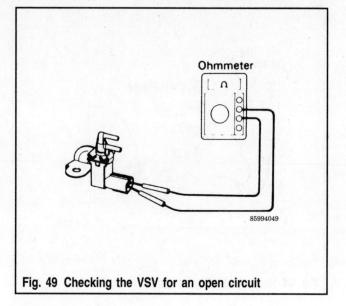

Fig. 49 Checking the VSV for an open circuit

Throttle Positioner Diaphragm

▶ **See Figures 50 and 51**

Check that the linkage moves in accordance with applied vacuum.

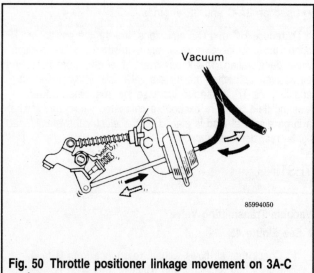

Fig. 50 Throttle positioner linkage movement on 3A-C engines

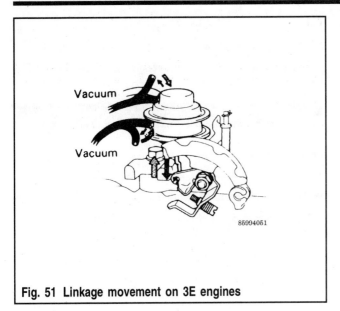

Fig. 51 Linkage movement on 3E engines

Jet

▶ **See Figure 52**

➡**Used on 3E engines.**

Check the jet by blowing air through both sides. Air should pass freely both ways.

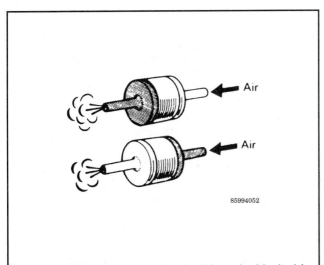

Fig. 52 Airflow through the jet should not be blocked in either direction

High Altitude Compensation

OPERATION

➡**Used on 3A-C and 3E engines.**

As altitude increases, air density decreases. This causes the air/fuel mixture to become richer (the same amount of fuel is mixing with less air). The high altitude compensation (HAC) system insures a proper air/fuel mixture by supplying additional air to the primary low and high speed circuits of the carburetor and advancing the ignition timing to improve driveability at altitudes above 3,930 feet (1,200 m). At altitudes below 2,570 feet (783 m), normal operation is resumed.

TESTING

HAC Valve

▶ **See Figures 53 and 54**

1. Check the HAC valve as follows:
   a. Above 3,930 ft. (1,200 m), blow into any one of the two ports on top of the HAC valve with the engine idling and check that the HAC valve is open (air flows through the bottom of the valve).
   b. Below 2,570 ft. (783 m), blow into any one of the two ports on top of the HAC valve with the engine idling and check that the HAC valve is closed (no air flow through the bottom of the valve).

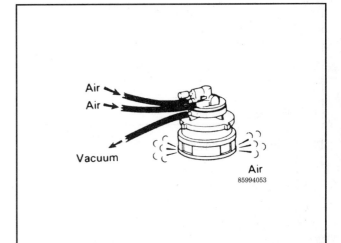

Fig. 53 Air should flow through the bottom of the HAC valve at high altitiudes

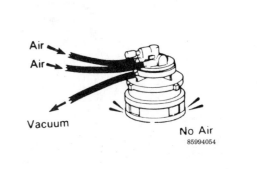

Fig. 54 Air should not flow through the bottom of the valve at low altitudes

Check Valve
▶ See Figure 55

1. Check the valve by blowing air into each pipe:
2. Check that air flows from the orange pipe to the black pipe.
3. Check that air does not flow from the black pipe to the orange pipe.

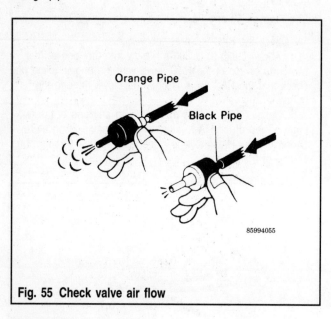

Fig. 55 Check valve air flow

Distributor Vacuum Advance
▶ See Figure 56

➡Used on 3A-C engines.

Remove the distributor cap and rotor. Plug one port of the sub-diaphragm. Using a hand-held vacuum pump, apply vacuum to the diaphragm, checking that the vacuum advance moves when the vacuum is applied. Reinstall the rotor and distributor cap.

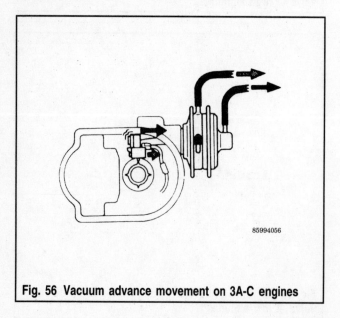

Fig. 56 Vacuum advance movement on 3A-C engines

Jet
➡Used on 3E engines.

Check the jet by blowing air through both sides. Air should pass freely both ways.

Hot Air Intake

OPERATION

➡Used on 3A-C and 3E engines.

This system directs hot air to the carburetor in cold weather to improve driveability and to prevent carburetor icing. When the air temperature in the air cleaner is cold, the atmospheric port in the hot idle compensation (HIC) valve is closed, sending vacuum to the hot air intake (HAI) diaphragm. The HAI diaphragm moves, opening the air control valve which directs the heated air (from the exhaust manifold) into the air cleaner.

Once the air cleaner temperature is warm, the HIC valve atmospheric port is open. This keeps the air control valve closed, allowing the intake air to come directly down the air cleaner's snorkel from outside the car. This air is cooler than the air from around the exhaust manifold.

TESTING

▶ See Figures 57 and 58

1. Remove the air cleaner cover and cool the HIC valve by blowing compressed air on it.
2. Check that the air control valve closes the cool air passage.
3. Reinstall the air cleaner cover and warm up the engine.
4. Check that the air control valve opens the cool air passage at idle.
5. Visually check the hoses and connections for cracks, leaks or damage.

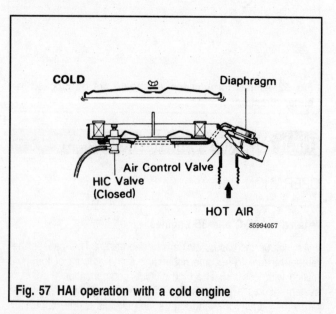

Fig. 57 HAI operation with a cold engine

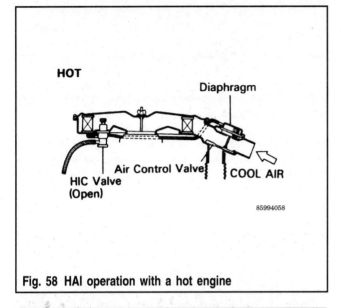

Fig. 58 HAI operation with a hot engine

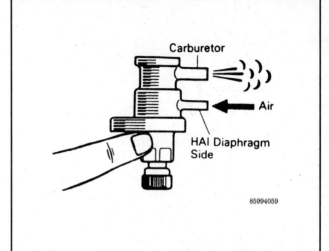

Fig. 59 With the atmospheric port closed, air should flow from the HAI diaphragm to the carburetor

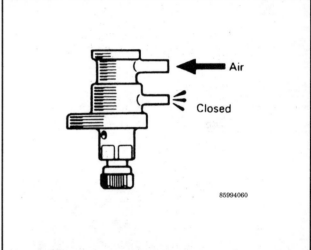

Fig. 60 Air should not flow from the carburetor to the HAI diaphragm with the atmospheric port open

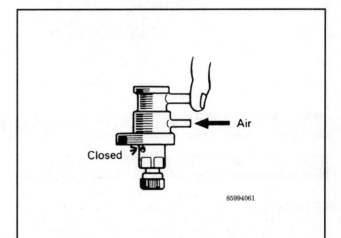

Fig. 61 When below its calibrated temperature, air should not flow from the HAI diaphragm to the atmospheric port with the carburetor side closed

Hot Idle Compensation

OPERATION

➡ Used on 3A-C and 3E engines.

The hot idle compensation (HIC) system allows additional air to enter the intake manifold, maintaining a proper air/fuel mixture during idle at high temperatures. It also controls the vacuum supplied to the HAI valve, allowing heated air to enter the air cleaner during cold operation.

TESTING

▶ See Figures 59, 60, 61 and 62

1. Check that air flows from the HAI diaphragm side to the carburetor side while closing the atmospheric port.
2. Check that air does not flow from the carburetor side to the HAI diaphragm side with the atmospheric port open.
3. Check that air does NOT flow from the HAI diaphragm side to the atmosphere port while closing the carburetor side below these temperatures:
   a. 72°F (22°C) — 3A-C engines
   b. 79°F (26°C) — 3E engines
4. Using a water bath, heat the HIC valve to above 84°F (29°C) on 3A-C engines or 93°F (34°C) on 3E engines.

➡ Do not allow water to get inside the valve.

5. Check that air flows from the HAI diaphragm side to the atmospheric port while closing the carburetor side.

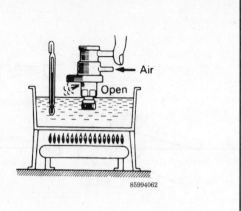

Fig. 62 When above its calibrated temperature, air should flow from the HAI diaphragm to the atmospheric port with the carburetor side closed

Heat Control Valve

OPERATION

➡Used on 3A-C engines.

When the engine is cold, the heat control valve improves fuel vaporization for better driveability by quickly heating the intake manifold. Once the engine has warmed up, it helps keep the intake manifold at proper temperature.

With the engine cold, the bi-metal spring positions the heat control valve to direct some of the engine's hot exhaust gases under the intake manifold which quickly brings it to the proper operating temperature.

When the engine is hot, the bi-metal spring contracts, moving the position of the heat control valve to direct most of the exhaust under the valve and away from direct contact with the intake manifold.

TESTING

▶ See Figure 63

The valve is within the exhaust system and has a counterweight on the outside of the pipe. With the engine cold, check that the counterweight is in the upper position. After the engine has been warmed up, check that the weight has moved to the lower position.

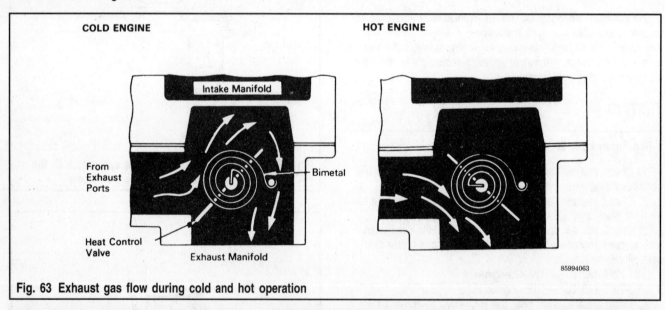

Fig. 63 Exhaust gas flow during cold and hot operation

ELECTRONIC ENGINE CONTROLS

Computerized Engine Systems

OPERATION

Engines equipped with a feedback carburetor use a simple system designed to keep the air/fuel ratio at an optimum of 14.7:1; excluding warm-up and acceleration. The carburetor is designed to run richer than it normally should. This sets up a rich limit of system operation. When a leaner operation is desired, the computer (ECM) energizes the electronic air bleed control valve (EBCV) to introduce additional air into the carburetor's main metering system and into the carburetor's primary bore. Once the air/fuel ratio is detected as being too lean by the oxygen sensor, the ECM will de-energize the EBCV and close both bleed ports. By shutting off the air, the mixture begins moving back towards the rich limit. The system is operating in the 'closed loop" mode, during which it will adjust itself and react to these adjustments. On these engines, the ECM receives information from the oxygen sensor, vacuum switches and the distributor.

The Electronic Fuel Injection (EFI) system precisely controls fuel injection to match engine requirements. This in turn reduces emissions and increases driveability. The ECM receives input from various sensors to determine engine operating conditions. These sensors provide the input to the control unit which determines the amount of fuel to be injected as well as other variables such as idle speed. These inputs and their corresponding sensors include:

• Intake manifold absolute pressure — MAP or Vacuum Sensor
• Intake air temperature — Intake Air Temperature Sensor
• Coolant temperature — Water Temperature Sensor
• Engine speed — Pulse signal from the distributor
• Throttle valve opening — Throttle Position Sensor
• Exhaust oxygen content — Oxygen Sensor

COMPONENT TESTING

Oxygen Sensor

➡ Used on 3A-C, 3E and 3E-E engines.

The oxygen (O_2) sensor is located on the exhaust manifold to detect the concentration of oxygen in the exhaust gas. Using highly refined metals (zirconia and platinum), the sensor uses changes in the oxygen content to generate an electrical signal which is transmitted to the ECM. The computer in turn reacts to the signal by adjusting the fuel metering at the injectors or at the carburetor. More or less fuel is delivered into the cylinders and the correct oxygen level is maintained.

3A-C ENGINES

▶ See Figure 64

1. Warm up the engine to normal operating temperature.
2. Connect the voltmeter to the service connector. This round connector is usually located on the right fender apron below the wiper motor. Connect the positive probe to the OX terminal and the negative probe to the E terminal.
3. Run the engine at 2,500 rpm for 90 seconds or more. This allows the sensor to achieve a stable temperature and the exhaust flow to stabilize.
4. Maintain the engine at 2,500 rpm and check the meter. The meter needle should fluctuate within a 0-7 volt range at least 8 times in 10 seconds. This indicates that the sensor is working properly.
5. If the sensor fails the test, perform a careful inspection of all the wiring and connectors in the system. A loose connection can cause the sensor to fail this test. Repeat the voltage test after the inspection.

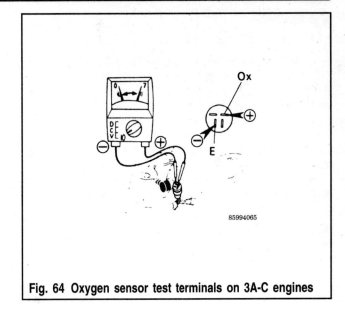

Fig. 64 Oxygen sensor test terminals on 3A-C engines

3E ENGINES

▶ See Figure 65

1. Warm up the engine to normal operating temperature.
2. Connect the voltmeter to the service connector. This is usually located on the left side of the firewall. Connect the positive probe to the OX terminal and the negative probe to the E1 terminal.
3. Run the engine at 2,500 rpm for 90 seconds or more. This allows the sensor to achieve a stable temperature and the exhaust flow to stabilize.
4. Maintain the engine at 2,500 rpm and check the meter. The meter needle should fluctuate 8 times or more in 10 seconds within a 1-5 volt range. This indicates that the sensor is working properly.
5. If the sensor fails the test, perform a careful inspection of all the wiring and connectors in the system. A loose connection can cause the sensor to fail this test. Repeat the voltage test after the inspection.

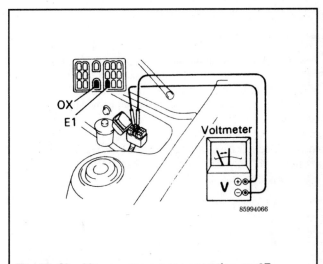

Fig. 65 Checking oxygen sensor operation on 3E engines

3E-E ENGINES

▶ **See Figure 66**

1. Warm up the engine to normal operating temperature.

2. Connect the voltmeter to the check connector on the left fender apron. Hook the positive probe to terminal **VF** and the negative probe to terminal **E1**.

3. Run the engine at 2,500 rpm for at least 120 seconds.

4. With the engine speed being maintained at 2,500 rpm, use a jumper wire to connect terminals **T** and **E1** at the check connector.

5. Watch the voltmeter and note the number of times the needle fluctuates in 10 seconds. If it moves eight times or more, the sensor is working properly.

➡**Perform a careful inspection of all the wiring and connectors in the system. A loose connection can cause the sensor to fail these tests.**

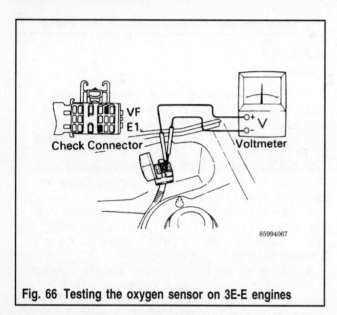

Fig. 66 Testing the oxygen sensor on 3E-E engines

Electronic Air Bleed Control Valve

▶ **See Figures 67, 68, 69 and 70**

➡**Used on 3A-C and 3E engines.**

1. Check for a short circuit. Using an ohmmeter, check that there is no continuity between the positive (+) terminal and the EBCV body. If there is continuity, replace the EBCV.

2. Check for an open circuit. Using an ohmmeter, measure the resistance between the two terminals. The resistance should be between 11-13Ω at 68°F (20°C). If the resistance is not within specification, replace the EBCV. Remember that the resistance will vary slightly with temperature. Resistance (ohms) will decrease as the temperature drops.

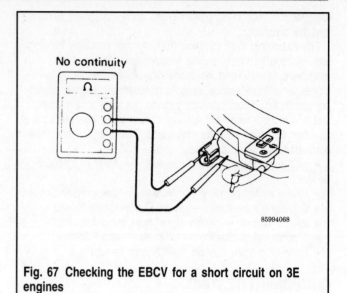

Fig. 67 Checking the EBCV for a short circuit on 3E engines

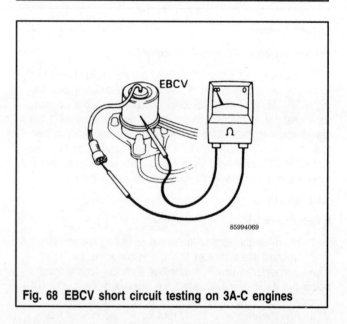

Fig. 68 EBCV short circuit testing on 3A-C engines

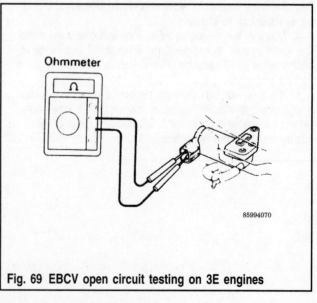

Fig. 69 EBCV open circuit testing on 3E engines

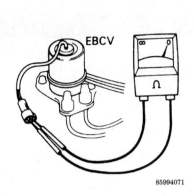

Fig. 70 Testing the EBCV for an open circuit on 3A-C engines

Vacuum Switch (A)

▶ See Figures 71 and 72

➡Used on 3A-C engines.

1. Using an ohmmeter, check that there is continuity between the switch terminal and the switch body.
2. Start the engine and run it until normal operating temperature is reached.
3. Using an ohmmeter, check that there is NO continuity between the switch terminal and the switch body.
4. If either test is failed, replace the switch.

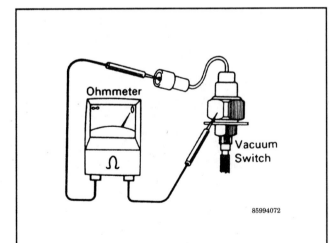

Fig. 71 With the engine off and cold, vacuum switch (A) should have continuity between its terminal and body

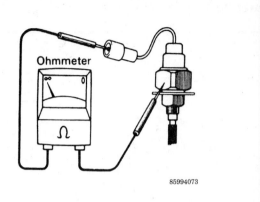

Fig. 72 With the engine warm and running, vacuum switch (A) should not have continuity between its terminal and body

Vacuum Switch (B)

▶ See Figure 73

➡Used on 3A-C engines.

1. Using an ohmmeter, check that there is NO continuity between the switch terminal and the switch body.
2. Start the engine and run until normal operating temperature is reached.
3. Using an ohmmeter, check that there is continuity between the switch terminal and the body.
4. If either test is failed, replace the switch.

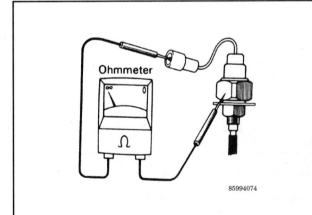

Fig. 73 With the engine off and cold, vacuum switch (B) should not have continuity between its terminal and body. It should have continuity when the engine is warm and running

Vacuum Switch

▶ See Figures 74 and 75

➡Used on 3E engines.

1. Using an ohmmeter, check for no continuity between the switch terminals.
2. Apply a vacuum of 5 in.Hg (12mm H_2O) or greater to the port on the switch.

3. Using an ohmmeter, check that there is continuity between the switch terminals.

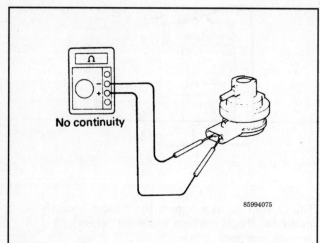

Fig. 74 On 3E engines, the switch should not have continuity between the terminals without vacuum applied

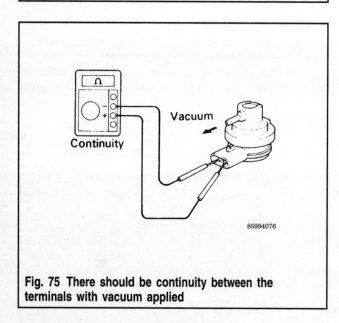

Fig. 75 There should be continuity between the terminals with vacuum applied

Deceleration Fuel Cut-Off Systems

➡Used on 3A-C, 3E and 3E-E engines.

This system cuts off fuel flow to the idle circuit of the carburetor or to the fuel injectors to prevent overheating and afterburning in the exhaust system when the vehicle is decelerating from a certain engine speed.

✳✳WARNING

Perform these tests quickly to avoid overheating the catalytic converter. Also, on 3E engines, be careful not to damage the switch tip with the screwdriver.

3A-C ENGINES

▶ **See Figures 76 and 77**

On 3A-C engines with a feedback carburetor system, follow this procedure:

1. Connect a tachometer the engine.
2. Start the engine and check that it runs normally.
3. Unplug the electrical connector from vacuum switch (A).
4. Gradually increase the engine speed to 2,300 rpm. Check that the engine speed is fluctuating.
5. Reconnect the vacuum hose and again gradually increase the engine speed to 2,300 rpm. Check that the engine operation returns to normal.

On 3A-C engines without a feedback carburetor system, follow this procedure:

6. Start the engine.
7. Disconnect the hose from the vacuum switch and plug the hose end.
8. Check that you can feel a click from the fuel cut solenoid valve when the vacuum hose is connected and disconnected at idle.
9. Stop the engine and connect the hose.

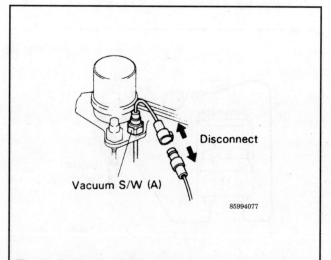

Fig. 76 Testing the fuel cut-off system on 3A-C engines with a feedback carburetor

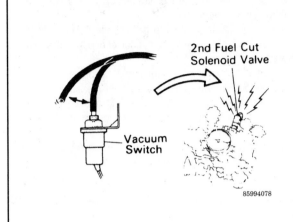

Fig. 77 Testing the fuel cut-off system on 3A-C engines without a feedback carburetor

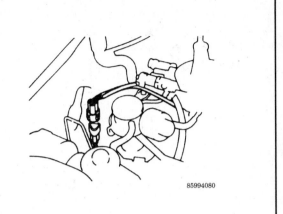

Fig. 79 With the solenoid valve disconnected, the engine should run rough, then die out

3E ENGINES

▶ **See Figures 78 and 79**

1. Connect a tachometer the engine.
2. Start the engine and check that it runs normally.
3. Gradually increase the engine speed to 2,100 rpm or less. Check that the engine speed is steady.
4. Raise the engine speed to 2,950 rpm or more. Using a screwdriver, press the tip of the throttle position switch. Check that the engine hesitates.
5. Release the throttle position switch and check that the engine speed returns to 2,950 rpm or more.
6. Unplug the solenoid valve connector at idle. Check that the idling becomes rough and that the engine eventually stops.

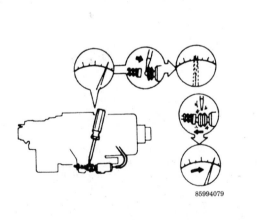

Fig. 78 Engine speed should fluctuate with the throttle position switch depressed on 3E engines

3E-E ENGINES

▶ **See Figures 80 and 81**

1. Allow the engine to reach normal operating temperature.
2. On 1990 models, follow this procedure:
   a. Unplug the connector from the throttle position sensor.
   b. Connect terminals **IDL** and **E2** on the wiring harness side.
   c. Gradually raise the engine speed and check that there is fluctuation between the fuel cut and fuel return points. The fuel cut speed is 2,300 rpm, fuel return speed is 1,700 rpm.
3. On models after 1990, follow this procedure:
   a. Connect the test probe of a tachometer to terminal **IG** (-) of the check connector.

✳✳WARNING

Never allow the tachometer terminal to touch ground as it could result in damage to the igniter and/or ignition coil. As some tachometers are not compatible with this ignition system, we recommend that you confirm the compatibility of yours before use.

   b. Increase the engine speed to at least 2,500 rpm. Check the injectors for operating (clicking) sound.
   c. Release the throttle lever, check that the injector sound stops momentarily and then resumes at approximately 1,300 rpm.
4. Remove the tachometer.

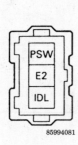

Fig. 80 Throttle position switch terminals on 1990 3E-E engines

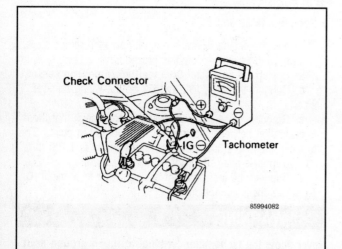

Fig. 81 Testing the fuel cut-off system on 1991 and later 3E-E engines

Manifold Absolute Pressure Sensor

▶ See Figures 82, 83, 84 and 85

➡Used on 3E-E engines.

This sensor advises the ECM of pressure changes in the intake manifold. It consists of a semi-conductor pressure converting element which converts a pressure change into an electrical signal. The ECM sends a reference signal to the MAP sensor; the change in air pressure changes the resistance within the sensor. The ECM reads the change from its reference voltage and signals its systems to react accordingly.

➡Use only a 10 megaohm digital multi-meter when testing. The use of any other type of equipment may damage the ECM and other components.

1. Unplug the vacuum sensor connector.
2. Turn the ignition switch ON.
3. Using a voltmeter, measure the voltage between terminals **VCC** and **E2** of the vacuum sensor connector. It should be between 4-6 volts.
4. Push the electrical connector back into place.
5. Disconnect the vacuum hose from the sensor.
6. Connect a voltmeter to terminals **PIM** and **E2** of the ECM. Measure and record the output voltage under ambient atmospheric pressure.
7. Apply vacuum to the sensor according to the segments show on the chart. Measure each voltage drop and compare to the chart.

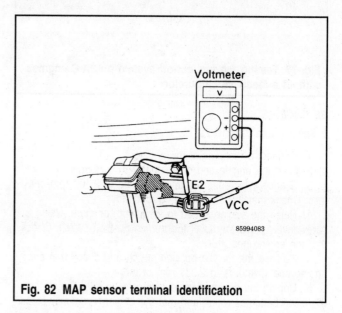

Fig. 82 MAP sensor terminal identification

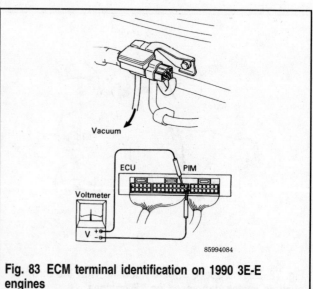

Fig. 83 ECM terminal identification on 1990 3E-E engines

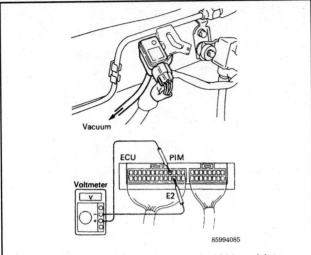

Fig. 84 ECM terminal identification on 1991 and later 3E-E engines

Voltage drop

Applied Vacuum mm HG $\left(\begin{array}{c}\text{in.Hg,}\\ \text{kPa}\end{array}\right)$	100 $\left(\begin{array}{c}3.94\\ 13.3\end{array}\right)$	200 $\left(\begin{array}{c}7.87\\ 26.7\end{array}\right)$	300 $\left(\begin{array}{c}11.81\\ 40.0\end{array}\right)$	400 $\left(\begin{array}{c}15.75\\ 53.3\end{array}\right)$	500 $\left(\begin{array}{c}19.69\\ 66.7\end{array}\right)$
Voltage drop V	0.3–0.5	0.7–0.9	1.1–1.3	1.5–1.7	1.9–2.1

Fig. 85 MAP sensor voltage drop chart

Intake Air Temperature Sensor

▶ **See Figures 86 and 87**

➡ **Used on 3E-E engines.**

The IAT sensor advises the ECM of changes in intake air temperature (and therefore air density). As air temperature of the intake varies, the ECM, by monitoring the voltage change, adjusts the amount of fuel injection according to the air temperature.

1. Unplug the electrical connector from the IAT sensor.
2. Using an ohmmeter, measure the resistance between both terminals. Refer to the chart for the proper resistance reading.
3. If the resistance is not as specified, replace the sensor.

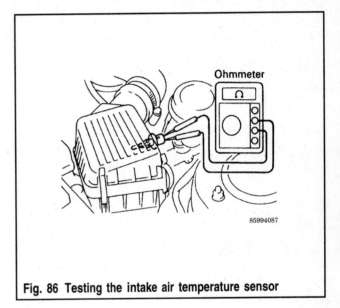

Fig. 86 Testing the intake air temperature sensor

INTAKE AIR TEMP. SENSOR

Thermistor

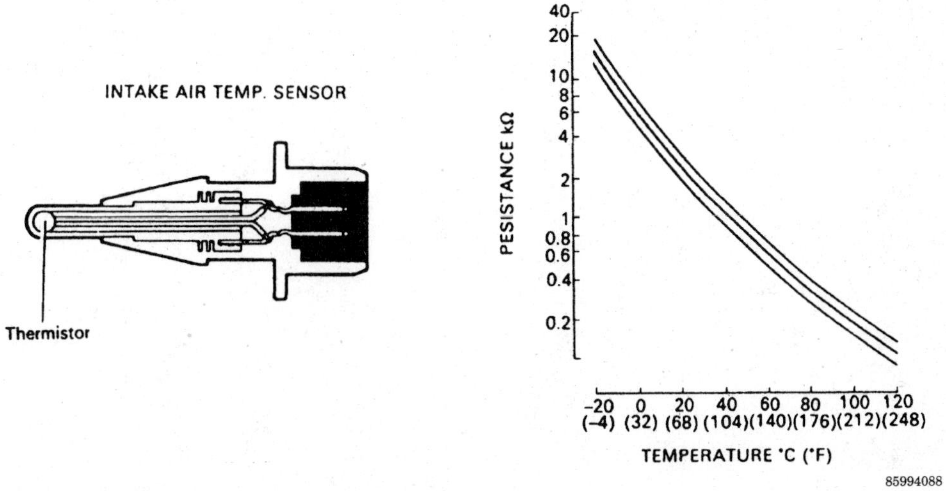

Fig. 87 IAT sensor resistance chart

Water Temperature Sensor

▶ See Figures 88 and 89

➡Used on 3E-E engines.

The water temperature sensor's function is to advise the ECM of changes in engine temperature by monitoring the changes in coolant temperature. The sensor must be handled carefully during removal. It can be damaged (thereby affecting engine performance) by impact.

1. Unplug the electrical connector from the sensor.
2. Using an ohmmeter, measure the resistance between both terminals. Refer to the chart for the proper resistance reading.
3. If the resistance is not as specified, replace the sensor.

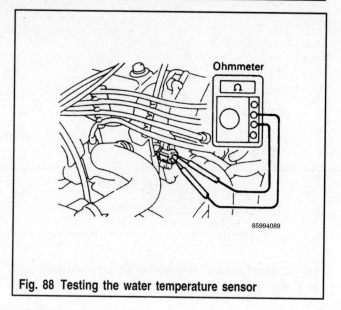

Fig. 88 Testing the water temperature sensor

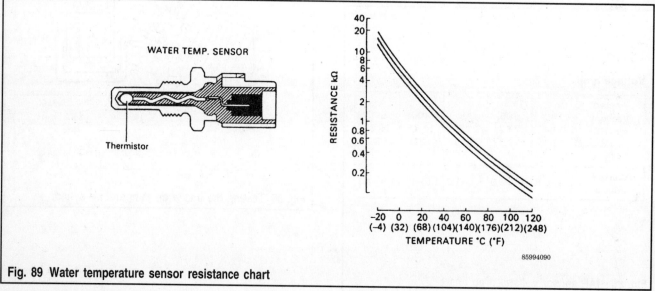

Fig. 89 Water temperature sensor resistance chart

Throttle Position Sensor

▶ See Figures 90, 91, 92, 93 and 94

➡Used on 3E-E engines.

1. Unplug the sensor connector.
2. Insert a thickness gauge between the throttle stop screw and the stop lever.
3. Using an ohmmeter, measure the resistance between each terminal. Compare the readings to the chart.

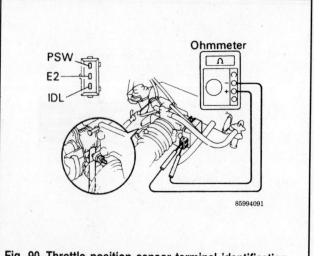

Fig. 90 Throttle position sensor terminal identification on 1990 3E-E engines

Clearance between lever and stop screw	Continuity between terminals		
	IDL – E2	PSW – E2	IDL – PSW
0.60 mm (0.0236 in.)	Continuity	No continuity	No continuity
0.80 mm (0.0315 in.)	No continuity	No continuity	No continuity
Throttle valve fully opened position	No continuity	Continuity	No continuity

85994092

Fig. 91 TPS test chart for 1990 3E-E engines

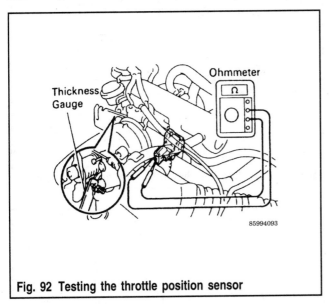

85994093

Fig. 92 Testing the throttle position sensor

Clearance between lever and stop screw	Between terminals	Resistance
0 mm (0 in.)	VTA – E2	0.2 – 0.8 kΩ
0.5 mm (0.020 in.)	IDL – E2	2.3 kΩ or less
0.70 mm (0.028 in.)	IDL – E2	Infinity
throttle valve fully opened	VTA – E2	3.3 – 10 kΩ
—	VC – E2	3 – 7 kΩ

85994095

Fig. 94 TPS test chart for 1991 and later 3E-E engines

Cold Start Injector Time Switch

▶ See Figure 95

➡Used on 3E-E engines.

Some 3E-E engines utilize a cold start injector to improve starting ability. This switch controls the length of time the injector will stay on depending on engine temperature.

1. Using an ohmmeter, measure the resistance between each of the terminals. They should be as follows:

a. Terminals **STA** and **STJ** — 20-40Ω below 86°F (30°C) or 40-60Ω when above 104°F (40°C)

b. Terminal **STA** and ground — 20-80Ω

2. If the resistance is not as specified, replace the switch.

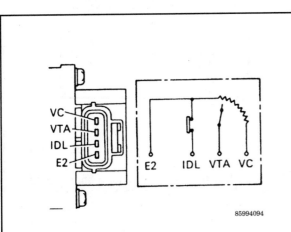

85994094

Fig. 93 TPS terminal identification on 1991 and later 3E-E engines

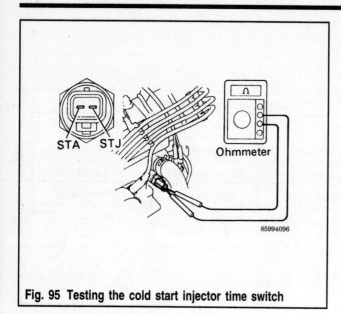

Fig. 95 Testing the cold start injector time switch

EGR Gas Temperature Sensor

▶ See Figure 96

➡Used on 3E-E engines.

1. Using an ohmmeter, measure the resistance between the two terminals. It should be as follows:
   a. 69.40-88.50kΩ at 122°F(50°C)
   b. 11.89-14.37kΩ at 212°F(100°C)
2. If the resistance is not as specified, replace the sensor.

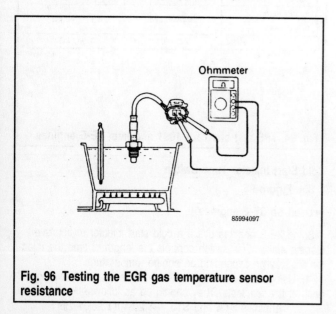

Fig. 96 Testing the EGR gas temperature sensor resistance

Idle-Up Controls

▶ See Figures 97, 98, 99 and 100

➡Used on 3E-E engines.

1. Test the water temperature sensor as described earlier.
2. Test the VSV using an ohmmeter. Check that there is continuity between the terminals. The resistance should be between 30-36Ω.
3. If it is not as specified, replace the VSV.
4. Using an ohmmeter, check that there is no continuity between each terminal and the VSV body. If there is continuity, replace the VSV.
5. Check that air does not blow from pipe E to F.
6. Apply battery voltage across the terminals. Check that air flows from pipe E to F.
7. If operation is not as specified, replace the VSV.

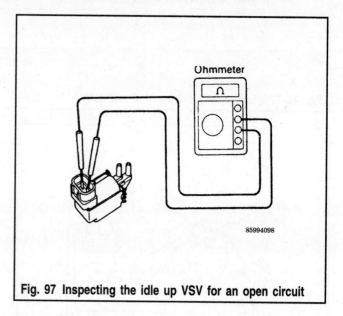

Fig. 97 Inspecting the idle up VSV for an open circuit

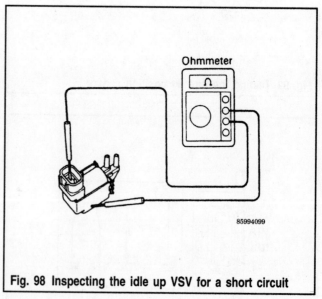

Fig. 98 Inspecting the idle up VSV for a short circuit

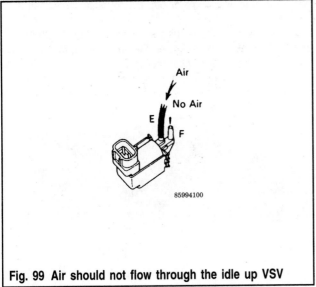

Fig. 99 Air should not flow through the idle up VSV

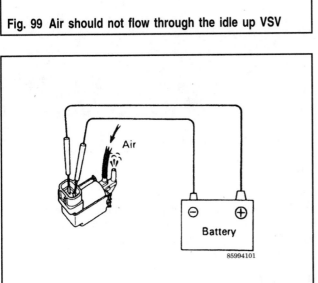

Fig. 100 Air should flow when battery voltage is applied to the idle up VSV

Fuel Pressure Controls

▶ See Figures 101, 102, 103 and 104

➡ Used on 3E-E engines.

1. Test the water temperature sensor as described earlier.
2. Test the VSV using an ohmmeter. Check that there is continuity between the terminals. The resistance should be between 30-39Ω.
3. If it is not as specified, replace the VSV.
4. Using an ohmmeter, check that there is no continuity between each terminal and the VSV body. If there is continuity, replace the VSV.
5. Check that air flows from pipe E to P.
6. Apply battery voltage across the terminals. Check that air flows from pipe E to F.
7. If operation is not as specified, replace the VSV.

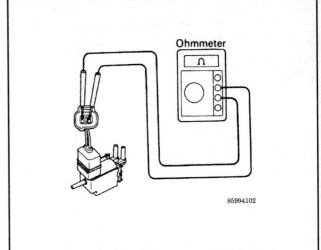

Fig. 101 Inspecting the fuel pressure VSV for an open circuit; throttle opener VSV is similar

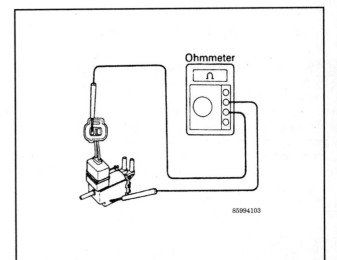

Fig. 102 Inspecting the fuel pressure VSV for a short circuit; throttle opener VSV is similar

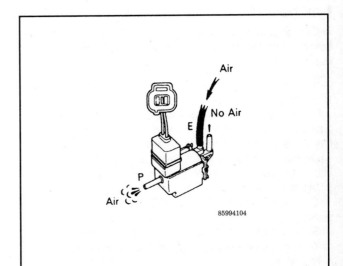

Fig. 103 No air should flow through the valve without battery voltage applied

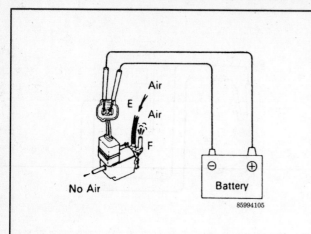

Fig. 104 Checking air flow on fuel pressure and throttle opener vacuum switching valves with battery voltage applied

Throttle Opener

➡**Used on 3E-E engines.**

1. Test the throttle position sensor as described earlier.
2. Test the VSV using an ohmmeter. Check that there is continuity between the terminals. The resistance should be between 33-39Ω.
3. If it is not as specified, replace the VSV.
4. Using an ohmmeter, check that there is no continuity between each terminal and the VSV body. If there is continuity, replace the VSV.
5. Check that air flows from pipe E to P.
6. Apply battery voltage across the terminals. Check that air flows from pipe E to F.
7. If operation is not as specified, replace the VSV.

REMOVAL & INSTALLATION

Oxygen Sensor

▶ **See Figure 105**

➡**Care should be used during the removal of the oxygen sensor. Both the sensor and its wire can be easily damaged.**

1. The best condition in which to remove the sensor is when the engine is moderately warm. This is generally achieved after two to five minutes (depending on outside temperature) of running after a cold start. The exhaust manifold has developed enough heat to expand and make the removal easier but is not so hot that it has become untouchable. Wearing heat resistant gloves is highly recommended during this repair.
2. With the ignition OFF, unplug the connector for the sensor.
3. Remove the two sensor attaching bolts.
4. Remove the oxygen sensor from the manifold.
To install:
5. During and after the removal, use great care to protect the tip of the sensor if it is to be reused. Do not allow it to come in contact with fluids or dirt. Do not attempt to clean it or wash it.
6. Apply a coat of anti-seize compound to the bolt threads but DO NOT allow any to get on the tip of the sensor.
7. Install the sensor in the manifold.
8. Reconnect the electrical connector and insure a clean, tight connection.

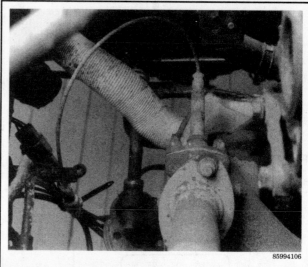

Fig. 105 A common oxygen sensor

MAP Sensor

Replacing the MAP sensor simply requires unplugging the vacuum and electrical connections, then unbolting the sensor. Inspect the vacuum hose over its entire length for any signs of cracking or splitting. The slightest leak can cause false messages to be send to the ECM.

IAT Sensor

To replace the IAT sensor:
1. Remove the air cleaner cover.
2. With the ignition OFF, unplug the electrical connector.
3. Push the IAT sensor out from inside the air cleaner housing.
To install:
4. Install the sensor, making sure it is properly placed and secure.
5. Connect the wiring harness, and install the air cleaner cover.

Water Temperature Sensor

➡**Perform this procedure only on a cold engine.**

1. Drain the cooling system as necessary.
2. With the ignition OFF, unplug the electrical connector to the sensor.
3. Using the proper sized wrench, carefully unscrew the sensor from the engine.
To install:
4. Coat the threads of the sensor with a sealant. Install the sensor and tighten it to 18 ft. lbs. (24 Nm).
5. Plug the electrical connector into the sensor.

6. Refill the coolant to the proper level. Road test the vehicle for proper operation.

Cold Start Injector Time Switch

➡**Perform this procedure only on a cold engine.**

1. Drain the cooling system as necessary.
2. With the ignition OFF, unplug the electrical connector to the switch.
3. Using the proper sized wrench, carefully unscrew the switch from the engine.

To install:

4. Coat the threads of the switch with a sealant and install it.
5. Plug the electrical connector into the switch.
6. Refill the coolant to the proper level. Road test the vehicle for proper operation.

EGR Gas Temperature Sensor

1. With the ignition OFF, unplug the electrical connector to the sensor.
2. Using the proper sized wrench, carefully unscrew the sensor from the engine.

To install:

3. Install the sensor.
4. Plug the electrical connector into the sensor.
5. Refill the coolant to the proper level. Road test the vehicle for proper operation.

Throttle Position Sensor

▶ **See Figures 106, 107, 108 and 109**

On 1990 models, follow this procedure:
1. Secure the throttle valve opening at approximately 45 degrees. Be careful not to damage any components.
2. Remove the two screws and the sensor.

To install:

3. Place the TPS over the throttle valve shaft. Do not turn the TPS when it is being installed.
4. Temporarily install the two screws. Remove the device securing the throttle valve angle.
5. Adjust the throttle position sensor, refer to Section 5.
On 1991-1994 models, follow this procedure:
6. Remove the two screws and the TPS.
7. To install, place the sensor on the throttle body as shown. Turn the sensor clockwise and install the two screws.
8. Adjust the TPS, refer to Section 5.

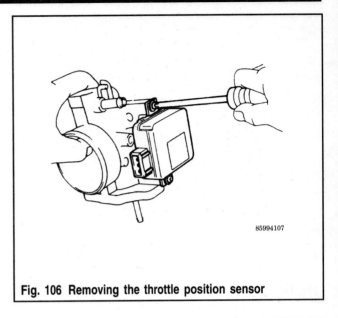

Fig. 106 Removing the throttle position sensor

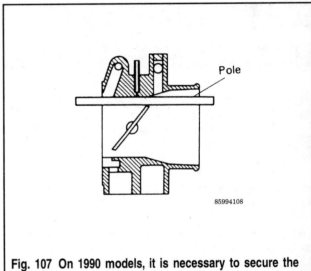

Fig. 107 On 1990 models, it is necessary to secure the throttle valve at an angle before TPS removal

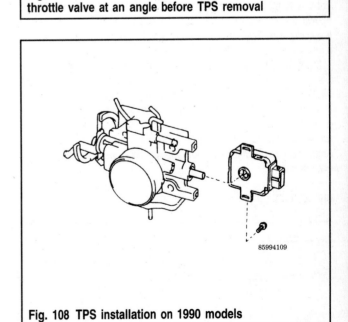

Fig. 108 TPS installation on 1990 models

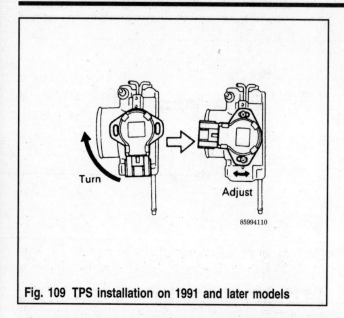

Fig. 109 TPS installation on 1991 and later models

Turn

Adjust

85994110

Vacuum Switches

Replacing the various vacuum switches simply requires unplugging the vacuum and/or electrical connections, then unbolting the switch. Inspect the vacuum hose over its entire length for any signs of cracking or splitting. The slightest leak can cause improper operation.

TROUBLE CODES

Self Diagnostics

The electronic control modules (ECM) on some 3E engines and all 3E-E engines contain a built-in self diagnosis system. When troubles with the engine control network are detected, the 'Check Engine" lamp on the dash panel will light. At the same time the trouble is identified by circuit and a diagnostic code is recorded within the ECM. This diagnostic code can be read by the number of flashes the Check Engine lamp displays when both check engine terminals are shorted together under the hood.

In the event of an internal computer malfunction, the ECM is programmed with back-up or default values. This allows the car to run on a fixed set of values for engine operation. Driveability may suffer since the driving conditions cannot be dealt with by the faulty computer. This back-up programming allows the computer to fail with out stranding the car, hence the nickname 'fail-safe". No computer is safe from failure, but a back-up system helps make the best of the situation.

Many problems in this system are the result of poor connections, vacuum leaks, charging system problems and other relatively minor conditions. Trouble code listings are included in this section as a guide to solving some of these simpler problems. However, if a problem cannot be found quickly and further diagnosis is necessary, it should be left to a qualified technician as they involve complex procedures and expensive equipment.

READING CODES

▶ See Figures 110 and 111

1. The following initial conditions must be met or the code will not be transmitted from the ECM:
   a. Battery voltage above 11 volts

   b. Throttle plate fully closed — keep your foot off the accelerator
   c. Transmission selector in neutral
   d. All accessory switches off
2. Turn the ignition switch ON, but DO NOT start the engine.
3. Use a service (jumper) wire to short together terminals **T** and **E1** of the engine check connector.

The diagnostic code(s) will be indicated by the number of flashes of the **Check Engine** light. If the system is normal, the light will blink repeatedly about every $\frac{1}{2}$ second. If a fault code is stored, its two digit code will be indicated in the pattern of the flashing. For example, code 21 would be indicated by two flashes, a pause, and one flash. There will be about a $1\frac{1}{2}$ second pause between the first and second digit of a code. If more than one code is stored, the next will be transmitted after a $2\frac{1}{2}$ second pause. Once all the codes have been flashed, the system will wait $4\frac{1}{2}$ seconds and repeat the entire series. It will continue sending the fault codes as long as the initial conditions are met and the engine check connector is shorted across terminal **T** and **E1**.

➡If more than one code is stored, they will be delivered in numerical order from the lowest to the highest, regardless of which code occurred first. The order of the codes DOES NOT indicate the order of occurrence.

4. After the code(s) have been read and recorded, turn the ignition switch to OFF and disconnect the jumper wire.

❋❋WARNING

Disconnecting the wire with the ignition ON may cause severe damage to the ECM.

Code No.	Number of check engine blinks	System	Diagnosis	Trouble area
—	 _⊓⊓⊓⊓⊓⊓⊓_ ON OFF	Normal	This appears when none of the other codes are identified.	—
12	 _⊓⊓⊓_	RPM Signal	No signal to ECU within several seconds after engine is cranked (TAC).	• Ignition coil circuit • Ignition coil • Igniter circuit • Igniter • ECU
21	 _⊓⊓⊓_	Oxygen Sensor Signal	During air-fuel ratio feedback correction, voltage output from the oxygen sensor does not exceed a set value on the lean side and the rich side continuously for a certain period.	• Oxygen sensor circuit • Oxygen sensor • ECU
22	 _⊓⊓⊓⊓_	Water Temp. Switch Signal	Open or short circuit in water temp. switch signal (TWS1, TWS2).	• No. 1 or No. 2 water temp. switch circuit • No. 1 or No. 2 water temp. switches • ECU
25	 _⊓⊓⊓⊓⊓⊓_	Lean Malfunction	• Open circuit in oxygen sensor signal (OX). • EBCV always open. • Short circuit in EBCV signal.	• Oxygen sensor circuit • Oxygen sensor • EBCV circuit • EBCV • Carburetor • ECU
26	 _⊓⊓⊓⊓⊓⊓_	Rich Malfunction	• EBCV always closed, or a clogged hose. • Open circuit in EBCV signal.	• EBCV circuit • EBCV hose • EBCV • Carburetor • ECU
31	 _⊓⊓⊓⊓_	Vacuum Switch Signal	Open or short circuit in vacuum switches signal (VSW1, VSW2).	• No. 1 or No. 2 vacuum switches signal • No. 1 or No. 2 vacuum switches • Vacuum hose • ECU
41	 _⊓⊓⊓⊓⊓_	Throttle Switch Signal	Open or short circuit in throttle switch signal (THS).	• Throttle switch circuit • Throttle switch • ECU
71	 ⊓⊓⊓⊓⊓⊓⊓_⊓	EGR Malfunction	• EGR valve normally closed, or a clogged hose. • Open circuit in EGR gas temp. sensor signal (THG).	• EGR valve • EGR hose • EGR gas temp. sensor circuit • EGR gas temp. sensor • ECU
72	 ⊓⊓⊓⊓⊓⊓_⊓⊓	Fuel cut Solenoid Signal	Open circuit in fuel cut solenoid signal (FCS).	• Fuel cut solenoid circuit • Fuel cut solenoid • ECU

85994111

Fig. 110 Trouble codes for 3E engines

Code No.	Number of "CHECK" engine blinks	System	Diagnosis	Trouble area
–	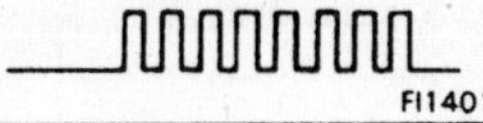 FI1401	Normal	This appears when none of the other codes are identified.	–
12	 FI1606	PRM Signal	No "NE" signal to ECU within 2 seconds after engine has been cranked.	• Distributor circuit • Distributor • Starter signal circuit • ECU
13	 FI1607	PRM Signal	No "NE" signal to ECU when engine speed is above 1,000 rpm.	• Distributor circuit • Distributor • ECU
14	 FI1608	Ignition Signal	No "IGF" signal to ECU 4 times in succession.	• Igniter and ignition coil circuit • Igniter and ignition coil • ECU
21	 FI1609	Oxygen Sensor Signal	During air-fuel ratio feedback correction, voltage output from the oxygen sensor does not exceed a set value on the lean side and the rich side continuously for a certain period.	• Oxygen sensor circuit • Oxygen sensor • ECU
22	 FI1610	Water Temp. Sensor Signal	Open or short circuit in water temp. sensor signal (THW).	• Water temp. sensor circuit • Water temp. sensor • ECU
24	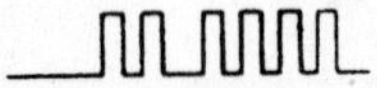 FI1611	Intake Air Temp. Sensor Signal	Open or short circuit in intake air temp. sensor signal (THA).	• Intake air temp. sensor circuit • Intake air temp. sensor • ECU
25	 FI2562	Air-Fuel Ratio Lean Malfunction	• When air-fuel ratio feedback correction value or adaptive control value continues at the upper (lean) or lower (rich) limit for a certain period of time of adaptive control value is not renewed for a certain period of time. • When marked variation is delected in engine revolutions for each cylinder during idle switch on and feedback condition. • Open or short circuit in oxygen sensor signal (ox).	• Injector circuit • Injector • Fuel line pressure • Vacuum Sensor • Air intake system • Oxygen sensor circuit • Oxygen sensor • Ignition system • Water temp. sensor • ECU
26	 FI2563	Air-Fuel Ratio Rich Malfunction		• Oxygen sensor circuit • Oxygen sensor • Injector circuit • Injector • Fuel line pressure • Cold start injector • Water temp. sensor • ECU

85994112

Fig. 111 Trouble codes for 3E-E engines

Code No.	Number of "CHECK" engine blinks	System	Diagnosis	Trouble area
31	 FI1612	Vacuum Sensor Signal	Open or short circuit intake manifold pressure signal (PIM).	• Vacuum sensor circuit • Vacuum sensor • ECU
41	 FI1614	Throttle Position Sensor Signal	The "IDL" and "PSW" signals are output simultaneously for several seconds.	• Throttle position sensor circuit • Throttle position sensor • ECU
42	 FI1615	Vehicle Speed Sensor Signal	No "SPD" signal to ECU for 8 seconds when engine speed is above 2,500 rpm and vacuum sensor pressure exceed a predetermined value [475 mm Hg (18.7 in.Hg, 63.3 kPa)]	• Vehicle speed sensor circuit • Vehicle speed sensor • ECU
43	 FI1616	Starter Signal	No "STA" signal to ECU until engine speed reaches 800 rpm with vehicle not moving.	• Ignition switch circuit • Ignition switch • ECU
71	 FI2622	EGR System Malfunction	• EGR gas temp. is below a predetermined level during operation. • Open circuit in EGR gas temp. sensor signal (THG).	• EGR valve • EGR hose • EGR gas temp. sensor circuit • EGR gas temp. sensor • VSV for EGR • VSV circuit for EGR • ECU
51	 FI1617	Switch Condition Signal	No "IDL" signal, "NSW" signal or "A/C" signal to ECU, with the check connector terminals T and E1 connected	• A/C switch circuit • A/C switch • A/C amplifier • Throttle position sensor circuit • Throttle position sensor • Neutral start switch circuit • Neutral start switch • Accelerator pedal and cable • ECU

8599412a

Fig. 112 Trouble codes for 3E-E engines

CLEARING CODES

Once the codes have been read and recorded, the memory on the ECM may be cleared of any stored codes by removing the power to the ECM for at least 1 minute. On 3E engines, remove the 15 amp RADIO No.1 fuse. On 3E-E engines, remove the 15 amp EFI fuse.

✳✳WARNING

The ignition MUST be OFF when the fuse is removed and reinstalled. Serious damage to the ECM may occur if this precaution is not followed.

VACUUM DIAGRAMS

Following is a listing of vacuum diagrams for most of the engine and emissions package combinations covered by this manual. Because vacuum circuits will vary based on various engine and vehicle options, always refer first to the vehicle emission control information label, if present. Should the label be missing, or should the vehicle be equipped with an engine

Remember that the codes are there to indicate a problem area. Don't clear the code just to get the dashboard light off — find the problem and fix it for keeps. If you erase the code and ignore the problem, the code will reset (when the engine is restarted) if the problem is still present.

The necessary time to clear the computer increases as the temperature drops. To be safe, remove the fuse for a full minute under all conditions. The system can also be cleared by disconnecting the negative battery cable, but this will require resetting other memory devices such as the clock and/or radio. If for any reason the memory does not clear, any stored codes will be retained. Any time the ECM is cleared, the car should be driven and then re-checked to confirm a normal signal from the ECM.

other than original equipment, refer to the diagrams below for the same or similar configuration.

If you wish to obtain a replacement emissions or vacuum label, most manufacturer's make these labels available for purchase. They can usually be ordered from a local dealer.

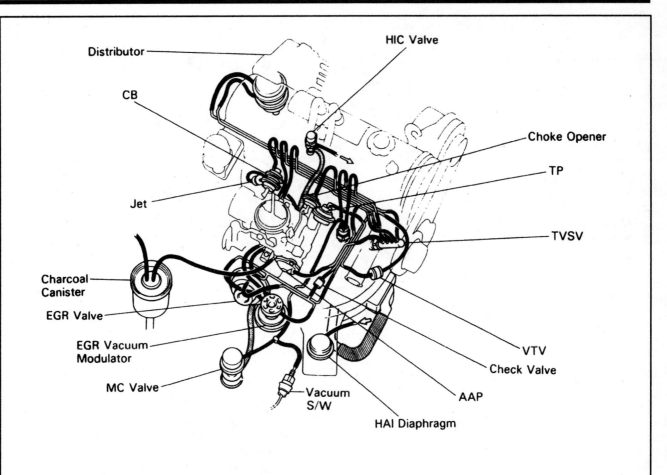

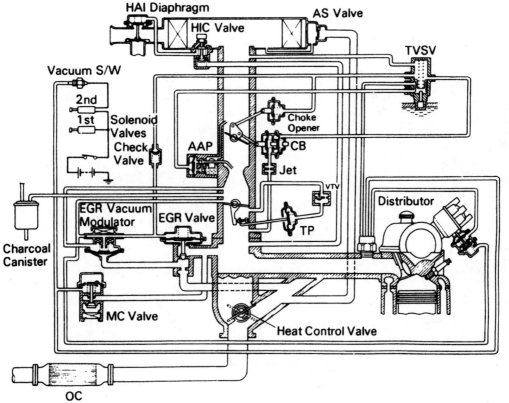

Fig. 113 Vacuum diagrams for 3A-C engines without a feedback carburetor system

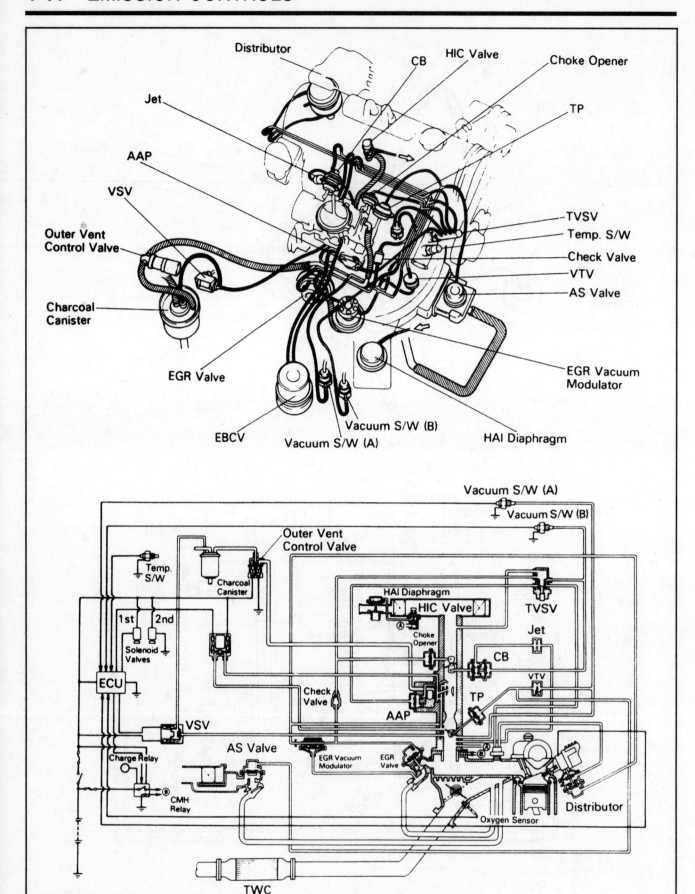

Fig. 114 Vacuum diagrams for California and Canada 3A-C engines

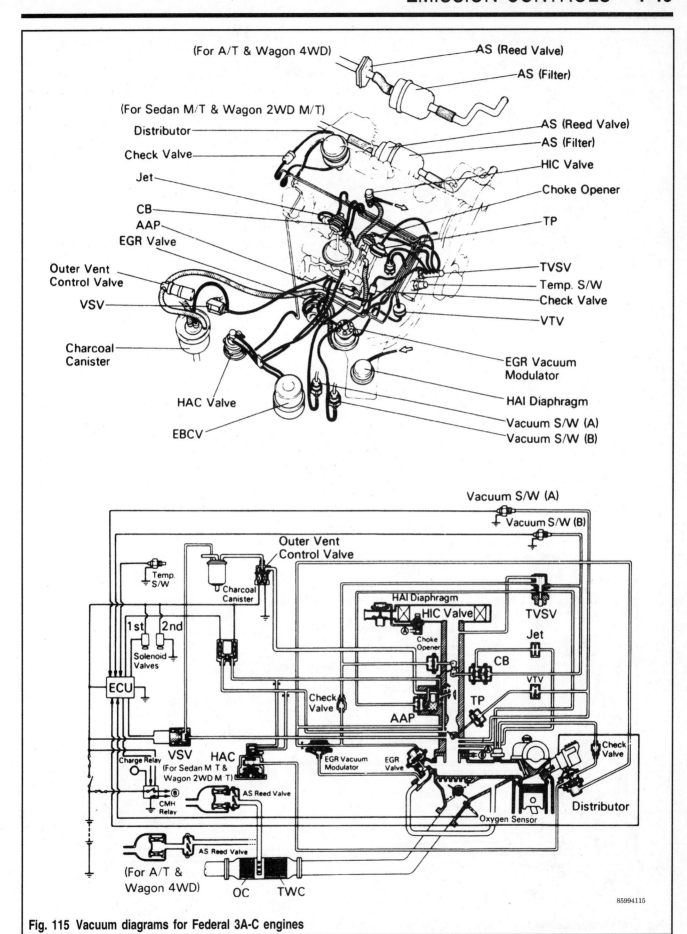

Fig. 115 Vacuum diagrams for Federal 3A-C engines

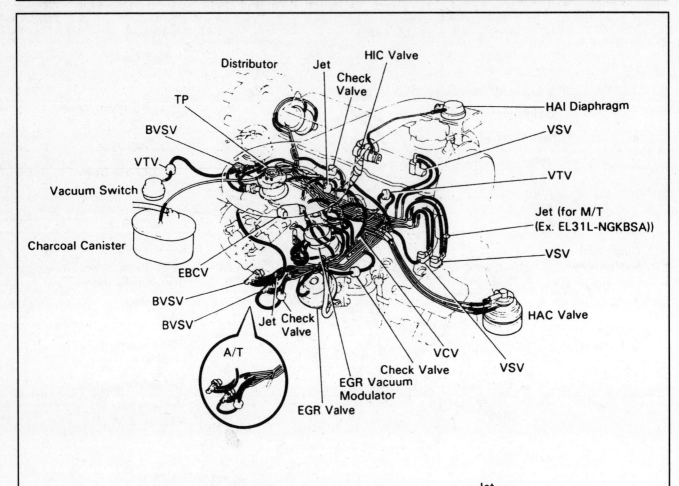

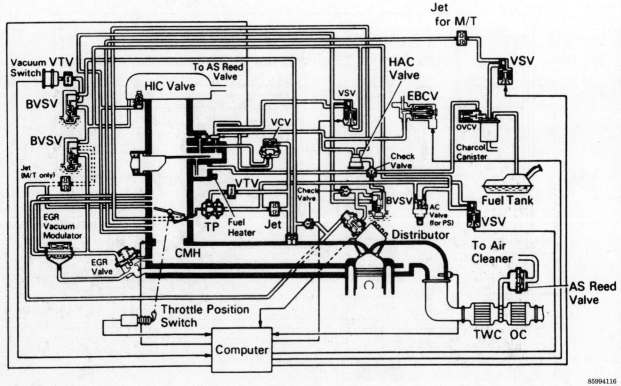

Fig. 116 Vacuum diagrams for Federal and Canada 3E engines

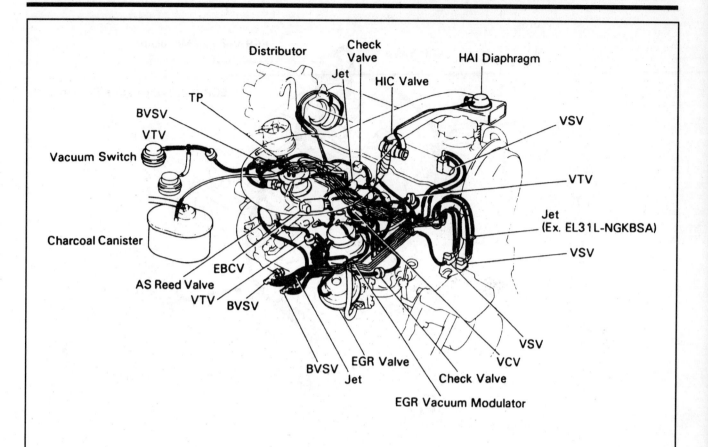

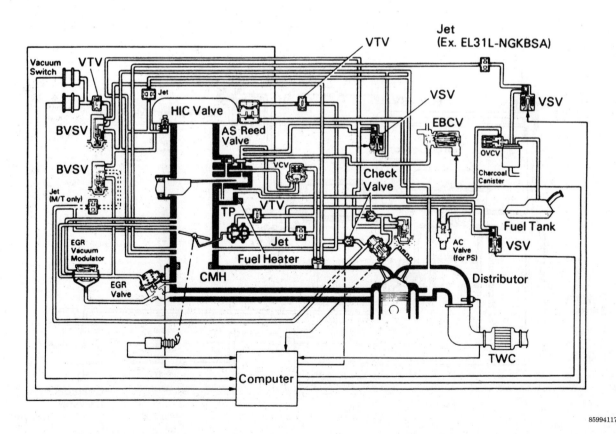

Fig. 117 Vacuum diagrams for California 3E engines

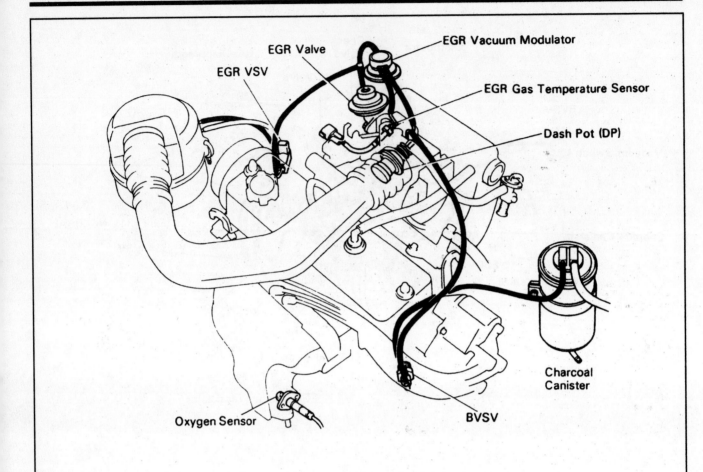

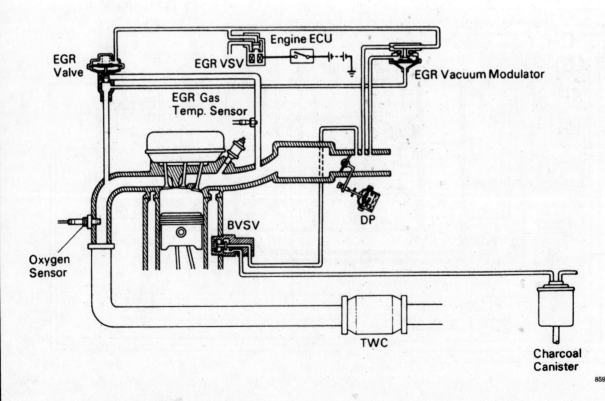

Fig. 118 Vacuum diagrams for 1990 3E-E engines

85994118

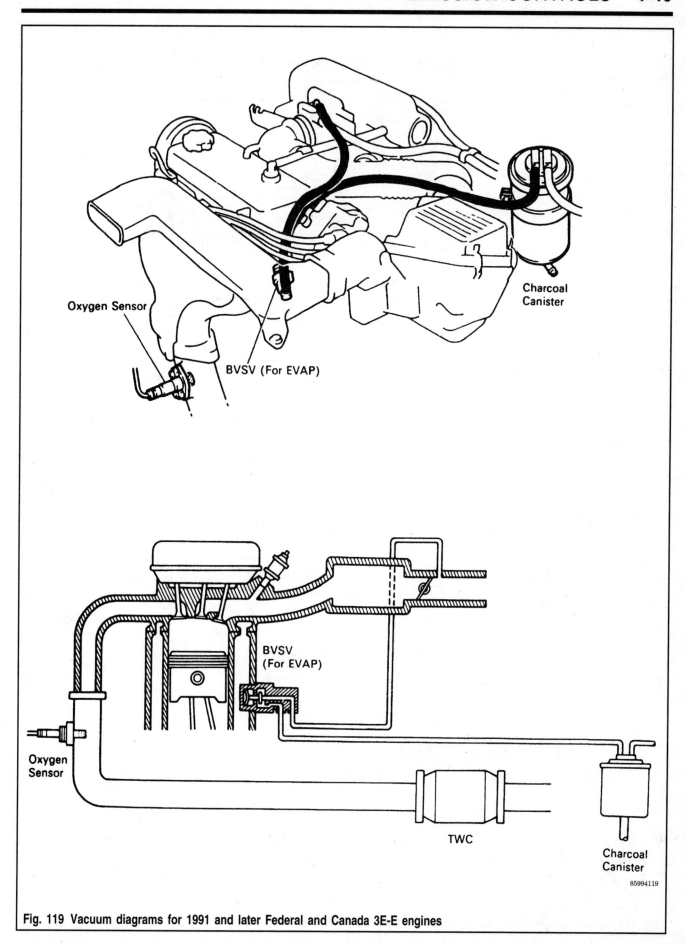

Oxygen Sensor

BVSV (For EVAP)

Charcoal Canister

BVSV (For EVAP)

Oxygen Sensor

TWC

Charcoal Canister

85994119

Fig. 119 Vacuum diagrams for 1991 and later Federal and Canada 3E-E engines

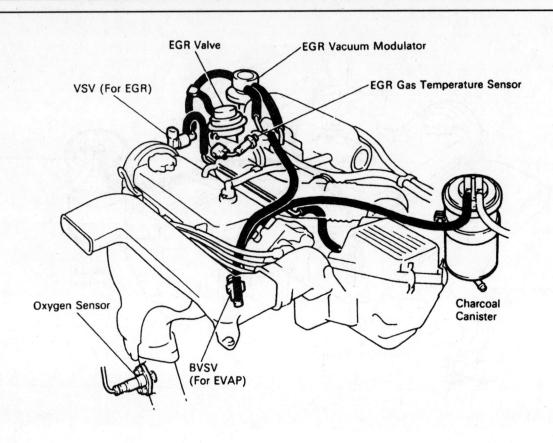

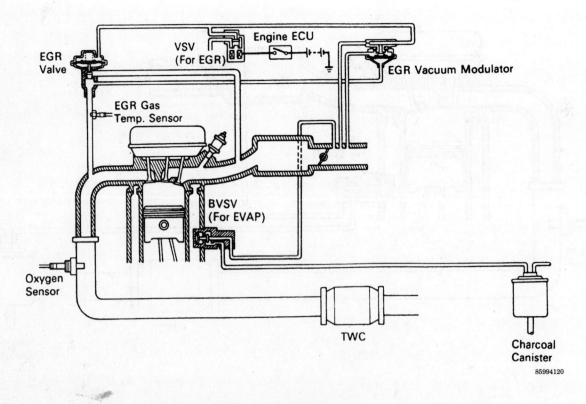

Fig. 120 Vacuum diagrams for 1991 and later California 3E-E engines

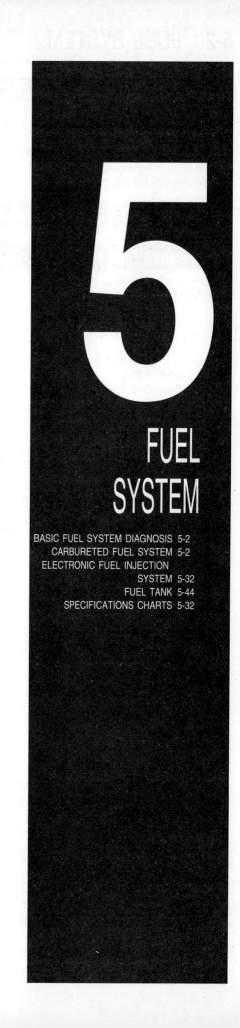

5

FUEL
SYSTEM

BASIC FUEL SYSTEM DIAGNOSIS

When there is a problem starting or driving a vehicle, two of the most important checks involve the ignition and the fuel systems. The questions most mechanics attempt to answer first, "is there adequate spark?" and "is there adequate fuel?" will often lead to solving most basic problems. For ignition system diagnosis and testing, please refer to Section 2 of this manual. If the ignition system checks out (there is spark), then you must determine if fuel system is operating properly (is there fuel?).

CARBURETED FUEL SYSTEM

Mechanical Fuel Pump

REMOVAL & INSTALLATION

▶ See Figures 1, 2, 3 and 4

The pump is located on the side of the cylinder head. To remove the fuel pump:

1. Disconnect the negative battery cable. With the engine cold and the key removed from the ignition, label and disconnect the fuel hoses from the fuel pump. Plug the lines as soon as they are removed.

✳✳CAUTION

The fuel system contains gasoline. Wear eye protection and contain spillage. Observe "no smoking/no open flame" precautions. Have a Class B-C (dry powder) fire extinguisher within arm's reach at all times.

2. Remove the mounting bolts holding the pump.
3. Remove the fuel pump.
4. Cover the fuel pump mounting face on the cylinder head.

To install:
5. Always use a new gasket. Place the fuel pump in position and install the two bolts. Tighten evenly to 13 ft. lbs. (18 Nm).
6. Connect the hoses to the fuel pump.
7. Start the engine and check for leaks.

TESTING

▶ See Figures 5, 6, 7, 8, 9, 10 and 11

Before performing any checks on the fuel pump, two conditions must be met. First, the pump must be internally "wet". Run a small amount of fuel into the pump so that the check valves will seal properly when tested. Dry valves may not seal and will yield false test results.

Hold the pump without blocking either pipe and operate the pump lever, noting the amount of force needed to move it. This is the reference point for all the tests. Do not apply more than this amount of force to the lever during the testing. Excessive force can damage an otherwise usable pump.

1. Block off the outlet and return pipes with your fingers. Operate the lever. There should be an increase in arm play and it should move freely.

Fig. 1 Label the hoses before disconnecting them. Most clamps can be loosened by pressing the tangs together and sliding the clamp upwards

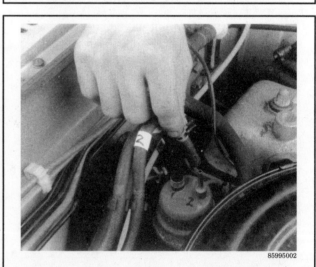

Fig. 2 Twist and pull, to remove the hoses from the fuel pump

2. Block the inlet port with your finger and operate the lever. The arm should lock when the normal amount of force is applied.

3. The diaphragm is checked by blocking the inlet, outlet and return pipes. When normal force is applied to the lever, the lever should lock and not move. Any lever motion indicates a ruptured diaphragm. This is a common cause of poor fuel

Fig. 3 The fuel pump is usually secured by two nuts or bolts

Fig. 4 Pull the fuel pump out of it's mounting boss on the cylinder head

mileage and poor acceleration since the correct amount of fuel is not being delivered to the carburetor.

➡**The fuel pump must pass all three of these tests to be considered usable. If the pump fails one or more tests, it must be replaced.**

4. Check the oil seal within the pump. Block off the vent hole in the lower part of the pump housing. The lever arm should lock when normal force is applied.

Carburetor

The carburetor is the most complex part of the fuel system. Carburetors vary in construction, but they all operate the same way; their job is to supply the correct mixture of fuel and air to the engine in response to varying conditions.

Despite their complexity, carburetors function on a simple physical principle known as the venturi principle. Air is drawn into the engine by the pumping action of the pistons. As the air enters the top of the carburetor, it passes through a venturi or restriction in the throttle bore. The air speeds up as it passes through the venturi, causing a slight drop in pressure. This pressure drop pulls fuel from the float bowl through a nozzle in the throttle bore. The air and fuel mix to form a fine mist, which is distributed to the cylinders through the intake manifold.

The carburetor used on 3A and 3A-C engines is a conventional 2-barrel, downdraft type similar to domestic carburetors. The circuits are: primary, for normal operational requirements; secondary, to supply high speed fuel needs; float, to supply fuel to the primary and secondary circuits; accelerator, to supply fuel for quick and safe acceleration; and finally, choke, for reliable starting in cold weather.

A variable venturi carburetor is used on 3E engines. A suction piston maintains the air flow velocity through the venturi at a nearly constant level by changing the cross-sectional area of the venturi according to the amount of intake air. The circuits in this V-type carburetor are: main, supplies fuel for normal operation requirements; by-pass, supplies fuel during idle; float, to supply fuel to the circuits; and accelerator, to supply additional fuel during quick acceleration.

It's important to remember that carburetors seldom give trouble during normal operation. Other than changing the fuel and air filters and making sure the idle speeds are proper at every tune-up, there's not much maintenance you can perform on the average carburetor.

PRELIMINARY ADJUSTMENTS

The following adjustments are performed with the carburetor removed from the engine. Adjustments on carburetors interrelate; if you change one setting you may affect other adjustments. Therefore, these procedures must performed in the order presented. Read the procedures thoroughly before continuing.

Float Level
▶ **See Figures 12, 13, 14, 15, 16 and 17**

➡**Performed on 3A, 3A-C and 3E engines.**

It will be necessary to remove the air horn from the carburetor to gain access to the float. Follow the procedures outlined in carburetor overhaul.

1. Remove the float, needle valve, spring and plunger.
2. Remove the pin clip from the needle valve.
3. Install the needle valve, spring and plunger onto the seat.
4. Install the float and pivot pin.
5. Allow the float to hang down by it's own weight. Check the clearance between the float tip and the carburetor body without the gasket on the air horn.
6. Clearance should be as follows:
   a. 3A and 3A-C engines — 0.283 in. (7.2mm)
   b. 3E engines — 0.169 in. (4.3mm)
7. Adjust, if necessary, by bending the portion of the float lip marked (A) in the illustration.
8. Lift up the float and check the clearance between the needle valve plunger and the float lip.

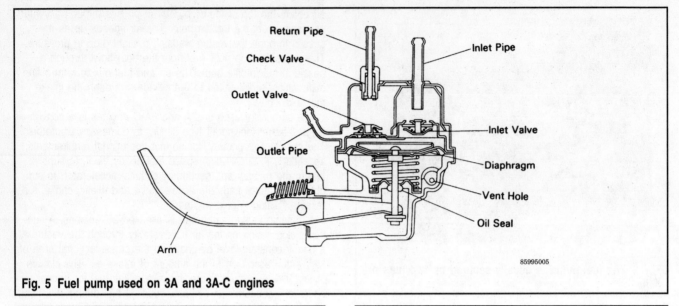

Fig. 5 Fuel pump used on 3A and 3A-C engines

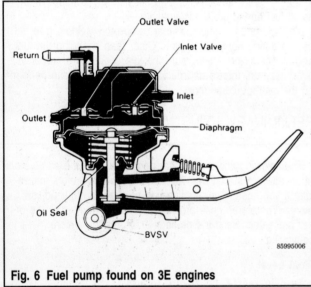

Fig. 6 Fuel pump found on 3E engines

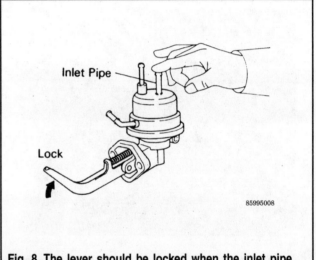

Fig. 8 The lever should be locked when the inlet pipe is blocked

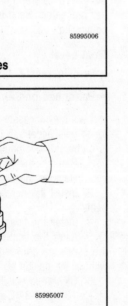

Fig. 7 With the return and outlet pipes blocked, the lever should not be locked

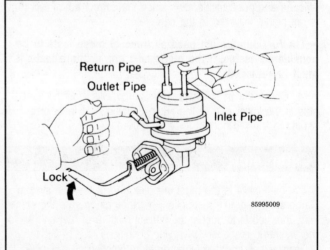

Fig. 9 The pump lever should be locked when all pipes are blocked

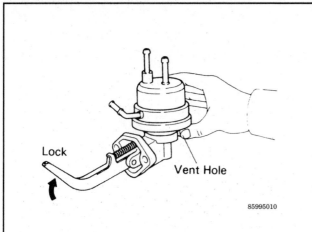

Fig. 10 The oil seal can be checked by blocking off the vent hole. The pump lever should be locked

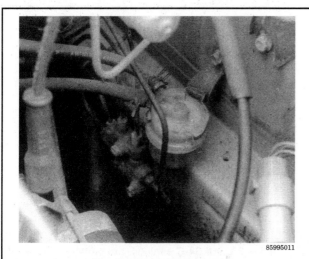

Fig. 11 The fuel filter and lines should also be checked for leaks and restrictions

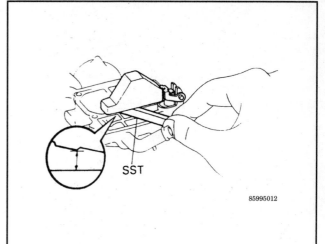

Fig. 12 Checking the float level raised position on 3A and 3A-C engines

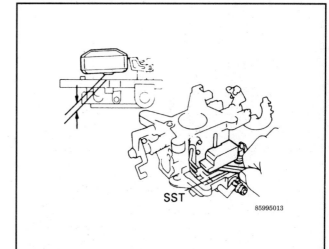

Fig. 13 Checking the float level raised position on 3E engines

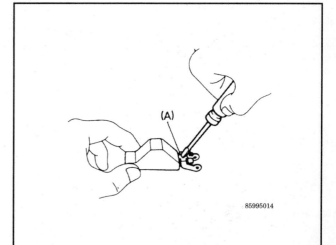

Fig. 14 Adjust the float level raised position by bending the portion of the float lip indicated

9. Clearance should be as follows:
   a. 3A and 3A-C engines — 0.0657-0.0783 in. (1.67-1.99mm)
   b. 3E engines — 0.035-0.043 in. (0.9-1.1mm)
10. Adjust by bending the portion of the float lip marked (B) in the illustration.
11. After adjusting the float level, remove the float, plunger, spring and needle valve.
12. Assemble the pin clip onto the needle valve.
13. Install the needle valve assembly, float and pivot pin. Assemble the carburetor following the procedures in carburetor overhaul.

Throttle Valve Opening

▶ See Figures 18, 19, 20, 21, 22 and 23

➡Performed on 3A, 3A-C and 3E engines.

1. Check the full opening angle of the throttle valve (primary throttle valve on 3A and 3A-C).

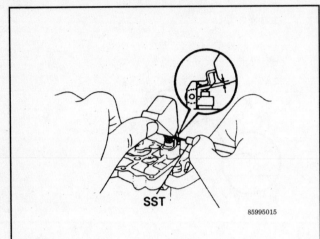

Fig. 15 Checking the float level lowered position on 3A and 3A-C engines

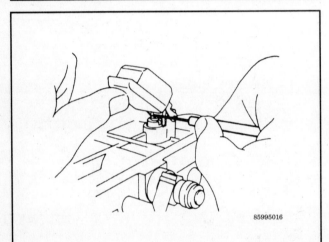

Fig. 16 Checking the float level lowered position on 3E engines

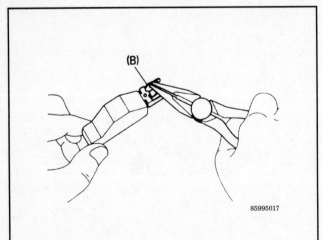

Fig. 17 Adjust the float level lowered position by bending the portion of the float lip shown

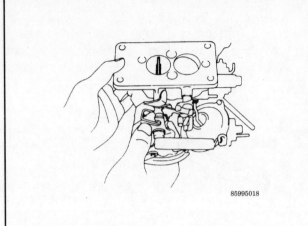

Fig. 18 Checking the primary throttle valve opening on 3A and 3A-C engines

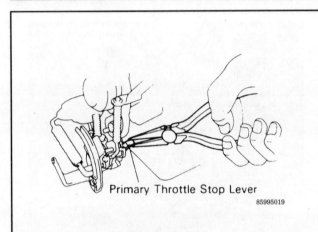

Fig. 19 On 3A and 3A-C engines, the primary throttle valve opening can be adjusted by bending the primary throttle stop lever

2. The throttle valve angle should be as follows:
   a. 3A and 3A-C engines — 90 degrees from horizontal
   b. 3E engines — 87-93 degrees from horizontal
3. Adjust by bending the throttle lever stop (primary stop on 3A and 3A-C).
4. On 3A and 3A-C engines, it will also be necessary to adjust the secondary throttle valve opening.
   a. Check the full opening angle of the secondary throttle valve.
   b. The secondary throttle valve angle should be 75 degrees from horizontal.
   c. Adjust by bending the secondary throttle lever stop.

Kick-Up Setting

▶ See Figures 24 and 25

➡ Performed on 3A and 3A-C engines.

1. With the primary throttle valve fully opened, check the clearance between the secondary throttle valve and the body.

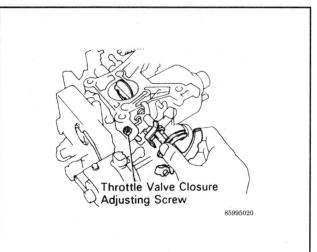

Fig. 20 Checking the throttle valve opening on 3E engines

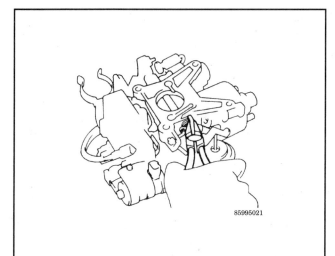

Fig. 21 Bend the throttle lever stopper on 3E engines to adjust the throttle valve opening

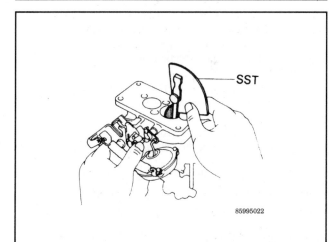

Fig. 22 On 3A and 3A-C engines, the secondary throttle valve opening should also be checked

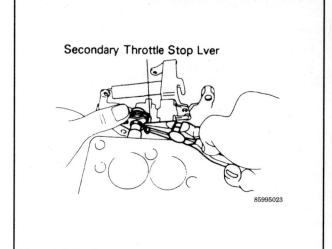

Fig. 23 Adjusting the secondary throttle valve opening on 3A and 3A-C engines

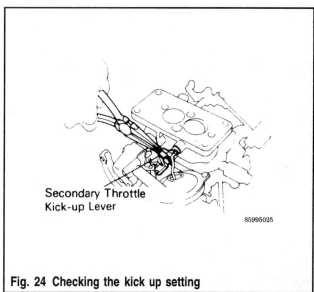

Fig. 24 Checking the kick up setting

2. The clearance should be as follows:
   a. Feedback carburetors — 0.0063 in. (0.16mm)
   b. Non-feedback carburetors — 0.0091 in. (0.23mm)
3. Adjust by bending the secondary throttle kick-up lever.

Secondary Touch Angle

▶ See Figures 26 and 27

➡ Performed on 3A and 3A-C engines.

1. Check the primary throttle valve opening angle at the point where the primary kick lever just touches the secondary kick lever.
2. The throttle valve opening angle should be 45 degrees from horizontal.
3. Adjust by bending the secondary throttle touch lever.

Automatic Choke

▶ See Figure 28

➡ Performed on 3A and 3A-C engines.

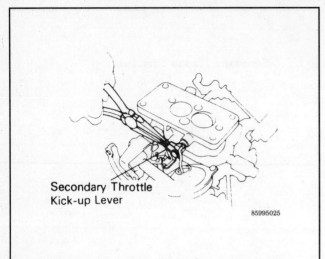

Fig. 25 The setting can be adjusted by bending the secondary throttle kick up lever

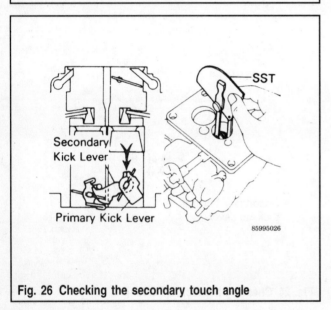

Fig. 26 Checking the secondary touch angle

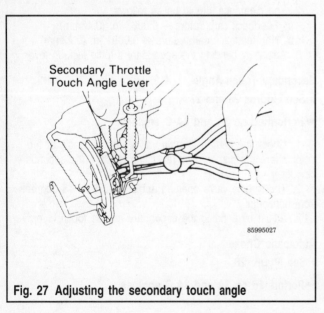

Fig. 27 Adjusting the secondary touch angle

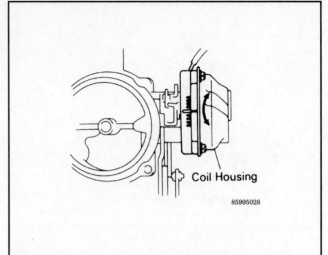

Fig. 28 The automatic choke can be adjusted on 3A and 3A-C engines with non-feedback carburetors

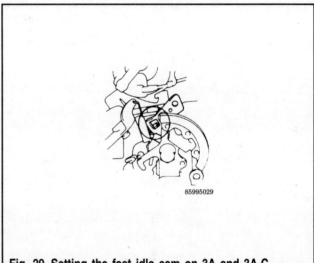

Fig. 29 Setting the fast idle cam on 3A and 3A-C engines

The automatic choke coil is adjustable on some 3A and 3A-C engines. If adjustment is possible, follow these procedures.

1. Set the coil housing index line so that it is aligned with the scale center line on the carburetor.

2. Depending on vehicle operating conditions, turn the coil housing to adjust. If the starting mixture is too rich, turn the housing clockwise. If this mixture is too lean, turn the housing counter-clockwise.

Remember, these are for starting mixtures only. This will not adjust idle or any other mixture settings.

Preliminary Fast Idle Adjustment

▶ **See Figures 29, 30, 31, 32, 33, 34, 35 and 36**

➡Performed on 3A, 3A-C and 3E engines.

3A AND 3A-C ENGINES

1. Set the throttle shaft lever to the first step of the fast idle cam.

2. With the choke valve fully closed, check the primary throttle valve angle.

3. The throttle valve angle should be as follows:
  a. Feedback carburetor — 20 degrees from horizontal
  b. Non-feedback carburetor — 21 degrees from horizontal
4. Adjust by turning the fast idle adjusting screw.

3E ENGINES

1. Set the fast idle adjusting cam to the roller of the throttle lever.
2. Measure the throttle valve angle. It should be as follows:
  a. Manual transaxle — 18.7 degrees from horizontal
  b. Automatic transaxle — 19 degrees from horizontal
3. Adjust by turning the No. 1 fast idle adjusting screw.
4. Separate the fast idle adjusting cam from the fast idle lever.
5. Using a screwdriver, pry open a gap of at least 0.20 in. (5mm) between the fast idle cam and the cold enrichment rod. Allow the gap to close again.
6. Flush out the compensator water pipe for 2-3 minutes with water. Do not allow water to enter the carburetor.
7. Apply vacuum to the throttle positioner diaphragms and measure the throttle angle.
8. Compare the temperature of the water used to flush the compensator to the chart and use the corresponding angles.
9. Adjust by turning the No. 2 fast idle adjusting screw.

Preliminary Throttle Positioner Adjustment

▶ See Figures 37, 38 and 39

➡Performed on 3E engines.

1. Remove the wax back springs. These must remain off for the remainder of the adjustments.
2. Measure the throttle valve angle.
3. It should be 13.2 degrees from horizontal. Adjust by turning the throttle positioner adjusting screw.

Unloader

▶ See Figures 40, 41 and 42

➡Performed on 3A, 3A-C and 3E engines.

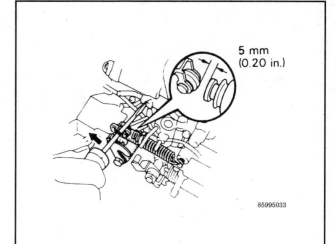
Fig. 33 Opening a gap between the fast idle cam and cold enrichment rod

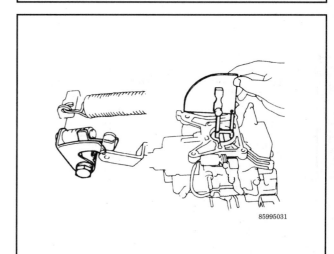
Fig. 31 Setting the fast idle adjusting cam and checking the throttle valve angle on 3E engines

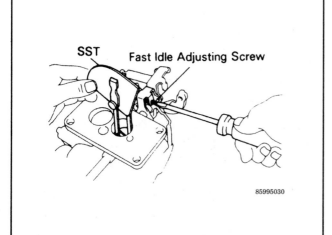
Fig. 30 Checking and setting the preliminary fast idle on 3A and 3A-C engines

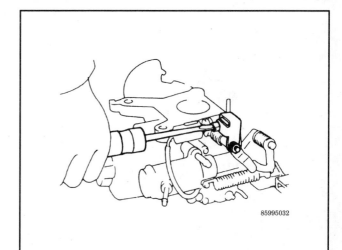
Fig. 32 No. 1 fast idle adjusting screw location on 3E engines

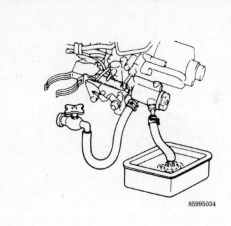

Fig. 34 Check the temperature of the water being used to flush the compensator

Water Temperature	Throttle Valve Angle
5°C (41°F)	15.5°
10°C (50°F)	15.0°
15°C (59°F)	14.5°
20°C (68°F)	14.0°
25°C (77°F)	13.5°

Fig. 35 Water temperature/throttle valve angle correlation chart

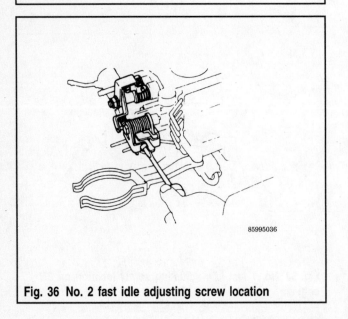

Fig. 36 No. 2 fast idle adjusting screw location

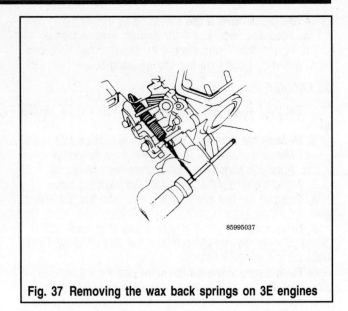

Fig. 37 Removing the wax back springs on 3E engines

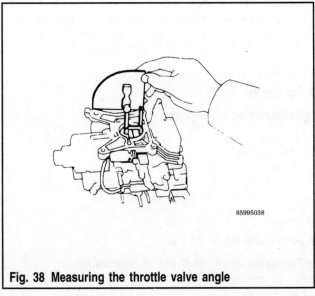

Fig. 38 Measuring the throttle valve angle

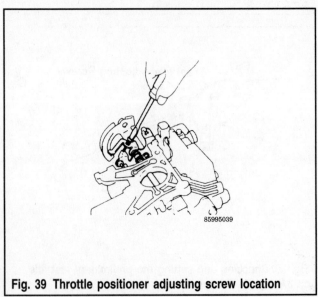

Fig. 39 Throttle positioner adjusting screw location

3A AND 3A-C ENGINES

1. With the primary throttle valve fully opened, check the choke valve angle.

2. The angle should be as follows:
  a. Feedback carburetor — 41 degrees from horizontal
  b. Non-feedback carburetor — 47 degrees from horizontal

3. Adjust by bending the unloader lever.

3E ENGINES

1. Apply vacuum to the throttle positioner diaphragms.

2. With the throttle valve fully opened, measure the piston lift stroke.

3. It should be more than 0.31 in. (8mm).

Choke Opener

▶ See Figures 43, 44 and 45

➡Performed on 3A and 3A-C engines.

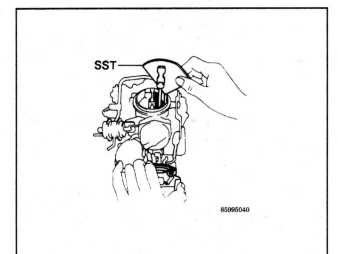

Fig. 40 Checking the choke valve angle on 3A and 3A-C engines

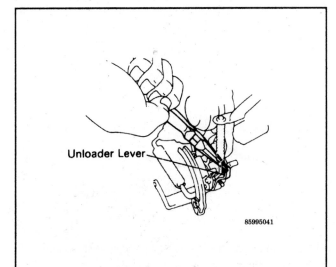

Fig. 41 Adjust by bending the unloader lever

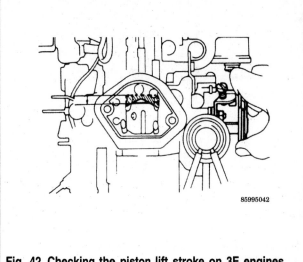

Fig. 42 Checking the piston lift stroke on 3E engines

1. Set the fast idle cam while holding the throttle slightly open.

2. Push the choke valve closed and hold it closed as you release the throttle valve.

3. Apply vacuum to the choke breaker diaphragm.

4. Check the choke valve angle. It should be 77 degrees from horizontal.

5. Adjust by bending the relief lever.

Choke Breaker

▶ See Figures 46, 47, 48 and 49

➡Performed on 3A and 3A-C engines.

1. Fully close the choke valve.

2. Apply vacuum to choke breaker diaphragm (A).

3. Check the choke valve angle. The angle should be as follows:
  a. Feedback carburetors — 38 degrees from horizontal
  b. Non-feedback carburetors — 39 degrees from horizontal

4. Adjust by bending the relief lever.

5. Apply vacuum to choke breaker diaphragms (A) and (B).

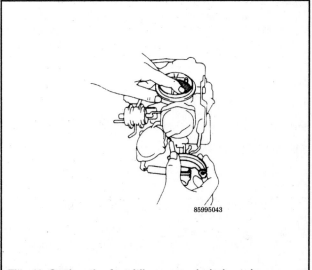

Fig. 43 Setting the fast idle cam and choke valve

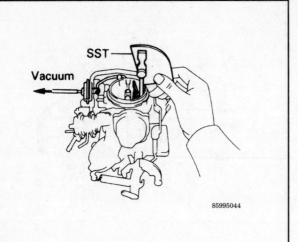

Fig. 44 Checking the choke valve angle with vacuum applied to the choke breaker

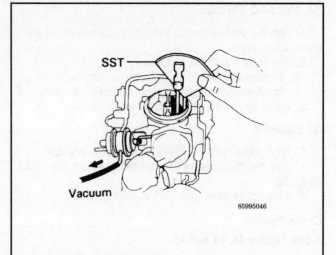

Fig. 46 With vacuum applied to diaphragm (A), measure the choke valve angle

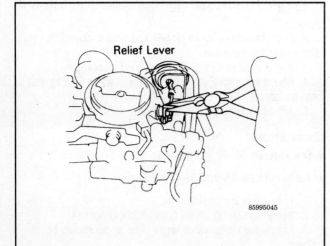

Fig. 45 Adjust the choke opener by bending the relief lever

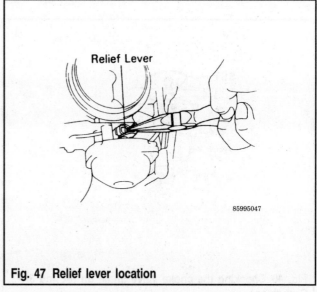

Fig. 47 Relief lever location

6. Check the choke valve angle. The angle should be as follows:
    a. Feedback carburetors — 55 degrees from horizontal
    b. Non-feedback carburetors — 50 degrees from horizontal
7. Adjust, if necessary, by turning the diaphragm adjusting screw.

Pump Stroke

▶ See Figures 50, 51 and 52

➡Performed on 3A, 3A-C and 3E engines.

3A AND 3A-C ENGINES

1. With the choke valve fully open, check the length of the pump stroke.
2. The length of the stroke should be as follows:
    a. Feedback carburetors — 0.157 in. (4mm)
    b. Non-feedback carburetors — 0.118 in. (3mm)
3. Adjust the pump stroke by bending the connecting link.

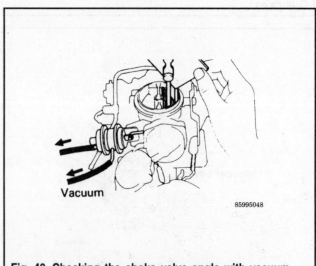

Fig. 48 Checking the choke valve angle with vacuum applied to both diaphragms (A) and (B)

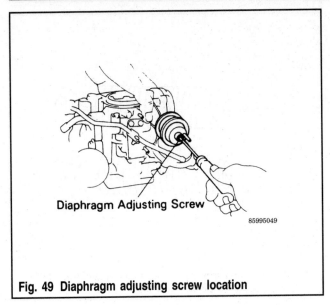

Fig. 49 Diaphragm adjusting screw location

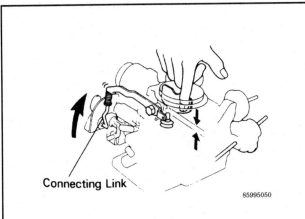

Fig. 50 Checking the pump stroke on 3A and 3A-C engines. It can be adjusted by bending the connecting link

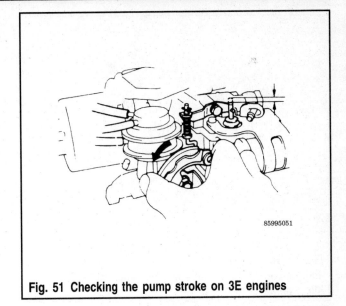

Fig. 51 Checking the pump stroke on 3E engines

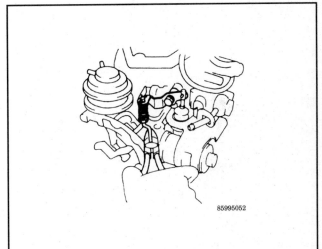

Fig. 52 On 3E engines, bend the connecting link here to adjust pump stroke

3E ENGINES

1. Measure the length of the pump stroke.
2. Length of the pump stroke should be 0.217 in. (5.5mm).
3. Adjust, if necessary, by bending the connecting link.

Preliminary Throttle Position Switch Adjustment

◆ **See Figures 53, 54, 55 and 56**

➡ **Performed on 3E engines.**

1. Check that the fast idle cam and the auxiliary fast idle cam do not move.
2. With the throttle valve fully opened, check that the switch has continuity.
3. Slowly return the from the full open position. At the point where there is no continuity through the switch, measure the throttle valve angle.
4. The angle should be 11.5 degrees from horizontal.

5. If necessary, adjust the throttle position switch adjusting screw.
6. The wax back springs, which were removed while performing the preliminary throttle positioner adjustment, can now be re-installed. Be sure the spring's hooks do not overlap.

FINAL ADJUSTMENTS

The following final adjustments are performed with the carburetor installed on the engine. Before making any adjustments to the carburetor, ALL of the following conditions must be met, unless otherwise noted:

- All accessories switched off.
- Ignition timing correctly set.
- Transmission in neutral, parking brake set, front and rear wheels blocked.

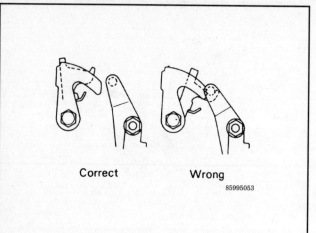

Fig. 53 When checking the throttle position switch adjustment, place the fast idle cam and auxiliary fast idle cam as shown

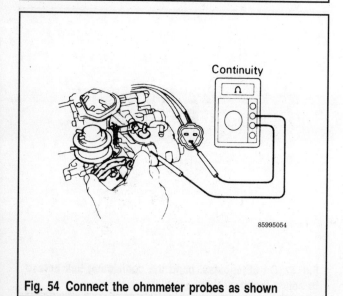

Fig. 54 Connect the ohmmeter probes as shown

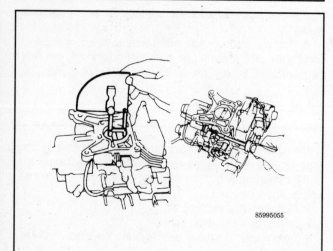

Fig. 55 Measuring the throttle valve angle and adjusting the throttle position switch

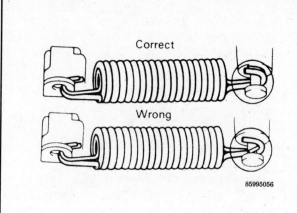

Fig. 56 When installing the wax back springs, be sure the spring's hooks do not overlap

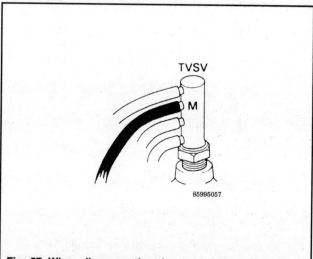

Fig. 57 When disconnecting the vacuum hose from port M, plug the port, not the hose

- Fuel level (float level) correctly set; view the fuel level in the small window on the right side of the carburetor, if equipped.
- Tachometer properly connected. See Section 2 for details.

❋❋CAUTION

The engine will be running during adjustments; be careful of moving parts and belts! Keep loose fitting clothes and long hair well away from the engine area!

Idle Speed

➥Performed on 3A, 3A-C and 3E engines.

Follow the procedures outlined in Section 2.

Fast Idle

➥Performed on 3A, 3A-C and 3E engines.

Follow the procedures outlined in Section 2.

Throttle Positioner

▶ See Figures 57, 58, 59, 60, 61, 62, 63 and 64

➡ Performed on 3A, 3A-C and 3E engines.

3A AND 3A-C ENGINES

1. Remove the air cleaner, then plug the Air Suction (AS) and Hot Idle Compensator (HIC) hoses.
2. Disconnect the hose from the Thermostatic Vacuum Switching Valve (TVSV) port **M** and plug the port. Disconnect the vacuum hose from Throttle Positioner (TP) diaphragm and plug the hose.
3. Check the engine speed. It should be at 1,400 rpm.
4. If necessary, adjust the TP adjusting screw.
5. Reconnect the vacuum hose to the TP diaphragm and check that the engine returns to normal idle.
6. Remove the plug and reconnect the vacuum hose to TVSV port **M**.

3E ENGINES

1. Disconnect the vacuum hose from the TP diaphragm (A) and plug the hose end.
2. Disconnect the vacuum hose from the EGR valve and plug the hose end.
3. Check that the TP is set at the first step. Engine speed should be at 1,100 rpm.
4. Adjust the TP screw, if necessary.

➡ Adjustment must be made with the cooling fan OFF.

5. Reconnect the vacuum hose to diaphragm (A).
6. Disconnect and plug the vacuum hose from diaphragm (B).
7. Check that the TP is set at the second step. Engine speed should be at 1,800-2,200 rpm.
8. Reconnect the vacuum hose to the diaphragm and the EGR valve.

Throttle Position (TP) Switch

▶ See Figures 65 and 66

➡ Performed on 3E engines.

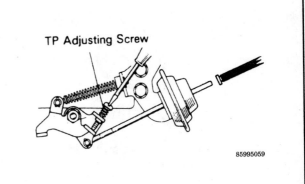

Fig. 59 Throttle positioner adjusting screw location on 3A and 3A-C engines

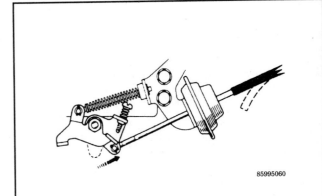

Fig. 60 Check that the idle speed returns to normal with the hose connected. Be sure to reconnect the hose to port M on the TVSV as well

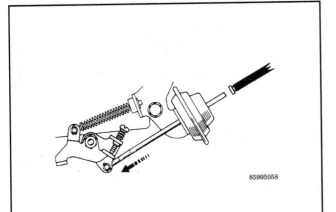

Fig. 58 With the vacuum hose disconnected from the diaphragm, the throttle positioner rod should move as shown

Fig. 61 Disconnecting and plugging the vacuum hose from diaphragm A

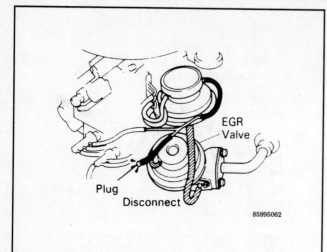

Fig. 62 The vacuum hose from the EGR valve should be disconnected and plugged as well

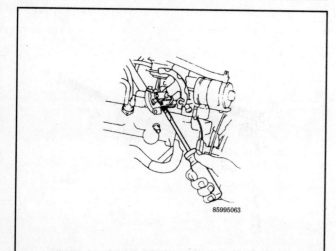

Fig. 63 Throttle positioner adjusting screw location on 3E engines

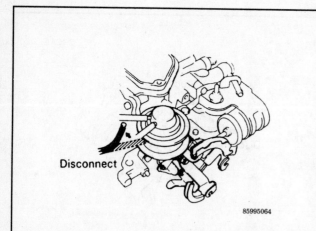

Fig. 64 Disconnecting and plugging the vacuum hose from diaphragm B

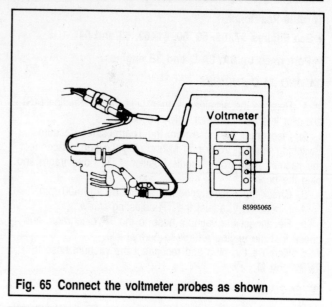

Fig. 65 Connect the voltmeter probes as shown

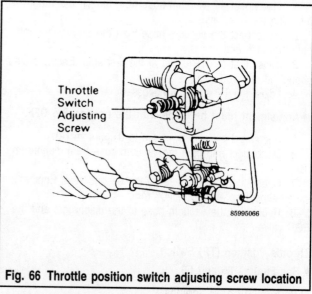

Fig. 66 Throttle position switch adjusting screw location

1. Using a voltmeter, place the positive probe to the TP switch terminal and the negative probe to the carburetor body.

2. From idle, open the throttle slowly.

3. As this is done, check the engine speed when the voltage drops from 12 to 0 volts. This should occur at 1,400 rpm.

4. Adjust the the throttle position switch adjusting screw, if necessary.

Idle Mixture

➡**Performed on 3A, 3A-C and 3E engines.**

This procedure should be performed only if the idle mixture screws were disturbed during overhaul. Refer to Section 2 for procedures.

REMOVAL & INSTALLATION

▶ See Figures 67, 68, 69, 70, 71, 72, 73, 74, 75, 76 and 77

➡Each fuel and vacuum line must be tagged or labeled individually during disassembly to assure correct installation. Never tilt the carburetor assembly during removal or installation. Review these procedures entirely before continuing.

1. Remove the air cleaner assembly.
2. Disconnect the accelerator cable from the carburetor.
3. If equipped with an automatic transaxle, disconnect the throttle valve cable.
4. Unplug the wiring connectors.
5. Label and disconnect the:
   a. carburetor vacuum hoses
   b. fuel inlet hoses
   c. charcoal canister hose

❋❋CAUTION

The carburetor contains gasoline. Wear eye protection and contain spillage. Observe "no smoking/no open flame" precautions. Have a Class B-C (dry powder) fire extinguisher within arm's reach at all times.

6. Remove the carburetor mounting nuts.
7. Remove the cold mixture heater wire clamp and lift out the EGR vacuum modulator bracket.
8. Lift the carburetor off the engine and place it on a clean cloth on the workbench. If desired, the insulator (base gasket) may also be removed.
9. Cover the inlet area of the manifold with clean rags or a plastic bag. This will prevent the entry of dust, dirt and loose parts.

To install:
10. Remove the rags/bag, then place the insulator on the manifold, making sure it is correctly positioned. Always use new gaskets.
11. Install the carburetor onto the manifold.

Fig. 67 The air intake duct can easily be removed after loosening the clamp bolt

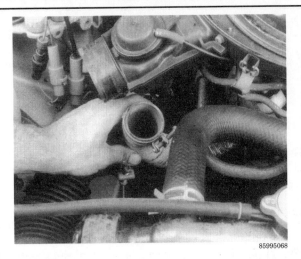

Fig. 68 The heated air intake hose should be replaced if it is damaged or missing

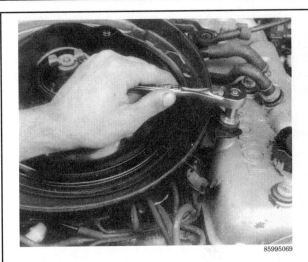

Fig. 69 The air cleaner is usually secured to the valve cover with small bolts

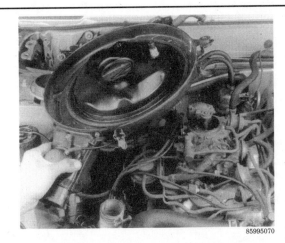

Fig. 70 Be sure to tag and disconnect all vacuum/electrical connections from the air cleaner before removal

Fig. 71 As you can see from this tangle of wires and hoses, it is advantageous to label all vacuum/electrical connections before removing the carburetor as well

12. Install the EGR vacuum modulator bracket. Clamp the cold mixture heater wire into place.

13. Tighten the carburetor mounting nuts to 13 ft. lbs. (18 Nm).

14. Reconnect the fuel inlet hose, the charcoal canister hose and the vacuum hoses.

15. Engage the wiring connector.

16. Connect the accelerator cable; connect the throttle valve cable if equipped with automatic transmission.

17. Reinstall the air cleaner.

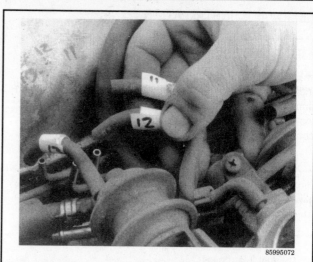

Fig. 72 Twist and pull the vacuum hoses from their connections

Fig. 73 Disconnecting the accelerator cable from the carburetor linkage

Fig. 74 Loosen the two nuts, then slide the cable from it's mounting bracket

Fig. 75 An extension is helpful for reaching the carburetor attaching nuts/bolts

Fig. 76 Make sure all connections are labeled and unplugged, then carefully remove the carburetor

Fig. 77 It's a good idea to clean the heat insulator while the carburetor is removed. The opening in the intake manifold should also be covered with a clean rag to prevent the entry of foreign objects

OVERHAUL

Efficient carburetion depends greatly on careful cleaning and inspection during overhaul since dirt, gum, water, or varnish in or on the carburetor parts are often responsible for poor performance.

Overhaul your carburetor in a clean, dust-free area. Carefully disassemble the carburetor, referring often to the exploded views. Keep all similar and look-alike parts segregated during disassembly and cleaning to avoid accidental interchange during assembly. Make a note of all jet sizes.

When the carburetor is disassembled, wash all parts (except diaphragms, electric choke units, pump plunger, and any other plastic, leather, fiber, or rubber parts) in clean carburetor solvent. Do not leave parts in the solvent any longer than necessary to sufficiently loosen the deposits. Excessive cleaning may remove the special finish from the float bowl and check valve bodies leaving these parts unfit for service. Rinse all parts in clean solvent and blow them dry with compressed air or allow them to air dry. Wipe clean all cork, plastic, and fiber parts with clean, lint-free cloth.

Blow out all passages and jets with compressed air and be sure that there are no restrictions or blockages. Never use wire or similar tools to clean jets, fuel passages, or air bleeds. Clean all jets and valves separately to avoid accidental interchange.

Check all parts for wear or damage. If wear or damage is found, replace the defective parts. Pay special attention to the following areas:

1. Check the float needle and seat for wear. If wear is found, replace the complete assembly.

2. Check the float hinge pin for wear and the float(s) for dents or distortion. Replace the float (the float assembly could have a pin-hole in it) if fuel has leaked into it.

3. Check the throttle and choke shaft bores for wear or an out-of-round condition. Damage or wear to the throttle arm, shaft or shaft bore will often require the replacement of the throttle body. These parts require a close tolerance of fit; wear may allow air leakage, which could affect starting and idling.

➡Throttle shafts and bushings are not usually included in overhaul kits. They may be available separately.

4. Inspect the idle mixture adjusting needles for burrs or grooves. Any such condition requires replacement of the needle, since you will not be able to obtain a satisfactory idle.

➡If idle mixture screws plugs are going to be removed (drilled out for a complete overhaul), refer to Section 2 for the necessary service procedure after the carburetor assembly is removed from the vehicle.

5. Test the accelerator pump check valves. They should pass air one way but not the other. Replace the valve if necessary.

6. Check the bowl cover for warped surfaces with a straightedge.

7. Closely inspect the valves and seats for wear and damage, replacing as necessary.

8. After the carburetor is assembled, check the choke valve (plate) for freedom of operation.

Carburetor overhaul kits are recommended for each overhaul. These kits contain all the gaskets and new parts to replace those that deteriorate most rapidly. Failure to replace all parts supplied with the kit (especially gaskets) can result in poor performance later.

Some carburetor manufacturers supply overhaul kits of 3 basic types: minor repair; major repair; and gasket kits. Generally, they contain the following:

Minor Repair Kits:
- All gaskets
- Float needle valve
- Volume control screw
- All diaphragms
- Spring for the pump diaphragm

Major Repair Kits:
- All jets and gaskets
- All diaphragms
- Float needle valve
- Volume control screw
- Pump ball valve
- Float(s)

Gasket Kits:
- All gaskets

After cleaning and checking all components, reassemble the carburetor, using new parts and referring to the exploded view. When reassembling, make sure that all screws and jets are tight in their seats, but do not overtighten, as the tips will be distorted. Tighten all screws gradually, in rotation. Do not tighten the needle valve(s) into their seats; uneven jetting will result. Always use new gaskets. Be sure to adjust the float level when reassembling.

➡**The following instructions are organized so that only one component group is worked on at a time. This helps avoid confusion and interchange of parts. To make reassembly easier, always arrange disassembled parts in order on the workbench. Be very careful not to mix up or lose small pieces such as balls, clips or springs. Reassembly and adjustment of the carburetor requires accurate measuring equipment capable of checking clearances and angles. These specialized carburetor clearance and angle gauges are available at reputable tool retailers, but may be difficult to find.**

Read the following procedures thoroughly before continuing.

3A and 3A-C Engines

▶ **See Figures 78, 79, 80, 81, 82, 83, 84, 85, 86, 87, 88, 89, 90, 91, 92, 93, 94, 95, 96 and 97**

1. Remove the carburetor as outlined previously.

➡**If idle mixture screws plugs are going to be drilled out, refer to Section 2 for the necessary service procedure.**

Fig. 78 Removing the needle valve and seat. Always use new gaskets when reassembling

2. Disconnect the choke link and the pump connecting rod.
3. Remove the pump arm pivot screw and the pump arm.
4. Remove the fuel hose and union.

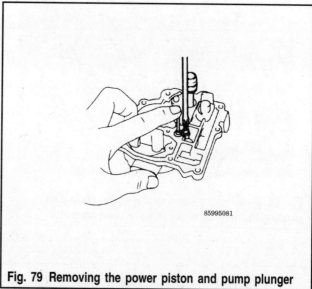

Fig. 79 Removing the power piston and pump plunger

5. Remove the eight air horn screws. Be careful to identify and collect the external parts attached to the screws, such as wire clamps, brackets and the steel number plate.
6. Disconnect the choke opener link.
7. Lift the air horn with its gasket from the body of the carburetor.
8. Remove the primary and secondary solenoid valves from the carburetor body.
9. Remove the float pivot pin, float and needle valve assembly.
10. Remove the needle valve seat and gasket.
11. Remove the power piston retainer, power piston and spring.
12. Pull out the pump plunger and remove the boot.
13. Begin disassembly of the carburetor body by removing the throttle positioner. Disconnect the link and remove the two bolts.

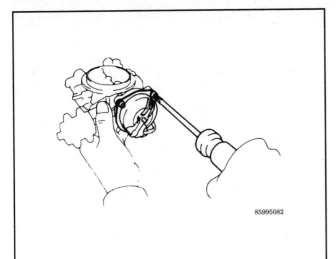

Fig. 80 On non-feedback carburetors, the choke housing is removable

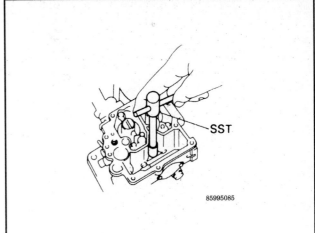

Fig. 82 A special tool is needed to remove the power valve and jet

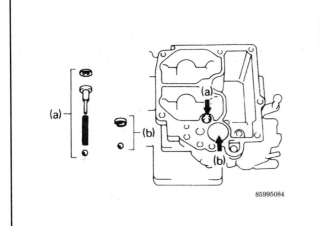

Fig. 81 Make a note of the accelerator pump check ball locations

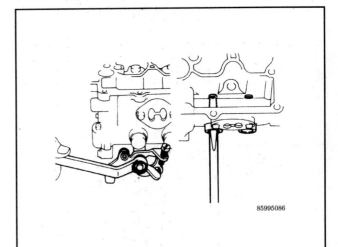

Fig. 83 Once the throttle positioner levers are removed, the primary and secondary main jets can be removed

14. Remove the stopper gasket, the pump discharge weight, the long spring and the large discharge ball.

15. Using a pair of tweezers, remove the plunger retainer and the small ball.

16. Remove the slow jet from the body.

17. Remove the power valve with the jet.

18. Disassemble the power valve and jet.

19. Remove the throttle positioner levers. Remove the primary main passage plug, primary main jet and the gasket. Then, do the same for the secondaries.

20. Remove the Auxiliary Accelerator Pump (AAP) housing, spring and diaphragm.

21. Remove the inlet plug and the small ball for the AAP.

22. Remove the outlet plug, short spring and the small ball.

23. Remove the primary and secondary venturis.

24. Remove the sight glass retainer, the glass and its O-ring.

25. Remove the throttle return spring and the throttle back spring.

26. Remove the nut and the throttle lever.

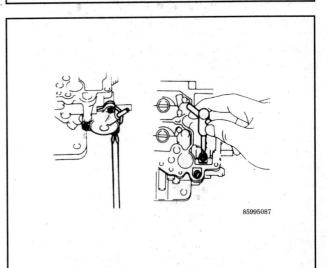

Fig. 84 Removing the auxiliary acceleration pump housing and inlet plug

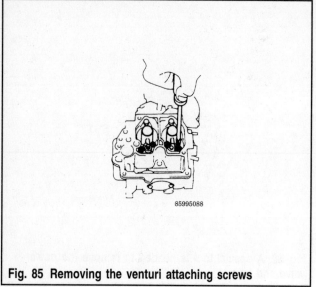

Fig. 85 Removing the venturi attaching screws

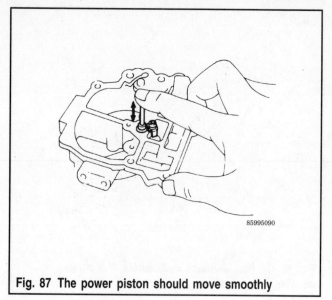

Fig. 87 The power piston should move smoothly

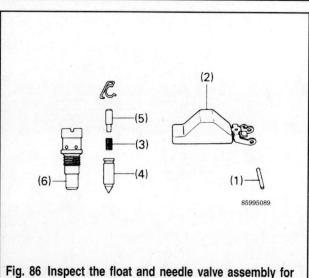

Fig. 86 Inspect the float and needle valve assembly for signs of wear or damage

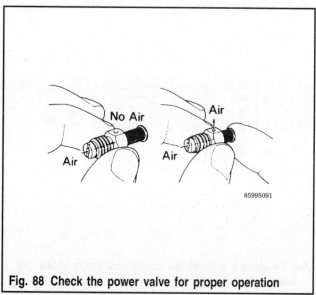

Fig. 88 Check the power valve for proper operation

27. Remove the bolt and the fast idle cam.

28. Remove the secondary throttle valve diaphragm by disconnecting the linkage and removing the assembly with its gasket.

29. Remove the three bolts and the vacuum passage bolt. Separate the carburetor body from the carburetor flange.

30. Clean all the disassembled parts before inspecting them. Wash and clean the cast metal parts with a soft brush in carburetor cleaner. Clean off the carbon around the throttle plates. Wash the other parts thoroughly in cleaner. Blow all dirt and other foreign matter from the jets, fuel passages and restrictions within the body. .

31. Inspect the float and needle valve. Check the pivot pin for scratches and excessive wear. Inspect the float for breaks in the lip and wear in the pivot pin holes. Check the needle valve plunger for wear or damage and the spring for deformation. The strainer should be checked for rust or breaks.

32. Make certain the power piston moves smoothly within its bore.

33. Check the power valve for proper air flow. In its normal (expanded) condition, no air should pass through it. When compressed at one end, air should enter the end, then exit through the side vent.

34. Inspect the choke heater by using an ohmmeter to measure its resistance. Correct resistance is 18 Ω. If a problem is found, the air horn assembly must be replaced.

To install:

35. Reassembly begins by placing a new gasket and the carburetor body onto the flange.

36. Install the vacuum passage bolt, then install the three retaining bolts. Be sure the vacuum passage bolt is placed in the correct location.

37. Assemble the secondary throttle diaphragm, position new gasket and install the assembly. Connect the linkage.

38. Install the fast idle cam with the bolt.

39. Install the throttle lever with its nut.

40. Install the throttle back spring and the throttle return spring.

41. Install the sight glass with a new O-ring.

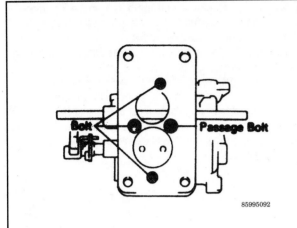

Fig. 89 Be sure to install the vacuum passage bolt in the correct location when assembling the carburetor

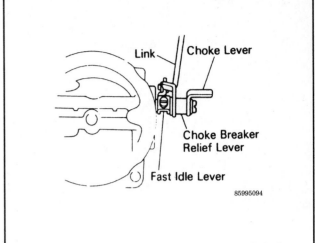

Fig. 91 Correct installation of the fast idle and choke levers

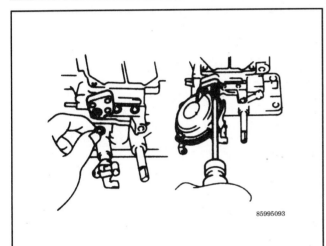

Fig. 90 Always use new gaskets and O-rings when assembling the carburetor

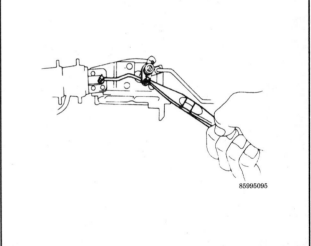

Fig. 92 Be sure to reinstall the retaining clips on the links

42. Install the primary and secondary venturis with new gaskets. Install a new O-ring on the primary venturi.

43. Install the auxiliary accelerator pump. First install the small ball and short spring with the outlet plug. Install the small ball with the inlet plug, followed by the AAP housing, spring and diaphragm.

44. Install the primary main jet and passage plug with a new gasket.

45. Install the secondary main jet and passage plug with a new gasket.

46. Install the throttle positioner levers.

47. Install the slow jet.

48. Assemble the power valve and jet and install them in position.

49. Install the discharge large ball, long spring, pump discharge weight and the stopper gasket.

50. Use tweezers to insert the plunger small ball and the retainer.

51. Reinstall the throttle positioner and connect its linkage.

52. On the air horn, install the valve seat over the gasket into the fuel inlet.

53. Measure and adjust the float level by following the procedures outlined earlier in this section.

54. Install the power piston spring and piston into its bore and install the retainer.

55. Install the acceleration pump plunger and its boot.

56. Place a new gasket onto the air horn.

57. Install the needle valve assembly, the float and the pivot pin. Insert the float lip between the plunger and the clip when installing the float.

58. Install the solenoid valves with new gaskets and O-rings into the body of the carburetor.

59. Assemble the air horn and body. Install the eight screws, paying particular attention to the various brackets, wire clamps and steel number plate. Tighten the screws evenly, in steps, using a criss-cross pattern.

60. Install the accelerator pump arm. Install the pump arm to the air horn with the pump plunger hole and lever aligned.

61. Connect the choke link and the pump connecting link.

62. Install the fuel pipe and union.

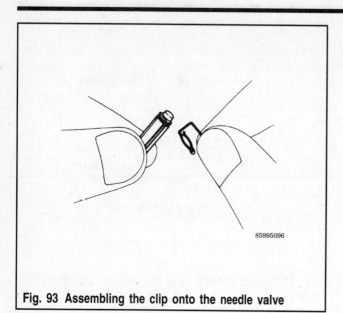

Fig. 93 **Assembling the clip onto the needle valve**

63. With the carburetor still on the bench, move the various linkages by hand, checking for smooth operation. Follow the adjustment procedures outlined earlier.

64. Reinstall the carburetor on the intake manifold, following the procedure outlined earlier.

65. Start the engine and allow it to warm up normally. During this time, pay careful attention to the high idle speed, the operation of the choke and its controls and the idle quality. If you worked carefully and accurately, and performed the bench set-up properly, the carburetor should need very little adjustment after reinstallation.

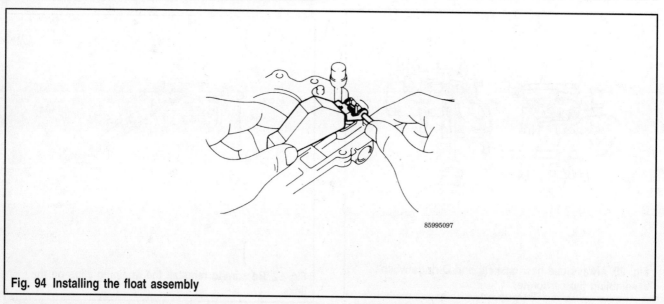

Fig. 94 **Installing the float assembly**

Fig. 95 **The air horn screws should be tightened evenly, in steps, using a criss-cross pattern**

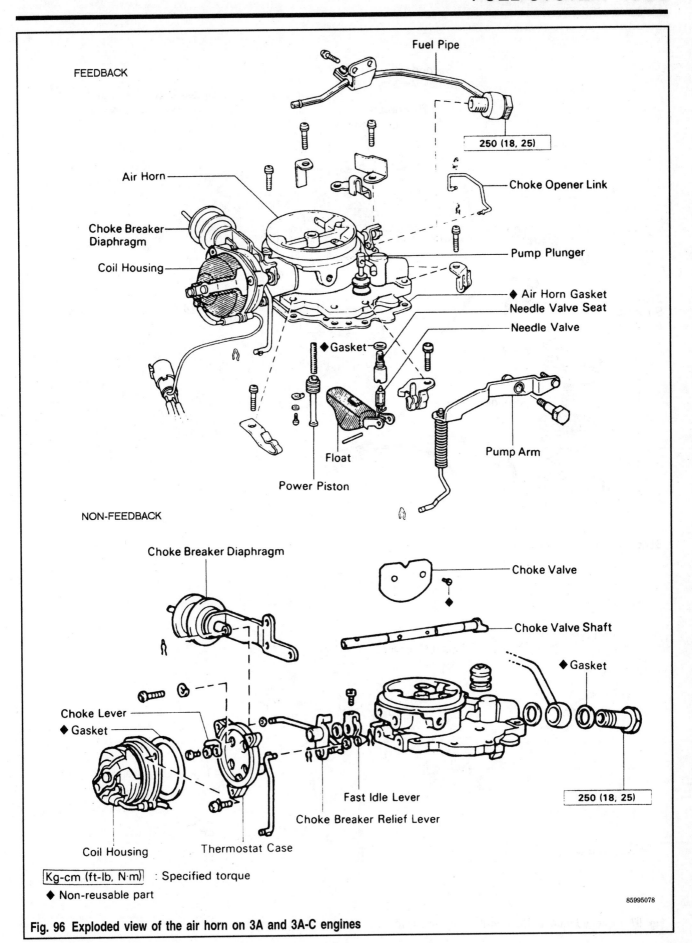

FEEDBACK

Fuel Pipe

250 (18, 25)

Air Horn

Choke Breaker Diaphragm

Coil Housing

Choke Opener Link

Pump Plunger

◆ Air Horn Gasket
Needle Valve Seat

Needle Valve

◆ Gasket

Pump Arm

Float

Power Piston

NON-FEEDBACK

Choke Breaker Diaphragm

Choke Valve

Choke Valve Shaft

◆ Gasket

Choke Lever
◆ Gasket

250 (18, 25)

Fast Idle Lever

Choke Breaker Relief Lever

Coil Housing

Thermostat Case

Kg-cm (ft-lb, N·m) : Specified torque

◆ Non-reusable part

85995078

Fig. 96 Exploded view of the air horn on 3A and 3A-C engines

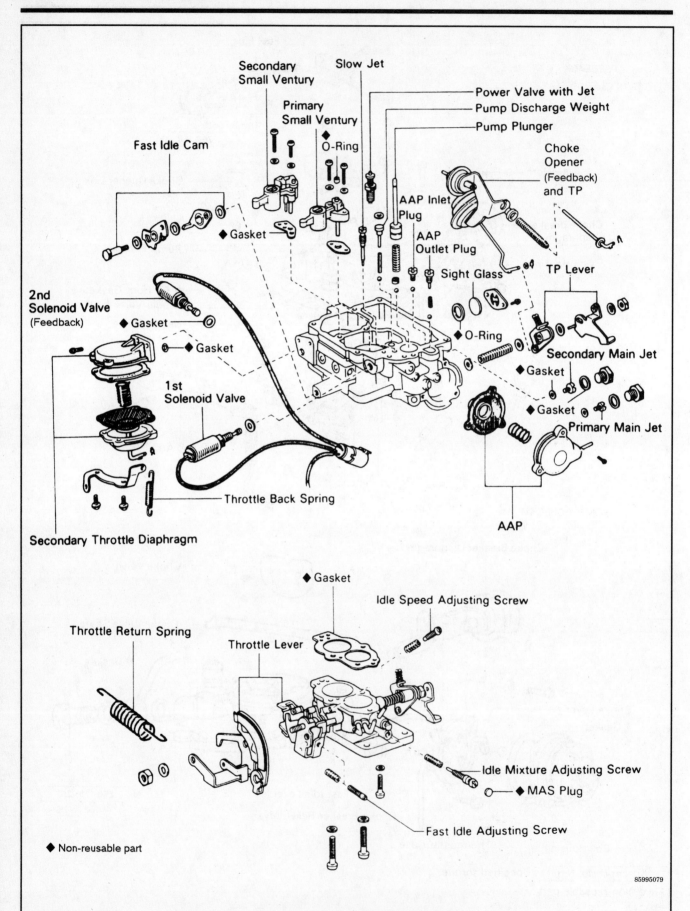

Fig. 97 Exploded view of the throttle body and float bowl on 3A and 3A-C engines

3E Engines

▶ **See Figures 98, 99, 100, 101, 102, 103, 104, 105, 106, 107, 108, 109, 110, 111 and 112**

1. Remove the carburetor from the engine.

➥**If idle mixture screws plugs are going to be drilled out, refer to Section 2 for the necessary service procedure.**

2. Remove the air cleaner support.
3. Remove the throttle position switch.
4. Remove the fuel cut solenoid valve and discard the gasket. Remove the clamps retaining the wires.
5. Remove the fuel nipple union and gaskets.
6. If the compensator must be replaced, remove the attaching screws and separate it from the carburetor body.
7. Install a small bolt into the suction chamber adjusting pin plug.
8. Pry off the plug with two small prybars, then remove the O-ring.

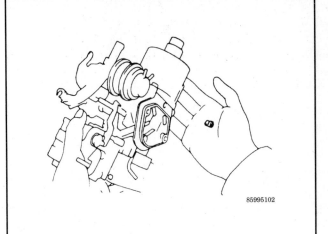

Fig. 100 With the plug removed, the adjusting pin can now be shaken out

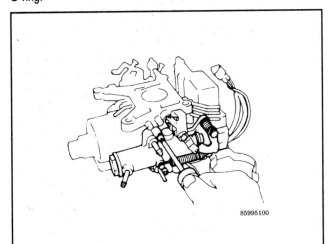

Fig. 98 Remove the compensator only if it is necessary to replace it

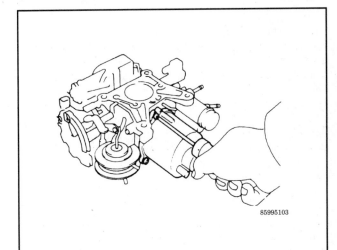

Fig. 101 Be careful not to damage the suction chamber when removing it

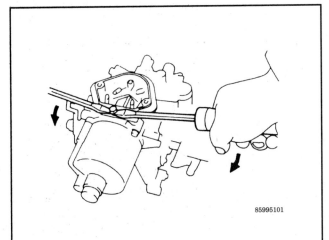

Fig. 99 The suction chamber adjusting pin plug can be removed using two small prybars

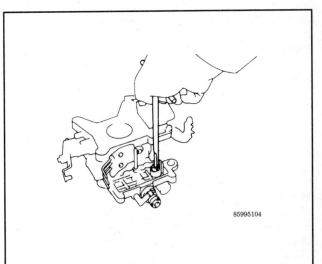

Fig. 102 Using improper tools or excessive force can easily damage brass components

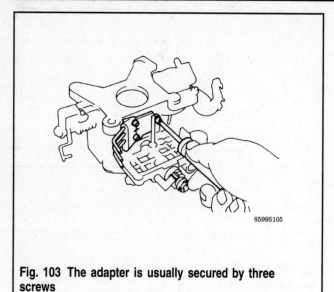

Fig. 103 The adapter is usually secured by three screws

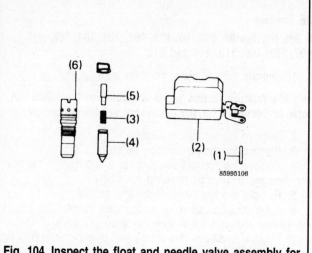

Fig. 104 Inspect the float and needle valve assembly for signs of wear or damage

9. Turn the carburetor over, then shake the pin out.

10. Remove the three suction chamber attaching screws. Pull out the suction chamber, spring and piston from the carburetor body.

11. Remove the pump arm clip, pivot screw and pump arm. Remove the bushing and spring from the connecting rod.

12. Remove the fuel heater wire from the clamp.

13. Remove the float bowl attaching screws, union nipple clamp, throttle valve solenoid, wire clamp, washer, number plate, EGR vacuum modulator bracket and the float bowl.

14. Remove the pump plunger and boots.

15. Remove the float pivot pin, float and needle assembly.

16. Remove the float bowl gasket, needle valve seat and gasket.

17. Remove the throttle positioner.

18. Remove the adapter and gasket.

19. Remove the three bolts and the vacuum passage bolt. Separate the carburetor body from the carburetor flange.

20. Clean all the disassembled parts before inspecting them. Wash and clean the cast metal parts with a soft brush in carburetor cleaner. Clean off the carbon around the throttle plates. Wash the other parts thoroughly in cleaner. Blow all dirt and other foreign matter from the jets, fuel passages and restrictions within the body.

21. Inspect the float and needle valve. Check the pivot pin for scratches and excessive wear. Inspect the float for breaks in the lip and wear in the pivot pin holes. Check the needle valve plunger for wear or damage and the spring for deformation. The strainer should be checked for rust or breaks.

22. Inspect the suction chamber and piston for scratches, damage and wear. Do the same for the metering needle.

23. Inspect the fuel heater and cold mixture heater. Using an ohmmeter, measure the resistance between the terminals of the float bowl wiring connector. It should be between 2-6 Ω. If not, replace the float bowl. Measure the resistance between the terminals of the cold mixture heater. It should be between 0.5-2.2 Ω. If not, replace the float bowl.

To install:

24. Install the adapter with a new gasket.

25. Install the throttle positioner.

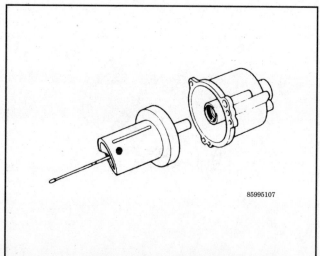

Fig. 105 The suction chamber, piston and metering needle should also be inspected for damage or wear

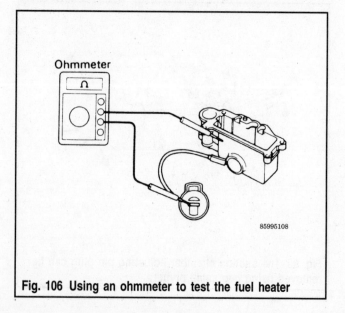

Ohmmeter

Ω

Fig. 106 Using an ohmmeter to test the fuel heater

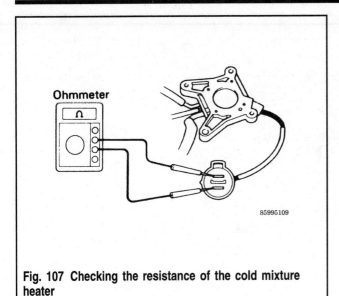

Fig. 107 Checking the resistance of the cold mixture heater

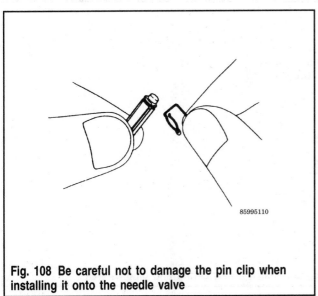

Fig. 108 Be careful not to damage the pin clip when installing it onto the needle valve

26. Install the needle valve seat over a new gasket into the fuel inlet.

27. Install the needle valve, spring and plunger onto the seat. Then install the float and pivot pin.

28. Perform the float adjustment procedures. After adjusting the float, remove the float, plunger, spring and needle valve.

29. Place a new gasket on the carburetor body.

30. Assemble the pin clip onto the needle valve, then reinstall needle valve assembly, float and pivot pin. Insert the float lip between the plunger and clip when installing the float.

31. Install the boots and pump plunger.

32. Assemble the pump damping spring to the float bowl.

33. Install the float bowl, union nipple clamp, solenoid valve clamp, EGR vacuum modulator bracket and number plate with the attaching screws.

34. Install the pump arm with the pivot screw. Install the retaining clip.

35. Install the suction piston into the carburetor body. Then, install the spring and suction chamber with the attaching screws.

36. Insert the suction chamber adjusting pin into the groove on the suction piston. Install a new O-ring with the plug.

37. Install the compensator with a new gasket. Be sure to install the throttle position switch wiring clamp and tighten the screws using the correct sequence.

38. Install the wax back springs. Be sure the spring's hooks do not overlap.

39. Install the union nipple with new gaskets.

40. Install the solenoid valve with a new gasket into the carburetor body.

41. Connect the solenoid valve and throttle position switch wire to the clamp. Install the two clamps.

42. Install the throttle position switch and air cleaner support.

43. With the carburetor still on the bench, move the various linkages by hand, checking for smooth operation. Follow the adjustment procedures outlined earlier.

44. Reinstall the carburetor on the intake manifold, following the procedure outlined earlier.

45. Start the engine and allow it to warm up normally. During this time, pay careful attention to the high idle speed, the operation of the choke and its controls and the idle quality. If you worked carefully and accurately, and performed the bench set-up properly, the carburetor should need very little adjustment after reinstallation.

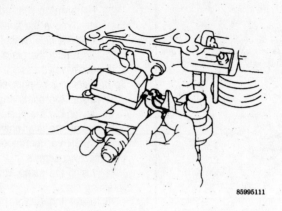

Fig. 109 Installing the float and needle valve assembly

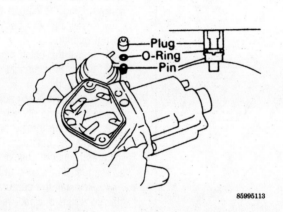

Fig. 110 Insert the suction pin into the groove on the suction piston. Install a new O-ring and plug as well

Fig. 111 If the compensator was removed, tighten the screws using this sequence

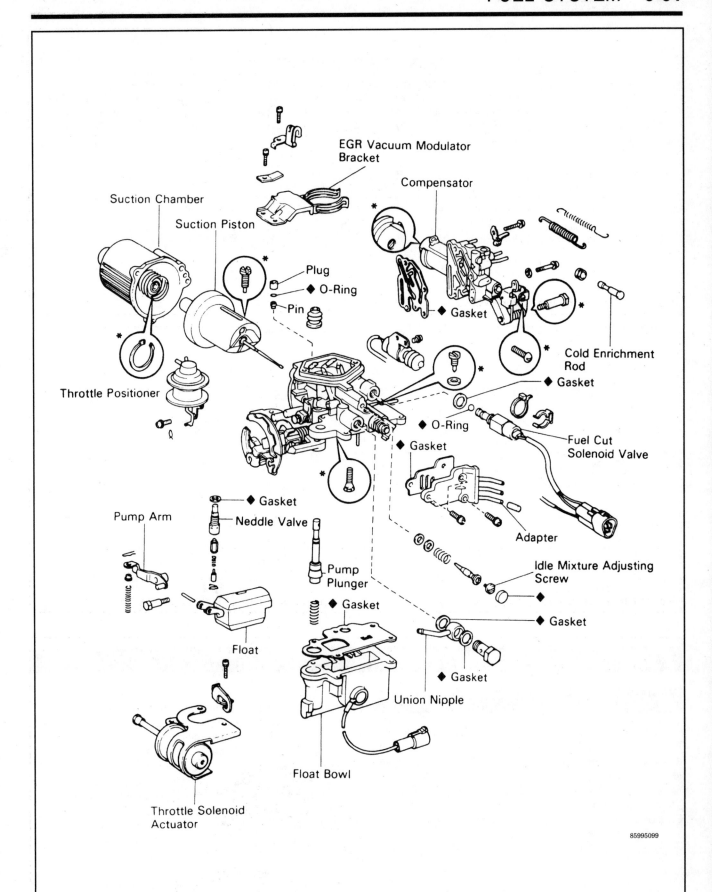

Fig. 112 Exploded view of the carburetor used on 3E engines

CARBURETOR SPECIFICATIONS

Year	Application	Float Level Raised (in.)	Float Level Lowered (in.)	Throttle Valve Opening Angle Primary (deg.)	Throttle Valve Opening Angle Secondary (deg.)	Kick Up Setting (in.)	Secondary Touch Angle (deg.)	Fast Idle Angle (deg.)	Unloader Angle (deg.)	Choke Opener Angle (deg.)	Choke Breaker A (deg.)	Choke Breaker A+B (deg.)	TP Pump Stroke (in.)	Setting Angle (deg.)
1984	3A-C Feedback	0.283	0.0657–0.0783	90	75	0.0063	45	20	41	77	38	55	0.157	—
	3A, 3A-C Non-Feedback	0.283	0.0657–0.0783	90	75	0.0091	45	21	47	77	39	50	0.118	—
1985	3A-C Feedback	0.283	0.0657–0.0783	90	75	0.0063	45	20	41	77	38	55	0.157	—
	3A, 3A-C Non-Feedback	0.283	0.0657–0.0783	90	75	0.0091	45	21	47	77	39	50	0.118	—
1986	3A-C Feedback	0.283	0.0657–0.0783	90	75	0.0063	45	20	41	77	38	55	0.157	—
	3A, 3A-C Non-Feedback	0.283	0.0657–0.0783	90	75	0.0091	45	21	47	77	39	50	0.118	—
1987	3A-C Feedback	0.283	0.0657–0.0783	90	75	0.0063	45	20	41	77	38	55	0.157	—
	3A, 3A-C Non-Feedback	0.283	0.0657–0.0783	90	75	0.0091	45	21	47	77	39	50	0.118	—
	3E	0.169	0.035–0.043	87–93	—	—	—	18.7①	②	—	—	—	0.217	13.2
1988	3A-C Feedback	0.283	0.0657–0.0783	90	75	0.0063	45	20	41	77	38	55	0.157	—
	3A, 3A-C Non-Feedback	0.283	0.0657–0.0783	90	75	0.0091	45	21	47	77	39	50	0.118	—
	3E	0.169	0.035–0.043	87–93	—	—	—	18.7①	②	—	—	—	0.217	13.2
1989	3E	0.169	0.035–0.043	87–93	—	—	—	18.7①	②	—	—	—	0.217	13.2
1990	3E	0.169	0.035–0.043	87–93	—	—	—	18.7①	②	—	—	—	0.217	13.2

① 18.7 on manual transaxle,
   19 on automatic transaxle
② 0.31 in. on 3E engines

8599CARB

ELECTRONIC FUEL INJECTION SYSTEM

System Description

The Electronic Fuel Injection (EFI) system precisely controls fuel injection to match engine requirements, reducing emissions and increasing driveability. The electric fuel pump supplies fuel to the pressure regulator. The fuel injectors are electric solenoid valves which open and close by signals from the Electronic Control Module (ECM). The ECM is also known as the Electronic Control Unit (ECU).

The ECM receives input from various sensors to determine engine operating conditions. This allows the ECM to determine the correct amount of fuel to be injected by it's preset program. These inputs and their corresponding sensors are:

• Intake manifold absolute pressure — Manifold Absolute Pressure (MAP) or vacuum sensor
• Intake air temperature — Intake Air Temperature (IAT) sensor
• Coolant temperature — Water temperature sensor
• Engine speed — reference pulse from the distributor
• Throttle valve opening angle — Throttle Position Sensor (TPS)
• Exhaust oxygen content — Oxygen sensor

Relieving Fuel System Pressure

✳✳CAUTION

Safety is very important when preforming fuel system maintenance.The fuel system is under pressure. Fuel pressure must be relieved before performing service procedures on fuel injection system components. Failure to conduct fuel system maintenance and repairs in a safe manner may result in serious personal injury.

1. Disconnect the negative battery cable. Unbolt the retaining screws and remove the protective shield for the fuel filter (if so equipped).
2. Place a pan under the delivery pipe (large connection) to catch the dripping fuel, then SLOWLY loosen the union bolt to bleed off the fuel pressure.

Electric Fuel Pump

REMOVAL & INSTALLATION

◆ **See Figures 113, 114, 115, 116, 117, 118, 119, 120, 121 and 122**

The electric fuel pump is contained within the fuel tank. On 1990 models, it is necessary to remove the fuel tank from the vehicle in order to reach the pump. On 1991-1994 models, the fuel pump can be accessed by removing the rear seat cushion and service hole cover.

➡**Before disconnecting fuel system lines, clean the fittings with a spray-type engine cleaner. Follow the instructions on the cleaner. Do not soak fuel system parts in liquid cleaning solvent.**

✳✳CAUTION

The fuel injection system is under pressure. Release pressure slowly and contain spillage. Observe "no smoking/no open flame" precautions. Have a Class B-C (dry powder) fire extinguisher within arm's reach at all times.

1990 Models

1. Disconnect the negative battery cable and relieve the fuel pressure. Remove the filler cap.
2. Remove the fuel tank from the vehicle.
3. Remove the fuel pump bracket attaching screws, then remove the fuel pump/bracket assembly from the tank.
4. Pull the lower side of the fuel pump from the bracket.
5. Remove the nuts attaching the wires to the fuel pump.
6. Disconnect the hose from the pump.
7. Separate the filter from the pump. Use a small screwdriver to remove the attaching clip.
8. While the tank is out and disassembled, inspect it for any signs of rust, leakage or metal damage. If any problem is found, replace the tank.
9. Inspect all of the lines, hoses and fittings for any sign of corrosion, wear or damage to the surfaces. Check the pump outlet hose and the filter for restrictions.

10. When reassembling, ALWAYS replace the sealing gaskets with new ones. Also replace any rubber parts showing any sign of deterioration.
To install:
11. Install the pump filter using a new clip. Install the rubber cushion under the filter.
12. Connect the outlet hose to the pump, then attach the pump to the bracket.
13. Connect the wires to the fuel pump with the nuts.
14. Install the fuel pump and bracket assembly onto the tank. Use new gaskets.
15. Install the fuel tank.
16. Start the engine and check carefully for any sign of leakage around the tank and lines. Road test the vehicle for proper operation.

1991-1994 Models

1. Disconnect the negative battery cable and relieve the fuel pressure. Remove the filler cap.
2. Remove the rear seat cushion from the vehicle.
3. Unplug the fuel pump and sending unit connector.
4. Remove the service hole cover.
5. Using SST 09631-22020 or an equivalent line (flare nut) wrench, disconnect the outlet pipe from the pump bracket.
6. Remove the pump bracket attaching screws.
7. Disconnect the return hoses from the pump bracket, then pull out the pump/bracket assembly.
8. Remove the fuel cut-off valve from the bracket assembly.
9. Remove the nut and spring washer, then disconnect the wires from the pump bracket.
10. Remove the sending unit attaching screws, then remove the unit from the bracket.
11. Pull the lower side of the fuel pump from the bracket.
12. Unplug the connector to the fuel pump.
13. Disconnect the hose from the pump.
14. Separate the filter from the pump. Use a small screwdriver to remove the attaching clip.
15. Inspect all of the lines, hoses and fittings for any sign of corrosion, wear or damage to the surfaces. Check the pump outlet hose and the filter for restrictions.
16. When reassembling, ALWAYS replace the sealing gaskets with new ones. Also replace any rubber parts showing any sign of deterioration.
To install:
17. Install the pump filter using a new clip. Install the rubber cushion under the filter.
18. Connect the outlet hose to the pump, then attach the pump to the bracket.
19. Engage the connector to the fuel pump.
20. Install the fuel sending unit to the pump bracket.
21. Install the fuel cut-off valve to the fuel pump bracket with a new gasket.
22. Install the fuel pump and bracket assembly onto the tank. Use new gaskets.
23. Connect the return hoses to the pump bracket.
24. Install the service hole cover, then the engage the fuel pump and sending unit connector.
25. Install the rear seat cushion.
26. Start the engine and check carefully for any sign of leakage around the tank and lines. Road test the vehicle for proper operation.

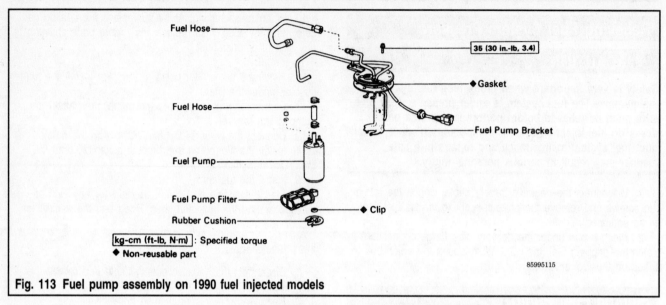

Fig. 113 Fuel pump assembly on 1990 fuel injected models

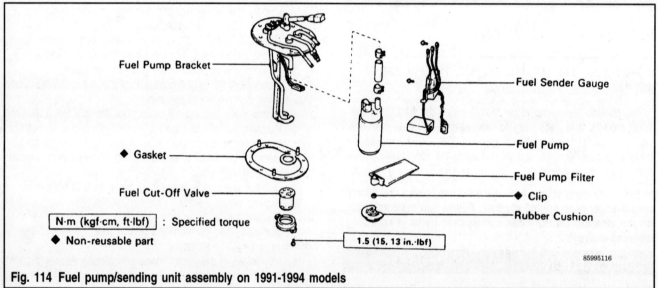

Fig. 114 Fuel pump/sending unit assembly on 1991-1994 models

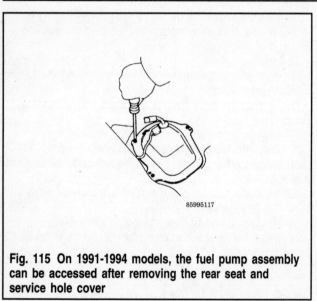

Fig. 115 On 1991-1994 models, the fuel pump assembly can be accessed after removing the rear seat and service hole cover

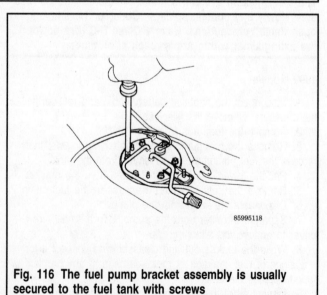

Fig. 116 The fuel pump bracket assembly is usually secured to the fuel tank with screws

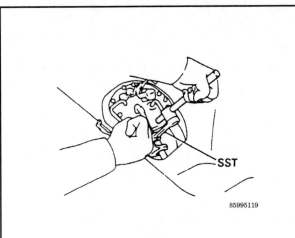

Fig. 117 A special tool is needed to disconnect the outlet pipe from the pump bracket — 1991-1994 models

Fig. 118 Removing the fuel pump from the pump bracket on 1990 fuel injected models

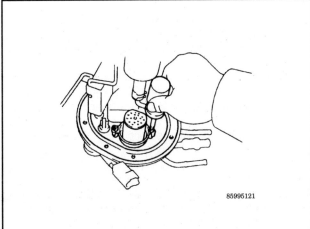

Fig. 119 Fuel cut-off valve removal on 1991-1994 models

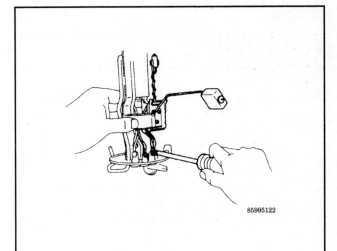

Fig. 120 The sending unit is secured to the pump bracket assembly on 1991-1994 models

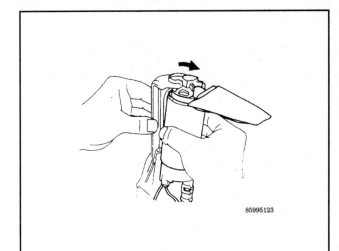

Fig. 121 Removing the fuel pump from the pump bracket assembly on 1991-1994 models

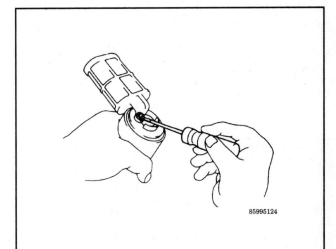

Fig. 122 The pump filter retaining clip can be removed using a small screwdriver

TESTING

▶ See Figures 123 and 124

Pump Operation

1. Turn the ignition switch **ON**, but do not start the motor.
2. Using a jumper wire, short terminals FP and +B of the check connector.
3. Feel that there is pressure in the hose running to the delivery pipe. You should hear the pump at the rear of the car.
4. Remove the jumper wire.
5. Turn the ignition to **OFF**. If the fuel pump failed to function, it may indicate a faulty pump, but before removing the pump, check the following items within the pump system:
   a. Fusible links
   b. Fuses
   c. Fuel injection main relay
   d. Fuel pump circuit opening relay
   e. All wiring connections and grounds

Fuel Pressure

1. Check that the battery voltage is approximately 12 volts.
2. Disconnect the negative battery cable.
3. Relieve the fuel system pressure.
4. Disconnect the hose from the fuel filter outlet.
5. Connect the hose and a fuel pressure gauge to the fuel filter outlet with three new gaskets and the union bolt.
6. Wipe any spilled gasoline.
7. Connect the negative battery cable.
8. Using a jumper wire, short terminals FP and +B of the check connector.
9. Turn the ignition switch **ON**, but do not start the car.
10. The fuel pressure should read 38-44 psi (265-304 kpa).
11. If the pressure is too high, the pressure regulator is probably defective. If it is too low, check for the following:
   a. Fuel hoses and connections for leaks or restrictions.
   b. Defective fuel pump.
   c. Clogged fuel filter.
   d. Defective pressure regulator.

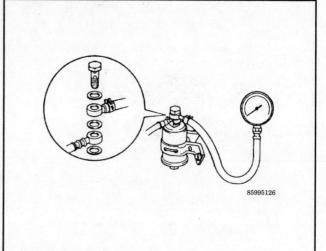

Fig. 124 The fuel pressure gauge should be connected to the fuel filter outlet

12. After checking the fuel pressure, turn the ignition **OFF** and remove the jumper wire from the check connector.
13. Disconnect the negative battery cable.
14. Relieve the fuel system pressure and remove the pressure gauge.
15. Connect the hose to the fuel filter outlet using new gaskets.
16. Wipe any fuel spillage.
17. Connect the negative battery cable, then start the engine and check for leaks.

Throttle Body

REMOVAL & INSTALLATION

▶ See Figures 125 and 126

1. Disconnect the negative battery cable.
2. Drain the cooling system to a level below the throttle body.
3. Remove the intake duct assembly.
4. Unplug the electrical connectors from the throttle body.
5. Disconnect the accelerator cable.
6. If so equipped, disconnect the transaxle shift cable (automatic transmission) and/or the cruise control cable.
7. Label and unplug the vacuum hoses to the throttle body.
8. Label and disconnect the coolant hoses from the throttle body.
9. Remove the nuts/bolts securing the throttle body, then carefully remove the throttle body.
   To install:
10. When reinstalling, always use a new gasket between the throttle body and the intake. Do not use sealants of any kind on the gasket. Place the throttle body in position, then install the nuts/bolts and tighten them to 9 ft. lbs. (13 Nm). Make certain that the throttle body is properly positioned with a new gasket before tightening; no air leaks are acceptable.
11. Connect the accelerator cable.
12. If so equipped, reattach the transaxle cable and/or the cruise control cable.

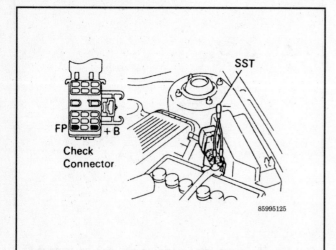

Fig. 123 Fuel pump test terminals of the check connector

13. Connect the vacuum and coolant hoses to the throttle body.

14. Engage the electrical connectors to the throttle body. Install the intake duct assembly.

15. Fill the cooling system.

16. Connect the negative battery cable.

ADJUSTMENTS

▶ **See Figures 127 and 128**

Throttle Position Sensor

Adjustment should only be performed if the sensor has been replaced, or if the testing procedure in Section 4 indicates the need for adjustment.

1. Loosen the screws securing the sensor.

2. On California models equipped with a throttle opener diaphragm on the throttle body, apply vacuum to it.

3. On 1990 models, insert a 0.0276 in. (0.70 mm) thickness gauge between the throttle stop screw and lever. On 1991 and later models, insert a 0.024 in. (0.60 mm) thickness gauge between the throttle stop screw and lever.

4. Connect the probes of an ohmmeter to terminals IDL and E2 of the sensor.

5. Gradually turn the sensor clockwise until the ohmmeter deflects, then tighten the screws.

6. Insert the following thickness gauges between the throttle stop screw and lever, then check the continuity between terminals IDL and E2 of the sensor.

    a. 1990 models — 0.0236 in (0.60 mm) thickness gauge, continuity

    b. 1990 models — 0.0315 in. (0.80 mm) thickness gauge, no continuity

    c. 1991-1994 models — 0.020 in. (0.50 mm) thickness gauge, continuity

    d. 1991-1994 models — 0.028 in. (0.70 mm) thickness gauge, no continuity

7. If the sensor did not perform as indicated, readjust the sensor.

Idle Speed

Follow the procedure outlined in Section 2 for idle speed adjustment.

Fuel Injectors

The injectors deliver a measured quantity of fuel according to signals from the ECM. As driving conditions change, the computer signals each injector to stay open a longer or shorter period of time. The injector, being an electric component, is either on or off (open or closed); there is no variable control for an injector other than duration.

Cleanliness is important when working on a fuel injected system. Every component must be treated with the greatest care and be protected from dust, grime and impact damage. The injectors are easily damaged by improper handling. Additionally, care must be used in dealing with electrical connectors. Look for and release any locking mechanisms on the connector before separating it from the injector. When reattach-

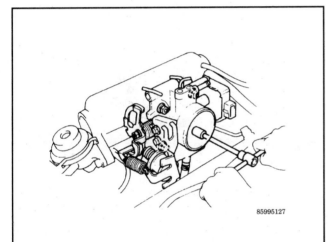

Fig. 125 An extension is helpful when removing the throttle body attaching nuts/bolts

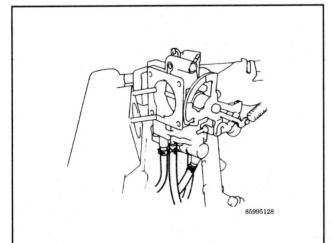

Fig. 126 Always use a new gasket when installing the throttle body

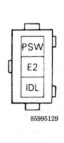

Fig. 127 Throttle position sensor terminal identification on 1990 fuel injected models

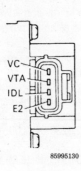

85995130

Fig. 128 Throttle position sensor terminal identification on 1991-1994 models

ing, make sure each pin is properly lined up and seated before pushing the connector closed.

REMOVAL & INSTALLATION

▶ **See Figures 129, 130, 131, 132 and 133**

❋❋CAUTION

The fuel system is under pressure. Release pressure slowly and contain spillage. Observe "no smoking/no open flame" precautions. Have a Class B-C (dry powder) fire extinguisher within arm's reach at all times.

1. Disconnect the negative battery cable.
2. Unplug the injector electrical connections. Be sure to release the locking tabs before attempting to unplug the connector.
3. Remove the fuel rail assembly.
4. Pull the injectors free of the delivery pipe. Certain engines may use injectors with color-coded collars. Note these positions for correct placement during installation.
   To install:

➡**Always use new O-rings and gaskets when installing fuel system components.**

5. Install a new grommet and O-ring on each injector. Apply a thin coat of gasoline to the O-ring (NEVER use oil of any sort), then install the injectors into the fuel rail. Make certain each injector can be smoothly rotated. If they do not rotate smoothly, the O-ring is not seated correctly and should be replaced. On injectors with color-coded collars, be sure they are installed in the proper order.
6. Install the fuel rail assembly.
7. Once again, check that the injectors rotate smoothly.
8. Engage the electrical connectors to each injector. On color-coded injectors, engage the gray connectors to the dark blue injectors, then the brown connectors to the brown injectors.

9. Connect the battery cable to the negative battery terminal. Start the engine and check for leaks.

❋❋CAUTION

If there is a leak at any fitting, the line will be under pressure and the fuel may spray in a fine mist. This mist is extremely explosive. Shut the engine off immediately if any leakage is detected. Use rags to wrap the leaking fitting until the pressure diminishes and wipe up any fuel from the engine area.

TESTING

▶ **See Figures 134 and 135**

The simplest way to test the injectors is to listen to them with the engine running. Use a stethoscope-type tool to touch each injector while the engine is idling. You should hear a distinct clicking as each injector opens and closes.

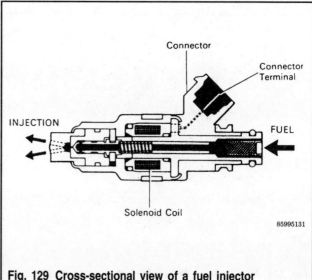

85995131

Fig. 129 Cross-sectional view of a fuel injector

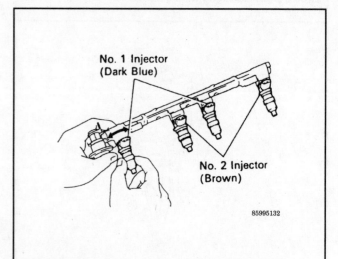

85995132

Fig. 130 If equipped, position color-coded injectors in this sequence

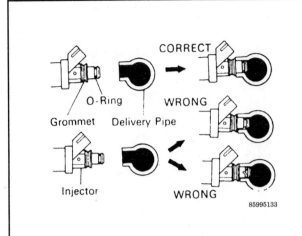

Fig. 131 The fuel injectors must be installed properly into the fuel rail

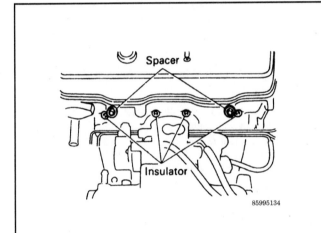

Fig. 132 Make sure the insulators and spacers are correctly positioned on the cylinder head

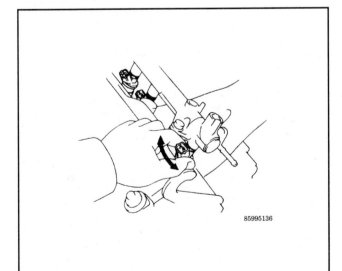

Fig. 133 The injectors should rotate smoothly

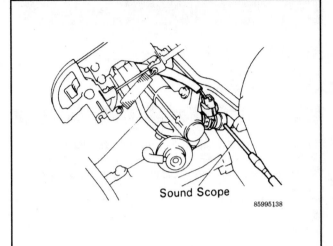

Fig. 134 Use a stethoscope-type tool to listen for injector operation

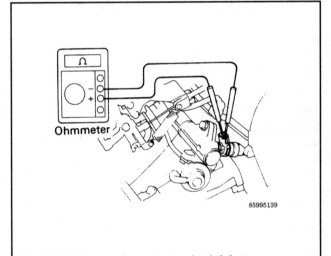

Fig. 135 Using an ohmmeter to check injector resistance

Additionally, the resistance of the injector can be easily checked. Disconnect the negative battery cable and unplug the electrical connector from the injector to be tested. Use an ohmmeter to check the resistance across the terminals of the injector. Correct resistance is approximately 13.8Ω at 68°F (20°C); slight variations are acceptable due to temperature conditions.

Bench testing of the injectors can only be done using expensive special equipment. Generally this equipment can be found at a dealership and sometimes at a well-equipped machine or performance shop. There is no provision for field testing the injectors by the owner/mechanic. DO NOT attempt to test the injector by removing it from the engine and making it spray into a jar.

Never attempt to check a removed injector by hooking it directly to the battery. The injector runs on a smaller voltage and the 12 volts from the battery will destroy it internally.

Fuel Rail Assembly

REMOVAL & INSTALLATION

◗ See Figures 136 and 137

✳✳CAUTION

The fuel system is under pressure. Release pressure slowly and contain spillage. Observe "no smoking/no open flame" precautions. Have a Class B-C (dry powder) fire extinguisher within arm's reach at all times.

1. Disconnect the negative battery cable, then relieve fuel system pressure.
2. Disconnect the PCV hoses.
3. Remove the air intake duct. Disconnect the accelerator cable.
4. If so equipped, disconnect the transaxle shift cable (automatic transmission) and/or the cruise control cable.
5. Label and unplug the vacuum hose from the pressure regulator.
6. Remove the dash pot and link bracket, if equipped.
7. Disconnect the fuel inlet and return hoses.
8. If equipped, remove the cold start injector.

➠Not all engines are equipped with a cold start injector.

9. Unplug the injector electrical connections. Be sure to release the locking tabs before attempting to unplug the connector.
10. At the fuel rail, remove the attaching bolts. Lift the delivery pipe and the injectors free of the engine. DON'T drop the injectors.

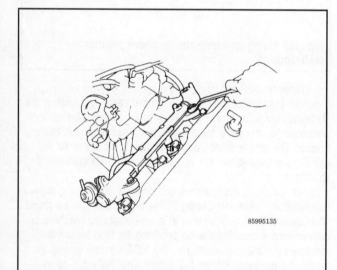

Fig. 136 Removing the fuel rail attaching bolts

Fig. 137 Always use new gaskets and O-rings

11. Remove the insulators and spacers from the cylinder head. Note the correct placement along with the amount of spacers and insulators used.

To install:

➥Always use new O-rings and gaskets when installing fuel system components.

12. Install the insulators into each injector hole. Place the spacers on the fuel rail mounting holes in the cylinder head.
13. Position the fuel rail on the cylinder head. Install the bolts, then tighten them to 14 ft. lbs. (19 Nm).
14. Engage the electrical connectors to each injector. On color-coded injectors, engage the gray connectors to the dark blue injectors, then the brown connectors to the brown injectors.
15. If equipped, install the cold start injector with new gaskets.
16. Connect the fuel inlet and return hoses. Tighten to 22 ft. lbs. (29 Nm).
17. Install the dashpot with the link bracket, if equipped.
18. Connect the vacuum hose to the pressure regulator. Attach the PCV hose.
19. Reconnect the accelerator, transaxle control and cruise control cables, then install the air intake duct.
20. Connect the battery cable to the negative battery terminal. Start the engine and check for leaks.

✳✳CAUTION

If there is a leak at any fitting, the line will be under pressure and the fuel may spray in a fine mist. This mist is extremely explosive. Shut the engine off immediately if any leakage is detected. Use rags to wrap the leaking fitting until the pressure diminishes and wipe up any fuel from the engine area.

Fuel Pressure Regulator

REMOVAL & INSTALLATION

▶ **See Figures 138, 139, 140 and 141**

1. Disconnect the negative battery cable, then relieve fuel system pressure.

❈❈CAUTION

The fuel system is under pressure. Release pressure slowly and contain spillage. Observe "no smoking/no open flame" precautions. Have a Class B-C (dry powder) fire extinguisher within arm's reach at all times.

2. Unplug the vacuum sensing hose from the fuel pressure regulator.
3. Disconnect the fuel pipe from the regulator.
4. Remove the two retaining bolts and pull the regulator out of the fuel rail.

To install:

5. Apply a light coat of gasoline to a new O-ring, then install it on the regulator.
6. Rotate the regulator to the left and right while installing it in the fuel rail. Make certain it can be smoothly rotated. If it does not rotate smoothly, the O-ring is not seated correctly and should be replaced.
7. Install the two retaining bolts. Tighten them to 69 inch lbs. (7.8 Nm).
8. Connect the fuel and vacuum hoses.
9. Start the engine and check carefully for leaks.

Air Bypass Valve

REMOVAL & INSTALLATION

▶ **See Figures 142 and 143**

1. Disconnect the negative battery cable.
2. Remove the throttle body.
3. Remove the bypass valve from the throttle body by loosening it's attaching screws.
4. Installation is the reverse of removal. Be sure to use a new O-ring and gasket.

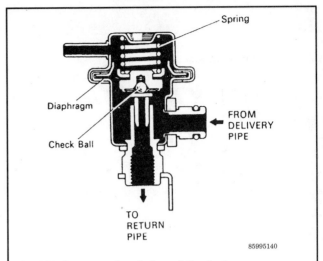

Fig. 138 Cross-sectional view of the fuel pressure regulator

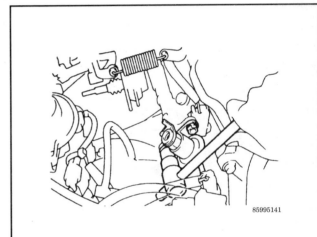

Fig. 139 The fuel pressure regulator is usually secured by two bolts

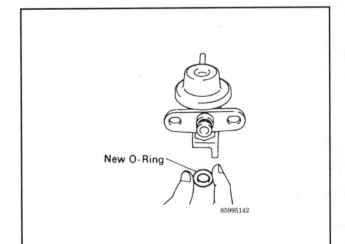

Fig. 140 Always use a new O-ring when installing the regulator

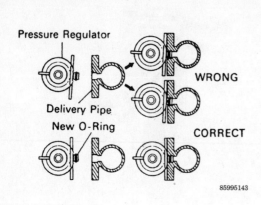

Fig. 141 Correct installation is critical to prevent fuel leaks

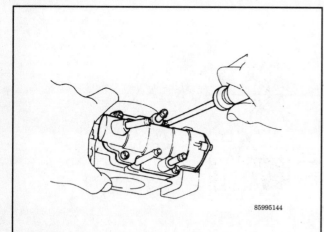

Fig. 142 The air bypass valve is usually secured to the throttle body by four screws

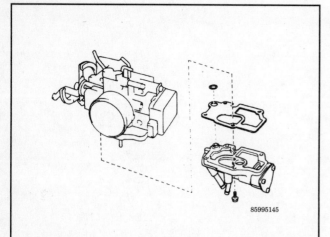

Fig. 143 Always use a new gasket and O-ring when installing the bypass valve

Cold Start Injector

REMOVAL & INSTALLATION

◗ **See Figures 144, 145 and 146**

1. Disconnect the negative battery cable, then unplug the wiring connector from the injector.

✳✳CAUTION

The fuel system is under pressure. Release pressure slowly and contain spillage. Observe "no smoking/no open flame" precautions. Have a Class B-C (dry powder) fire extinguisher within arm's reach at all times.

2. Wrap the fuel pipe connection in a rag or towel. Remove the two union bolts and the cold start injector pipe with its gaskets.
3. Remove the two retaining bolts, then remove the cold start injector with it's gaskets.
   To install:
4. Install the injector with a new gasket, then tighten the two mounting bolts to 69 inch lbs. (7.8 Nm).
5. Again using new gaskets, install the cold start injector pipe. Tighten the bolts to 14 ft. lbs. (20 Nm).
6. Engage the cold start injector connector.
7. Connect the negative battery cable, then start the engine and check for leaks.

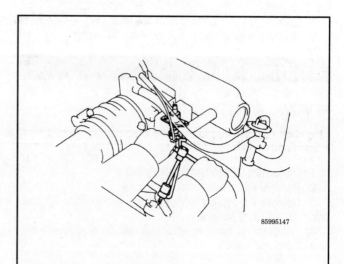

Fig. 144 An extension is helpful when removing the cold start injector fuel pipe

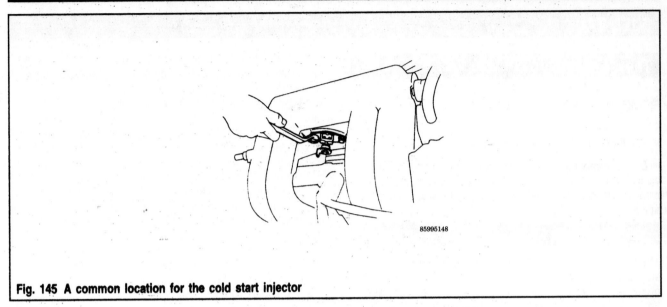

Fig. 145 A common location for the cold start injector

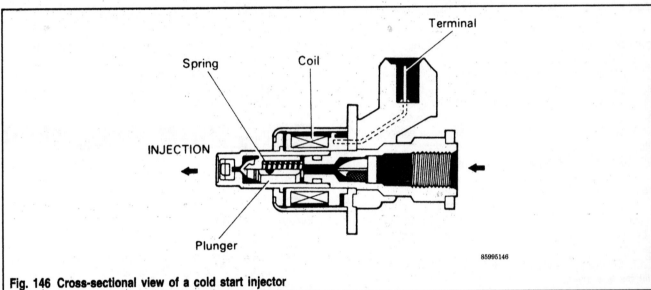

Fig. 146 Cross-sectional view of a cold start injector

FUEL TANK

Tank Assembly

REMOVAL & INSTALLATION

▶ **See Figures 147, 148, 149 and 150**

➡Before removing fuel system parts, clean them with a spray-type engine cleaner. Follow the instructions on the cleaner. Do not soak fuel system parts in liquid cleaning solvent.

✳✳CAUTION

The fuel injection system is under pressure. Release pressure slowly and contain spillage. Observe "no smoking/no open flame" precautions. Have a Class B-C (dry powder) fire extinguisher within arm's reach at all times.

1. Disconnect the negative battery cable. On fuel injected engines, properly relieve the fuel system pressure.
2. Remove the filler cap.
3. Using a siphon or pump, drain the fuel from the tank and store it in a proper metal container with a tight cap.
4. On 1991-1994 models, remove the rear seat cushion and service hole cover to gain access to the electrical wiring.
5. Unplug the connector(s) for the fuel pump and/or sending unit.
6. Raise the vehicle and safely support it on jackstands.
7. Loosen the clamp and remove the filler neck and overflow pipe from the tank.
8. Remove the supply hose from the tank. Wrap a rag around the fitting to collect escaping fuel. Disconnect the breather hose from the tank, again using a rag to control spillage.
9. Cover or plug the end of each disconnected line to keep dirt out and fuel in.
10. Support the fuel tank with a floor jack or transmission jack. Use a broad piece of wood to distribute the load. Be careful not to deform the bottom of the tank.
11. Remove the fuel tank support strap bolts.
12. Swing the straps away from the tank and lower the jack. Balance the tank with your other hand or have a helper assist you. The tank is bulky and may have some fuel left in it. If its balance changes suddenly, the tank may fall.

➡The fuel tank will release strong fuel vapors while it is removed from the vehicle. Be sure to store it in a safe, well ventilated area.

13. Remove the fuel filler pipe extension, the breather pipe assembly and the sending unit assembly. Keep these items in a clean, protected area away from the car.

To install:

14. While the tank is out and disassembled, inspect it for any signs of rust, leakage or metal damage. If any problem is found, replace the tank.

15. Inspect all of the lines, hoses and fittings for any sign of corrosion, wear or damage to the surfaces. Check the pump outlet hose and the filter for restrictions.
16. When reassembling, ALWAYS replace the sealing gaskets with new ones. Also replace any rubber parts showing any sign of deterioration.
17. Connect the breather pipe assembly and the filler pipe extension.
18. Place the fuel tank on the jack and elevate it into place within the car. Attach the straps and install the strap bolts, tightening them to 29 ft. lbs. (39 Nm).
19. Connect the breather, return and supply hoses to the tank.
20. Connect the filler neck and overflow pipe to the tank. Make sure the clamps are properly seated and secure.
21. Lower the vehicle to the ground.
22. Connect the pump and/or sending unit electrical connector(s) to the harness.
23. Install the rear seat cushion and service hole cover, if applicable.
24. Using a funnel, pour the fuel that was drained from its container into the fuel filler.
25. Install the fuel filler cap.
26. Start the engine and check carefully for any sign of leakage around the tank and lines.

Sending Unit

REMOVAL & INSTALLATION

Except 1991-1994 Models

1. Disconnect the negative battery cable.
2. Remove the fuel tank assembly from the vehicle.
3. Remove the sending unit attaching screws, then pull the assembly out from the tank.
4. Installation is the reverse of removal. Always use new gaskets.

1991-1994 Models

1. Disconnect the negative battery cable.
2. Remove the fuel pump/sending unit assembly from the vehicle. Refer to the electric fuel pump procedure in this section.
3. Remove the fuel cut-off valve from the bracket assembly.
4. Remove the nut and spring washer, then disconnect the wires from the pump bracket.
5. Remove the sending unit attaching screws, then remove the unit from the bracket.
6. Installation is the reverse of removal. Always use new gaskets.

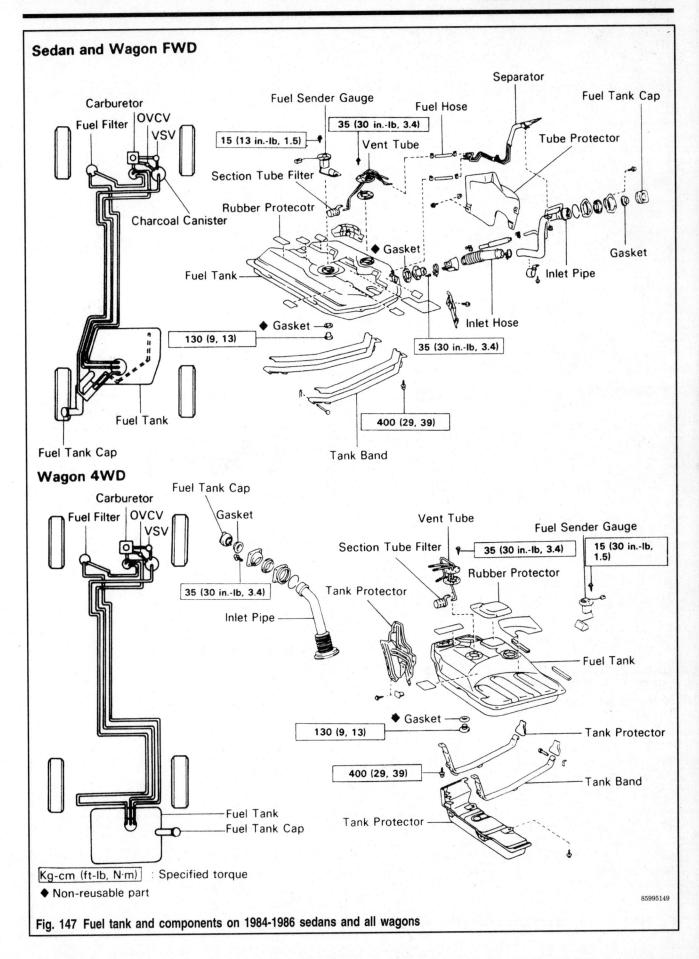

Sedan and Wagon FWD

Carburetor
Fuel Filter
OVCV
VSV
Charcoal Canister
Fuel Tank

Fuel Sender Gauge
35 (30 in.-lb, 3.4)
15 (13 in.-lb, 1.5)
Section Tube Filter
Vent Tube
Rubber Protecotr

Fuel Hose
Separator
Fuel Tank Cap
Tube Protector
◆ Gasket
Gasket
Inlet Pipe
Inlet Hose
35 (30 in.-lb, 3.4)

130 (9, 13)
◆ Gasket

400 (29, 39)
Tank Band

Fuel Tank
Fuel Tank Cap

Wagon 4WD

Carburetor
Fuel Filter
OVCV
VSV

Fuel Tank Cap
Gasket
35 (30 in.-lb, 3.4)
Inlet Pipe

Section Tube Filter
Tank Protector
Vent Tube
35 (30 in.-lb, 3.4)
Rubber Protector

Fuel Sender Gauge
15 (30 in.-lb, 1.5)

Fuel Tank

Fuel Tank
Fuel Tank Cap
130 (9, 13)
◆ Gasket
Tank Protector
400 (29, 39)
Tank Band
Tank Protector

Kg-cm (ft-lb, N·m) : Specified torque
◆ Non-reusable part

Fig. 147 Fuel tank and components on 1984-1986 sedans and all wagons

85995149

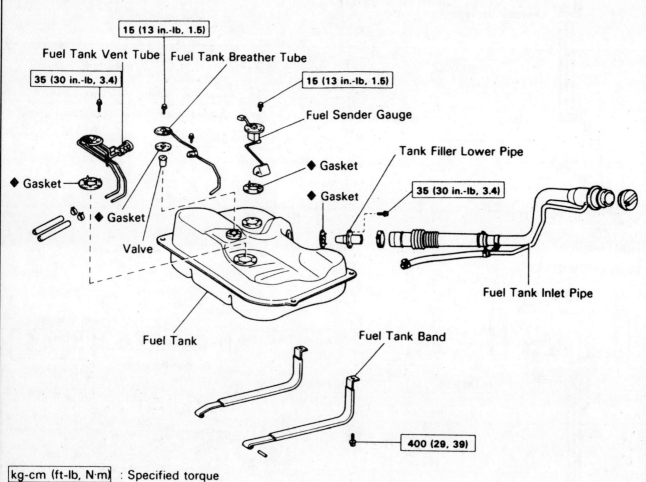

15 (13 in.-lb, 1.5)

Fuel Tank Vent Tube | Fuel Tank Breather Tube

35 (30 in.-lb, 3.4)

15 (13 in.-lb, 1.5)

Fuel Sender Gauge

Tank Filler Lower Pipe

◆ Gasket

◆ Gasket

35 (30 in.-lb, 3.4)

◆ Gasket

◆ Gasket

Valve

Fuel Tank Inlet Pipe

Fuel Tank

Fuel Tank Band

400 (29, 39)

kg-cm (ft-lb, N·m) : Specified torque

◆ Non-reusable part

85995150

Fig. 148 Fuel tank and components on 1987-1990 sedans equipped with 3E engines

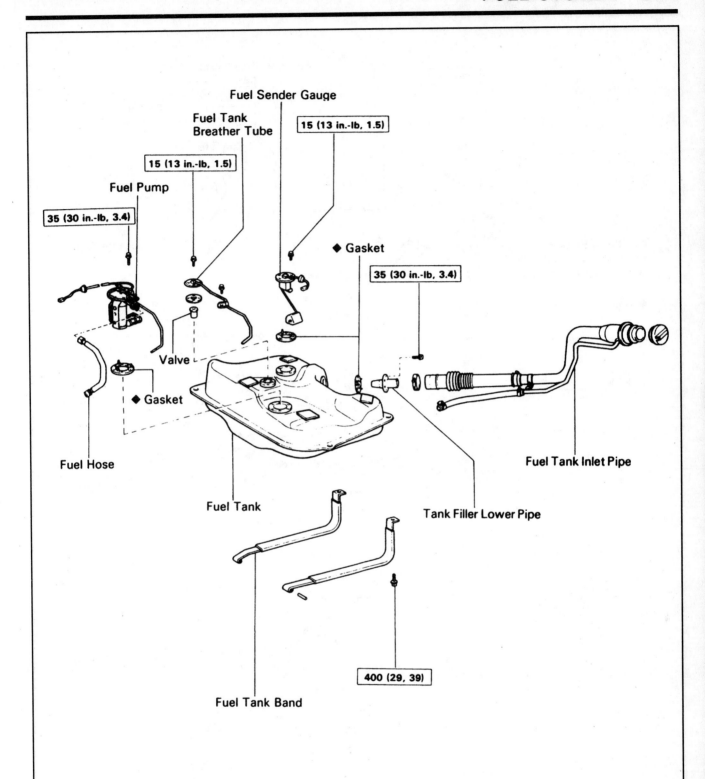

Fuel Sender Gauge

Fuel Tank
Breather Tube

15 (13 in.-lb, 1.5)

15 (13 in.-lb, 1.5)

Fuel Pump

35 (30 in.-lb, 3.4)

◆ Gasket

35 (30 in.-lb, 3.4)

Valve

◆ Gasket

Fuel Tank Inlet Pipe

Fuel Hose

Fuel Tank

Tank Filler Lower Pipe

Fuel Tank Band

400 (29, 39)

kg-cm (ft-lb, N·m) : Specified torque

◆ Non-reusable part

85995151

Fig. 149 Fuel tank and components on 1990 models equipped with fuel injected engines

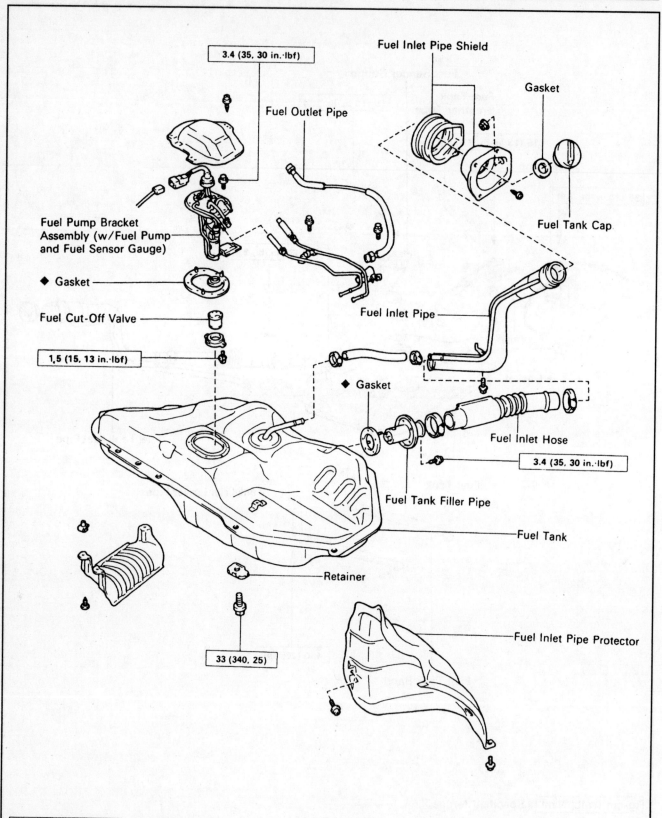

3.4 (35, 30 in.·lbf)

Fuel Inlet Pipe Shield

Gasket

Fuel Outlet Pipe

Fuel Tank Cap

Fuel Pump Bracket
Assembly (w/Fuel Pump
and Fuel Sensor Gauge)

◆ Gasket

Fuel Cut-Off Valve

Fuel Inlet Pipe

1.5 (15, 13 in.·lbf)

◆ Gasket

Fuel Inlet Hose

3.4 (35, 30 in.·lbf)

Fuel Tank Filler Pipe

Fuel Tank

Retainer

Fuel Inlet Pipe Protector

33 (340, 25)

N·m (kgf·cm, ft·lbf) : Specified torque

◆ Non-reusable part

85995152

Fig. 150 Fuel tank and components on 1991-1994 models

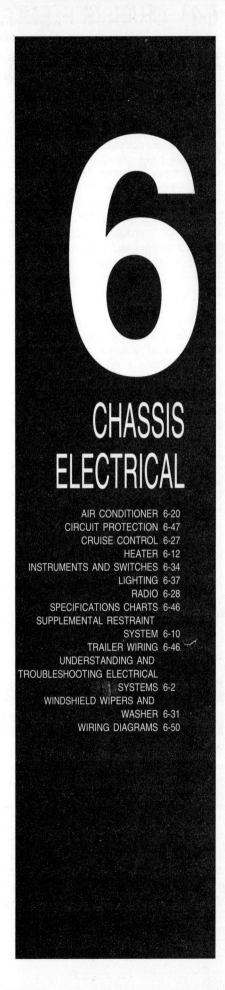

6

CHASSIS
ELECTRICAL

UNDERSTANDING AND TROUBLESHOOTING ELECTRICAL SYSTEMS

At the rate which both import and domestic manufacturers have incorporated electronic control systems into their production lines, most new vehicles are equipped with one or more on-board computer. These electronic components (with no moving parts) should theoretically last the life of the vehicle, provided nothing external happens to damage the circuits or memory chips.

While it is true that electronic components should never wear out, in the real world malfunctions do occur. It is also true that any computer-based system is extremely sensitive to electrical voltages and cannot tolerate careless or haphazard testing or service procedures. An inexperienced individual can literally do major damage looking for a minor problem by using the wrong kind of test equipment or connecting test leads or connectors with the ignition switch **ON**. When selecting test equipment, make sure the manufacturer's instructions state that the tester is compatible with whatever type of system is being serviced. Read all instructions carefully and double check all test points before installing probes or making any test connections.

The following section outlines basic diagnosis techniques for dealing with automotive electrical systems. Along with a general explanation of the various types of test equipment available to aid in servicing modern automotive systems, basic repair techniques for wiring harnesses and connectors are also given. Read the basic information before attempting any repairs or testing. This will provide the background of information necessary to avoid the most common and obvious mistakes that can cost both time and money. Although the replacement and testing procedures are simple in themselves, the systems are not, and unless one has a thorough understanding of all components and their function within a particular system, the logical test sequence these systems demand cannot be followed. Minor malfunctions can make a big difference, so it is important to know how each component affects the operation of the overall system to find the ultimate cause of a problem without replacing good components unnecessarily. It is not enough to use the correct test equipment; the test equipment must be used correctly.

Safety Precautions

✳✳CAUTION

Whenever working on or around any electrical or electronic systems, always observe these general precautions to prevent the possibility of personal injury or damage to electronic components.

• Never install or remove battery cables with the key ON or the engine running. Jumper cables should be connected with the key OFF to avoid power surges that can damage electronic control units. Engines equipped with computer controlled systems should avoid both giving and getting jump starts due to the possibility of serious damage to components from arcing in the engine compartment when connections are made with the ignition ON.

• Always remove the battery cables before charging the battery. Never use a high output charger on an installed battery or attempt to use any type of "hot shot" (24 volt) starting aid.

• Exercise care when inserting test probes into connectors to insure good contact without damaging the connector or spreading the pins. Always probe connectors from the rear (wire) side, NOT the pin side, to avoid accidental shorting of terminals during test procedures.

• Never remove or attach wiring harness connectors with the ignition switch ON, especially to an electronic control unit.

• Do not drop any components during service procedures and never apply 12 volts directly to any component (like a solenoid or relay) unless instructed specifically to do so. Some component electrical windings are designed to safely handle only 4 or 5 volts and can be destroyed in seconds if 12 volts are applied directly to the connector.

• Remove the electronic control unit if the vehicle is to be placed in an environment where temperatures exceed approximately 176°F (80°C), such as a paint spray booth or when arc or gas welding near the control unit location in the car.

Add-On Electrical Equipment

The electrical system in your car is designed to perform under reasonable operating conditions without interference between components. Before any additional electrical equipment is installed, it is recommended that you consult your Toyota dealer or a reputable repair facility familiar with the vehicle and its systems.

If the vehicle is equipped with mobile radio equipment and/or mobile telephone, it may have an effect upon the operation of the ECM. Radio Frequency Interference (RFI) from the communications system can be picked up by the car's wiring harnesses and conducted into the ECM, giving it the wrong messages at the wrong time. Although well shielded against RFI, the ECM should be further protected through the following steps:

1. Install the antenna as far as possible from the ECM. Since the ECM is located behind the center console area, the antenna should be mounted at the rear of the car.

2. Keep the antenna wiring a minimum of eight inches away from any wiring running to the ECM and from the ECM itself. NEVER wind the antenna wire around any other wiring.

3. Mount the equipment as far from the ECM as possible. Be very careful during installation not to drill through any wires or short a wire harness with a mounting screw.

4. Insure that the electrical feed wire(s) to the equipment are properly and tightly connected. Loose connectors can cause interference.

5. Make certain that the equipment is properly grounded to the car. Poor grounding can damage expensive equipment.

Organized Troubleshooting

When diagnosing a specific problem, organized troubleshooting is a must. The complexity of a modern automobile demands that you approach any problem in a logical, organized manner. There are certain troubleshooting techniques that are standard:

1. Establish when the problem occurs. Does the problem appear only under certain conditions? Were there any noises, odors, or other unusual symptoms?

2. Isolate the problem area. To do this, make some simple tests and observations; then eliminate the systems that are working properly. Check for obvious problems such as broken wires, dirty connections or split/disconnected vacuum hoses. Always check the obvious before assuming something complicated is the cause.

3. Test for problems systematically to determine the cause once the problem area is isolated. Are all the components functioning properly? Is there power going to electrical switches and motors? Is there vacuum at vacuum switches and/or actuators? Is there a mechanical problem such as bent linkage or loose mounting screws? Doing careful, systematic checks will often turn up most causes on the first inspection without wasting time checking components that have little or no relationship to the problem.

4. Test all repairs after the work is done to make sure that the problem is fixed. Some causes can be traced to more than one component, so a careful verification of repair work is important to pick up additional malfunctions that may cause a problem to reappear or a different problem to arise. A blown fuse, for example, is a simple problem that may require more than another fuse to repair. If you don't look for a problem that caused a fuse to blow, a shorted wire for example, may go undetected.

Experience has shown that most problems tend to be the result of a fairly simple and obvious cause, such as loose or corroded connectors or air leaks in the intake system. This makes careful inspection of components during testing essential to quick and accurate troubleshooting.

TEST EQUIPMENT

➡Pinpointing the exact cause of trouble in an electrical system can sometimes only be accomplished by the use of special test equipment. The following describes commonly used test equipment and explains how to put it to best use in diagnosis. In addition to the information covered below, the manufacturer's instructions booklet provided with the tester should be read and clearly understood before attempting any test procedures.

Jumper Wires

Jumper wires are simple, yet extremely valuable, pieces of test equipment. Jumper wires are merely wires that are used to bypass sections of a circuit. The simplest type of jumper wire is a length of multi-strand wire with an alligator clip at each end. Jumper wires are usually fabricated from lengths of standard automotive wire and whatever type of connector (alligator clip, spade connector or pin connector) that is required for the particular vehicle being tested. The well

equipped tool box will have several different styles of jumper wires in several different lengths. Some jumper wires are made with three or more terminals coming from a common splice for special purpose testing. In cramped, hard-to-reach areas it is advisable to have insulated boots over the jumper wire terminals in order to prevent accidental grounding, sparks, and possible fire, especially when testing fuel system components.

Jumper wires are used primarily to locate open electrical circuits, on either the ground (-) side of the circuit or on the hot (+) side. If an electrical component fails to operate, connect the jumper wire between the component and a good ground. If the component operates only with the jumper installed, the ground circuit is open. If the ground circuit is good, but the component does not operate, the circuit between the power feed and component may be open. By moving the jumper wire successively back from the lamp toward the power source, you can isolate the area of the circuit where the open is located. When the component stops functioning, or the power is cut off, the open is in the segment of wire between the jumper and the point previously tested.

You can sometimes connect the jumper wire directly from the battery to the hot terminal of the component, but first make sure the component uses 12 volts in operation. Some electrical components, such as fuel injectors, are designed to operate on about 4 volts and running 12 volts directly to the injector terminals can burn out the wiring.

By inserting an in-line fuse holder between a set of test leads, a fused jumper wire can be used for bypassing open circuits. Use a 5 amp fuse to provide protection against voltage spikes. When in doubt, use a voltmeter to check the voltage input to the component and measure how much voltage is being applied normally.

✳✳CAUTION

Never use jumpers made from wire that is of lighter gauge than used in the circuit under test. If the jumper wire is of too small gauge, it may overheat and possibly melt. Never use jumpers to bypass high resistance loads in a circuit. Bypassing resistances, in effect, creates a short circuit. This may, in turn, cause damage and fire. Jumper wires should only be used to bypass lengths of wire.

Unpowered Test Light

The 12 volt test light is used to check circuits and components while electrical current is flowing through them. It is used for voltage and ground tests. Twelve volt test lights come in different styles but all have three main parts; a ground clip, a probe, and a light. The most commonly used 12 volt test lights have pick-type probes. To use a 12 volt test light, connect the ground clip to a good ground and probe wherever necessary with the pick. The pick should be sharp so that it can penetrate wire insulation to make contact with the wire, without making a large hole in the insulation. The wrap-around light is handy in hard to reach areas or where it is difficult to support a wire to push a probe pick into it. To use the wrap around light, hook the wire to probed with the hook and pull the trigger. A small pick will be forced through the wire insulation into the wire core.

✳✳CAUTION

Do not use a test light to probe electronic ignition spark plug or coil wires. Never use a pick-type test light to probe wiring on computer controlled systems unless specifically instructed to do so. Any wire insulation that is pierced by the test light probe should be taped and sealed with silicone after testing.

Like the jumper wire, the 12 volt test light is used to isolate opens in circuits. But, whereas the jumper wire is used to bypass the open to operate the load, the 12 volt test light is used to locate the presence of voltage in a circuit. If the test light glows, you know that there is power up to that point; if the 12 volt test light does not glow when its probe is inserted into the wire or connector, you know that there is an open circuit (no power). Move the test light in successive steps back toward the power source until the light in the handle does glow. When it does glow, the open is between the probe and point which was probed previously.

➡**The test light does not detect that 12 volts (or any particular amount of voltage) is present; it only detects that some voltage is present. It is advisable before using the test light to touch its terminals across the battery posts to make sure the light is operating properly.**

Self-Powered Test Light

The self-powered test light usually contains a 1.5 volt penlight battery. One type of self-powered test light is similar in design to the 12 volt unit. This type has both the battery and the light in the handle, along with a pick-type probe tip. The second type has the light toward the open tip, so that the light illuminates the contact point. The self-powered test light is a dual purpose piece of test equipment. It can be used to test for either open or short circuits when power is isolated from the circuit (continuity test). A powered test light should not be used on any computer controlled system or component unless specifically instructed to do so. Many engine sensors can be destroyed by even this small amount of voltage applied directly to the terminals.

Voltmeter

A voltmeter is used to measure voltage at any point in a circuit, or to measure the voltage drop across any part of a circuit. It can also be used to check continuity in a wire or circuit by indicating current flow from one end to the other. Voltmeters usually have various scales on the meter dial and a selector switch to allow the selection of different voltages. The voltmeter has a positive and a negative lead. To avoid damage to the meter, always connect the negative lead to the negative (-) side of circuit (to ground or nearest the ground side of the circuit) and connect the positive lead to the positive (+) side of the circuit (to the power source or the nearest power source). Note that the negative voltmeter lead will always be black and that the positive voltmeter will always be some color other than black (usually red). Depending on how the voltmeter is connected into the circuit, it has several uses.

A voltmeter can be connected either in parallel or in series with a circuit and it has a very high resistance to current flow. When connected in parallel, only a small amount of current will flow through the voltmeter current path; the rest will flow through the normal circuit current path and the circuit will work normally. When the voltmeter is connected in series with a circuit, only a small amount of current can flow through the circuit. The circuit will not work properly, but the voltmeter reading will show if the circuit is complete or not.

Ohmmeter

The ohmmeter is designed to read resistance (Ω) in a circuit or component. Although there are several different styles of ohmmeters, all will usually have a selector switch which permits the measurement of different ranges of resistance (usually the selector switch allows the multiplication of the meter reading by 10, 100, 1,000, and 10,000). A calibration knob allows the meter to be set at zero for accurate measurement. Since all ohmmeters are powered by an internal battery (usually 9 volts), the ohmmeter can be used as a self-powered test light. When the ohmmeter is connected, current from the ohmmeter flows through the circuit or component being tested. Since the ohmmeter's internal resistance and voltage are known values, the amount of current flow through the meter depends on the resistance of the circuit or component being tested.

The ohmmeter can be used to perform continuity test for opens or shorts (either by observation of the meter needle or as a self-powered test light), and to read actual resistance in a circuit. It should be noted that the ohmmeter is used to check the resistance of a component or wire while there is no voltage applied to the circuit. Current flow from an outside voltage source (such as the vehicle battery) can damage the ohmmeter, so the circuit or component should be isolated from the vehicle electrical system before any testing is done. Since the ohmmeter uses its own voltage source, either lead can be connected to any test point.

➡**When checking diodes or other solid state components, the ohmmeter leads can only be connected one way in order to measure current flow in a single direction. Make sure the positive (+) and negative (-) terminal connections are as described in the test procedures to verify the one-way diode operation.**

In using the meter for making continuity checks, do not be concerned with the actual resistance readings. Zero resistance, or any reading, indicates continuity in the circuit. Infinite resistance indicates an open in the circuit. A high resistance reading where there should be none indicates a problem in the circuit. Checks for short circuits are made in the same manner as checks for open circuits except that the circuit must be isolated from both power and normal ground. Infinite resistance indicates no continuity to ground, while zero resistance indicates a dead short to ground.

Ammeters

An ammeter measures the amount of current flowing through a circuit in units called amperes or amps. Amperes are units of electron flow which indicate how fast the electrons are flowing through the circuit. Since Ohms Law dictates that current flow in a circuit is equal to the circuit voltage divided by the total circuit resistance, increasing voltage also increases the current level (amps). Likewise, any decrease in resistance will increase the amount of amps in a circuit. At normal operating voltage, most circuits have a characteristic amount of amperes, called "current draw" which can be measured using an ammeter. By referring to a specified current draw rating, measuring the amperes, and comparing the two values, one can determine what is happening within the circuit to aid in diagnosis. An open circuit, for example, will not allow any current to flow so the ammeter reading will be zero. More current flows through a heavily loaded circuit or when the charging system is operating.

An ammeter is always connected in series with the circuit being tested. All of the current that normally flows through the circuit must also flow through the ammeter; if there is any other path for the current to follow, the ammeter reading will not be accurate. The ammeter itself has very little resistance to current flow and therefore will not affect the circuit, but it will measure current draw only when the circuit is closed and electricity is flowing. Excessive current draw can blow fuses and drain the battery, while a reduced current draw can cause motors to run slowly, lights to dim and other components to not operate properly. The ammeter can help diagnose these conditions by locating the cause of the high or low reading.

Multimeters

Different combinations of test meters can be built into a single unit designed for specific tests. Some of the more common combination test devices are known as Volt/Amp testers, Tach/Dwell meters, or Digital Multimeters. The Volt/Amp tester is used for charging system, starting system or battery tests and consists of a voltmeter, an ammeter and a variable resistance carbon pile. The voltmeter will usually have at least two ranges for use with 6, 12 and/or 24 volt systems. The ammeter also has more than one range for testing various levels of battery loads and starter current draw and the carbon pile can be adjusted to offer different amounts of resistance. The Volt/Amp tester has heavy leads to carry large amounts of current and many later models have an inductive ammeter pickup that clamps around the wire to simplify test connections. On some models, the ammeter also has a zero-center scale to allow testing of charging and starting systems without switching leads or polarity. A digital multimeter is a voltmeter, ammeter and ohmmeter combined in an instrument which gives a digital readout. These are often used when testing solid state circuits because of their high input impedance (usually 10 megohms or more).

The tach/dwell meter that combines a tachometer and a dwell (cam angle) meter is a specialized kind of voltmeter. The tachometer scale is marked to show engine speed in rpm and the dwell scale is marked to show degrees of distributor shaft rotation. In most electronic ignition systems, dwell is determined by the control unit, but the dwell meter can also be used to check the duty cycle (operation) of some electronic engine control systems. Some tach/dwell meters are powered by an internal battery, while others take their power from the car battery in use. The battery powered testers usually require calibration much like an ohmmeter before testing.

TESTING

Open Circuits

To use the self-powered test light to check for open circuits, first isolate the circuit from the vehicle's 12 volt power source by disconnecting the battery or wiring harness connector. Connect the test light ground clip to a good ground and probe sections of the circuit sequentially with the test light. (start from either end of the circuit). If the light is out, the open is between the probe and the circuit ground. If the light is on, the open is between the probe and end of the circuit toward the power source.

Short Circuits

By isolating the circuit both from power and from ground, and using a self-powered test light, you can check for shorts to ground in the circuit. Isolate the circuit from power and ground. Connect the test light ground clip to a good ground and probe any easy-to-reach test point in the circuit. If the light comes on, there is a short somewhere in the circuit. To isolate the short, probe a test point at either end of the isolated circuit (the light should be on). Leave the test light probe connected and open connectors, switches, remove parts, etc., sequentially, until the light goes out. When the light goes out, the short is between the last circuit component opened and the previous circuit opened.

➡**The 1.5 volt battery in the test light does not provide much current. A weak battery may not provide enough power to illuminate the test light even when a complete circuit is made (especially if there are high resistances in the circuit). Always make sure that the test battery is strong. To check the battery, briefly touch the ground clip to the probe; if the light glows brightly the battery is strong enough for testing. Never use a self-powered test light to perform checks for opens or shorts when power is applied to the electrical system under test. The 12 volt vehicle power will quickly burn out the 1.5 volt light bulb in the test light.**

Available Voltage Measurement

Set the voltmeter selector switch to the 20V position and connect the meter negative lead to the negative post of the battery. Connect the positive meter lead to the positive post of the battery and turn the ignition switch ON to provide a load. Read the voltage on the meter or digital display. A well charged battery should register over 12 volts. If the meter reads below 11.5 volts, the battery power may be insufficient to operate the electrical system properly. This test determines voltage available from the battery and should be the first step in any electrical trouble diagnosis procedure. Many electrical problems, especially on computer controlled systems, can be caused by a low state of charge in the battery. Excessive corrosion at the battery cable terminals can cause a poor contact that will prevent proper charging and full battery current flow.

Normal battery voltage is 12 volts when fully charged. When the battery is supplying current to one or more circuits it is said to be "under load". When everything is off the electrical system is under a "no-load" condition. A fully charged battery may show about 12.5 volts at no load; will drop to 12 volts under medium load; and will drop even lower under heavy load. If the battery is partially discharged the voltage decrease under heavy load may be excessive, even though the battery shows 12 volts or more at no load. When allowed to discharge further, the battery's available voltage under load will decrease more severely. For this reason, it is important that the battery be fully charged during all testing procedures to avoid errors in diagnosis and incorrect test results.

Voltage Drop

When current flows through a resistance, the voltage beyond the resistance is reduced (the larger the current, the greater the reduction in voltage). When no current is flowing, there is no voltage drop because there is no current flow. All points in the circuit which are connected to the power source are at the same voltage as the power source. The total voltage drop always equals the total source voltage. In a long circuit with many connectors, a series of small, unwanted voltage drops due to corrosion at the connectors can add up to a total loss of voltage which impairs the operation of the normal loads in the circuit.

INDIRECT COMPUTATION OF VOLTAGE DROPS

1. Set the voltmeter selector switch to the 20 volt position.
2. Connect the meter negative lead to a good ground.
3. Probe all resistances in the circuit with the positive meter lead.
4. Operate the circuit in all modes and observe the voltage readings.

DIRECT MEASUREMENT OF VOLTAGE DROPS

1. Set the voltmeter switch to the 20 volt position.
2. Connect the voltmeter negative lead to the ground side of the resistance load to be measured.
3. Connect the positive lead to the positive side of the resistance or load to be measured.
4. Read the voltage drop directly on the 20 volt scale.

Too high a voltage indicates too high a resistance. If, for example, a blower motor runs too slowly, you can determine if there is too high a resistance in the resistor pack. By taking voltage drop readings in all parts of the circuit, you can isolate the problem. Too low a voltage drop indicates too low a resistance. Take the blower motor for example again. If a blower motor runs too fast in the MED and/or LOW position, the problem can be isolated in the resistor pack by taking voltage drop readings in all parts of the circuit to locate a possibly shorted resistor. The maximum allowable voltage drop under load is critical, especially if there is more than one high resistance problem in a circuit because all voltage drops are cumulative. A small drop is normal due to the resistance of the conductors.

HIGH RESISTANCE TESTING

1. Set the voltmeter selector switch to the 4 volt position.
2. Connect the voltmeter positive lead to the positive post of the battery.
3. Turn on the headlights and heater blower to provide a load.
4. Probe various points in the circuit with the negative voltmeter lead.

5. Read the voltage drop on the 4 volt scale. Some average maximum allowable voltage drops are:
- FUSE PANEL: 7 volts
- IGNITION SWITCH: 5 volts
- HEADLIGHT SWITCH: 7 volts
- IGNITION COIL (+): 5 volts
- ANY OTHER LOAD: 1.3 volts

➡**Voltage drops are all measured while a load is operating; without current flow, there will be no voltage drop.**

Resistance Measurement

The batteries in an ohmmeter will weaken with age and temperature, so the ohmmeter must be calibrated or "zeroed" before taking measurements. To zero the meter, place the selector switch in its lowest range and touch the two ohmmeter leads together. Turn the calibration knob until the meter needle is exactly on zero.

➡**All analog (needle) type ohmmeters must be zeroed before use, but some digital ohmmeter models are automatically calibrated when the switch is turned on. Self-calibrating digital ohmmeters do not have an adjusting knob, but its a good idea to check for a zero readout before use by touching the leads together. All computer controlled systems require the use of a digital ohmmeter with at least 10 megohms impedance for testing. Before any test procedures are attempted, make sure the ohmmeter used is compatible with the electrical system or damage to the on-board computer could result.**

To measure resistance, first isolate the circuit from the vehicle power source by disconnecting the battery cables or the harness connector. Make sure the key is OFF when disconnecting any components or the battery. Where necessary, also isolate at least one side of the circuit to be checked in order to avoid reading parallel resistances. Parallel circuit resistances will always give a lower reading than the actual resistance of either of the branches. When measuring the resistance of parallel circuits, the total resistance will always be lower than the smallest resistance in the circuit. Connect the meter leads to both sides of the circuit (wire or component) and read the actual measured ohms on the meter scale. Make sure the selector switch is set to the proper ohm scale for the circuit being tested to avoid misreading the ohmmeter test value.

❊❊WARNING

Never use an ohmmeter with power applied to the circuit. Like the self-powered test light, the ohmmeter is designed to operate on its own power supply. The normal 12 volt automotive electrical system current could damage the meter!

Wiring Harnesses

The average automobile contains about ½ mile of wiring, with hundreds of individual connections. To protect the many wires from damage and to keep them from becoming a confusing tangle, they are organized into bundles, enclosed in plastic or taped together and called wiring harnesses. Different harnesses serve different parts of the vehicle. Individual wires are color coded to help trace them through a harness where sections are hidden from view.

Automotive wiring or circuit conductors can be in any one of three forms:

1. Single strand wire
2. Multi-strand wire
3. Printed circuitry

Single strand wire has a solid metal core and is usually used inside such components as alternators, motors, relays and other devices. Multi-strand wire has a core made of many small strands of wire twisted together into a single conductor. Most of the wiring in an automotive electrical system is made up of multi-strand wire, either as a single conductor or grouped together in a harness. All wiring is color coded on the insulator, either as a solid color or as a colored wire with an identification stripe. A printed circuit is a thin film of copper or other conductor that is printed on an insulator backing. Occasionally, a printed circuit is sandwiched between two sheets of plastic for more protection and flexibility. A complete printed circuit, consisting of conductors, insulating material and connectors for lamps or other components is called a printed circuit board. Printed circuitry is used in place of individual wires or harnesses in places where space is limited, such as behind instrument panels.

Since automotive electrical systems are very sensitive to changes in resistance, the selection of properly sized wires is critical when systems are repaired. A loose or corroded connection or a replacement wire that is too small for the circuit will add extra resistance and an additional voltage drop to the circuit. A ten percent voltage drop can result in slow or erratic motor operation, for example, even though the circuit is complete. The wire gauge number is an expression of the cross section area of the conductor. The most common system for expressing wire size is the American Wire Gauge (AWG) system.

Gauge numbers are assigned to conductors of various cross section areas. As gauge number increases, area decreases and the conductor becomes smaller. A 5 gauge conductor is smaller than a 1 gauge conductor and a 10 gauge is smaller than a 5 gauge. As the cross section area of a conductor decreases, resistance increases and so does the gauge number. A conductor with a higher gauge number will carry less current than a conductor with a lower gauge number.

➡Gauge wire size refers to the size of the conductor, not the size of the complete wire. It is possible to have two wires of the same gauge with different diameters because one may have thicker insulation than the other.

12 volt automotive electrical systems generally use 10, 12, 14, 16 and 18 gauge wire. Main power distribution circuits and larger accessories usually use 10 and 12 gauge wire. Battery cables are usually 4 or 6 gauge, although 1 and 2 gauge wires are occasionally used. Wire length must also be considered when making repairs to a circuit. As conductor length increases, so does resistance. An 18 gauge wire, for example, can carry a 10 amp load for 10 feet without

excessive voltage drop; however if a 15 foot wire is required for the same 10 amp load, it must be a 16 gauge wire.

An electrical schematic shows the electrical current paths when a circuit is operating properly. It is essential to understand how a circuit works before trying to figure out why it doesn't. Schematics break the entire electrical system down into individual circuits and show only one particular circuit. In a schematic, no attempt is made to represent wiring and components as they physically appear on the vehicle; switches and other components are shown as simply as possible. Face views of harness connectors show the cavity or terminal locations in all multi-pin connectors to help locate test points.

If you need to backprobe a connector while it is on the component, the order of the terminals must be mentally reversed. The wire color code can help in this situation, as well as a keyway, lock tab or other reference mark.

WIRING REPAIR

Soldering is a quick, efficient method of joining metals permanently. Everyone who has the occasion to make wiring repairs should know how to solder. Electrical connections that are soldered are far less likely to come apart and will conduct electricity much better than connections that are only "pig-tailed" together. The most popular (and preferred) method of soldering is with an electrical soldering gun. Soldering irons are available in many sizes and wattage ratings. Irons with higher wattage ratings deliver higher temperatures and recover lost heat faster. A small soldering iron rated for no more than 50 watts is recommended, especially on electrical systems where excess heat can damage the components being soldered.

There are three ingredients necessary for successful soldering; proper flux, good solder and sufficient heat. A soldering flux is necessary to clean the metal of tarnish, prepare it for soldering and to enable the solder to spread into tiny crevices. When soldering, always use a rosin core solder which is non-corrosive and will not attract moisture once the job is finished. Other types of flux (acid core) will leave a residue that will attract moisture and cause the wires to corrode. Tin is a unique metal with a low melting point. In a molten state, it dissolves and alloys easily with many metals. Solder is made by mixing tin with lead. The most common proportions are 40/60, 50/50 and 60/40, with the percentage of tin listed first. Low priced solders usually contain less tin, making them very difficult for a beginner to use because more heat is required to melt the solder. A common solder is 40/60 which is well suited for all-around general use, but 60/40 melts easier and is preferred for electrical work.

Soldering Techniques

Successful soldering requires that the metals to be joined be heated to a temperature that will melt the solder, usually 360-460°F (182-238°C). Contrary to popular belief, the purpose of the soldering iron is not to melt the solder itself, but to heat the parts being soldered to a temperature high enough to melt the solder when it is touched to the work. Melting flux-cored solder on the soldering iron will usually destroy the effectiveness of the flux.

➡ **Soldering tips are made of copper for good heat conductivity, but must be "tinned" regularly for quick transference of heat to the project and to prevent the solder from sticking to the iron. To "tin" the iron, simply heat it and touch the flux-cored solder to the tip; the solder will flow over the hot tip. Wipe the excess off with a clean rag, but be careful as the iron will be hot.**

After some use, the tip may become pitted. If so, simply dress the tip smooth with a smooth file and "tin" the tip again. Flux-cored solder will remove oxides but rust, bits of insulation and oil or grease must be removed with a wire brush or emery cloth. For maximum strength in soldered parts, the joint must start off clean and tight. Weak joints will result in gaps too wide for the solder to bridge.

If a separate soldering flux is used, it should be brushed or swabbed on only those areas that are to be soldered. Most solders contain a core of flux and separate fluxing is unnecessary. Hold the work to be soldered firmly. It is best to solder on a wooden board, because a metal vise will only rob the piece to be soldered of heat and make it difficult to melt the solder. Hold the soldering tip with the broadest face against the work to be soldered. Apply solder under the tip close to the work, using enough solder to give a heavy film between the iron and the piece being soldered, while moving slowly and making sure the solder melts properly. Keep the work level or the solder will run to the lowest part and favor the thicker parts, because these require more heat to melt the solder. If the soldering tip overheats (the solder coating on the face of the tip burns up), it should be retinned. Once the soldering is completed, let the soldered joint stand until cool. Tape and seal all soldered wire splices after the repair has cooled.

Wire Harness Connectors

Most connectors in the engine compartment or otherwise exposed to the elements are protected against moisture and dirt which could create oxidation and deposits on the terminals.

These special connectors are weather-proof. All repairs require the use of a special terminal and the tool required to service it. This tool is used to remove the pin and sleeve terminals. If removal is attempted with an ordinary pick, there is a good chance that the terminal will be bent or deformed. Unlike standard blade type terminals, these weather-proof terminals cannot be straightened once they are bent. Make certain that the connectors are properly seated and all of the sealing rings are in place when connecting leads. On some models, a hinge-type flap provides a backup or secondary locking feature for the terminals. Most secondary locks are used to improve connector reliability by retaining the terminals if the small terminal lock tangs are not positioned properly.

Molded-on connectors require complete replacement of the connection. This means splicing a new connector assembly into the harness. All splices should be soldered to insure proper contact. Use care when probing the connections or replacing terminals in them as it is possible to short between opposite terminals. If this happens to the wrong terminal pair, it is possible to damage certain components. Always use

jumper wires between connectors for circuit checking and never probe through weatherproof seals.

Open circuits are often difficult to locate by sight because corrosion or terminal misalignment are hidden by the connectors. Merely wiggling a connector on a sensor or in the wiring harness may correct the open circuit condition. This should always be considered when an open circuit or a failed sensor is indicated. Intermittent problems may also be caused by oxidized or loose connections. When using a circuit tester for diagnosis, always probe connections from the wire side. Be careful not to damage sealed connectors with test probes.

All wiring harnesses should be replaced with identical parts, using the same gauge wire and connectors. When signal wires are spliced into a harness, use wire with high temperature insulation only. It is seldom necessary to replace a complete harness. If replacement is necessary, pay close attention to insure proper harness routing. Secure the harness with suitable plastic wire clamps to prevent vibrations from causing the harness to wear in spots or contact any hot components.

➡ **Weatherproof connectors cannot be replaced with standard connectors. Instructions are provided with replacement connector and terminal packages. Some wire harnesses have mounting indicators (usually pieces of colored tape) to mark where the harness is to be secured.**

In making wiring repairs, it's important that you always replace damaged wires with wires that are the same gauge as the wire being replaced. The heavier the wire, the smaller the gauge number. Wires are color-coded to aid in identification and whenever possible the same color coded wire should be used for replacement. A wire stripping and crimping tool is necessary to install solderless terminal connectors. Test all crimps by pulling on the wires; it should not be possible to pull the wires out of a good crimp.

Wires which are open, exposed or otherwise damaged are repaired by simple splicing. Where possible, if the wiring harness is accessible and the damaged place in the wire can be located, it is best to open the harness and check for all possible damage. In an inaccessible harness, the wire must be bypassed with a new insert, usually taped to the outside of the old harness.

When replacing fusible links, be sure to use fusible link wire, NOT ordinary automotive wire. Make sure the fusible segment is of the same gauge and construction as the one being replaced and double the stripped end when crimping the terminal connector for a good contact. The melted (open) fusible link segment of the wiring harness should be cut off as close to the harness as possible, then a new segment spliced in as described. In the case of a damaged fusible link that feeds two harness wires, the harness connections should be replaced with two fusible link wires so that each circuit will have its own separate protection.

➡ **Most of the problems caused in the wiring harness are due to bad ground connections. Always check all vehicle ground connections for corrosion or looseness before performing any power feed checks to eliminate the chance of a bad ground affecting the circuit.**

Hard Shell Connectors

Unlike molded connectors, the terminal contacts in hard shell connectors can be replaced. Weatherproof hard-shell connectors with the leads molded into the shell have non-replaceable terminal ends. Replacement usually involves the use of a special terminal removal tool that depress the locking tangs (barbs) on the connector terminal and allow the connector to be removed from the rear of the shell. The connector shell should be replaced if it shows any evidence of burning, melting, cracks, or breaks. Replace individual terminals that are burnt, corroded, distorted or loose.

➡**The insulation crimp must be tight to prevent the insulation from sliding back on the wire when the wire is pulled. The insulation must be visibly compressed under the crimp tabs, and the ends of the crimp should be turned in for a firm grip on the insulation.**

The wire crimp must be made with all wire strands inside the crimp. The terminal must be fully compressed on the wire strands with the ends of the crimp tabs turned in to make a firm grip on the wire. Check all connections with an ohmmeter to insure a good contact. There should be no measurable resistance between the wire and the terminal when connected.

Fusible Links

The fuse link is a short length of special, Hypalon (high temperature) insulated wire, integral with the engine compartment wiring harness and should not be confused with standard wire. It is several wire gauges smaller than the circuit which it protects. Under no circumstances should a fuse link replacement repair be made using a length of standard wire cut from bulk stock or from another wiring harness.

To repair any blown fuse link use the following procedure:
1. Determine which circuit is damaged, its location and the cause of the open fuse link. If the damaged fuse link is one of three fed by a common No. 10 or 12 gauge feed wire, determine the specific affected circuit.
2. Disconnect the negative battery cable.
3. Cut the damaged fuse link from the wiring harness and discard it. If the fuse link is one of three circuits fed by a single feed wire, cut it out of the harness at each splice end and discard it.
4. Identify and procure the proper fuse link with butt connectors for attaching the fuse link to the harness.
5. To repair any fuse link in a 3-link group with one feed:
   a. After cutting the open link out of the harness, cut each of the remaining undamaged fuse links close to the feed wire weld.
   b. Strip approximately ½ in. (13mm) of insulation from the detached ends of the two good fuse links, Then insert two wire ends into one end of a butt connector and carefully push one stripped end of the replacement fuse link into the

same end of the butt connector and crimp all three firmly together.

➡**Care must be taken when fitting the three fuse links into the butt connector as the internal diameter is a snug fit for three wires. Make sure to use a proper crimping tool. Pliers, side cutter, etc. will not apply the proper crimp to retain the wires and withstand a pull test.**

   c. After crimping the butt connector to the three fuse links, cut the weld portion from the feed wire and strip approximately ½ in. (13mm) of insulation from the cut end. Insert the stripped end into the open end of the butt connector and crimp very firmly.
   d. To attach the remaining end of the replacement fuse link, strip approximately ½ in. (13mm) of insulation from the wire end of the circuit from which the blown fuse link was removed, and firmly crimp a butt connector or equivalent to the stripped wire. Then, insert the end of the replacement link into the other end of the butt connector and crimp firmly.
   e. Using rosin core solder with a consistency of 60 percent tin and 40 percent lead, solder the connectors and the wires at the repairs then insulate with electrical tape or heat shrink tubing.

➡**Heat shrink tubing must be slipped over the wire before crimping and soldering the connection.**

6. To replace any fuse link on a single circuit in a harness, cut out the damaged portion, strip approximately ½ in. (13mm) of insulation from the two wire ends and attach the appropriate replacement fuse link to the stripped wire ends with two proper size butt connectors. Solder the connectors and wires, then insulate.
7. To repair any fuse link which has an eyelet terminal on one end such as the charging circuit, cut off the open fuse link behind the weld, strip approximately ½ in. (13mm) of insulation from the cut end and attach the appropriate new eyelet fuse link to the cut stripped wire with an appropriate size butt connector. Solder the connectors and wires at the repair, then insulate.
8. Connect the negative battery cable to the battery and test the system for proper operation.

➡**Do not mistake a resistor wire for a fuse link. The resistor wire is generally longer and has print stating, "Resistor-don't cut or splice".**

When attaching a single No. 16, 17, 18 or 20 gauge fuse link to a heavy gauge wire, always double the stripped wire end of the fuse link before inserting and crimping it into the butt connector for positive wire retention.

SUPPLEMENTAL RESTRAINT SYSTEM

General Information

SYSTEM OPERATION

▶ See Figure 1

The Supplemental Restraint System (SRS), together with the seat belt, is designed to help protect the driver during frontal impact.

When the vehicle is involved in a frontal collision within the activation area and the shock is greater than a predetermined level, the SRS is automatically activated. A safing sensor is designed to close at a deceleration rate less then the front and center air bag sensors. Air bag activation occurs when the safing sensor and either a front air bag sensor and/or the center air bag sensor contacts close simultaneously.

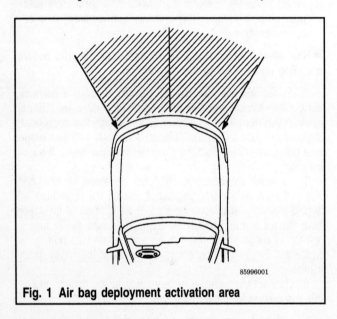

Fig. 1 Air bag deployment activation area

SYSTEM COMPONENTS

Air bag

▶ See Figures 2 and 3

The air bag of the SRS is stored in the steering wheel pad and cannot be disassembled. A gas generant inflates the air bag during a frontal collision of sufficient force. The bag de-

flates as the gas is discharged through the vent holes at the bag's rear or side.

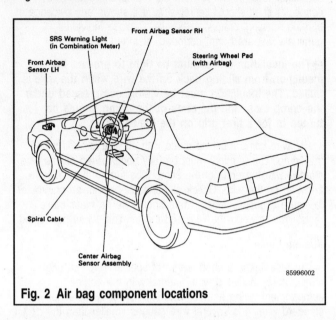

Fig. 2 Air bag component locations

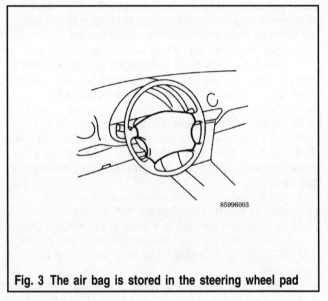

Fig. 3 The air bag is stored in the steering wheel pad

Spiral Cable

▶ See Figure 4

A spiral cable is used as an electrical joint from the air bag controls to the steering wheel.

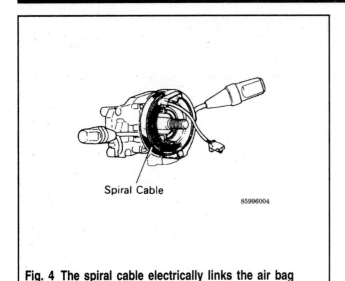

Fig. 4 The spiral cable electrically links the air bag controls to the air bag

SRS Warning Light
▶ See Figure 5

The SRS warning light is located in the combination meter. It goes on to alert the driver when a malfunction is detected by the center air bag sensor assembly during system self-diagnosis. Under normal operating conditions, the light goes ON for about 6 seconds, then goes OFF when the ignition key is turned to the **ACC** or **ON** position.

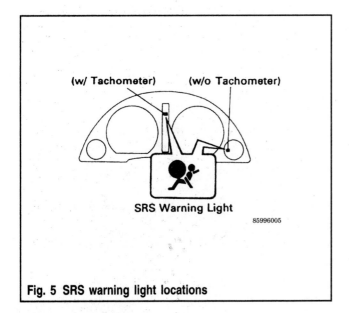

Fig. 5 SRS warning light locations

Front Air bag Sensors
▶ See Figure 6

A front air bag sensor is mounted inside each of the front fenders. The sensor unit is basically a mechanical switch. When the sensor detects a deceleration force above a predetermined level in a collision, the contacts in the sensor close,

sending a signal to the center air bag sensor assembly. The sensor cannot be disassembled.

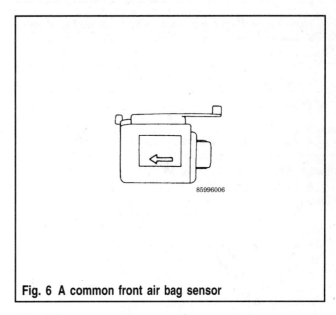

Fig. 6 A common front air bag sensor

Center Air bag Sensor Assembly
▶ See Figure 7

The center air bag sensor assembly is mounted on the floor inside the console. The center air bag sensor assembly consists of a center air bag sensor, safing sensors, air bag ignition control and a self-diagnosis circuit. It receives signals from the air bag sensors and determines whether or not the SRS must be activated.

SRS Connectors

All connectors in the SRS are colored yellow to distinguish them from other connectors and are specifically designed for use in the SRS.

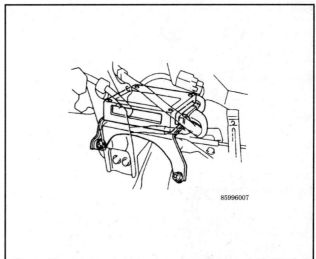

Fig. 7 The center air bag sensor assembly consists of several control circuits

SYSTEM PRECAUTIONS

The following service precautions should always be followed:
• Always disarm the system before performing any work on the vehicle
• Do not disassemble any air bag system components
• SRS service and diagnosis should only be performed by a certified technician
• The SRS must be inspected 10 years after the vehicle's date of manufacture
• Always have the SRS inspected when the vehicle has been involved in a collision (even in cases of minor collisions) where the air bag did not deploy
• Any visible damage to SRS components requires replacement
• Never strike or jar a sensor, air bag deployment could occur
• Never subject the vehicle to temperatures higher than 200°F (93°C), such as in a paint booth, without first disabling the system and having the SRS components removed by a certified technician
• Always touch a vehicle ground after sliding across the seat or walking across vinyl/carpeted floors to avoid static discharge damage to the SRS

DISARMING THE SYSTEM

1. Turn the ignition switch to the **LOCK** position.
2. Disconnect the negative battery cable, then insulate it by wrapping it with electrical tape.
3. Wait at least 90 seconds from the time the ignition switch is turned to the **LOCK** position and the battery is disconnected before performing any further work. The SRS is equipped with a back-up power source. If work is started before 90 seconds have elapsed, air bag deployment may occur.

ARMING THE SYSTEM

1. Connect the negative battery cable.
2. Perform a SRS check by turning the ignition key to the **ON** or **ACC** position, but do not start the engine.
3. The warning lamp should illuminate for about 6 seconds. If no malfunctions are detected, the lamp should turn OFF. If it stays ON, have the vehicle serviced immediately by a certified technician.

HEATER

Blower Motor

❊❊CAUTION

On models equipped with a Supplemental Restraint System (SRS) or "air bag," work must NOT be started until at least 90 seconds have passed from the time that both the ignition switch is turned to the LOCK position and the negative cable is disconnected from the battery.

REMOVAL & INSTALLATION

▸ **See Figures 8, 9 and 10**

1. Disconnect the negative battery cable. Remove the screws attaching the under-dash cover, if equipped.
2. Remove any obstructions which may interfere with blower motor removal.
3. Unplug the blower motor connector.
4. Remove the bolts/screws attaching the blower motor to the heater/air conditioning unit.
5. With the blower removed, check the case for any debris or signs of fan contact. Inspect the fan for wear spots, cracked blades or hub, loose retaining nut or poor alignment.

To install:

6. Place the blower motor in position, making sure it is properly aligned within the case. Install bolts/screws, then tighten them.

7. Engage the connector to the blower motor. Install any other components removed for access to the blower motor assembly.
8. Install the under-dash cover, if equipped. Connect the negative battery cable, then check for proper operation of the blower motor.

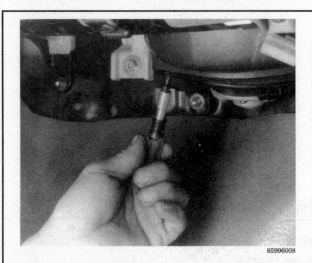

Fig. 8 The blower motor is usually secured by several screws to the housing

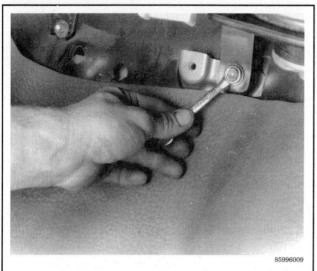

Fig. 9 Some blower motors also have a grounding strap

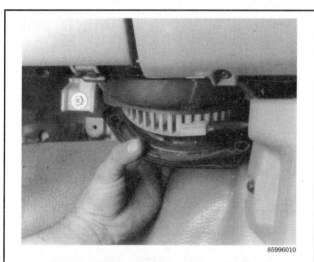

Fig. 10 Make sure the sealing gasket is in place before installing the motor

Heater Unit

✳✳CAUTION

On models equipped with a Supplemental Restraint System (SRS) or "air bag," work must NOT be started until at least 90 seconds have passed from the time that both the ignition switch is turned to the LOCK position and the negative cable is disconnected from the battery.

REMOVAL & INSTALLATION

▶ See Figures 11, 12, 13, 15, 14, 16, 17, 18, 19 and 20

1. Disconnect the negative battery cable.
2. Drain the cooling system.
3. Remove the glove compartment and the lower trim panels.

4. Remove the cooling unit on air conditioned models. Refer to the appropriate procedure later in this section.
5. In the engine compartment, disconnect the hoses from the heater core pipes. Also, remove the pipe grommets from the firewall.
6. Remove the control panel. Refer to the appropriate procedure.
7. Loosen the center duct attaching screws, then remove the duct.
8. Remove the instrument panel reinforcement braces.
9. Loosen the heater unit extension attaching screws, then remove the heater unit extension. This applies to vehicles without air conditioning only.
10. Label and disconnect any control cables attached to the heater unit.
11. Label and unplug any electrical connections on the heater unit.
12. Loosen the heater unit attaching screws, then remove the unit from the vehicle. On some models, removing the left

Fig. 11 Make sure you disconnect the hoses from the heater core before attempting to remove the heater unit

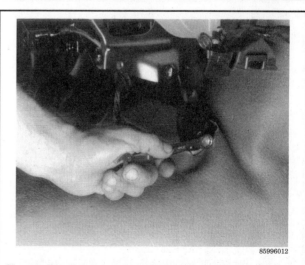

Fig. 12 The instrument panel reinforcement brace is secured by several small bolts

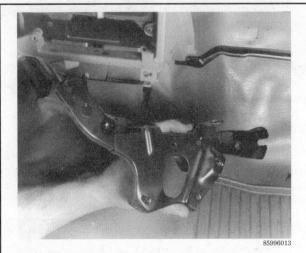
Fig. 13 Make sure you remove the brace; do not attempt to bend it out of the way

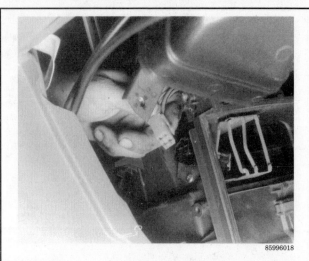
Fig. 16 Be sure to unplug the resistor block connector before attempting to remove the heater unit

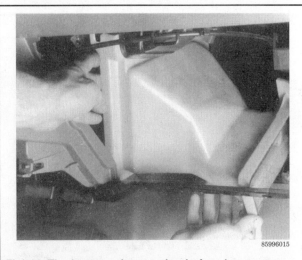
Fig. 14 The heater unit extension is found on cars without air conditioning

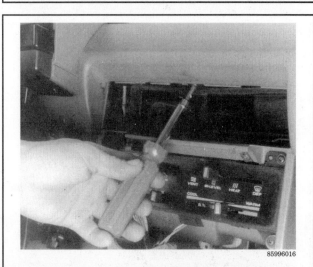
Fig. 17 The heater unit has many hidden attaching screws

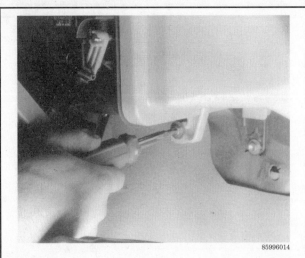
Fig. 15 The heater unit extension is secured by several screws

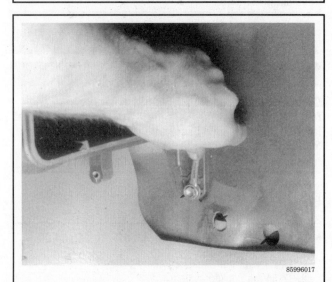
Fig. 18 Removing the heater unit lower attaching bolt

side duct may make removal easier. Be careful not to spill any coolant from the heater core inside the vehicle.

To install:

13. Install the heater unit to the vehicle. Engage any electrical and/or cable connections applicable. Also, install the left side duct if removed earlier.

14. Install the heater unit extension on cars without A/C.

15. Install the instrument panel reinforcement braces.

16. Install the center duct and the control panel.

17. Install the cooling unit on models equipped with A/C.

18. Install the lower trim panels and the glove compartment.

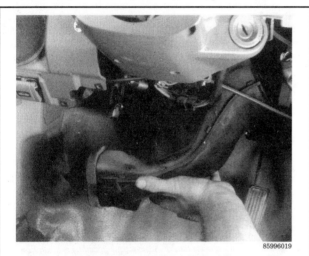

Fig. 19 On some models, removing the left side duct may make removal easier

Fig. 20 Carefully lower the heater unit, be sure not to damage it and other components

19. Install the grommets and hoses to the heater core pipes.

20. Fill the cooling system. Start the engine and check for leaks as well as proper heater operation.

Heater Core

REMOVAL & INSTALLATION

▶ **See Figures 21 and 22**

1. Disconnect the negative battery cable, then drain the cooling system.

2. On models equipped with air conditioning, remove the cooling unit. Refer to the appropriate procedure later in this section.

3. On models not equipped with air conditioning, remove the heater unit extension. Follow the procedures outlined in this section.

4. Remove the heater unit from the vehicle following the procedures outlined in this section.

Fig. 21 The heater core retaining clamp should be loosened or removed

5. Remove the heater core retaining screw(s) and clamp(s).

6. Carefully pull the core from the heater unit assembly.

7. Remove any debris which may be in the heater unit.

To install:

8. Position the heater core into the unit, then install the retaining clamp(s) and screws(s).

9. Install the heater unit.

10. Install the heater unit extension on cars without A/C or the cooling unit on cars with A/C.

11. Fill the cooling system. Start the engine and check for leaks as well as proper heater operation.

Fig. 22 With the core removed, the inside of the heater unit should be cleaned

Water Control Valve

REMOVAL & INSTALLATION

▶ See Figure 23

➡ Not all models use water control valves.

The water control valve is usually located in the engine compartment, connected in-line with the heater core inlet hose.

1. Disconnect the negative battery cable.
2. Drain the cooling system.
3. Disconnect the control cable from the valve.
4. Remove the hose clamps, then remove the water valve from the hose.
5. Installation is the reverse of removal. Adjust the cable.

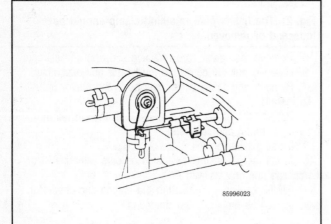

Fig. 23 A common water control valve found on some models

Control Panel

REMOVAL & INSTALLATION

1984-1986 Sedans and All Wagons
▶ See Figures 24 and 25

1. Disconnect the negative battery cable.
2. Loosen the lower console/radio trim box retaining screws, then remove the panel.
3. Loosen the center trim panel attaching screws, then remove the panel.
4. Loosen the control panel attaching screws, then pull the panel out from the dash. Disconnect the control cables and unplug the electrical connections from the back of the control panel.
5. Installation is the reverse of removal.

Fig. 24 Once the lower console/radio trim box has been removed, the center trim panel attaching screws can be accessed

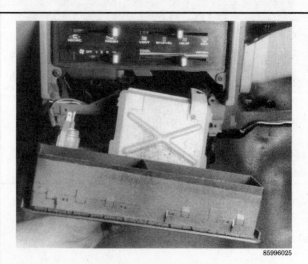

Fig. 25 The control panel can be removed after the center trim panel has been removed

1987-1990 Sedans

▶ See Figure 26

1. Disconnect the negative battery cable.
2. Loosen and remove the driver's side lower trim panel attaching screws, then remove the panel.
3. Loosen and remove the center trim panel attaching screw. This trim panel extends to under the instrument cluster and is secured by several clips. Do not use excessive force on the panel when prying it from the dash.
4. Loosen and remove the control panel attaching screws, then pull the panel out from the dash. Disconnect the control cables and unplug the electrical connections from the back of the control panel.
5. Installation is the reverse of removal.

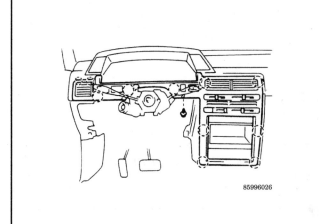

Fig. 26 The center trim panel on 1987-1990 sedans extends to under the instrument cluster

1991-1994 Models

▶ See Figure 27

✳✳CAUTION

On models equipped with a Supplemental Restraint System (SRS) or "air bag," work must NOT be started until at least 90 seconds have passed from the time that both the ignition switch is turned to the LOCK position and the negative cable is disconnected from the battery.

1. Disconnect the negative battery cable.
2. Remove the instrument panel. Refer to Section 10 for the appropriate procedure.
3. Disconnect the control cables and unplug the electrical connections from the back of the control head.
4. Installation is the reverse of removal.

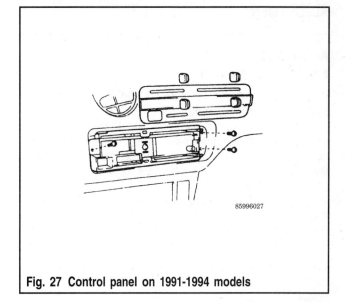

Fig. 27 Control panel on 1991-1994 models

Control Cables

REMOVAL & INSTALLATION

▶ See Figure 28

1. Remove the control panel.
2. Disengage the adjusting clip at the heater/cooling unit end of the cable.
3. Disengage the end of the control cable from the control lever.
4. Remove the cable from the vehicle.
5. Installation is the reverse of removal. Adjust the cable.

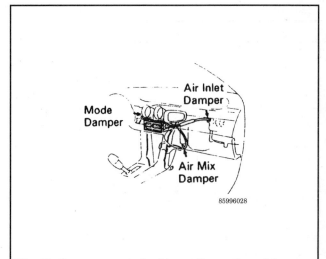

Fig. 28 Common control cable routings, all models similar

ADJUSTMENT

Air Inlet Door
♦ **See Figures 29 and 30**

1. Disengage the control cable from the lever at the heater/cooling unit end of the cable.

2. On all 1984-1990 models and 1991-1994 right hand drive models, set both the air inlet door and the control panel to the FRESH position. Then, slide the control cable through the adjusting clip until the eyelet on the cable end can be engaged to the lever.

3. On 1991-1994 left hand drive models, set both the air inlet door and the control panel to the RECIRC position. Then, slide the control cable through the adjusting clip until the eyelet on the cable end can be engaged to the lever.

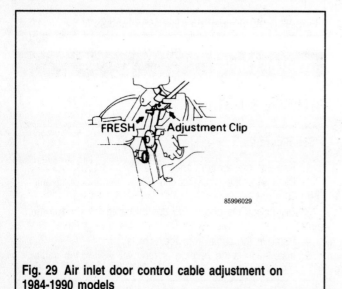

Fig. 29 Air inlet door control cable adjustment on 1984-1990 models

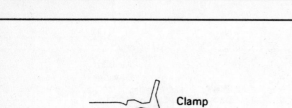
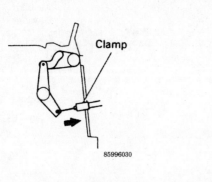

Fig. 30 Air inlet door control cable adjustment on 1991-1994 models

Mode Selector Door
♦ **See Figures 31 and 32**

1. Disengage the control cable from the lever at the heater/cooling unit end of the cable.

2. Set both the mode selector door and the control panel to the FACE position. Then, slide the control cable through the adjusting clip until the eyelet on the cable end can be engaged to the lever.

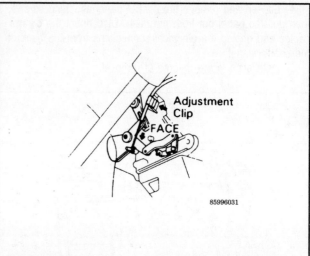

Fig. 31 Mode selector cable adjustment on 1984-1990 models

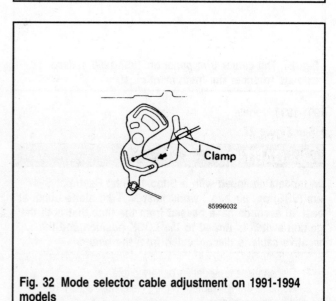

Fig. 32 Mode selector cable adjustment on 1991-1994 models

Air Mix Door
♦ **See Figures 33 and 34**

1. Disengage the control cable from the lever at the heater/cooling unit end of the cable.

2. Set both the air mix door and the control panel to the COOL position. Then, slide the control cable through the adjusting clip until the eyelet on the cable end can be engaged to the lever.

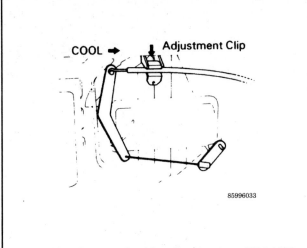

Fig. 33 Air mix control cable adjustment on 1984-1990 models

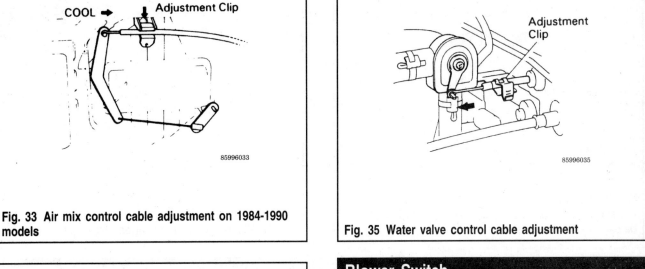

Fig. 35 Water valve control cable adjustment

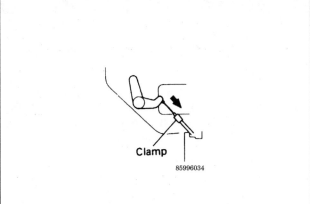

Fig. 34 Air mix control cable adjustment on 1991-1994 models

Water Control Valve
▶ **See Figure 35**

1. Disengage the adjusting clip.
2. Place the water valve lever on the COOL position while pushing the outer cable in the COOL direction. Clamp the outer cable to the water valve bracket with the adjusting clip.

Blower Switch

REMOVAL & INSTALLATION

▶ **See Figures 36 and 37**

✳✳CAUTION

On models equipped with a Supplemental Restraint System (SRS) or "air bag," work must NOT be started until at least 90 seconds have passed from the time that both the ignition switch is turned to the LOCK position and the negative cable is disconnected from the battery.

1. Disconnect the negative battery cable.
2. On 1984-1990 models, remove the control panel. Then, remove the blower switch retaining screws or disengage it from the retaining clips.
3. On 1991-1994 models:
   a. Remove the control panel knobs and face plate.
   b. Remove the radio and ashtray.
   c. Remove the illumination light from the control head.
   d. Using a small screwdriver, carefully pry loose the clip and push out the blower switch to the rear of the control assembly.
   e. Unplug the connector from the blower switch.
4. Installation is the reverse of removal.

Fig. 36 A/C switch removal on 1991-1994 models. Tape the end of the tool before use, this will help prevent damage to the face plate

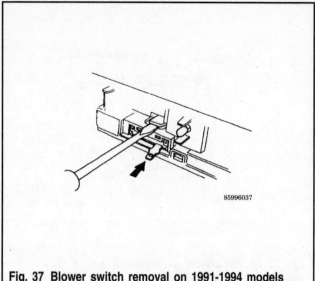

Fig. 37 Blower switch removal on 1991-1994 models

AIR CONDITIONER

Compressor

REMOVAL & INSTALLATION

▶ **See Figures 38, 39 and 40**

✳✳CAUTION

On models equipped with a Supplemental Restraint System (SRS) or "air bag," work must NOT be started until at least 90 seconds have passed from the time that both the ignition switch is turned to the LOCK position and the negative cable is disconnected from the battery.

➡**In certain areas it may be illegal to service air conditioning components unless you are certified, consult with your local authorities.**

1. Recover the refrigerant from the system. Please refer to Section 1.
2. Disconnect the negative battery cable.
3. Remove the engine under cover, if applicable.
4. Unplug the electrical connections from the compressor.
5. Label and disconnect the hoses from the compressor. Cap the openings immediately to keep moisture and dirt out of the system.

6. Loosen and remove the compressor drive belt.
7. Remove the compressor mounting bolts, then the compressor.
   To install:
8. If the compressor is to be replaced, drain the compressor oil into a measuring cup. Record the amount drained, then pour this amount of new oil into the new compressor. On 1984-1986 sedans and all wagons, use Densoil 6, Suniso 5GS or equivalent. On 1987-1993 sedans, use Densoil 7 or equivalent. On 1994 models, use ND-Oil 9, made expressly for use with R134a. Do not use R-12 refrigerant, oil or components on R134a systems and vice versa. Expensive system damage will result, as they are not compatible.
9. Install the compressor with the mounting bolts. Torque to 18 ft. lbs. (25 Nm).
10. Install the drive belt.
11. Connect the hoses to the compressor. On 1984-1986 sedans and all wagons, torque the discharge line to 16 ft. lbs. (22 Nm) and the suction line to 24 ft. lbs. (32 Nm). On 1987-1993 sedans, torque the suction and discharge lines to 18 ft. lbs. (25 Nm). On 1994 models, torque the suction and discharge lines to 8 ft. lbs. (10 Nm). Always use new O-rings, if applicable.
12. Engage the compressor electrical connections.
13. Install the engine under cover, then connect the negative battery cable.
14. Evacuate, charge and leak test the system.

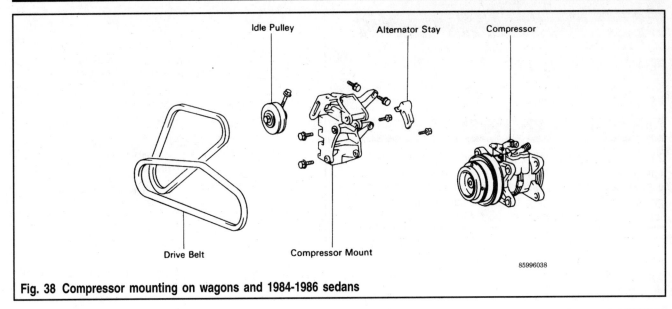

Fig. 38 Compressor mounting on wagons and 1984-1986 sedans

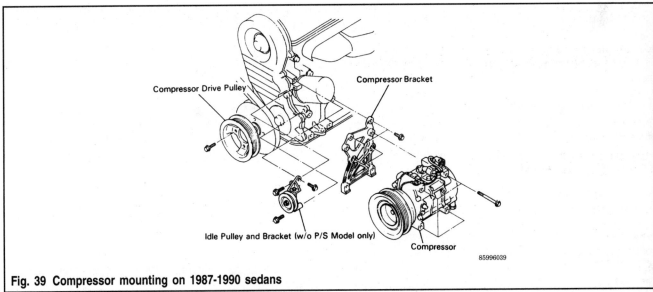

Fig. 39 Compressor mounting on 1987-1990 sedans

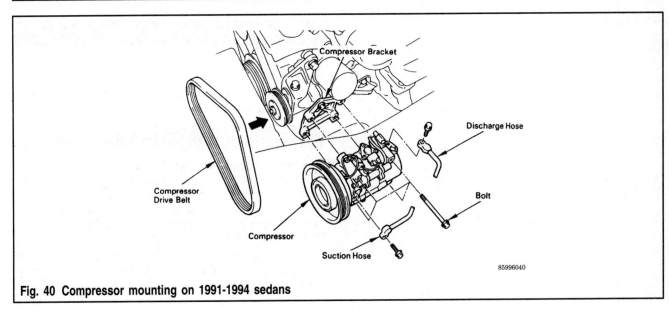

Fig. 40 Compressor mounting on 1991-1994 sedans

Condenser

REMOVAL & INSTALLATION

▶ See Figures 41 and 42

> **※※CAUTION**
>
> On models equipped with a Supplemental Restraint System (SRS) or "air bag," work must NOT be started until at least 90 seconds have passed from the time that both the ignition switch is turned to the LOCK position and the negative cable is disconnected from the battery.

➡In certain areas it may be illegal to service air conditioning components unless you are certified, consult with your local authorities.

1. Recover the refrigerant from the system. Please refer to Section 1.
2. Disconnect the negative battery cable.
3. Remove the front grille, hood lock and center brace. On 1987-1994 sedans, also remove the horn and condenser fan.
4. Disconnect the refrigerant lines from the condenser. Cap the openings immediately to keep moisture and dirt out of the system.
5. On some models, it will be necessary to remove the receiver/drier and its bracket from the condenser. Refer to the appropriate procedure outlined later in this section.
6. Remove the attaching bolts, then remove the condenser from the vehicle.

To install:

7. Install the condenser with the attaching bolts.
8. If applicable, install the receiver/drier with its bracket.
9. If the condenser is being replaced, add 1.4-1.7 fl. oz. (40-50 cc) of refrigerant oil to the system. On 1984-1986 sedans and all wagons, use Densoil 6, Suniso 5GS or equivalent. On 1987-1993 sedans, use Densoil 7 or equivalent. On 1994 models, use ND-Oil 9, made expressly for use with R134a. Do not use R-12 refrigerant, oil or components on R134a systems and vice versa. Expensive system damage will result, as they are not compatible.
10. Connect the refrigerant lines to the condenser. On 1984-1986 sedans and all wagons, torque the liquid line tube to 10 ft. lbs. (13 Nm) and the flexible hose to 16 ft. lbs. (22 Nm). On 1987-1990 sedans, torque the hold-down bolts to 4 ft. lbs. (5 Nm). On 1991-1993 models, torque the hold-down bolt to 9 ft. lbs. (13 Nm). On 1994 models, torque the hold-down bolt to 48 inch lbs. (5.4 Nm). Always use new O-rings, if applicable.
11. Install all components removed for access to the condenser.
12. Evacuate, charge and leak test the system.

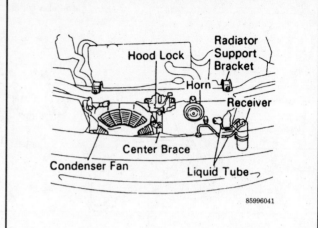

Fig. 41 On some models, it will be necessary to remove the horn, condenser fan and receiver/drier

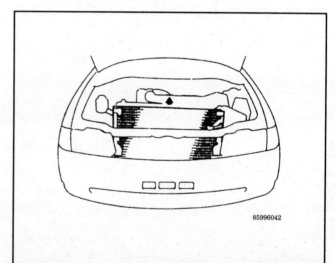

Fig. 42 Pull the condenser straight up, be careful not to damage it

Receiver/Drier

REMOVAL & INSTALLATION

▶ See Figure 43

> **※※CAUTION**
>
> On models equipped with a Supplemental Restraint System (SRS) or "air bag," work must NOT be started until at least 90 seconds have passed from the time that both the ignition switch is turned to the LOCK position and the negative cable is disconnected from the battery.

➡In certain areas it may be illegal to service air conditioning components unless you are certified, consult with your local authorities.

1. Recover the refrigerant from the system. Please refer to Section 1.

2. Disconnect the negative battery cable.

3. On some models it will be necessary to remove the front grille.

4. Disconnect the refrigerant lines from the receiver/drier unit.

5. Remove the unit from its bracket.

To install:

6. Install the unit in its bracket.

7. If the receiver/drier unit is being replaced, add 0.71 fl. oz. (20 cc) of refrigerant oil to the system. On 1984-1986 sedans and all wagons, use Densoil 6, Suniso 5GS or equivalent. On 1987-1993 sedans, use Densoil 7 or equivalent. On 1994 models, use ND-Oil 9, made expressly for use with R134a. Do not use R-12 refrigerant, oil or components on R134a systems and vice versa. Expensive system damage will result, as they are not compatible.

8. Connect the refrigerant lines to the unit. On 1984-1986 sedans and all wagons, torque to 10 ft. lbs. (13 Nm). On 1987-1990 sedans, torque to 4 ft. lbs. (5 Nm). On 1991-1994 models, torque to 48 inch lbs. (5.4 Nm). Always use new O-rings, if applicable.

9. Install all components removed for access to the receiver/drier.

10. Evacuate, charge and leak test the system.

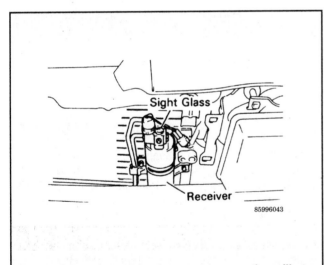

Fig. 43 On some models, you must remove the grille to access the receiver/drier unit

Cooling Unit

REMOVAL & INSTALLATION

▶ See Figures 44, 45, 46, 47 and 48

✳✳CAUTION

On models equipped with a Supplemental Restraint System (SRS) or "air bag," work must NOT be started until at least 90 seconds have passed from the time that both the ignition switch is turned to the LOCK position and the negative cable is disconnected from the battery.

➡ **In certain areas it may be illegal to service air conditioning components unless you are certified, consult with your local authorities.**

1. Recover the refrigerant from the system. Please refer to Section 1.

2. Disconnect the negative battery cable.

3. In the engine compartment, disconnect the refrigerant lines from the assembly. Cap the open fittings immediately to prevent the entry of dirt and moisture.

4. Remove the grommets in the firewall from the inlet and outlet fittings, if applicable.

5. Remove the lower trim panel from under the dashboard and the glove box.

6. Unplug the electrical connectors.

7. Remove the air duct and A/C amplifier, if necessary.

8. Remove the bolts securing the cooling assembly and remove the from the car.

To install:

9. Position the cooling unit in place inside the car, then install the retaining nuts/bolts.

10. Install the A/C amplifier and air duct.

11. Engage the wiring connectors.

12. Install the glove box and the under-dash cover.

13. Install the grommets on the inlet and outlet fittings.

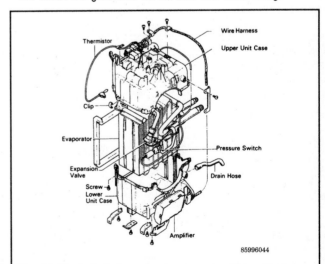

Fig. 44 Exploded view of a common cooling unit and components

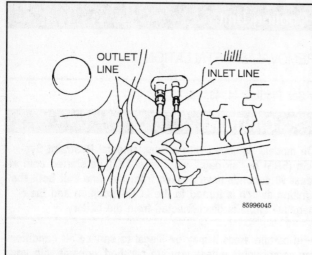

Fig. 45 The refrigerant must be recovered before opening the system's lines

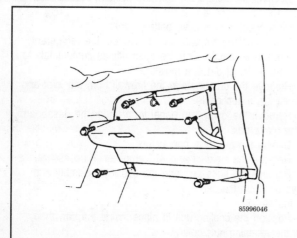

Fig. 46 The glove box is commonly attached by a series of small bolts and/or screws

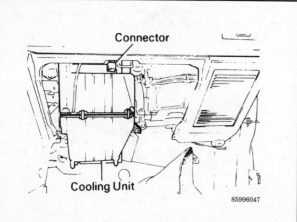

Fig. 47 Make sure you unplug the cooling unit electrical connections before attempting to remove the unit from the vehicle

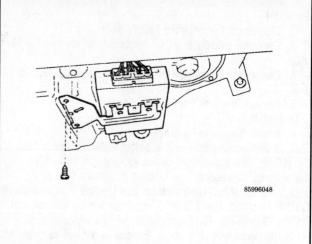

Fig. 48 Remove any components which may impede cooling unit removal

14. Connect the refrigerant lines to the cooling unit. Torque the cooling unit inlet line (smaller one) to 10 ft. lbs. (14 Nm). Torque the outlet line (bigger one) to 24 ft. lbs. (32 Nm). Use new O-rings, if applicable.

15. Evacuate, charge and leak test the air conditioning system.

Evaporator Core

REMOVAL & INSTALLATION

▶ **See Figures 49 and 50**

❋❋CAUTION

On models equipped with a Supplemental Restraint System (SRS) or ''air bag,'' work must NOT be started until at least 90 seconds have passed from the time that both the ignition switch is turned to the LOCK position and the negative cable is disconnected from the battery.

➡In certain areas it may be illegal to service air conditioning components unless you are certified, consult with your local authorities.

1. Recover the refrigerant from the system. Please refer to Section 1.

2. Disconnect the negative battery cable.

3. Remove the cooling unit.

4. Separate the upper and lower halves of the cooling unit case. It is usually retained by screws and clips.

5. Remove the expansion valve from the evaporator, if necessary. Refer to the appropriate procedure later in this section.

6. Inspect the evaporator fins for blockage.

To install:

7. Connect the expansion valve to the evaporator.

8. Install the upper and lower case of the cooling unit.

9. Install the cooling unit in the car.

10. If the evaporator is being replaced, add 1.4-1.7 fl. oz. (40-50 cc) of refrigerant oil to the system. On 1984-1986 sedans and all wagons, use Densoil 6, Suniso 5GS or

equivalent. On 1987-1993 sedans, use Densoil 7 or equivalent. On 1994 models, use ND-Oil 9, made expressly for use with R134a. Do not use R-12 refrigerant, oil or components on R134a systems and vice versa. Expensive system damage will result, as they are not compatible.

11. Evacuate, charge and leak test the air conditioning system.

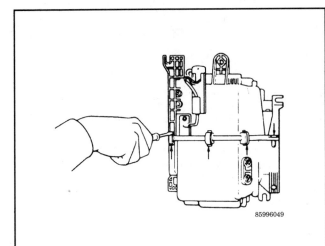

Fig. 49 A small prybar can be used to release the retaining clamps

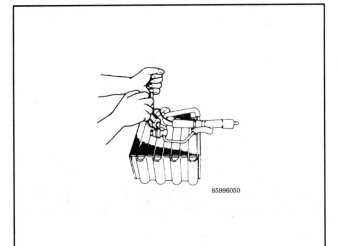

Fig. 50 Always use a back-up wrench when disconnecting threaded fittings

Expansion Valve

REMOVAL & INSTALLATION

▶ See Figures 51 and 52

✳✳CAUTION

On models equipped with a Supplemental Restraint System (SRS) or "air bag," work must NOT be started until at least 90 seconds have passed from the time that both the ignition switch is turned to the LOCK position and the negative cable is disconnected from the battery.

➡In certain areas it may be illegal to service air conditioning components unless you are certified, consult with your local authorities.

1. Recover the refrigerant from the system. Please refer to Section 1.
2. Disconnect the negative battery cable.
3. Remove the cooling unit.
4. Remove the evaporator from the cooling unit.
5. Remove the expansion valve from the evaporator. On threaded-type expansion valves, always use a back-up wrench on the other fitting to avoid bending the tube.

To install:
6. On threaded-type valves, connect the expansion valve to the inlet fitting of the evaporator. Torque to 16 ft. lbs. (22 Nm). Connect the refrigerant tube to the inlet fitting of the expansion valve. Torque to 10 ft. lbs. (13 Nm). Always use new O-rings.
7. On block-type valves, torque the attaching bolts to 48 inch lbs. (5.4 Nm). Use new O-rings as necessary.
8. Install the evaporator in the cooling unit.
9. Install the cooling unit in the vehicle.
10. Evacuate, charge and leak test the air conditioning system.

Fig. 51 Removing a threaded-type expansion valve. Note the use of a back-up wrench on the other fitting

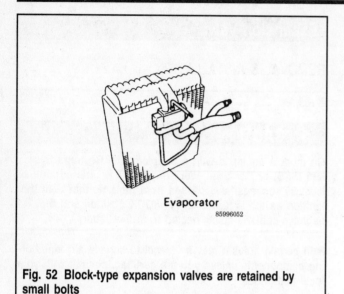

Fig. 52 Block-type expansion valves are retained by small bolts

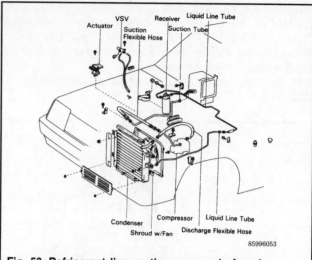

Fig. 53 Refrigerant line routing commonly found on wagons and 1984-1986 sedans

Refrigerant Lines

REMOVAL & INSTALLATION

▶ See Figures 53 and 54

❋❋CAUTION

On models equipped with a Supplemental Restraint System (SRS) or "air bag," work must NOT be started until at least 90 seconds have passed from the time that both the ignition switch is turned to the LOCK position and the negative cable is disconnected from the battery.

➡In certain areas it may be illegal to service air conditioning components unless you are certified, consult with your local authorities.

Refrigerant lines are secured with either threaded-type fittings or block-type fittings. It is very important to use a back-up wrench on threaded-type fittings to avoid twisting the line. Block-type fittings are simply secured by attaching bolts.

Apply a few drops of clean refrigerant oil to O-rings (always use new ones) and torque their fittings or attaching bolts to proper specifications. Failure to do so can result in broken O-rings, cracked fittings, stripped threads and poor sealing. All of these lead to refrigerant leaks and eventual air conditioning system destruction. It is also important to note that R-12 system components cannot be used in R134a systems. This includes O-rings! The use of improper refrigerant and/or oil will only result in improper cooling and total system destruction.

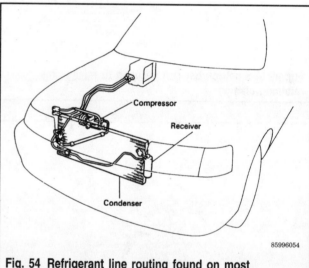

Fig. 54 Refrigerant line routing found on most 1987-1994 sedans

Pressure Switch

REMOVAL & INSTALLATION

▶ See Figure 55

❋❋CAUTION

On models equipped with a Supplemental Restraint System (SRS) or "air bag," work must NOT be started until at least 90 seconds have passed from the time that both the ignition switch is turned to the LOCK position and the negative cable is disconnected from the battery.

➡In certain areas it may be illegal to service air conditioning components unless you are certified, consult with your local authorities.

1. Recover the refrigerant from the system. Please refer to Section 1.

2. Disconnect the negative battery cable.

3. Remove the cooling unit.

4. Remove the evaporator.

5. Remove the pressure switch from the refrigerant line. On some models, it is necessary to replace to refrigerant line as the switch itself is not removable.

To install:

6. Install the pressure switch and torque to 10 ft. lbs. (13 Nm).

7. Install the evaporator in the cooling unit.

8. Install the cooling unit.

9. Evacuate, charge and leak test the system.

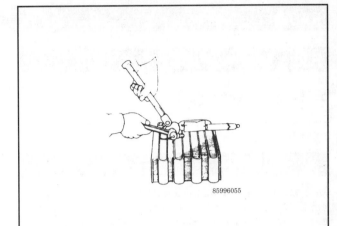

Fig. 55 Removing the pressure switch. On some models, it is necessary to replace to refrigerant line as the switch itself is not removable

CRUISE CONTROL

Control Switches

REMOVAL & INSTALLATION

▶ **See Figure 56**

Main Switch

Refer to the procedure for dash mounted switches outlined later in this section.

Selector Switch

Refer to the procedure for the combination switch outlined later in this section.

Speed Sensor

REMOVAL & INSTALLATION

The speed sensor is integral with the speedometer unit. Refer to the procedure for speedometer, tachometer and gauges outlined later in this section.

Actuator

REMOVAL & INSTALLATION

1. Disconnect the negative battery cable.

2. Label and disconnect the vacuum hoses, then unplug the electrical connector.

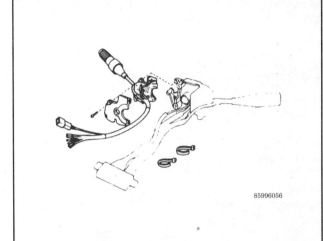

Fig. 56 The cruise control selector switch is part of the combination switch assembly

3. Disconnect the cable from the actuator linkage.

4. Remove the actuator bracket attaching bolts/nuts, then remove the actuator assembly from the vehicle.

5. Installation is the reverse of removal. Check and adjust the cable free-play.

ADJUSTMENT

1. Check that the cable free-play (slack) is less than 0.39 in. (10 mm).

2. If necessary, loosen the cable lock-nuts, then adjust for proper free-play.

RADIO

Radio Receiver/Tape Player

REMOVAL & INSTALLATION

▶ See Figures 57, 58, 59 and 60

✳✳CAUTION

On models equipped with a Supplemental Restraint System (SRS) or "air bag," work must NOT be started until at least 90 seconds have passed from the time that both the ignition switch is turned to the LOCK position and the negative cable is disconnected from the battery.

1. Disconnect the negative battery cable.
2. On 1984-1986 sedans and all wagons, remove the radio console box. On all other models, remove the center trim panel. These trim panels are usually secured by screws and/or clips. Be sure you have removed all of the attaching screws before prying the panel from the dash. Do not use excessive force on the panel as this will only lead to damage.

Fig. 58 The radio is usually secured to its mounting bracket by small screws and/or bolts

4. Pull the radio from the dash until the wiring connectors are exposed.

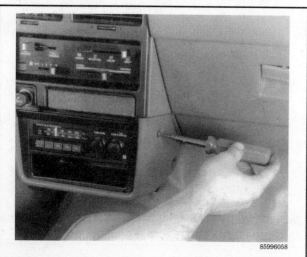
Fig. 57 The radio console box is usually secured by small screws

3. Remove the mounting screws from the radio.

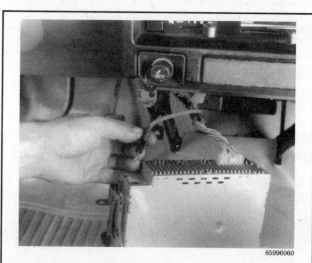
Fig. 59 Pull the radio out far enough to reach the connectors, then unplug them

5. Unplug the electrical connectors and the antenna cable, then remove the radio from the car.
   To install:
6. Connect the wiring and the antenna cable, then place the radio in position within the dash.
7. Install the attaching screws.
8. Install the trim panel (make sure all the spring clips engage), then install the screws.
9. Check the radio for proper operation.

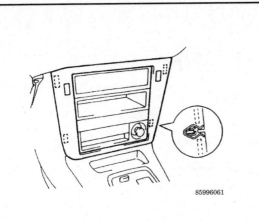

Fig. 60 The center trim panel, on some models, is retained by small clips and can be removed by carefully pulling it out from the dash

Speakers

REMOVAL & INSTALLATION

✳✳CAUTION

On models equipped with a Supplemental Restraint System (SRS) or "air bag," work must NOT be started until at least 90 seconds have passed from the time that both the ignition switch is turned to the LOCK position and the negative cable is disconnected from the battery.

Dash Mounted
▶ See Figure 61

Dash mounted speakers can be accessed after removing the appropriate trim panel. These panels are usually retained by screws and clips. Be sure you have removed all of the attaching screws before prying the panel from the dash. Do not use excessive force on the panel as this will only lead to damage. Once the panel has been removed, loosen the speaker attach-

ing bolts/screws, then pull the speaker from the dash and unplug the electrical connection. Always disconnect the negative battery cable first.

Door Mounted

Door mounted speakers can be accessed after removing the door panel. These panels are usually retained by screws and clips. Be sure you have removed all of the attaching screws before prying the panel from the door. A special tool can be purchased for this purpose. Do not use excessive force on the panel as this will only lead to damage. Once the panel has been removed, loosen the speaker attaching bolts/screws, then pull the speaker from its mount and unplug the electrical connection. Always disconnect the negative battery cable first.

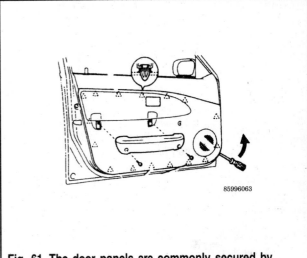

Fig. 61 The door panels are commonly secured by several hidden clips

Rear Speakers
▶ See Figure 62

Removing the rear speakers involves basically the same procedure as the front speakers. Remove the appropriate trim panel, then remove the speaker. The rear speakers on some models can be accessed from inside the trunk. Always disconnect the negative battery cable first.

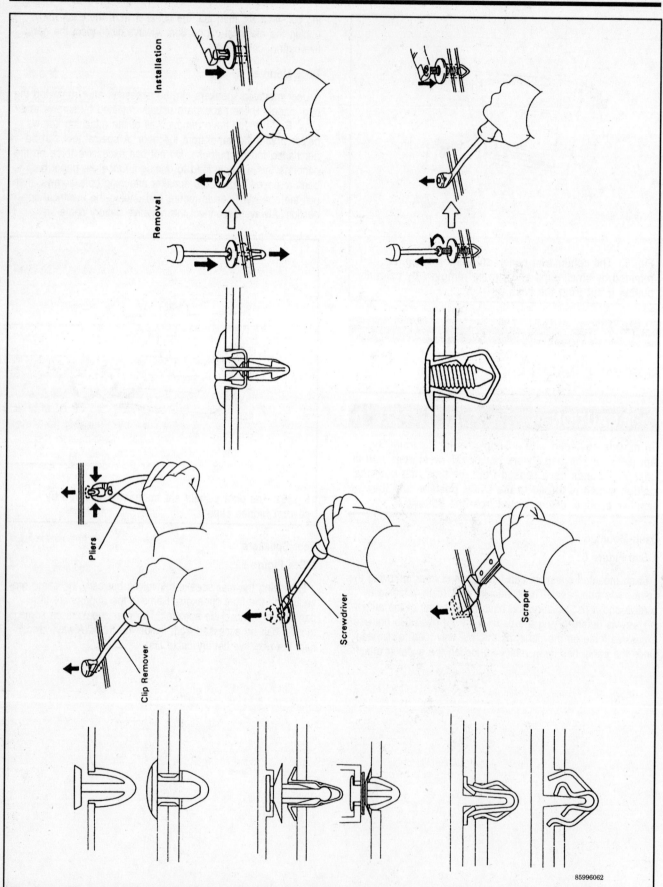

Fig. 62 Various clips are commonly used to secure trim panels. The tips of the removal tools should be taped to prevent damage to the trim panel finish

85996062

WINDSHIELD WIPERS AND WASHER

Blade and Arm

REMOVAL & INSTALLATION

▶ **See Figures 63, 64, 65, 66 and 67**

1. To remove the wiper blades, lift up on the spring release tab on the wiper blade-to-wiper arm connector.
2. Pull the blade assembly off the wiper arm.
3. Press the old wiper blade insert down, away from the blade assembly, to free it from the retaining clips on the blade ends. Slide the insert out of the blade. Slide the new insert into the blade assembly and bend the insert upward slightly to engage the retaining clips.

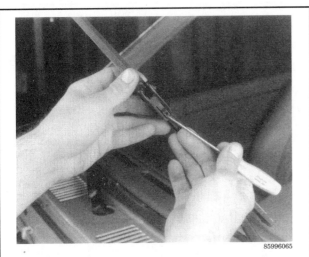

Fig. 63 Be careful not to break the release tab when disengaging it

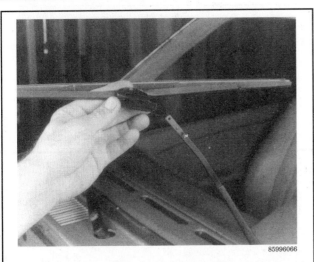

Fig. 64 The wiper blade can be slipped off the arm after the release tab is disengaged

4. To replace a wiper arm, remove the nut/bolt (on some models, a cap covers this retaining nut at the bottom of the wiper arm) which secures it to the pivot and carefully pull the arm upward and off the pivot. Install the arm by placing it on the pivot and tightening the nut. Remember that the arm MUST BE reinstalled in its EXACT previous position or it will not cover the correct area during use.

➡ **If one wiper arm does not move when turned on or only moves a little bit, check the retaining nut at the bottom of the arm. The extra effort of moving wet snow or leaves off the glass can cause the nut to come loose; the pivot will turn without moving the arm.**

Windshield Wiper Motor

REMOVAL & INSTALLATION

▶ **See Figures 68, 69, 70 and 71**

❊❊CAUTION

On models equipped with a Supplemental Restraint System (SRS) or "air bag," work must NOT be started until at least 90 seconds have passed from the time that both the ignition switch is turned to the LOCK position and the negative cable is disconnected from the battery.

Front Wiper Assembly

1. Disconnect the negative battery cable.
2. Unplug the electrical connector from the wiper motor.
3. Remove the mounting bolts, then remove the motor from the firewall.
4. Pry the wiper linkage socket from the motor arm assembly.
5. Installation is the reverse of removal.

Fig. 65 A small cap usually covers the wiper arm retaining nut/bolt

Fig. 66 Once the retaining nut/bolt is removed, carefully pull the wiper arm from its pivot

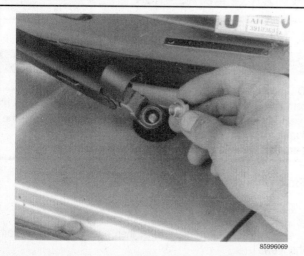

Fig. 67 Make sure the wiper arm is correctly positioned before installing the retaining nut/bolt

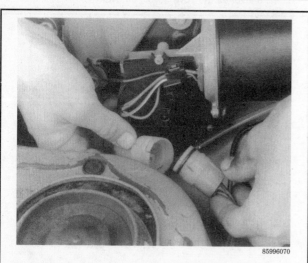

Fig. 68 Be careful not to break the locking tab when separating the electrical connector

Fig. 69 The wiper motor is usually held by three bolts

Fig. 70 A small prybar can be used to separate the linkage from the wiper motor

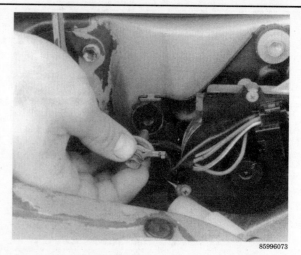

Fig. 71 Make sure the rubber mounting insulators and the ground wire are installed before tightening the bolts

Rear Wiper Assembly

▶ See Figure 72

1. Remove the wiper arm from the pivot, then remove the spacer and washer on the pivot.
2. Remove the cover (trim) panel on the inside of the hatch lid.
3. Remove the plastic cover on the wiper motor and unplug the wiring connector from the motor.
4. Remove the mounting nuts/bolts, then remove the wiper motor.

To install:
5. Position the motor and secure it to the hatch lid.
6. Connect the wiring harness, then install the plastic cover.
7. Install the inner trim panel on the hatch lid.
8. Install the wiper arm with its washer and spacer. Make sure the arm is correctly positioned before tightening the nut.

Wiper Linkage

REMOVAL & INSTALLATION

✳✳CAUTION

On models equipped with a Supplemental Restraint System (SRS) or "air bag," work must NOT be started until at least 90 seconds have passed from the time that both the ignition switch is turned to the LOCK position and the negative cable is disconnected from the battery.

1. Remove the windshield wiper motor as previously outlined.
2. Remove the wiper arms.
3. Unfasten the wiper pivot retaining nuts/bolts, then remove the linkage assembly through the access hole.

To install:
4. Place the linkage through the access hole and line up the pivots in their holes.

5. Install the pivot retaining nuts onto the pivots. Before final tightening, make sure the linkage is aligned in all its holes.
6. Reinstall the wiper motor and arms. Check the wipers for proper operation.

Washer Fluid Reservoir

REMOVAL & INSTALLATION

▶ See Figure 73

1. Drain the washer fluid from the reservoir.
2. Disconnect the hoses, then remove the reservoir attaching bolts.
3. Remove the reservoir from the vehicle.
4. Installation is the reverse of removal.

Fig. 73 Don't confuse the washer fluid reservoir with the coolant overflow tank. They are separate units

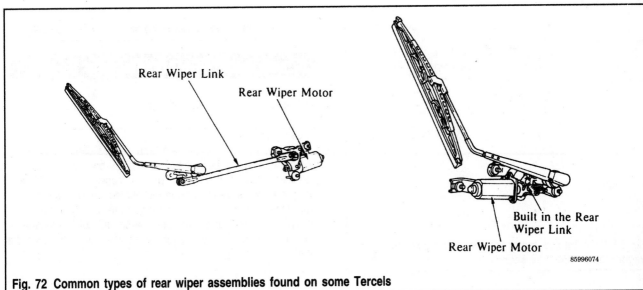

Fig. 72 Common types of rear wiper assemblies found on some Tercels

INSTRUMENTS AND SWITCHES

Combination Meter

REMOVAL & INSTALLATION

♦ See Figures 74, 75, 76, 77 and 78

❋❋CAUTION

On models equipped with a Supplemental Restraint System (SRS) or "air bag," work must NOT be started until at least 90 seconds have passed from the time that both the ignition switch is turned to the LOCK position and the negative cable is disconnected from the battery.

1. Disconnect the negative battery cable.
2. Remove the combination meter trim panel. This is usually retained by a series of screws and clips. Do not use excessive force when pulling the trim panel from the dash, it is easily damaged. On 1987-1990 sedans, the driver's side lower trim panel and the center trim panel must be removed first.
3. Remove the attaching screws from the combination meter, then disconnect the speedometer cable and unplug the wiring connectors. Remove the meter assembly from the instrument panel. On some models, removal of the combination switch first will ease removal. Refer to the appropriate procedure.

To install:
4. Connect the wiring harnesses and the speedometer cable to the meter. Place the meter in the dash, then secure it with the attaching screws. Make certain the wiring is properly placed to prevent it from becoming pinched or crushed.
5. Install the combination meter trim panel.
6. Install the center and lower trim panel, if applicable.
7. Road test the vehicle and check for proper operation.

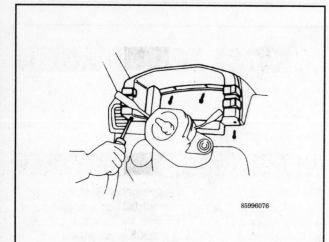

Fig. 74 Combination meter trim panel removal on wagons and 1984-1986 sedans

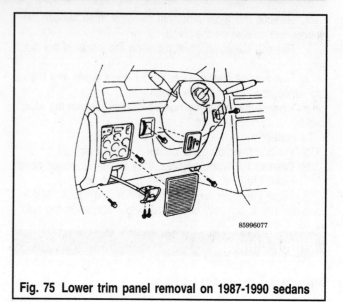

Fig. 75 Lower trim panel removal on 1987-1990 sedans

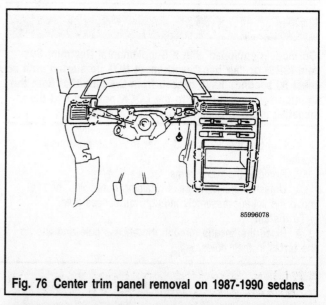

Fig. 76 Center trim panel removal on 1987-1990 sedans

Speedometer, Tachometer and Gauges

REMOVAL & INSTALLATION

The speedometer, tachometer and gauges can usually be replaced using the same basic procedure, once the combination meter has been removed. In most cases, removal of the gauges involves disassembling the printed circuit board and front lens from the meter. The gauges are usually secured by a series of small screws or bolts. Be careful not to damage the indicator needles and gauge faces when disassembling the meter.

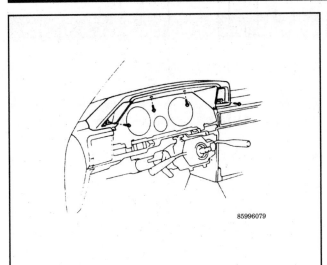

Fig. 77 Combination meter trim panel removal on 1987-1990 sedans

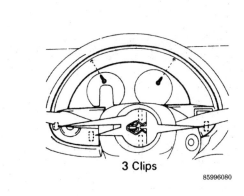

3 Clips

Fig. 78 Combination meter trim panel removal on 1991-1994 sedans

Speedometer Cable

REMOVAL & INSTALLATION

1. Disconnect the negative battery cable.
2. Follow the appropriate procedure given previously for removal of the combination meter.
3. Safely raise the car and support it on jackstands.

➡**Depending on the length of your arm, you may be able to reach the cable connection at the transmission/transaxle without raising the car, but it is usually easier with the car elevated.**

4. Disconnect the cable fitting at the transmission/transaxle and lift the cable and case away from the transmission/transaxle.
5. Follow the cable back to the firewall, releasing any clips or retainers.

6. From inside the car, work the speedometer cable through the grommet in the firewall into the engine compartment. It may be necessary to pop the grommet out of the firewall and transfer it to the new cable.
   To install:
7. When installing, track the new cable into position, remembering to attach the grommet to the firewall securely. Make absolutely certain that the cable is not kinked, or routed near hot or moving parts. All curves in the cable should be very gentle and not located near the ends. The speedometer cable inside the housing should be lubricated before installing it.
8. Attach any retaining clips, brackets or retainers, beginning from the middle of the cable and working towards each end.
9. Attach the cable to the transmission/transaxle. Remember that the cable has a formed, square end on it. This shaped end must fit into a matching hole in the transmission/transaxle mount. Don't try to force the cable collar (screw fitting) into place if the cable isn't seated properly.
10. Lower the car to the ground.
11. Attach the speedometer cable to the combination meter, again paying close attention to the fit of the square-cut end into the square hole. Don't force the cable retainer or you'll break the clips.
12. Reinstall the combination meter following procedures outlined previously. Road test the vehicle and check for proper operation.

Printed Circuit Board

REMOVAL & INSTALLATION

The printed circuit board is attached to the back of the combination meter. It is usually secured by a series of screws/nuts and by the bulb sockets. These sockets can usually be removed by first twisting, then pulling them from the meter. Do not force any components as they are easily damaged

Combination Switch

REMOVAL & INSTALLATION

♦ **See Figures 79 and 80**

✻✻CAUTION

On models equipped with a Supplemental Restraint System (SRS) or "air bag," work must NOT be started until at least 90 seconds have passed from the time that both the ignition switch is turned to the LOCK position and the negative cable is disconnected from the battery.

1. Disconnect the negative battery cable.
2. Remove the steering wheel.
3. Remove the driver's side lower trim panel.

4. Remove their attaching screws, then separate the upper and lower steering column covers.

5. Unplug the connector from the combination switch to the dashboard wiring harness.

6. Remove the mounting bolts/screws, then remove the combination switch.

To install:

7. Position the switch carefully onto the column, then secure the mounting screws.

8. Connect the wiring harness from the switch to the dashboard harness.

9. Install the upper and lower column covers.

10. Install the driver's lower trim panel.

11. Install the steering wheel. Check the combination switch for proper operation in all modes.

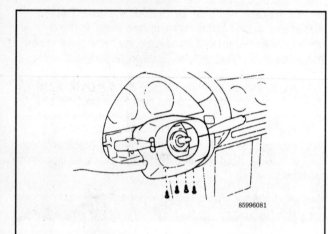

85996081

Fig. 79 Removing the steering column upper and lower covers

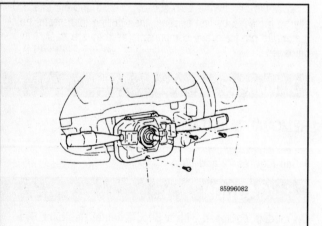

85996082

Fig. 80 The combination switch is usually retained by small screws

Dash-Mounted Switches

REMOVAL & INSTALLATION

❋❋CAUTION

On models equipped with a Supplemental Restraint System (SRS) or "air bag," work must NOT be started until at least 90 seconds have passed from the time that both the ignition switch is turned to the LOCK position and the negative cable is disconnected from the battery.

Most dash-mounted switches can be removed using the same basic procedure. Remove the trim panel which the switch is secured to. Trim panels are usually secured by a series of screws and/or clips. Make sure you remove all attaching screws before attempting to pull on the panel. Do not use excessive force as trim panels are easily damaged. Once the trim panel has been removed, unplug the switch connector, then remove its retaining screws or pry it from the mounting clip. Always disconnect the negative battery cable first.

Ignition Switch

REMOVAL & INSTALLATION

▶ See Figure 81

❋❋CAUTION

On models equipped with a Supplemental Restraint System (SRS) or "air bag," work must NOT be started until at least 90 seconds have passed from the time that both the ignition switch is turned to the LOCK position and the negative cable is disconnected from the battery.

1. Disconnect the negative battery cable.

2. Remove the screws which secure the steering column upper and lower covers.

3. Turn the ignition key to the **ACC** position.

4. Push the lock cylinder stop in with a small punch or screwdriver.

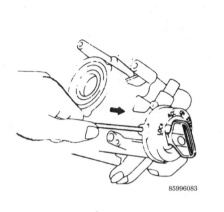

Fig. 81 Depressing the lock cylinder stop tab

➡️On some vehicles, it may be necessary to remove the steering wheel and combination switch first.

5. Withdraw the lock cylinder from the housing while depressing the stop tab.

6. Remove the ignition switch retaining screws, then withdraw the switch from the lock housing.

To install:

7. Align the locking cam with the hole in the ignition switch, then insert the switch into the lock housing.

8. Secure the switch with its screws.

9. Make sure both the lock cylinder and the column lock are in the **ACC** position. Slide the cylinder into the lock housing until the stop tab engages the hole in the lock.

10. Install the steering column covers.

11. Engage the ignition switch connector.

12. Check the ignition switch operation in all positions.

LIGHTING

Headlights

REMOVAL & INSTALLATION

▶ See Figures 82, 83, 84 and 85

Sealed Beam Type

1. Remove the headlight bezel (trim) and/or the radiator grille, as necessary. It may also be necessary to remove the front turn signal/parking light on some models.

2. The headlight is held in place by a retainer secured by small screws. Identify these screws before applying any tools. Do not confuse the small retaining screws with the larger aiming screws.

3. Using a small screwdriver (preferably magnetic), remove the small screws in the head lamp retainer.

Fig. 83 Apply some penetrating oil on the retaining screw threads. This will ease their removal as they are usually rusted

4. The head lamp may be gently pulled free from its mount. Unplug the connector from the back of the headlight, then remove the unit from the car.

To install:

5. Place the new head lamp in position and connect the wiring harness. Make sure the headlight is right-side up.

6. Turn on the headlights and check the new lamp for proper function. Check both high and low beams before final assembly.

7. Install the retainer.

8. Install the headlight bezel and/or grille.

Semi-Sealed Beam Type

▶ See Figures 86 and 87

➡️This type of light is replaced from behind the unit. The lens is not removed or loosened.

1. Open and support the hood.

Fig. 82 On some models, it is necessary to remove the grille before removing the headlight bezel

Fig. 84 The grease inside the connector helps prevent terminal corrosion

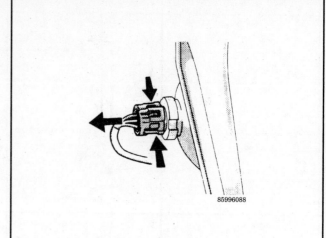

Fig. 86 On semi-sealed beams, depress the sides of the connector to release the lock tab

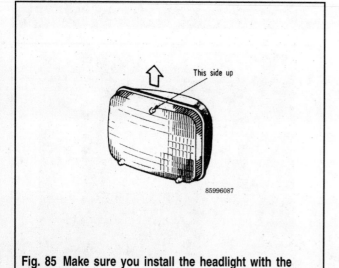

This side up

Fig. 85 Make sure you install the headlight with the correct side up

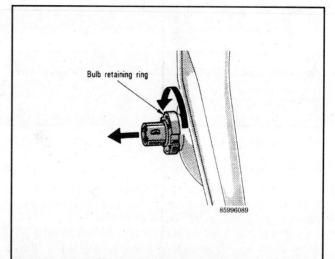

Bulb retaining ring

Fig. 87 Turn the bulb retaining ring, then remove the bulb

2. Unplug the wiring connector from the back the lamp. Be careful to release the locking tab completely before removal.

3. Grasp the base of the bulb holder and collar, twist it, then carefully remove the bulb holder and bulb from the housing.

4. Release the clip on the holder, then remove the bulb.

To install:

5. Install the new bulb in the holder and make sure the clip engages firmly.

➡**Hold the new bulb with a clean cloth or a piece of paper. DO NOT touch or grasp the bulb with your fingers. The oils from your skin will produce a hot spot on the glass envelope, shortening bulb life by up to 50 percent. If the bulb is touched accidentally, clean it with alcohol and a clean rag before installation.**

6. Install the holder and bulb into the housing. Note that the holder has guides which must align with the housing. When the holder is correctly seated, turn the collar to lock the holder in place.

7. Connect the wiring harness. Turn on the headlights and check the function of the new bulb on both high and low beam.

AIMING

▶ **See Figures 88 and 89**

The head lamps should be aimed using a special alignment tool, however this procedure may be used for temporary adjustment. Local regulations may vary regarding head lamp aiming, consult with your local authorities.

1. Verify the tires are at their proper inflation pressure. Clean the head lamp lenses and make sure there are no heavy loads in the trunk. The gas tank should be filled.

2. Position the vehicle on a level surface facing a flat wall 25 ft. (7.7 m) away.

3. Measure and record the distance from the floor to the center of the head lamp. Place a strip of tape across the wall at this same height.

4. Place strips of tape on the wall, perpendicular to the first measurement, indicating the vehicle centerline and the centerline of both head lamps.

5. Rock the vehicle side-to-side a few times to allow the suspension to stabilize.
6. Turn the lights ON, adjust the head lamps to achieve a high intensity pattern in the areas shown in the illustrations.

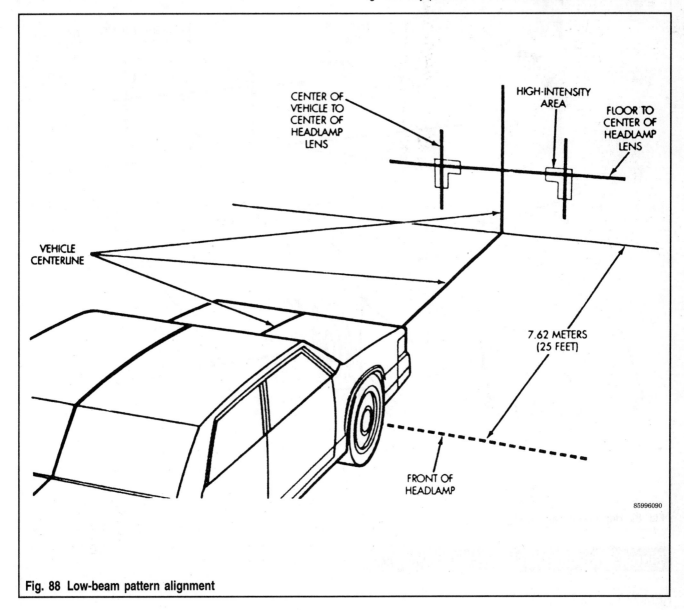

Fig. 88 Low-beam pattern alignment

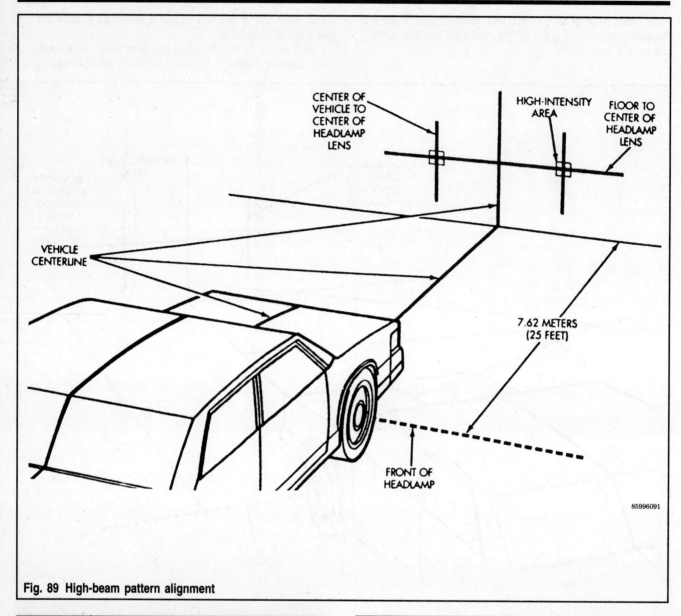

Fig. 89 High-beam pattern alignment

Signal and Marker Lights

REMOVAL & INSTALLATION

Front Turn Signals

▶ See Figure 90

➡ On 1991-1994 models, the front turn signals are also the front marker and parking lights.

1. Remove the lens attaching screws, then remove the lens. On 1991-1994 models open the hood to access the attaching screw.

2. Single-end bulbs are removed by first pressing in, then turning counterclockwise. On double-end (wedge base) bulbs, pull the bulb straight out of its socket.

3. Installation is the reverse of removal. Check turn signal light operation.

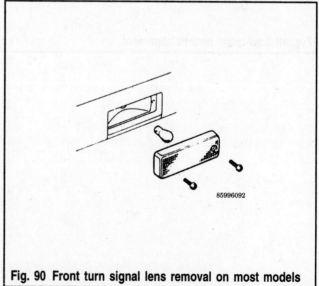

Fig. 90 Front turn signal lens removal on most models

Side Marker Lights (Parking Lights)

▶ See Figures 91, 92, 93 and 94

FRONT

➡On 1991-1994 models, the front turn signals are also the front marker and parking lights.

1. Remove the lens retaining screw(s). On 1991-1994 models open the hood to access the attaching screw.
2. Single-end bulbs are removed by first pressing in, then turning counterclockwise. On double-end (wedge base) bulbs, pull the bulb straight out of its socket.
3. Installation is the reverse of removal. Check for proper light operation.

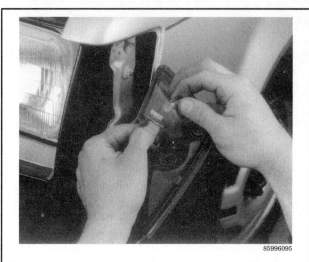

Fig. 93 On wedge base bulbs, remove by pulling the bulb straight out of the socket

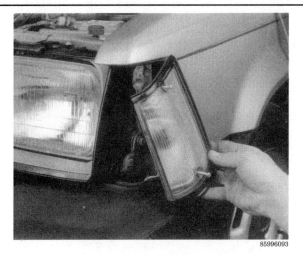

Fig. 91 The side marker lens is usually retained by screws

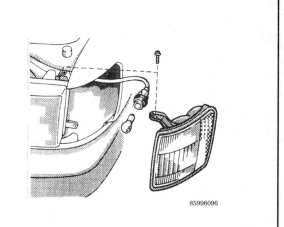

Fig. 94 Side marker/front turn signal lens removal on 1991-1994 models

REAR

▶ See Figure 95

➡On 1991-1994 models, follow the procedure for rear turn signal, brake and parking lights.

1. Remove the lens retaining screw(s).
2. Single-end bulbs are removed by first pressing in, then turning counterclockwise. On double-end (wedge base) bulbs, pull the bulb straight out of its socket.
3. Installation is the reverse of removal. Check for proper light operation.

Fig. 92 Removing the bulb/socket assembly from the lens

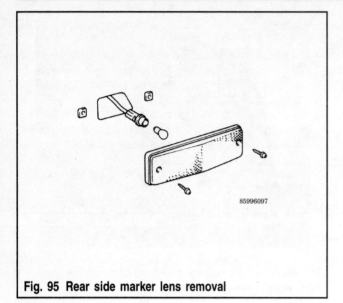

Fig. 95 Rear side marker lens removal

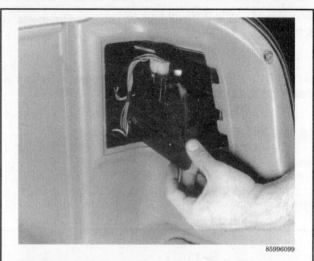

Fig. 97 The bulb/socket assembly can be removed by pressing this release clip

Rear Turn Signal, Brake and Parking Lights
▶ See Figures 96, 97 and 98

1984-1986 SEDANS, ALL WAGONS

1. Remove the light access panel from inside the hatch area.
2. Remove the bulb/socket assembly from the lens.
3. Single-end bulbs are removed by first pressing in, then turning counterclockwise. On double-end (wedge base) bulbs, pull the bulb straight out of its socket.
4. Installation is the reverse of removal. Check for proper light operation.

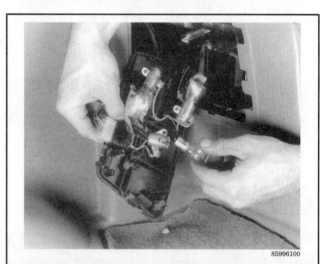

Fig. 98 Single-end bulbs are removed by first pressing in, then turning counterclockwise

1987-1994 SEDANS

▶ See Figures 99 and 100

1. Raise the trunk lid, then remove the lens attaching screws/nuts.
2. Carefully pull the lens from the body far enough to allow you to disconnect the appropriate bulb/socket from the assembly.
3. Single-end bulbs are removed by first pressing in, then turning counterclockwise. On double-end (wedge base) bulbs, pull the bulb straight out of its socket.
4. Installation is the reverse of removal. Check for proper light operation.

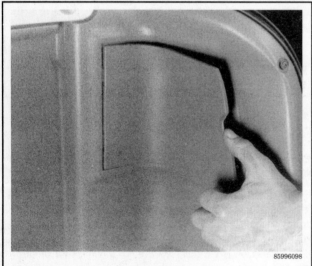

Fig. 96 Removing the light access panel

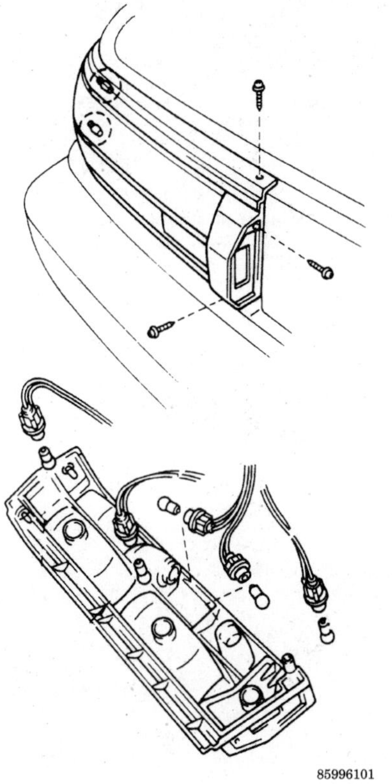

Fig. 99 Rear turn signal, brake and parking light lens removal on 1987-1990 sedans

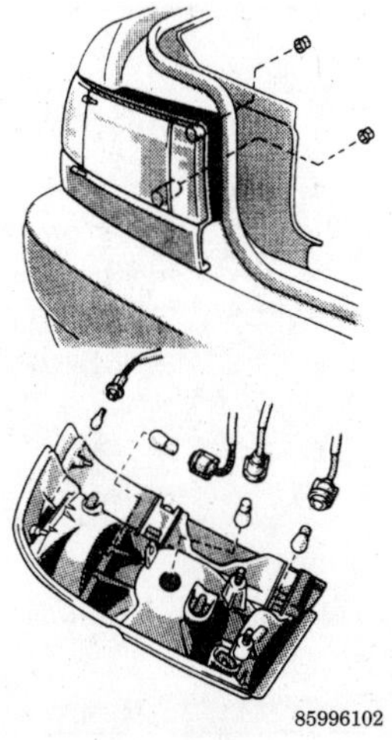

Fig. 100 Rear turn signal, brake and parking light lens removal on 1991-1994 sedans

High-Mount Brake Light

➧ See Figure 101

1. Remove the high-mount brake light plastic housing. The push-pin clips can be removed by first pushing in the center pin with a small punch, then pulling the clip from the housing. Be careful not to damage the clip or housing.
2. Once the housing is removed, replace the bulb. Single-end bulbs are removed by first pressing in, then turning counterclockwise. On double-end (wedge base) bulbs, pull the bulb straight out of its socket.
3. Installation is the reverse of removal. Check for proper light operation.

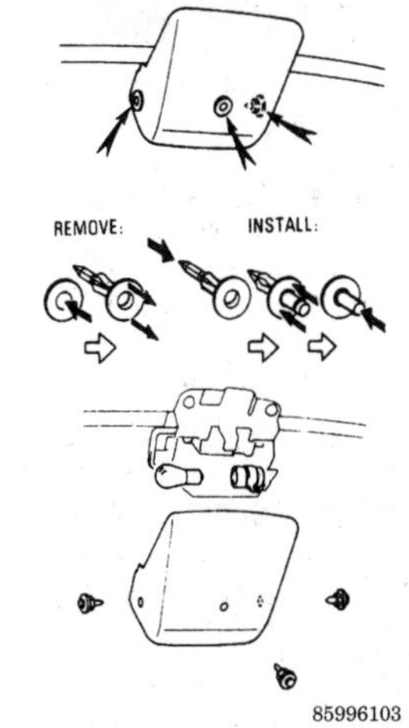

Fig. 101 High-mount brake light housing removal and bulb replacement

Dome Light

➧ See Figure 102

1. Carefully pry the dome light lens from the housing.
2. Release the bulb from the housing.
3. Installation is the reverse of removal. Check for proper bulb operation.

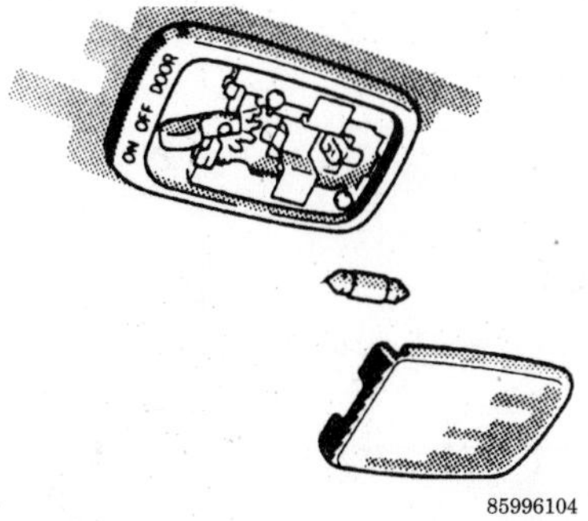

Fig. 102 Dome light replacement on most models

Cargo and Passenger Area Lamps

▶ See Figure 103

1. Remove the lens housing retaining screw(s).
2. Release the bulb from the housing.
3. Installation is the reverse of removal. Check for proper bulb operation.

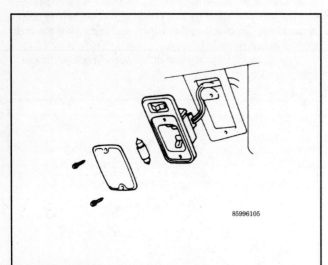

Fig. 103 Cargo and passenger area light replacement on most models

License Plate Lights

1984-1986 SEDANS

▶ See Figures 104, 105, 106, 107 and 108

1. It will be necessary to remove the hatch-lid trim panel first. This is usually secured by a series of screws and pull clips.
2. Remove the lamp assembly attaching nuts/bolts.
3. Unplug the electrical connector, then withdraw the lamp assembly from the hatch lid.
4. Separate the rear cover from the lens assembly. Remove the bulb/socket assembly attaching screw(s), then remove it from the lens assembly.
5. Remove the bulb from its socket.
6. Installation is the reverse of removal. Check for proper bulb operation.

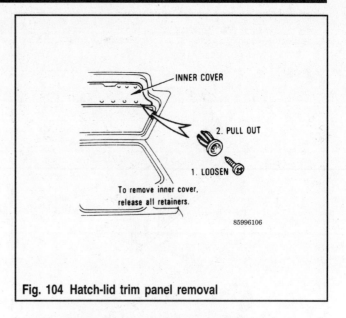

Fig. 104 Hatch-lid trim panel removal

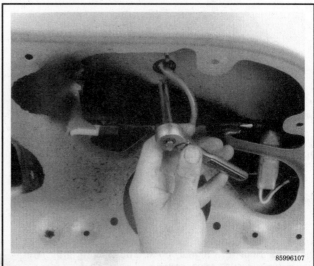

Fig. 105 Removing the lamp assembly attaching nuts

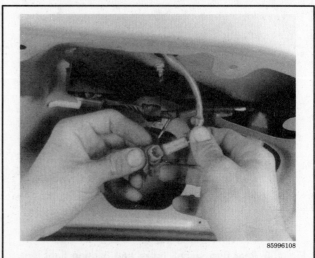

Fig. 106 Unplug the electrical connection, then remove the assembly from the vehicle

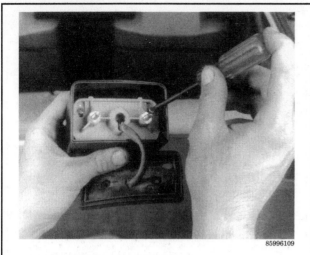

Fig. 107 Removing the bulb/socket assembly from the housing

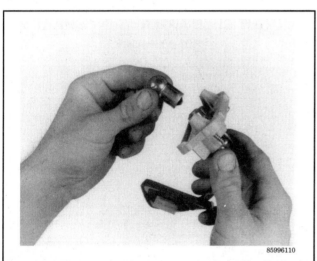

Fig. 108 Single-end bulbs are removed by first pressing in, then turning counterclockwise

WAGONS

▶ See Figure 109

1. Remove the lens attaching screws/nuts, then remove the lens.

2. Single-end bulbs are removed by first pressing in, then turning counterclockwise. On double-end (wedge base) bulbs, pull the bulb straight out of its socket.

3. Installation is the reverse of removal. Check for proper light operation.

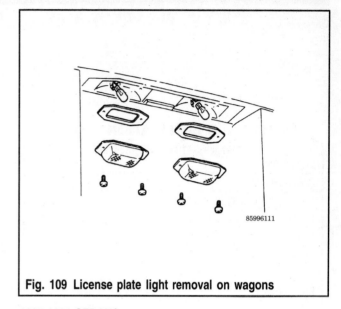

Fig. 109 License plate light removal on wagons

1987-1990 SEDANS

On 1987-1990 sedans, follow the rear turn signal, brake and parking light procedure, then replace the appropriate bulb.

1991-1994 MODELS

▶ See Figure 110

1. Carefully push the lens assembly to the side, then pull down. Remove the bulb by pulling it from its socket

2. Gently press the retaining clips in, then push the lens assembly in to its mounting hole.

3. Check for proper bulb operation.

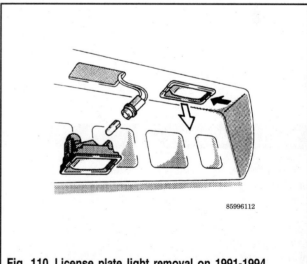

Fig. 110 License plate light removal on 1991-1994 models

LIGHT BULB APPLICATION CHART

All Wagons—1984–1986 Sedans	
Light Bulbs	Bulb No.
Parking lights	194
Front turn signal lights	1156
Rear side marker lights	194
Rear turn signal lights	1156
Stop and tail lights	1157
Stop light	1157
Back-up lights	1156
License plate lights Sedan	89
Station wagon	—
Interior light	—
Personal lights	1853
Luggage compartment light	—
Sealed beam	6052 H6052 H6054
Semi-sealed beam	9004

85996300

LIGHT BULB APPLICATION CHART

1987–1990 Sedans	
Light Bulbs	Bulb No.
Parking and front side marker lights	168
Front turn signal lights	1156
Interior light	—
Rear side marker lights	194
Rear turn signal lights	1156
Stop and tail lights	1157
Back-up lights	1156
License plate lights	89
Stop light	1156
Semi-sealed beam	9004

85996301

LIGHT BULB APPLICATION CHART

1991–1994 Models	
Light Bulbs	Bulb No.
Parking, front side marker and front turn signal lights	1157
Rear side marker lights	168
Rear turn signal lights	1156
Stop and tail lights	1157
Back-up lights	1156
License plate lights	168
Interior light	—
Trunk room light	194
High mounted stop-light	921
Sealed beam	H4666
Semi-sealed beam	9004

85996302

TRAILER WIRING

Wiring the car for towing is fairly easy. There are a number of good wiring kits available and these should be used, rather than trying to design your own. All trailers will need brake lights and turn signals as well as tail lights and side marker lights. Most states require back-up lights for trailers as well as extra marker lights for overly wide trailers. Some trailers are also equipped electric brakes. Others can be fitted with them as an option, depending on the weight to be carried. Add to this an accessory wire to operate trailer internal equipment or to charge the trailer's battery, and you can have as many as seven wires in the harness.

Determine the equipment on your trailer and buy the wiring kit necessary. The kit should contain all the wires needed, plus a plug adapter set which includes the female plug, mounted on the bumper or hitch, and the male plug to be wired into the trailer harness. When installing the kit, follow the manufac- turer's instructions. The color coding of the wires is usually standard throughout the industry.

One point to note: some domestic vehicles, and most imported vehicles, have separate turn signals at the rear. On most domestic vehicles, the brake lights and rear turn signals operate with the same bulb. For those vehicles with separate turn signals, you can purchase an isolation unit so that the brake lights won't blink whenever the turn signals are operated. You can also go to your local electronics supply house and buy four diodes to wire in series with the brake and turn signal bulbs. Diodes will isolate the brake and turn signals. The choice is yours. The isolation units are simple and quick to install, but far more expensive than the diodes. The diodes, however, require more work to install properly, since they require the cutting of each bulb's wire and soldering the diode into place.

The best wiring kits are those with a spring loaded cover on the vehicle mounted socket. This cover prevents dirt and moisture from corroding the terminals. Never let the vehicle socket hang loosely. Always mount it securely to the bumper or hitch.

If you don't get a connector with a cover, at least put a piece of tape over the end of the connector when not in use. Most trailer lighting failures can be traced to corroded connectors and/or poor ground connections.

CIRCUIT PROTECTION

Fuses

▶ See Figures 111, 112, 113, 114, 115, 116 and 117

REPLACEMENT

Most models have fuses found in two locations. One fuse box is located inside the car, just under the extreme left side of the dashboard. This fuse box generally contains the fuses for the body and electrical circuits such as the wipers, rear defogger, ignition, cigarette lighter, etc. In addition, various relays and circuit breakers for accessories are also mounted on or around this fuse box.

The second fuse block is found under the hood usually on the forward part of the left wheelhouse. Some models use a combination fuse block and relay board while other models have an additional relay board next to the fuse box. The fuses and relays generally control the engine and major electrical systems on the car, such as headlights (separate fuses for left and right), air conditioning, horns, fuel injection, ECM, and fans.

Each fuse location is labeled on the fuse block identifying its primary circuit, but designations such as "Engine", "CDS Fan" or "ECU-B" may not tell you what you need to know. A fuse can control more than one circuit, so check related fuses. For example, on some vehicles, you'll find the cruise control drawing its power through the fuse labeled "ECM-IG". This sharing of fuses is necessary to conserve space and wiring.

The individual fuses are made of plastic and connect into the fusebox with two small blades, similar to a household wall plug. Removing the fuse with the fingers can be difficult; there isn't a lot to grab onto. For this reason, the fuse box contains a small plastic fuse remover which can be clipped over the back of the fuse and used as a handle to pull it free.

Once the fuse is out, view the fusible element through the clear plastic of the fuse case. An intact fuse will show a continuous horseshoe-shaped wire within the plastic. This element simply connects one blade with the other; if it's intact, power can pass. If the fuse is blown, the link inside the fuse will show a break, possibly accompanied by a small black mark. This shows that the link broke when the electrical current exceeded the wires ability to carry it.

Once removed, any fuse may be checked for continuity with an ohmmeter. A reliable general rule is to always replace a suspect fuse with a new one. Doing so eliminates one variable in the diagnostic path and may cure the problem outright. Remember, however, that a blown fuse is rarely the cause of

a problem; the fuse is opening to protect the circuit from some other malfunction either in the wiring or the component itself. Always replace a fuse or other electrical component with one of equal amperage rating; NEVER increase the ampere rating of the circuit. The number on the back of the fuse body (5, 7.5, 10, 15, etc.) indicates the rated amperage of the fuse.

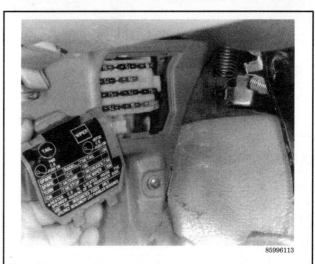
Fig. 111 Fuse panel located in the driver's side kick panel

Fig. 112 Fuse/relay/circuit breaker center in the engine compartment

Fig. 113 Replacing the fuse is a simple procedure

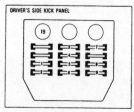
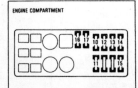
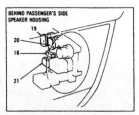

Fuses

1. TURN 7.5 A: Turn signal lights

2. IGN 7.5 A: Charging system, discharge warning light, electric underhood cooling fan

3. RADIO No.2 7.5 A: Radio, cassette tape player

4. CIG 15 A: Cigarette lighter, digital clock display

5. DOME 7.5 A: Interior light, personal light, luggage compartment light, clock, open door warning light, key reminder buzzer

6. STOP 15 A: Stop lights

7. TAIL 15 A: Tail lights, parking lights, side marker lights, license plate lights, instrument panel lights

8. GAUGES 7.5 A: Gauges and meters, warning lights and buzzers (except discharge and open door warning lights), back-up lights, cruise control system

9. WIPER 20 A: Windshield wipers and washer, rear window wiper and washer

10. ENGINE 15 A: Charging system, emission control system

11. RADIO 15 A: No circuit

12. HEAD (RH) 15 A: Right-hand headlight

13. HEAD (LH) 15 A: Left-hand headlight

14. CHARGE 7.5 A: Charging system, discharge warning light, automatic choke, emission control system

15. HAZ-HORN 15 A: Emergency flashers, horns

16. SPARE: Spare fuse

17. SPARE: Spare fuse

18. 10 A: Environmental cooling system

Circuit breakers

19. 30 A: Electric sun roof

20. 30 A: Rear window defogger

21. 30 A: Environmental control system

85996116

Fig. 114 Fuse application on wagons and 1984-1986 sedans

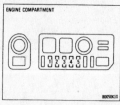
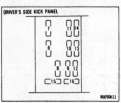
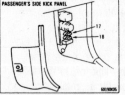
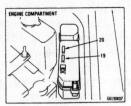
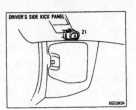

Fuses

1. CHARGE 7.5 A: Charging system, emission control system, discharge warning light, automatic choke

2. HEAD (LH) 15 A: Left-hand headlight

3. HEAD (RH) 15 A: Right-hand headlight

4. RADIO (No. 1) 15 A: Radio, cassette tape player

5. HAZ-HORN 15 A: Emergency flashers, horns

6. STOP 20 A: Stop lights, cruise control system cancel device, parking lights

7. RADIO (No. 2) 7.5 A: Radio, cassette tape player

8. DOME 7.5 A: Interior light, clock, open door warning light

9. ECU, IG 10 A: Cruise control system, electronically controlled automatic transmission system

10. CIG 15 A: Cigarette lighter

11. IGN 15 A: Charging system, discharge warning light, emission control system, electric underhood cooling fans

12. ENGINE 10 A: Charging system

13. GAUGES 7.5 A: Gauges and meters, warning lights and buzzers (except discharge and open door warning lights), back-up lights, environmental control system, environmental cooling system, rear window defogger

14. TURN 7.5 A: Turn signal lights

15. TAIL 15 A: Tail lights, parking lights, side marker lights, license plate lights, instrument panel lights

16. WIPER 20 A: Windshield wipers and washer, rear window wiper and washer

17. HEATER 30 A: Environmental control system

18. A/C 10 A: Environmental cooling system

19. 7.5 A: Spare fuse

20. 15 A: Spare fuse

Circuit breaker

21. 30 A: Rear window defogger

85996117

Fig. 115 Fuse application on 1987-1990 sedans

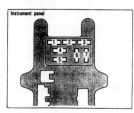 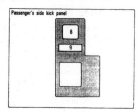 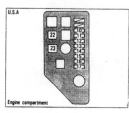 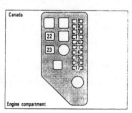

1. **CIG/RADIO 15A:** Cigarette lighter, radio, clock

2. **TURN 10A:** Turn signal lights

3. **WIPER 20A:** Windshield wipers and washer

4. **TAIL 15A:** Tail lights, parking lights, license plate lights, instrument panel lights

5. **STOP 10A:** Stop lights, high mounted stoplight

6. **DEF 30A:** Rear window defogger (without timer)

7. **GAUGE 15A:** Gauges and meters, warning lights (except discharge and open door warning lights), back-up lights

8. **HTR 30A:** Air conditioning system, "A/C" fuse, rear window defogger (with timer)

9. **A/C 10A:** Air conditioning system

10. **CDS FAN 30A:** Electric underhood cooling fan

11 **RAD FAN 30A:** Electric underhood cooling fan

12. **HEAD (LH) 10A:** Left-hand headlight

13. **HEAD (RH) 10A:** Right-hand headlight

14. **DOME 15A:** Interior light, open door warning light, trunk room light, clock, radio

15. **AM2 15A:** Ignition system

16. **HAZ-HORN 15A:** Horns, turn signal lights

17. **EFI 15A:** Electronic fuel injection system

18. **HEAD (LH-UPR) 10A:** Left-hand headlight (high beam)

19. **HEAD (RH-UPR) 10A:** Right-hand headlight (high beam)

20. **HEAD (LH-LWR) 10A:** Left-hand headlight (low beam)

21. **HEAD (RH-LWR) 10A:** Right-hand headlight (low beam)

22. **AM1 50A:** Ignition system

23.**ALT 100A:** Charging system, "HTR", "TAIL", "STOP", "DEF" fuses

85996118

Fig. 116 Fuse application on 1991-1992 sedans

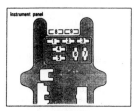 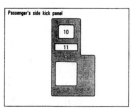 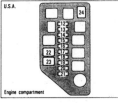 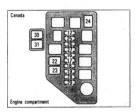

1. **CIG/RADIO 15A:** Cigarette lighter, radio, clock

2. **TURN 10A:** Turn signal lights

3. **WIPER 20A:** Windshield wipers and washer

4. **TAIL 15A:** Tail lights, parking lights, license plate lights, instrument panel lights

5. **STOP 10A:** Stop lights, high mounted stoplight

6. **DEF 30A:** Rear window defogger (without timer)

7. **GAUGE 15A:** Gauges and meters, service reminder indicators and warning buzzers (except discharge and open door warning lights), back-up lights

8. **IGN 7.5 A:** SRS airbag system (U.S.A.)

9. **ECU IG 7.5 A:** Anti-lock brake sysem

10. **HTR 30A:** Air conditioning system, "A/C" fuse, rear window defogger (with timer)

11. **A/C 10A:** Air conditioning system

12. **ALT-S 7.5 A:** Charging system

13. **HEAD (LH) 10A:** Left-hand headlight

14. **HEAD (RH) 10A:** Right-hand headlight

15. **ECU-B 10 A:** SRS airbag system

16. **DOME 15A:** Interior light, open door warning light, trunk room light, clock, radio

17. **AM2 15A:** Electronic ignition system/ distributor ignition system

18. **HAZ-HORN 15A:** Horns, turn signal lights

19. **EFI 15A:** Multiport fuel injection system/ sequential multiport fuel injection system

20. **CDS FAN 30A:** Electric cooling fan

21 **RAD FAN 30A:** Electric cooling fan

22. **AM1 50A:** Electronic ignition system/ distributor ignition system

23.**ALT 100A:** Charging system, "HTR", "TAIL", "STOP", "DEF" fuses

24. **ABS 60 A:** Anti-lock brake system

25. **HEAD (LH-UPR) 10A:** Left-hand headlight (high beam)

26. **HEAD (RH-UPR) 10A:** Right-hand headlight (high beam)

27. **DRL 7.5 A:** Daytime running light system

28. **HEAD (LH-LWR) 10A:** Left-hand headlight (low beam)

29. **HEAD (RH-LWR) 10A:** Right-hand headlight (low beam)

30. **RDI FAN 30 A:** Electric cooling fan

31. **CDS FAN 30 A:** Electric cooling fan

85996119

Fig. 117 Fuse application on 1993-1994 sedans

Fusible Links

REPLACEMENT

The fuse link is a short length of special, Hypalon (high temperature) insulated wire, integral with the engine compartment wiring harness and should not be confused with standard wire. It is several wire gauges smaller than the circuit which it protects. Under no circumstances should a fuse link replacement repair be made using a length of standard wire cut from bulk stock or from another wiring harness. Please refer to the beginning of this section for details on fusible link repair.

Circuit Breakers

REPLACEMENT

The circuit breakers found on the fuse and relay boards are mounted with blades similar to the fuses. Before removing a breaker, always disconnect the negative battery cable to prevent potentially damaging electrical spikes within the system. Simply remove the breaker by pulling it straight out from the relay board. Do not twist the relay; damage may occur to the connectors inside the housing.

➡**Some circuit breakers do not reset automatically. Once tripped, they must be reset by hand. Use a small screwdriver or similar tool; insert it in the hole in the back of the breaker and push gently. Once the breaker is reset, either check it for continuity with an ohmmeter or reinstall it and check the circuit for function.**

Reinstall the circuit breaker by pressing it straight into its mount. Make certain the blades line up correctly and that the circuit breaker is fully seated. Reconnect the negative battery cable and check the circuit for function.

Turn Signal and Hazard Flasher

REPLACEMENT

The combination turn signal and hazard flasher unit is usually located under the dash on the left side near the fuse box.

WIRING DIAGRAMS

The average automobile contains about ½ mile of wiring, with hundreds of individual connections. To protect the many wires from damage and to keep them from becoming a confusing tangle, they are organized into bundles, enclosed in plastic or taped together and called wiring harnesses. Different harnesses serve different parts of the vehicle. Individual wires are color coded to help trace them through a harness where sections are hidden from view.

Automotive wiring or circuit conductors can be in any one of three forms:

1. Single strand wire
2. Multi-strand wire
3. Printed circuitry

Single strand wire has a solid metal core and is usually used inside such components as alternators, motors, relays and other devices. Multi-strand wire has a core made of many small strands of wire twisted together into a single conductor. Most of the wiring in an automotive electrical system is made up of multi-strand wire, either as a single conductor or grouped together in a harness. All wiring is color coded on the insulator, either as a solid color or as a colored wire with an identification stripe. A printed circuit is a thin film of copper or other conductor that is printed on an insulator backing. Occasionally, a printed circuit is sandwiched between two sheets of plastic for more protection and flexibility. A complete printed circuit, consisting of conductors, insulating material and connectors for lamps or other components is called a printed circuit board. Printed circuitry is used in place of individual wires or harnesses in places where space is limited, such as behind instrument panels.

Since automotive electrical systems are very sensitive to changes in resistance, the selection of properly sized wires is critical when systems are repaired. A loose or corroded connection or a replacement wire that is too small for the circuit will add extra resistance and an additional voltage drop to the circuit. A ten percent voltage drop can result in slow or erratic motor operation, for example, even though the circuit is com-

plete. The wire gauge number is an expression of the cross section area of the conductor. The most common system for expressing wire size is the American Wire Gauge (AWG) system.

Gauge numbers are assigned to conductors of various cross section areas. As gauge number increases, area decreases and the conductor becomes smaller. A 5 gauge conductor is smaller than a 1 gauge conductor and a 10 gauge is smaller than a 5 gauge. As the cross section area of a conductor decreases, resistance increases and so does the gauge number. A conductor with a higher gauge number will carry less current than a conductor with a lower gauge number.

➡**Gauge wire size refers to the size of the conductor, not the size of the complete wire. It is possible to have two wires of the same gauge with different diameters because one may have thicker insulation than the other.**

12 volt automotive electrical systems generally use 10, 12, 14, 16 and 18 gauge wire. Main power distribution circuits and larger accessories usually use 10 and 12 gauge wire. Battery cables are usually 4 or 6 gauge, although 1 and 2 gauge wires are occasionally used. Wire length must also be considered when making repairs to a circuit. As conductor length increases, so does resistance. An 18 gauge wire, for example, can carry a 10 amp load for 10 feet without excessive voltage drop; however if a 15 foot wire is required for the same 10 amp load, it must be a 16 gauge wire.

An electrical schematic shows the electrical current paths when a circuit is operating properly. It is essential to understand how a circuit works before trying to figure out why it doesn't. Schematics break the entire electrical system down into individual circuits and show only one particular circuit. In a schematic, no attempt is made to represent wiring and components as they physically appear on the vehicle; switches and other components are shown as simply as possible. Face views of harness connectors show the cavity or terminal locations in all multi-pin connectors to help locate test points.

The flasher unit is not the classic round can found on many domestic cars; instead, it is a small box-shaped unit easily mistaken for another relay. Depending on the year and model of your vehicle, the flasher may be plugged directly into the fuse and relay panel or it may be plugged into its own connector and mounted near the fuse panel. The flasher unit emits the familiar ticking sound when the signals are in use and may be identified by touching the case and feeling for the click as the system functions.

The flasher unit simply unplugs from its connector and a replacement may be installed. Very rapid flashing on one side only or no flashing on one side generally indicates a failed bulb rather than a failed flasher.

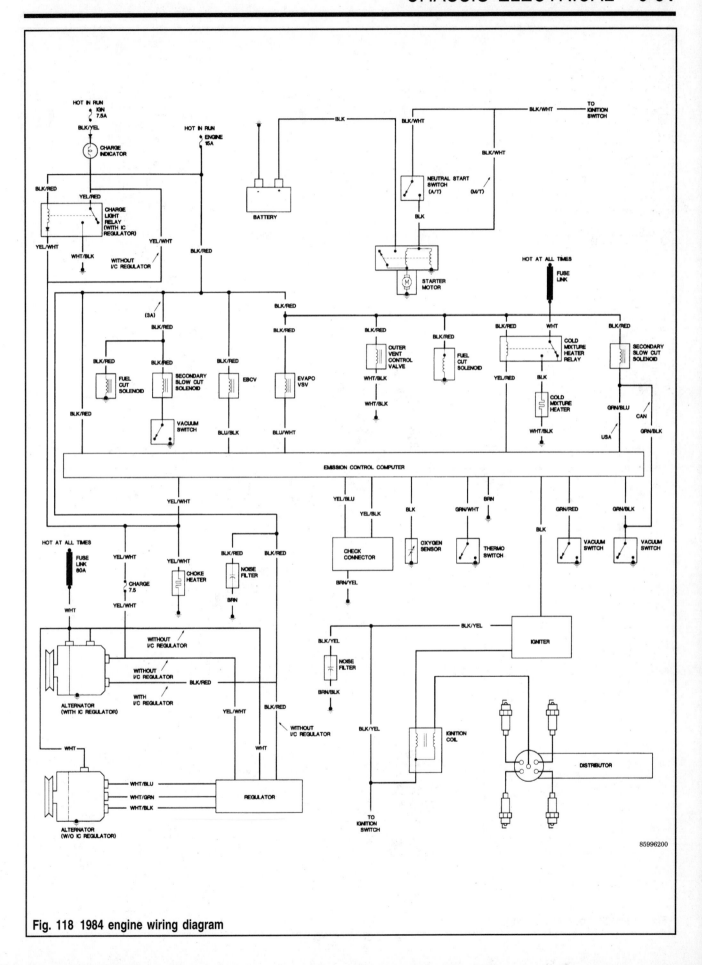

Fig. 118 1984 engine wiring diagram

85996200

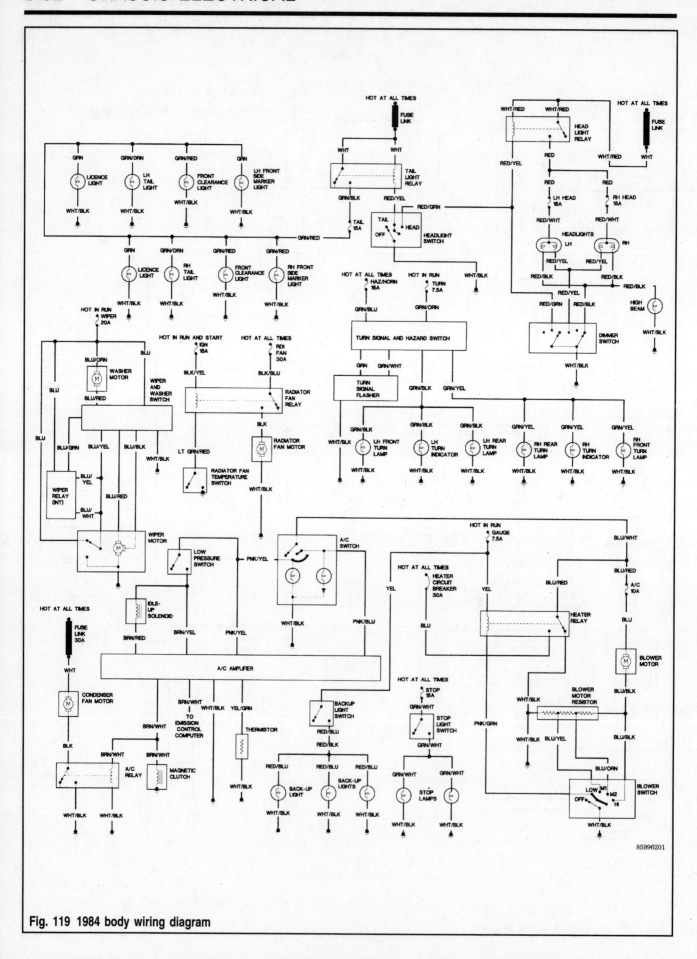

Fig. 119 1984 body wiring diagram

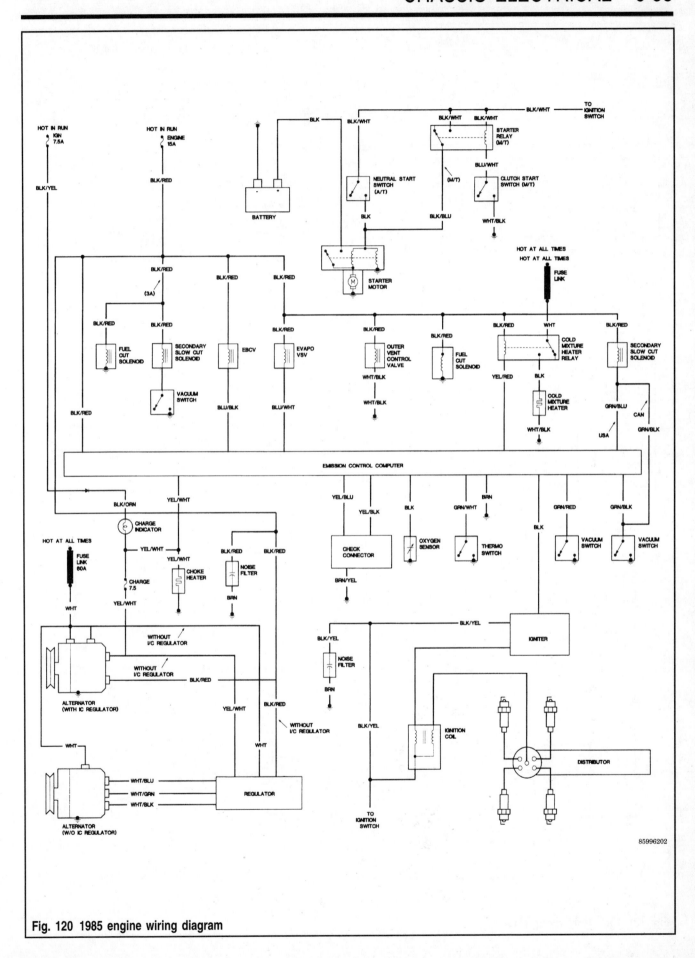

Fig. 120 1985 engine wiring diagram

85996202

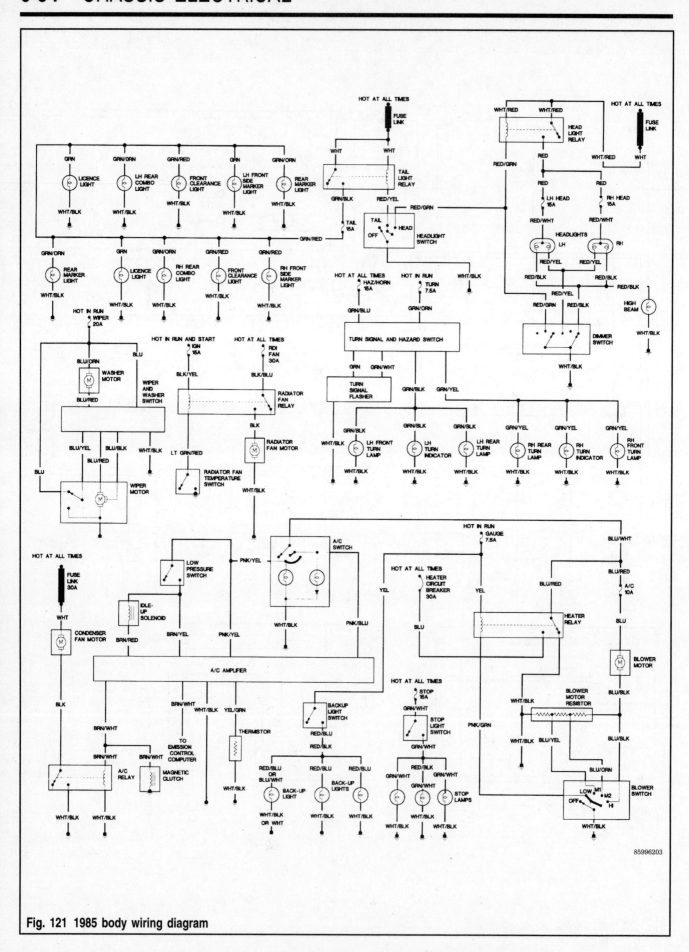

Fig. 121 1985 body wiring diagram

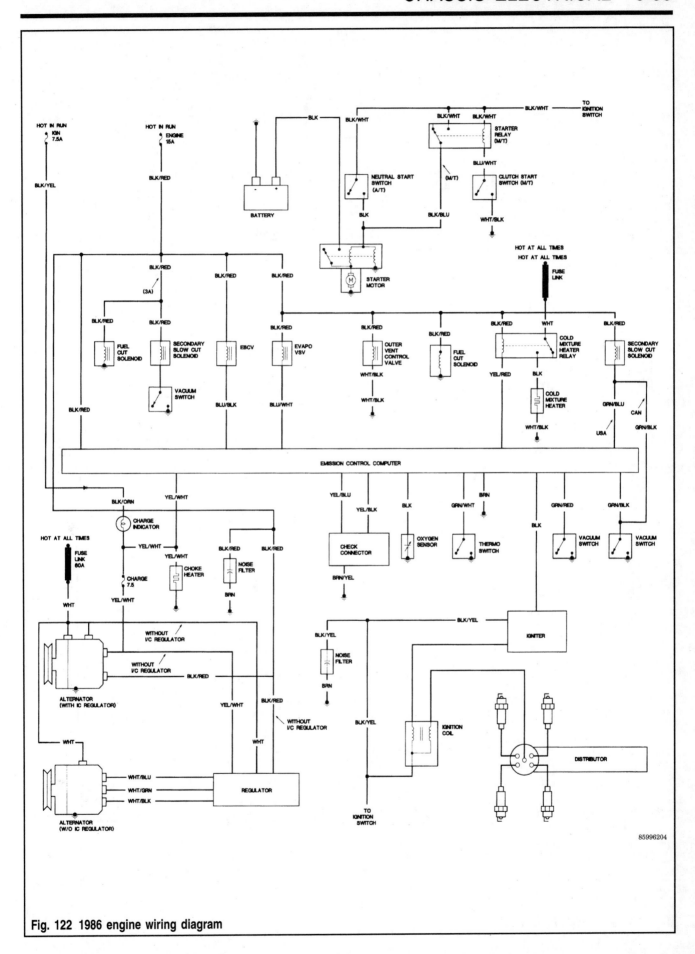

Fig. 122 1986 engine wiring diagram

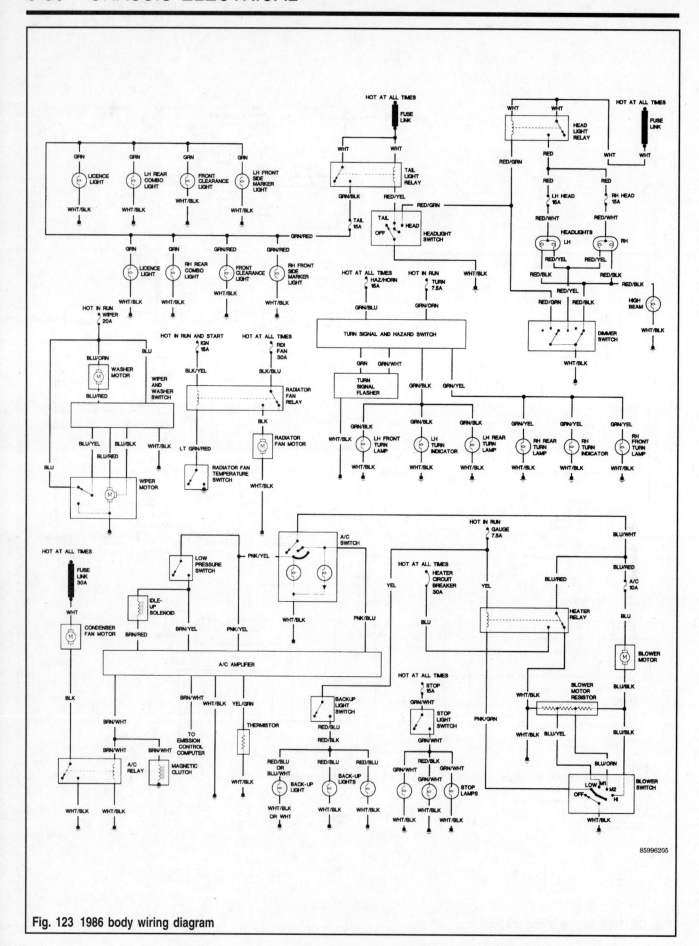

Fig. 123 1986 body wiring diagram

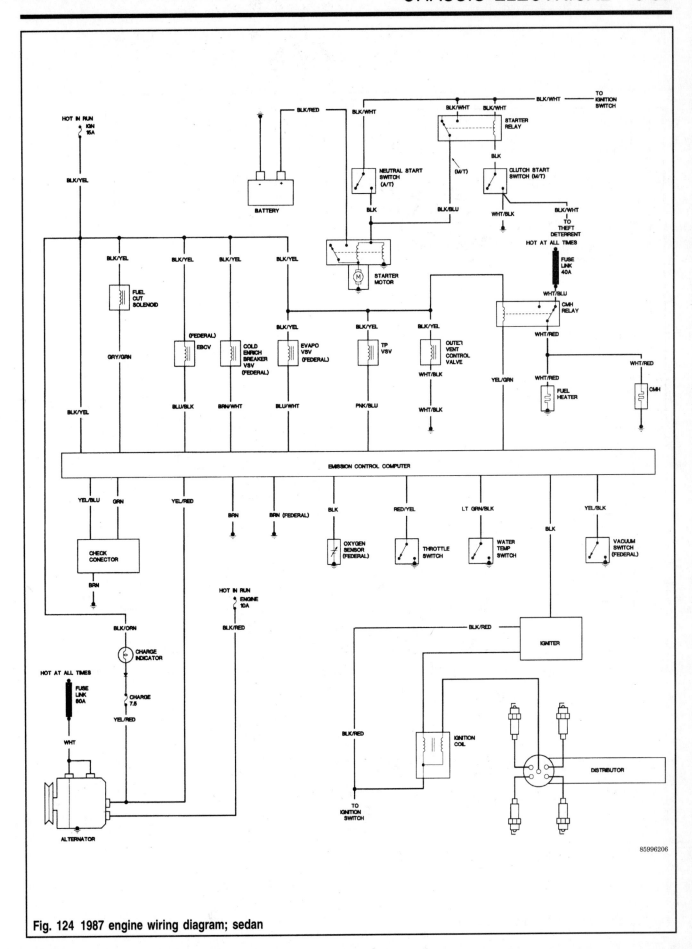

Fig. 124 1987 engine wiring diagram; sedan

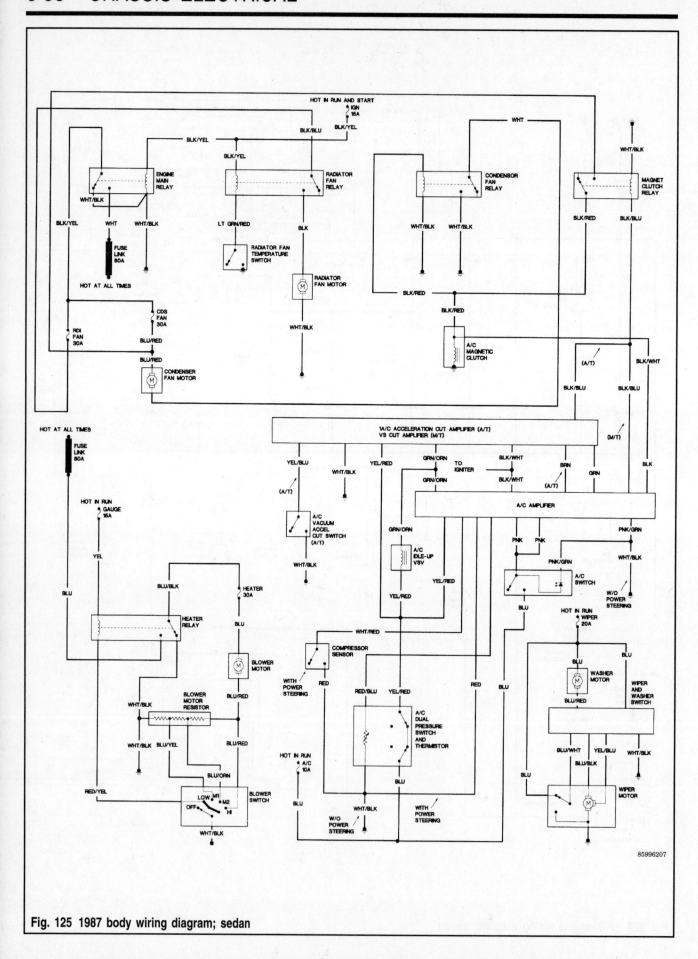

Fig. 125 1987 body wiring diagram; sedan

85996207

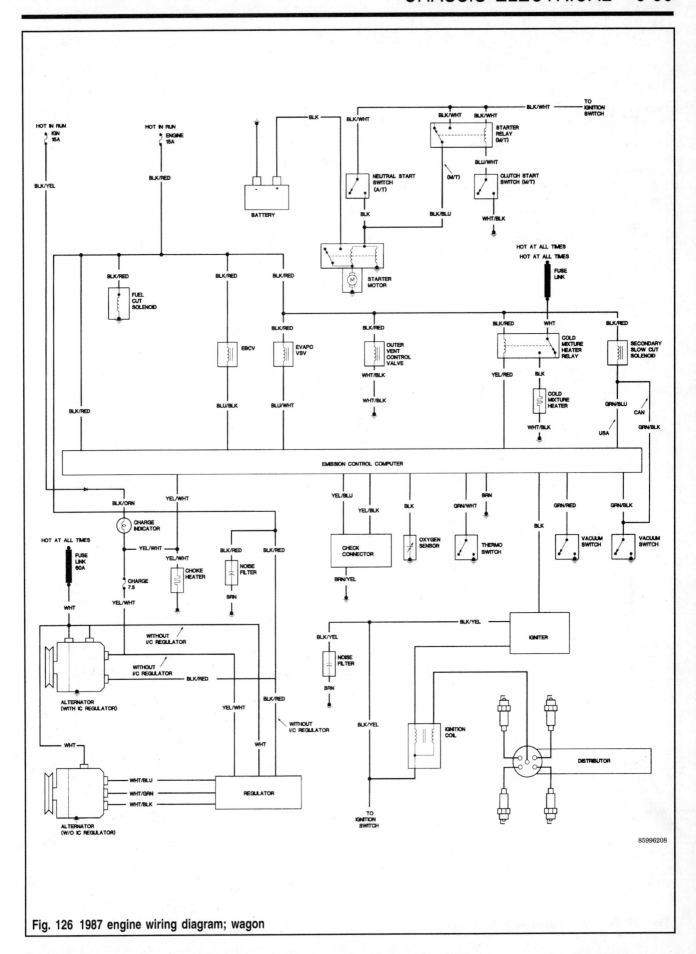

Fig. 126 1987 engine wiring diagram; wagon

85996208

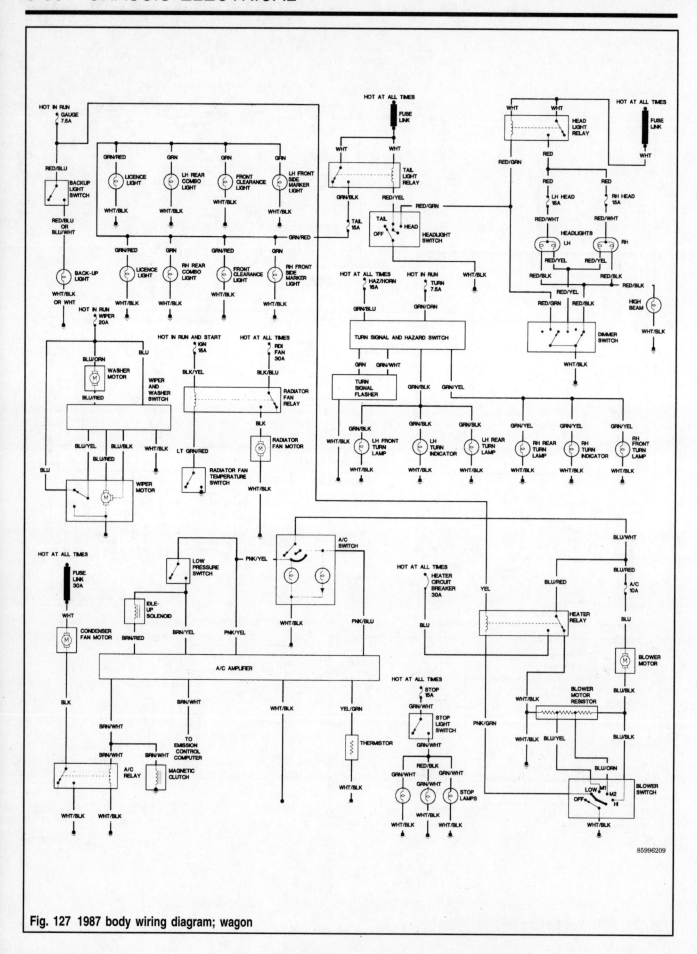

Fig. 127 1987 body wiring diagram; wagon

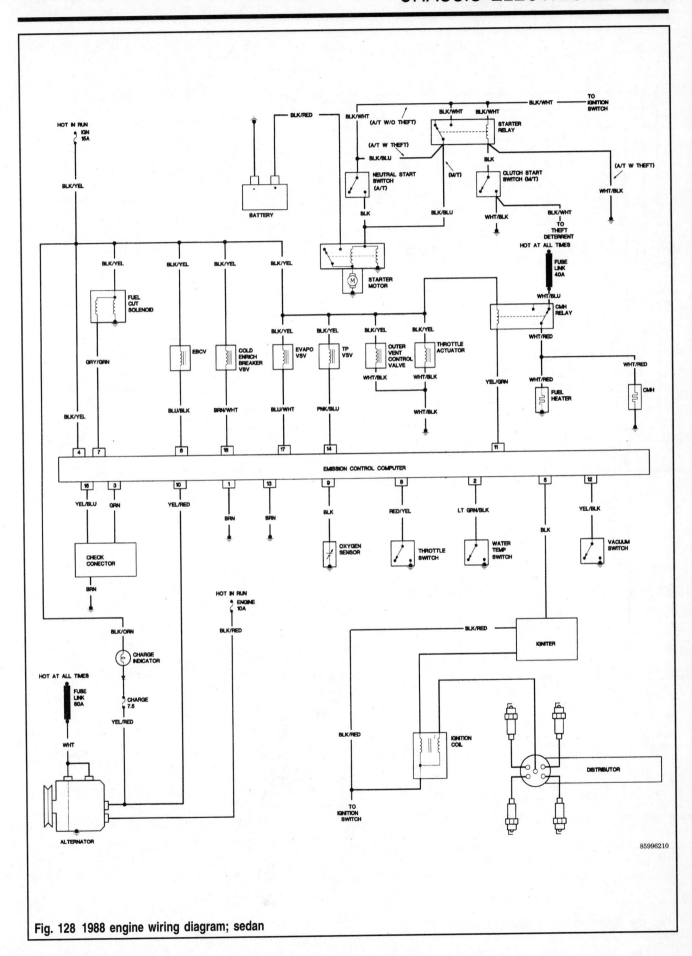

Fig. 128 1988 engine wiring diagram; sedan

85996210

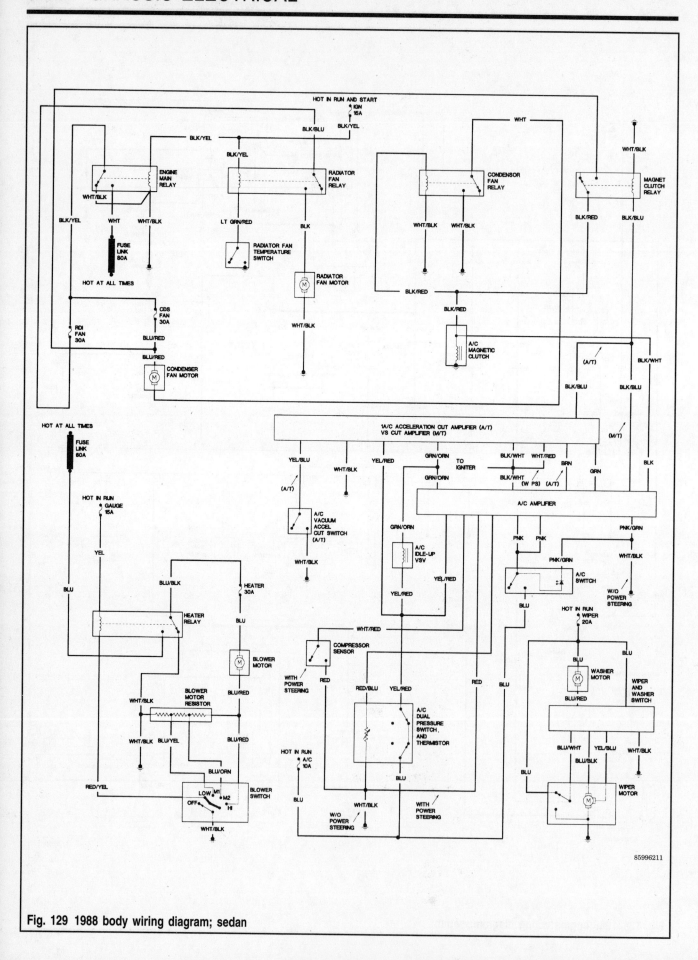

Fig. 129 1988 body wiring diagram; sedan

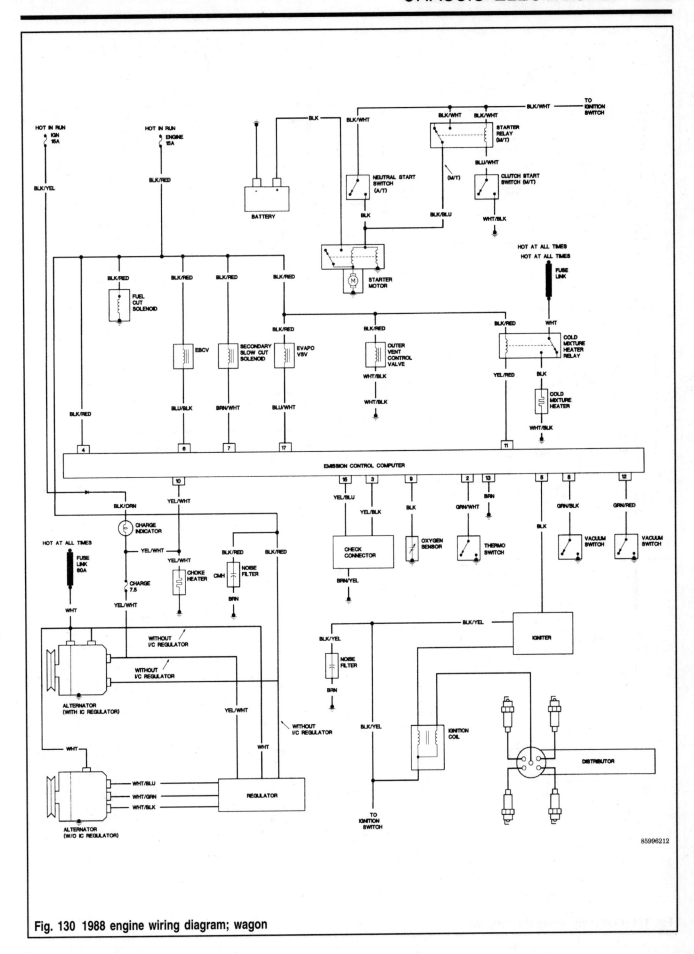

Fig. 130 1988 engine wiring diagram; wagon

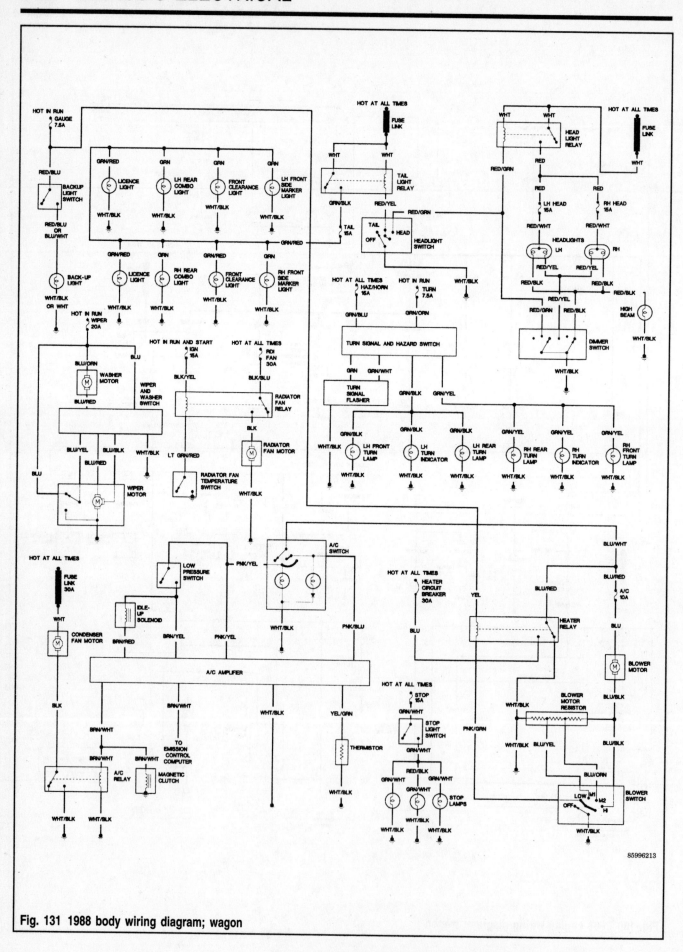

Fig. 131 1988 body wiring diagram; wagon

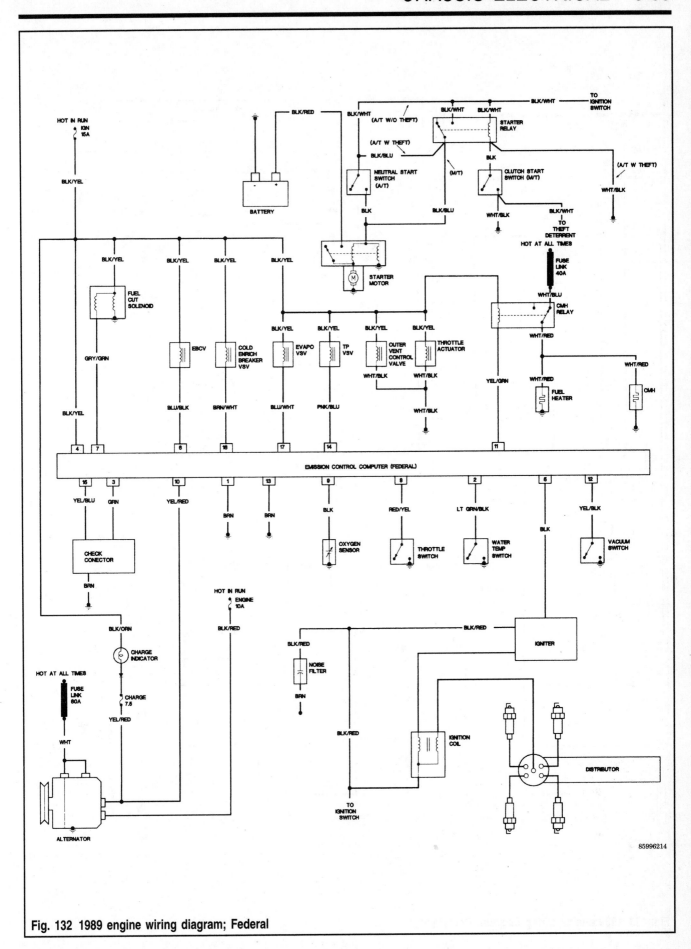

Fig. 132 1989 engine wiring diagram; Federal

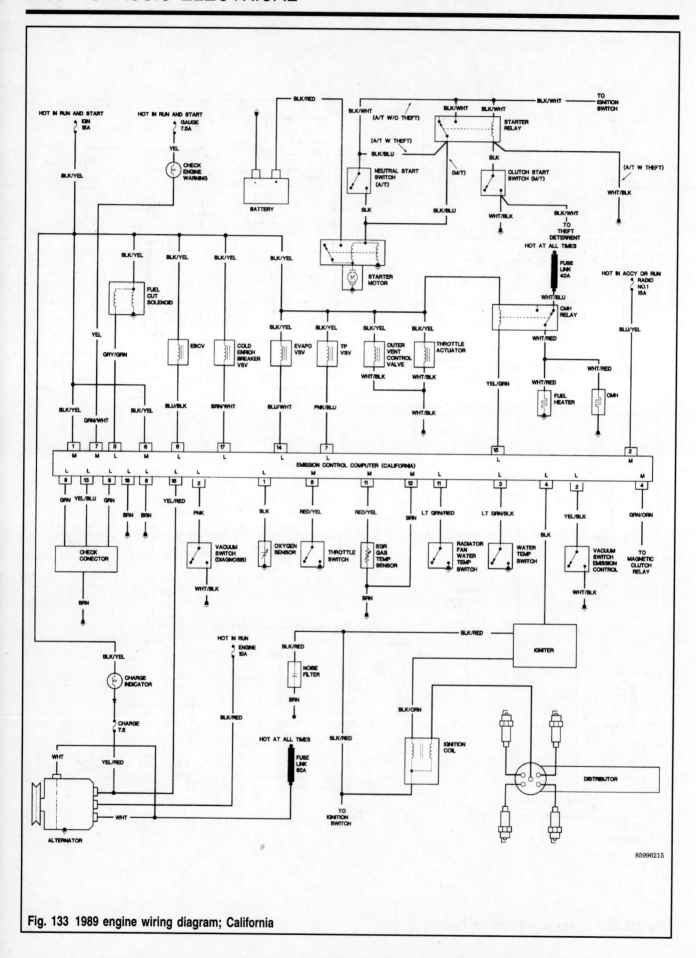

Fig. 133 1989 engine wiring diagram; California

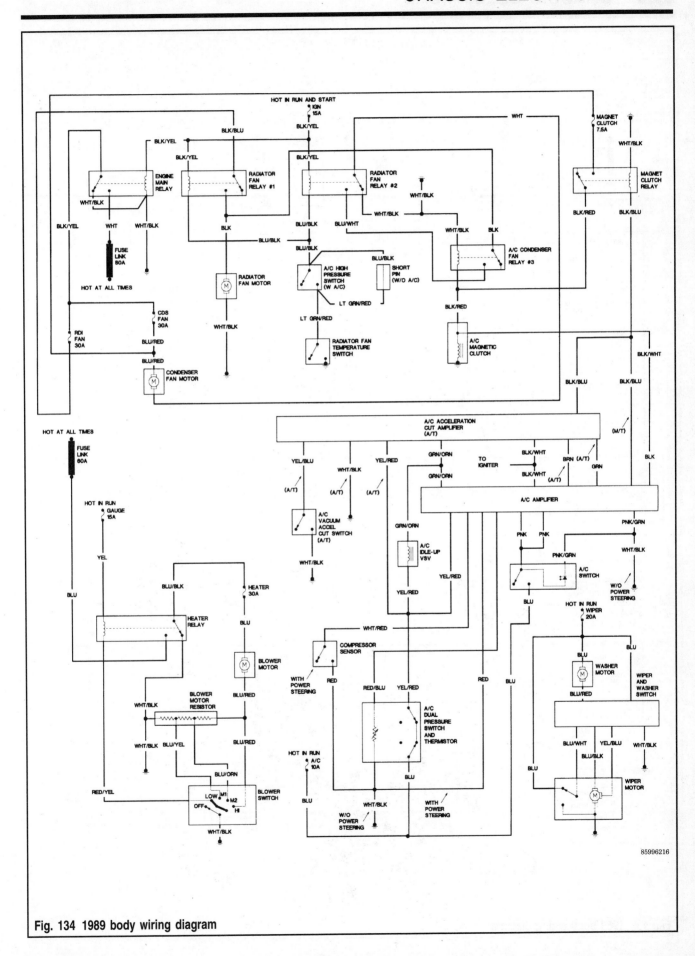

Fig. 134 1989 body wiring diagram

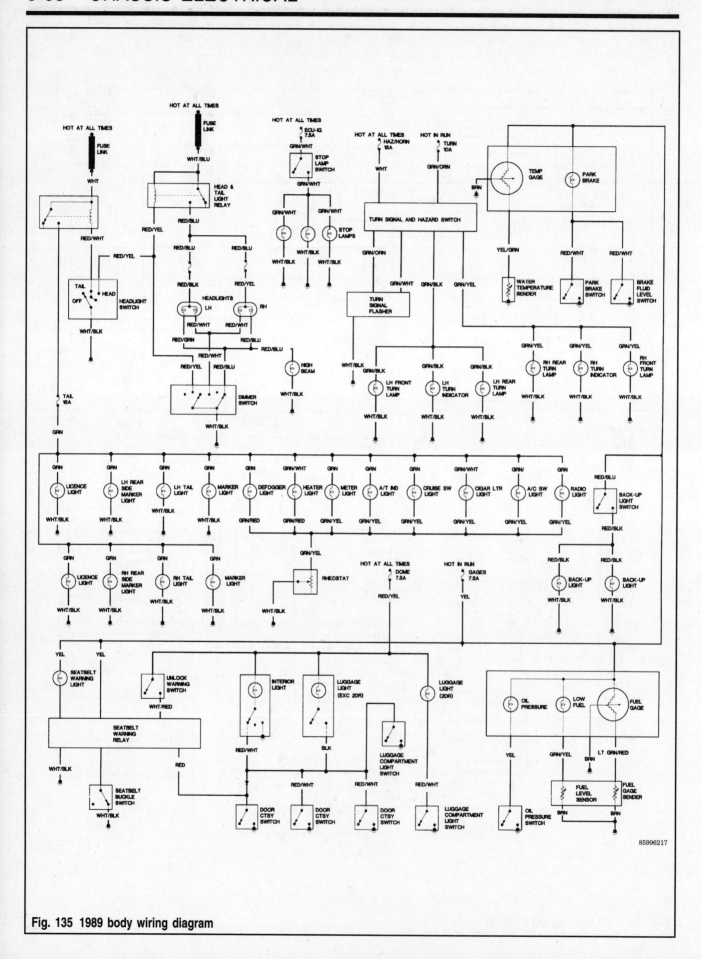

Fig. 135 1989 body wiring diagram

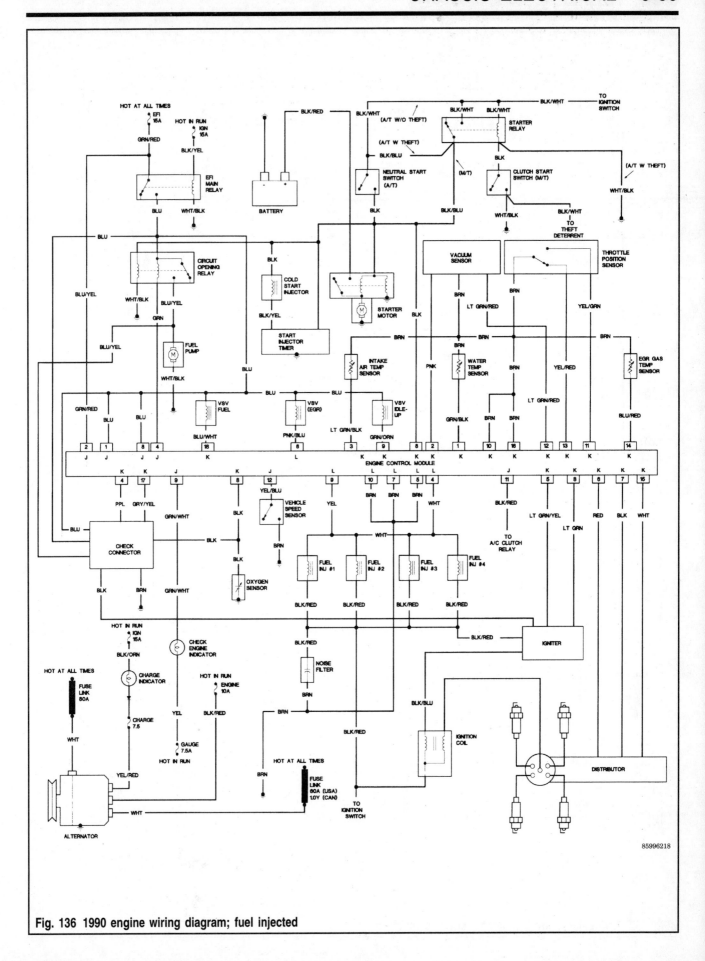

Fig. 136 1990 engine wiring diagram; fuel injected

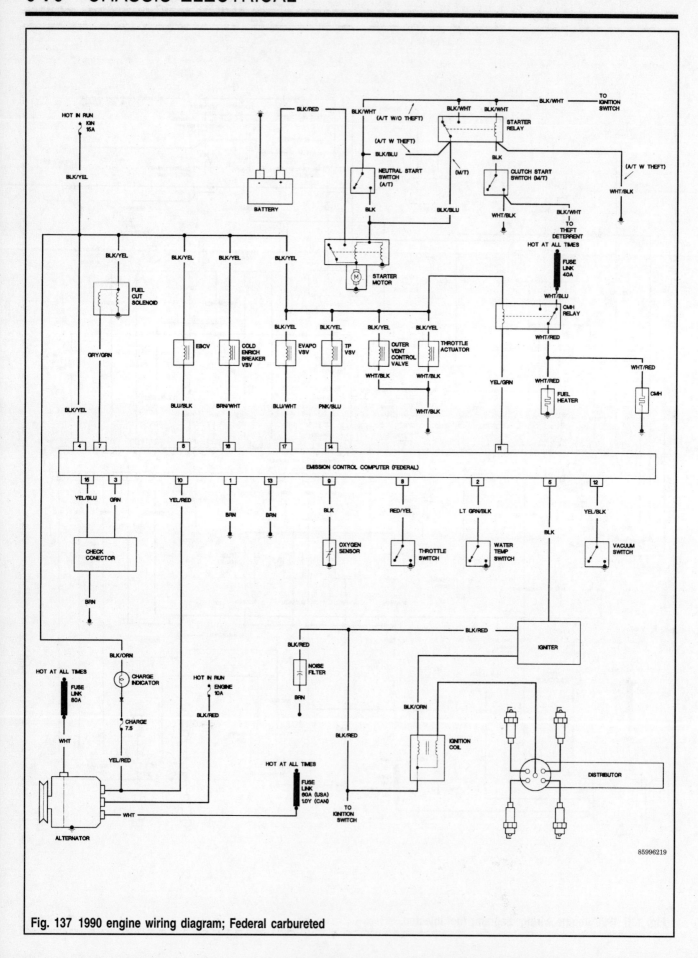

Fig. 137 1990 engine wiring diagram; Federal carbureted

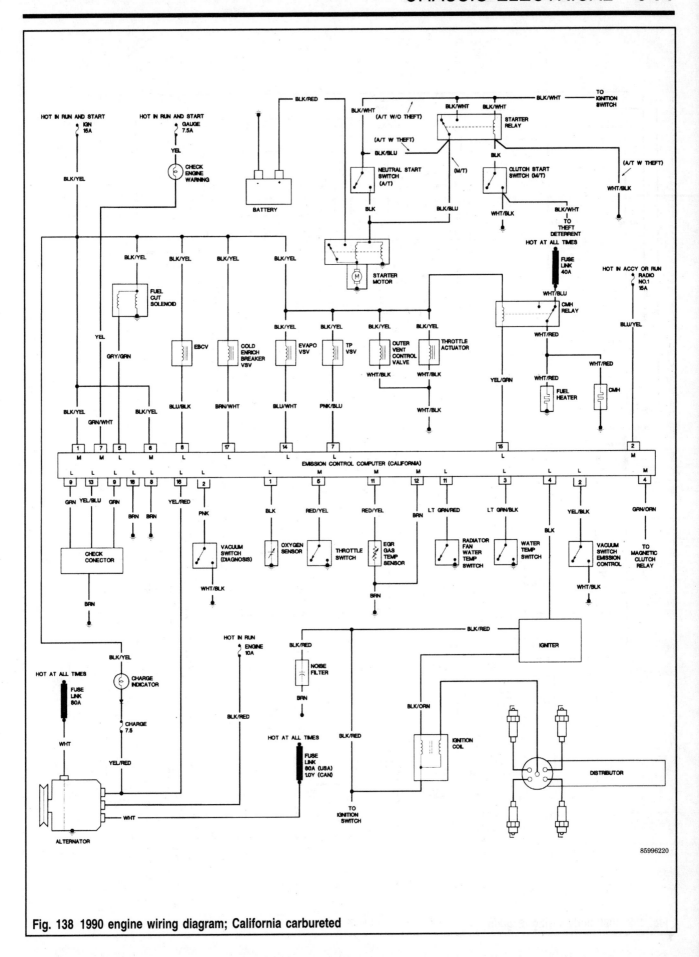

Fig. 138 1990 engine wiring diagram; California carbureted

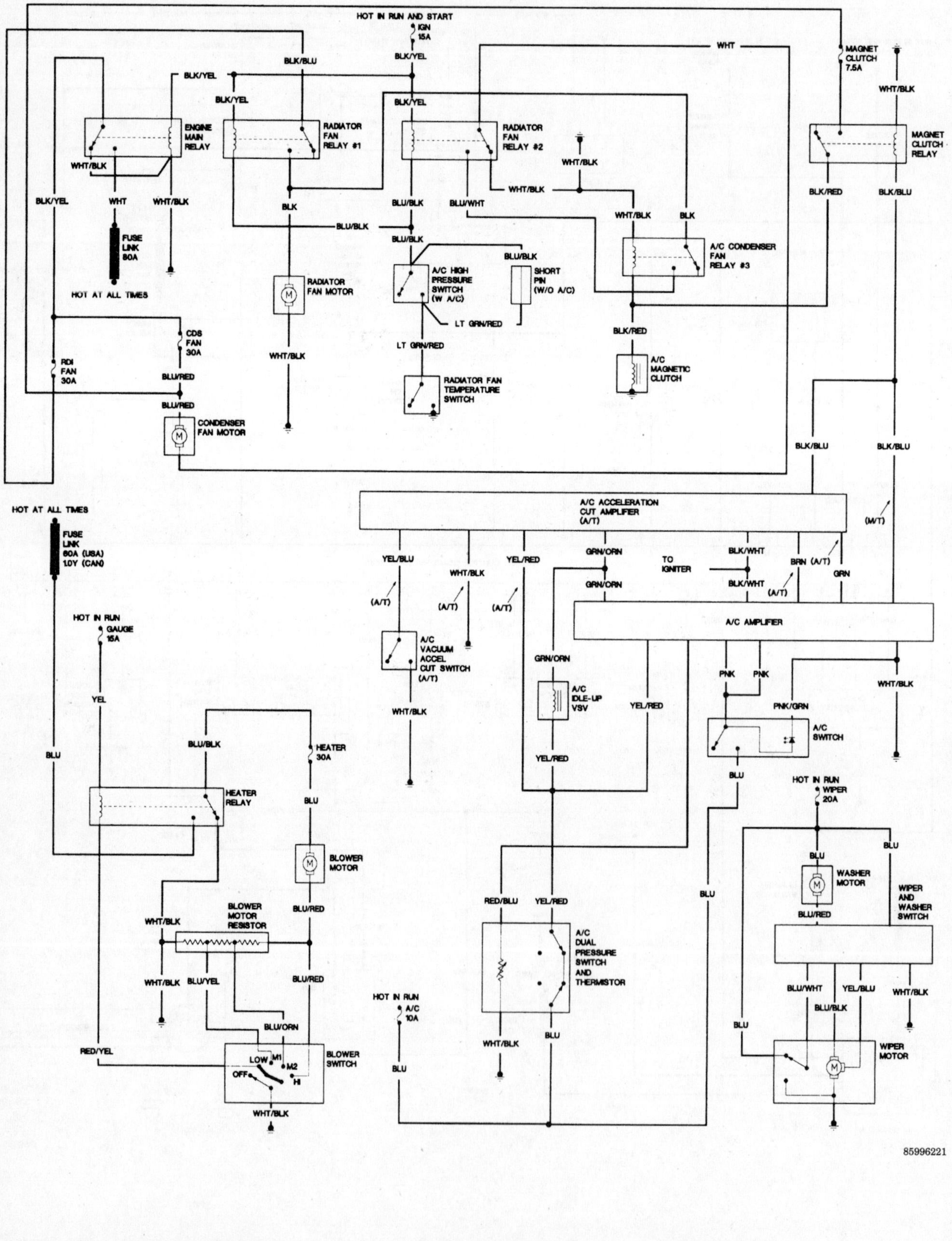

Fig. 139 1990 body wiring diagram

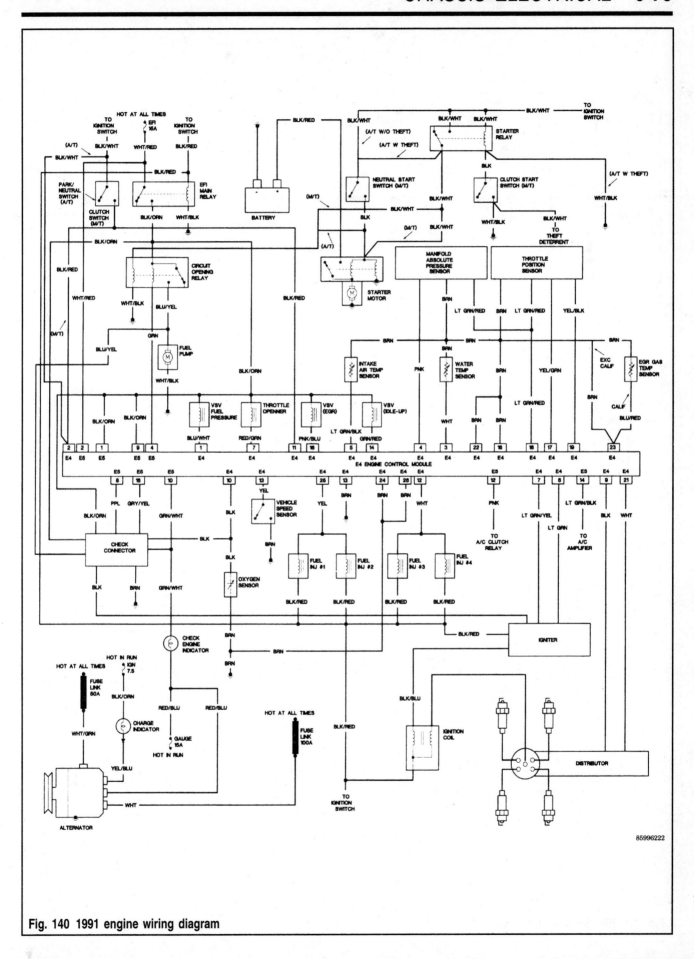

Fig. 140 1991 engine wiring diagram

85996222

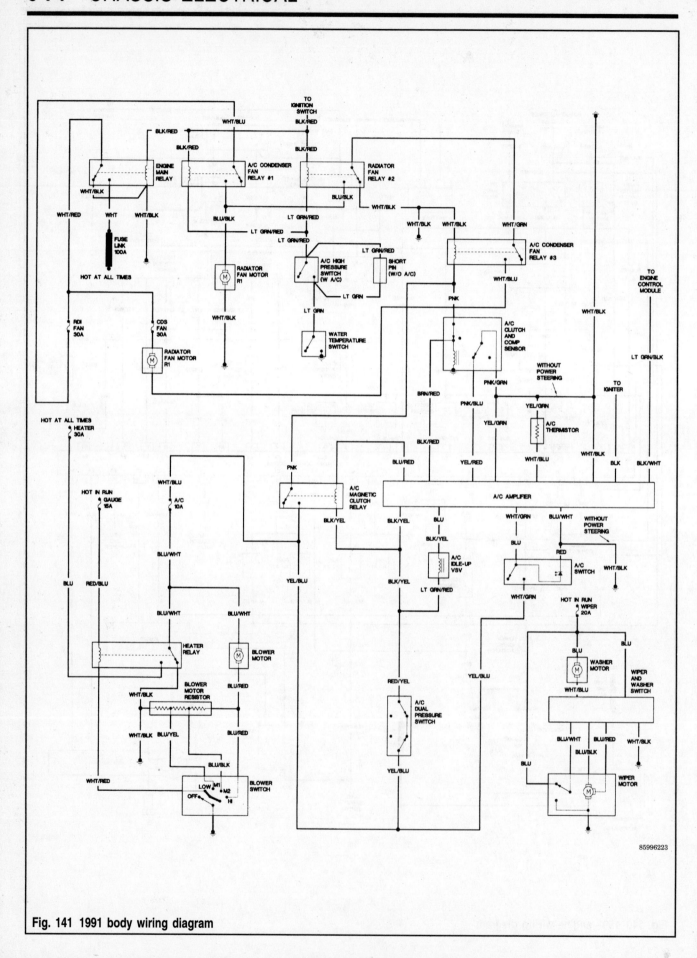

Fig. 141 1991 body wiring diagram

85996223

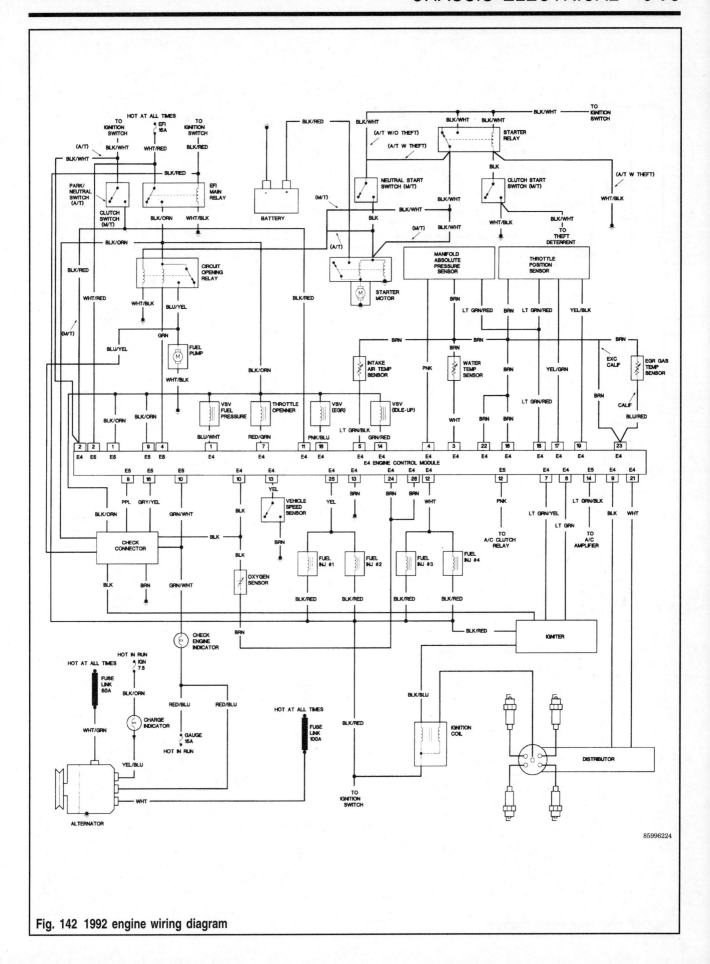

Fig. 142 1992 engine wiring diagram

85996224

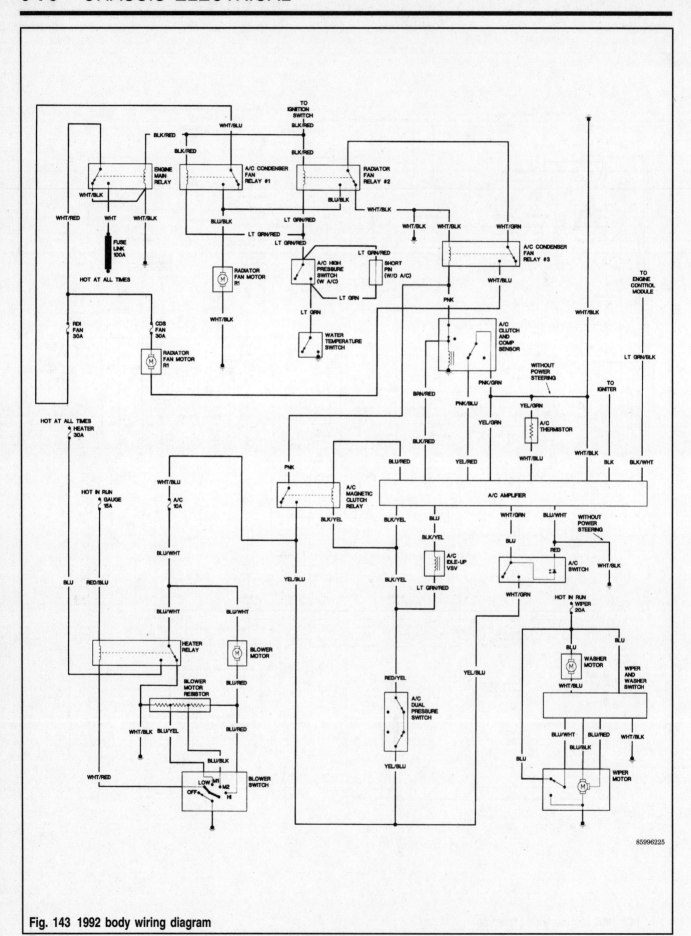

Fig. 143 1992 body wiring diagram

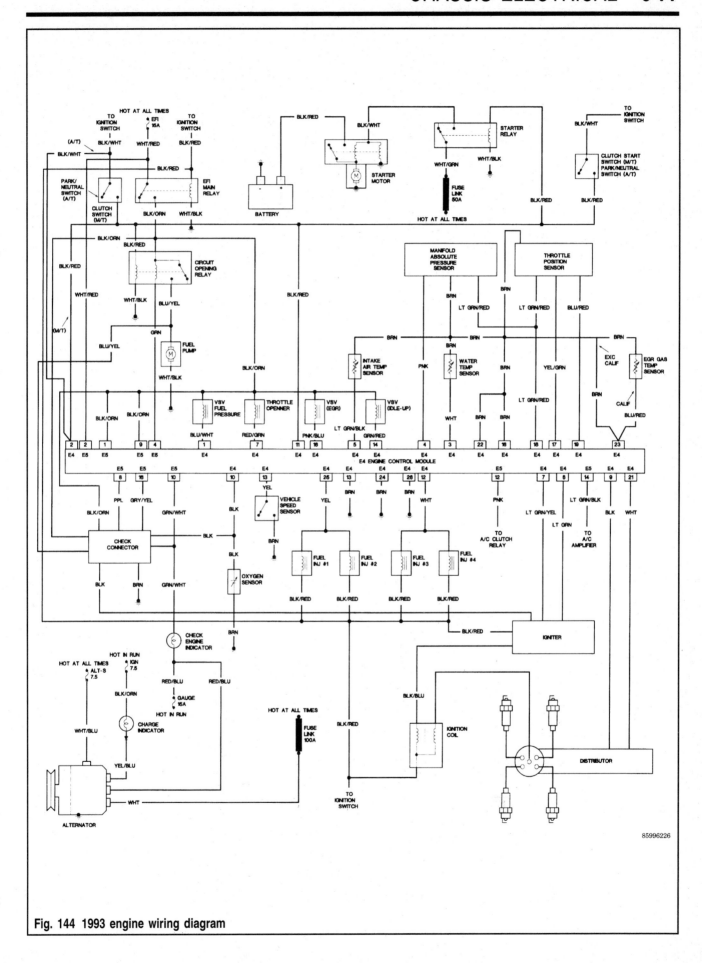

Fig. 144 1993 engine wiring diagram

85996226

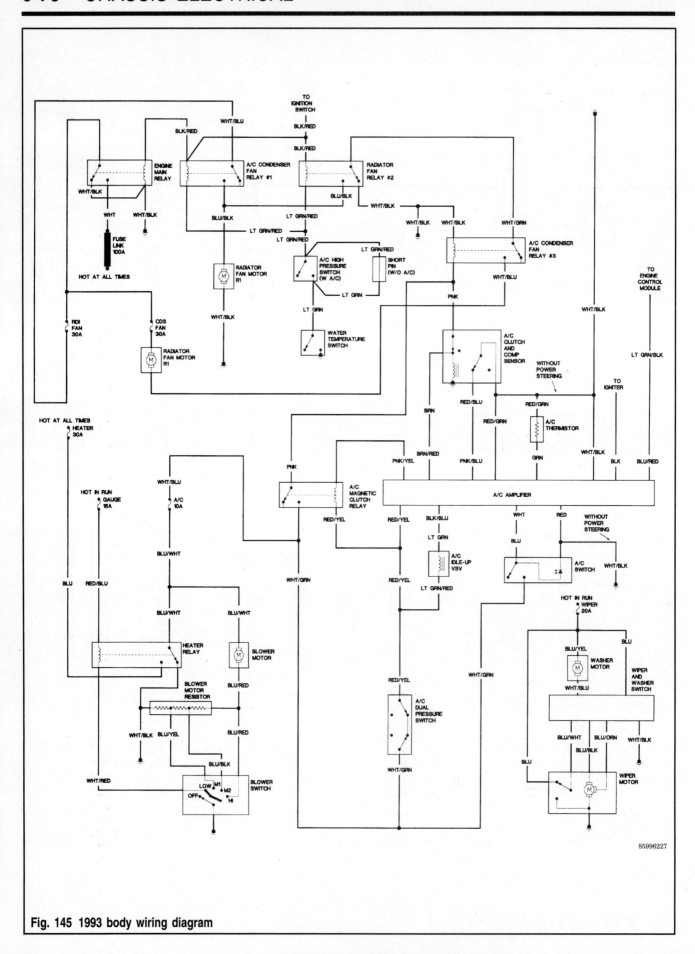

Fig. 145 1993 body wiring diagram

85996227

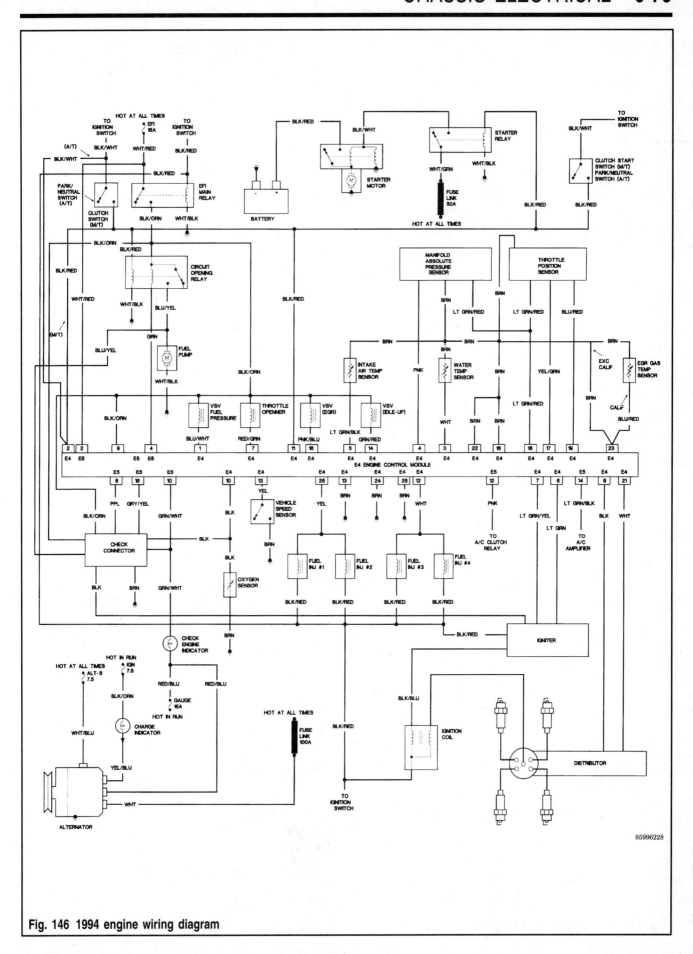

Fig. 146 1994 engine wiring diagram

85996228

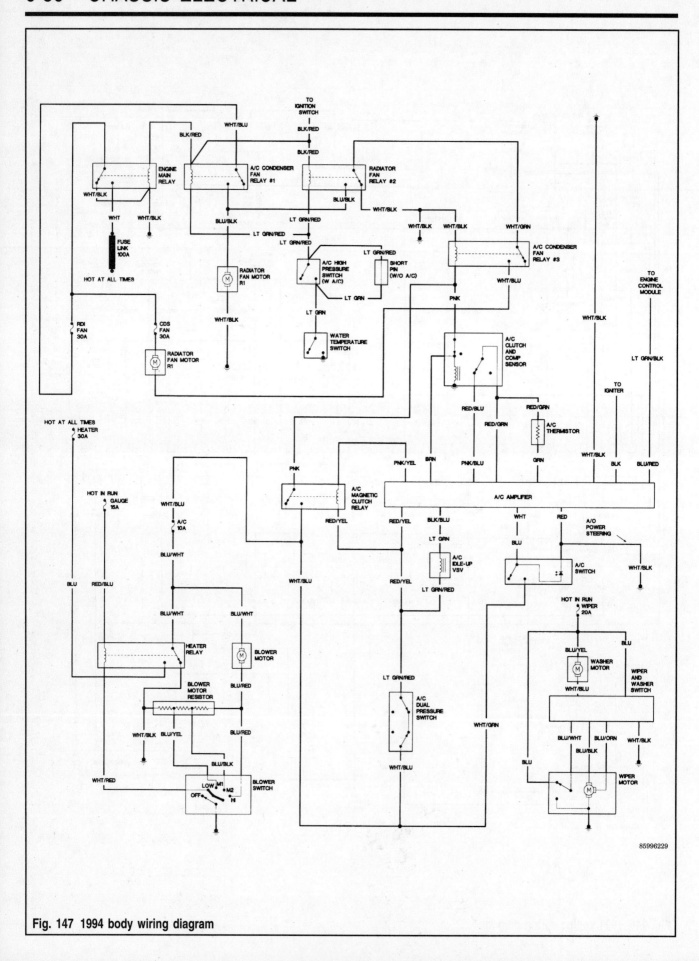

Fig. 147 1994 body wiring diagram

85996229

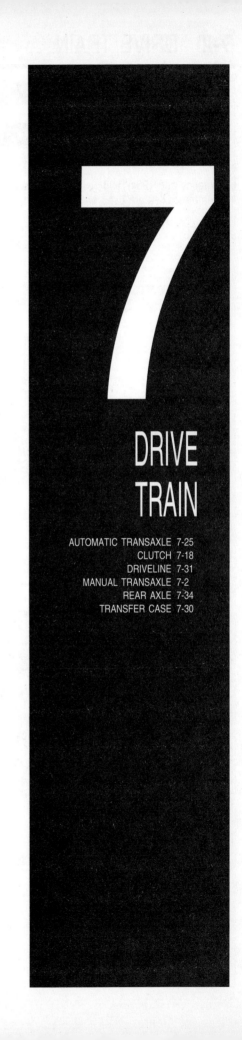

7

DRIVE
TRAIN

MANUAL TRANSAXLE

Identification

▶ **See Figures 1 and 2**

Wagons and 1984-1986 sedans use Z-series transaxles. C-series transaxles are used on 1987-1994 sedans.

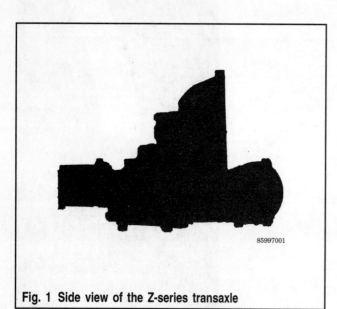

85997001

Fig. 1 Side view of the Z-series transaxle

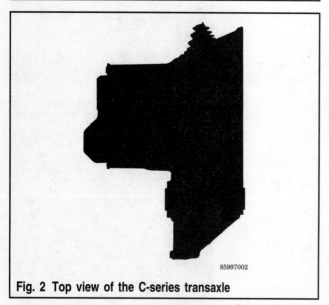

85997002

Fig. 2 Top view of the C-series transaxle

Adjustments

SHIFT LEVER VERTICAL FREE-PLAY

▶ **See Figures 3 and 4**

This procedure applies to 1987-1990 sedans only. Check the shift lever vertical play. If greater than 0.0059 in. (0.15mm), replace the shift lever bushing using the following procedure.

1. Remove the shift lever knob and cover.

➡ **On some models, it may be necessary to remove the center console.**

2. Remove the snapring securing the shift lever ball seat to the shift lever retainer.
3. Disconnect the shift lever from the selecting lever.
4. Pull the shift lever assembly from it's seat, then replace the bushing.
5. Installation is the reverse of removal.

SHIFT LINKAGE/CABLES

The shift linkage/cables are precisely adjusted at the factory during assembly and cannot be adjusted in the field. Cable stretch, bracket damage or excessive bushing wear can cause misadjustment. The individual cable, bracket or bushing must be replaced. Any attempt to adjust the shift cables can cause poor shifting and/or transaxle damage.

CLUTCH SWITCH

▶ **See Figure 5**

The clutch switch is used to prevent the vehicle from starting unless the clutch pedal is fully depressed. This is a safety feature which helps prevent personal injury and/or property damage which may occur if the vehicle's starter is engaged when the transaxle is in gear. On some models equipped with cruise control, it also disengages the cruise control feature.

1. Place the transaxle in the neutral position. Set the parking brake firmly and block the drive wheels.
2. Check that the engine does not start with the clutch pedal released.
3. Check that the engine starts with the clutch pedal fully depressed.
4. If necessary, adjust by loosening the lock-nuts and repositioning the switch. On 1987-1990 sedans with cruise control, check the pedal height (refer to the procedure in this section).

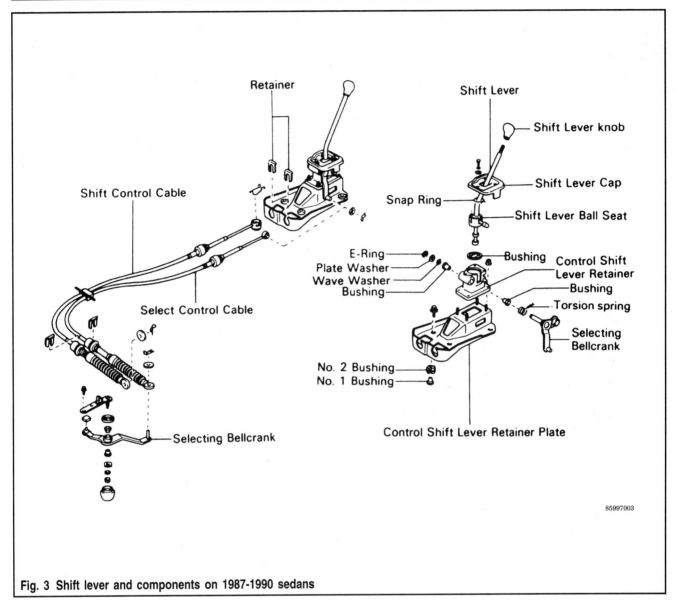

Fig. 3 Shift lever and components on 1987-1990 sedans

Retainer

Shift Lever

Shift Lever knob

Shift Control Cable

Snap Ring

Shift Lever Cap

Shift Lever Ball Seat

E-Ring

Plate Washer

Wave Washer

Bushing

Bushing

Control Shift Lever Retainer

Bushing

Torsion spring

Selecting Bellcrank

Select Control Cable

No. 2 Bushing

No. 1 Bushing

Control Shift Lever Retainer Plate

Selecting Bellcrank

85997003

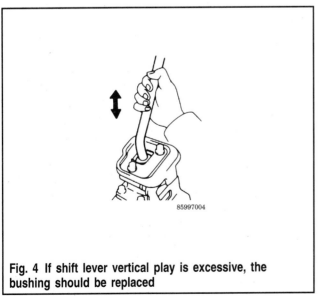

Fig. 4 If shift lever vertical play is excessive, the bushing should be replaced

85997004

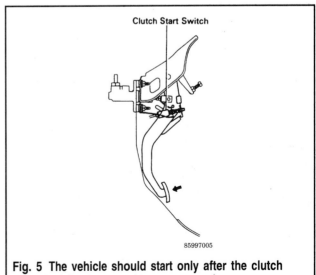

Clutch Start Switch

Fig. 5 The vehicle should start only after the clutch pedal is fully depressed

85997005

Back-up Light Switch

REMOVAL & INSTALLATION

This light switch is mounted on the manual transaxle housing. Its removal and replacement is accomplished by unplugging the wiring connector from the switch, then unscrewing the switch from the case (always replace the mounting gasket below it). A special socket with a slit cut in the side of it (for the wiring to feed through) is necessary for this service operation.

Install the new switch and torque to 19 ft. lbs. (25 Nm) for Z-series transaxles and 30 ft. lbs. (40 Nm) for C-series transaxles. Engage the electrical connector. Turn the ignition key to the **ON** position, then depress clutch pedal and place shifter in the Reverse position. Check the operation of the back-up lights.

Transaxle

REMOVAL & INSTALLATION

✳✳CAUTION

On models equipped with a Supplemental Restraint System (SRS) or "air bag," work must NOT be started until at least 90 seconds have passed from the time that both the ignition switch is turned to the LOCK position and the negative cable is disconnected from the battery.

➡Make sure to identify the correct manual transaxle type of your vehicle. Read the entire procedure applicable to your vehicle before continuing.

Z-Series Type — All Wagons and 1984-1986 Sedans
▶ See Figures 6, 7, 8, 9, 10, 11, 12, 13, 14, 15, 16, 17, 18, 19, 20 and 21

2-WHEEL DRIVE MODELS

1. Disconnect the negative battery cable. Drain the transaxle fluid.
2. On 1984 models, drain the cooling system, then remove the upper radiator hose and the air cleaner inlet duct.
3. Disconnect the clutch cable.
4. Remove the transaxle upper attaching bolts.
5. Remove both halfshafts. Refer to the procedure in this section.
6. Raise and securely support the vehicle.
7. If equipped, remove air inlet pipe from the converter.
8. Remove the front exhaust pipe and the stiffener plate.
9. Disconnect the gear shift and shift lever housing rods.
10. Unplug the back-up light switch connector, then disconnect the speedometer cable from the transaxle.
11. Remove the transaxle lower attaching bolts.
12. Using a floor jack, position it under the transaxle. Secure the transaxle to the jack to support it's weight.
13. Using a block of wood, position it between the engine and the cowl. This is done to prevent damage to the distributor

unit as it could make contact with the brake booster when the rear crossmember is removed.
14. Remove the transaxle from the engine. Draw it out and pull it towards the rear of the vehicle.

➡The transaxle is a fairly heavy assembly, have an assistant help you.

To install:
15. Apply molybdenum disulfide lithium base grease to the input shaft splines, then apply multi-purpose grease to the input shaft tip and the front of the release bearing.
16. Align the input shaft spline with the clutch disc, then push the transaxle fully into position.
17. Install the lower transaxle attaching bolts. Torque the 14mm bolts to 29 ft. lbs. (39 Nm) and the 17mm bolts to 43 ft. lbs. (59 Nm).
18. Install the rear support crossmember, then torque the bolts to 70 ft. lbs. (95 Nm). Remove the floor jack and the wooden block.
19. Connect the speedometer cable, then engage the back-up light switch connector.
20. Connect the shift lever housing and gear shift rods.
21. Install the front exhaust pipe. Torque the exhaust pipe-to-manifold nuts to 46 ft. lbs. (62 Nm).
22. If equipped with an air inlet pipe, connect it to the converter.
23. Connect the clutch cable.
24. Install both halfshafts.
25. Install the upper transaxle attaching bolts. Torque the 14mm bolts to 29 ft. lbs. (39 Nm) and the 17mm bolts to 43 ft. lbs. (59 Nm).
26. On 1984 models, connect the upper radiator hose and the air cleaner inlet duct. Refill the cooling system.
27. Connect the negative battery cable. Refill the transaxle with the appropriate fluid (refer to Section 1), then road test the vehicle.

4-WHEEL DRIVE MODELS

1. Disconnect the negative battery cable. Drain the transaxle fluid.

Fig. 6 Drain the transaxle fluids before starting the service procedures

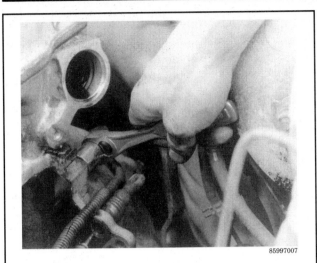

Fig. 7 Disengage the clutch cable from the hook on the release lever

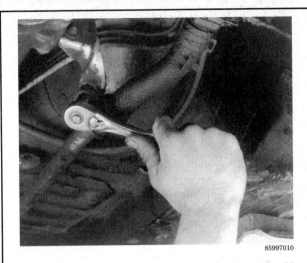

Fig. 10 If equipped, the converter air inlet pipe should be disconnected from the transaxle

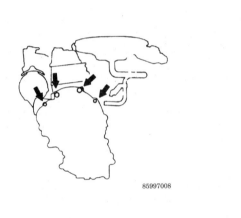

Fig. 8 Transaxle upper attaching bolt locations

Fig. 11 Excessive wear or damage to the gear selector rod bushings can cause difficult shifting

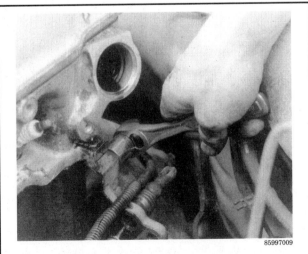

Fig. 9 The upper attaching bolts can usually be accessed from the engine compartment

Fig. 12 The speedometer cable is usually threaded into the side of the transaxle case

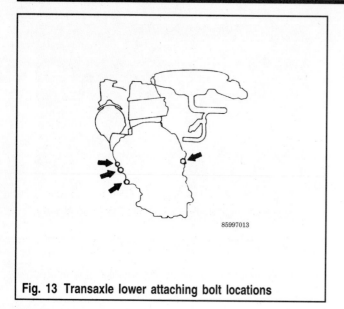

85997013

Fig. 13 Transaxle lower attaching bolt locations

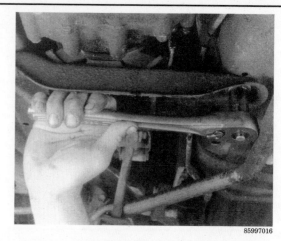

85997016

Fig. 16 Block engine movement and support the transaxle with a jack before removing the rear crossmember

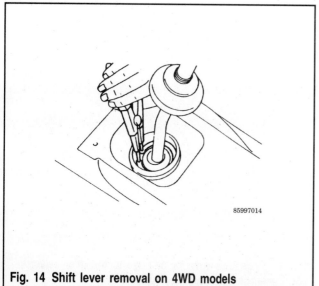

85997014

Fig. 14 Shift lever removal on 4WD models

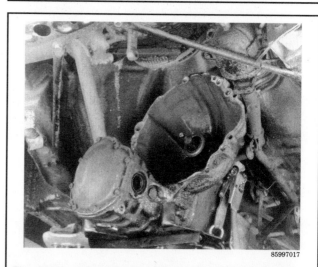

85997017

Fig. 17 It's a good idea to secure the transaxle with a strap to prevent it from tipping or falling off the jack

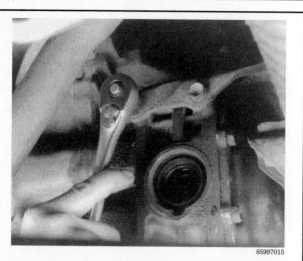

85997015

Fig. 15 Remove the bolts securing the transaxle to the front mounting brackets as well

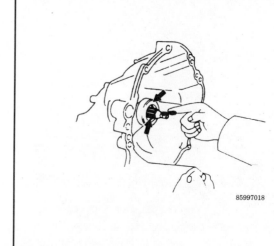

85997018

Fig. 18 Multi-purpose grease should be applied to the front of the release bearing and to the input shaft tip

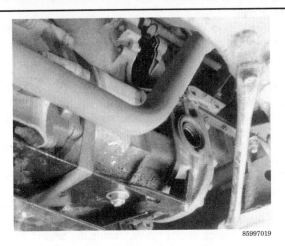

Fig. 19 Align the dowel pins on the transaxle with the holes on the engine mating surface, then push the assembly together

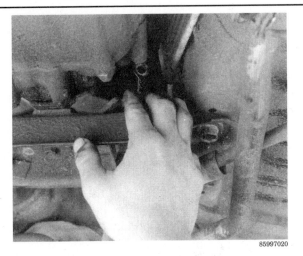

Fig. 20 The ground wire eyelet and mating surfaces should be cleaned before attaching it

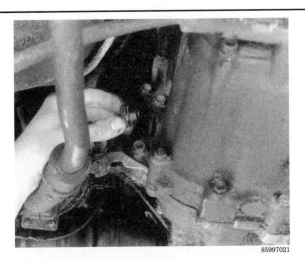

Fig. 21 Remember to fill the transaxle assembly with the proper fluid(s)

2. On 1984 models, drain the cooling system. Remove the upper radiator hose from the engine, then the air cleaner inlet duct.

3. Remove the console box and the shift lever from inside the vehicle. The shift lever is retained by a snapring.

4. Disconnect the clutch cable.

5. Remove the upper transaxle attaching bolts.

6. Raise and securely support the vehicle.

7. Remove both halfshafts. Refer to the appropriate procedure in this section.

8. Remove the rear driveshaft. Refer to the appropriate procedure in this section.

9. If equipped, remove air inlet pipe from the converter.

10. Remove the front exhaust pipe and the stiffener plate, if equipped.

11. Disconnect the selecting rod from the rear drive shift link lever.

12. Unplug the electrical connectors from the back-up light switch, the 4WD indicator switch and the extra low gear (EL) indicator. Disconnect the speedometer cable from the transaxle.

13. Remove the transaxle lower attaching bolts.

14. Using a floor jack, position it under the transaxle. Secure the transaxle to the jack in order to support it's weight.

15. Using a block of wood, position it between the engine and the cowl. This is done to prevent damage to the distributor unit as it could make contact with the brake booster when the rear crossmember is removed.

16. Remove the rear support crossmember.

17. Remove the transaxle from the engine. Draw it out and pull it towards the rear of the vehicle.

➡The transaxle is a fairly heavy assembly, have an assistant help you.

To install:

18. Apply molybdenum disulfide lithium base grease to the input shaft splines, then apply multi-purpose grease to the input shaft tip and the front of the release bearing.

19. Align the input shaft spline with the clutch disc, then push the transaxle fully into position.

20. Install the lower transaxle attaching bolts. Torque the 14mm bolts to 29 ft. lbs. (39 Nm) and the 17mm bolts to 43 ft. lbs. (59 Nm).

21. Install the rear support crossmember, then torque the bolts to 70 ft. lbs. (95 Nm). Remove the floor jack and the wooden block.

22. Connect the speedometer cable. Engage the back-up light, 4WD indicator, and Extra Low (EL) gear indicator switch connectors.

23. Connect the selecting rod to the rear drive shift link lever.

24. Install the front exhaust pipe. Torque the exhaust pipe-to-manifold nuts to 46 ft. lbs. (62 Nm).

25. If equipped with an air inlet pipe, connect it to the converter.

26. Connect the clutch cable.

27. Install both halfshafts.

28. Install the upper transaxle attaching bolts. Torque the 14mm bolts to 29 ft. lbs. (39 Nm) and the 17mm bolts to 43 ft. lbs. (59 Nm).

29. Install the shift lever and console box inside the vehicle.

30. On 1984 models, connect the upper radiator hose and the air cleaner inlet duct. Refill the cooling system, if necessary.

31. Connect the negative battery cable. Refill the transaxle with GL-4 or GL-5 (oil grade) 75W-90 or 80W-90 (viscosity) lubricant, then road test the vehicle. Refer to Section 1 for details.

C-Series Type — 1987-1994 Sedans

▶ **See Figures 22, 23 and 24**

1. Disconnect the negative battery cable.
2. Remove the air cleaner with the air inlet duct. Unplug the back-up light switch connector.
3. If equipped with cruise control, remove the battery and cruise control actuator with it's bracket.
4. Remove the clutch release cylinder. Refer to the appropriate procedure later in this section.
5. Disconnect the speedometer cable at the transaxle. Remove the shift control cable clips, washers and the cable ends.

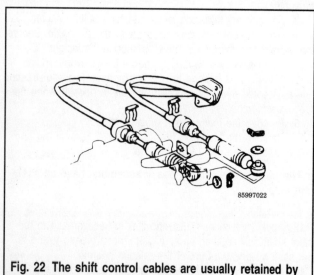

Fig. 22 The shift control cables are usually retained by small clips

6. Remove the selecting bellcrank with it's bracket from the transaxle case.
7. Remove the transaxle upper attaching bolts.
8. Raise and securely support the vehicle, then remove the engine undercover(s).
9. Drain the transaxle oil.
10. Remove both halfshafts. Refer to the appropriate procedure later in this section.
11. On 1987-1990 sedans, remove the front and rear engine mounting brackets. On 1991-1994 sedans, remove the rear engine mount only.
12. Remove the starter.
13. Raise the transaxle and engine slightly using a jack and wooden block, then disconnect the left engine mount.
14. Using a floor jack, position it under the transaxle. Secure the transaxle to the jack to support it's weight.
15. Remove the lower transaxle mounting bolts. Slightly lower the left side of the engine, then remove the transaxle.

➡The transaxle is a fairly heavy assembly, have an assistant help you.

To install:

16. Apply molybdenum disulfide lithium base grease to the input shaft splines. Apply multi-purpose grease to the front surface of the release bearing.

17. Align the input shaft spline with the clutch disc, then install the transaxle to the engine. Torque bolts (A) to 47 ft. lbs. (64 Nm), bolts (B) to 34 ft. lbs. (46 Nm) and bolts (C) to 65 inch lbs. (7.4 Nm). For bolt locations, please refer to the accompanying illustration.

18. Install the front and rear engine mounting brackets on 1987-1990 sedans. Torque the front bracket bolts to 43 ft. lbs. (58 Nm) and the rear bracket to 21 ft. lbs. (28 Nm). Do not install the mount bolts at this time.

19. On 1991-1994 sedans, install the rear engine mount and torque the bolts to 58 ft. lbs. (78 Nm).

20. Install the left engine mount. Torque the bolts to 35 ft. lbs. (48 Nm).

21. Install the starter.

22. On 1987-1990 sedans, install the front and rear mounting bolts. Confirm that the mount insulator is in the middle of

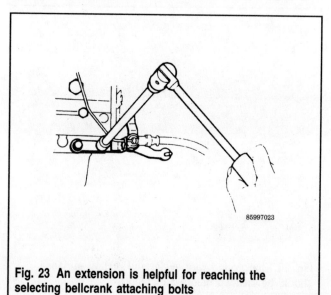

Fig. 23 An extension is helpful for reaching the selecting bellcrank attaching bolts

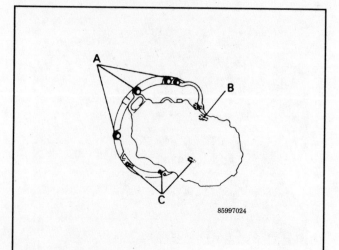

Fig. 24 Transaxle attaching bolts. Refer to the text for proper torque specifications

the insulator mount bracket. Torque the bolts to 47 ft. lbs. (64 Nm).

23. Install the halfshafts.
24. Connect the speedometer cable to the transaxle.
25. Fill the transaxle with GL-4 or GL-5 (oil grade) 75W-90 or 80W-90 (viscosity) lubricant. Refer to Section 1 for details.
26. Install the engine under cover(s).
27. Lower the vehicle, then connect the shift control cables.
28. Engage the back-up light switch connector, then install the clutch release cylinder.
29. Install the selecting bellcrank with it's bracket.
30. Install the cruise control actuator and battery, if applicable.
31. Install the air cleaner and air inlet hose.
32. Connect the negative battery cable, then road test the vehicle and check for proper operation.

Halfshafts

REMOVAL & INSTALLATION

▶ See Figures 25, 26, 27, 28, 29, 30, 31, 32, 33, 34, 35, 36, 37, 38, 39, 40, 41, 42 and 43

❋❋CAUTION

On models equipped with a Supplemental Restraint System (SRS) or "air bag," work must NOT be started until at least 90 seconds have passed from the time that both the ignition switch is turned to the LOCK position and the negative cable is disconnected from the battery.

Wagons and 1984-1986 Sedans

1. Disconnect the negative battery cable.
2. Remove the wheel cover.
3. Remove the cotter pin, hub nut cap, hub nut and washer.
4. Loosen the wheel nuts.
5. Raise and safely support the car. Remove the wheel.
6. Remove the brake caliper from the steering knuckle, then suspend it with a wire. Remove the disc. Refer to the appropriate procedures in this manual.
7. Remove the cotter pin and nut from the tie rod end. Using SST 09610-20012 or it's equivalent tie rod separator, disconnect the tie rod end from the steering knuckle.
8. Matchmark the position of the shock absorber lower bracket and camber adjusting cam to the steering knuckle.
9. Remove the nuts and bolts, then disconnect the steering knuckle.
10. Using SST 09950-20016 or it's equivalent hub puller, press the axle hub from the halfshaft outboard joint. Cover the halfshaft boot with a shop rag to protect it from damage.
11. Remove the stiffener plate from the transaxle assembly and engine (left side only).
12. Using SST 09648-16010 or it's equivalent halfshaft removal tool, tap the halfshaft out of the transaxle.
    To install:
13. Apply multi-purpose grease to the oil seal lip on the transaxle.

14. Using SST 09648-16010 or it's equivalent halfshaft installation tool, tap the halfshaft into the transaxle until it contacts the pinion shaft in the transaxle and the snapring engages in the side gear. The halfshaft should not pull out of the transaxle by hand.
15. Install the stiffener plate (left side only). Torque the bolts to 29 ft. lbs. (39 Nm).
16. Install the halfshaft to the axle hub with the washer and hub nut. Be careful not to damage the oil lip seal and the halfshaft boot.
17. Install the disc to the axle hub.
18. Lower the stabilizer bar, then assemble the shock absorber lower bracket to the steering knuckle.
19. Insert the bolts from the front side, then align the matchmarks of the camber adjusting cam. Torque the bolts to 105 ft. lbs. (142 Nm).
20. Install the brake caliper to the steering knuckle. Refer to the appropriate procedure in this manual.
21. Connect the tie rod end to the steering knuckle. Torque the nut to 36 ft. lbs. (49 Nm), then secure it with a new cotter pin.
22. Torque the hub nut to 137 ft. lbs. (186 Nm). Install the hub nut cap, then install a new cotter pin.
23. Install the wheel.
24. Lower the vehicle to the ground.
25. Have the front wheel alignment checked and/or adjusted by a reputable service facility. Road test the vehicle for proper operation.

1987-1990 Sedans

➡The hub bearing could be damaged if it is subjected to the vehicle weight, such as when moving the vehicle with the halfshaft removed. If it is necessary to place the vehicle weight on the hub bearing, support it with SST 09608-16041, 09608-02020, 09608-02040 or a equivalent hub bearing support tool.

1. Disconnect the negative battery cable.
2. Remove the engine under cover.
3. Drain the transaxle fluid.
4. Remove the wheel cover.

85997026

Fig. 25 Heavy grease around the inside of the wheel or on the brake caliper usually indicates a torn boot

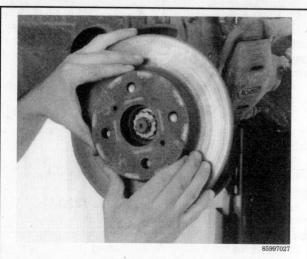

Fig. 26 Remove the brake disc, if necessary, for increased working space

Fig. 27 Needle nose pliers are useful for removing cotter pins

Fig. 28 On some models, it will be necessary to remove the left side stiffener plate

Fig. 29 Remove the cotter pin before removing the nut which secures the outer tie rod end

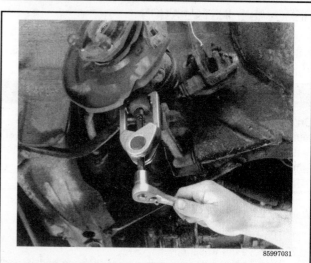

Fig. 30 Separating the outer tie rod end from the steering knuckle

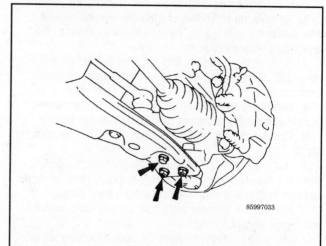

Fig. 31 On 1991-1994 models, disconnect the lower control arm from the steering knuckle

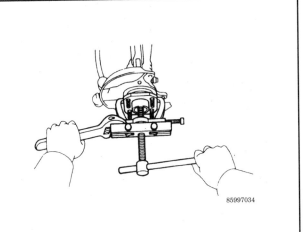

Fig. 32 A special tool is required to press the halfshaft from the hub on wagons and 1984-1986 sedans

Fig. 33 On other models, thread the hub nut onto the shaft, then tap it loose

Fig. 34 Be careful not to damage the oil seal when separating the driveshaft from the hub

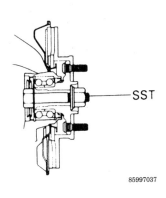

Fig. 35 A special tool is used to prevent hub bearing damage on 1987-1990 sedans

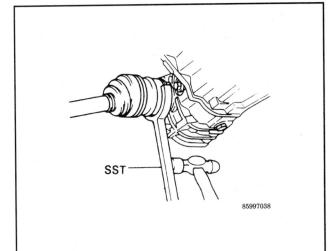

Fig. 36 Removing the halfshaft on wagons and 1984-1986 sedans

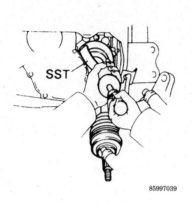

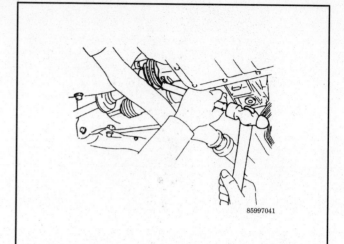

Fig. 39 A brass drift and hammer can be used to remove the right side halfshaft on 1991-1994 models

Fig. 37 A special tool is used to remove and install the halfshafts on 1987-1990 sedans

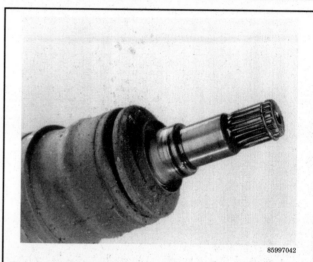

Fig. 40 Always replace the snapring on the transaxle end of the halfshaft

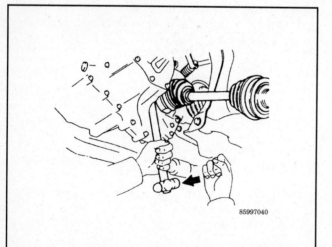

Fig. 38 Use a prybar or hammer handle to remove the left side halfshaft on 1991-1994 models

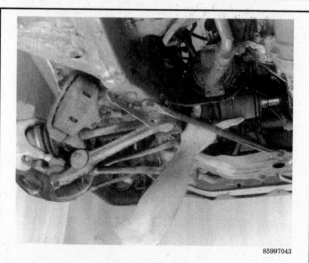

Fig. 41 Be careful not to damage the oil seal in the transaxle when installing the halfshaft

Fig. 42 A new hub nut should always be used. The hub nut cap and cotter pin should be installed to ensure the hub nut retains it's proper torque

5. Remove the cotter pin, hub nut cap, hub nut and washer.

6. Loosen the wheel nuts.

7. Raise and safely support the car. Remove the wheel.

8. Remove the brake caliper from the steering knuckle, then suspend it with a wire. Remove the disc. Refer to the appropriate procedures in this manual.

9. Remove the cotter pin and nut from the tie rod end. Using SST 09610-55012 or it's equivalent tie rod separator, disconnect the tie rod end from the steering knuckle.

10. Matchmark the position of the shock absorber lower bracket and camber adjusting cam to the steering knuckle.

11. Remove the nuts and bolts, then disconnect the steering knuckle.

12. Thread the hub nut part way onto the halfshaft. Using a brass faced hammer, tap the halfshaft outboard joint loose from the axle hub. Remove the nut, then slide the outboard joint out of the hub. Cover the halfshaft boot with a shop rag to protect it from damage.

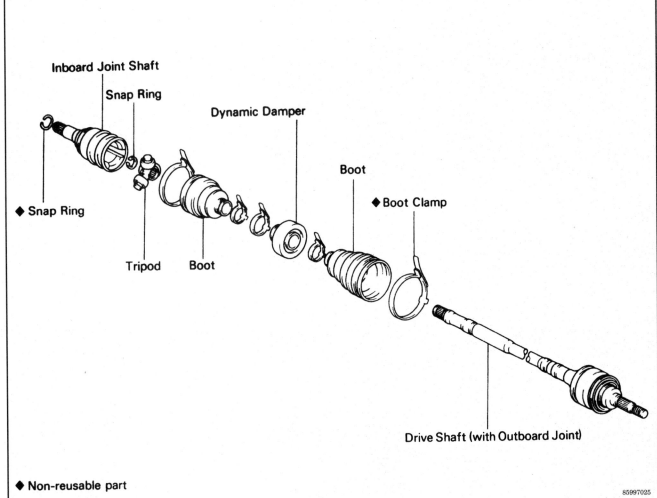

Inboard Joint Shaft
Snap Ring
Dynamic Damper
Boot
◆ Boot Clamp
◆ Snap Ring
Tripod
Boot
Drive Shaft (with Outboard Joint)

◆ Non-reusable part

Fig. 43 Exploded view of a common halfshaft

13. Using SST 09520-10021 or it's equivalent halfshaft removal/installation tool (slide hammer type), drive the halfshaft out of the transaxle.

To install:

14. Apply multi-purpose grease to the oil seal lip on the transaxle.

15. Using SST 09520-10021 or it's equivalent halfshaft removal/installation tool (slide hammer type), drive the halfshaft into the transaxle until it contacts the pinion shaft in the transaxle and the snapring engages in the side gear. Check that there is between 0.008-0.12 in. (2-3mm) of axial play. The halfshaft should not pull out of the transaxle by hand.

16. Install the halfshaft to the axle hub. Be careful not to damage the oil lip seal and the halfshaft boot.

17. Assemble the shock absorber lower bracket to the steering knuckle, then align the matchmarks of the camber adjusting cam. Torque the bolts to 166 ft. lbs. (226 Nm).

18. Connect the tie rod end to the steering knuckle. Torque the nut to 36 ft. lbs. (49 Nm), then secure it with a new cotter pin.

19. Install the disc and caliper to the steering knuckle.

20. Torque the hub nut to 137 ft. lbs. (186 Nm). Install the hub nut cap, then install a new cotter pin.

21. Fill the transaxle with the appropriate fluid. For details please refer to Section 1.

22. Install the wheel.

23. Lower the vehicle to the ground.

24. Have the front wheel alignment checked and/or adjusted by a reputable service facility. Road test the vehicle for proper operation.

1991-1994 Sedans

1. Disconnect the negative battery cable.

2. Remove the engine under cover.

3. Drain the transaxle fluid.

4. Remove the wheel cover.

5. Remove the cotter pin, hub nut cap, hub nut and washer.

6. Loosen the wheel nuts.

7. Raise and safely support the car. Remove the wheel.

8. Remove the cotter pin and nut from the tie rod end. Using SST 09628-62011 or an equivalent tie rod separator, disconnect the tie rod end from the steering knuckle.

9. Disconnect the lower ball joint from the lower control arm by removing the attaching nuts/bolts.

10. Thread the hub nut part way onto the halfshaft. Using a brass faced hammer, tap the halfshaft outboard joint loose from the axle hub. Remove the nut, then slide the outboard joint out of the hub. Cover the halfshaft boot with a shop rag to protect it from damage.

11. To remove the left side halfshaft, use a prybar or hammer handle to disconnect the driveshaft from the transaxle. To remove the right side halfshaft, use a brass drift and hammer to tap the shaft out of the transaxle.

To install:

12. Install a new snapring on the end of the halfshaft.

13. Install the halfshaft to the transaxle, then, using a brass drift and hammer, drive halfshaft into the transaxle until it contacts the pinion shaft in the transaxle and the snapring engages in the side gear. Check that there is between

0.008-0.12 in. (2-3mm) of axial play. The halfshaft should not pull out of the transaxle by hand.

14. Connect the halfshaft to the axle hub.

15. Connect the lower ball joint to the lower control arm and torque the bolts/nuts to 59 ft. lbs. (80 Nm).

16. Connect the tie rod end to the steering knuckle, then torque the nut to 36 ft. lbs. (49 Nm). Install a new cotter pin.

17. Install the hub nut, then torque to 137 ft. lbs. (186 Nm) on 1991 models, 166 ft. lbs. (226 Nm) on 1992-1993 models, and 159 ft. lbs. (216 Nm) on 1994 models. Install the lock-cap and a new cotter pin.

18. Fill the transaxle with the appropriate fluid. Please refer to Section 1 for details.

19. Install the wheel.

20. Lower the vehicle to the ground.

21. Have the front wheel alignment checked and/or adjusted by a reputable service facility. Road test the vehicle for proper operation.

CV JOINT OVERHAUL

▶ **See Figures 44, 45, 46, 47, 48, 49, 50, 51, 52, 53, 54, 55, 56, 57 and 58**

The halfshaft assembly is a flexible unit consisting of an inner and outer Constant Velocity (CV) joint joined by an axle shaft. Care must be taken not to over-extend the joint assembly during repairs or handling. When either end of the shaft is disconnected from the car, any over-extension could result in separation of the internal components and possible joint failure.

The CV joints are protected by rubber boots designed to keep the high-temperature grease in, while keeping the road grime and water out. The most common cause of joint failure is a ripped boot (tow hooks on halfshaft when car is being towed) which allows the lubricant to leave the joint, thus causing heavy wear. The boots are exposed to road hazards all the time and should be inspected frequently. Any time a boot is found to be damaged or slit, it should be replaced immediately.

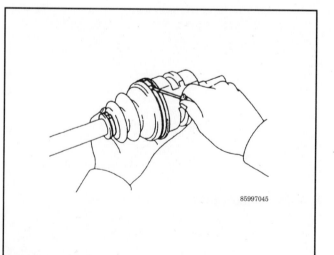

85997045

Fig. 44 A small prybar can be used to remove the boot clamps

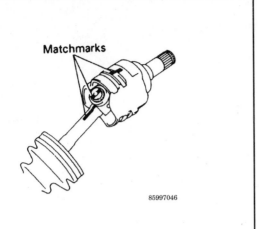

Fig. 45 Paint matchmarks to ensure assembly in the original position

➡Whenever the driveshaft is held in a vise, use pieces of wood in the jaws to protect the components from damage or deformation. Read the entire procedure before continuing and refer to the exploded view of the halfshaft assembly components as a guide.

1. Remove the halfshaft and securely mount it in a vise.
2. Using snapring pliers, remove the snapring from the transaxle end of the halfshaft. This is the inboard joint.
3. Remove the inboard boot retaining clamps. Slide the boot out of the way, exposing the joint.
4. Paint matchmarks on the inboard joint tulip and tripod. Do not use a punch to make the matchmarks.
5. Remove the inboard joint tulip from the halfshaft. Clean all grease from the tripod joint and rollers.
6. Use snapring pliers to remove the tripod joint retaining ring.
7. Paint matchmarks on the shaft and tripod. Do not use a punch to make these marks.
8. Tape the rollers together to prevent them from falling off the tripod joint.

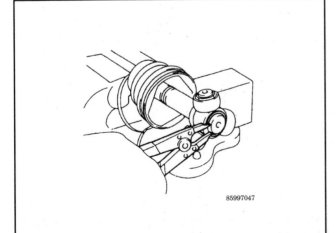

Fig. 46 Removing the snapring. A new snapring should be used during reassembly

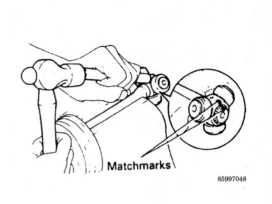

Fig. 47 Matchmarks should be painted on the shaft and tripod before removal. Do not tap on the rollers

9. Using a brass drift, uniformly tap the tripod joint from the shaft. Do not tap on the rollers.
10. Remove the boot from the shaft. Remove the clamp and dynamic damper, if applicable.
11. Remove the boot clamps from the outboard joint, then remove the boot.

➡Do not remove or disassemble the outboard CV joint. If it is worn or damaged, the joint/shaft assembly must be replaced with a new unit.

12. Clean all parts thoroughly and inspect for wear, damage or corrosion. Look for any scratches, cracks or galling of the metal. Replace any components, as necessary.
   To assemble:
13. Slide a new outboard joint boot onto the shaft. Wrap vinyl or teflon tape around the spline of the shaft to prevent damaging the boot.
14. Install the dynamic damper and clamp, if applicable. Make sure the damper is installed in the correct location on the shaft.

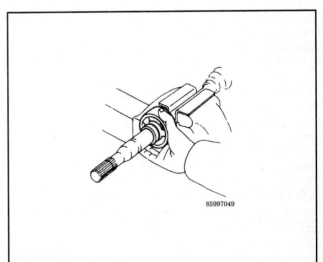

Fig. 48 Mark the position of the damper before removing it

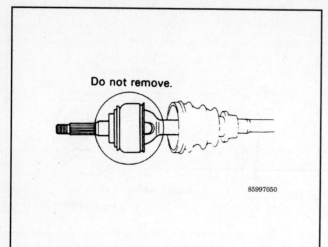

85997050

Fig. 49 The outboard joint should not be removed or disassembled

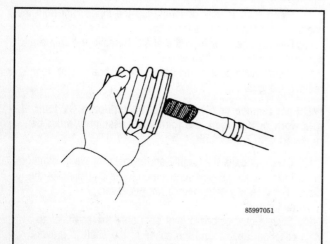

85997051

Fig. 50 Tape the end of the shaft to prevent damaging the boot

15. Slide a new inboard joint boot onto the shaft, then remove the tape from the splines.

16. Assemble the tripod joint onto the shaft. Align the matchmarks, then place the beveled side of the tripod axial spline toward the outboard joint and install it onto the shaft.

17. Use a brass drift and hammer to seat the tripod the correct distance onto the shaft. The retaining ring groove should be exposed.

18. Using snapring pliers, install a new tripod joint retaining ring.

19. Assemble the boot to the outboard joint shaft. On all wagons and 1984-1986 sedans, pack 0.5 lb. (240 g) of grease into the joint. On 1987-1994 sedans, pack 0.26-0.29 lb. (120-130 g) of grease into the joint. This grease is usually supplied in the boot kit. If not, use grease specifically formulated for CV joint use.

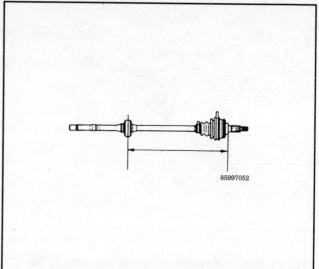

85997052

Fig. 51 Make sure the damper is installed in the proper location

20. Align the matchmarks, then assemble the inboard joint to the shaft. On all wagons and 1984-1986 sedans, pack 0.2 lb. (90 g) of grease into the joint and 0.1 lb. (50 g) of grease into the boot. On 1987-1994 sedans, pack 0.31-0.33 lb. (140-150 g) of grease into the joint and/or boot.

21. Assemble the clamps onto the boots. Be sure the boot is properly positioned on the shaft groove, then bend the band and lock it.

22. Check the shaft for correct length. Insure that the boot is not stretched or contracted when the halfshaft is at it's specified length. The right side halfshaft on wagons and 1984-1986 sedans should be approximately 24.41 in. (620mm) in length. The left side should be approximately 28.43 in. (722mm). On 1987-1994 sedans, the left side halfshaft should be approximately 21.815 in. (554mm) in length. The right side halfshaft should be 30.882 in. (784mm) in length.

23. Install a new snapring to the inboard joint shaft.

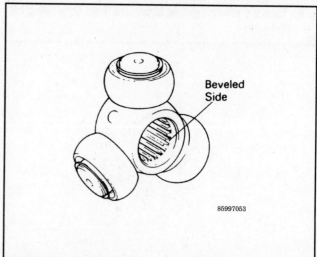

Beveled Side

85997053

Fig. 52 The beveled side of the joint should be installed towards the outboard joint

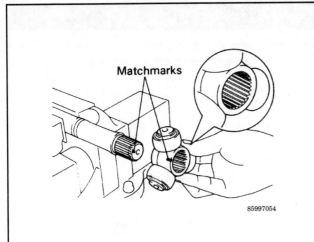

Fig. 53 Align the matchmarks, then install the joint on the shaft

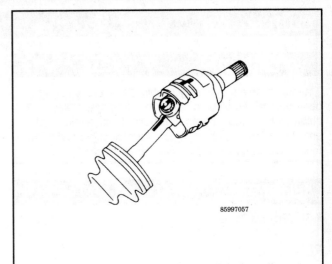

Fig. 56 Align the matchmarks, then slide the tulip assembly onto the tripod

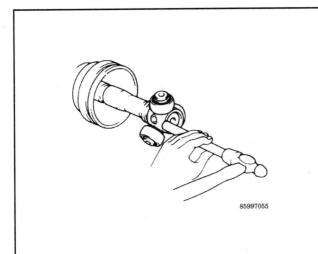

Fig. 54 Use a hammer and brass drift to seat the joint the correct distance on the shaft

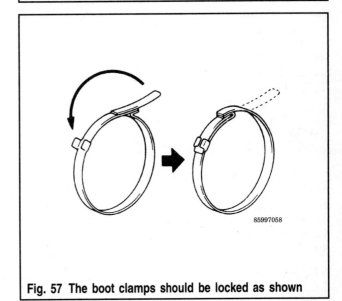

Fig. 57 The boot clamps should be locked as shown

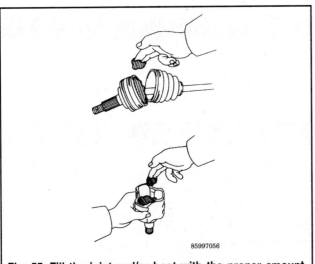

Fig. 55 Fill the joint and/or boot with the proper amount of grease

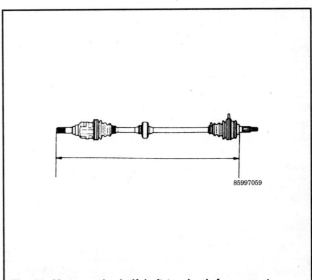

Fig. 58 Measure the halfshaft to check for correct overall length

CLUTCH

❋❋CAUTION

The clutch driven disc may contain asbestos which has been determined to be a cancer causing agent. Never clean clutch surfaces with compressed air. Avoid inhaling any dust from any clutch area! When cleaning clutch surfaces, use commercially available brake cleaning fluids.

Adjustments

♦ See Figures 59, 60 and 61

PEDAL HEIGHT

1. Measure the pedal height from the asphalt sheet, except Tercel EZ models, on which the pedal height is measured from the dash panel. Pedal height should be as follows:

    a. Wagons and 1984-1986 sedans — 7.13-7.44 in. (181-189mm)

    b. 1987-1990 Sedans (except Tercel EZ) — 6.14-6.54 in. (156-166mm)

    c. Tercel EZ models — 6.38-6.77 in. (162-172 mm)

    d. 1991-1994 4-speed Sedans — 5.69-6.08 in. (144.5-154.5mm)

    e. 1991-1994 5-speed Sedans — 5.51-5.91 in. (140-150 mm)

2. If the pedal height is not as indicated, loosen the lock-nut, then turn the adjusting bolt until the height is correct. On 1987-1990 sedans with cruise control, pedal height is adjusted by turning the clutch switch (loosen the lock-nut and unplug the switch connector first). When pedal height is correct, tighten the lock-nut.

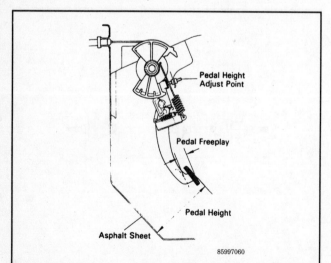

Fig. 59 Pedal adjustments on wagons and 1984-1986 sedans

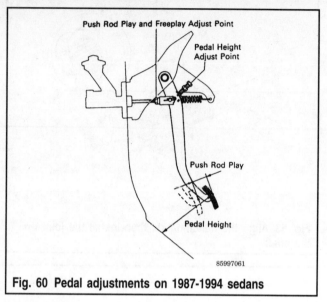

Fig. 60 Pedal adjustments on 1987-1994 sedans

FREE-PLAY

Push rod free-play adjustment is not applicable to wagons and 1984-1986 sedans.

1. Check the push rod play. Push in on the pedal softly with your finger until the resistance begins to increase a little. Play at the pedal top should be 0.039-0.197 in. (1-5mm).

2. Check the pedal free-play. Push in on the pedal until the beginning of clutch resistance is felt. Pedal free-play should be between 0.08-0.98 in. (2-25mm) on wagons and 1984-1986 sedans, or 0.20-0.59 in. (5-15mm) on 1987-1994 sedans.

3. If necessary, adjust the pedal and/or push rod free-play. If free-play is not within specifications on wagons and 1984-1986 sedans, check the release sector and pawl position. If there are less than six notches remaining, replace the clutch disc. On 1987-1994 sedans, loosen the lock-nut and turn the push rod until play is correct, then tighten the lock-nut. Recheck the pedal height.

Clutch Pedal

REMOVAL & INSTALLATION

♦ See Figure 62

❋❋CAUTION

Always wear safety glasses when removing the return and/or tension springs from the pedal assembly. Failure to do so could result in serious injury.

Wagons and 1984-1986 Sedans

1. Disconnect the negative battery cable.

2. Carefully remove the pedal return and sector tension springs.

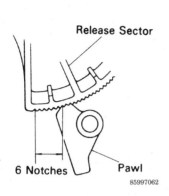

Fig. 61 On wagons and 1984-1986 sedans, replace the clutch disc if less than six notches remain on the sector

3. Remove the pedal through-bolt and nut.

4. Disconnect the clutch cable from the release sector, then remove the pedal.

To install:

5. Install the pedal in the vehicle, then connect the clutch cable to the release sector. Torque the nut to 27 ft. lbs. (37 Nm).

6. Install the sector tension and pedal return springs.

7. Check and adjust the clutch pedal.

1987-1994 Sedans

✶✶CAUTION

On models equipped with a Supplemental Restraint System (SRS) or "air bag," work must NOT be started until at least 90 seconds have passed from the time that both the ignition switch is turned to the LOCK position and the negative cable is disconnected from the battery.

1. Disconnect the negative battery cable.

2. Remove the push rod clevis pin retaining clip and the clevis pin.

3. Carefully remove the pedal return spring.

4. Remove the pedal through-bolt and nut, then remove the pedal.

To install:

5. Install the pedal in the vehicle. Tighten the nut until snug.

6. Install the pedal return spring, clevis pin and retaining clip.

7. Check and adjust the clutch pedal.

Driven Disc and Pressure Plate

REMOVAL & INSTALLATION

▶ **See Figures 63, 64, 65, 66, 67, 68, 69, 70, 71, 72 and 73**

✶✶CAUTION

On models equipped with a Supplemental Restraint System (SRS) or "air bag," work must NOT be started until at least 90 seconds have passed from the time that both the ignition switch is turned to the LOCK position and the negative cable is disconnected from the battery.

➡**Do not allow grease or oil to get on the disc, pressure plate, or flywheel surfaces.**

1. Remove the transaxle from the vehicle as outlined in this section.

2. Paint matchmarks on the flywheel and pressure plate.

3. Loosen each pressure plate attaching bolt one turn at a time until the spring tension is released.

4. Remove the attaching bolts, then pull off the clutch cover with the clutch disc. Make a note as to which side of the disc faces the flywheel; it is imperative for it to be installed facing the right direction. Be careful not to drop the clutch disc.

5. On wagons and 1984-1986 sedans, remove the bearing clip, then pull off the release bearing and hub. Remove the release bearing together with the fork on 1987-1994 sedans.

6. Inspect the parts for wear or deterioration. It is strongly recommended that the driven disc, pressure plate and release bearing be replaced as a unit if any part is worn. The slight additional cost of the parts is more than offset by not having to disassemble it again to replace another component later.

7. Inspect the release fork/lever and return springs for damage. Replace as necessary.

8. Inspect the flywheel for any signs of cracking, bluing in the steel (a sign of extreme heat) or scoring. Any bluing or cracks which are found requires replacement of the flywheel. The flywheel should be free of all but the slightest ridges and valleys or scores. A scored flywheel will immediately attack a new clutch disc, causing slippage and vibration. Replace or resurface the flywheel as necessary.

9. On wagons and 1984-1986 sedans:

a. Inspect the pilot bearing for smooth rotation. If necessary, replace it. Use SST 09303-35011 or it's equivalent pilot bearing puller to remove the bearing and SST 09304-30012 or it's equivalent pilot bearing driver to install it.

b. If replacing the release bearing, SST 09315-00010 or it's equivalent release bearing removal/installation tool must be used to press the bearing off and onto the hub. After installing, check that there is no drag on the bearing when it is turned under pressure.

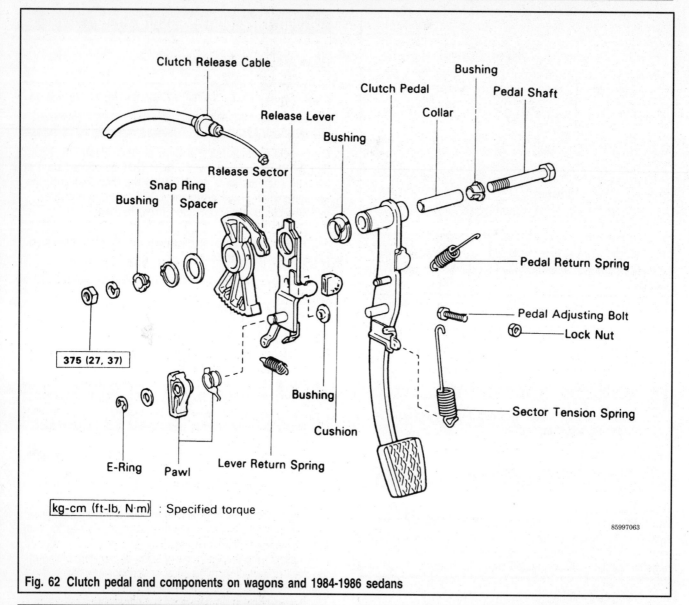

Clutch Release Cable

Release Lever

Release Sector

Snap Ring

Bushing

Spacer

Bushing

Clutch Pedal

Collar

Bushing

Pedal Shaft

Pedal Return Spring

375 (27, 37)

Pedal Adjusting Bolt

Lock Nut

Bushing

Sector Tension Spring

Cushion

E-Ring

Pawl

Lever Return Spring

kg-cm (ft-lb, N·m) : Specified torque

85997063

Fig. 62 Clutch pedal and components on wagons and 1984-1986 sedans

85997064

Fig. 63 Matchmarks should be painted on the pressure plate and flywheel before removal

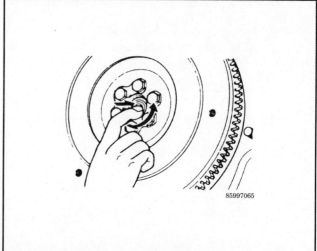

85997065

Fig. 64 On wagons and 1984-1986 sedans, check the pilot bearing for smooth rotation

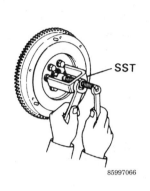

Fig. 65 A special puller is used to remove the pilot bearing

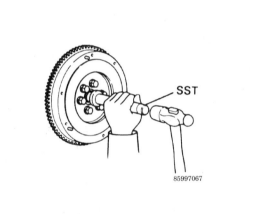

Fig. 66 Carefully drive the new bearing into the flywheel

To install:

10. Install the disc with the correct side facing the flywheel. Center the clutch disc by using a clutch pilot tool (pilot tools are usually available at most automotive parts stores).

❊❊WARNING

The clutch disc must be installed with the correct side facing the flywheel and properly centered by using a pilot tool. Failure to do so will result in improper clutch/transaxle installation as well as severe clutch and transaxle assembly damage.

11. Align the matchmarks on the pressure plate and flywheel, then finger-tighten the attaching bolts. Tighten the bolts evenly and gradually using the correct sequence until the pressure plate is snug. Final torque (using the correct sequence) is 14 ft. lbs. (19 Nm). Make sure the clutch disc is still centered, then remove the pilot tool.

12. On wagons and 1984-1986 sedans, apply multi-purpose grease to the front of the release bearing and the tip of the

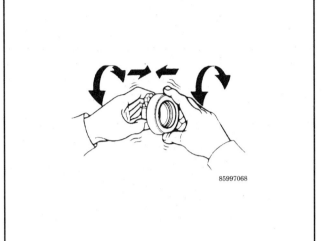

Fig. 67 Check the release bearing for smooth rotation

input shaft. Apply molybdenum disulfide lithium base grease to the following:

a. Release fork and hub contact points.
b. Release fork and fork lever contact points.
c. Release fork lever and bushing contact points.
d. Release fork lever and oil seal contact points.
e. Inside the release bearing hub.
f. Input shaft splines.

13. On 1987-1994 sedans, apply molybdenum disulfide lithium base grease to the following:

a. Release fork and hub contact points.
b. Release fork and push rod contact points.
c. Release fork pivot point.
d. Input shaft splines.

14. On wagons and 1984-1986 sedans, install the release bearing and hub, then engage the bearing clip.
15. On 1987-1994 sedans, install the release bearing to the fork, then install the assembly to the transaxle.
16. Install the transaxle in the vehicle.
17. Road test the vehicle for proper operation.

Fig. 68 Make sure the clutch disc is installed with the proper side facing the flywheel

Fig. 69 A pilot tool is used to center the disc

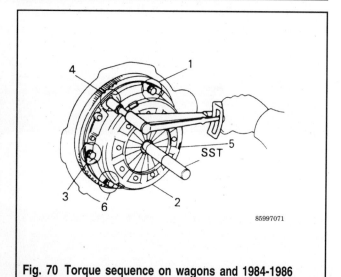

Fig. 70 Torque sequence on wagons and 1984-1986 sedans

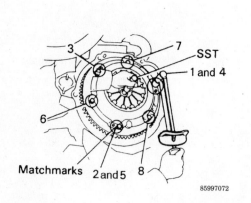

Fig. 71 Pressure plate attaching bolt torque sequence on 1987-1994 sedans

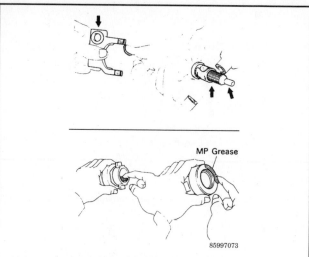

Fig. 72 Apply the appropriate grease to these points on wagons and 1984-1986 sedans

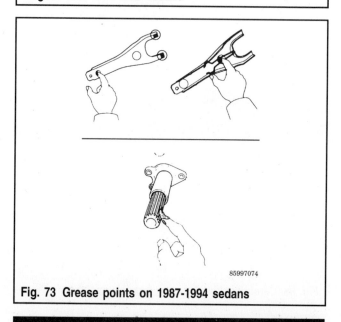

Fig. 73 Grease points on 1987-1994 sedans

Clutch Master Cylinder

REMOVAL & INSTALLATION

❈❈CAUTION

On models equipped with a Supplemental Restraint System (SRS) or "air bag," work must NOT be started until at least 90 seconds have passed from the time that both the ignition switch is turned to the LOCK position and the negative cable is disconnected from the battery.

1. Disconnect the negative battery cable.
2. Drain or siphon the fluid from the clutch master cylinder.
3. On 1987-1990 models, remove the reservoir tank.

4. Using a flare nut or line wrench, disconnect the hydraulic line to the clutch release from the master cylinder.

➡Do not spill brake fluid on the painted surfaces of the vehicle. If this occurs, wash it off immediately using plenty of clean water.

5. From inside the car, remove the clevis pin clip and the clevis pin. If necessary, remove the underdash panel and the air duct for more clearance.
6. Unfasten the bolts which secure the clutch master cylinder to the firewall. Withdraw the assembly from the firewall side.

To install:

7. Install the master cylinder with its retaining nuts to the firewall. Torque them to 9 ft. lbs. (13 Nm).
8. Connect the hydraulic line from the clutch release cylinder to the master cylinder.
9. Connect the clevis, then install the clevis pin and clip.
10. Fill the reservoir with clean, fresh brake fluid, then bleed the system.
11. Check the cylinder and the hose connection for leaks.
12. Adjust the clutch pedal.
13. Reinstall the air duct and underdash cover panel, if applicable.

OVERHAUL

➧ See Figure 74

Refer to the exploded view of clutch master cylinder components as a guide for the overhaul procedure.

1. Clamp the master cylinder body in a vise with protected jaws.
2. On 1991-1994 models, use a pin punch and hammer to drive out the slotted spring pin retaining the reservoir. Do the same for 1987-1990 models to remove the inlet union.
3. Remove the snapring and remove the pushrod/piston assembly.
4. Inspect the master cylinder bore for scoring, grooves or corrosion. If any of these conditions are observed, replace the cylinder. Inspect the piston, spring, push rod and boot for damage or wear. Replace any parts which are worn or defective.

To assemble:

5. Before reassembly, coat all internal parts with clean brake fluid.
6. Install the piston assembly in the cylinder bore.
7. Install the pushrod, then secure it with the snapring.
8. Install the reservoir or inlet union. Drive in the slotted spring pin using a pin punch and hammer.

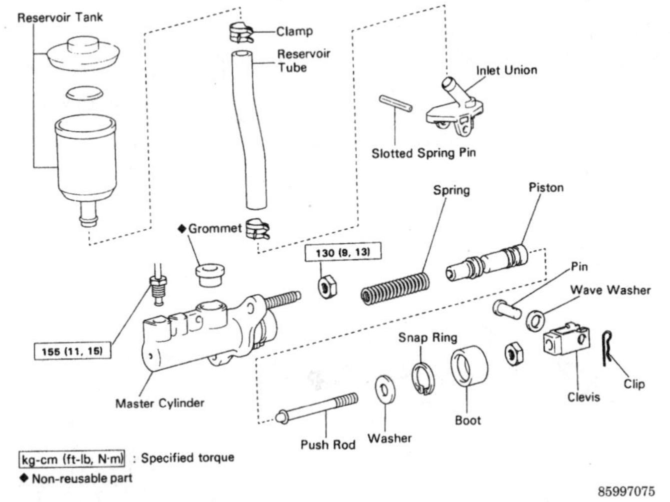

Fig. 74 Exploded view of the clutch master cylinder components

Clutch Release Cylinder

REMOVAL & INSTALLATION

⁂CAUTION

On models equipped with a Supplemental Restraint System (SRS) or "air bag," work must NOT be started until at least 90 seconds have passed from the time that both the ignition switch is turned to the LOCK position and the negative cable is disconnected from the battery.

➡Do not spill brake fluid on the painted surfaces of the vehicle. If this occurs, wash it off immediately using plenty of clean water.

1. Disconnect the negative battery cable.
2. Using a flare nut or line wrench, disconnect the hydraulic line on the clutch release from it's master cylinder. Use a container to catch the fluid.
3. Remove the release cylinder retaining nuts/bolts, then remove the cylinder.

To install:

4. Install the cylinder to the clutch housing, then tighten the bolts to 9 ft. lbs. (12 Nm).
5. Connect the hydraulic line.
6. Bleed the system and remember to top up the fluid in the clutch master cylinder when finished.

OVERHAUL

▶ **See Figure 75**

Refer to the exploded view of the release cylinder and components as a guide for the overhaul procedure.

1. Remove the pushrod assembly and the rubber boot.
2. Withdraw the piston, complete with its cup; don't separate the cup from the piston unless it is being replaced.
3. Wash all the parts in brake fluid.
4. Replace any worn or damaged parts. Inspect the cylinder bore carefully for any sign of damage, wear or corrosion.

To assemble:

5. Before reassembly, coat all internal parts in clean brake fluid. Insert the spring and piston into the cylinder.
6. Install the boot and insert the pushrod.

Hydraulic System Bleeding

▶ **See Figure 76**

1. Fill the clutch master cylinder reservoir with brake fluid.

➡ **Do not spill brake fluid on the painted surfaces of the vehicle. If this occurs, wash it off immediately using plenty of clean water.**

2. Fit a tube over the bleeder plug (usually on the release cylinder), then place the other end into a clean jar half-filled with brake fluid.

3. Depress the clutch pedal, loosen the bleeder plug with a wrench, and allow the fluid to flow into the jar.
4. Tighten the plug and then release the clutch pedal.
5. Repeat these steps until no air bubbles are visible in the bleeder tube.
6. When no air bubbles are seen, tighten the plug with the clutch pedal still fully depressed.
7. Top off the fluid in the clutch master cylinder reservoir.
8. Check the system for leaks.

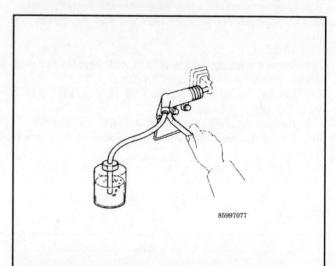

85997077

Fig. 76 The clutch system bleed screw is usually located on the release cylinder

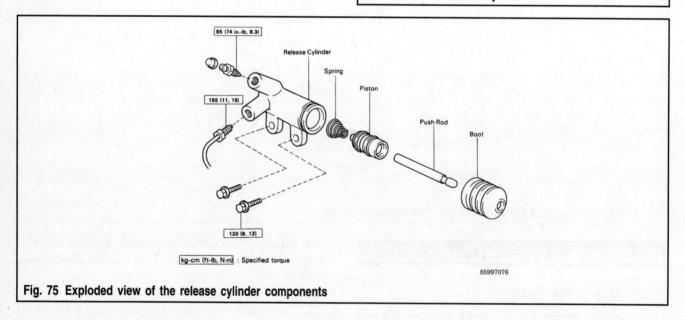

85997076

Fig. 75 Exploded view of the release cylinder components

AUTOMATIC TRANSAXLE

Identification

On most models, the transaxle identification tag is located at the top front of the transaxle case.

Fluid Pan

REMOVAL & INSTALLATION

♦ See Figure 77

1. Raise and safely support the vehicle.
2. If equipped with a plug, drain the transmission fluid.
3. Carefully loosen and remove the bolts holding the oil pan. Tap around the pan lightly with a plastic mallet, breaking the gasket tension by vibration. Do not pry the pan down with a screwdriver or similar tool; the pan is lightweight metal and may deform, causing leaks.
4. Remove all traces of gasket material from the pan and the transaxle mating faces. Clean them carefully with a plastic or wooden scraper. Do not gouge the metal.
5. Clean the pan thoroughly of all oil and sediment.
6. Install a new gasket on the pan, then bolt the pan into place. Snug the bolts in a criss-cross pattern, working from the center out. Tighten the pan bolts to 43 inch lbs. (4.9 Nm).

➡If the mating surfaces of the oil pan and transaxle are clean and straight, there is no need for gasket sealer during reassembly. The use of sealer is generally not recommended on these transmissions.

7. Lower the vehicle to the ground and refill the transaxle using Dexron II® automatic transmission fluid. Please refer to Section 1 for details.

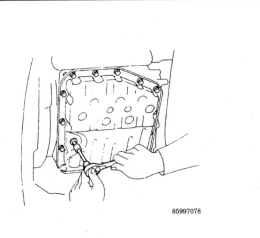

Fig. 77 Most fluid pans are equipped with a drain plug

85997078

FILTER SERVICE

1. With the pan removed, the transaxle filter is visible. Remove the bolts holding the filter, then remove the filter and gasket, if so equipped.

➡On some models, the filter retaining bolts are different lengths and MUST BE reinstalled in their correct locations. Take great care not to interchange them.

2. Clean the mating surfaces of the filter; make sure all traces of the old gasket material are removed.
3. Install the new filter assembly (some models use a gasket under the filter). Install the retaining bolts in their correct locations and tighten only to 7 ft. lbs. (10 Nm).
4. Install the pan.

Adjustments

SHIFT LINKAGE/CABLE

♦ See Figure 78

Wagons and 1984-1986 Sedans

1. Inspect the connecting rod bushing for wear or deformation, replace as necessary. Loosen the nut on the connecting rod.
2. Push the manual lever fully rearward, then return the lever two notches forward to the NEUTRAL position.
3. Set the shift selector to N.
4. While having an assistant holding the shift selector slightly forward against it's stop (towards the R position), tighten the connecting rod nut.
5. Check for proper operation.

1987-1994 Sedans

1. Loosen the swivel nut on the manual lever, then push the lever fully towards the right side of the vehicle.
2. Return the manual lever two notches to the NEUTRAL position, then set the shift selector lever to N.
3. While having an assistant holding the shift selector slightly forward against it's stop (towards the R position), tighten the swivel nut.
4. Check for proper operation.

THROTTLE VALVE (TV) LINKAGE/CABLE

♦ See Figures 79 and 80

1. With the ignition **OFF**, depress the accelerator pedal all the way. Check that the throttle plate(s) in the carburetor or throttle body are fully open. If not, adjust the accelerator linkage.
2. On wagons and 1984-1986 sedans:
   a. Check that the throttle valve lever lines up with the mark on the transmission case.

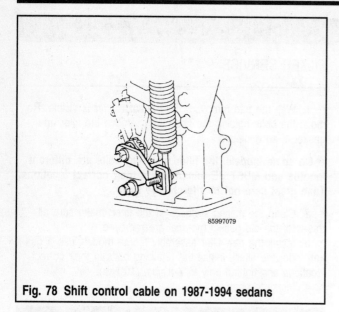

Fig. 78 Shift control cable on 1987-1994 sedans

b. If necessary, loosen the turnbuckle lock-nut, then adjust the turnbuckle until the throttle lever lines up with the mark on the transmission.

3. On 1987-1994 sedans:

a. Peel the rubber dust boot back from the throttle valve cable, if present.

b. Loosen the adjustment nut(s).

c. Adjust the outer cable so that the distance between the end of the boot and stopper on the cable is 0-0.04 in. (0-1.0mm).

4. Tighten the adjustment nut(s). Make sure that the adjustment hasn't changed. If applicable, install the dust boot.

Neutral Safety/Back-Up Light Switch

The reverse or back-up light function is controlled by the neutral safety switch. When the switch is properly adjusted, the

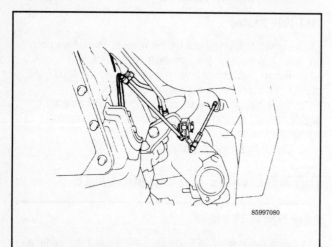

Fig. 79 On wagons and 1984-1986 sedans, the throttle lever should line up with the mark on the transaxle case

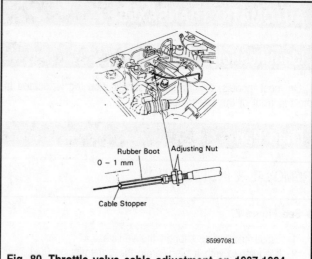

Fig. 80 Throttle valve cable adjustment on 1987-1994 sedans

white lamps at the rear will only come on when the car is in reverse.

REMOVAL & INSTALLATION

✳✳CAUTION

On models equipped with a Supplemental Restraint System (SRS) or "air bag," work must NOT be started until at least 90 seconds have passed from the time that both the ignition switch is turned to the LOCK position and the negative cable is disconnected from the battery.

1. Disconnect the negative battery cable.

2. Remove the bolt/nut attaching the manual lever to the control shaft, then remove the lever.

3. Unplug the electrical connector, then remove the switch attaching bolts.

To install:

4. Install the switch, then engage the electrical connection.

5. Connect the manual lever to the control shaft, then adjust the switch.

6. Check for proper operation.

ADJUSTMENT

▶ See Figure 81

1. Move the shift selector to the N position.

2. Locate the neutral safety switch on the side of the transaxle, then loosen the switch retaining bolts.

3. Align the groove on the safety switch shaft with the line which is scribed on the housing. Hold the switch position, then tighten the switch bolt(s) to 9 ft. lbs. (13 Nm) on wagons and 1984-1986 sedans or 48 inch lbs. (5.4 Nm) on 1987-1994 sedans.

4. Check the switch for proper operation.

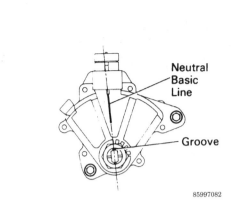

Fig. 81 Align the groove on the safety switch shaft with the line which is scribed on the housing

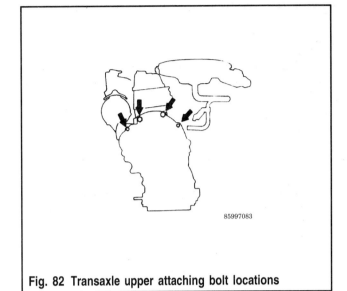

Fig. 82 Transaxle upper attaching bolt locations

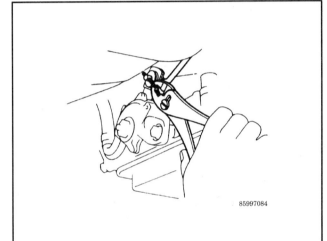

Fig. 83 Pliers can be used to remove the clip retaining the shift control rod

Transaxle

REMOVAL & INSTALLATION

✳✳CAUTION

On models equipped with a Supplemental Restraint System (SRS) or "air bag," work must NOT be started until at least 90 seconds have passed from the time that both the ignition switch is turned to the LOCK position and the negative cable is disconnected from the battery.

Wagons and 1984-1986 Sedans

♦ See Figures 82, 83, 84, 85 and 86

1. Disconnect the negative battery cable.
2. Drain the radiator, then remove the upper radiator hose. Remove the air cleaner assembly.
3. Remove the transaxle upper attaching bolts.
4. Drain the fluid from the transaxle.
5. Remove both halfshafts. Refer to the procedure in this section.
6. Remove the front exhaust pipe.
7. Disconnect the speedometer cable, then label and unplug all electrical connectors on the transaxle.
8. Disconnect the oil cooler inlet and outlet pipes, if equipped.
9. Disconnect the throttle valve linkage and the shift control rod.
10. On 4WD vehicles, remove the rear driveshaft.
11. Remove the torque converter cover, then remove the converter attaching bolts. Turn the crankshaft to gain access to each bolt.
12. Remove the transaxle lower attaching bolts.
13. Place a wooden block between the engine and cowl. This is done since the distributor may make contact with the brake booster when the rear support member is removed.
14. Support the transaxle with a jack, then remove the engine rear support member.

15. Separate the transaxle from the engine and carefully remove it from the vehicle.

To install:

16. Apply multi-purpose grease to the center hub of the torque converter.
17. Install a guide pin in the converter.
18. Position the transaxle for installation. Do not tilt the transaxle forward as the torque converter could slide out.
19. Align the guide pin with one of the drive plate holes. Connect the transaxle to the engine.
20. Install the transaxle lower attaching bolts. Torque the 10mm bolts to 29 ft. lbs. (39 Nm) and the 12mm bolts to 43 ft. lbs. (59 Nm).
21. Remove the guide pin, then install the rear support member. Torque the bolts to 70 ft. lbs. (95 Nm).
22. Install the torque converter mount bolts finger-tight. Uniformly torque the bolts to 13 ft. lbs. (18 Nm).
23. Install the converter cover and dust seal with the ground wire. Torque the 14mm bolt to 17 ft. lbs. (24 Nm) and the 17mm bolt to 48 inch lbs. (5.4 Nm).

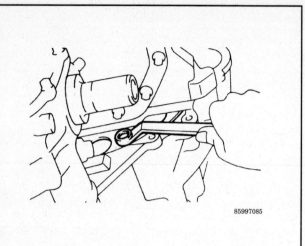

85997085

Fig. 84 The torque converter bolts can be accessed after removing the cover

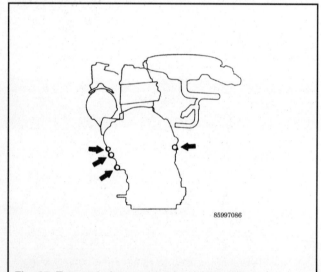

85997086

Fig. 85 Transaxle lower attaching bolt locations

24. On 4WD vehicles, install the rear driveshaft.

25. Connect the shift control rod and throttle linkage, then connect the oil cooler lines.

26. Install the front exhaust pipe and both halfshafts.

27. Install the transaxle upper attaching bolts. Torque the 14 mm bolts to 29 ft. lbs. (39 Nm) and the 17 mm bolts to 43 ft. lbs. (59 Nm).

28. Engage all electrical connectors on the transaxle.

29. Adjust the throttle linkage, then install the air cleaner.

30. Fill the transaxle with Dexron II® automatic transmission fluid.

31. Fill the front differential with GL-5 SAE 90 oil. Refer to Section 1 for details.

32. Install the upper radiator hose and fill the cooling system. Connect the negative battery cable.

33. Adjust the throttle valve and shift linkages.

34. Road test the vehicle for proper operation. Recheck the fluid levels.

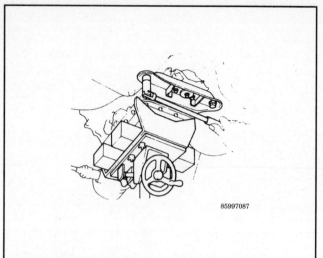

85997087

Fig. 86 Support the transaxle with a jack before removing the rear crossmember

1987-1994 Sedans

▶ See Figures 87, 88, 89, 90, 91, 92, 93 and 94

1. Disconnect the negative battery cable.

2. Unplug the electrical connections, then disconnect the speedometer cable.

3. Disconnect the throttle valve cable from the throttle linkage.

4. Remove the starter.

5. Remove the transaxle upper attaching bolts.

6. Remove the engine under cover, then disconnect the oil cooler lines.

7. Disconnect the shift control cable, then remove both halfshafts.

8. Remove the exhaust front pipe.

9. Remove the torque converter attaching bolts. Turn the crankshaft to gain access to each bolt.

10. Disconnect the left side engine mounting bracket. Hold the engine and transaxle with two jacks or a chain block and jack, then remove the rear engine mounting bracket. Remove the bolts attaching the bracket to the body first.

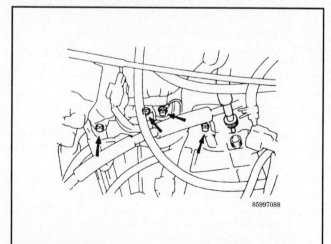

85997088

Fig. 87 Transaxle upper attaching bolt locations. Be sure to reconnect the ground wire when installing the transaxle

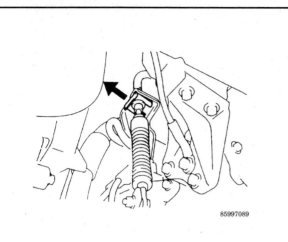

Fig. 88 Remove the control cable retaining clip, then disconnect the cable from the control lever

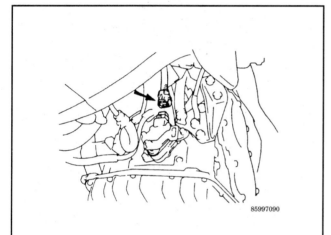

Fig. 89 Make sure all electrical connections are disengaged before removing the transaxle

11. Remove the transaxle mounting bolts, then separate the transaxle from the engine. Have an assistant help you, the transaxle is a heavy component.

To install:

12. Position the transaxle for installation. Align the pins in the block with the converter housing. Temporarily install one bolt.

13. Install the transaxle attaching bolts. Torque the mounting bolts to 47 ft. lbs. (64 Nm).

14. Install the left side engine mounting bracket. Torque to 32 ft. lbs. (43 Nm).

15. Install the rear engine mounting bracket. Torque the engine bolts to 43 ft. lbs. (58 Nm) and the body bolts to 54 ft. lbs. (73 Nm).

16. Install the torque converter attaching bolts. Torque the bolts evenly to 13 ft. lbs. (18 Nm).

17. Install the front exhaust pipe.

18. Install the halfshafts.

19. Connect the shift control cable, then install the oil cooler lines.

20. Install the engine under cover.

21. Install the upper transaxle attaching bolts. Torque the mounting bolts to 47 ft. lbs. (64 Nm).

22. Install the starter, then connect the throttle valve cable.

23. Connect the speedometer cable, then engage the electrical connectors.

24. Adjust the throttle valve and shift control cable.

25. Fill the transaxle and differential with Dexron II® automatic transmission fluid. Road test the vehicle for proper operation, then recheck the fluid levels. Refer to Section 1 for details.

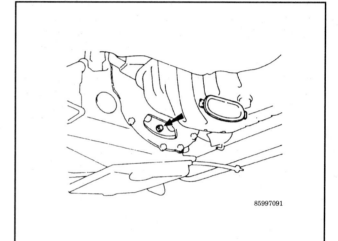

Fig. 90 Remove the torque converter attaching bolts through the access hole

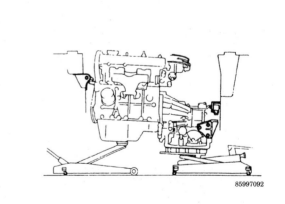

Fig. 91 Secure both the engine and the transaxle with jacks

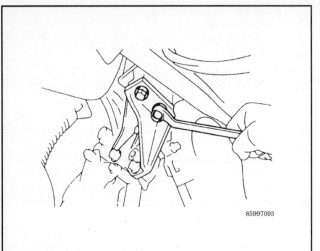

Fig. 92 The left side mounting bracket is usually secured to the body by two bolts

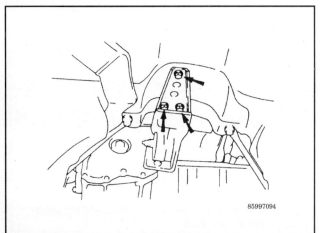

Fig. 93 Remove the bolts attaching the rear mounting bracket to the body first, then remove the bracket from the transaxle

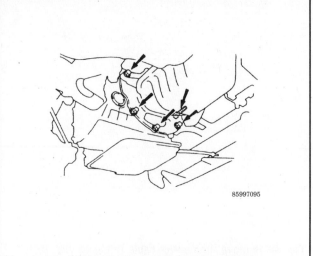

Fig. 94 Transaxle lower attaching bolt locations

Halfshafts

The halfshafts used on automatic transaxles are almost identical to those used on manual transaxles. Therefore, removal/installation and overhaul procedures are accomplished in the same manner. Please refer to the procedures outlined in the manual transaxle section for service procedures.

TRANSFER CASE

On Tercel 4WD vehicles, the transfer case is integral with the transaxle assembly.

Extra Low Gear and 4WD Indicator Switches

REMOVAL & INSTALLATION

▶ See Figure 95

These switches are found on vehicles with manual transaxles. They indicate when the vehicle is in 4WD mode and when the extra low gear has been engaged.
1. Disconnect the negative battery cable.
2. Raise and safely support the vehicle.

3. Unplug the switch electrical connection, then remove the switch from the transaxle housing using a wrench.
To install:
4. Install the switch in the transaxle. Always use new gaskets and O-rings.
5. Engage the electrical connection.
6. Lower the vehicle and check the operation of the switch.

4WD Change-Over Solenoid

REMOVAL & INSTALLATION

▶ See Figure 96

This solenoid is found on vehicles with automatic transaxles.
1. Disconnect the negative battery cable.
2. Raise and safely support the vehicle.

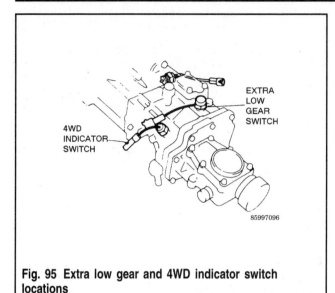

Fig. 95 Extra low gear and 4WD indicator switch locations

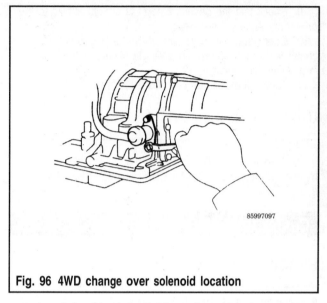

Fig. 96 4WD change over solenoid location

3. Unplug the switch electrical connections, then remove the switch attaching screws.

4. Pull the solenoid out from the transaxle housing.

To install:

5. Install the switch in the transaxle, then engage the electrical connection. Always use new gaskets and O-rings.

6. Lower the vehicle and check switch operation.

Rear Output Shaft Seal

REMOVAL & INSTALLATION

▶ **See Figure 97**

1. Disconnect the negative battery cable.

2. Remove the driveshaft. Refer to the procedures in this section.

3. Using SST 09308-10010 or an equivalent seal puller, remove the oil seal from the extension housing.

To install:

4. Using a seal driver, tap the seal in until it's surface is flush with the extension housing edge.

DRIVELINE

Rear Driveshaft and U-Joints

REMOVAL & INSTALLATION

▶ **See Figures 98, 99, 100, 101 and 102**

1. Disconnect the negative battery cable.

2. Raise the vehicle and safely support it with jackstands.

3. Matchmark the driveshaft and companion flanges, then unfasten the bolts which attach the flanges to the differential.

4. Remove the bolts attaching the center support bearing to the body. Some vehicles may use height washers between the

5. Install the driveshaft. Road test the vehicle for proper operation.

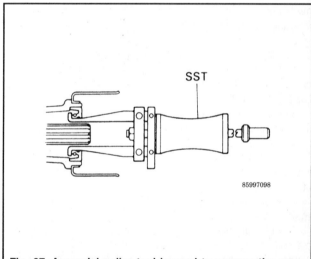

Fig. 97 A special puller tool is used to remove the rear output shaft seal

bearing and the body. Make a note as to their location for proper installation later.

5. Pull driveshaft assembly out from the transaxle. Insert SST 09325-12010 or an equivalent extension housing plug into the transaxle to prevent fluid leakage.

To install:

6. Apply multi-purpose grease to the outside diameter and splines of the yoke. Remove the SST, then install the driveshaft assembly into the transaxle.

7. Align the matchmarks on the flanges, then connect them with the attaching bolts/nuts. Torque the nuts to 31 ft. lbs. (42 Nm).

8. Connect the center support bearing to the body. Remember to place the height washers between the body and bearing, if applicable. Install the two mount bolts finger-tight.

9. Check that the bearing bracket is at right angles to the driveshaft. Adjust, if necessary.

10. Check that the center line of the bearing is set to the center line of the bracket. The vehicle should not have a load in it. Adjust, if necessary.

11. Torque the bolts to 27 ft. lbs. (37 Nm).

U-JOINT REPLACEMENT

The U-joints on 4WD Tercels are not serviceable, the intermediate shaft and/or propeller shaft must be replaced in the event of U-joint failure.

Center Support Bearing

REMOVAL & INSTALLATION

▶ **See Figures 103, 104, 105, 106 and 107**

1. Remove the driveshaft from the vehicle.

2. Make alignment marks across the two flanges then remove the attaching nuts/bolts. Separate the propeller shaft from the intermediate shaft.

3. Paint alignment marks on the flange (attached to the center support bearing) and the intermediate shaft.

4. Using a hammer and chisel, carefully loosen staked part of nut. Use SST 09330-00021 or an equivalent flange securing bar to hold the flange, then remove the nut.

5. Clamp the flange yoke in a vise, then tap the intermediate shaft out using a brass drift.

To install:

6. Slide the center support bearing and the flange onto the intermediate shaft. If equipped with cut out marks on the bracket, they should face the rear of the vehicle.

7. Align the matchmarks on the flange and the intermediate shaft.

8. Place the flange in a soft jawed vise, then thread a new nut onto the shaft. Use SST 09330-00021 or an equivalent flange securing bar to hold the flange, then torque the nut to

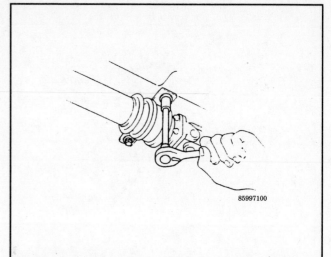
Fig. 99 The center support bearing is usually secured to the body by two bolts

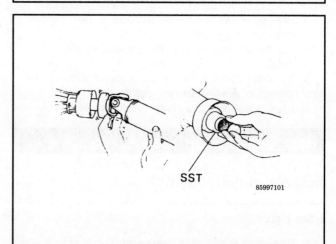
Fig. 100 Carefully side the driveshaft out from the transaxle, then plug the end of the transaxle to prevent fluid leakage

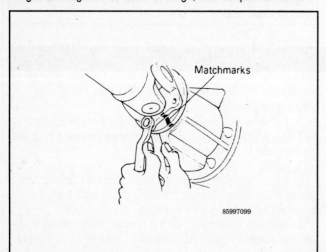
Fig. 98 Paint matchmarks on the flanges before removing the bolts

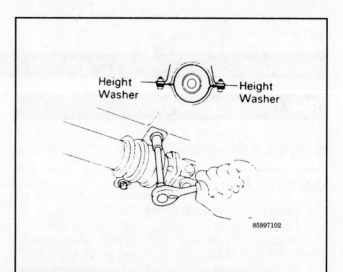
Fig. 101 Be sure to install the height washers, if equipped

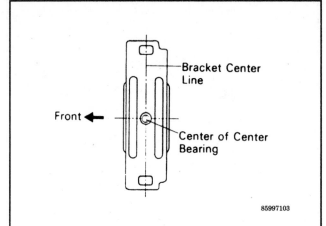

Fig. 102 Make sure that the bearing center lines are correctly set. Note that the notches in the bracket face the rear of the vehicle

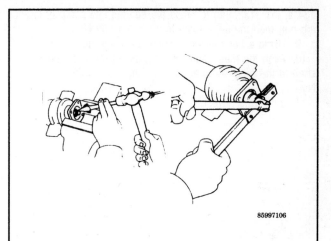

Fig. 105 A hammer and chisel can be used to remove the staked part of the nut. Use a special tool to hold the flange while removing the nut

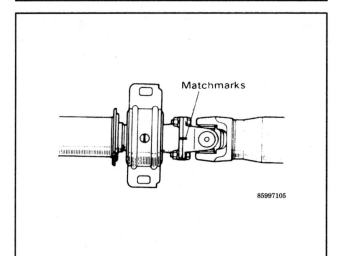

Fig. 104 Paint matchmarks on the flanges before removing the attaching bolts/nuts

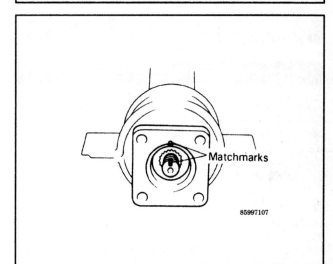

Fig. 106 Paint matchmarks on the flange and shaft before removing the center support bearing

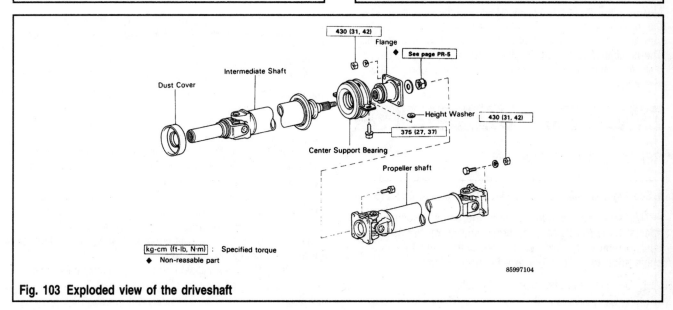

Fig. 103 Exploded view of the driveshaft

134 ft. lbs. (182 Nm) to press the bearing into position. Loosen the nut, then torque it again to 22 ft. lbs. (30 Nm).

9. Using a hammer and punch, stake the nut.

10. Align the matchmarks, then connect the intermediate shaft to the propeller shaft. Tighten the nuts to 42 ft. lbs. (31 Nm).

11. Install the driveshaft.

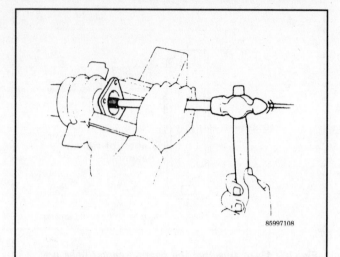

Fig. 107 Use a brass drift and hammer to tap the shaft out of the bearing

REAR AXLE

Determining Axle Ratio

The drive axle of a car has a certain ratio. This number (usually a whole number and a decimal fraction) is actually a comparison of the number of gear teeth on the ring gear and the pinion gear. For example, a 4.11 rear means that theoretically, there are 4.11 teeth on the ring gear for each tooth on the pinion gear. Said another way, the driveshaft must turn 4.11 times to turn the wheels once. Actually, on a 4.11 rear, there might be 37 teeth on the ring gear and 9 teeth on the pinion gear. By dividing the number of teeth on the pinion gear into the number of teeth on the ring gear, the numerical axle ratio (4.11) is obtained. This provides a good method of determining exactly which axle ratio you are dealing with.

Another method of determining gear ratio is to raise and support the car so that both rear wheels are off the ground. Make a chalk mark on the rear wheel and the driveshaft. Put the transmission in neutral. Turn the rear wheel one complete turn and count the number of turns that the driveshaft makes. The number of turns that the driveshaft makes in one complete revolution of the rear wheel is an approximation of the rear axle ratio.

Axle Shaft, Bearing and Seal

REMOVAL & INSTALLATION

◆ See Figures 108, 109, 110, 111, 112, 113, 114 and 115

➡This service procedure requires the use of expensive special tools (machine shop press and an oil bath). It is best to remove the axle shaft, then send it out to a machine shop to replace the axle bearing assembly.

1. Disconnect the negative battery cable.

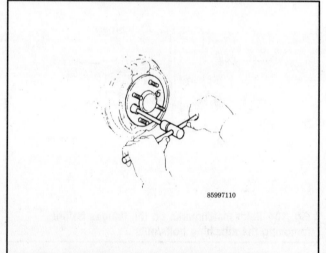

Fig. 108 The backing plate attaching nuts can be accessed through the hole in the rear axle shaft flange

2. Raise and safely support the vehicle.

3. Remove the wheel cover, unfasten the lug nuts, then remove the wheel.

4. Remove the brake drum.

5. Remove the backing plate attachment nuts through the access holes in the rear axle shaft flange.

6. Use SST 09520-00031 or an equivalent slide hammer puller to withdraw the axle shaft from it's housing. Use care not to damage the oil seal when removing the axle shaft.

7. Disconnect the brake line, then remove the brake backing plate. Remove the end gasket from the axle housing.

8. Grind the axle bearing inner retainer, then cut it off using a hammer and chisel. Be careful not to damage the axle shaft by grinding through the retainer.

9. Using SST 09527-20011 or an equivalent bearing support plate, press the bearing off the axle shaft.

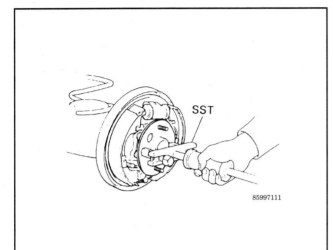

Fig. 109 A special tool is used to remove the axle shaft from the housing

10. Position the bearing outer retainer and a new bearing onto the shaft. Using SST 09515-20010 or it's equivalent, press the bearing to the correct location.

11. Heat the inner bearing retainer to about 302°F (150°C) in an oil bath. Press the inner retainer onto the axle shaft. Face the non-beveled side of the inner retainer toward the bearing.

✳✳CAUTION

Use extreme caution when working with the heated bearing retainer. Wear asbestos gloves, goggles and heavy, protective clothing the avoid injury and burns. Use tongs or a similar tool to handle the bearing retainer.

12. Remove the oil seal from the axle housing using SST 09308-00010 or an equivalent oil seal puller.

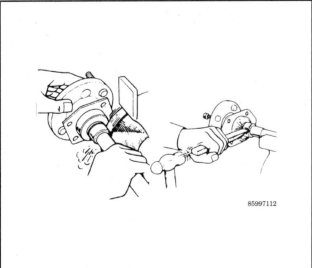

Fig. 110 Removing the bearing retainer

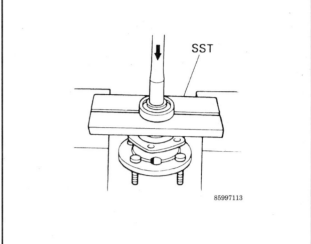

Fig. 111 A press must be used to remove and install the bearing

13. Install the oil seal in the axle housing housing. Drive the oil seal into the axle housing to a depth of 0.220 in. (5.6mm) using SST 09517-12010 or an equivalent seal driver.

14. Clean the flange of the axle housing and backing plate. Apply sealer to the end gasket and retainer gasket as necessary.

15. Place new end and retainer gaskets in position. Face the notch of gasket downward.

16. Install the backing plate to the axle housing and all necessary components.

17. Insert the axle shaft straight in, not at an angle. Be careful not to damage the oil seal and/or oil deflector inside the axle housing. Secure the rear axle shaft with new self-locking nuts. Torque them to 48 ft. lbs. (66 Nm).

18. Install the brake drum and wheel.

19. Bleed the brake system, then road test for proper operation.

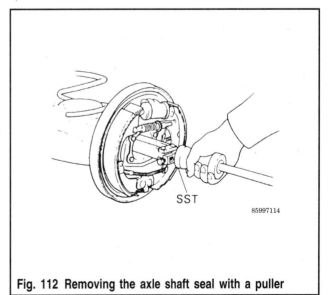

Fig. 112 Removing the axle shaft seal with a puller

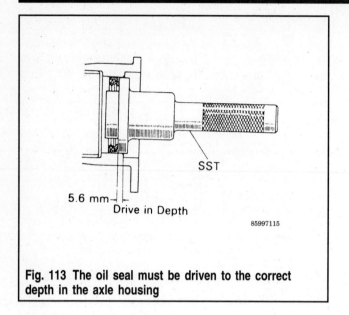

85997115

Fig. 113 The oil seal must be driven to the correct depth in the axle housing

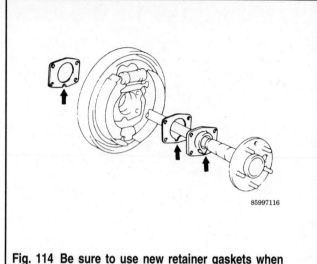

85997116

Fig. 114 Be sure to use new retainer gaskets when installing the axle shaft

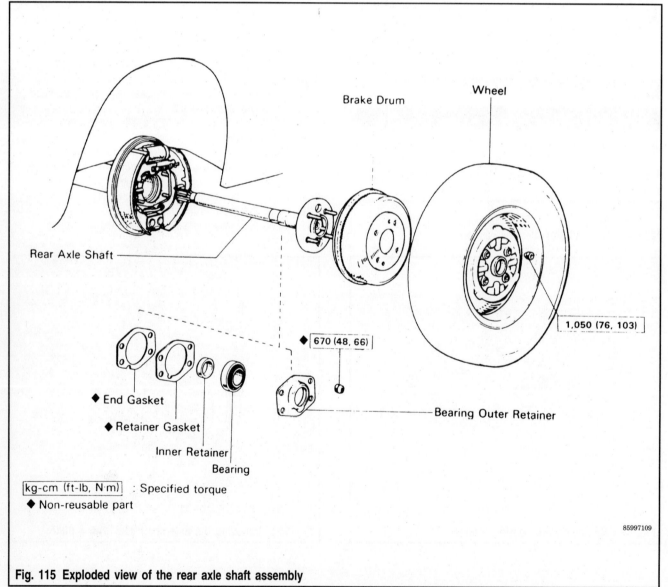

Fig. 115 Exploded view of the rear axle shaft assembly

Differential Carrier

REMOVAL & INSTALLATION

▶ **See Figure 116**

1. Disconnect the negative battery cable.
2. Raise and safely support the vehicle. Drain the differential fluid.
3. Remove the rear axle shafts as outlined in this section.
4. Disconnect the driveshaft from the differential assembly. Refer to the appropriate procedure.
5. Remove the differential carrier retaining bolts, then remove the carrier assembly.
6. Installation is the reverse of removal. Use a new gasket and torque the differential carrier retaining bolts to 23 ft. lbs. (31 Nm). Refill the differential unit with GL-5 SAE 90 oil, refer to Section 1 for details.

Pinion Seal

REMOVAL & INSTALLATION

▶ **See Figures 117, 118, 119, 120, 121, 122 and 123**

1. Disconnect the negative battery cable.
2. Disconnect the driveshaft from the differential companion flange. Refer to the appropriate procedure in this section.
3. Using a hammer and chisel, loosen the staked part of the companion flange nut. Use SST 09330-00021 or an equivalent flange securing bar to hold the flange while removing the nut and washer. Remove the companion flange.
4. Using SST 09308-10010 or an equivalent seal puller, remove the oil seal from the housing.
5. Using SST 09556-12010 or an equivalent bearing puller, remove the front bearing from the drive pinion. Remove the bearing spacer.

➡ **The bearing must be removed in order to replace the bearing spacer. This is done since proper bearing preload is lost when the companion flange nut is loosened. It is imperative for proper bearing preload to be achieved.**

To install:
6. Slide a new bearing spacer and bearing onto the pinion shaft.
7. Install the oil slinger and a new seal. Using SST 09554-30011 or an equivalent seal driver, drive the seal to a depth of 0.039 in. (1mm). Apply some multi-purpose grease to the oil seal lip.
8. Using SST 09557-22022 or an equivalent puller, install the companion flange.
9. Use SST 09330-00021 or an equivalent flange securing bar to hold the flange. Install the washer, then coat the threads with multi-purpose grease. Tighten the nut to 103 ft. lbs. (140 Nm).

10. Using a beam-type torque wrench, measure the bearing preload. Smoothly rotate the wrench and record an average reading. Do not record the break-away torque (the amount of force necessary to start the assembly moving) as it is not indicative of true preload. It should be between 5.6-10.9 inch lbs. (0.6-1.2 Nm).
11. If preload exceeds specification, replace the bearing spacer and repeat the preload procedure. Do not back off the pinion nut to reduce preload. If preload is less than specification, retighten the nut in 9 ft. lbs. (13 Nm) steps until the specified preload is reached. Do not exceed 174 ft. lbs. (235 Nm). If this maximum torque is exceeded, replace the bearing spacer and repeat the preload procedure.
12. Stake the nut, then connect the driveshaft to the companion flange.
13. Check the fluid level, add if necessary.
14. Road test and check for proper operation.

Axle Housing

REMOVAL & INSTALLATION

1. Disconnect the negative battery cable.
2. Raise and safely support the vehicle. Drain the differential fluid.
3. If necessary, remove the rear axle shafts as outlined in this section. Label and disconnect all lines and/or hoses that are necessary to remove the axle housing assembly from the vehicle.
4. Disconnect the driveshaft from the differential companion flange. If necessary, remove the differential carrier from the axle housing. Refer to the appropriate procedure(s) in this section.
5. Support the rear axle assembly with a pair of floor jacks. Strap the axle assembly securely to the jacks.
6. Disconnect the rear shock absorbers from the axle, then remove the coil springs. Refer to Section 8 for details.
7. Remove the rear stabilizer bar and the upper/lower control arms. Refer to Section 8 for the appropriate procedures.
8. Slowly lower the rear axle assembly, then remove the assembly from under the vehicle.
To install:
9. Position the axle assembly under the vehicle, then connect the upper/lower control arms and the rear stabilizer bar.
10. Install the coil springs, then connect the shock absorbers to the axle. Remove the floor jacks secured to the axle.
11. If applicable, install the differential carrier. Align the matchmarks, then connect the driveshaft to the companion flange. Connect all lines and/or hoses to the rear axle assembly.
12. If applicable, install the axle shafts.
13. Lower the vehicle, then refill the differential unit with GL-5 SAE 90 oil. Refer to Section 1 for details.
14. Make sure all fasteners are tightened to their specified torque. Refer to Section 8 for all rear suspension components.

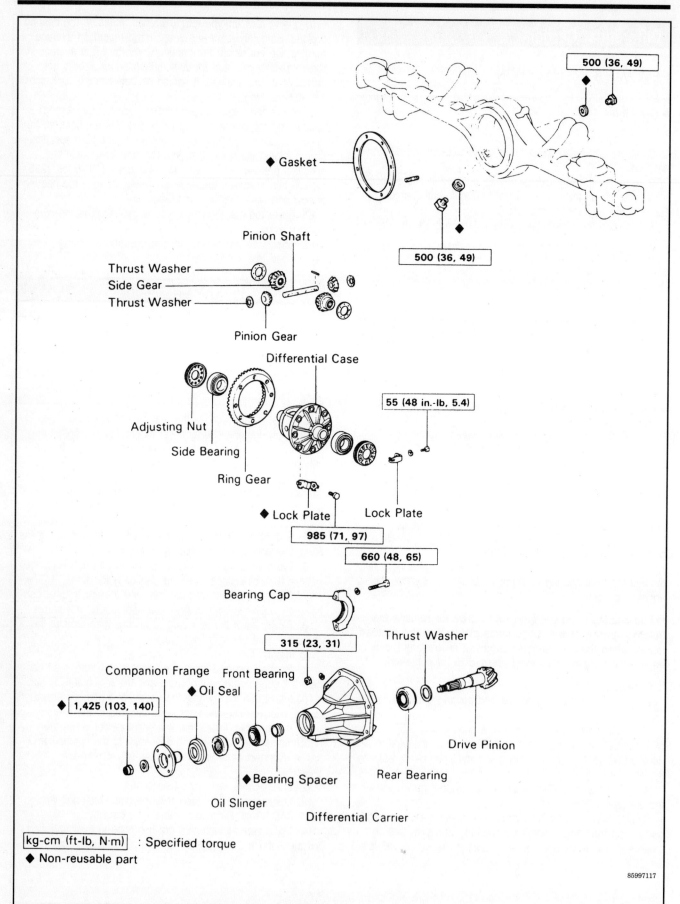

500 (36, 49)

◆ Gasket

500 (36, 49)

Pinion Shaft

Thrust Washer

Side Gear

Thrust Washer

Pinion Gear

Differential Case

55 (48 in.-lb, 5.4)

Adjusting Nut

Side Bearing

Ring Gear

◆ Lock Plate   Lock Plate

985 (71, 97)

660 (48, 65)

Bearing Cap

Thrust Washer

315 (23, 31)

Companion Frange   Front Bearing

◆ Oil Seal

◆ 1,425 (103, 140)

Drive Pinion

◆ Bearing Spacer

Rear Bearing

Oil Slinger

Differential Carrier

kg-cm (ft-lb, N·m) : Specified torque

◆ Non-reusable part

85997117

Fig. 116 Exploded view of the differential carrier assembly

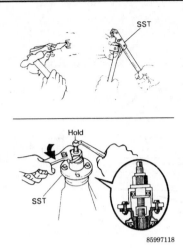

Fig. 117 Removing the companion flange. A special tool is used to separate the flange from the shaft once the nut is removed

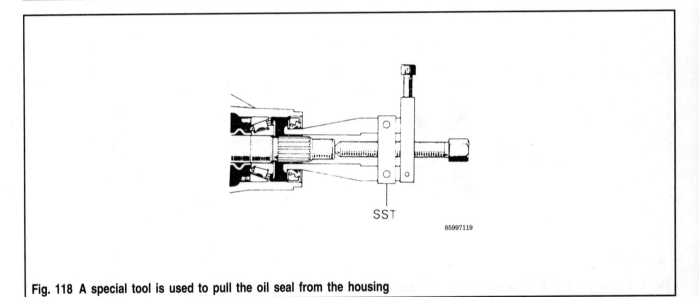

Fig. 118 A special tool is used to pull the oil seal from the housing

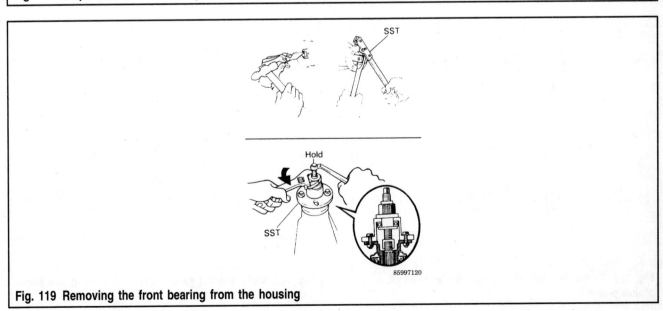

Fig. 119 Removing the front bearing from the housing

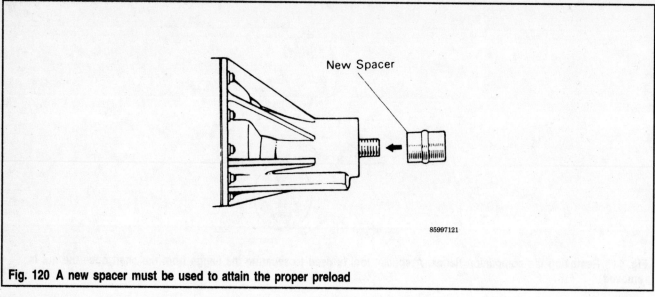

Fig. 120 A new spacer must be used to attain the proper preload

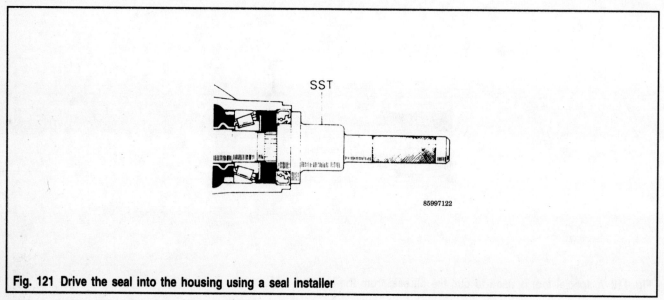

Fig. 121 Drive the seal into the housing using a seal installer

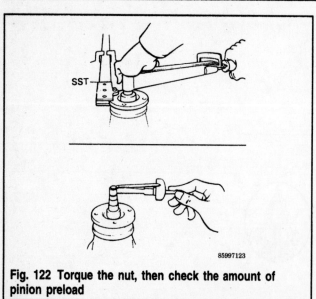

Fig. 122 Torque the nut, then check the amount of pinion preload

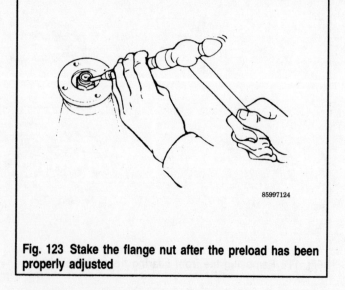

Fig. 123 Stake the flange nut after the preload has been properly adjusted

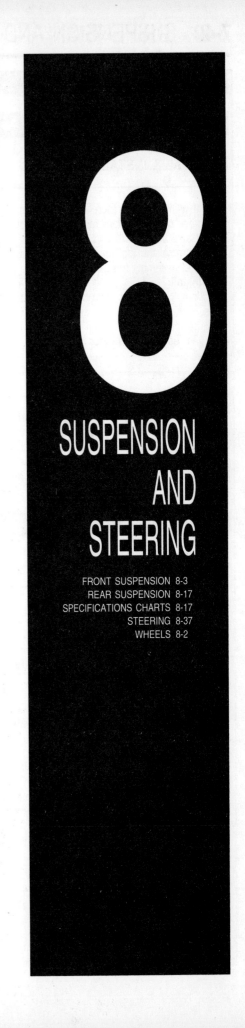

8

SUSPENSION AND STEERING

WHEELS

Wheel Assembly

REMOVAL & INSTALLATION

1. If using a lug wrench, loosen the lug nuts slightly, in a criss-cross pattern, before raising the vehicle.
2. Raise the vehicle and safely support it with jackstands.
3. Remove the lug nuts in a criss-cross pattern, then pull the wheel assembly from the vehicle.

To install:

4. Install the wheel, then thread the lug nuts onto the studs. Tighten the nuts until snug.
5. Lower the vehicle, then torque the nuts to 76 ft. lbs. (103 Nm) using a criss-cross pattern.

INSPECTION

Before installing the wheels, check for any cracks or enlarged bolt holes. Remove any corrosion on the mounting surfaces with a wire brush. Installation of the wheels without a good metal-to-metal contact can cause wheel nuts to loosen. Recheck the wheel nut torque after 1,000 miles (1,610 km) of driving.

Wheel Studs

REPLACEMENT

Front Wheels

◆ **See Figures 1 and 2**

1. Remove the front wheel.
2. Remove the brake caliper and disc. Refer to the procedures outlined in this manual.
3. Turn the hub so that the broken stud is in the area of the open portion of the disc brake dust cover.
4. Using SST 09628-10011 or its equivalent, remove the stud.

To install:

5. Insert the new stud into the hole in the hub flange. Align the splines on the stud with the grooves in the hole.
6. Install a washer, then thread a lug nut onto the stud. Tighten the nut until the stud is pulled fully into the hub flange.
7. Install the brake disc and caliper.
8. Install the wheel.

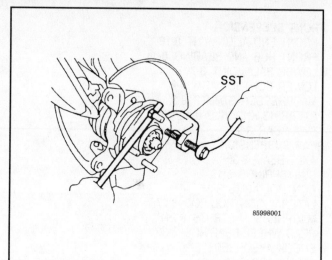

Fig. 1 A special tool is used to press the stud out of the hub flange

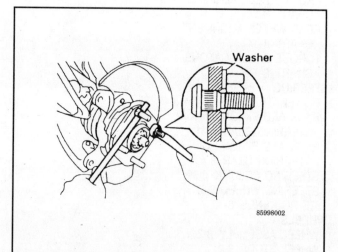

Fig. 2 Install a washer and nut, then draw the stud into the hub flange

Rear Wheels

◆ **See Figure 3**

SEDANS

1. Remove the rear drum/hub assembly. Refer to the procedures in this manual.
2. Using a press, remove the wheel stud.

To install:

3. Align the splines on the stud with the grooves in the hub, then press the stud into the hub.
4. Install the rear drum/hub assembly.

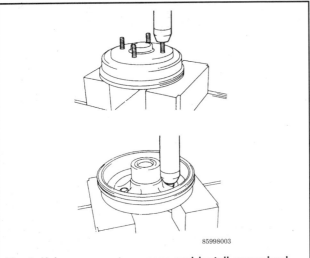

Fig. 3 Using a press to remove and install rear wheel studs on sedans

FRONT SUSPENSION

MacPherson Struts

✻✻CAUTION

Exercise great caution when working with the front suspension. Coil springs and other suspension components are under extreme tension and result in severe injury if released improperly. Never remove the nut on the top of the shock absorber piston without using the proper spring compressor tool.

REMOVAL & INSTALLATION

▶ See Figures 4 and 5

✻✻CAUTION

The suspension on any vehicle is assembled with high grade, hardened fasteners. NEVER substitute a fastener of inferior load rating when assembling a suspension component!

✻✻CAUTION

On models equipped with a Supplemental Restraint System (SRS) or "air bag," work must NOT be started until at least 90 seconds have passed from the time that both the ignition switch is turned to the LOCK position and the negative cable is disconnected from the battery.

1. Disconnect the negative battery cable.
2. Raise and safely support the front of the vehicle with jackstands.

WAGONS

1. Remove the rear drum assembly. Refer to the procedures in this manual.
2. On some applications, you may be able to press the stud from the hub using SST 09628-10011 or its equivalent. Check that the necessary clearance exists. If the clearance is not adequate, remove the axle shaft as described in this manual, then position the shaft on a press and carefully remove the stud.

To install:
3. Insert the new stud into the hole in the hub flange. Align the splines on the stud with the grooves in the hole.
4. Install a washer, then thread a lug nut onto the stud. Tighten the nut until the stud is pulled fully into the hub flange.
5. Install the axle shaft, as necessary.
6. Install the rear drum assembly.

3. On 1987-94 sedans, disconnect the brake hose from the caliper, then plug the fittings. Remove the brake hose from the strut lower attaching bracket.
4. Cover the halfshaft boot to protect it from fluids and impact damage.
5. Paint or use a scribing tool to make matchmarks on the steering knuckle and the strut lower attaching bracket.

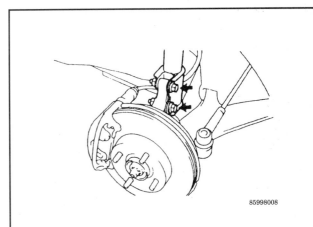

Fig. 4 Mark the position of the strut lower bracket and the steering knuckle before removing the attaching bolts

6. Remove the bolts which attach the strut assembly to the steering knuckle.
7. Remove the nuts attaching the strut assembly to the shock tower. DO NOT remove the center nut. This nut is usually covered by a plastic cap in the center of the shock tower.

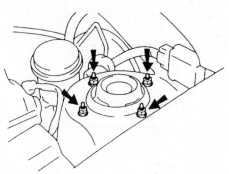

85998009

Fig. 5 Upper strut assembly attaching nut locations. Do not remove the center nut

8. Remove the strut assembly from the vehicle. Remember that the spring is still under tension. It should stay in place as long as the nut on the shock piston shaft is not removed.

To install:

9. Install the strut assembly to the vehicle. Torque the attaching nuts to the following:
   a. 1984-85 models — 17 ft. lbs. (24 Nm)
   b. 1986 models — 13 ft. lbs. (17 Nm)
   c. 1987-90 models — 23 ft. lbs. (31 Nm)
   d. 1991-94 models — 29 ft. lbs. (39 Nm)

10. Connect the lower strut attaching bracket to the steering knuckle. Proceed as follows:
   a. On wagons and 1984-86 sedans, insert the bolts through the front of the steering knuckle, then align the matchmarks. Torque the nuts to 105 ft. lbs. (142 Nm).
   b. On 1987-94 sedans, insert the bolts through the rear of the steering knuckle, then align the matchmarks. Coat the threads with oil, then torque the nuts to 166 ft. lbs. (226 Nm) on 1987-90 sedans and 181 ft. lbs. (245 Nm) on 1991-94 sedans.

11. Connect the brake hose to the caliper and strut assembly, as applicable. Bleed the brake system.

12. Pack the bearing in the shock tower with multi-purpose grease, then reinstall the dust cover.

13. Install the wheel(s), then lower the car.

14. Have the wheel alignment checked by a reputable shop. Road test the vehicle for proper operation.

OVERHAUL

▶ **See Figures 6, 7, 8, 9, 10, 11, 12 and 13**

✳✳CAUTION

The suspension on any vehicle is assembled with high grade, hardened fasteners. NEVER substitute a fastener of inferior load rating when assembling a suspension component!

✳✳CAUTION

This procedure requires the use of a spring compressor; it cannot be performed without one. IF YOU DO NOT HAVE ACCESS TO THIS SPECIAL TOOL, DO NOT ATTEMPT TO DISASSEMBLE THE STRUT! The coil springs are retained under considerable pressure. They exert enough force to cause serious personal injury and component damage. Exercise extreme caution when disassembling the strut.

1. Remove the strut assembly from the vehicle. Refer to the appropriate procedure.

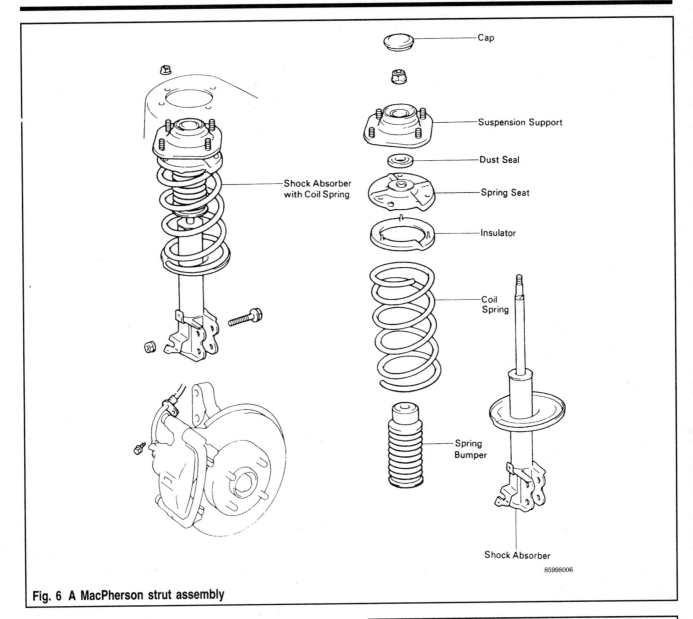

Cap

Suspension Support

Dust Seal

Spring Seat

Insulator

Shock Absorber
with Coil Spring

Coil
Spring

Spring
Bumper

Shock Absorber

85998006

Fig. 6 A MacPherson strut assembly

2. Install a bolt and two nuts to the lower strut attaching bracket, then secure the assembly in a vise. Do not over-tighten the strut assembly in the vise, as this will result in damage to the strut tube.

3. Using SST 09727-22032, 09727-30020 or their equivalent, compress the spring until the upper spring retainer is free of any spring tension. Do not over-compress the spring.

4. Use a spring seat holder (SST 09727-22032, 09727-30020, 09729-22031 or their equivalent) so that the spring seat will not turn as you remove the nut on the end of the shock piston rod.

5. Remove the bearing plate, the support and the upper spring retainer. Make a note as to their correct order of assembly.

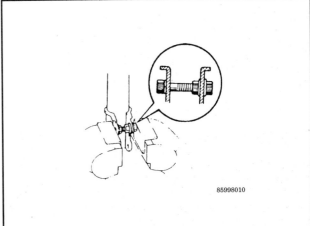

85998010

Fig. 7 Install a bolt and two nuts before securing the strut assembly in a vise. This will prevent damage to the bracket

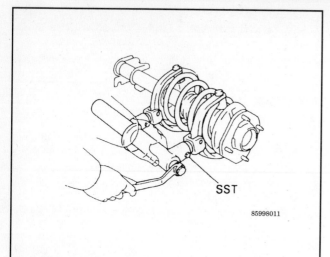

Fig. 8 A spring compressor must be used before disassembling the strut

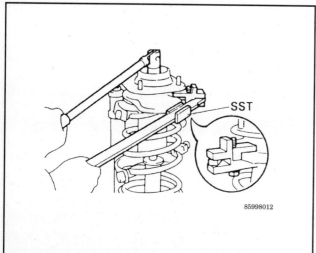

Fig. 9 A special tool can be used to hold the spring seat while loosening the center nut

6. If replacing the spring, slowly and CAUTIOUSLY unscrew the spring compressor until all spring tension is relieved. Remove the spring and the dust cover.

➡ If the piston rod to retracts into the shock absorber, screw a nut onto the rod and pull the rod out by the nut. Do not use pliers to grip the rod as they will damage its surface, resulting in leaks, uneven operation or seal damage. Be extremely careful not to stress or hit the rod.

Check the shock absorber by moving the piston rod through its full range of travel. It should move smoothly and evenly throughout its entire travel without any trace of binding or notching. If a shock absorber is to be replaced, the internal gas should be vented to make the unit safe for disposal. On models up to 1990, use SST 09720-00011 to loosen the ring nut two or three turns and vent the gas completely. On 1991-94 models, fully extend the shock absorber rod, then drill a small hole between the spring lower seat and the lower strut attaching bracket. Wear safety goggles to protect your eyes from metal chips which may fly up when drilling.

Check the upper strut mount assembly for any abnormal noise, binding or restricted motion. Lubricate the upper bearing with multi-purpose grease before reinstallation.

To assemble:

➡ **Never reuse the nut on the end of the shock piston rod. Always replace this nut.**

7. Assemble the spring bumper, coil spring, insulator, spring seat and dust seal onto the the strut.

8. Compress the spring, if necessary. Align the coil spring end with the groove or hollow in the lower seat. Do not over-compress the spring; compress it just enough to allow installation of the piston rod nut.

9. Thread a new nut onto the piston rod, then tighten it until the rod begins to rotate.

10. Double check that the spring is correctly seated in the upper and lower mounts and reposition it as needed. Slowly release the tension on the spring compressor, then remove it from the coil spring.

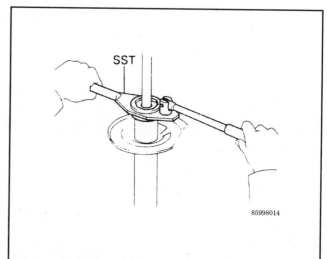

Fig. 10 On other models, the ring nut can be loosened to relieve the gas before disposal

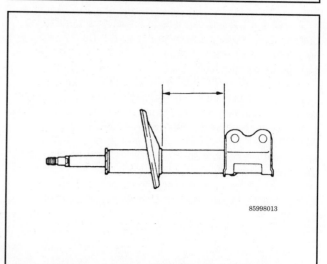

Fig. 11 On some models, the strut must be drilled in the area shown to relieve the gas before disposal

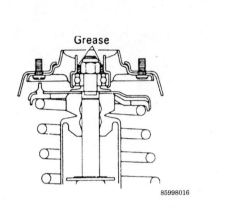

Fig. 12 Multi-purpose grease should be packed into the support bearing

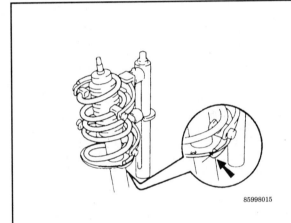

Fig. 13 Make sure the coil spring is correctly positioned on the spring seat

11. On 1987-94 sedans, torque the shaft nut to 34 ft. lbs. (47 Nm) at this time. Use a spring seat holder (SST 09727-22032, 09727-30020, 09729-22031 or their equivalent) so that the spring seat will not turn as you tighten the nut on the end of the piston rod.

12. Place the strut assembly in position, then install it following the procedures outlined in this section. On wagons and 1984-86 sedans the piston rod nut can now be tightened to 34 ft. lbs. (47 Nm).

Lower Ball Joint

INSPECTION

♦ See Figure 14

Vertical Play

➡ **Performed on 1984-90 models**

1. Raise the front of the vehicle, then place a wooden block with a height of 7.09-7.87 in. (180-200mm) under the tire of the side to be checked.

2. Lower the jack until there is about half a load on the front coil springs. Place the stands under the vehicle for safety.

3. Make sure the front wheels are in a straight-forward position, then block them with chocks.

4. Move the lower arm up and down and check that there is no vertical play.

5. If vertical play is found, replace the ball joint.

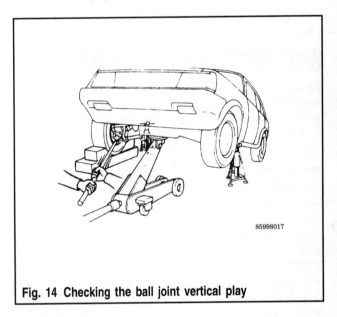

Fig. 14 Checking the ball joint vertical play

Turning Torque

♦ See Figure 15

➡ **Performed on 1984-94 models**

1. Remove the ball joint. Refer to the procedures in this section.

2. Move the ball joint stud back and forth five times, then thread a nut onto the stud.

3. Using a torque wrench, turn the nut slowly and continuously (each turn should take between 2-4 seconds). On the fifth turn, take a torque reading.

4. The turning torque on 1984-90 models should be between 6.9-21.7 inch lbs. (0.8-2.5 Nm). A reading between 8.7-26 inch lbs. (1-2.9 Nm) should be found on 1991-94 models.

5. Replace the ball joint, if necessary.

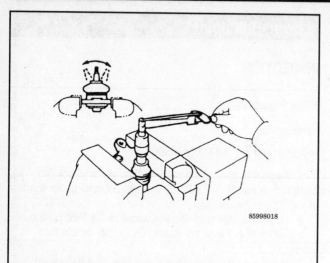

85998018

Fig. 15 Move the ball joint stud back and forth several times, then check the turning torque

REMOVAL & INSTALLATION

▶ **See Figures 16 and 17**

> ※※**CAUTION**
>
> On models equipped with a Supplemental Restraint System (SRS) or "air bag," work must NOT be started until at least 90 seconds have passed from the time that both the ignition switch is turned to the LOCK position and the negative cable is disconnected from the battery.

> ※※**CAUTION**
>
> The suspension on any vehicle is assembled with high grade, hardened fasteners. NEVER substitute a fastener of inferior load rating when assembling a suspension component!

➡The use of the special tools is required for this procedure. A ball joint separator is a commonly available tool which prevents damage to the joint and knuckle. Do not attempt to separate the joint with hammers, prybars or similar tools.

Wagons and 1984-86 Sedans

1. Disconnect the negative battery cable.
2. Raise and safely support the front of the vehicle with jackstands.
3. Remove the nuts/bolts attaching the lower ball joint to the steering knuckle.
4. Remove the cotter pin and nut from the ball joint stud.
5. Use SST 09950-20016 or its equivalent to press the ball joint out of the control arm.

To install:

6. Install the lower ball joint to the control arm. Thread the nut onto the shaft, then torque to 58 ft. lbs. (78 Nm). Install a new cotter pin.

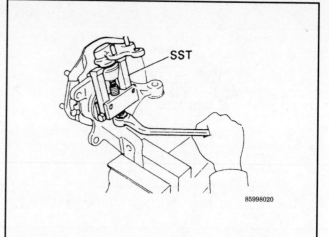

85998020

Fig. 17 On some models, it is necessary to remove the axle hub/steering knuckle assembly to access the lower ball joint

7. Connect the lower control arm to the steering knuckle. Torque the nuts/bolts to 59 ft. lbs. (80 Nm).
8. Lower the vehicle and check for proper operation.

1987-94 Sedans

1. Disconnect the negative battery cable.
2. Remove the axle hub/steering knuckle assembly. Refer to the procedure in this section.
3. Remove the cotter pin and nut from the ball joint stud.
4. Using SST 09610-55012 (1987-90), 09628-62011 (1991-94) or their equivalent, press the ball joint from the knuckle assembly.

To install:

5. Install the lower ball joint to the steering knuckle, then torque the nut to 72 ft. lbs. (98 Nm). Install a new cotter pin.
6. Install the axle hub/steering knuckle assembly on the vehicle.
7. Lower the vehicle and check for proper operation.

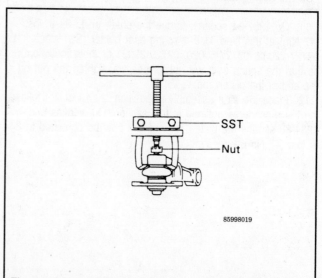

85998019

Fig. 16 A special tool is used to remove the ball joint

Sway Bar

REMOVAL & INSTALLATION

▶ See Figures 18 and 19

➡Not all models are equipped with a sway bar

✳✳CAUTION

The suspension on any vehicle is assembled with high grade, hardened fasteners. NEVER substitute a fastener of inferior load rating when assembling a suspension component!

Wagons and 1984-86 Sedans

1. Disconnect the negative battery cable.
2. Remove the engine under cover.
3. Remove the bolts attaching the sway bar brackets to the crossmember.
4. Remove the nuts connecting the sway bar ends to the control arm.
5. Remove the sway bar. Do not lose the spacers.

To install:

6. Replace any bushings which may be damaged or deformed.
7. Install the sway bar ends to the lower control arms. Make sure the spacers, retainers and bushings are installed properly. Thread a new nut onto the sway bar end.
8. Install the brackets to the crossmember. It may be necessary to pry the bar forward.
9. Install the bolts and torque to 32 ft. lbs. (43 Nm).
10. Bounce the vehicle to stabilize the suspension. Torque the nuts on the sway bar ends to 78 ft. lbs. (105 Nm).

Other Models

1. Remove the nuts/bolts attaching the sway bar to the lower control arm.
2. Remove the bolts attaching the sway bar brackets.

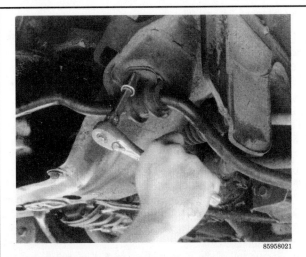

Fig. 18 Removing the bolts attaching the sway bar to the crossmember

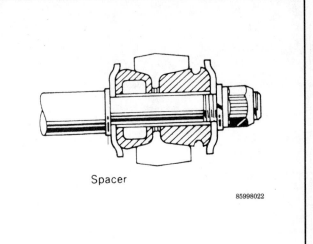

Spacer

85998022

Fig. 19 Make sure the spacer, bushings and retainers are correctly installed before tightening the nut

3. Disconnect the exhaust pipe from the exhaust manifold.
4. Remove the sway bar.

To install:

5. Replace any bushings which are damaged or deformed.
6. Position the sway bar, then install both brackets. Torque the bolts to 14 ft. lbs. (19 Nm).
7. Connect the sway bar to the control arms. Use a new nut and torque to 13 ft. lbs. (18 Nm).

Lower Control Arm

REMOVAL & INSTALLATION

✳✳CAUTION

The suspension on any vehicle is assembled with high grade, hardened fasteners. NEVER substitute a fastener of inferior load rating when assembling a suspension component!

✳✳CAUTION

On models equipped with a Supplemental Restraint System (SRS) or ''air bag,'' work must NOT be started until at least 90 seconds have passed from the time that both the ignition switch is turned to the LOCK position and the negative cable is disconnected from the battery.

Wagons and 1984-86 Sedans

▶ See Figures 20, 21, 22 and 23

1. Disconnect the negative battery cable.
2. Raise and safely support the vehicle.
3. Remove the nuts/bolts attaching the ball joint to the steering knuckle.
4. Remove the nut holding the sway bar end to the control arm.
5. Place a jack under the wheel and raise the car until the body lifts off the stand.

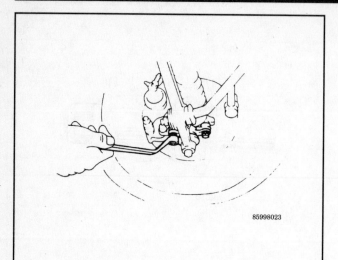

Fig. 20 The ball joint is attached to the steering knuckle by two bolts

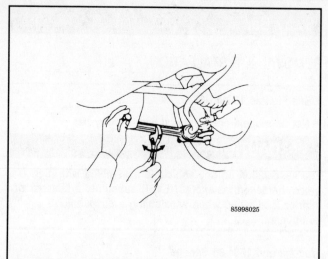

Fig. 22 Pry the lower arm back and forth, while pulling out the attaching bolt

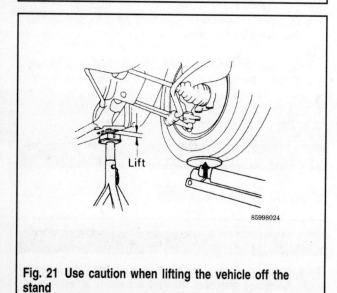

Fig. 21 Use caution when lifting the vehicle off the stand

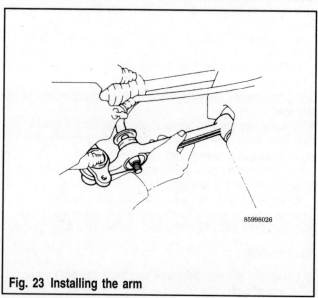

Fig. 23 Installing the arm

6. Loosen the lower control arm pivot bolt. Pry the lower arm and pull out the bolt.

7. Disconnect the arm from the sway bar, then remove it from the vehicle. Be careful not to lose the caster adjusting spacer.

8. Lower the vehicle onto the stand.

To install:

9. Check the rubber bushings and replace it if any sign of damage or deformation is found.

10. Insert the sway bar into the control arm. Install the sway bar and control arm bolt/nut. Do not torque the nut/bolt yet.

11. Connect the ball joint to the steering knuckle, then torque the nuts to 59 ft. lbs. (80 Nm).

12. Lower the vehicle and bounce it to stabilize the suspension.

13. Torque the sway bar nut to 78 ft. lbs. (105 Nm) and the control arm bolt to 83 ft. lbs. (113 Nm).

14. Have the wheel alignment checked by a reputable shop.

1987-94 Sedans

▶ **See Figures 24 and 25**

1. Disconnect the negative battery cable.

2. Remove the nuts/bolts attaching the ball joint to the lower control arm.

3. Remove the single bolt securing the front of the control arm and the two rear bolts securing the control arm bracket.

4. Remove the control arm from the vehicle.

To install:

5. If the bushings appear damaged or deformed, the entire lower control arm must be replaced.

6. Install the control arm and tighten the attaching bolts until just snug.

7. Connect the control arm to the ball joint. Torque the nuts to 59 ft. lbs. (80 Nm).

8. Lower the vehicle, then bounce it up and down to stabilize the suspension.

9. Torque the single front control arm bolt to 108 ft. lbs. (147 Nm) and the rear bracket bolts to 64 ft. lbs. (87 Nm).

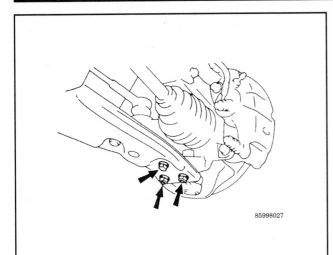

Fig. 24 Remove the nuts/bolts securing the ball joint to the lower control arm

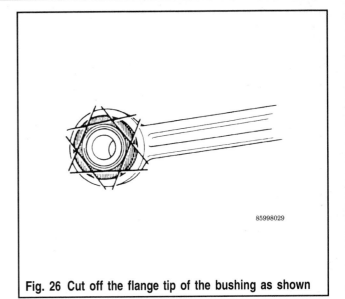

Fig. 26 Cut off the flange tip of the bushing as shown

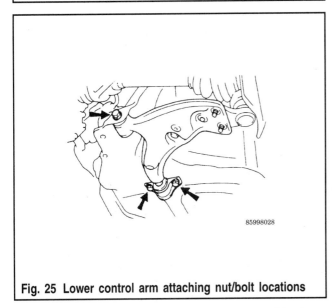

Fig. 25 Lower control arm attaching nut/bolt locations

10. Have the wheel alignment checked by a reputable shop.

BUSHING REPLACEMENT

▶ See Figures 26, 27, 28 and 29

❊❊CAUTION

The suspension on any vehicle is assembled with high grade, hardened fasteners. NEVER substitute a fastener of inferior load rating when assembling a suspension component!

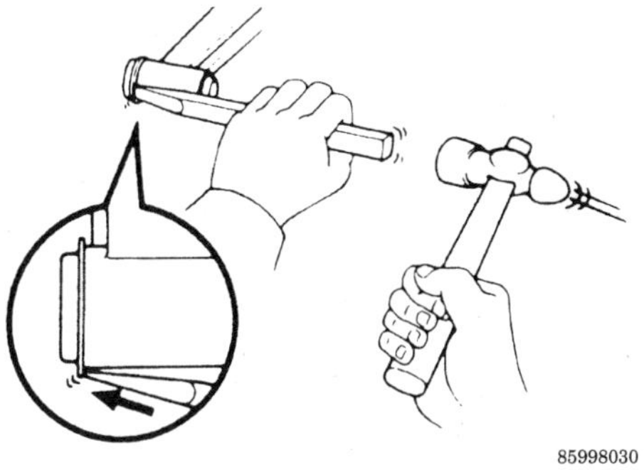

Fig. 27 Bending the flange tips with a hammer and chisel

➡Bushing replacement is possible on wagons and 1984-86 sedans only. On 1987-94 sedans, the entire lower control arm must be replaced as an assembly.

1. Remove the control arm from the vehicle.
2. Cut the flange tip of the bushing as shown, then bend the remaining positions inward with a hammer and chisel.
3. Bend in the flange tips, then pull off the flange with a pair of pliers.
4. Remove the bushing out of the control arm using SST 09726-32010 or its equivalent and a press.
5. Install the bushing using SST 09726-32010 or its equivalent and a press. Do not allow grease or oil to get on the bushing.
6. Install the control arm.

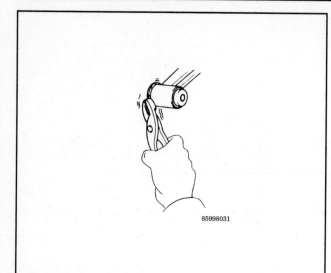

Fig. 28 Use a pair of pliers to pull off the flange

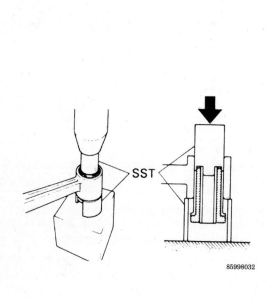

Fig. 29 A press is used to remove and replace the bushings in the control arm

Steering Knuckle

REMOVAL & INSTALLATION

▶ See Figure 30

> **✳✳CAUTION**
>
> On models equipped with a Supplemental Restraint System (SRS) or "air bag," work must NOT be started until at least 90 seconds have passed from the time that both the ignition switch is turned to the LOCK position and the negative cable is disconnected from the battery.

> **✳✳CAUTION**
>
> The suspension on any vehicle is assembled with high grade, hardened fasteners. NEVER substitute a fastener of inferior load rating when assembling a suspension component!

1. Disconnect the negative battery cable.
2. Remove the wheel, then remove the cotter pin, lock cap and hub nut.
3. Remove the brake caliper and disc. Refer to the procedures outlined in this manual.
4. Remove the tie rod end cotter pin and nut. Separate the tie rod from the steering knuckle using a suitable puller.
5. Matchmark the position of the strut lower attaching bracket and the steering knuckle.
6. Disconnect the lower control arm from the steering knuckle. This is usually accomplished by removing the lower ball joint attaching nuts/bolts.
7. Remove the nuts/bolts attaching the steering knuckle to the strut lower attaching bracket.
8. Separate the steering knuckle/hub assembly from the halfshaft. On wagons and 1984-86 sedans, use SST 09950-20016 or its equivalent. On other models, tap the driveshaft with a soft-faced hammer.
   To install:
9. Install the steering knuckle to the halfshaft. Thread the hub nut onto the shaft to hold the assembly. Be careful not to damage the halfshaft boot and the oil seal lip.
10. Install the lower ball joint attaching nuts/bolts. Do not torque them at this time.
11. Connect the steering knuckle to the strut lower attaching bracket. Refer to the strut procedures outlined in this section.
12. Torque the lower ball joint attaching nuts/bolts. Refer to the appropriate procedure outlined in this section.
13. Connect the tie rod end to the steering knuckle. Torque the nut to 36 ft. lbs. (49 Nm), then install a new cotter pin.
14. Install the brake disc and caliper.
15. Install the hub nut, lock cap and cotter pin. Refer to the halfshaft procedures outlined in this manual.
16. Lower the vehicle and check for proper operation. Have the alignment checked by a reputable shop.

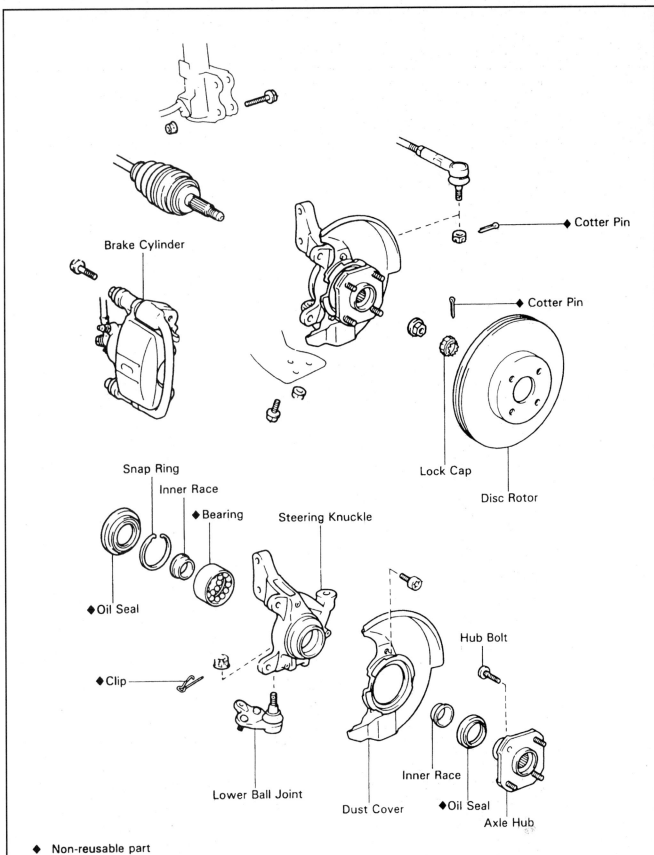

Brake Cylinder

◆ Cotter Pin

◆ Cotter Pin

Lock Cap

Disc Rotor

Snap Ring

Inner Race

◆ Bearing

Steering Knuckle

◆ Oil Seal

Hub Bolt

◆ Clip

Lower Ball Joint

Dust Cover

Inner Race

◆ Oil Seal

Axle Hub

◆   Non-reusable part

85998033

Fig. 30 A steering knuckle/hub assembly

Front Hub and Bearing

REMOVAL & INSTALLATION

▶ See Figures 31, 32, 33, 34, 35, 36 and 37

✳✳CAUTION

On models equipped with a Supplemental Restraint System (SRS) or "air bag," work must NOT be started until at least 90 seconds have passed from the time that both the ignition switch is turned to the LOCK position and the negative cable is disconnected from the battery.

✳✳CAUTION

The suspension on any vehicle is assembled with high grade, hardened fasteners. NEVER substitute a fastener of inferior load rating when assembling a suspension component!

Wagons and 1984-86 Sedans

1. Remove the steering knuckle. Refer to the procedures in this section.
2. Using a small prybar, remove the dust deflector.

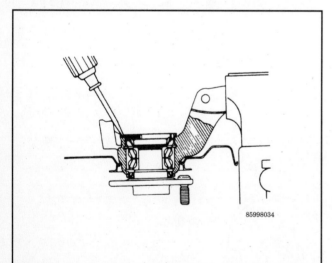

Fig. 31 A small prybar can be used to remove the dust deflector

3. Using SST 09308-00010 or its equivalent, remove the inner oil seal from the steering knuckle.
4. Remove the hole snapring using a pair of snapring pliers.

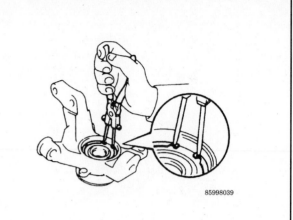

Fig. 32 Snapring pliers should be used when removing the snapring

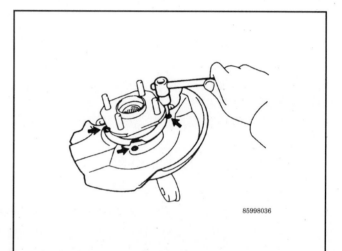

Fig. 33 The disc brake dust cover is usually retained by three small screws

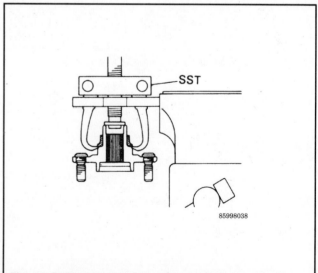

Fig. 34 Pulling the inner bearing races from the hub

5. Remove the disc brake dust cover.

6. Using SST 09950-20016 or its equivalent, remove the axle hub from the steering knuckle.

7. Remove the inside bearing inner race.

8. Using SST 09950-20016 or its equivalent, remove the outside bearing inner race.

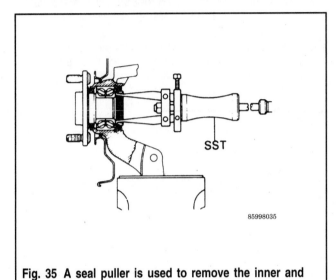

Fig. 35 A seal puller is used to remove the inner and outer oil seals

9. Using SST 09308-00010 or its equivalent, remove the outer oil seal.

10. Place the inner race of the outside bearing in the bearing. Using SST 09228-22020 and 09950-20016, press out the bearing.

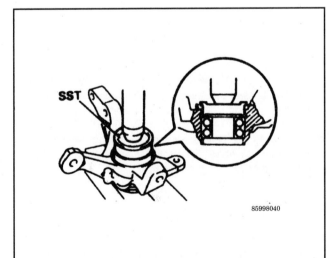

Fig. 36 A press is used to remove and install bearings in the hub

To install:

11. Using SST 09309-35010 or its equivalent, press in a new bearing. Note that there are two types of bearings, KOYO and NSK. Identify the original bearing and replace it with the same type.

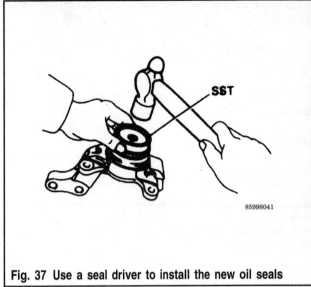

Fig. 37 Use a seal driver to install the new oil seals

12. Install the outside bearing inner race. Using a seal driver, install a new outer oil seal into the steering knuckle. Apply multi-purpose grease to the seal lip.

13. Install the disc brake dust cover to the knuckle.

14. Install new inner races into the inner bearing. Using SST 09228-22020 and 09310-35010 or their equivalent, press in the inner race until it is tightly against the shoulder of the hub. Be sure not to switch the inner and outer races when installing.

15. Install the hole snapring. Using a seal driver, install the inner oil seal to a depth of 0.130 in. (3.3mm) from the end of the surface.

16. Drive in a new dust seal into the steering knuckle. Install the knuckle assembly to the vehicle.

1987-90 Sedans

1. Remove the steering knuckle. Refer to the procedures in this section.

2. Remove the ball joint, refer to the procedures in this section.

3. Using a small prybar, remove the inner oil seal from the steering knuckle.

4. Remove the hole snapring using a pair of snapring pliers.

5. Remove the disc brake dust cover.

6. Using SST 09950-20017 or its equivalent, remove the axle hub from the steering knuckle.

7. Remove the inside bearing inner race.

8. Using SST 09950-20017 or its equivalent, remove the outside bearing inner race.

9. Remove the outer oil seal using a small prybar.

10. Place the inner race of the outside bearing in the bearing. Using a brass drift and hammer, drive out the bearing.

To install:

11. Using SST 09316-60010 or its equivalent, press in a new bearing.

12. Install the outside bearing inner race. Using a seal driver, install a new outer oil seal into the steering knuckle. Apply multi-purpose grease to the seal lip.

13. Install the disc brake dust cover to the knuckle.

14. Install a new inner race to the inside bearing. Using SST 09310-35010 or its equivalent, install the axle hub onto the knuckle.

15. Install the hole snapring. Using a seal driver, install the inner oil seal.

16. Install the ball joint to the steering knuckle. Install the knuckle assembly to the vehicle.

1991-94 Sedans

1. Remove the steering knuckle. Refer to the procedures in this section.

2. Remove the ball joint, refer to the procedures in this section.

3. Using a small prybar, remove the inner oil seal from the steering knuckle.

4. Using SST 09950-20017 or its equivalent, remove the axle hub from the steering knuckle.

5. Remove the disc brake dust cover.

6. Using SST 09950-20017 or its equivalent, remove the outside bearing inner race.

7. Remove the outer oil seal using a small prybar.

8. Remove the hole snapring using a pair of snapring pliers.

9. Place the inner race of the outside bearing in the bearing. Using a brass drift and hammer, drive out the bearing.

To install:

10. Using SST 09608-10010 or its equivalent, press in a new bearing. If the inner race and balls come loose from the outer race, be sure to install them on the same side as before.

11. Install the hole snapring. Using a seal driver, install the outer oil seal.

12. Install the disc brake dust cover to the knuckle.

13. Using SST 09608-10010, 09950-20017 or their equivalent, install the axle hub onto the knuckle.

14. Install the lower ball joint.

15. Using a seal driver, install a new inner oil seal into the steering knuckle. Apply multi-purpose grease to the seal lip.

16. Install the knuckle assembly to the vehicle.

Front End Alignment

Alignment of the front wheels is essential if your car is to go, stop and turn as designed. Alignment can be altered by collision, overloading, poor repair or bent components.

If you are diagnosing bizarre handling and/or poor road manners, the first place to look is the tires. Although the tires may wear as a result of an alignment problem, worn or poorly inflated tires can make you chase alignment problems which don't exist.

Once you have eliminated all other causes (always check and repair front end parts BEFORE wheel alignment), unload everything from the trunk except the spare tire, set the tire pressures to the correct level and take the car to a reputable alignment facility. Since the alignment settings are measured in very small increments, it is almost impossible for the home mechanic to accurately determine the settings. The explanations that follow will help you understand the three dimensions of alignment: caster, camber and toe.

CASTER

Caster is the tilting of the steering axis either forward or backward from the vertical, when viewed from the side of the vehicle. A backward tilt is said to be positive and a forward tilt is said to be negative.

CAMBER

Camber is the tilting of the wheels from the vertical (leaning in or out) when viewed from the front of the vehicle. When the wheels tilt outward at the top, the camber is said to be positive. When the wheels tilt inward at the top the camber is said to be negative. The amount of tilt is measured in degrees from the vertical. This measurement is called camber angle.

TOE

Toe is the turning in or out (parallelism) of the wheels. The actual amount of toe setting is normally only a fraction of an inch. The purpose of toe-in (or out) specification is to ensure parallel rolling of the wheels. Toe-in also serves to offset the small deflections of the steering support system which occur when the vehicle is rolling forward or under braking.

Changing the toe setting will radically affect the overall 'feel' of the steering, the behavior of the car under braking, tire wear and even fuel economy. Excessive toe (in or out) causes excessive drag or scrubbing on the tires.

FRONT WHEEL ALIGNMENT

Year	Model	Caster Range (deg.)	Caster Preferred Setting (deg.)	Camber Range (deg.)	Camber Preferred Setting (deg.)	Toe-in (in.)
1984	Sedan wo/P.S.	$2/3$P–$1^2/3$P	$1^1/6$P	$1/6$N–$5/6$P	$1/3$P	0.06 out–0.04 in
	Sedan w/P.S.	$2^1/6$P–$3^1/6$P	$2^2/3$P	$1/6$N–$5/6$P	$1/3$P	0.06 out–0.04 in
	Wagon wo/P.S.	$1/6$N–$1^1/3$P	$2/3$P	$1/4$N–$3/4$P	$1/4$P	0.04 out–0.04 in
	Wagon w/P.S.	$1^1/4$P–3P	$2^1/4$P	$1/4$N–$3/4$P	$1/4$P	0.04 out–0.04 in
	4WD	2P–3P	$2^1/2$P	$1/3$P–$2^1/3$P	$1^1/3$P	0.04 out–0.04 in
1985	Sedan wo/P.S.	$2/3$P–$1^2/3$P	$1^1/6$P	$1/6$N–$5/6$P	$1/3$P	0.06 out–0.04 in
	Sedan w/P.S.	$2^1/6$P–$3^1/6$P	$2^2/3$P	$1/6$N–$5/6$P	$1/3$P	0.06 out–0.04 in
	Wagon wo/P.S.	$1/6$N–$1^1/3$P	$2/3$P	$1/4$N–$3/4$P	$1/4$P	0.04 out–0.04 in
	Wagon w/P.S.	$1^1/4$P–3P	$2^1/4$P	$1/4$N–$3/4$P	$1/4$P	0.04 out–0.04 in
	4WD	2P–3P	$2^1/2$P	$1/3$P–$2^1/3$P	$1^1/3$P	0.04 out–0.04 in
1986	Sedan wo/P.S.	$2/3$P–$1^2/3$P	$1^1/6$P	$1/6$N–$5/6$P	$1/3$P	0.06 out–0.04 in
	Sedan w/P.S.	$2^1/6$P–$3^1/6$P	$2^2/3$P	$1/6$N–$5/6$P	$1/3$P	0.06 out–0.04 in
	Wagon wo/P.S.	$1/6$N–$1^1/3$P	$2/3$P	$1/4$N–$3/4$P	$1/4$P	0.04 out–0.04 in
	Wagon w/P.S.	$1^1/4$P–3P	$2^1/4$P	$1/4$N–$3/4$P	$1/4$P	0.04 out–0.04 in
	4WD	$1^{15}/_{16}$P–$2^{15}/_{16}$P	$2^7/_{16}$P	$1/_{16}$P–$1^{11}/_{16}$P	$9/_{16}$P	0.08 out–0
1987	Sedan wo/P.S.	$1/4$P–$1^3/4$P	1P	$3/4$N–$3/4$P	0	0.08 out–0.08 in
	Sedan w/P.S.	$1^3/4$P–$3^1/4$P	$2^1/2$P	$3/4$N–$3/4$P	0	0.08 out–0.08 in
	Wagon wo/P.S.	$1/6$N–$1^1/3$P	$2/3$P	$3/4$N–$3/4$P	0	0.12 out–0.04 in
	Wagon w/P.S.	$1^1/4$P–3P	$2^1/4$P	$3/4$N–$3/4$P	0	0.12 out–0.04 in
	4WD	$1^{11}/_{16}$P–$3^3/_{16}$P	$2^1/4$P	$3/_{16}$N–$1^5/_{16}$P	$9/_{16}$P	0.12 out–0.04 in
1988	Sedan wo/P.S.	$1/4$P–$1^3/4$P	1P	$3/4$N–$3/4$P	0	0.08 out–0.08 in
	Sedan w/P.S.	$1^3/4$P–$3^1/4$P	$2^1/2$P	$3/4$N–$3/4$P	0	0.08 out–0.08 in
	4WD	$1^{11}/_{16}$P–$3^3/_{16}$P	$2^1/4$P	$3/_{16}$N–$1^5/_{16}$P	$9/_{16}$P	0.12 out–0.04 in
1989	Sedan wo/P.S.	$1/4$P–$1^3/4$P	1P	$3/4$N–$3/4$P	0	0.08 out–0.08 in
	Sedan w/P.S.	$1^3/4$P–$3^1/4$P	$2^1/2$P	$3/4$N–$3/4$P	0	0.08 out–0.08 in
1990	Sedan wo/P.S.	$1/4$P–$1^3/4$P	1P	$3/4$N–$3/4$P	0	0.08 out–0.08 in
	Sedan w/P.S.	$1^3/4$P–$3^1/4$P	$2^1/2$P	$3/4$N–$3/4$P	0	0.08 out–0.08 in
1991	Sedan	$1^3/4$P–$3^1/4$P	$2^1/2$P	$3/4$N–$3/4$P	0	0.08 out–0.08 in
1992	Sedan	$1^3/4$P–$3^1/4$P	$2^1/2$P	$3/4$N–$3/4$P	0	0.08 out–0.08 in
1993	Sedan	$1^3/4$P–$3^1/4$P	$2^1/2$P	$3/4$N–$3/4$P	0	0.08 out–0.08 in
1994	Sedan	$1^3/4$P–$3^1/4$P	$2^1/2$P	$3/4$N–$3/4$P	0	0.08 out–0.08 in

85998300

REAR SUSPENSION

▶ See Figures 38 and 39

Coil Springs

REMOVAL & INSTALLATION

▶ See Figures 40, 41, 42 and 43

❋❋CAUTION

The suspension on any vehicle is assembled with high grade, hardened fasteners. NEVER substitute a fastener of inferior load rating when assembling a suspension component!

This procedure applies to 4WD vehicles only. Refer to the overhaul section of the MacPherson strut procedures for coil spring removal on other models.

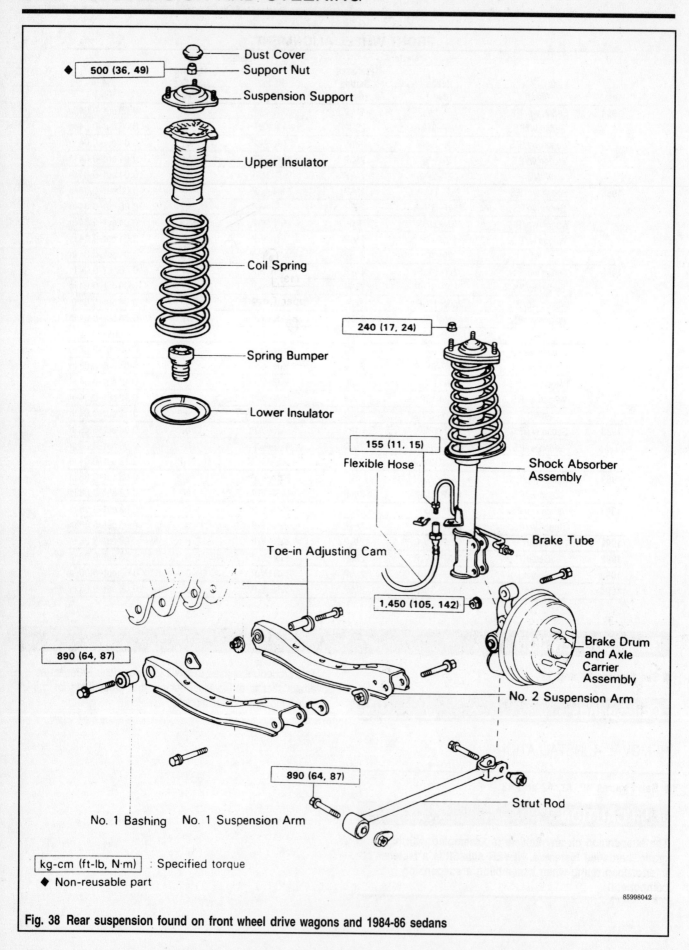

Dust Cover

◆ 500 (36, 49) — Support Nut

Suspension Support

Upper Insulator

Coil Spring

Spring Bumper

Lower Insulator

240 (17, 24)

155 (11, 15)

Flexible Hose

Shock Absorber Assembly

Toe-in Adjusting Cam

Brake Tube

1,450 (105, 142)

Brake Drum and Axle Carrier Assembly

890 (64, 87)

No. 2 Suspension Arm

Strut Rod

890 (64, 87)

No. 1 Bashing   No. 1 Suspension Arm

kg-cm (ft-lb, N·m) : Specified torque

◆ Non-reusable part

85998042

Fig. 38 Rear suspension found on front wheel drive wagons and 1984-86 sedans

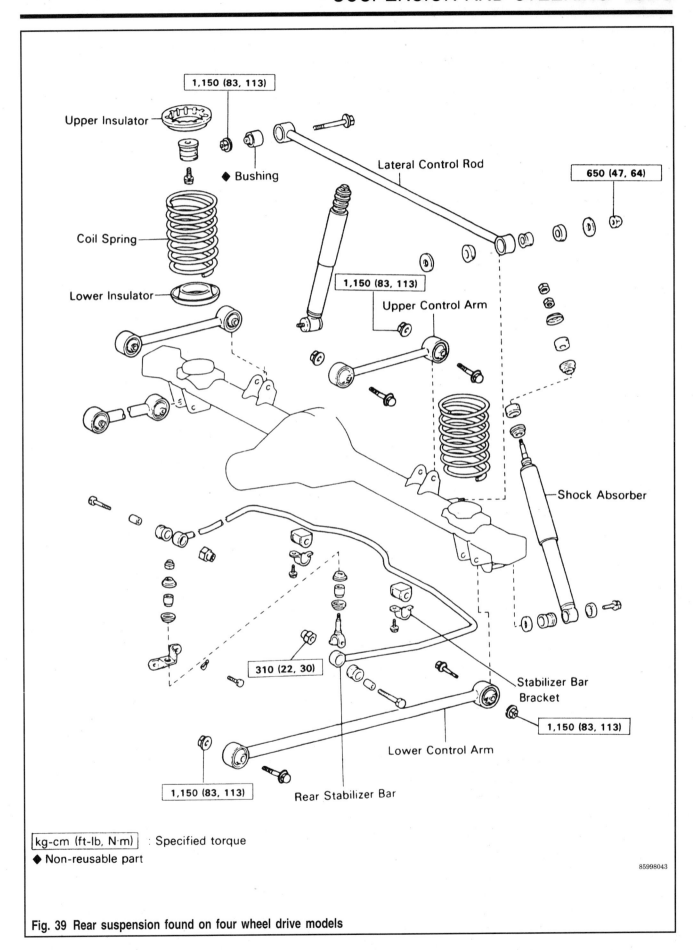

Fig. 39 Rear suspension found on four wheel drive models

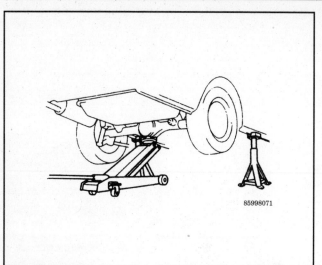

Fig. 40 Support the body with jackstands and the rear axle with a jack

1. Jack up the rear axle housing, then support the frame (not rear axle housing) with jackstands. Leave the jack in place under the rear axle housing.
2. Remove the rear wheel(s).
3. Remove the bolt securing the shock absorber to the axle housing.
4. Remove the bolts holding the sway bar brackets to the axle housing.
5. Disconnect the lateral control rod from the rear axle housing by removing the attaching bolt/nut.
6. Slowly lower the jack under the rear axle housing until the spring tension is relieved. Be careful not to stretch the parking brake cables and brake lines. Disconnect them, if necessary

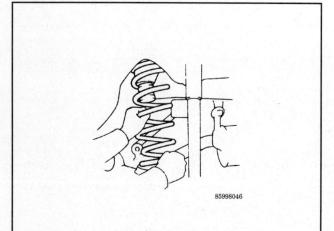

Fig. 41 When removing the coil spring, pull the spring out, then down

7. Withdraw the coil spring, complete with its insulators.
To install:
8. Inspect the coil spring and insulators for wear and cracks, or weakness; replace either or both as necessary.

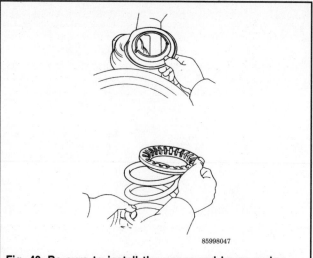

Fig. 42 Be sure to install the upper and lower spring seats

9. Install the lower insulator on the axle housing, then put the upper insulator on the coil spring.
10. Install the spring. Jack up the rear axle housing and check the position of the lower insulator and spring. If incorrect, lower the axle and reposition.

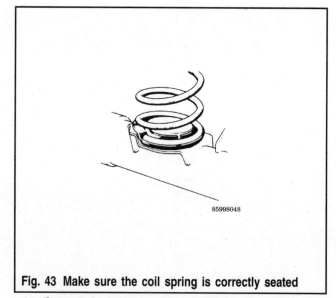

Fig. 43 Make sure the coil spring is correctly seated

11. Connect the lateral control rod. Tighten the nut/bolt until it is just snug.
12. Connect the shock absorber to the rear axle housing. Torque the bolt to 27 ft. lbs. (37 Nm).
13. Connect the sway bar to the axle housing.
14. Remove the stands, then lower the vehicle and bounce it to stabilize the suspension.
15. Torque the lateral control rod nut/bolt to 47 ft. lbs. (64 Nm).

Shock Absorbers

This procedure applies to 4WD models only. Refer to the MacPherson strut procedures on other models.

TESTING

A good way to test the shock absorbers is to intermittently apply downward pressure to the side of the car until it is moving up and down for almost its full suspension travel. Release it and observe its recovery. If the car bounces once or twice after having been released and then comes to a rest, the shocks are all right. If the car continues to bounce, the shocks will probably require replacement. If oil is leaking from the cylinder portion of the assembly, the shock absorber must be replaced.

REMOVAL & INSTALLATION

▶ See Figures 44 and 45

✷✷CAUTION

The suspension on any vehicle is assembled with high grade, hardened fasteners. NEVER substitute a fastener of inferior load rating when assembling a suspension component!

1. Raise the rear of the car and support the rear axle with jackstands.

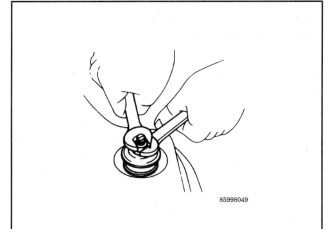

Fig. 44 Removing the shock absorber upper retaining nuts

2. Remove the shock absorber upper retaining nuts. These are usually accessed form inside the vehicle.

➡**On some models, upper retaining nut removal may require removing the rear seat.**

3. Remove the bolt securing the shock absorber to the rear axle housing.

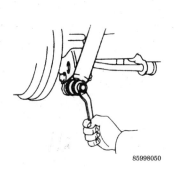

Fig. 45 Removing the bolt securing the shock to the rear axle housing

4. Remove the shock absorber.
To install:
5. Inspect the shock for wear, leaks or other signs of damage.
6. Install the shock absorber, then thread the upper retaining nut onto the shaft.
7. Hold the shaft with an adjustable wrench, then torque the nut to 18 ft. lbs. (25 Nm).
8. Connect the shock absorber to the rear axle housing, then torque the bolt to 27 ft. lbs. (37 Nm).
9. Lower the vehicle and check for proper operation.

MacPherson Struts

REMOVAL & INSTALLATION

▶ See Figures 46, 47 and 48

✷✷CAUTION

On models equipped with a Supplemental Restraint System (SRS) or ''air bag,'' work must NOT be started until at least 90 seconds have passed from the time that both the ignition switch is turned to the LOCK position and the negative cable is disconnected from the battery.

✷✷CAUTION

The suspension on any vehicle is assembled with high grade, hardened fasteners. NEVER substitute a fastener of inferior load rating when assembling a suspension component!

Wagons and 1984-86 Sedans

1. Working from inside the car, remove the trim plate covering the strut attaching nuts.
2. Raise the rear of the vehicle and support it with jackstands (do not place stands under the suspension arms). Remove the wheel.

3. Disconnect the brake line and flexible hose at the mounting bracket on the strut tube. Plug the open lines. Remove flexible hose from the strut.

4. If you will be overhauling the strut assembly, loosen the support nut from inside the car. DO NOT remove it at this time.

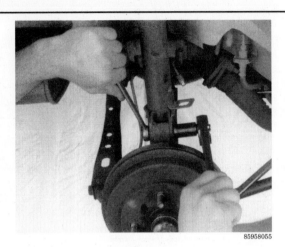

Fig. 46 On wagons and 1984-86 sedans, matchmark the position of the strut assembly to the axle carrier before removing the attaching bolts

5. Matchmark the position of the strut to the axle carrier, then remove the strut lower attaching bolts/nuts.

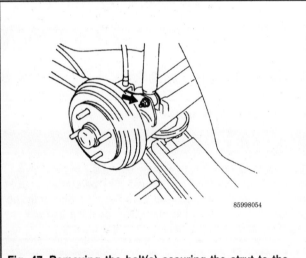

Fig. 47 Removing the bolt(s) securing the strut to the rear axle assembly

6. From inside the car, remove the nuts holding the strut assembly to the body.

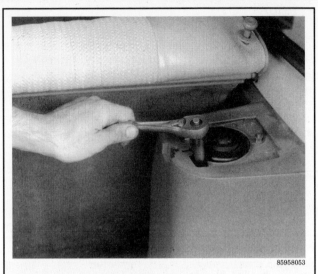

Fig. 48 Removing the upper attaching nuts

To install:

7. Position the strut assembly on the vehicle. Install the nuts attaching the strut assembly to the body, then torque the bolts to 17 ft. lbs. (24 Nm).

8. Connect the strut assembly to the axle carrier. Torque the nuts to 105 ft. lbs. (142 Nm).

9. Torque the support nut to 36 ft. lbs. (49 Nm), if applicable.

10. Connect the brake tubes and install the flexible hose to the strut assembly. Bleed the brake system.

11. Lower the vehicle and check for proper operation. Have the alignment checked by a reputable shop.

1987-94 Sedans

1. On some models, it will necessary to remove the rear seat to gain access to the strut upper attaching bolts/nuts.

2. Raise the rear of the vehicle and support the body with jackstands. Remove the wheel(s).

3. Remove the nut/bolt securing the bottom of the strut to the axle beam.

4. Remove the nuts securing the strut to the body from inside the vehicle, then remove the strut assembly.

To install:

5. Connect the strut assembly to the body. Torque the nuts to 23 ft. lbs. (31 Nm).

6. Connect the strut assembly to the axle beam. Tighten the bolt until it is just snug.

7. Install the wheel(s), then lower the vehicle. Bounce the vehicle to stabilize the suspension.

8. Torque the nut attaching the strut to the axle beam to 50 ft. lbs. (68 Nm).

OVERHAUL

▶ See Figures 49, 50, 51, 52, 53 and 54

✳✳CAUTION

This procedure requires the use of a spring compressor; it cannot be performed without one. IF YOU DO NOT HAVE ACCESS TO THIS SPECIAL TOOL, DO NOT ATTEMPT TO DISASSEMBLE THE STRUT! The coil springs are retained under considerable pressure. They exert enough force to cause serious personal injury and component damage. Exercise extreme caution when disassembling the strut.

✳✳CAUTION

The suspension on any vehicle is assembled with high grade, hardened fasteners. NEVER substitute a fastener of inferior load rating when assembling a suspension component!

1. Remove the strut from the vehicle. Refer to the appropriate procedure in this section.

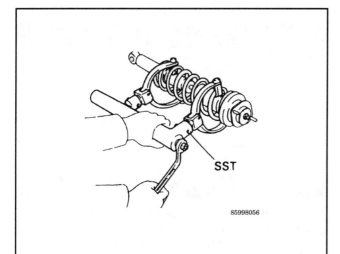

Fig. 49 Compress the coil spring before removing the support nut

2. Compress the coil spring. Use SST 09727-22032 on 1984-90 models and SST 09727-30020 on 1991-94 models.
3. Hold the upper support, then remove the nut on the end of the shock piston rod.

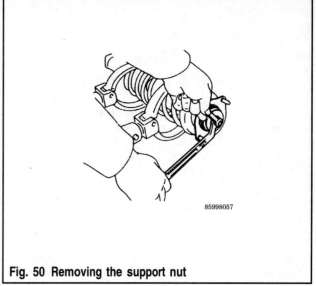

Fig. 50 Removing the support nut

4. Remove the support, coil spring, insulator and bumper. Make a note as to their order.
Check the shock absorber by moving the piston shaft through its full range of travel. It should move smoothly and evenly throughout its entire travel without any trace of binding or notching. Inspect the spring for any sign of deterioration or cracking. The waterproof coating on the coils should be intact to prevent rusting.

➡Do not turn the piston rod within the cylinder if the piston rod is fully extended. Never reuse the support nut.

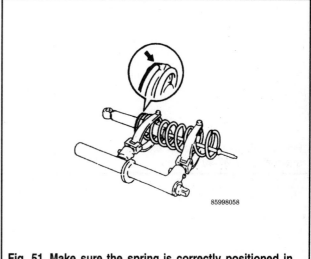

Fig. 51 Make sure the spring is correctly positioned in its seat

5. Assemble all components in order onto the the strut assembly. Make sure the spring end aligns with the hollow in the lower seat.

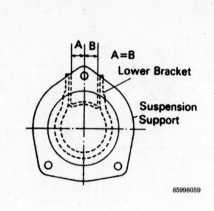

Fig. 52 Aligning the lower bracket with the suspension support on wagons and 1984-86 sedans

6. Align the suspension support with the strut lower bracket. This assures the spring will be properly seated top and bottom.

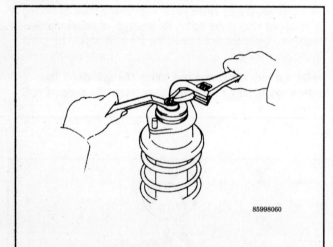

Fig. 53 Aligning the lower bracket with the suspension support on 1987-90 sedans

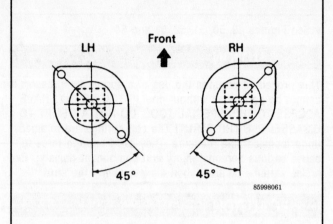

Fig. 54 Aligning the lower bracket with the suspension support on 1991-94 sedans

7. Thread a new support nut onto the piston rod, then tighten it to 40 ft. lbs. (54 Nm) on 1987-94 Sedans. Do not torque the support nut on wagons and 1984-86 sedans at this time.

8. Install the strut on the vehicle.

Control Arms

Control arms are found on wagons and 1984-86 sedans.

REMOVAL & INSTALLATION

Front Wheel Drive Models
▶ See Figures 55, 56 and 57

❊❊CAUTION

The suspension on any vehicle is assembled with high grade, hardened fasteners. NEVER substitute a fastener of inferior load rating when assembling a suspension component!

These vehicles use two control arms on each rear wheel. To avoid confusion, the arm closest to the front of the car will be referred to as the front arm. Refer to the exploded view of the suspension components.

FRONT ARM

1. Raise and safely support the vehicle, then remove the wheel.

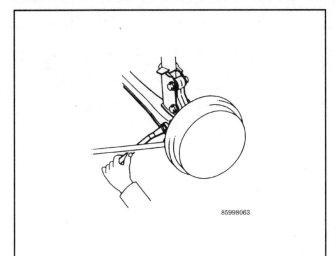

Fig. 55 Removing the bolt securing the front control arm to the axle carrier

2. Remove the nut/bolt securing the arm to the axle carrier.

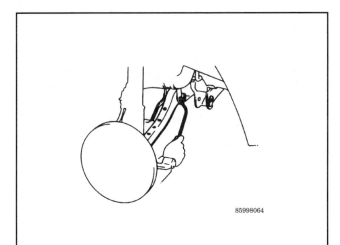

Fig. 56 Removing the bolt securing the front control arm to the body

3. Remove the nut/bolt holding the arm to the body.
4. Remove the arm from the vehicle.
5. If the arm shows any signs of bending or cracking, it must be replaced. Any attempt to straighten a bent arm will damage it.

To install:

6. Place the arm in position, install the arm-to-body nut/bolt. Tighten the nut until it is just snug. Make sure the lip of the nut is resting on the flange of the bracket, not over it.

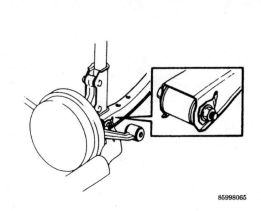

Fig. 57 Make sure the lip of the nut is resting correctly when installing the front arm

7. Connect the arm to the axle carrier, tighten the nut until it is just snug.
8. Install the wheel.
9. Lower the car to the ground. Bounce the car rear and front several times to position the suspension.
10. Torque the bolts, with the vehicle's weight on the suspension, to 64 ft. lbs. (87 Nm).
11. Have a reputable shop check rear wheel alignment.

REAR ARM

▶ See Figures 58, 59, 60 and 61

1. Raise and safely support the vehicle, then remove the wheel.

Fig. 58 Matchmark the position of the cam bolt before removing it

2. Observe and matchmark the position of the adjusting cam at the arm-to-body mounting bolt.

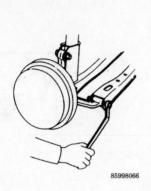

85998066

Fig. 59 Removing the bolt securing the rear control arm to the axle carrier

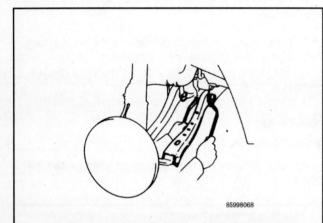

85998068

Fig. 60 When removing the bolt attaching the rear arm to the body, be sure to loosen the bolt, not the cam

3. Remove the nut/bolt holding the arm to the axle carrier.

4. Remove the cam and bolt holding the arm to the body. Loosen the bolt, do not turn the cam.

5. Remove the arm.

6. If the arm shows any signs of bending or cracking, it must be replaced. Any attempt to straighten a bent arm will damage it.

To install:

7. Place the arm in position. Install the cam and body bolt, then align the marks made earlier. Tighten the bolt until it is just snug.

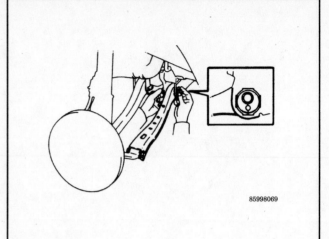

85998069

Fig. 61 Align the matchmarks on the cam when installing the rear arm

8. Install the arm to the axle carrier, then tighten the bolt until it is just snug. Make sure the lip of the nut is resting on the flange of the bracket, not over it.

9. Install the wheel.

10. Lower the car to the ground. Bounce the car rear and front several times to position the suspension.

11. Torque the bolts, with the vehicle's weight on the suspension, to 64 ft. lbs. (87 Nm). Make sure the marks on the cam are still properly aligned.

12. Have a reputable shop check rear wheel alignment.

Four Wheel Drive Models

▶ **See Figures 62 and 63**

UPPER CONTROL ARM

1. Raise the rear of the vehicle and support the body with jackstands. Support the rear axle housing with a jack.

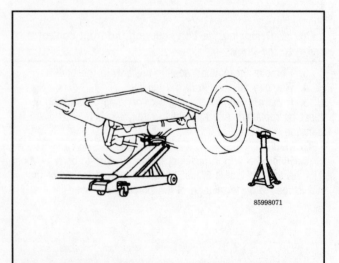

85998071

Fig. 62 Support the body with jackstands, then place a jack under the rear axle

2. Remove the bolt holding the upper control arm to the body.

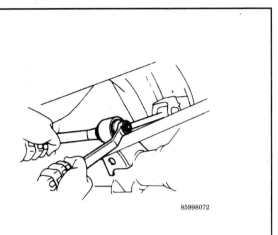

Fig. 63 Removing the bolt securing the upper control arm to the axle housing; lower control arm similar

3. Remove the bolt holding the upper control arm to the axle housing, then remove the upper control arm.

To install:

4. Position the upper control arm, then install the arm-to-body and arm-to-axle housing bolts. Tighten the nut until just snug.

5. Lower the vehicle and bounce it a few times to stabilize the suspension.

6. Raise and support the vehicle once again. Raise the rear axle housing until the body is just free from the jackstands.

7. Tighten the upper arm-to-body bolt to 83 ft. lbs. (113 Nm). Do the same for the upper arm-to-axle housing bolt.

LOWER CONTROL ARM

▶ See Figure 64

1. Raise the rear of the vehicle and support the body with jackstands. Support the rear axle housing with a jack.

2. Remove the bolt holding the lower control arm to the body.

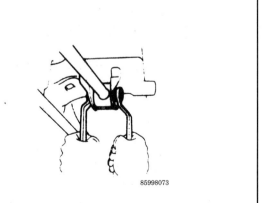

Fig. 64 Removing the bolt securing the lower control arm to the body; upper control arm similar

3. Remove the bolt holding the lower control arm to the rear axle housing, then remove the lower control arm.

To install:

4. Position the lower control arm, then install the arm-to-body and arm-to-axle housing bolts. Tighten the nuts until they are just snug.

5. Lower the vehicle and bounce it a few times to stabilize the suspension.

6. Raise and support the vehicle once again. Raise the rear axle housing until the body is just free from the jackstands.

7. Tighten the lower arm-to-body bolt to 83 ft. lbs. (113 Nm). Do the same for the lower arm-to-axle housing bolt.

Lateral Control Rod

The lateral control rod can be found on 4WD models and 1987-94 sedans.

REMOVAL & INSTALLATION

▶ See Figures 65 and 66

✳✳CAUTION

On models equipped with a Supplemental Restraint System (SRS) or "air bag," work must NOT be started until at least 90 seconds have passed from the time that both the ignition switch is turned to the LOCK position and the negative cable is disconnected from the battery.

✳✳CAUTION

The suspension on any vehicle is assembled with high grade, hardened fasteners. NEVER substitute a fastener of inferior load rating when assembling a suspension component!

1. Disconnect the negative battery cable.

2. Raise the rear of the vehicle, then support the axle with jackstands.

3. Remove the nut/bolt securing the rod to the axle, then disconnect the lateral rod from the rear axle.

4. Remove the nut/bolt securing the rod to the body, then disconnect the lateral rod from the body. Remove the rod.

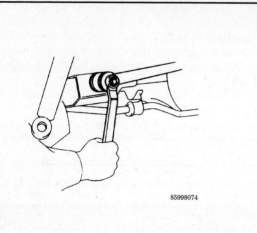

Fig. 65 Removing the nut securing the lateral control rod to the axle housing

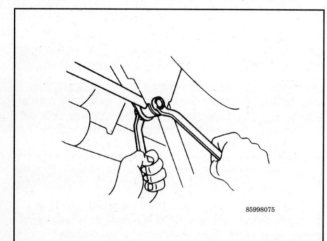

Fig. 66 Removing the nut securing the lateral control rod to the body

To install:

5. Install the rod to the body with the nut, then finger-tighten it. Make sure the bushing, washer and spacer are correctly installed.

6. Position the arm on the axle with the nut, then finger-tighten it.

7. Lower the vehicle and bounce it a few times to stabilize the suspension.

8. Raise and support the rear of the vehicle again, then tighten the rod-to-body nut to 83 ft. lbs. (113 Nm) and the rod-to-axle nut to 47 ft. lbs. (64 Nm).

Strut Rod

The strut rod can be found on FWD wagons and 1984-86 sedans.

REMOVAL & INSTALLATION

▶ See Figures 67, 68, 69 and 70

❊❊CAUTION

The suspension on any vehicle is assembled with high grade, hardened fasteners. NEVER substitute a fastener of inferior load rating when assembling a suspension component!

1. Raise the rear of the vehicle and support the body with stands.

2. Remove the bolt/nut securing the rod to the axle carrier.

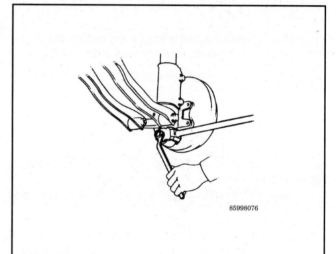

Fig. 67 Removing the nut securing the strut rod to the axle carrier

3. Remove the bolt/nut securing the rod to the body, then remove the rod.

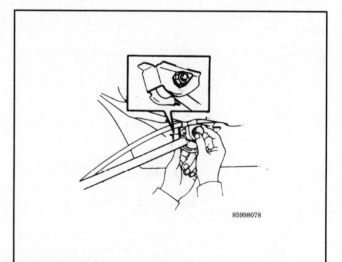

Fig. 68 Removing the nut securing the strut rod to the body

To install:

4. Position the strut rod, then install the bolts. Tighten them until they are just snug. Make sure that the lip of the nut is resting on the flange of the bracket. When connecting the strut

rod to the axle carrier, make sure that the lip of the nut is aligned with the groove in the bracket.

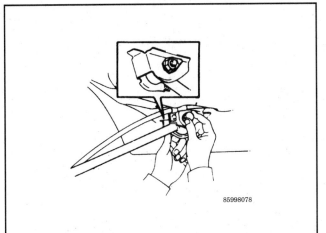

Fig. 69 When installing the strut rod to the body, be sure the lip of the nut is resting on the flange of the bracket

5. Lower the vehicle, then bounce it to stabilize the suspension. Torque the bolts to 64 ft. lbs. (87 Nm).

6. Have a reputable shop check the rear wheel alignment.

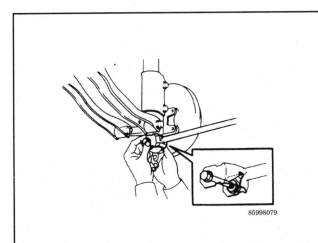

Fig. 70 Proper installation of the strut rod to the axle carrier

Sway Bar

The sway bar can be found on 4WD models.

REMOVAL & INSTALLATION

▶ See Figures 71 and 72

✳✳CAUTION

The suspension on any vehicle is assembled with high grade, hardened fasteners. NEVER substitute a fastener of inferior load rating when assembling a suspension component!

1. Remove the sway bar bushing brackets.
2. Remove the bolts/nuts holding both ends of the sway bar, then remove the bar.
   To install:
3. Assemble the ends of the bar to the body links. Torque to 22 ft. lbs. (30 Nm).
4. Install the sway bar bushing brackets. Torque to 27 ft. lbs. (37 Nm).

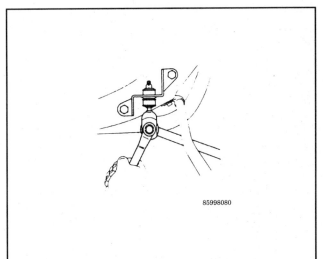

Fig. 71 Removing the bolt securing the sway bar to the link

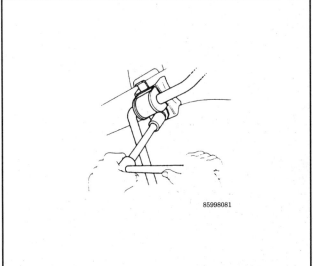

Fig. 72 Removing the sway bar bushing brackets

Axle Beam

This procedure applies to 1987-94 models.

REMOVAL & INSTALLATION

▶ **See Figures 73 and 74**

❊❊CAUTION

On models equipped with a Supplemental Restraint System (SRS) or "air bag," work must NOT be started until at least 90 seconds have passed from the time that both the ignition switch is turned to the LOCK position and the negative cable is disconnected from the battery.

❊❊CAUTION

The suspension on any vehicle is assembled with high grade, hardened fasteners. NEVER substitute a fastener of inferior load rating when assembling a suspension component!

1. Disconnect the negative battery cable.
2. Raise the rear of the vehicle, then support the body with jackstands. Remove the wheels.
3. Disconnect and plug the brake lines from the wheel cylinders.
4. Disengage the attaching clips, then remove the brake lines/hoses from the axle beam.
5. Remove the brake shoes, then disengage the parking brake cable from the backing plate. Refer to the appropriate procedures in this manual.
6. Remove the brake backing plate, if necessary.
7. Remove the lateral control rod.
8. Make sure all hoses, cables or lines are disconnected from the axle beam.
9. Support the axle beam with a jack, then remove the nut/bolts attaching the strut assemblies to the axle beam.
10. Remove the nuts/bolts securing the axle beam assembly to the body, then carefully lower and remove the axle beam.

To install:

11. Position the axle beam in place, then install the attaching bolts/nuts. Tighten the nuts until just snug.
12. Connect the strut assemblies to the axle beam. Tighten the nuts until just snug.
13. Install the lateral control rod. Tighten the nuts until just snug.
14. Install the rear brake components, then connect the lines.
15. Install the wheels, then lower the vehicle and bounce it to stabilize the suspension.
16. Torque the axle beam-to-body bolts to 105 ft. lbs. (142 Nm). Refer to the appropriate procedures for the lateral control rod and strut assembly torque specifications.
17. Bleed the brake system.

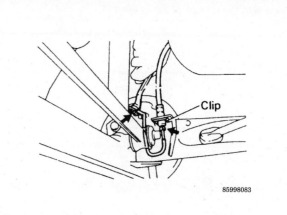

Fig. 74 Make sure all lines, hoses and cables are disconnected from the axle beam before removal

Rear Wheel Bearings

This procedure applies to front wheel drive models. For rear axle bearing procedures on four wheel drive models, please refer to Section 7.

REMOVAL & INSTALLATION

❊❊CAUTION

The suspension on any vehicle is assembled with high grade, hardened fasteners. NEVER substitute a fastener of inferior load rating when assembling a suspension component!

Sedans

▶ **See Figures 75, 76, 77, 78, 79, 80, 81, 82, 83, 84 and 85**

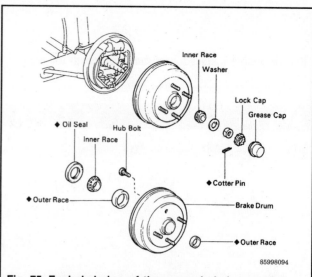

Fig. 75 Exploded view of the rear axle hub on sedans

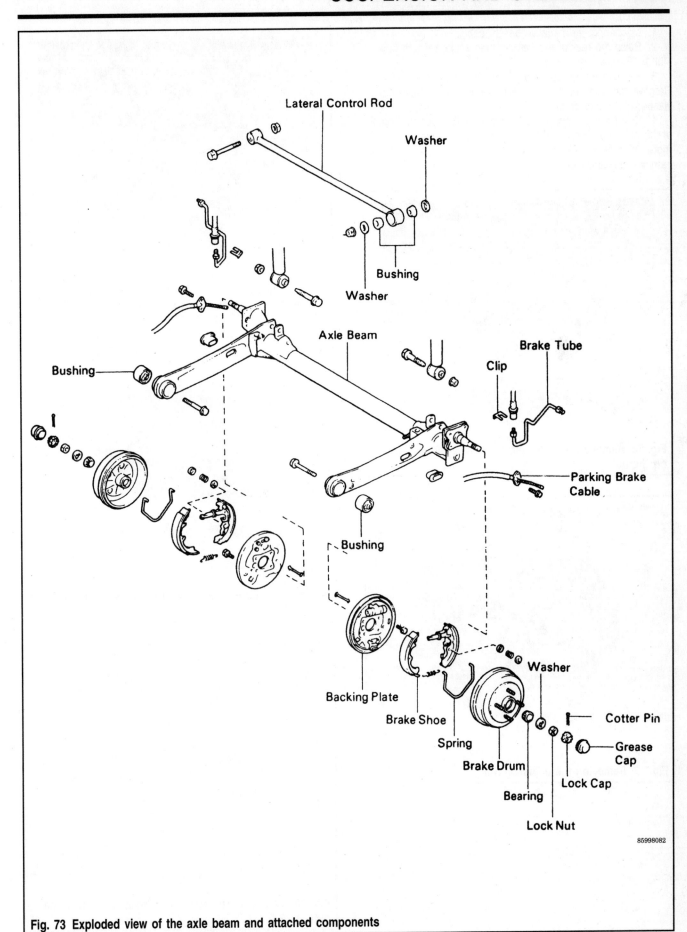

Fig. 73 Exploded view of the axle beam and attached components

1. Disconnect the negative battery cable.

2. Raise the rear of the vehicle, then support it with jackstands. Remove the wheel.

3. Remove the grease cap, cotter pin, lock cap and nut. Remove the axle hub together with the outer bearing, thrust washer and brake drum.

4. Using a small prybar, pry out the oil seal from the back of the hub, then remove the inner bearing. Remove the races (note depth for correct installation) by driving them out with a hammer and brass drift.

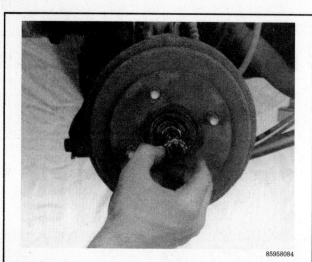

Fig. 76 Remove the cotter pin, then slide the lock cap off the nut

Fig. 77 Removing the adjusting nut

Fig. 78 Once the nut has been removed, slide the washer and the bearing out from the hub

Fig. 79 A small prybar can be used to remove the oil seal

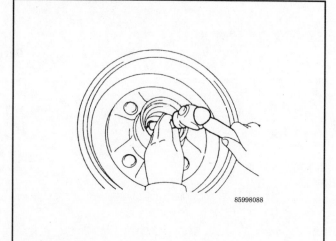

Fig. 80 Using a brass drift and hammer to remove the outer races

To install:

5. Carefully press the new races into the hub using a press and the appropriate SST. On 1984-86 sedans, use SST 09608-16011 and 09608-20012 or their equivalent. On 1991-94 sedans, use SST 09608-30012 and 09550-10012 or their equivalent.

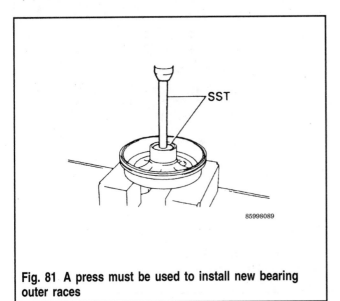

Fig. 81 A press must be used to install new bearing outer races

6. Place some wheel bearing grease onto the palm of your hand, then take one bearing at a time and work the grease into it until it begins to ooze out the other side. Coat the inside of the axle hub and bearing cap with the same grease.

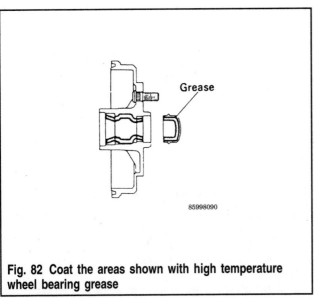

Fig. 82 Coat the areas shown with high temperature wheel bearing grease

7. Install the inner bearing, then install a new oil seal using a seal driver.

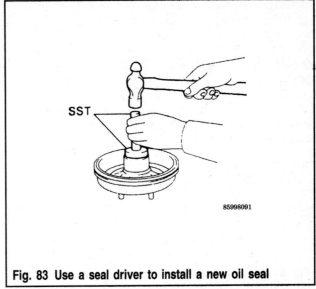

Fig. 83 Use a seal driver to install a new oil seal

8. Place the axle hub and outer bearing on the axle shaft. Fill the space between the outer bearing and washer with wheel bearing grease, then install the washer and nut.

9. Tighten the nut to 22 ft. lbs. (29 Nm). Seat the bearing by turning the hub several times. Loosen the nut until it can be turned by hand, then confirm that there is no brake drag.

10. Measure and make note of the rotation frictional force of the oil seal using spring scale.

11. Tighten the adjusting nut until the correct preload is obtained. On 1984-90 sedans, preload should equal 0.9-2.2 lbs. (3.9-9.8 N) in addition to rotation frictional force of the oil seal. On 1991-94 sedans, preload should equal 0-2.6 lbs. (0-11.8 N) in addition to the rotation frictional force of the oil seal.

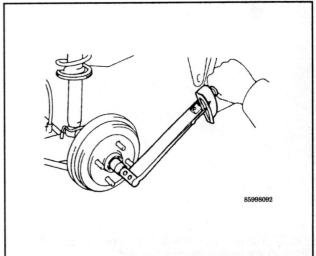

Fig. 84 Torque the adjusting nut while turning the drum, then back out the nut until loosened

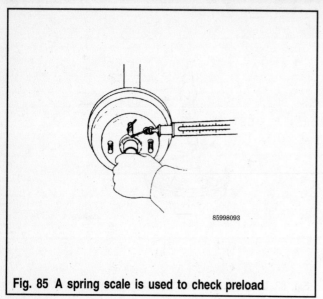

Fig. 85 A spring scale is used to check preload

12. Insure that the hub rotates smoothly. Use a new cotter pin when installing the lock cap.

13. Install all necessary components as required.

Wagons

▶ **See Figures 86, 87, 88, 89, 90, 91, 92 and 93**

1. Raise and safely support the vehicle. Remove the wheel.
2. Remove the brake drum.
3. Remove the bolts holding the hub to the axle carrier, then remove the hub. These bolts can be accessed through the hole in the hub flange.

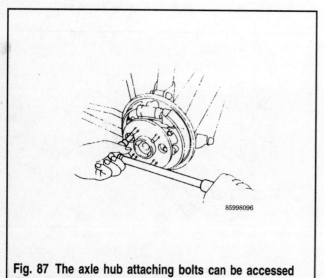

Fig. 87 The axle hub attaching bolts can be accessed through the hole in the hub flange

4. Clamp the hub in a vise. Do not overtighten and use protective jaws to prevent damage to the hub flange.

5. Using a hammer and chisel. remove the stake on the nut. Remove the nut.

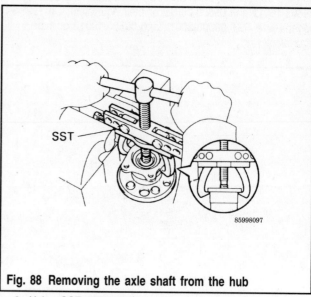

Fig. 88 Removing the axle shaft from the hub

6. Using SST 09950-20016 or its equivalent, separate the axle shaft and hub. Remove the inside bearing inner race.

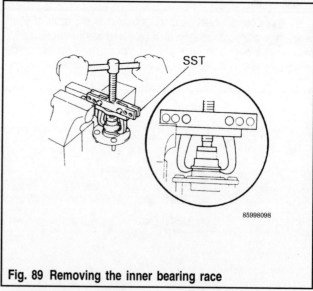

Fig. 89 Removing the inner bearing race

7. Using the same SST, pull off the outside bearing inner race from the axle shaft. Remove the oil seal.

8. Install the inner race of the removed bearing. Using SST 09636-20010 or its equivalent, press out the bearing.

To install:

9. Apply multi-purpose grease around the bearing outer race.

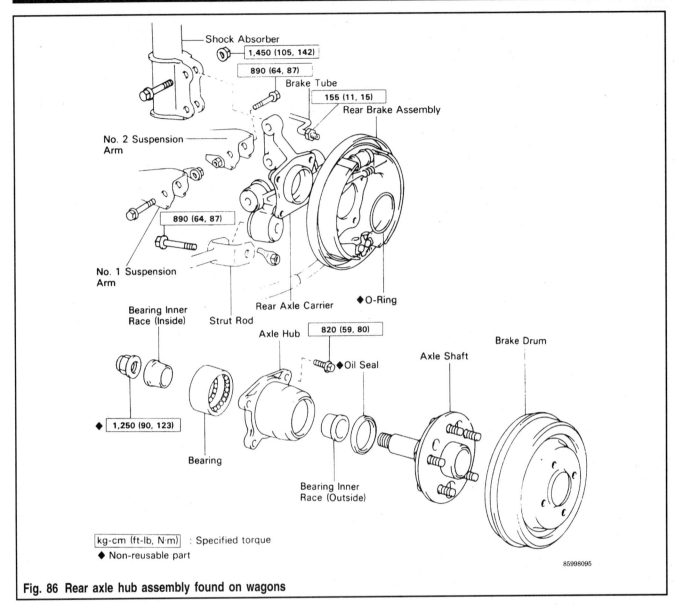

kg-cm (ft-lb, N·m) : Specified torque
◆ Non-reusable part

85998095

Fig. 86 Rear axle hub assembly found on wagons

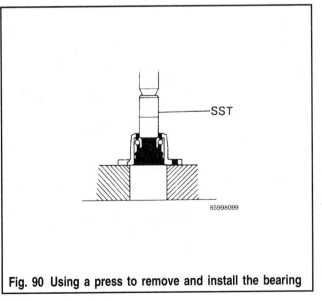

85998099

Fig. 90 Using a press to remove and install the bearing

10. Using SST 09316-60010 or its equivalent, press in a new bearing.

11. Using a seal driver, install a new oil seal. Apply multi-purpose grease to the oil seal lip.

12. Install the inner race of both bearings. Using SST 09636-20010 or its equivalent, press the assembly onto the axle shaft.

13. Thread a new nut onto the shaft, then torque it to 90 ft. lbs. (123 Nm). Stake the nut with a hammer and chisel.

14. Install a new O-ring onto the hub, then install the assembly to the axle carrier. Torque the bolts to 59 ft. lbs. (80 Nm).

15. Install the brake drum and rear wheel. Check for proper operation.

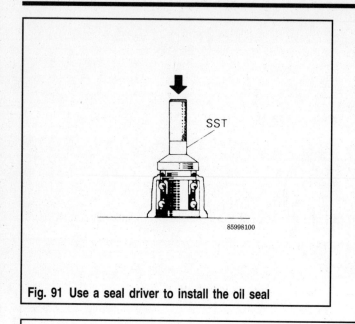

85998100

Fig. 91 Use a seal driver to install the oil seal

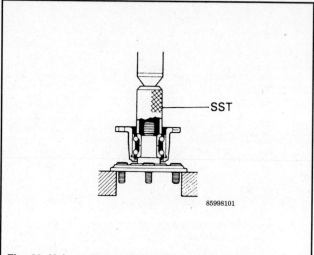

85998101

Fig. 92 Using a press to install the hub to the axle shaft

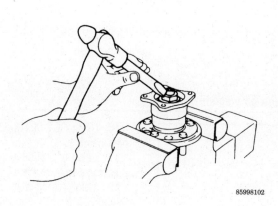

85998102

Fig. 93 Stake the nut using a hammer and chisel

REAR WHEEL ALIGNMENT

| Year | Model | Caster | | Camber | | Toe (in.) |
		Range (deg.)	Preferred Setting (deg.)	Range (deg.)	Preferred Setting (deg.)	
1984	Sedan	—	—	$3/16$N–$13/16$P	$5/16$P	0
1985	Sedan	—	—	$9/16$N–$7/16$P	$1/16$P	0
1986	Sedan	—	—	$9/16$N–$7/16$P	$1/16$P	0

85998301

STEERING

Steering Wheel

REMOVAL & INSTALLATION

▶ See Figures 94, 95, 96 and 97

✳✳CAUTION

On models equipped with a Supplemental Restraint System (SRS) or "air bag," work must NOT be started until at least 90 seconds have passed from the time that both the ignition switch is turned to the LOCK position and the negative cable is disconnected from the battery.

✳✳CAUTION

The steering system on any vehicle is assembled with high grade, hardened fasteners. NEVER substitute a fastener of inferior load rating when assembling a suspension component!

➡Do not attempt to remove or install the steering wheel by hammering on it. Damage to the energy-absorbing steering column could result.

Without Air Bag

1. Disconnect the negative battery cable.
2. Loosen the horn pad retaining screws, if applicable, then pull the pad from the steering wheel.

Fig. 94 Remove the horn pad retaining screw, if applicable, then remove the pad

3. Remove the steering wheel hub retaining nut and washer.

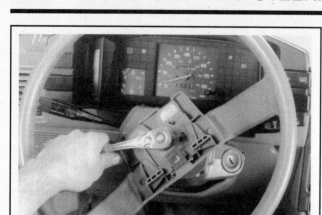

Fig. 95 Removing the steering wheel retaining nut

4. Paint matchmarks on the hub and shaft to aid in correct installation.

Fig. 96 Matchmark the position of the steering wheel to aid in installation

5. Use SST 09609-20011 or its equivalent, to remove the steering wheel.

Fig. 97 A steering wheel puller must be used to remove the steering wheel

6. Installation is performed in the reverse order of removal. Tighten the steering wheel retaining nut to 25 ft. lbs. (34 Nm). This will draw the steering wheel onto the shaft.

With Air Bag

▶ **See Figures 98 and 99**

✳✳WARNING

Be sure the air bag system is disarmed before attempting any service procedures. Failure to do so may result in serious personal injury and component damage.

1. Disconnect the negative battery cable.
2. Make sure the wheels are in the straight ahead position.
3. Remove the two small covers on the back of the steering wheel to access the steering wheel pad retaining screws.
4. Using a T30 Torx® bit, loosen the screws until the collar on the screw is bottomed against the screw case.
5. Pull the steering wheel pad out of the steering wheel, then unplug the SRS connector. Take care not to pull on the air bag wire harness.

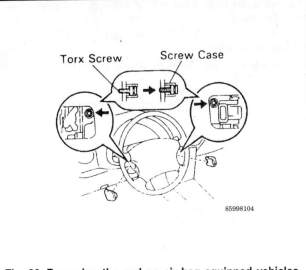

Fig. 98 Removing the pad on air bag equipped vehicles

➡When storing the pad, keep the finished side (facing the driver) of the pad facing upwards. Carry the pad with the finished side facing away from you. Never attempt to disassemble the pad.

6. Remove the steering wheel hub retaining nut and washer.
7. Paint matchmarks on the hub and shaft to aid in correct installation.
8. Use SST 09609-20011 or its equivalent, to remove the steering wheel.

To install:
9. Align the matchmarks, then install the steering wheel onto the shaft. Tighten the retaining nut to 26 ft. lbs. (35 Nm). This will draw the steering wheel onto the shaft.

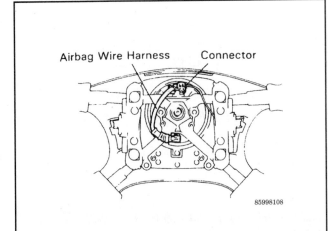

Fig. 99 Make sure the harness is not pinched on air bag equipped vehicles

10. Confirm that the collar on the screw is bottomed against the screw case. Engage the SRS connector, then install the pad on the wheel.

11. Tighten the screws to 78 inch lbs. (8.8 Nm). Note the following:
   a. Make sure that the pad retaining screws are tightened to their specified torque.
   b. Replace the air bag if the pad has been dropped, or if there are cracks, dents or other defects in the pad (front and back) or connector.
   c. When installing the pad, make sure that the wiring will not interfere with other components and are not pinched between other parts.
12. Install the covers on the back of the steering wheel.
13. Connect the negative battery cable, then check for proper air bag warning lamp operation.

Steering Column

REMOVAL & INSTALLATION

▶ See Figure 100

✳✳CAUTION

On models equipped with a Supplemental Restraint System (SRS) or "air bag," work must NOT be started until at least 90 seconds have passed from the time that both the ignition switch is turned to the LOCK position and the negative cable is disconnected from the battery.

✳✳CAUTION

The steering system on any vehicle is assembled with high grade, hardened fasteners. NEVER substitute a fastener of inferior load rating when assembling a suspension component!

1. Disconnect the negative battery cable.
2. Remove the left side under dash panel and air duct, as necessary. Unplug the combination switch and all other electrical connections attached to the steering column.
3. Remove the hole cover screws to gain access to the steering column yoke. Remove the bolt securing the yoke to the steering column shaft.
4. Remove the nuts/bolts securing the lower column mounting brackets, then remove the nuts/bolts securing the upper column mounting bracket to the instrument panel.
5. Carefully pull the column out to disengage it from the yoke, then remove the column from the car.

To install:
6. Place the column assembly into position, then install the upper and lower bracket nuts/bolts finger-tight. Make sure the column shaft is engaged in the yoke.
7. Torque the upper and lower mounting nuts/bolts to 19 ft. lbs. (25 Nm).
8. Torque the steering column-to-yoke bolt to 26 ft. lbs. (35 Nm) on 1984-90 models and 21 ft. lbs. (28 Nm) on 1991-94 models.
9. Install the hole cover.
10. Engage the combination switch and all other electrical connections.
11. Install air duct and trim panel, as necessary.

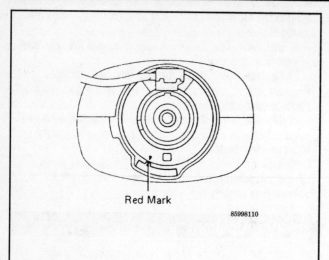

Fig. 100 The spiral cable must be centered on air bag equipped vehicles

12. Center the spiral cable on vehicles equipped with air bags as follows:

a. Check the the front wheels are in the straight ahead position.

b. Remove the steering wheel and combination switch.

c. Turn the spiral cable counter-clockwise by hand until it becomes harder to turn the cable.

d. Turn the spiral cable clockwise about three turns and align the red mark. The spiral cable will rotate about three turns to either left or right of center.

➡The spiral cable must be centered to prevent air bag component damage and accidental deployment.

13. On vehicles equipped with an air bag, check for proper air bag warning lamp operation.

Tie Rod Ends

REMOVAL & INSTALLATION

✳✳CAUTION

On models equipped with a Supplemental Restraint System (SRS) or "air bag," work must NOT be started until at least 90 seconds have passed from the time that both the ignition switch is turned to the LOCK position and the negative cable is disconnected from the battery.

✳✳CAUTION

The steering system on any vehicle is assembled with high grade, hardened fasteners. NEVER substitute a fastener of inferior load rating when assembling a suspension component!

Outer Tie Rod

▶ **See Figures 101 and 102**

1. Disconnect the negative battery cable.

2. Raise the front of the vehicle and support it safely. Remove the wheel.

3. Remove the cotter pin and nut securing the tie rod to the steering knuckle.

4. Using a tie rod separator, disengage the tie rod from the steering knuckle.

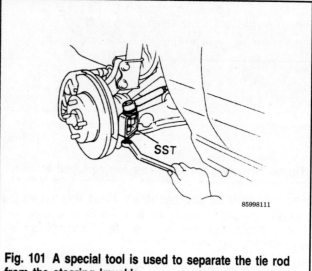

Fig. 101 A special tool is used to separate the tie rod from the steering knuckle

➡Use only the correct tool to separate the tie rod. Replace the joint if the rubber boot is cracked or ripped.

5. Matchmark the position of the tie rod on the steering rack.

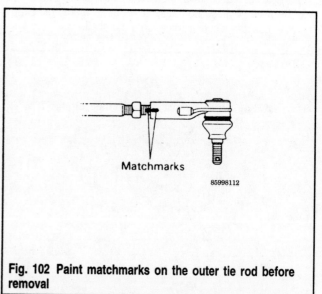

Fig. 102 Paint matchmarks on the outer tie rod before removal

6. Loosen the lock-nut or clamp bolt, then remove the tie rod from the steering rack (the tie rod is threaded onto the shaft).

To install:

7. Thread the tie rod onto the rack until the matchmarks made earlier align.

8. Tighten the lock-nuts to 41 ft. lbs. (56 Nm) on 1984-90 models and 35 ft. lbs. (47 Nm) on 1991-94 models.

9. Connect the tie rod end to the steering knuckle. Tighten the nut to 36 ft. lbs. (49 Nm), then install a new cotter pin.

10. Install the wheel, then lower the vehicle to the ground. Have the alignment checked at a reputable repair facility.

Inner Tie Rod

▶ **See Figures 103 and 104**

1. Disconnect the negative battery cable.

2. Remove the rack and pinion assembly from the vehicle. Refer to the appropriate procedure in this section.

3. If necessary, remove the outer tie rod end.

4. Secure the rack assembly in a vise. Do not overtighten and use protective jaws to prevent damaging the unit.

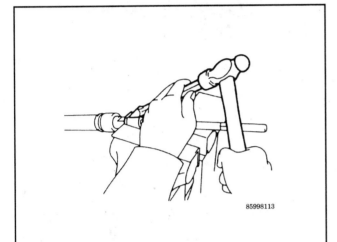

85998113

Fig. 103 Use a hammer and chisel to unstake the claw washer

5. Using a hammer and chisel, unstake the claw washer.

6. While holding the rack shaft flats with an adjustable wrench, use SST 09612-10092 or its equivalent, on wagons and 1984-86 sedans and SST 09617-10020 or its equivalent on 1987-94 sedans to remove the inner tie rod end.

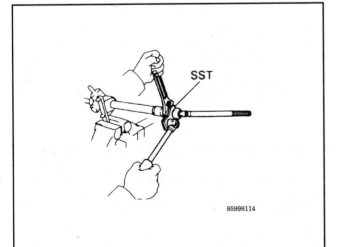

SST

85998114

Fig. 104 A special tool is used to remove and install the inner tie rods

To install:

7. Install a new claw washer. Align the groove in the shaft with the claw on the washer, then thread the inner tie rod onto the shaft.

8. While holding the rack shaft flats with an adjustable wrench, use SST 09612-10092 or its equivalent, on wagons and 1984-86 sedans and SST 09617-10020 or its equivalent on 1987-94 sedans to install the inner tie rod end. Torque to 61 ft. lbs. (83 Nm) on wagons and 1984-86 sedans and 38 ft. lbs. (51 Nm) on 1987-94 sedans.

9. Stake the claw washer over the flats on the inner tie rod, not the rack shaft.

10. Install the outer tie rod end, if necessary.

11. Install the rack assembly on the vehicle.

12. Bleed the system on vehicles equipped with power steering.

13. Check for proper operation. Have a reputable shop check the wheel alignment.

Rack and Pinion Manual Steering Gear

ADJUSTMENTS

Adjustments to the manual steering gear/rack and pinion assembly are not necessary during normal service.

REMOVAL & INSTALLATION

▶ **See Figures 105, 106 and 107**

✳✳CAUTION

On models equipped with a Supplemental Restraint System (SRS) or "air bag," work must NOT be started until at least 90 seconds have passed from the time that both the ignition switch is turned to the LOCK position and the negative cable is disconnected from the battery.

✳✳CAUTION

The steering system on any vehicle is assembled with high grade, hardened fasteners. NEVER substitute a fastener of inferior load rating when assembling a suspension component!

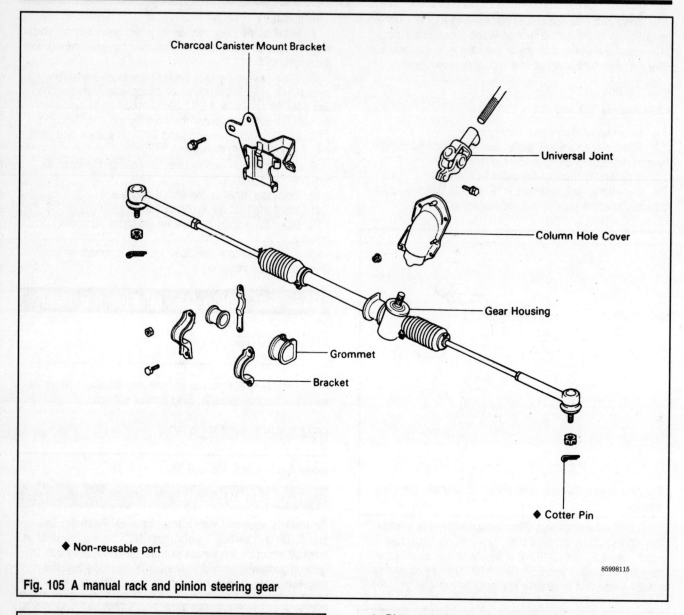

Charcoal Canister Mount Bracket

Universal Joint

Column Hole Cover

Gear Housing

Grommet

Bracket

Cotter Pin

◆ Non-reusable part

85998115

Fig. 105 A manual rack and pinion steering gear

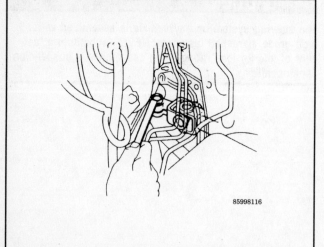

85998116

Fig. 106 Removing the bolt securing the yoke to the steering gear

1. Disconnect the negative battery cable.
2. Remove the hole cover screws to gain access to the steering column/steering gear yoke. Remove the bolt securing the yoke to the steering gear assembly.

➡**On vehicles equipped with air bags, secure the steering wheel so that it will not turn.**

3. Elevate and safely support the vehicle, then remove both front wheels.
4. Remove the cotter pins from both tie rod ends, then remove the nuts.
5. Using a tie rod separator, disengage the tie rod ends from the steering knuckles.
6. Remove the nuts/bolts attaching the steering rack to the body.

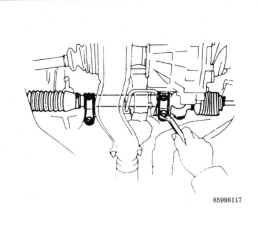

Fig. 107 Removing the brackets securing the steering gear

7. Lower the rack assembly or, if possible, slide the assembly out through the wheel well opening. Remove any components necessary to gain additional working space.

To install:

8. Install the rack assembly. Secure it with the retaining bolts/nuts, then tighten them to 43 ft. lbs. (59 Nm).

9. Torque the steering gear-to-yoke bolt to 26 ft. lbs. (35 Nm) on 1984-90 models and 21 ft. lbs. (28 Nm) on 1991-94 models.

10. Connect the tie rod ends to each steering knuckle. Tighten the nuts to 36 ft. lbs. (49 Nm), then install new cotter pins.

11. Install the front wheels.

12. Lower the car to the ground.

➡On vehicles equipped with air bags, the spiral cable in the steering column must be centered if the steering wheel has been turned. Refer to the steering column procedure in this section.

13. Install the hole cover. Have a reputable shop check the front end alignment.

Rack and Pinion Power Steering Gear

ADJUSTMENTS

Adjustments to the power steering gear/rack and pinion assembly are not necessary during normal service.

REMOVAL & INSTALLATION

▶ See Figures 108, 109, 110, 111 and 112

> ✳✳**CAUTION**
>
> On models equipped with a Supplemental Restraint System (SRS) or "air bag," work must NOT be started until at least 90 seconds have passed from the time that both the ignition switch is turned to the LOCK position and the negative cable is disconnected from the battery.

> ✳✳**CAUTION**
>
> The steering system on any vehicle is assembled with high grade, hardened fasteners. NEVER substitute a fastener of inferior load rating when assembling a suspension component!

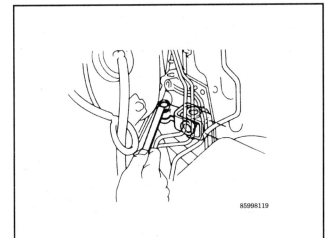

Fig. 108 Removing the bolt securing the yoke to the steering gear

1. Disconnect the negative battery cable.

2. Remove the hole cover screws to gain access to the steering column/steering gear yoke. Remove the bolt securing the yoke to the steering gear assembly.

➡On vehicles equipped with air bags, secure the steering wheel so that it will not turn.

3. Place a drain pan below the power steering rack assembly. Clean the area around the line fittings on the rack.

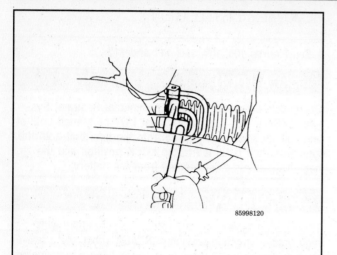

85998120

Fig. 109 Disconnecting the fluid lines from the steering gear

4. Elevate and safely support the vehicle, then remove both front wheels.

5. Remove the cotter pins from both tie rod ends, then remove the nuts.

6. Using a tie rod separator, disengage the tie rod ends from the steering knuckles.

7. Label and disconnect the fluid pressure and return lines at the rack.

8. Remove the nuts/bolts attaching the steering rack to the body.

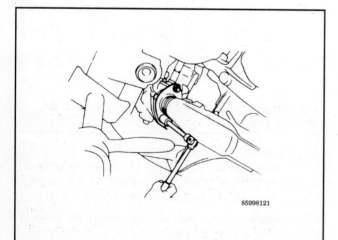

85998121

Fig. 110 It may be necessary to remove the front exhaust pipe on some models to gain additional clearance

9. On some models it may be necessary to remove the front exhaust pipe and the rear engine mounting bracket/crossmember. Support the transaxle with a jack before removing the engine mounting bracket/crossmember.

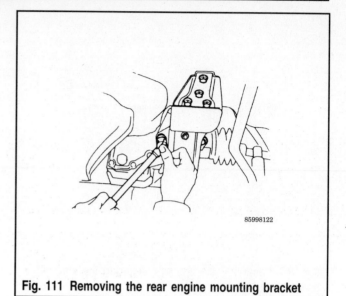

85998122

Fig. 111 Removing the rear engine mounting bracket

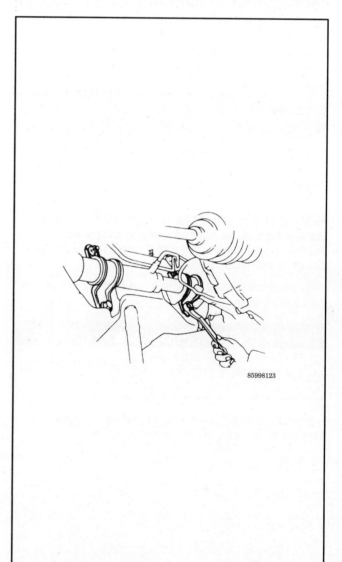

85998123

Fig. 112 Removing the bolts securing the assembly to the vehicle

10. Lower the rack assembly or, if possible, slide the assembly to the right and lower the left side. Remove any components necessary to gain additional working space.

To install:

11. Install the rack assembly. Secure it with the retaining bolts/nuts, then torque them to the following:

    a. Wagons and 1984-86 sedans — 43 ft. lbs. (59 Nm)

    b. 1987-90 sedans — 32 ft. lbs. (43 Nm)

    c. 1991-94 sedans — 43 ft. lbs. (59 Nm)

12. Install the front exhaust pipe and rear engine mounting bracket, if applicable.

13. Connect the fluid lines. Always start the threads by hand before using a tool.

14. Torque the steering gear-to-yoke bolt to 26 ft. lbs. (35 Nm) on 1984-90 models and 21 ft. lbs. (28 Nm) on 1991-94 models.

15. Connect the tie rod ends to each steering knuckle. Tighten the nuts to 36 ft. lbs. (49 Nm), then install new cotter pins.

16. Install the front wheels.

17. Lower the car to the ground.

18. Install the hole cover. Add fluid and bleed the system.

➡️**On vehicles equipped with air bags, the spiral cable in the steering column must be centered if the steering wheel has been turned. Refer to the steering column procedure in this section.**

19. Have a reputable shop check the front end alignment.

Power Steering Pump

REMOVAL & INSTALLATION

♦ See Figure 113

❋❋CAUTION

On models equipped with a Supplemental Restraint System (SRS) or "air bag," work must NOT be started until at least 90 seconds have passed from the time that both the ignition switch is turned to the LOCK position and the negative cable is disconnected from the battery.

❋❋CAUTION

The steering system on any vehicle is assembled with high grade, hardened fasteners. NEVER substitute a fastener of inferior load rating when assembling a suspension component!

1. Disconnect the negative battery cable.

2. Drain the power steering fluid from the reservoir. Disconnect pressure line and return hose.

3. Remove the power steering pump belt.

4. If necessary to access the pump from under the vehicle, remove the engine under cover then safely raise and support the vehicle.

5. Remove the bolts from the mount bracket. Remove the power steering pump assembly from the vehicle.

6. Installation is the reverse of the removal. Tighten the retaining bolts to 32 ft. lbs. (43 Nm). Adjust drive belt tension, bleed power steering and check for leaks.

BLEEDING

Any time the power steering system has been opened or disassembled, the system must be bled to remove any air which may be trapped in the lines. Air will prevent the system from providing the correct pressures to the rack. Also, the correct fluid level reading will not be obtained if the system is not bled.

1. With the engine running, turn the wheel all the way to the left, then shut off the engine.

2. Add power steering fluid to the appropriate mark on the indicator.

3. Start the engine and run at fast idle for about 15 seconds. Stop the engine and recheck the fluid level. Add to the appropriate mark as needed.

4. Start the engine and bleed the system by turning the wheels from full left to full right 3 or 4 times.

5. Stop the engine and check the fluid level and condition. Fluid with air in it has many tiny bubbles. This air must be eliminated from the system before normal operation can be obtained. Repeat the steps until the fluid is clear of air bubbles.

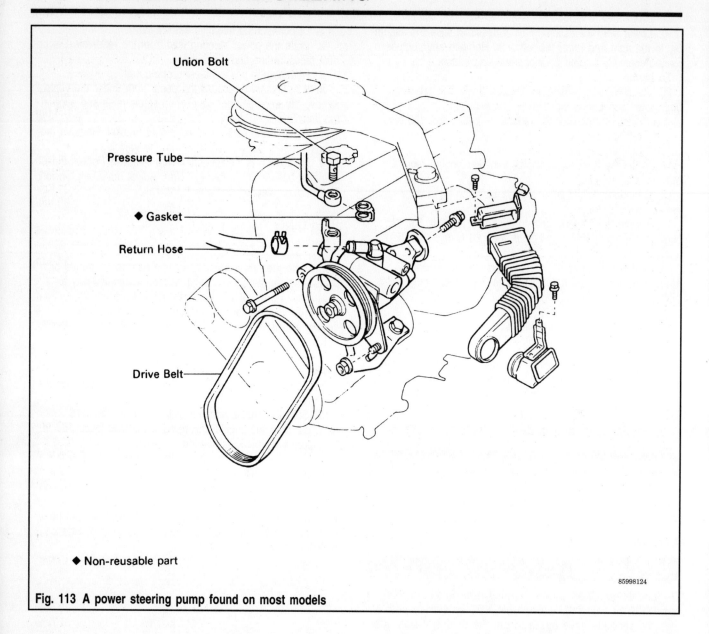

Fig. 113 A power steering pump found on most models

TORQUE SPECIFICATIONS

Component	English	Metric
Wheel lug nuts	76 ft. lbs.	103 Nm
Front struts		
Upper attaching bolts/nuts		
1984–1985 models	17 ft. lbs.	24 Nm
1986 models	13 ft. lbs.	17 Nm
1987–1990 models	23 ft. lbs.	31 Nm
1991–1994 models	29 ft. lbs.	39 Nm
Lower attaching bolts/nuts		
Wagons and 1984–1986 sedans	105 ft. lbs.	142 Nm
1987–1990 sedans	166 ft. lbs.	226 Nm
1991–1994 sedans	181 ft. lbs.	245 Nm
Shaft (support) nut	34 ft. lbs.	47 Nm
Rear struts		
Upper attaching nuts/bolts		
Wagons and 1984–1986 sedans	17 ft. lbs.	24 Nm
1987–1994 sedans	23 ft. lbs.	31 Nm
Lower attaching nuts/bolts		
Wagons and 1984–1986 sedans	105 ft. lbs.	142 Nm
1987–1994 sedans	50 ft. lbs.	68 Nm
Shaft (support) nut		
Wagons and 1984–1986 sedans	36 ft. lbs.	49 Nm
1987–1994 sedans	40 ft. lbs.	54 Nm
Rear shock absorbers		
Upper nuts	18 ft. lbs.	25 Nm
Lower nuts	27 ft. lbs.	37 Nm
Front sway bar		
Wagons and 1984–1986 sedans		
Bracket bolts	32 ft. lbs.	43 Nm
End nuts	78 ft. lbs.	105 Nm
Other models		
Bracket bolts	14 ft. lbs.	19 Nm
Sway bar-to-control arm	13 ft. lbs.	18 Nm
Rear sway bar		
Body link	22 ft. lbs.	30 Nm
Brackets	27 ft. lbs.	37 Nm
Front control arms		
Wagons and 1984–1986 sedans	83 ft. lbs.	113 Nm
1987–1994 sedans		
Front bolts	108 ft. lbs.	147 Nm
Bracket bolts	64 ft. lbs.	87 Nm
Rear control arms		
Front wheel drive		
Front arm	64 ft. lbs.	87 Nm
Rear arm	64 ft. lbs.	87 Nm
Four wheel drive		
Upper arm	83 ft. lbs.	113 Nm
Lower arm	83 ft. lbs.	113 Nm
Ball joints		
Stud nut		
Wagons and 1984–1986 sedans	58 ft. lbs.	78 Nm
1987–1994 sedans	72 ft. lbs.	98 Nm
Attaching nuts/bolts	59 ft. lbs.	80 Nm

85998302

TORQUE SPECIFICATIONS

Component	English	Metric
Lateral control rod		
Rod-to-body nut/bolt	83 ft. lbs.	113 Nm
Rod-to-axle nut/bolt	47 ft. lbs.	64 Nm
Strut rod	64 ft. lbs.	87 Nm
Axle beam	105 ft. lbs.	142 Nm
Steering wheel		
Non-airbag vehicles		
Retaining nut	25 ft. lbs.	34 Nm
Airbag vehicles		
Retaining nut	26 ft. lbs.	35 Nm
Pad attaching screws	78 inch lbs.	8.8 Nm
Steering column		
Upper and lower attaching nuts/bolts	19 ft. lbs.	28 Nm
Column-to-yoke bolt		
1984–1990 models	26 ft. lbs.	35 Nm
1991–1994 models	21 ft. lbs.	28 Nm
Outer tie rods		
Lock nuts		
1984–1990 models	41 ft. lbs.	56 Nm
1991–1994 models	35 ft. lbs.	47 Nm
Stud nut	36 ft. lbs.	49 Nm
Inner tie rods		
Wagons 1984–1986 sedans	61 ft. lbs.	83 Nm
1987–1994 sedans	38 ft. lbs.	51 Nm
Manual rack and pinion	43 ft. lbs.	59 Nm
Power rack and pinion		
Wagons 1984–1986 sedans	43 ft. lbs.	59 Nm
1987–1990 sedans	32 ft. lbs.	43 Nm
1991–1994 sedans	43 ft. lbs.	59 Nm

8599832a

9

BRAKES

BRAKE OPERATING SYSTEM

Adjustments

DRUM BRAKES

▶ **See Figures 1 and 2**

The rear drum brakes are equipped with automatic adjusters actuated by the brake mechanism. No periodic adjustment of the drum brakes is necessary if this mechanism is working properly. If the pedal travel is greater than normal, it may be due to a lack of adjustment at the rear. In a safe location, drive the car backwards at low speed. While backing, pump the brake pedal slowly several times (neither the speed of the car or the speed of pumping the pedal has any effect on the adjustment, the idea is to apply the brakes several times while backing). Drive forward and check the pedal feel by braking from moderate speed. It may take 2 or 3 passes in reverse to bring the pedal to the correct travel; each brake application moves the adjuster very little.

If brake shoe-to-drum clearance is incorrect and applying and releasing the brakes in reverse does not adjust it properly, the parts will have to be disassembled for repair.

An alternate method of adjustment can be used when the brakes have been disassembled or when the reversing method does not work.

1. Elevate and safely support the vehicle. If only the rear wheels are elevated, block the front wheels with chocks. Once the vehicle is firmly on stands, release the parking brake.

2. Remove the rear wheels.

3. Remove the brake drum. It will not come off if the parking brake is applied.

✳✳CAUTION

Brake pads and shoes may contain asbestos, which has been determined to be a cancer causing agent. Never clean the brake surfaces with compressed air! Avoid inhaling any dust from brake surfaces! When cleaning brakes, use commercially available brake cleaning fluids.

4. If the brake drum cannot be removed easily:

a. Insert a screwdriver through the hole in the backing plate and hold the adjusting lever away from the star wheel.

b. Using a brake adjusting tool, turn the wheel to reduce the tension (increase the clearance) on the brake shoes.

5. Use a brake drum measuring tool with both inside diameter and outside diameter capability. Measure the inside diameter of the brake drum and record the reading.

6. Measure the diameter of the brake shoe assembly at the friction surface. Use the adjusting wheel to adjust the brake shoes until the diameter of the shoes is 0.024 in. (0.6mm) less than the diameter of the drum. This small clearance is important; over-adjusted brakes cause drag and premature wear on the shoes.

7. Install the brake drum(s) and install the rear wheel(s).

8. Apply the parking brake and lower the car to the ground.

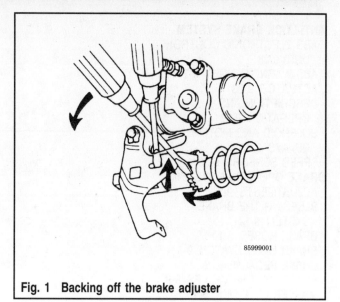

Fig. 1 Backing off the brake adjuster

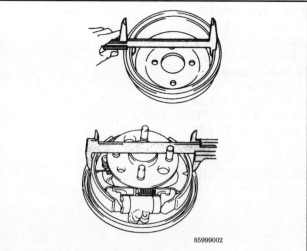

Fig. 2 Measuring the diameters of the drum and shoe assemblies

BRAKE PEDAL

▶ **See Figures 3, 4 and 5**

The correct adjustment of the brake pedal height, free-play and reserve distance is critical to the correct operation of the brake system. These three measurements interrelate and should be performed in sequence.

Pedal Height

1. Measure the pedal height from the top of the pedal pad to the asphalt sheet. Correct distances are as follows:

a. Wagons and 1984-1986 sedans — 7.24-7.64 in. (184-194mm)

b. 1987-1990 Sedans — 5.79-6.18 in. (147-157mm)

c. 1991-1994 manual transaxle sedans — 5.63-6.02 in. (143-153mm)

d. 1991-1994 automatic transaxle sedans — 5.45-5.85 in. (138.5-148.5mm)

2. If it is necessary to adjust the pedal height, loosen the brake light switch and back it off so that some clearance exists between it and the pedal arm.

➡**On some models, it may be necessary to remove the lower dash trim panel and air duct for access.**

3. Adjust the pedal height by loosening the locknut and turning the pedal pushrod.

4. On 1984-1990 models, return the brake light switch to a position in which it lightly contacts the stopper on the pedal arm.

5. On 1991-1994 models, return the switch to a position in which it lightly contacts the stopper on the pedal arm, then back it out one turn. Check the clearance between the switch and the pedal. It should be between 0.02-0.09 in. (0.5-2.4mm). Adjust, if necessary.

Pedal Free-play

1. With the engine **OFF**, depress the brake pedal several times.

2. Pedal free-play is the distance between the "at rest" pedal position and the position at which the beginning of pedal resistance is felt. This represents the distance the pedal pushrod moves before actuating the booster air valve. Correct free-play is 0.12-0.24 in. (3-6mm) on 1984-1990 models and 0.04-0.24 in. (1-6mm) on 1991-1994 models.

3. If necessary, adjust the pedal pushrod to achieve the proper free-play. After adjusting the free-play, recheck the pedal height.

Pedal Reserve Distance

1. With the transaxle in PARK or NEUTRAL and the parking brake fully released, start the engine and apply normal braking effort to the pedal. Depress the pedal fully, but don't try to put it through the floor.

2. While the pedal is depressed, have an assistant measure the distance from the top of the pedal pad to the floor. Specifications are as follows:

a. Wagons and 1984-1986 sedans — 3.54 in. (90mm)

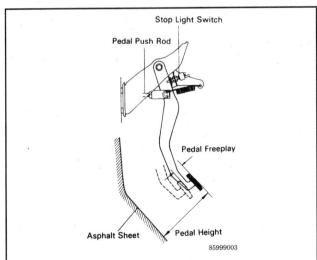

Fig. 3 Pedal height and free-play adjustment measurements

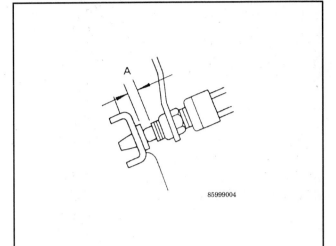

Fig. 4 Measuring the clearance between the brake switch and pedal on 1991-1994 models

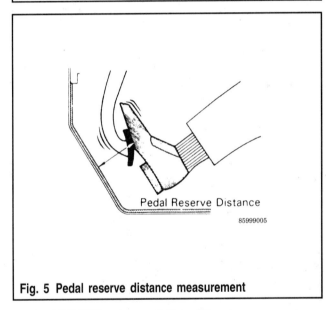

Fig. 5 Pedal reserve distance measurement

b. 1987-1990 sedans — 2.20 in. (56mm)
c. 1991-1994 sedans — 1.97 in. (50mm)

3. The reserve distance can be greater than specified but must not be less. If the reserve distance is less than specification, the brake system must be diagnosed for leaks or component failure.

Brake Light Switch

REMOVAL & INSTALLATION

1. Disconnect the negative battery cable.
2. Unplug the wiring from the switch terminals. On some models, it may be necessary to remove the lower dash trim panel and air duct for access.
3. Loosen the locknut closest to the brake pedal arm. Unscrew the switch from the nut, then remove it from the bracket.

To install:

4. Position the switch so the plunger is lightly compressed against the stopper on the pedal, then finger-tighten the locknut.

5. Connect an ohmmeter across the terminals of the switch. Adjust the switch so that continuity is displayed on the ohmmeter just as the brakes are applied, but no sooner.

6. Tighten the locknut to hold the switch in position. Engage the electrical connection.

7. Connect the negative battery cable, then test the operation of the brake lights.

Brake Pedal

REMOVAL & INSTALLATION

✳✳CAUTION

On models equipped with a Supplemental Restraint System (SRS) or an "air bag," work must NOT be started until at least 90 seconds have passed from the time that both the ignition switch is turned to the LOCK position and the negative cable is disconnected from the battery.

1. Disconnect the negative battery cable.

2. Remove the lower dash trim panel and air duct, if necessary.

3. Remove the brake pedal return spring and brake light switch.

4. Remove the clevis pin clip and pin.

5. Unbolt and remove the brake pedal from the vehicle.

To install:

6. Position the pedal in the vehicle, then tighten the retaining nut/bolt.

7. Install the clevis pin and clip.

8. Install the brake return spring.

9. Install the brake light switch, then adjust the pedal and switch.

10. Install the lower dash trim panel and air duct.

11. Test the brake pedal and light for proper operation.

Master Cylinder

REMOVAL & INSTALLATION

▶ See Figures 6, 7, 8, 9 and 10

✳✳CAUTION

On models equipped with a Supplemental Restraint System (SRS) or an "air bag," work must NOT be started until at least 90 seconds have passed from the time that both the ignition switch is turned to the LOCK position and the negative cable is disconnected from the battery.

➡Be careful not to spill brake fluid on the painted surfaces of the vehicle; it will damage the paint. If spillage occurs, rinse the area immediately with water. Handle the steel brake lines with care. Once they are bent or kinked, they cannot be straightened.

1. Disconnect the negative battery cable.

2. Clean the area around the reservoir and brake lines to prevent entry of dirt into the system.

3. Disconnect the wiring from the brake fluid level warning switch. Release the harness from any clips.

4. Remove the air intake duct, if necessary.

5. Use a clean syringe to remove the fluid from the reservoir.

6. Disconnect the brake lines from the master cylinder using a line or flare nut wrench. Plug or tape the lines immediately to keep dirt and moisture out of the system.

7. Remove the nuts securing the master cylinder to the brake booster.

8. If necessary, remove the union bracket.

9. Remove the master cylinder and gasket.

To install:

10. Always use a new gasket or seal. On some models, confirm that the UP mark on the master cylinder boot is in the correct position.

11. Install the master cylinder.

12. Install the union bracket, if applicable.

13. Thread the nuts onto the studs, then tighten them to 9 ft. lbs. (13 Nm).

14. Connect the brake lines to the master cylinder. Make certain each fitting is correctly threaded, then tighten each fitting. Do not overtighten.

15. Install the air intake duct, as necessary.

16. Connect the wiring to the brake fluid sensing switch, then attach any harness clips.

17. Fill the master cylinder reservoir with fresh DOT 3 brake fluid.

18. Connect the negative battery cable. Bleed the brake system.

Fig. 6 Be careful not to break the lock tab when unplugging the electrical connector

Fig. 7 Always use a flare nut or line wrench when disconnecting brake lines

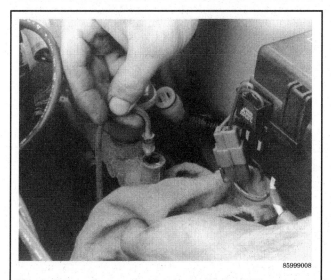

Fig. 8 Use a shop rag to catch any brake fluid

Fig. 9 Some brake lines may be hard to reach. Be careful not to bend them

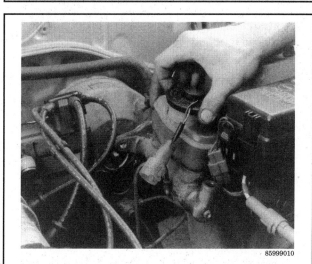

Fig. 10 After the retaining nuts have been removed, carefully pull the master cylinder away from it's mount

OVERHAUL

▶ See Figures 11, 12, 13, 14, 15, 16, 17 and 18

1. Remove master cylinder from the car. Remove the cap and strainer from the reservoir.

2. Remove the reservoir retaining screw, then carefully pull the reservoir from the assembly.

3. Mount the cylinder (protect the cylinder from damage using a cloth or block of wood) in a vise.

4. Remove the two grommets from the cylinder.

5. Tape the tip of a brass drift, then push the pistons all the way into the bore and remove the piston stopper bolt with it's gasket.

6. Hold the piston into the bore, then remove the snapring with snapring pliers.

7. Place a rag on two wooden blocks. Remove the master cylinder from the vise and tap the cylinder flange between the blocks until the piston tip protrudes.

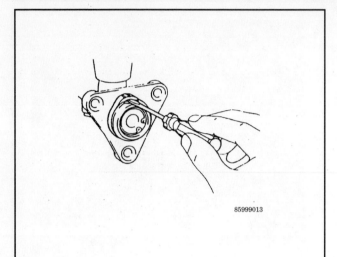

85999013

Fig. 11 A small screwdriver can be used to remove the master cylinder boot

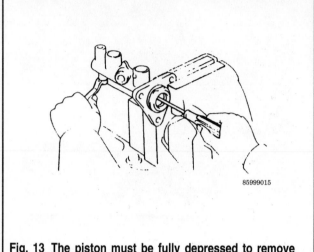

85999015

Fig. 13 The piston must be fully depressed to remove the stopper bolt

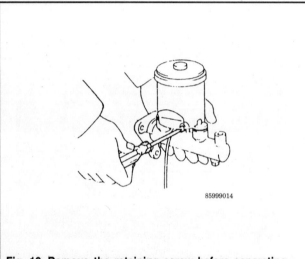

85999014

Fig. 12 Remove the retaining screw before separating the reservoir from the cylinder body

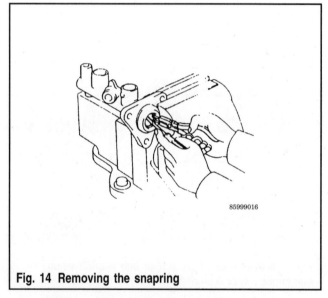

85999016

Fig. 14 Removing the snapring

8. Remove the piston by pulling it straight out.

➡**If the piston is removed at an angle, the cylinder bore may become damaged.**

9. Inspect all parts of the pistons, grommets and bore for any sign of wear, cuts, corrosion or scoring. Check the inlet port and return port for obstructions. Use compressed air to clear any dirt or foreign matter from the area.

To assemble:
10. Apply clean brake fluid to the rubber parts of the pistons.
11. Insert the springs and pistons straight into the bore. Do not angle them during installation.

➡**Be careful not to damage the rubber lips on the pistons.**

12. Install the snapring while pushing in the piston.
13. Push the pistons all the way in, then install the piston stopper bolt and gasket. Tighten it to 7 ft. lbs. (10 Nm).
14. Install the reservoir grommets.
15. Install the cap and strainer onto the reservoir, then push the reservoir into position on the cylinder.
16. Install the retaining screw while pushing on the reservoir. Tighten the screw to 15 inch lbs. (1.7 Nm).

➡**There may be a slight bit of play in the reservoir after the screw is installed. This is normal and no washers or spacers should be installed.**

17. Install the master cylinder.

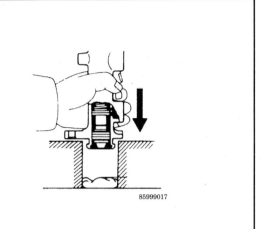

Fig. 15 Carefully tap the cylinder body on wooden blocks until the piston can be extracted

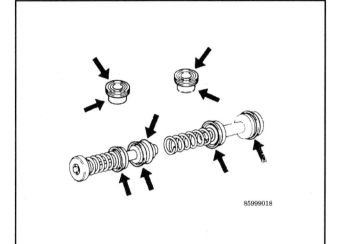

Fig. 16 Apply fresh brake fluid to these parts before assembling

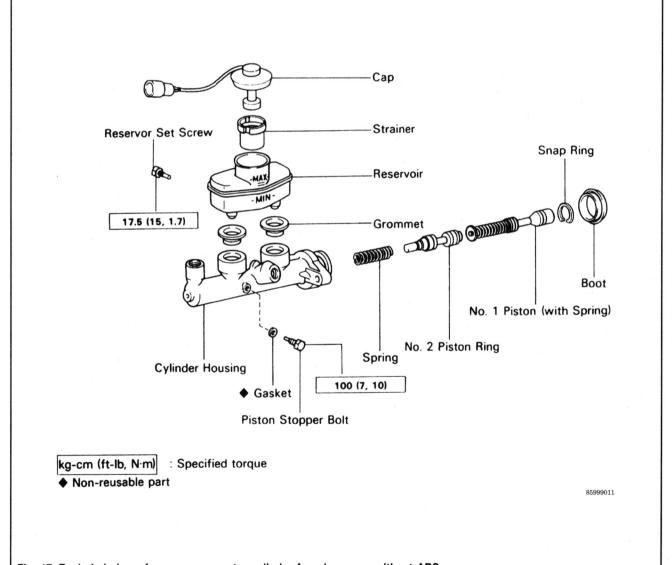

Cap
Strainer
Reservoir
Snap Ring
Reservor Set Screw
17.5 (15, 1.7)
Grommet
Boot
No. 1 Piston (with Spring)
No. 2 Piston Ring
Spring
Cylinder Housing
100 (7, 10)
♦ Gasket
Piston Stopper Bolt

kg-cm (ft-lb, N·m) : Specified torque
♦ Non-reusable part

Fig. 17 Exploded view of a common master cylinder found on cars without ABS

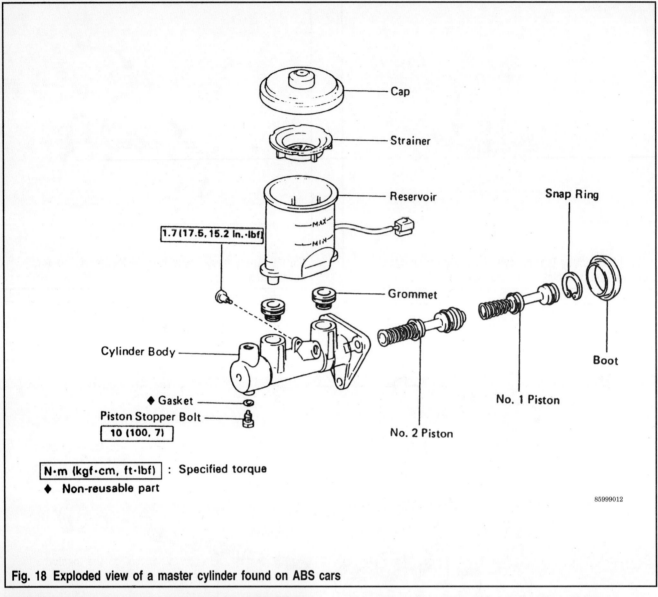

Fig. 18 Exploded view of a master cylinder found on ABS cars

Power Brake Booster

REMOVAL & INSTALLATION

▶ See Figures 19, 20 and 21

1. Disconnect the negative battery cable.
2. Remove any components necessary to gain working access.
3. Remove the brake master cylinder from the booster. Refer to the necessary service procedures.
4. Remove the vacuum hose from the booster.
5. From inside the car, disconnect the pedal return spring, clevis pin clip and pin.
6. Remove the brake booster retaining nuts. It will be helpful to have an assistant support the booster while the nuts are loosened.

7. Remove the booster from the engine compartment.
To install:
8. Have an assistant hold the booster in position while you install the retaining nuts. Tighten the nuts to 9 ft. lbs. (13 Nm).
9. Install the clevis pin and clip, then install the pedal return spring.
10. Connect the vacuum hose to the booster.
11. Install any other components necessary.
12. Adjust the pushrod length.
13. Install the master cylinder.
14. Adjust the brake pedal.
15. Bleed the brake system. Refer to the necessary service procedure.

ADJUSTMENTS

▶ See Figures 22 and 23

1. Install the gasket on the master cylinder.

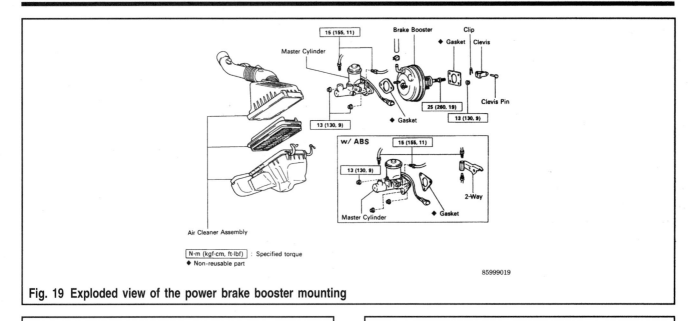

Fig. 19 Exploded view of the power brake booster mounting

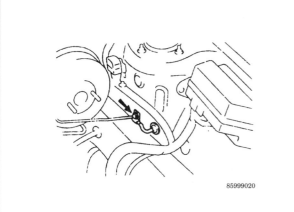

Fig. 20 Brake lines and other components may have to be repositioned to gain access for removal of the brake booster

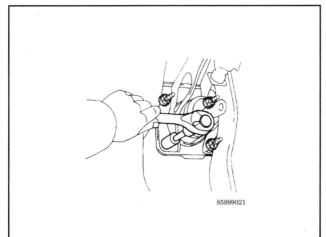

Fig. 21 After the clevis has been disconnected from the brake pedal, the attaching nuts can be removed

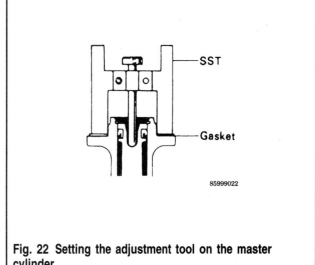

Fig. 22 Setting the adjustment tool on the master cylinder

2. Set SST 09737-00010 or an equivalent gauging tool on the gasket, then lower the pin until it's tip slightly touches the piston.

3. Turn the tool upside down and set it on the booster.

4. Measure the clearance between the booster pushrod and the pin head. There should be no clearance. Adjust the pushrod length until the pushrod slightly touches the pin head.

Brake System Valves

REMOVAL & INSTALLATION

▶ See Figures 24 and 25

Proportioning Valve

The proportioning valve is located on the center of the firewall under the hood. Except for leakage or impact damage, it rarely needs replacement. If it must be removed, all brake

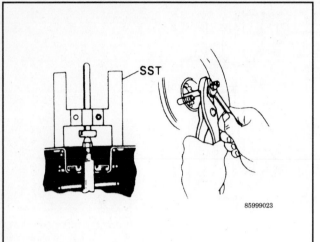

Fig. 23 There should be no clearance between the tool and the pushrod. Adjust, as necessary

lines must be labeled and removed and the valve removed from its mount. Clean the fittings before removal to prevent dirt from entering the ports. After the lines are reconnected, carefully tighten the fittings to 11 ft. lbs. (15 Nm) using a torque wrench with a crow's foot attachment. The entire brake system must be bled.

Vacuum Check Valve

This check valve allows vacuum to flow out of the brake booster, but will not allow back-flow. This maintains a supply of vacuum within the booster during periods of high manifold pressure. The valve can be removed from the hose by hand. Once removed, the valve can be tested by gently blowing through it. It should allow airflow in one direction but not the other. When installing a new valve, make sure it is positioned so that the air can flow from the booster to the engine. Most replacement valves have an arrow showing the direction of airflow. If in doubt of it's condition, replace it.

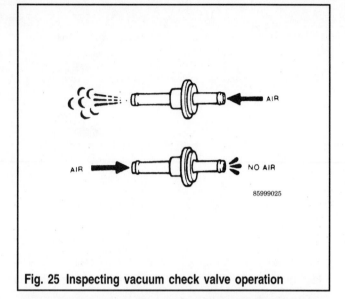

Fig. 25 Inspecting vacuum check valve operation

Brake Hoses

INSPECTION

▶ See Figure 26

1. Inspect the lines and hoses in a well lit area. Use a small mirror to allow you to see concealed parts of the hose or line. Check the entire length and circumference of each line or hose.
2. Look for any sign of wear, deformation, corrosion, cracking, bends, swelling or thread damage.
3. The slightest sign of leakage requires immediate attention.
4. Check all clamps for tightness, then check that all lines and hoses have sufficient clearance from moving parts and heat sources.
5. Check that any lines passing through grommets are routed through the center of the grommet and are not forced against the side of the hole. Relieve any excess tension.

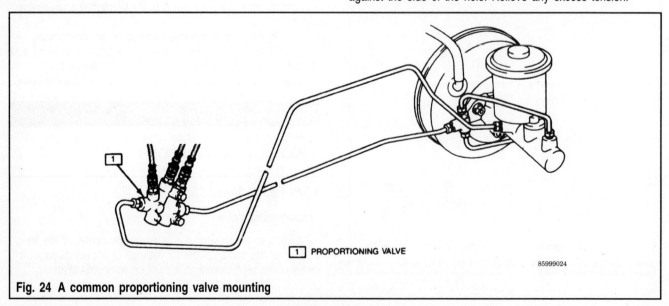

1 PROPORTIONING VALVE

Fig. 24 A common proportioning valve mounting

6. Some metal lines may contain spring-like coils. These coils absorb vibration and prevent the line from cracking under strain. Do not attempt to straighten the coils or change their diameter.

REMOVAL & INSTALLATION

▶ **See Figures 27 and 28**

1. Elevate and safely support the vehicle.
2. Remove the wheel.
3. Clean all dirt from the hose junctions.
4. Place a catch pan under the hose area.
5. Using 2 wrenches (one should be line or flare nut wrench), disconnect the flexible hose from the steel brake line at the strut assembly.
6. If equipped with disc brakes, disconnect the brake hose union bolt at the brake caliper. If equipped with drum brakes, disconnect the hose from the steel pipe running to the wheel cylinder.
7. Remove the hose retaining clips and remove the hose from the vehicle.
8. If the system is to remain disconnected for more than the time it takes to swap hoses, tape or plug the line and caliper to prevent dirt and moisture from entering.
   To install:
9. Install the new brake hose into the retaining clips.
10. Connect the hose to the caliper (disc brakes) and tighten the union bolt to 22 ft. lbs. (30 Nm) or connect the hose to the short line running into the wheel cylinder (drum brakes) and tighten the fitting to 11 ft. lbs. (15 Nm).
11. Connect the steel brake line to the hose at the strut. Start the threads by hand and make sure the joint is properly threaded before tightening. Tighten the fitting to 11 ft. lbs. (15 Nm).
12. Install the wheel. Bleed the brake system. Refer to the necessary service procedures.

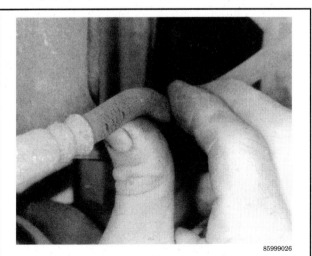

Fig. 26 Hoses showing signs of cracking should be replaced

Fig. 27 Always use a line or flare nut wrench to disconnect brake lines

Fig. 28 Needle nose pliers can be used to remove retaining clips

13. Lower the car to the ground.

BRAKE PIPE FLARING

Flaring steel lines is a skill which needs to be practiced before it should be done on a line which is to be used on a vehicle. A special flaring kit with double flaring adapters is required. It is essential that the flare is formed evenly to prevent any leaks when the brake system is under pressure. Only steel lines, not copper lines, should be used. It is also mandatory that the flare be a double flare. With the supply of parts available today, a pre-flared steel brake line should be available to fit your needs. Due to the high pressures in the brake system and the serious injuries that could occur if the flare should fail, it is strongly advised that pre-flared lines should be installed when repairing the braking system. If a line were to leak brake fluid due to a defective flare, and the leak were to go undetected, brake failure would result.

✳✳WARNING

A double flaring tool must be used as single flaring tools cannot produce a flare strong enough to hold the necessary pressure.

1. Determine the length of pipe needed. Allow ⅛ in. (3.2 mm) for each flare. Cut using an appropriate tool.
2. Square the end of the tube with a file and chamfer the edges. Remove any burrs.
3. Install the required fittings on the pipe.
4. Install the flaring tool into a vice and install the handle into the operating cam.
5. Loosen the die clamp screw and rotate the locking plate to expose the die carrier.
6. Select the required die set and install in the carrier.
7. Insert the prepared line through the rear of the die and push forward until the line end is flush with the die face.
8. Make sure the rear of both halves of the die are resting against the hexagon die stops. Then rotate the locking plate to the fully closed position and clamp the die firmly by tightening the clamp screw.
9. Rotate the punch turret until the appropriate size points towards the open end of the line to be flared.
10. Pull the operating handle against the line resistance in order to create the flare, then return the handle to the original position.
11. Release the clamp screw and rotate the locking plate to the open position.
12. Remove the die set and the line then separate by gently tapping both halves on the bench. Inspect the flare for proper size and shape.

Bleeding the Brake System

▶ **See Figures 29, 30 and 31**

It is necessary to bleed the hydraulic system any time system has been opened or when air has become trapped within the fluid lines. It may be necessary to bleed the system at all four brakes if air has been introduced through a low fluid level or by disconnecting brake pipes at the master cylinder.

If a line is disconnected at one wheel only, generally only that brake needs bleeding. If lines are disconnected at any fitting between the master cylinder and the brake, the system components served by the disconnected pipe must be bled.

➡**Do not allow brake fluid to splash or spill onto painted surfaces; the paint will be damaged. If spillage occurs, flush the area immediately with clean water.**

1. Fill the master cylinder reservoir to the MAX line with brake fluid and keep it full throughout the bleeding procedure.
2. If the master cylinder has been removed or disconnected, it must be bled before any brake unit is bled. To bleed the master cylinder:
   a. Disconnect the front brake line from the master cylinder and allow fluid to flow from the front connector port.

Fig. 29 Make sure the master cylinder has a **sufficient** amount of fluid in the reservoir

   b. Reconnect the line to the master cylinder and tighten until just snug.
   c. Have a helper press the brake pedal down one time and hold it down.
   d. Loosen the front brake line connection at the master cylinder. This will allow trapped air to escape, along with some fluid.
   e. Again tighten the line, release the pedal slowly and repeat the sequence until only fluid runs from the port. No air bubbles should be present in the fluid.
   f. Final tighten the line fitting at the master cylinder to 11 ft. lbs. (15 Nm).
   g. After all the air has been bled from the front connection, bleed the master cylinder at the rear connection by repeating the steps.
3. Place the correct size box-end or line wrench over the bleeder valve, then attach a tight-fitting transparent hose over the bleeder. Allow the tube to hang submerged in a transparent container of clean brake fluid. The fluid must remain above the end of the hose at all times, otherwise the system will ingest air instead of fluid.
4. Have an assistant pump the brake pedal several times slowly, then hold it down.
5. Slowly unscrew the bleeder valve (¼-½ turn is usually enough). After the initial rush of air and/or fluid, tighten the bleeder. Have the assistant slowly release the brake pedal.
6. Repeat the steps until no air bubbles are seen in the hose or container. If air is constantly appearing after repeatedly bleeding, the system must be examined for the source of the leak or loose fitting.
7. If the entire system must be bled, begin with the right rear, then the left front, left rear and right front brake in that order. After each brake is bled, check and top off the fluid level in the reservoir.

➡**Do not reuse brake fluid which has been bled from the brake system.**

8. After bleeding, check the pedal for sponginess. Repeat the bleeding procedure as necessary to correct.

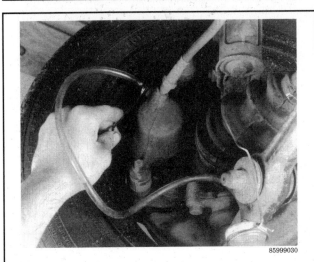

Fig. 30 Position a box wrench over the bleeder screw at the top of the caliper

Fig. 31 The bleeder screw for rear drum brakes is next to the inlet line for the wheel cylinder

FRONT DISC BRAKES

✳✳CAUTION

Brake pads may contain asbestos, which has been determined to be a cancer causing agent. Never clean the brake surfaces with compressed air! Avoid inhaling any dust from brake surfaces! When cleaning brakes, use commercially available brake cleaning fluids.

Brake Pads

REMOVAL & INSTALLATION

✳✳CAUTION

On models equipped with a Supplemental Restraint System (SRS) or "air bag," work must NOT be started until at least 90 seconds have passed from the time that both the ignition switch is turned to the LOCK position and the negative cable is disconnected from the battery.

▶ See Figures 32, 33, 34, 35, 36 and 37

1. Raise and safely support the front of the vehicle on jackstands. Set the parking brake and block the rear wheels.
2. Siphon a sufficient quantity of brake fluid from the master cylinder reservoir to prevent the brake fluid from overflowing the master cylinder when removing or installing the brake pads. This is necessary as the piston must be forced into the cylinder bore to provide sufficient clearance to remove and/or install the pads.
3. Remove the wheel, then reinstall 2 lug nuts finger-tight to hold the disc in place.
4. Use a caliper compressor, a C-clamp or large pair of pliers to slowly press the caliper piston back into the caliper. If the piston is frozen, or if the caliper is leaking hydraulic fluid, the caliper must be overhauled or replaced.

➡**Disassemble brakes one wheel at a time. This will prevent parts confusion and also prevent the opposite caliper piston from popping out during pad installation.**

5. Remove the two caliper mounting bolts, then remove the caliper from the mounting bracket. Position the caliper out of the way and support it with wire so it doesn't hang by the brake line.
6. Remove the brake pads, wear indicators, anti-squeal shims, support plates and the anti-squeal springs. Disassemble slowly and take note of how the parts fit together (refer to exploded view of components). This will save time during reassembly.
7. Inspect the brake disc (both sides) for scoring or gouging. Measure the disc for both thickness and run-out. Refer to the inspection procedures in this section.

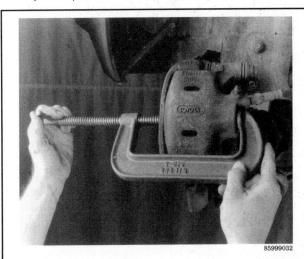

Fig. 32 A large C-clamp can be used to seat the caliper piston in it's bore

Fig. 33 The caliper is secured to the mounting bracket by two bolts

Fig. 34 Hang the caliper out of the way. Be sure not to stretch or kink the hose

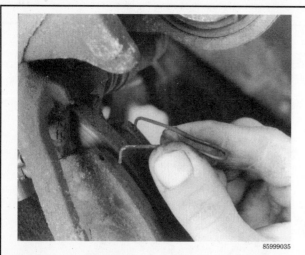

Fig. 35 Some models may be equipped with anti-squeal springs on the pads

Fig. 36 Note the position of the brake pads during removal to assure proper installation

8. Inspect the pads for remaining thickness and condition. Any sign of uneven wear, cracking, heat checking or spotting requires replacement. Compare the wear of the inner pad to the outer pad. While they will not wear at exactly the same rate, the remaining thickness should be about the same on both pads. If one is heavily worn and the other is not, suspect either a binding caliper piston or dirty slides in the caliper mount. Brake pads should always be replaced in sets (both wheels).

9. Examine the two caliper retaining bolts and the slide bushings in which they run. Everything should be clean and dry. If cleaning is needed, use spray solvents and a clean cloth. Do not wire brush or sand the bolts; this will cause grooves in the metal which will trap more dirt. Check the condition of the rubber dust boots and replace them if damaged.

To install:

10. Install the pad support plates onto the mounting bracket.

11. Install new pad wear indicators onto each pad, making sure the arrow on the tab points in the direction of disc rotation.

12. Install new anti-squeal pads to the back of the pads.

13. Install the pads into the mounting bracket, then install the anti-squeal springs.

14. Install the caliper assembly to the mounting plate. Before installing the retaining bolts, apply a thin, even coating of lithium soap base glycol grease or an equivalent high-temperature brake grease to the threads and slide surfaces. Tighten the bolts to 18 ft. lbs. (25 Nm).

15. Remove the 2 lugs holding the disc in place, then install the wheel.

16. Lower the vehicle to the ground. Check the level of the brake fluid in the master cylinder reservoir; it should be at least to the middle of the reservoir.

17. Depress the brake pedal several times and make sure that the movement feels normal. The first brake pedal application may result in a very long stroke due to the pistons being retracted. Always make several brake applications before starting the vehicle. Bleeding is not usually necessary after pad replacement.

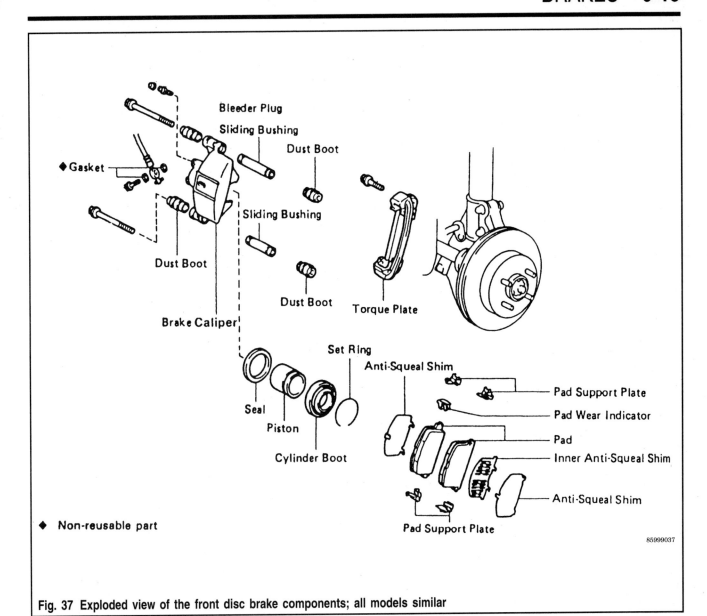

Fig. 37 Exploded view of the front disc brake components; all models similar

18. Recheck the fluid level and add to the MAX line, if necessary.

➡Braking should be moderate for the first 5 miles or so until the new pads seat correctly. The new pads will burnish best if put through several moderate heating and cooling cycles. Avoid hard braking until the brakes have experienced several long, slow stops with time to cool in between. Taking the time to properly burnish the brakes will yield quieter operation, more efficient stopping and contribute to extended brake life.

INSPECTION

◆ See Figures 38 and 39

The front brake pads may be inspected without removal. With the front end elevated and supported, remove the

wheel(s). Unlock the steering column lock and turn the wheel so that the brake caliper is out from under the fender.

View the pads through the cut-out in the center of the caliper. Remember to look at the thickness of the pad friction material (the part that actually presses on the disc) rather than the thickness of the backing plate which does not change with wear.

Remember that you are looking at the profile of the pad, not the whole thing. Brake pads can wear on a taper which may not be visible through the window. It is also not possible to check the contact surface for cracking or scoring from this position. This quick check can be helpful only as a reference; detailed inspection requires pad removal.

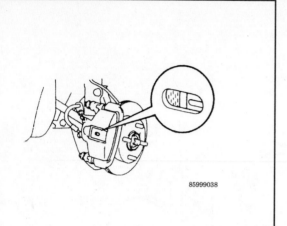

Fig. 38 Pad thickness can be seen through the caliper inspection hole

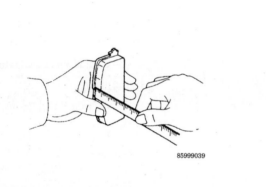

Fig. 39 Pads should be removed and measured for a more detailed inspection

Brake Caliper

REMOVAL & INSTALLATION

▶ See Figures 40 and 41

❊❊CAUTION

On models equipped with a Supplemental Restraint System (SRS) or "air bag," work must NOT be started until at least 90 seconds have passed from the time that both the ignition switch is turned to the LOCK position and the negative cable is disconnected from the battery.

1. Raise and safely support the front of the vehicle on jackstands. Set the parking brake and block the rear wheels.
2. Siphon a sufficient quantity of brake fluid from the master cylinder reservoir to prevent the brake fluid from overflowing the master cylinder when removing or installing the calipers. This is necessary as the piston must be forced into the cylinder bore to provide sufficient clearance to remove and/or install the caliper.
3. Remove the wheel, then reinstall 2 lug nuts finger-tight to hold the disc in place.
4. Use a caliper compressor, a C-clamp or large pair of pliers to slowly press the caliper piston back into the caliper.

➡**Disassemble brakes one wheel at a time. This will prevent parts confusion and also prevent the opposite caliper piston from popping out during installation.**

5. Disconnect the hose union at the caliper. Use a pan to catch any spilled fluid and immediately plug the disconnected hose.
6. Remove the two caliper mounting bolts and then remove the caliper from the mounting bracket.
   To install:
7. Install the caliper assembly to the mounting plate. Before installing the retaining bolts, apply a thin, even coating of lithium base glycol grease or an equivalent high-temperature brake grease to the threads and slide surfaces. Tighten the bolts to 18 ft. lbs. (25 Nm).
8. Install the brake hose to the caliper. Always use a new gasket and tighten the union to 22 ft. lbs. (30 Nm).
9. Bleed the brake system.
10. Remove the 2 lugs holding the disc in place and install the wheel.
11. Lower the vehicle to the ground. Check the level of the brake fluid in the master cylinder reservoir; it should be at least to the middle of the reservoir. Fill, as necessary

Fig. 40 The brake hose fitting should be loosened using a line or flare nut wrench

Fig. 41 After the mounting bolts and the brake hose have been unthreaded, the caliper can be removed from the vehicle

OVERHAUL

▶ See Figures 42, 43, 44, 45 and 46

➡For reasons of safety and reliability, we recommend that if one caliper requires replacement/overhaul, both calipers should be replaced/overhauled as a set.

1. Drain the remaining fluid from the caliper.
2. Carefully remove the dust boot from around the piston.
3. Grasp the piston and carefully extract it from the caliper bore (a turning/pulling motion may ease removal). If the piston will not come out of it's bore, it can usually be removed using compressed air. Cushion the inside arms of the caliper with a block of wood or rags. Apply compressed air into the brake line port; this will force the piston out.

❊❊CAUTION

Do not place fingers in front of the piston in an attempt to catch it or protect it when applying compressed air. Injury can result. Use just enough air pressure to ease the piston out of the bore.

4. Remove the seal from the inside of the caliper bore. Check all the parts for wear, scoring, deterioration, cracking or other abnormal conditions. Corrosion, generally caused by water in the system, will appear as white deposits on the metal (similar to what may be found on an old aluminum storm door on your house). Pay close attention to the condition of the inside of the caliper bore and the outside of the piston. Any sign of corrosion or scoring requires new parts; do not attempt to clean or resurface.

5. A caliper overhaul kit usually contains, at minimum, new seals and dust boots. A good kit will contain a new piston as well, but you may have to buy the piston separately. Any time the caliper is disassembled, a new piston is highly recommended in addition to the new seals.

6. Clean all the components to be reused with an aerosol brake solvent and dry them thoroughly. Use a clean, lint-free cloth to wipe moisture or water vapor from the parts.

Fig. 42 The dust boot is usually secured with a retaining ring

Fig. 43 The dust boot should be inspected for damage

Fig. 44 Protect the caliper before blowing the piston from it's bore

Fig. 45 Replace the piston if it is damaged

7. Coat all the caliper components with fresh brake fluid.

➡Some repair kits come with special assembly lubricant for the piston and seal. Use this lubricant according to directions with the kit.

8. Install the piston seal and piston into the caliper bore. This is an exacting job; the clearances are very small. Make sure that the seal is seated in its groove and that the piston is not cocked when inserted into the bore.

9. Install the dust boot and its clip or ring.

10. Install the slide bushings and rubber boots onto the caliper if they were removed during disassembly.

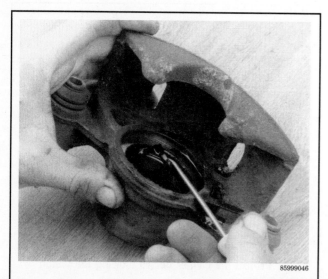

Fig. 46 Remove the piston seal and inspect the bore

Brake Disc (Rotor)

REMOVAL & INSTALLATION

✳✳CAUTION

On models equipped with a Supplemental Restraint System (SRS) or "air bag," work must NOT be started until at least 90 seconds have passed from the time that both the ignition switch is turned to the LOCK position and the negative cable is disconnected from the battery.

1. Elevate and safely support the car. If only the front end is supported, set the parking brake and block the rear wheels.

2. Remove the wheel.

3. Remove the brake caliper from its mount and suspend it out of the way. Don't disconnect the hose or let the caliper hang by the hose. Remove the brake pads with all the clips and shims.

4. Install all the lug nuts finger-tight to hold the rotor in place. If the nuts are open at both ends, it is helpful to install them backwards (tapered end out) to secure the disc.

5. Remove the two bolts holding the caliper mounting bracket to the steering knuckle. These bolts will be tight. Remove the lug nuts holding the rotor.

6. Remove the bracket from the knuckle. Before removing the rotor, make a mark on the rotor indexing one wheel stud to one hole in the rotor. This assures the rotor will be reinstalled in its original position.

To install:

7. Make certain the rotor is clean and free of any particles of rust or metal from resurfacing. Observe the index mark made earlier, then fit the rotor over the wheel lugs. Install the lug nuts to hold it in place.

8. Install the caliper mounting bracket in position, then tighten the bolts to 65 ft. lbs. (88 Nm).

9. Install the brake pads and the hardware (clips/shims).

10. Install the caliper.

11. Install the wheel, then lower the car to the ground.

INSPECTION

▶ See Figures 47 and 48

➡For reasons of safety and reliability, we recommend that if one rotor requires replacement, both rotors, along with new pads, should be replaced as a set.

Run-out

1. Elevate and safely support the car. If only the front end is supported, set the parking brake and block the rear wheels.

2. Remove the wheel.

3. Remove the brake caliper from its mount and suspend it out of the way. Don't disconnect the hose or let the caliper hang by the hose. Remove the brake pads with all the clips and shims.

4. Install all the lug nuts to hold the rotor in place. If the nuts are open at both ends, it is helpful to install them backwards (tapered end out) to secure the disc. Tighten the nuts a

bit tighter than finger-tight, but make sure all are at approximately the same clamp load.

5. Mount a dial indicator with a magnetic or universal base on the strut so that the tip of the indicator contacts the rotor about 0.39 in. (10mm) from the outer edge.

6. Zero the dial indicator. Turn the rotor one complete revolution and observe the total indicated run-out.

7. If run-out exceeds 0.0059 in. (0.15mm) on 1984-1990 models or 0.0035 in. (0.09mm) on 1991-1994 models, clean the wheel hub and rotor mating surfaces and remeasure. If the run-out still exceeds maximum, remove the rotor and remount it so that the wheel studs now run through different holes. If this re-indexing does not provide correct run-out measurements, the rotor should be considered warped beyond use and should be either resurfaced or replaced.

Thickness

The thickness of the rotor partially determines its ability to withstand heat and provide adequate stopping force. Every rotor has a minimum thickness established by the manufacturer. This minimum measurement MUST NOT be exceeded. A rotor which is too thin may crack under braking; if this occurs the wheel can lock instantly, resulting in sudden loss of control. If any part of the rotor measures below minimum thickness, the disc must be replaced. Additionally, a rotor which needs to be resurfaced may not allow sufficient cutting before reaching minimum. Since the allowable wear from new to minimum is about 0.04 in. (1mm), it is wise to replace the rotor rather than resurface it.

1. Thickness and thickness variation can be measured with a micrometer. All measurements must be made at the same

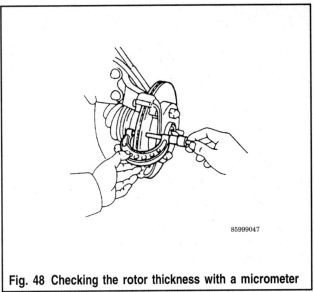

Fig. 48 Checking the rotor thickness with a micrometer

distance in from the edge of the rotor. Measure at four equally spaced points around the disc and record the measurements. Compare each measurement to the minimum thickness specifications found in the chart in this section.

2. Compare the four measurements to each other and find the difference between each pair. A rotor which does not meet these specifications should be resurfaced or replaced as applicable.

Condition

A new rotor will have a smooth even surface which rapidly changes during use. It is not uncommon for a rotor to develop very fine concentric scoring (like the grooves on a record) due to dust and grit being trapped by the brake pad. This slight irregularity is normal, but as the grooves deepen, wear and noise increase while stopping may be affected. As a general rule, any groove deep enough to snag a fingernail during inspection is cause for corrective action or replacement.

Any sign of blue spots, discoloration, heavy rusting or gouges require replacement of the rotor. If you are checking the disc on the car (such as during pad replacement or tire rotation) remember to turn the disc and check both the inner and outer faces completely. If anything looks questionable or requires consideration, choose the safer option and replace the rotors. The front brakes are a critical system and must be maintained at 100 percent reliability.

Any time rotors are replaced, the pads should also be replaced (as a set) so that the surfaces mate properly. The restored feel and accurate stopping make the extra investment worthwhile.

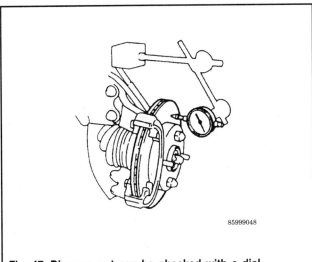

Fig. 47 Disc run-out can be checked with a dial indicator

REAR DRUM BRAKES

✳✳CAUTION

Brake shoes may contain asbestos, which has been determined to be a cancer causing agent. Never clean the brake surfaces with compressed air! Avoid inhaling any dust from brake surfaces! When cleaning brakes, use commercially available brake cleaning fluids.

Brake Drums

REMOVAL & INSTALLATION

✳✳CAUTION

On models equipped with a Supplemental Restraint System (SRS) or "air bag," work must NOT be started until at least 90 seconds have passed from the time that both the ignition switch is turned to the LOCK position and the negative cable is disconnected from the battery.

1. Elevate and safely support the vehicle. If only the rear wheels are elevated, block the front wheels with chocks. Once the vehicle is firmly on stands, release the parking brake.
2. Remove the rear wheel.
3. Make an index mark showing the relationship between one wheel lug and one hole in the drum. This will allow the drum to be reinstalled in its original position.
4. On sedans, remove the grease cap, cotter pin, lock cap, nut, washer and wheel bearing.
5. Tap the drum with a rubber mallet or wooden hammer handle. Remove the brake drum. It will not come off if the parking brake is applied. If the brake drum cannot be removed easily, follow these procedures:
    a. Insert a screwdriver through the hole in the backing plate and hold the adjusting lever away from the star wheel.
    b. Using a brake adjusting tool, turn the star wheel to reduce the tension (increase the clearance) on the brake shoes.

✳✳WARNING

Do not apply the brake pedal while the drum is removed.

To install:
6. Before reinstalling the drum, perform the measurements and adjustments explained in this section.
7. Install the drum, observing the matchmarks made earlier. Keep the drum straight while installing it; if it goes on crooked it can damage the brake shoes.
8. On sedans, install the adjust the wheel bearing(s). Refer to the procedures in this manual.
9. Install the wheel.
10. Lower the car to the ground.
11. Test drive the car at safe speeds and in a safe location to check the pedal feel and brake function. Adjust as necessary.

INSPECTION

▶ See Figure 49

➡For reasons of safety and reliability, we recommend that if one drum requires replacement, both drums, along with new shoes, should be replaced as a set.

1. Clean the drum.
2. Inspect the drum for scoring, cracks, grooves and out-of-roundness. Measure it to determine maximum diameter. A cracked drum must be replaced; do not attempt to weld a drum.
3. Light scoring may be removed by dressing the drum with fine emery cloth. If brake linings are replaced, always resurface a grooved drum.
4. Heavy scoring will require the use of a brake drum lathe to turn the drum.

➡During manufacture, weights are used to balance brake drums. These weights must not be removed. After a drum is refinished, or if there are vibration problems not traceable to wheel balance, the brake drums should be checked for balance. If the drum is out of balance, it must be replaced.

Brake Shoes

INSPECTION

▶ See Figures 50 and 51

➡For reasons of safety and reliability, we recommend that if any shoe requires replacement, all shoes should be replaced as a set.

An inspection hole is provided in the backing plate of each rear wheel which allows the brakes to be checked without removing the drum. Remove the hole plug, then check the

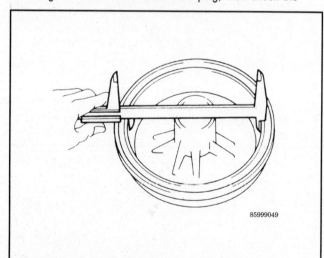

85999049

Fig. 49 The inside diameter of the brake drum should be measured

lining thickness through the hole. If below minimum, the shoes must be replaced. Always install the plug after inspection making certain it is properly seated and tight.

This method doesn't provide a lot of information about how the brakes are wearing since it only shows one part of one shoe, but is a quick and easy first check. The only way to see the friction faces of the shoes is to remove the brake drums. No generalities can be drawn between the left and right side shoes, so both drums must be removed to perform a proper inspection.

With the drums removed:

1. Liberally spray the entire brake assembly with aerosol brake cleaner. Do not use other solvents, compressed air or a dry brush.

2. Measure the thickness of the friction surface on each shoe at several different locations. If any measurement is below the minimum thickness, replace all the shoes (both sides) as a set.

3. Check the contact surfaces closely for any signs of scoring, cracking, uneven or tapered wear, discoloration or separa-

tion from the backing plate. Anything that looks unusual requires replacement.

4. If the shoes are in otherwise good condition except for glazing (a shiny, hard surface), the glaze may be removed by light sanding with emery cloth. Also lightly sand the inside of the drum to de-glaze its surface. Do not attempt to rub out grooves or ridges; this is best done with a resurfacing lathe. After sanding the components wash them thoroughly with aerosol brake cleaner to remove any grit.

REMOVAL & INSTALLATION

▶ **See Figures 52, 53, 54, 55, 56, 57, 58, 59, 60, 61 and 62**

➡**The brake shoes can be removed and replaced using everyday hand tools, but the use of brake spring tools and assorted specialty tools makes the job much easier. These common brake tools are available at low cost and can greatly reduce working time. Record the location of all brake hardware before starting this service procedure. Do one side at a time, so that the other side may be used as guide.**

1. Elevate and safely support the vehicle. If only the rear wheels are elevated, block the front wheels with chocks. Once the vehicle is firmly on stands, release the parking brake.

2. Remove the rear wheel.

3. Remove the brake drum.

✳✳WARNING

Do not apply the brake pedal while the drum is removed.

4. Remove the return spring.

5. Disconnect and remove the retainers, hold-down springs and pins.

6. Remove the anchor spring.

7. Use a pair of pliers to disconnect the parking brake cable from the parking brake lever.

8. Remove the adjusting lever spring.

9. Remove the shoes and adjuster as a unit.

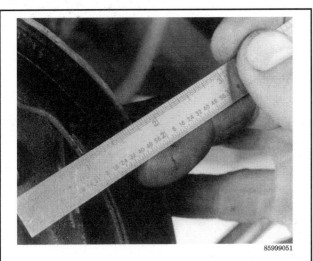

Fig. 51 The brake drums should be removed to allow pad thickness measurement at several different points

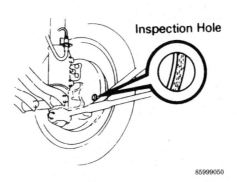

Fig. 50 An inspection hole is provided in the backing plate to observe shoe condition

Fig. 52 Make a note as to the position of the brake components before removal to assure proper installation

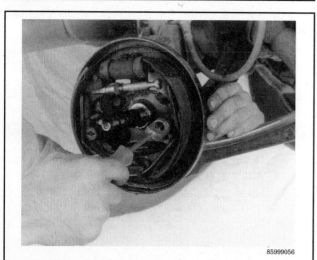

Fig. 53 A hold-down spring removal tool can be used to remove the brake shoe retaining springs

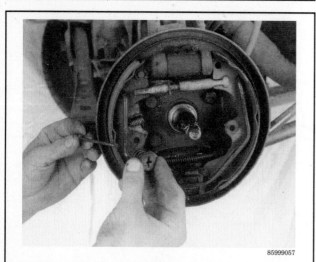

Fig. 54 A hold-down spring and pin is used to secure the brake shoes on most models

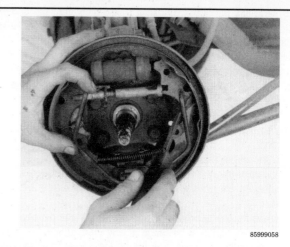

Fig. 55 A small prybar can be used to remove and install the return spring, but work carefully and wear safety glasses

Fig. 56 Remove the shoes and adjusting strut as a unit

10. Disassemble the adjustor, the parking brake lever and the automatic adjuster lever. The C-washer holding the shoe to the adjuster may need to be spread a little before removal.

11. Clean all the parts with aerosol brake solvent. Do not use other solvents.

12. Closely inspect all the parts. Any part of doubtful strength or quality must be replaced.

To install:

13. Apply a small amount of high-temperature grease to the points at which the brake shoes contact the backing plate and to both the contact and pivot points on the adjuster strut.

14. Install the parking brake lever and automatic adjusting lever to the rear (trailing) shoe.

15. Install a new C-washer and use pliers to close it. Do not bend it more than necessary to hold in place.

16. Install the adjuster (strut) and return spring in place on the rear shoe and install the adjusting lever spring.

➡ Do not allow oil or grease to get on the lining surface.

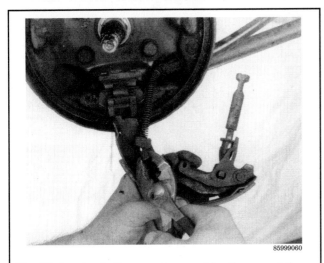

Fig. 57 A pair of pliers can be used to disconnect the parking brake cable from the lever

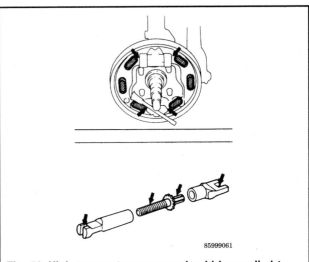

Fig. 58 High temperature grease should be applied to these parts

17. Using pliers, connect the parking brake cable to the lever.

18. Pass the parking brake cable through the notch in the anchor plate.

19. Set the rear shoe in position with the end of the shoe inserted in the wheel cylinder and the adjuster in place.

20. Install the hold-down spring, retainers and pin.

21. Install the anchor spring between the front (leading) and rear shoe.

22. Position the front shoe with the end of the shoe inserted in the wheel cylinder and the adjuster in place.

23. Install the hold-down spring, retainers and pin.

24. Connect the return spring.

25. Measure both the brake diameter and the drum diameter, then adjust the brake shoes to the proper clearance. Refer to the procedure outlined in this section.

26. Install the drum and wheel.

27. Lower the car to the ground.

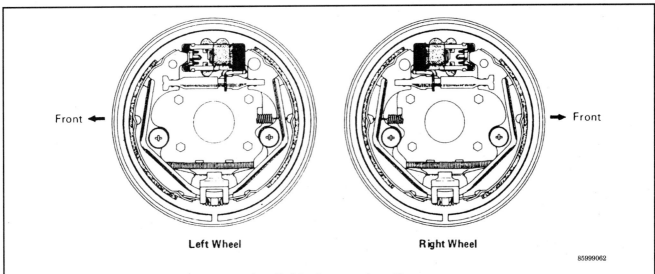

Left Wheel   Right Wheel

Fig. 59 Make sure the brake components are installed in the correct position

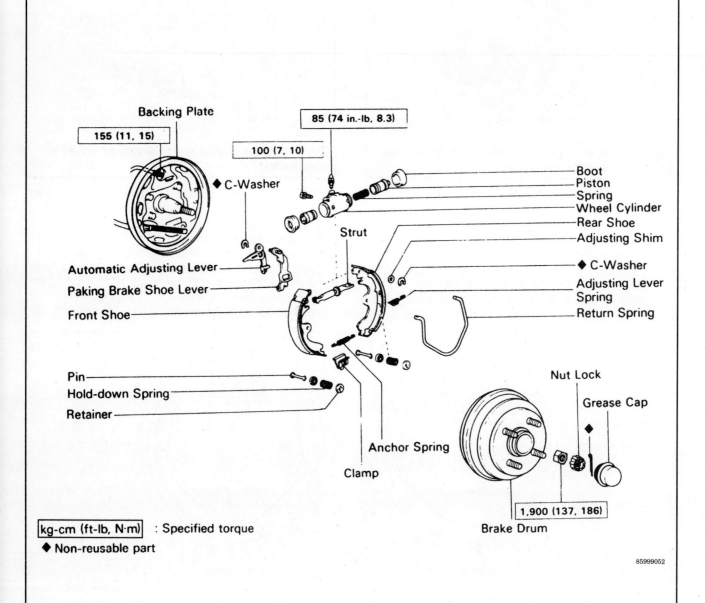

Backing Plate

155 (11, 15)

85 (74 in.-lb, 8.3)

100 (7, 10)

Boot
Piston
Spring
Wheel Cylinder
Rear Shoe
Adjusting Shim

◆ C-Washer

Strut

◆ C-Washer

Adjusting Lever
Spring

Return Spring

Automatic Adjusting Lever
Paking Brake Shoe Lever
Front Shoe

Pin
Hold-down Spring
Retainer

Nut Lock

Grease Cap

Anchor Spring

Clamp

Brake Drum

1,900 (137, 186)

kg-cm (ft-lb, N·m) : Specified torque
◆ Non-reusable part

85999052

Fig. 60 Exploded view of the rear brake components found on sedans

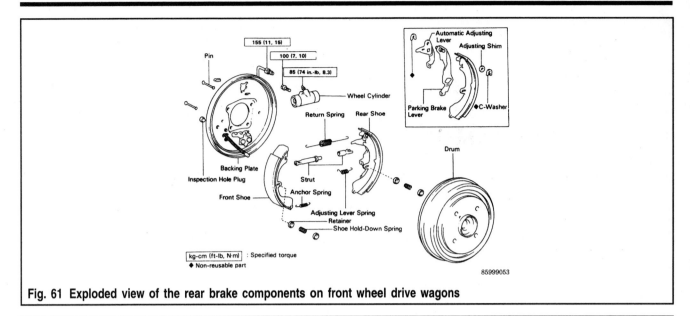

Fig. 61 Exploded view of the rear brake components on front wheel drive wagons

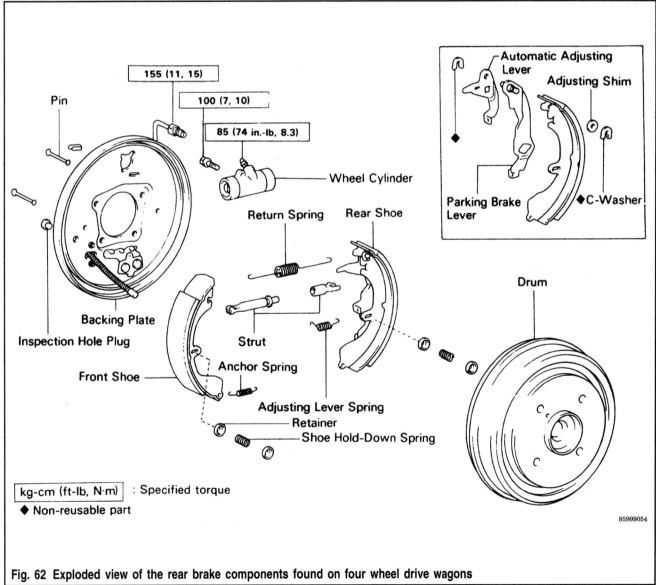

Fig. 62 Exploded view of the rear brake components found on four wheel drive wagons

Wheel Cylinders

REMOVAL & INSTALLATION

▶ See Figure 63

✳✳CAUTION

On models equipped with a Supplemental Restraint System (SRS) or "air bag," work must NOT be started until at least 90 seconds have passed from the time that both the ignition switch is turned to the LOCK position and the negative cable is disconnected from the battery.

➡For reasons of safety and reliability, we recommend that if one wheel cylinder requires replacement, both cylinders should be replaced as a set.

If wheel cylinders are leaking or seized, they should be replaced. The units are inexpensive enough to make replacement a better choice than repair. Even if the pistons and seals can be replaced, the internal bore can rarely be restored to perfect condition. A faulty repair can reduce braking force on the wheel or cause a leak which soaks the brake shoes in fluid.

When inspecting the cylinders on the car, the rubber boots must be lifted carefully and the inner area checked for leaks. A very slight moistness usually coated with dust is normal, but any accumulation of fluid is evidence of a leak and must be dealt with immediately.

1. Remove the rear brake shoes and hardware.
2. Using a line or flare nut wrench, disconnect the brake line from the back of the cylinder. This joint may be dirty or corroded. Clean it off and apply penetrating oil if necessary. Do not allow the threaded fitting to twist the brake line. Plug or tape the brake line to prevent leakage.
3. Loosen the bolts securing the wheel cylinder to the backing plate carefully (to prevent breaking the bolts), then remove the bolts.
4. Remove the wheel cylinder from the backing plate. Drain the remaining fluid into a container.
5. Install the cylinder onto the backing plate and tighten the mounting bolts to 7 ft. lbs. (10 Nm).
6. Carefully reinstall the brake line and tighten it to 11 ft. lbs. (15 Nm).
7. Install the shoes and hardware.
8. Install the brake drum and wheel.
9. Bleed the brake system. Repeat bleeding may be needed to eliminate all the air within the line and cylinder. Refer to the necessary service procedures in this section.

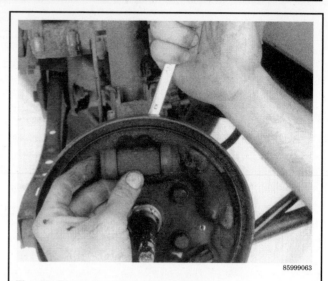

85999063

Fig. 63 Removing the wheel cylinder

Brake Backing Plate

REMOVAL & INSTALLATION

✳✳CAUTION

On models equipped with a Supplemental Restraint System (SRS) or "air bag," work must NOT be started until at least 90 seconds have passed from the time that both the ignition switch is turned to the LOCK position and the negative cable is disconnected from the battery.

1. Elevate and safely support the vehicle. If only the rear wheels are elevated, block the front wheels with chocks. Once the vehicle is firmly on stands, release the parking brake.
2. Remove the rear wheel.
3. Remove the brake drum.
4. Remove the brake shoes and hardware.
5. Disconnect the brake line from the wheel cylinder.
6. On four wheel drive models, remove the rear axle shaft(s). Refer to the procedures in this manual.
7. On front wheel drive models, remove the bolts securing the backing plate/axle assembly.
8. Remove the backing plate.
   To install:
9. Install the backing plate/axle assembly with new gaskets. Refer to any service procedures necessary.
10. Torque the bolts to the following:
    a. 1984-1986 sedans — 59 ft. lbs. (80 Nm)
    b. Front wheel drive wagons — 59 ft. lbs. (80 Nm)
    c. Four wheel drive wagons — 48 ft. lbs. (66 Nm)
    d. 1987-1990 sedans — 51 ft. lbs. (70 Nm)
    e. 1991-1994 sedans — 34 ft. lbs. (47 Nm)
11. Connect the brake line to the wheel cylinder. Tighten to 11 ft. lbs. (15 Nm).
12. Install the brake shoes and hardware.
13. Install the brake drum and rear wheel.
14. Bleed the brake system.
15. Lower the vehicle to the ground.

PARKING BRAKE

Cables

REMOVAL & INSTALLATION

▶ See Figure 64

❈❈CAUTION

On models equipped with a Supplemental Restraint System (SRS) or "air bag," work must NOT be started until at least 90 seconds have passed from the time that both the ignition switch is turned to the LOCK position and the negative cable is disconnected from the battery.

1. Elevate and safely support the car. If only the rear wheels are elevated, block the front wheels. Release the parking brake after the car is supported.
2. Remove the rear wheel(s).
3. Remove the brake drum and shoes.
4. Remove the parking brake cable from the backing plate. A box-end wrench can be slipped over the end of the cable and used to simultaneously depress all of the locking tangs on the cable retainer.
5. Remove any exhaust heat shields which may interfere with the removal of the cable.
6. Remove the cable retaining clip.
7. Remove the cable from the equalizer (yoke).

To install:
8. Fit the end of the new cable into the equalizer and make certain it is properly seated.
9. Install the cable retaining clip.

➥Make certain the cable is properly routed and does not contain any sharp bends or kinks.

10. Feed the cable through the backing plate.
11. Install the brake shoes and hardware.
12. Install the brake drums and wheels.
13. Lower the car to the ground, then adjust the parking brake.

Fig. 64 When removing the parking brake cable from the backing plate, use a box-end wrench to depress the retaining tangs

85999064

ADJUSTMENT

▶ See Figures 65 and 66

1. Pull the parking brake lever all the way up and count the number of clicks. The correct range is as follows:
   a. 1984-1986 sedans — 5-8 clicks
   b. Wagons — 6-8 clicks
   c. 1987-1990 sedans — 7-9 clicks
   d. 1991-1994 sedans — 4-7 clicks

➥Before adjusting the parking brake, make sure that the rear brakes are adjusted properly.

2. Remove the center console box or the brake lever cover.
3. At the rear of the handbrake lever, loosen the locknut on the brake cable.
4. Turn the adjusting nut until the parking brake travel is correct.
5. Tighten the locknut.
6. Reinstall the console.

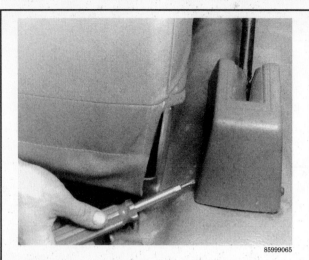

Fig. 65 The brake lever cover is secured by several screws

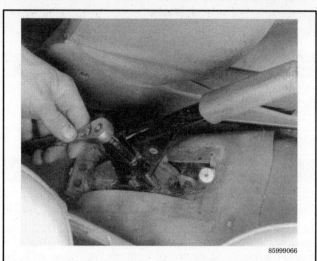

Fig. 66 Loosen the locknut, then turn the adjusting screw

ANTI-LOCK BRAKE SYSTEM

Description and Operation

▶ See Figure 67

This system is designed to prevent wheel lock-up during emergency braking or when braking on slick road conditions. By preventing wheel lock-up, maximum braking and steering capability is maintained. The system is a combination of electrical and hydraulic components working together to control the flow of brake fluid when necessary.

Under normal braking conditions, the anti-lock brake system (ABS) functions in the same manner as a standard brake system. During anti-lock braking, line pressures are controlled by the rapid cycling of electronic valves within the actuator. These valves can allow pressures in the system to increase, remain constant or decrease depending on the conditions determined by the ABS Electronic Control Unit (ECU).

The operator may feel the pedal pulsate and hear a clicking sound as the ABS is engaged. Although the ABS prevents wheel lock-up during hard braking, some tire chirp may be heard. This is an indication that the system is holding the wheel(s) just outside the point of lock-up. Additionally, the final few feet of an ABS-engaged stop may be completed with the wheels locked as the system does not function below 4 mph (6.5 kph). All of these conditions are normal and are not indicative of a system problem.

The ABS consists of speed sensors for each wheel, ABS warning light, solenoid and motor relays, actuator and the ABS electronic control unit. Due to the high-cost of the tools and the skill required, testing of the actuator and the ECU should only be performed by your dealer or a reputable shop.

ABS Warning Light

TESTING

▶ See Figure 68

The ABS warning light should turn on for 3 seconds, then turn off when the ignition switch is turned to the **ON** position. If the light does not come on, check the fuse, bulb and wiring harness. If the light turns on, but does not turn off after 3 seconds, turns on and off intermittently or stays on, have the vehicle serviced by your dealer or a reputable shop.

ABS Electronic Control Unit

REMOVAL & INSTALLATION

❈❈CAUTION

On models equipped with a Supplemental Restraint System (SRS) or "air bag," work must NOT be started until at least 90 seconds have passed from the time that both the ignition switch is turned to the LOCK position and the negative cable is disconnected from the battery.

1. With the ignition **OFF**, disconnect the negative battery cable.
2. Remove the appropriate trim panel.
3. Unplug the electrical connections.
4. Remove the retaining nuts.
5. Installation is the reverse of removal.

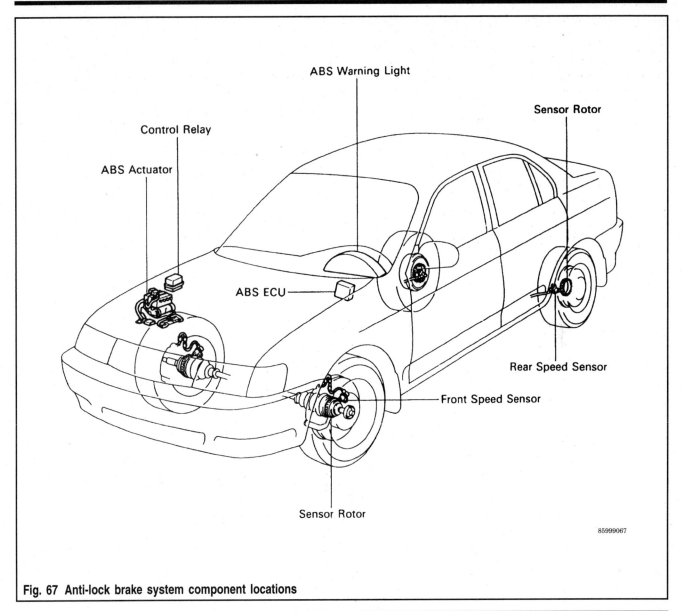

Fig. 67 Anti-lock brake system component locations

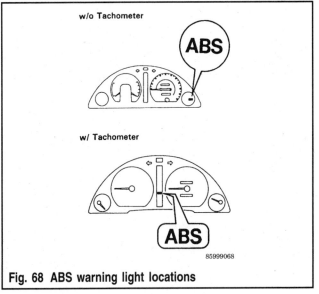

Fig. 68 ABS warning light locations

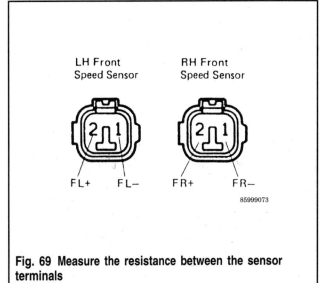

Fig. 69 Measure the resistance between the sensor terminals

Speed Sensors

TESTING

Front Speed Sensors

▶ See Figures 69, 70 and 71

1. Remove the fender shield.
2. Unplug the speed sensor connector.
3. Measure the resistance between the terminals. It should be between 0.92-1.22 kΩ.
4. Check that there is no continuity between each terminal and the sensor body.
5. Replace the sensor if the conditions are not as specified.
6. Engage the electrical connection, then install the fender shield.
7. Remove the front driveshaft. Refer to the appropriate procedure in this manual.
8. Inspect the sensor rotor serrations on the end of the driveshaft for scratches, cracks, warping or missing teeth. Replace, as applicable.
9. Install the driveshaft.

Rear Speed Sensors

▶ See Figures 70, 72 and 73

1. Remove the rear seat cushion.
2. Unplug the speed sensor connector.
3. Measure the resistance between the terminals. It should be between 0.9-1.3 kΩ. Replace the sensor if resistance is not as specified.
4. Check that there is no continuity between each terminal and the sensor body.
5. Replace the sensor if the conditions are not as specified.
6. Engage the electrical connection, then install the rear seat cushion.
7. Remove the brake drum. Refer to the appropriate procedure in this manual.
8. Inspect the sensor rotor serrations for scratches, cracks, warping or missing teeth. Replace, as applicable.

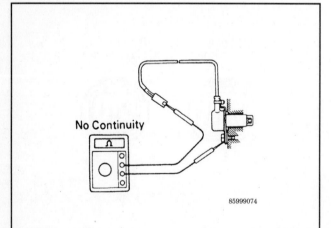

Fig. 70 Check that there is no continuity between the terminals and the sensor body

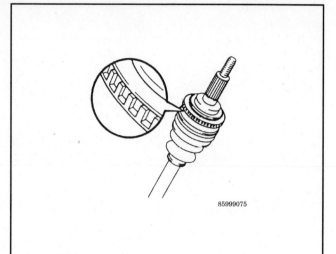

Fig. 71 Check the sensor rotor serrations on the halfshaft for damage

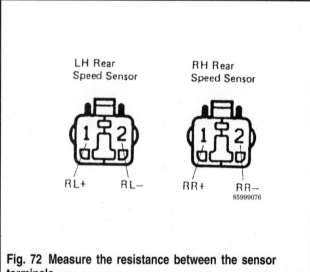

Fig. 72 Measure the resistance between the sensor terminals

9. Install the brake drum.

REMOVAL & INSTALLATION

✳✳CAUTION

On models equipped with a Supplemental Restraint System (SRS) or "air bag," work must NOT be started until at least 90 seconds have passed from the time that both the ignition switch is turned to the LOCK position and the negative cable is disconnected from the battery.

Front Sensors

▶ See Figures 74, 75, 76 and 77

1. Disconnect the negative battery cable.
2. Remove the fender shield, then unplug the electrical connection.

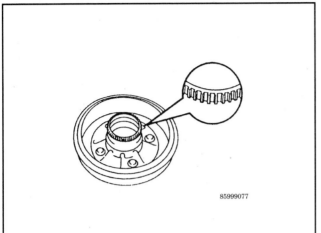

Fig. 73 Check the rotor serrations on the hub of the brake drum for damage

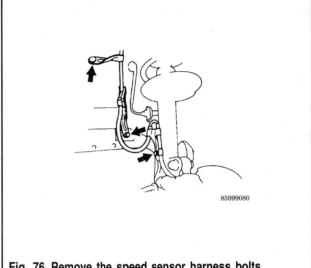

Fig. 76 Remove the speed sensor harness bolts

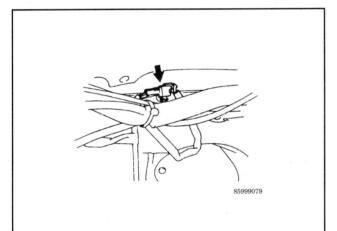

Fig. 75 Unplug the front speed sensor electrical connection. This is usually hidden under the fender shield

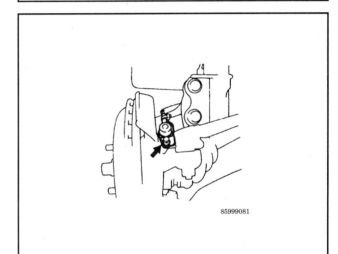

Fig. 77 Remove the bolt securing the speed sensor to the steering knuckle

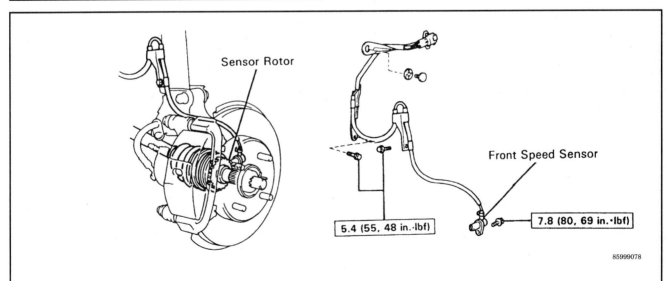

Fig. 74 Front speed sensor installation

3. Remove the clamp bolts and clip securing the sensor harness to the body and shock absorber.

4. Remove the speed sensor from the steering knuckle.

To install:

5. Install the speed sensor to the steering knuckle. Tighten to 69 inch lbs. (7.8 Nm).

6. Engage the sensor electrical connection. Tighten the sensor harness bolts to 48 inch lbs. (5.4 Nm).

7. Install the fender shield.

Rear Sensors

▶ **See Figures 78, 79, 80 and 81**

1. Disconnect the negative battery cable.

2. Remove the rear seat cushion.

3. Unplug the sensor connector, then pull out the sensor wire harness with the grommet.

4. Remove the bolts securing the harness to the suspension arm.

5. Remove the sensor attaching bolt, then remove the sensor.

To install:

6. Install the speed sensor. Tighten to 69 inch lbs. (7.8 Nm).

7. Pass the sensor harness through the body panel, then engage the electrical connection.

8. Install the grommet securely.

9. Tighten the sensor harness bolts to 48 inch lbs. (5.4 Nm). Install the rear seat cushion.

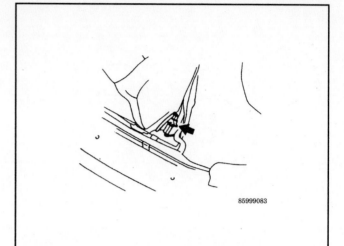

Fig. 79 Remove the seat cushion, then unplug the electrical connection for the rear speed sensor

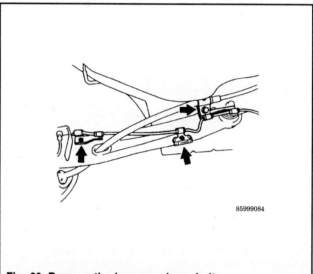

Fig. 80 Remove the harness clamp bolts

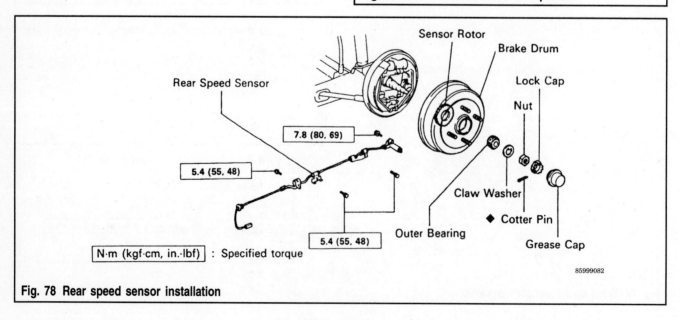

Fig. 78 Rear speed sensor installation

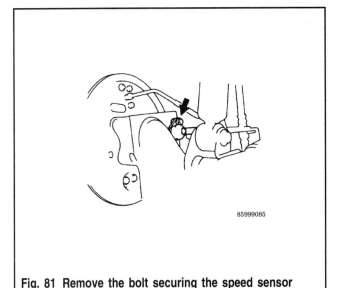

Fig. 81 Remove the bolt securing the speed sensor

Actuator

REMOVAL & INSTALLATION

♦ See Figures 82, 83, 84 and 85

✳✳CAUTION

On models equipped with a Supplemental Restraint System (SRS) or "air bag," work must NOT be started until at least 90 seconds have passed from the time that both the ignition switch is turned to the LOCK position and the negative cable is disconnected from the battery.

1. Disconnect the negative battery cable.
2. Remove the bolt securing the power steering hose (if equipped).
3. Remove the bolt securing the brake lines to the shock tower.
4. Unplug the electrical connections.
5. Disconnect the brake lines from the actuator using a line or flare nut wrench.
6. Remove the bolts securing the actuator bracket to the body, then remove the assembly from the vehicle.
7. Separate the actuator from the bracket assembly, if necessary.
   To install:
8. Install the actuator assembly to the vehicle. Tighten the side bracket bolts to 14 ft. lbs. (19 Nm) and the front bracket bolt to 9 ft. lbs. (13 Nm).
9. Thread the brake line fittings into the actuator. Tighten them to 11 ft. lbs. (15 Nm).
10. Engage the electrical connectors.
11. Install the bolts securing the brake lines and power steering hose.
12. Connect the negative battery cable, then bleed the brake system.

13. Inspect for leaks, then check for proper ABS warning light operation.

Solenoid and Motor Relays

TESTING

Motor Relay
♦ See Figures 86 and 87

1. Inspect the continuity of the relay as follows:
   a. Unplug the electrical connector.
   b. Check that there is continuity between terminals 9 and 10 of the relay.
   c. Check that there is no continuity between terminals 7 and 8 of the relay.
   d. Replace the relay if not as specified.
2. Inspect the operation of the motor relay as follows:
   a. Using jumper wires, connect the positive lead from the battery to terminal 10 and negative lead to terminal 9 of the relay.
   b. Check that there is continuity between terminals 7 and 8 of the relay.
   c. Replace the relay if operation is not as specified.
3. Engage the electrical connector.

Solenoid Relay
♦ See Figures 88 and 89

1. Inspect the continuity of the relay as follows:
   a. Unplug the electrical connector.
   b. Check that there is continuity between terminals 1 and 9 of the relay.
   c. Check that there is no continuity between terminals 2 and 5 of the relay.
   d. Replace the relay if not as specified.
2. Inspect the operation of the motor relay as follows:
   a. Using jumper wires, connect the positive lead from the battery to terminal 1 and negative lead to terminal 9 of the relay.
   b. Check that there is continuity between terminals 2 and 5 of the relay.
   c. Check that there is no continuity between terminals 2 and 6 of the relay.
   d. Replace the relay if operation is not as specified.

REMOVAL & INSTALLATION

♦ See Figure 90

1. Disconnect the negative battery cable.
2. Unplug the electrical connections from the control relays.
3. Remove the control relay assembly from the actuator bracket. Replace the appropriate relay, if necessary.
   To install:
4. Install the control relay assembly to the actuator bracket.
5. Engage the electrical connection.
6. Check for proper ABS warning light operation.

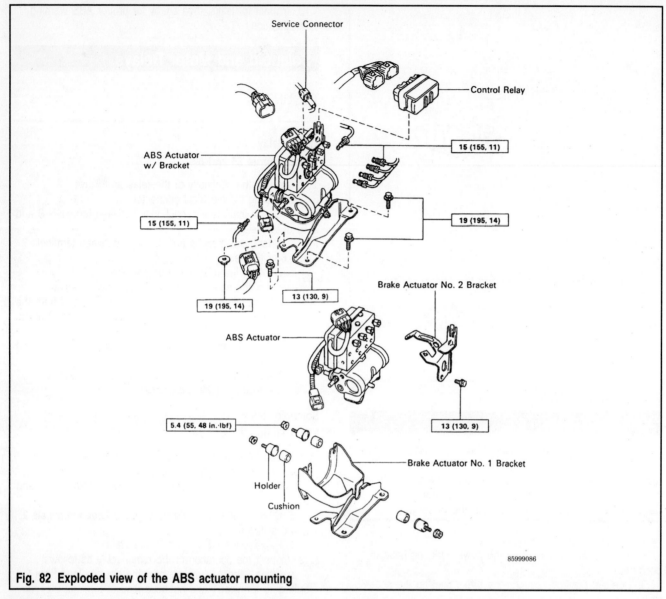

Fig. 82 Exploded view of the ABS actuator mounting

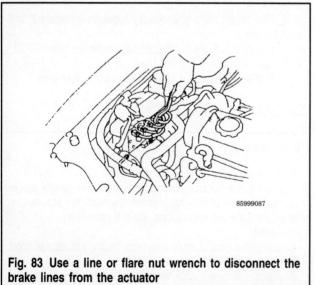

Fig. 83 Use a line or flare nut wrench to disconnect the brake lines from the actuator

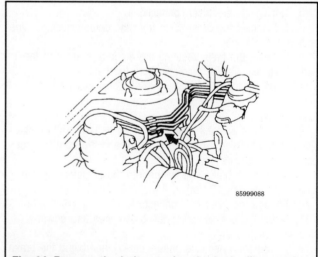

Fig. 84 Remove the bolt securing the brake lines to the shock tower

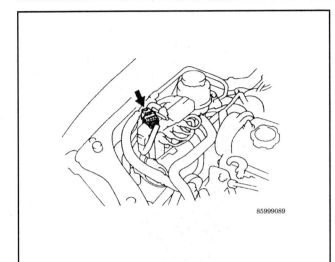

Fig. 85 Be careful not to break the lock-tabs when unplugging the electrical connections

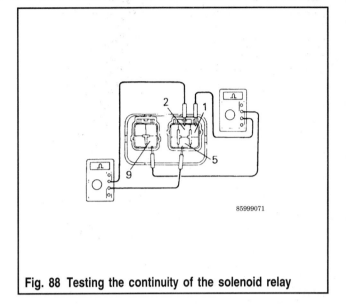

Fig. 88 Testing the continuity of the solenoid relay

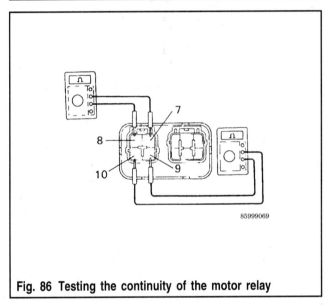

Fig. 86 Testing the continuity of the motor relay

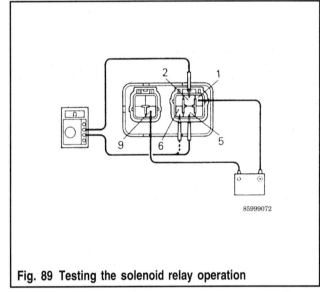

Fig. 89 Testing the solenoid relay operation

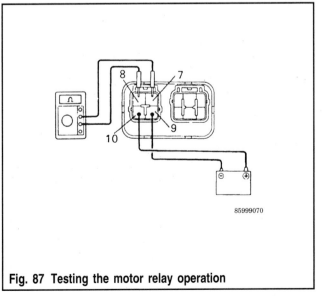

Fig. 87 Testing the motor relay operation

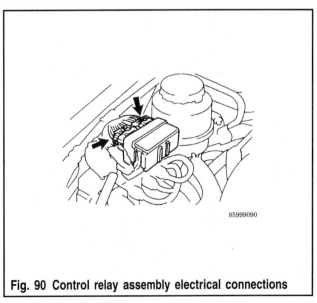

Fig. 90 Control relay assembly electrical connections

BRAKE SPECIFICATIONS

All measurements in inches unless noted.

Year	Model	Master Cylinder Bore	Brake Disc			Brake Drum Diameter			Minimum Lining Thickness	
			Original Thickness	Minimum Thickness	Maximum Runout	Original Inside Diameter	Max. Wear Limit	Maximum Machine Diameter	Front	Rear
1984	Tercel	①	0.433	0.394	0.006	7.087 ②	7.126 ③	7.126 ③	0.040	0.040
1985	Tercel	①	0.433	0.394	0.006	7.087 ②	7.126 ③	7.126 ③	0.040	0.040
1986	Tercel	①	0.433	0.394	0.006	7.087 ②	7.126 ③	7.126 ③	0.040	0.040
1987	Tercel	①	0.433	0.394	0.006	7.087 ②	7.126 ③	7.126 ③	0.040	0.040
1988	Tercel	①	0.433	0.394	0.006	7.087 ②	7.126 ③	7.126 ③	0.040	0.040
1989	Tercel	①	0.433	0.394	0.006	7.087	7.126 ③	7.126 ③	0.040	0.040
1990	Tercel	①	0.433	0.394	0.0059	7.087	7.126	7.126	0.394	0.039
1991	Tercel	①	0.709	0.669	0.0035	7.087	7.126	7.126	0.039	0.039
1992	Tercel	①	0.709	0.669	0.0035	7.087	7.126	7.126	0.039	0.039
1993	Tercel	①	0.709	0.669	0.0035	7.087	7.126	7.126	0.039	0.039
1994	Tercel	①	0.709	0.669	0.0035	7.087	7.126	7.126	0.039	0.039

① Not specified by the manufacturer
② Wagon—FWD & 4WD: 7.874
③ Wagon—FWD & 4WD: 7.913

85999300

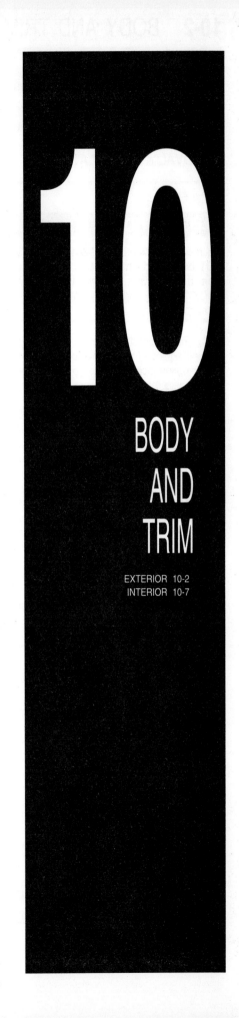

10

BODY
AND
TRIM

EXTERIOR

Doors

REMOVAL & INSTALLATION

▶ See Figure 1

✳✳CAUTION

On models equipped with an air bag (SRS), work must NOT be started until at least 90 seconds have passed from the time that both the ignition switch is turned to the LOCK position and the negative cable is disconnected from the battery.

1. Disconnect the negative battery cable.
2. If equipped with power door locks, windows or any other power option located in the door, remove the inner door panel then unplug the electrical connections. Remove the wire harness retainers, then extract the harness from the door.
3. Matchmark the hinge locations to aid in installation.
4. Pull the door stopper pin upward while pushing in on the claw. Leave the claw raised after removing the pin.
5. Place a wooden block or equivalent under the door for protection, then support it with a floor jack.
6. Remove the door mounting bolts, then remove the door.

To install:

7. Position the door on the vehicle and loosely install the hinge bolts.
8. Align the hinges with the matchmarks, then tighten the bolts.
9. Install and connect the door wire harness and trim panel, if applicable.
10. Slowly close the door and check for proper alignment. Adjust the door as necessary.

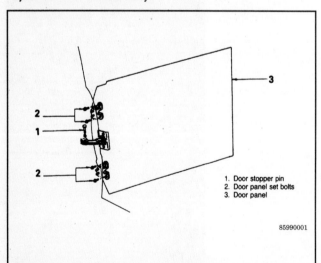

1. Door stopper pin
2. Door panel set bolts
3. Door panel

85990001

Fig. 1 Common door hinge assemblies found on most models

ADJUSTMENT

▶ See Figures 2, 3 and 4

1. To adjust the door in the forward/rearward and vertical directions, loosen the body side hinge bolts and move the door to the desired position.
2. To adjust the door in the left/right and vertical direction, loosen the door side hinge bolts and move the door to the desired position.
3. Adjust the door lock striker as necessary by slightly loosening the striker mounting screws, then tap the striker lightly with a soft-faced hammer. Tighten the striker mounting screws.

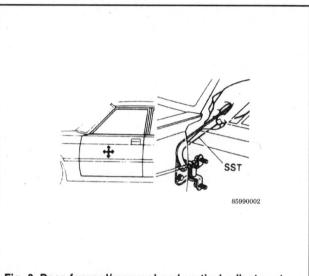

SST

85990002

Fig. 2 Door forward/rearward and vertical adjustment

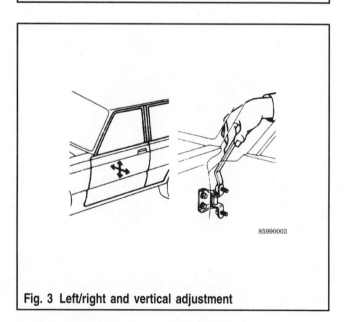

85990003

Fig. 3 Left/right and vertical adjustment

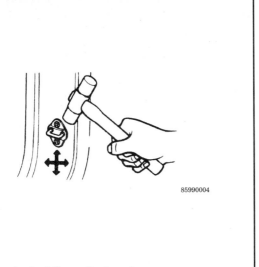

Fig. 4 Door lock striker adjustment

Hood

REMOVAL & INSTALLATION

▶ See Figure 5

❋❋CAUTION

On models equipped with an air bag (SRS), work must NOT be started until at least 90 seconds have passed from the time that both the ignition switch is turned to the LOCK position and the negative cable is disconnected from the battery.

1. Disconnect the negative battery cable.
2. Protect the painted areas such as the fenders with a cover.
3. Matchmark the position of the hinges on the hood. Loosen the hinge-to-hood retaining bolts.

Fig. 5 Have an assistant hold the hood while removing the attaching bolts

4. With the aid of an assistant remove the retaining bolts, then lift the hood away from the car. Use care not to damage the hood or vehicle during removal.
   To install:
5. Carefully install the hood on the vehicle and loosely install the bolts.
6. Align the matchmarks, then tighten the bolts.
7. Close the hood slowly to check for proper alignment. Do not slam the hood closed, alignment is usually required.
8. Align the hood so that all clearances are the same and the hood panel is flush with the body.

ALIGNMENT

▶ See Figures 6, 7, 8 and 9

➡On some models, a centering bolt is used as the hood hinge set bolt; the hood can not be adjusted with it on. Substitute a bolt with a washer for the centering bolt.

1. For forward/rearward and left/right adjustments, loosen the hinge bolts and move the hood the desired position.
2. For vertical adjustment of the hoods front edge, turn the cushion.
3. For vertical adjustment of the rear end of the hood, increase or decrease the number of washers or shims.
4. Adjust the hood lock if necessary by loosening the bolts, then repositioning.

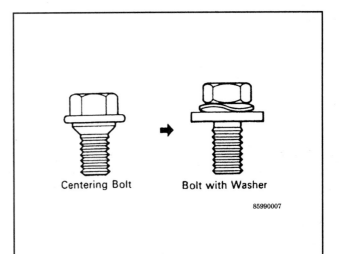

Centering Bolt   Bolt with Washer

Fig. 6 Substitute the centering bolt with a standard bolt and washer

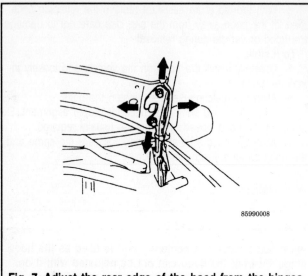

Fig. 7 Adjust the rear edge of the hood from the hinges

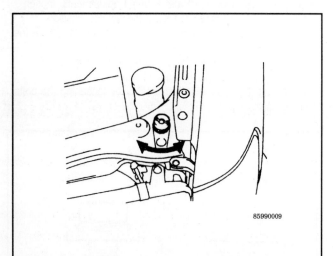

Fig. 8 The front of the hood can be adjusted by turning the cushions

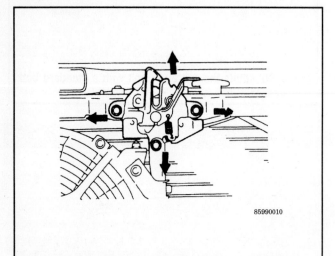

Fig. 9 If necessary, the hood lock can be adjusted by loosening the bolts, then repositioning it

Hatch or Trunk Lid

REMOVAL & INSTALLATION

▶ See Figures 10 and 11

✳✳CAUTION

On models equipped with an air bag (SRS), work must NOT be started until at least 90 seconds have passed from the time that both the ignition switch is turned to the LOCK position and the negative cable is disconnected from the battery.

Trunk Lid

1. Disconnect the negative battery cable.
2. If necessary, disconnect the wire harness from the trunk lid.
3. Matchmark the position of the trunk lid to the hinges.
4. Have an assistant hold the trunk lid, then remove the bolts securing the trunk lid to the hinges.
5. Carefully remove the trunk lid from the vehicle.
6. Installation is the reverse of removal. Adjust as necessary.

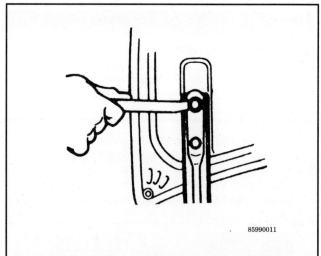

Fig. 10 Matchmark the position of the trunk lid before removing the attaching bolts

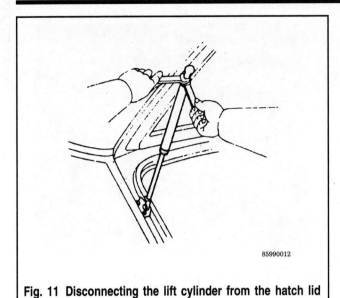

Fig. 11 Disconnecting the lift cylinder from the hatch lid

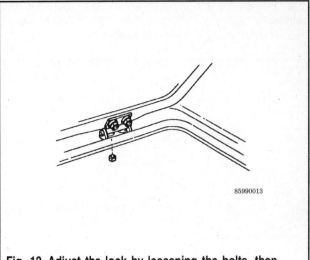

Fig. 12 Adjust the lock by loosening the bolts, then repositioning

Hatch Lid

1. Disconnect the negative battery cable.
2. If necessary, disconnect the wire harness from the hatch lid.
3. Matchmark the position of the hinges on the hatch.
4. Have an assistant hold the hatch, then disconnect the lift cylinder.
5. Remove the hinge bolts, then carefully remove the lid.
6. Installation is the reverse of removal. Adjust as necessary.

ADJUSTMENT

▶ See Figure 12

1. For forward/rearward and left/right adjustments, loosen the bolts then move the hood the desired position.
2. For vertical adjustment of the of the lid, increase or decrease the number of shims or washers on the hinges.
3. Adjust the lock or striker by loosening the bolts, then repositioning.

Bumpers

REMOVAL & INSTALLATION

✳✳CAUTION

On models equipped with an air bag (SRS), work must NOT be started until at least 90 seconds have passed from the time that both the ignition switch is turned to the LOCK position and the negative cable is disconnected from the battery.

1. Disconnect the negative battery cable.
2. Unplug all electrical connections at the bumper assembly.
3. Remove the bumper cover, if necessary. It may be necessary to remove the head or tail lamp assemblies to gain access to the attaching screws.
4. Remove the bumper mounting bolts and bumper assembly. Remove the shock absorbers from the bumper, as necessary.

➡**The shock absorber is filled with a high pressure gas and should not be disassembled.**

5. Install bumper assembly in the reverse order of the removal. Align the bumper assemblies, as necessary.

Grille

REMOVAL & INSTALLATION

▶ See Figures 13, 14 and 15

1. The grille is usually secured by a series of small screws. Raise the hood and look for screws securing the grille to the metalwork.

2. Remove the retaining screws, then lift the grille from the vehicle.

3. Installation is the reverse of removal.

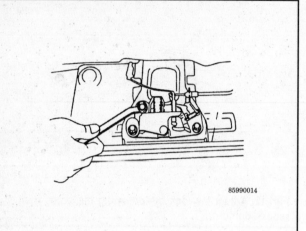

Fig. 13 Most of the grille attaching screws are easily accessed

Fig. 14 There may also be some hidden attaching screws or bolts

Fig. 15 Make sure all of the retainers are removed before removing the grille

Outside Mirrors

REMOVAL & INSTALLATION

▶ **See Figure 16**

1. Remove the setting screw and knob. Tape the end of a thin screwdriver or equivalent and pry retainer loose to remove the cover.

2. Remove the retaining screws, then remove the mirror assembly. Unplug the electrical connection on power mirrors.

3. Installation is the reverse of the removal procedure. Cycle the mirror several times to make sure that it works properly.

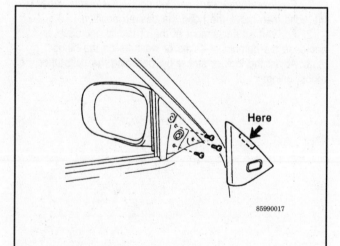

Fig. 16 The mirror retaining screws can be accessed after removing the cover

Antenna

➡On most applications, the mast and cable are one piece. If the mast is damaged or broken, the entire antenna assembly including the cable must be replaced.

REMOVAL & INSTALLATION

✱✱CAUTION

On models equipped with an air bag (SRS), work must NOT be started until at least 90 seconds have passed from the time that both the ignition switch is turned to the LOCK position and the negative cable is disconnected from the battery.

1. Disconnect the negative battery cable.
2. Remove the radio.
3. Remove the lower left dashboard trim and kick panel.
4. Attach a long piece of mechanic's wire or heavy string to the end of the antenna wire. This will track up through the pillar as you remove the old antenna and be available to pull the new line into place.
5. Remove the attaching screws at the antenna mast. Remove the antenna and carefully pull the cable up the pillar. Have an assistant insure the end inside the car does not snag or pull other wires.
   To install:
6. Remove the mechanic's wire or string from the old cable, then attach it to the new cable. Make sure it is tied so that the plug will stay straight during installation.
7. With an assistant, feed the new cable into the pillar while pulling gently on the guide wire or string. Route the antenna cable properly under the dash, making sure it will not snag on the steering column or pedal linkages. Route the cable high enough that there is no chance of it hanging around the driver's feet. Use tape or cable ties to secure it.
8. Install the attaching screws holding the mast to the pillar. Make sure the screws are properly threaded and that both the screws and their holes are free of dirt or corrosion. A poor connection at these screws can affect antenna and radio performance.
9. Remove the guide line from the antenna cable. Install the radio, then check for proper operation.
10. Install the lower left dashboard trim and the left side kick panel.

Fenders

REMOVAL & INSTALLATION

✱✱CAUTION

On models equipped with an air bag (SRS), work must NOT be started until at least 90 seconds have passed from the time that both the ignition switch is turned to the LOCK position and the negative cable is disconnected from the battery.

1. Disconnect the negative battery cable.
2. Remove the inner fender liner and bumper assembly, if necessary, for clearance.
3. Tape the edge of the door and hood to protect the paint finish.
4. Remove all bolts securing the fender, then carefully remove the fender from the vehicle.
5. Installation is the reverse of removal.

INTERIOR

Instrument Panel and Pad

REMOVAL & INSTALLATION

✱✱CAUTION

On models equipped with an air bag (SRS), work must NOT be started until at least 90 seconds have passed from the time that both the ignition switch is turned to the LOCK position and the negative cable is disconnected from the battery.

Wagons and 1984-1986 Sedans
▶ **See Figures 17, 18, 19 and 20**

1. Disconnect the negative battery cable.
2. Remove the steering wheel.
3. Remove the right and left front pillar trim. Pry the clips with a small prybar, then pull the trim pieces from the pillars.
4. Remove the right side speaker grille. The grille may be attached with a clip (which must be pulled loose to remove the grille) and/or with screws.

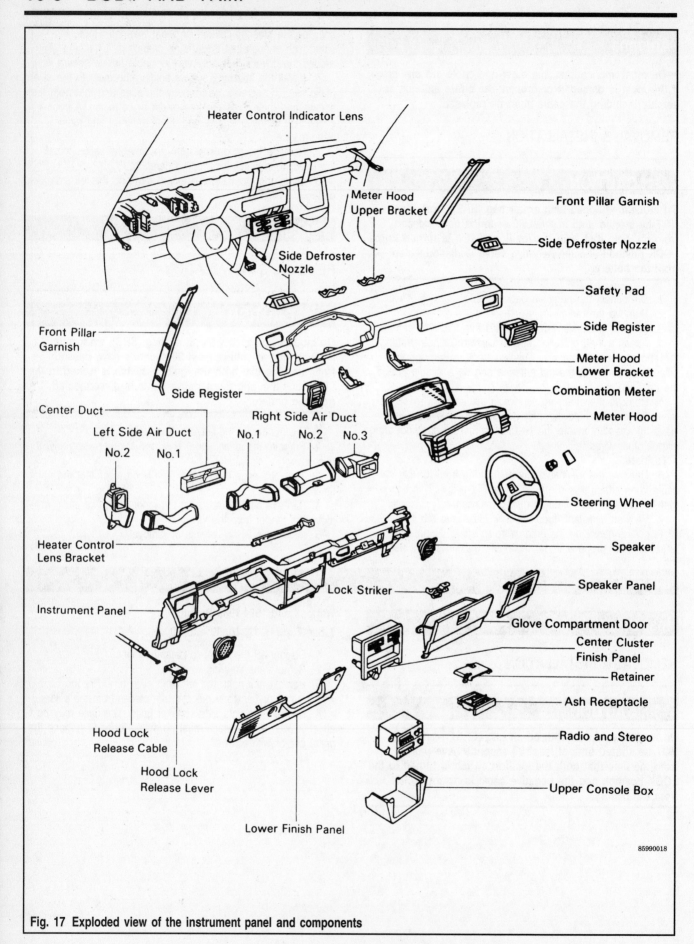

Heater Control Indicator Lens

Meter Hood Upper Bracket

Front Pillar Garnish

Side Defroster Nozzle

Side Defroster Nozzle

Safety Pad

Side Register

Front Pillar Garnish

Meter Hood Lower Bracket

Side Register

Combination Meter

Center Duct

Right Side Air Duct

Meter Hood

Left Side Air Duct

No.1   No.2   No.3

No.2   No.1

Steering Wheel

Heater Control Lens Bracket

Speaker

Speaker Panel

Lock Striker

Instrument Panel

Glove Compartment Door

Center Cluster Finish Panel

Retainer

Ash Receptacle

Hood Lock Release Cable

Radio and Stereo

Hood Lock Release Lever

Upper Console Box

Lower Finish Panel

85990018

Fig. 17 Exploded view of the instrument panel and components

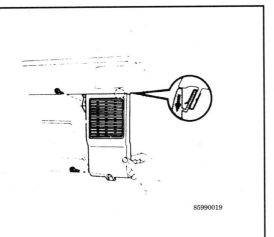

Fig. 18 The speaker panel is usually secured by clips and screws

5. Remove the glove compartment door. This is usually secured by screws on its hinge. Unplug the electrical connection for the right side speaker.

6. Remove the right side air ducts.

7. Remove the radio and heater control panel.

8. Remove the lower trim cover from the steering column.

9. Remove the hood release lever.

10. Remove the heater duct assembly.

11. Remove the combination meter (instrument cluster) assembly from the instrument panel.

12. Remove the side-window defroster nozzles. The grilles are snapped into place.

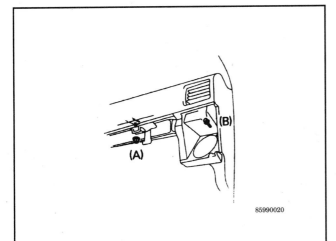

Fig. 19 Always look for hidden screws and nuts when removing the instrument panel

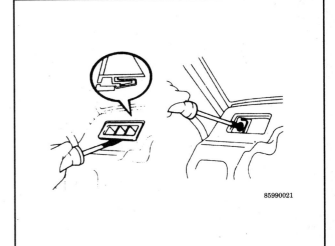

Fig. 20 There are some attaching screws hidden under the side window defroster and outlet ducts

13. Remove the mounting bolts for the dashboard assembly and remove the dash assembly from the car. Be careful of any wiring and/or hoses routed along the back of the dash. Do not damage any other components while the dash is being removed from the car.

To install:

14. Position the dashboard in the car. Attach any wiring harnesses to the inside of the dash before securing the mounting bolts.

15. Install the side defroster nozzles.

16. Install the heater control panel and connect its wiring and vacuum lines. Install the trim panel on the lower console.

17. Install the radio and accessory equipment and install its trim panel.

18. Engage the speaker electrical connection, then install the glove box door.

19. Install the heater ducts.

20. Install the instrument assembly, connecting the speedometer cable and the wiring connectors.

21. Install the hood for the instrument cluster and then install the air outlet grilles.

22. Install the steering column and front pillar trim covers.

23. Install the steering wheel. Connect the negative battery cable. Start the engine, then road test the vehicle for proper operation. Check the operation of all instrument dashboard components.

1987-1990 Sedans

▶ See Figures 21, 22, 23, 24, 25 and 26

1. Disconnect the negative battery cable.
2. Remove the steering wheel.
3. Remove the console.
4. Remove the steering column covers.

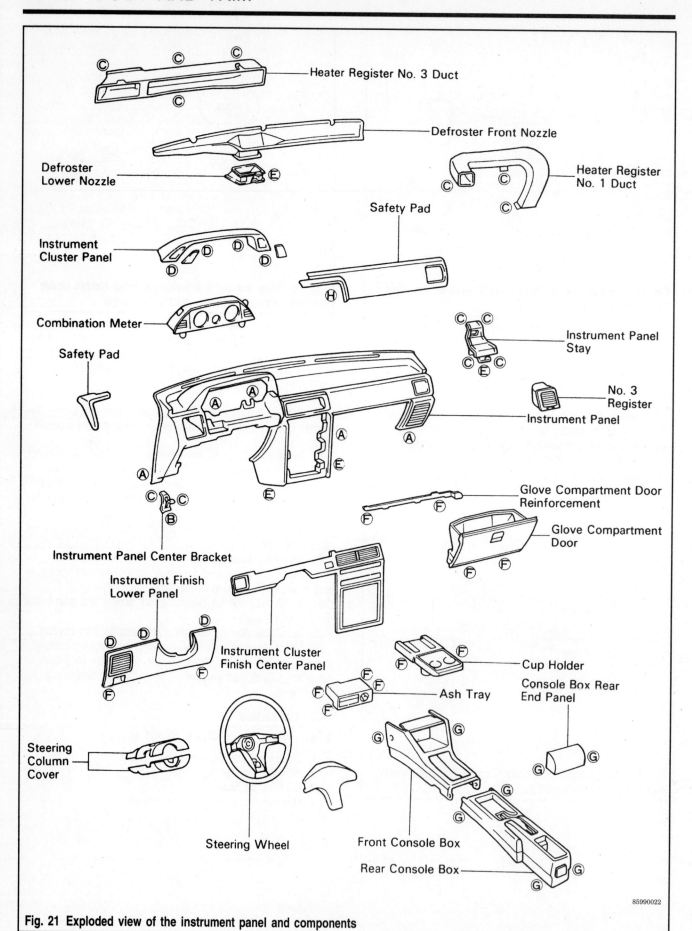

Heater Register No. 3 Duct

Defroster Front Nozzle

Defroster Lower Nozzle

Heater Register No. 1 Duct

Safety Pad

Instrument Cluster Panel

Combination Meter

Instrument Panel Stay

Safety Pad

No. 3 Register

Instrument Panel

Glove Compartment Door Reinforcement

Glove Compartment Door

Instrument Panel Center Bracket

Instrument Finish Lower Panel

Instrument Cluster Finish Center Panel

Cup Holder

Console Box Rear End Panel

Ash Tray

Steering Column Cover

Steering Wheel

Front Console Box

Rear Console Box

85990022

Fig. 21 Exploded view of the instrument panel and components

5. Remove the screws attaching the hood release lever.
6. Pull off the knob for the light control rheostat, then remove the retaining nut.
7. Remove the lower finish panel attaching screws, then remove the panel. Unplug the electrical connections.
8. Remove the heater control panel knobs and the screw attaching the center finish panel. Carefully pull the center finish panel from the dash.
9. Remove the combination meter (instrument cluster).
10. Remove the heater control panel and radio.
11. Remove the screws attaching the glove box door and reinforcement, then remove the door and reinforcement.
12. Remove the bolts/screws securing the dashboard. Pull out at an upward angle to remove the assembly from the vehicle

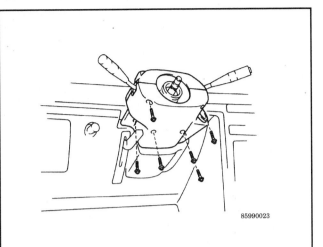

Fig. 22 The steering column cover is secured by a series of screws

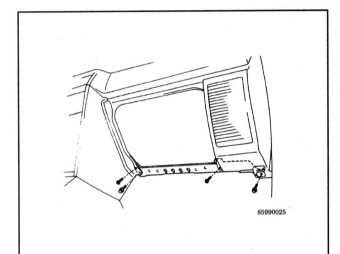

Fig. 24 The glovebox door reinforcement is secured by small screws

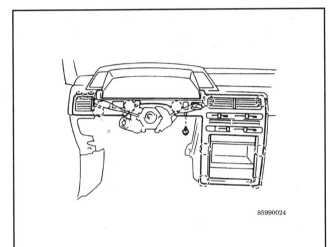

Fig. 23 The center finish panel is held by a small screw and several hidden clips

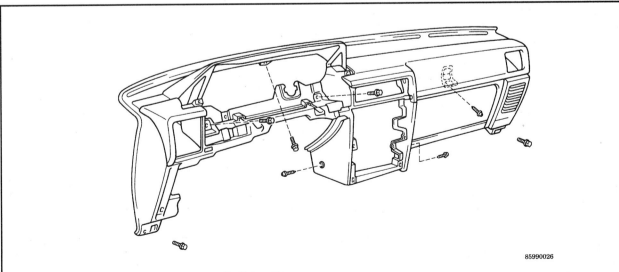

Fig. 25 Instrument panel attaching screw/bolt locations

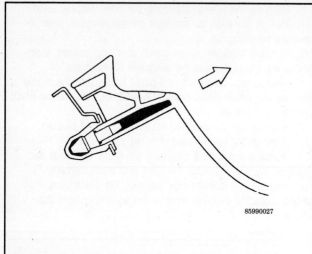

85990027

Fig. 26 When removing the instrument panel, pull it upwards at an angle to disengage it from its clips

To install:

13. Position the dashboard in the vehicle. Make sure the speedometer cable and wiring harnesses are correctly routed.

14. Install the glove box door and reinforcement.

15. Install the heater control panel and radio.

16. Install the combination meter.

17. Install the center finish and lower finish trim panels.

18. Install the hood release lever and rheostat knob.

19. Install the steering column cover, steering wheel and console.

20. Connect the negative battery cable. Start the engine, then road test the vehicle for proper operation. Check the operation of all instrument dashboard components.

1991-1994 Sedans

▶ **See Figures 27, 28, 29, 30, 31, 32 and 33**

1. Disconnect the negative battery cable.

2. Pull the front pillar trim panels from the retaining clips.

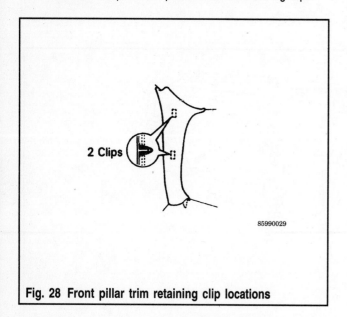

2 Clips

85990029

Fig. 28 Front pillar trim retaining clip locations

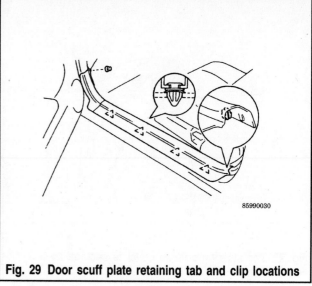

85990030

Fig. 29 Door scuff plate retaining tab and clip locations

3. Remove the door scuff plate and cowl trim panels as follows:

   a. Remove the plastic cap from the cowl side trim.

   b. Release the tab fitting in the rear edge of the scuff plate.

   c. Using a clip remover, remove the scuff plate clips from the rear side.

   d. Remove the cowl side trim from the scuff plate by carefully pulling it away.

4. Remove the steering wheel and the column covers.

5. Remove the console.

6. Remove the screws attaching the hood release lever. Pull it forward to remove it.

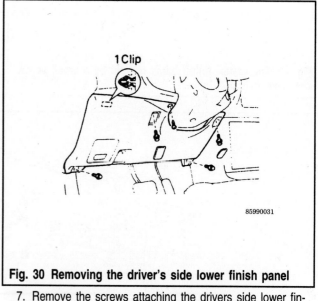

1 Clip

85990031

Fig. 30 Removing the driver's side lower finish panel

7. Remove the screws attaching the drivers side lower finish panel. Carefully pull the panel from the dash.

8. Remove the combination switch assembly.

9. Remove the combination meter (instrument cluster).

10. Remove the glovebox and lower finish panel attaching screws. Pull the assembly out from the dash.

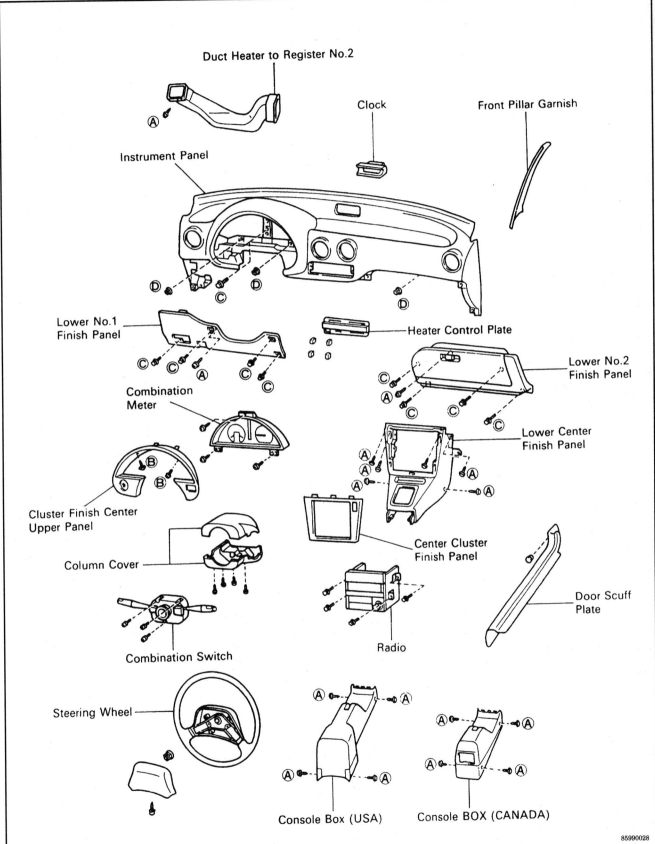

Duct Heater to Register No.2

Clock

Front Pillar Garnish

Instrument Panel

Lower No.1 Finish Panel

Heater Control Plate

Lower No.2 Finish Panel

Combination Meter

Lower Center Finish Panel

Cluster Finish Center Upper Panel

Column Cover

Center Cluster Finish Panel

Door Scuff Plate

Combination Switch

Radio

Steering Wheel

Console Box (USA)

Console BOX (CANADA)

85990028

Fig. 27 Exploded view of the instrument panel and components

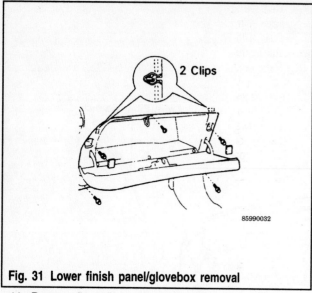

Fig. 31 Lower finish panel/glovebox removal

11. Remove the radio and heater control panel trim plate.
12. Remove the screws securing the center finish panel, then pull the assembly from the dash.
13. Remove the clock using a small prybar, then unplug the electrical connection.

14. Remove the heater ducts and the screws securing the electrical junction box.

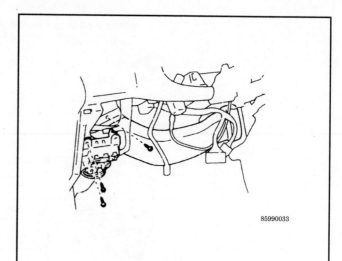

Fig. 32 Remove the electrical junction box screws, then hang it out of the way

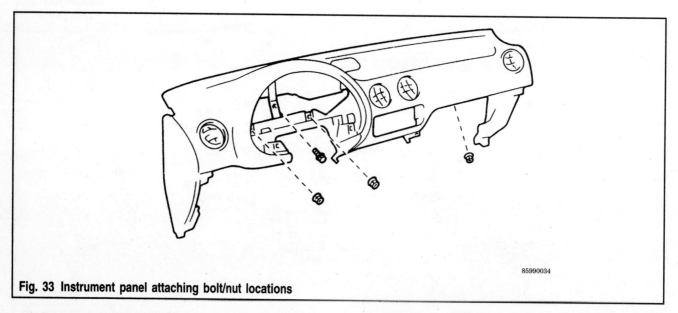

Fig. 33 Instrument panel attaching bolt/nut locations

15. Remove the bolts/nuts securing the dashboard, then remove the assembly from the vehicle.
   To install:
16. Position the dashboard assembly in the vehicle. Attach any wiring harnesses to the inside of the dash before securing the mounting bolts.
17. Install the heater ducts and the screws securing the electrical junction box.
18. Install the clock, then engage the electrical connection.
19. Install the center finish panel, heater control panel trim plate and radio.
20. Install the glovebox and lower finish panel.

21. Install the instrument cluster and combination switch assembly. Make sure the spiral cable is properly centered on air bag equipped vehicles, refer to the procedure in this manual.
22. Install the driver's side lower finish panel and hood release lever.
23. Install the console.
24. Install the steering column covers and steering wheel.
25. Install the cowl side trim and scuff plate.
26. Install the front pillar trim pieces.
27. Connect the negative battery cable. Start the engine and road test the vehicle for proper operation. Check the operation of all instrument dashboard components.

Console

REMOVAL & INSTALLATION

▶ See Figure 34

❈❈CAUTION

On models equipped with an air bag (SRS), work must NOT be started until at least 90 seconds have passed from the time that both the ignition switch is turned to the LOCK position and the negative cable is disconnected from the battery.

The consoles are usually removed by loosening the mounting screws and disengaging the retaining clips. Many of these screws are concealed by plastic covers which may be popped off with a small screwdriver or similar tool. The consoles can be lifted over the shifter handle and removed from the car. Be very careful not to lose any small parts between the floor pan and carpet while the console is out.

Once the console is removed, take an extra moment to clean it thoroughly and apply a vinyl protectant. You can now get all the crevices that have been blocked by the seats and hidden by the carpet. When the console is reinstalled, make sure that any wires in the area are not pinched by the console or pierced by the mounting screws.

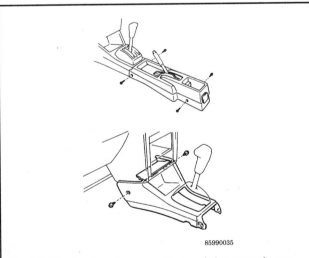

Fig. 34 The front and rear sections of the console are usually secured by several screws

Door Panels

REMOVAL & INSTALLATION

▶ See Figures 35, 36 and 37

1. Remove the screw securing the door opening lever, then pull the assembly out slightly. Disconnect the control link from the lever.

2. Remove the pull handle, arm rest and trim plate covering the outside mirror retaining screws.

3. Pull off the regulator handle snap ring with a shop rag, then remove the handle and plate.

4. Remove the door trim by prying between the retainers with a small prybar (tape the tip before use). On some models it may be necessary to remove the inner weatherstrip on the bottom of the door before removing the trim panel. Remove it by prying between the weatherstrip and the door panel.

5. Installation is the reverse of removal procedure. Handle the door trim panel with care after removal.

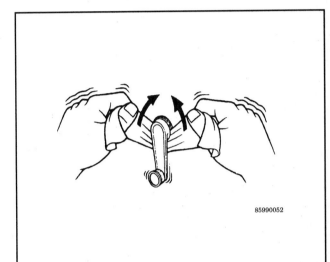

Fig. 35 A shop rag can be used to remove the snapring securing the regulator handle

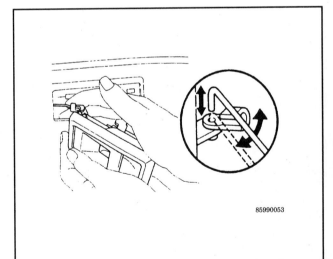

Fig. 36 Disengaging the links from the door handle lever

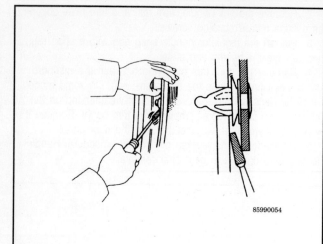

85990054

Fig. 37 Tape the tip of the tool before prying the door panel loose

Heater/AC Ducts and Outlets

REMOVAL & INSTALLATION

♦ **See Figure 38**

The lower heater ducts can be removed by first removing the lower finish trim panels, then remove the duct attaching screw and duct. To remove the ducts for the defroster and dash outlets, the instrument panel assembly must be removed first. The ducts can then be removed from the back of the dashboard by removing the attaching screws.

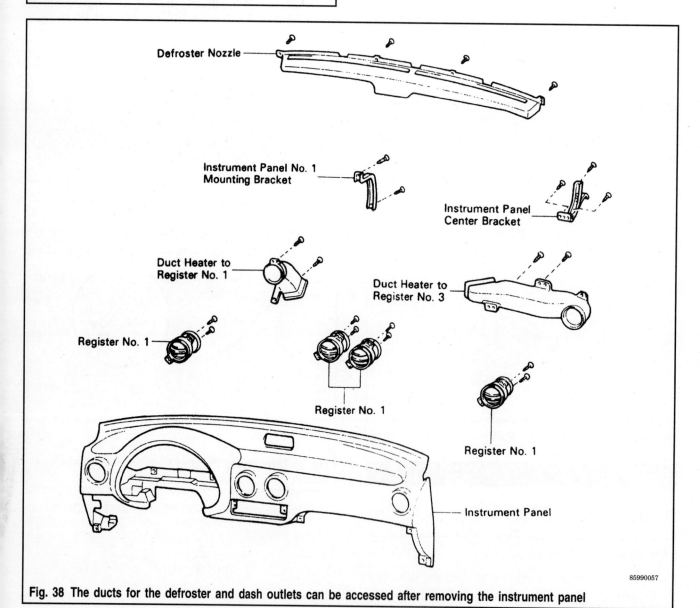

85990057

Fig. 38 The ducts for the defroster and dash outlets can be accessed after removing the instrument panel

Door Locks

REMOVAL & INSTALLATION

1. Remove the door trim panel.
2. Carefully remove the water deflector shield from inside the door. Take your time and don't rip it.
3. Disconnect the link rod running between the lock cylinder and the lock/latch mechanism.
4. Remove the lock retaining screws, the slide the assembly out through the access hole.
5. Installation is the reverse of removal.

Door Glass and Regulator

REMOVAL & INSTALLATION

▶ **See Figures 39, 40, 41, 42, 43, 44, 45, 46 and 47**

Front Doors

1. Remove the door trim panel.
2. Remove the water deflector shield and lower the window glass fully.
3. Carefully pry out the outer door glass weatherstrip from its retaining clips.
4. If necessary, remove the access hole cover.
5. Remove the window mounting nuts/bolts.

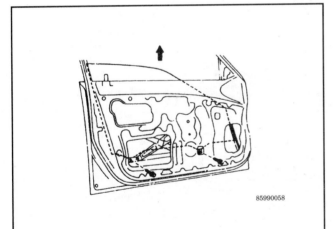

Fig. 46 Remove the nuts/bolts securing the window to the regulator, then carefully remove it from the front door

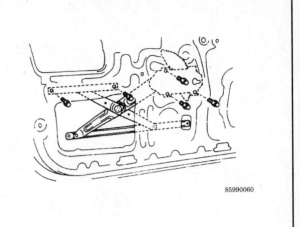

Fig. 47 Remove the bolts securing the regulator to the front door, then remove it through the access hole

6. Carefully remove the glass through the top of the door.
7. Remove the window regulator mounting bolts, then remove the regulator

To install:

8. If the window glass is to be replaced:
   a. Remove the sash channel from the glass.
   b. Apply a solution of soapy water to the sash channel.
   c. Install the channel to the new glass using a plastic hammer to tap the sash into place. Note that the sash channel must be exactly positioned on the glass or the bolt holes will not align at reinstallation.
9. Install the regulator and tighten the bolts evenly.
10. Install the window glass, then install the window mounting nuts/bolts.
11. Wind the window slowly up and down and observe its movement and alignment. The position of the glass can be adjusted by moving the equalizing arm bracket up or down.
12. Install the outer weatherstrip.
13. Install the access panel and water deflector, making sure it is intact and properly sealed.
14. Install the door trim panel.

Rear Doors

▶ **See Figures 48 and 49**

1. Remove the door trim panel.
2. Remove the water deflector shield and lower the window glass fully.
3. Carefully pry the outer door glass weatherstrip from its retaining clips.
4. On some models, it may be necessary to remove the stationary glass from the door. Refer to the appropriate service procedure in this section.
5. Disconnect the glass from the regulator arm.
6. Carefully remove the glass through the top of the door.
7. Remove the window regulator mounting bolts, then remove the regulator.

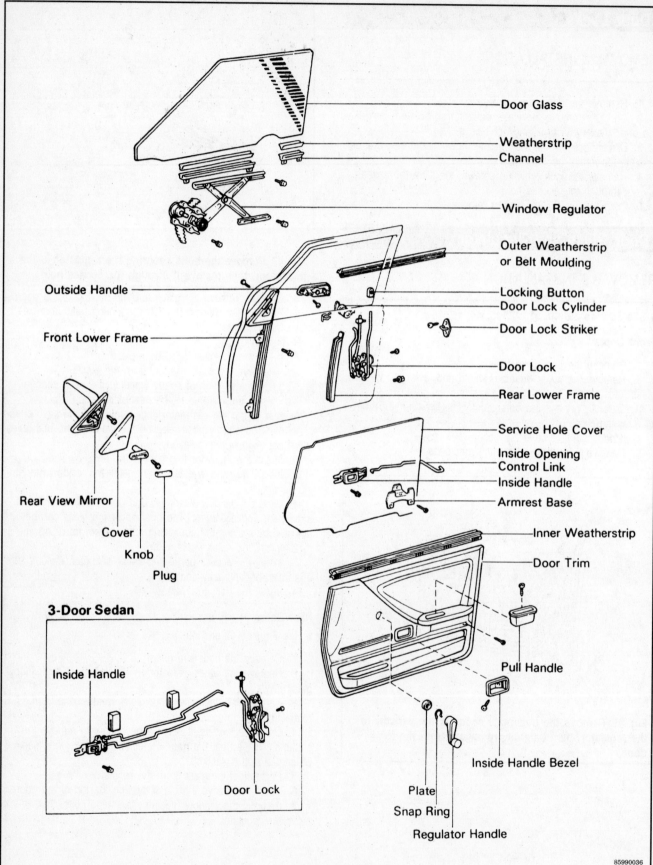

Door Glass

Weatherstrip

Channel

Window Regulator

Outer Weatherstrip
or Belt Moulding

Outside Handle

Locking Button

Door Lock Cylinder

Door Lock Striker

Front Lower Frame

Door Lock

Rear Lower Frame

Service Hole Cover

Inside Opening
Control Link

Inside Handle

Armrest Base

Rear View Mirror

Inner Weatherstrip

Cover

Door Trim

Knob

Plug

3-Door Sedan

Inside Handle

Pull Handle

Inside Handle Bezel

Door Lock

Plate

Snap Ring

Regulator Handle

85990036

Fig. 39 Front door components found on wagons and 1984-1986 sedans

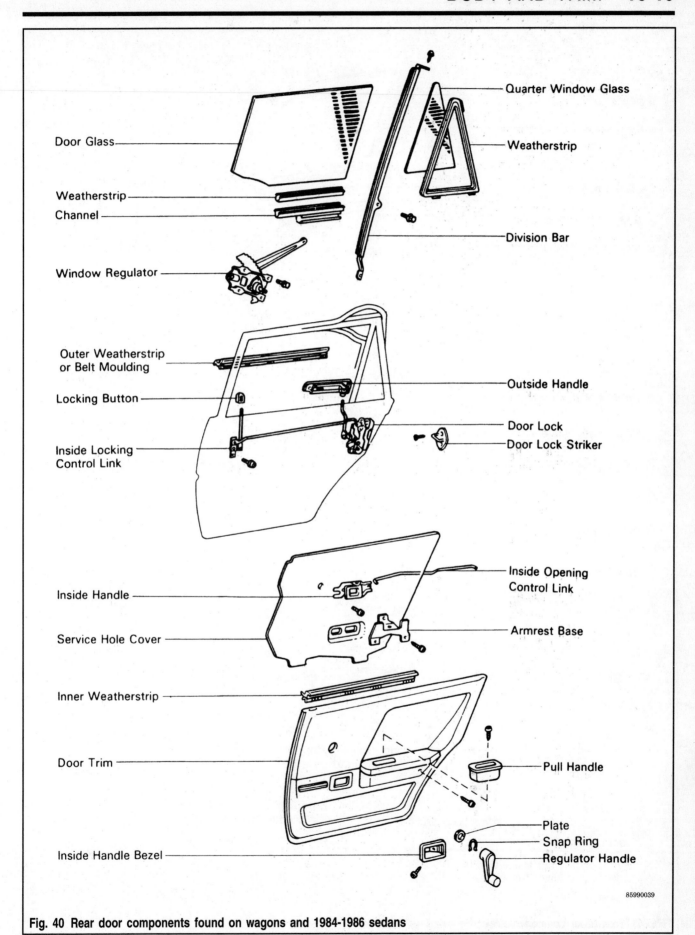

Fig. 40 Rear door components found on wagons and 1984-1986 sedans

Door Glass

Weatherstrip

Channel

Window Regulator

Outer Weatherstrip or Belt Moulding

Locking Button

Inside Locking Control Link

Inside Handle

Service Hole Cover

Inner Weatherstrip

Door Trim

Inside Handle Bezel

Quarter Window Glass

Weatherstrip

Division Bar

Outside Handle

Door Lock
Door Lock Striker

Inside Opening Control Link

Armrest Base

Pull Handle

Plate
Snap Ring
Regulator Handle

85990039

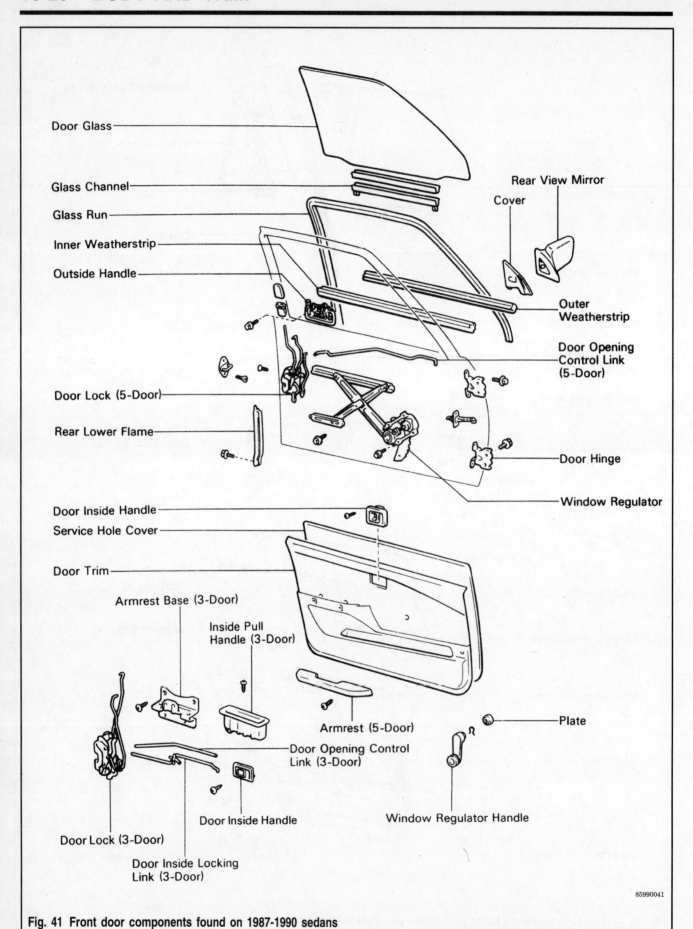

Door Glass

Glass Channel

Glass Run

Inner Weatherstrip

Outside Handle

Rear View Mirror

Cover

Outer Weatherstrip

Door Opening Control Link (5-Door)

Door Lock (5-Door)

Rear Lower Flame

Door Hinge

Window Regulator

Door Inside Handle

Service Hole Cover

Door Trim

Armrest Base (3-Door)

Inside Pull Handle (3-Door)

Armrest (5-Door)

Plate

Door Opening Control Link (3-Door)

Door Inside Handle

Window Regulator Handle

Door Lock (3-Door)

Door Inside Locking Link (3-Door)

85990041

Fig. 41 Front door components found on 1987-1990 sedans

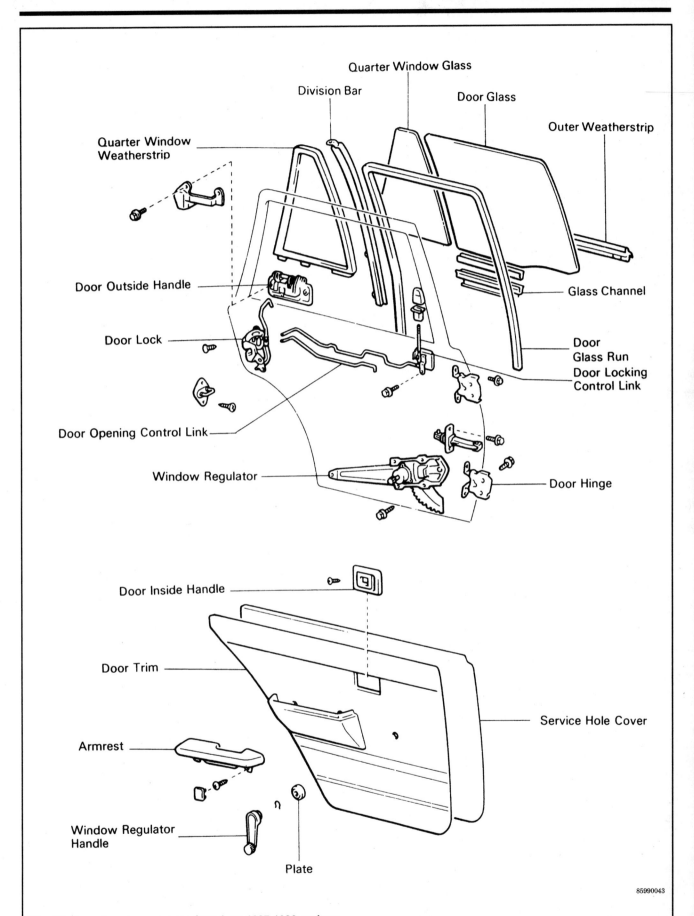

Quarter Window Glass

Division Bar

Door Glass

Outer Weatherstrip

Quarter Window
Weatherstrip

Door Outside Handle

Door Lock

Door Opening Control Link

Window Regulator

Glass Channel

Door
Glass Run
Door Locking
Control Link

Door Hinge

Door Inside Handle

Door Trim

Service Hole Cover

Armrest

Window Regulator
Handle

Plate

85990043

Fig. 42 Rear door components found on 1987-1990 sedans

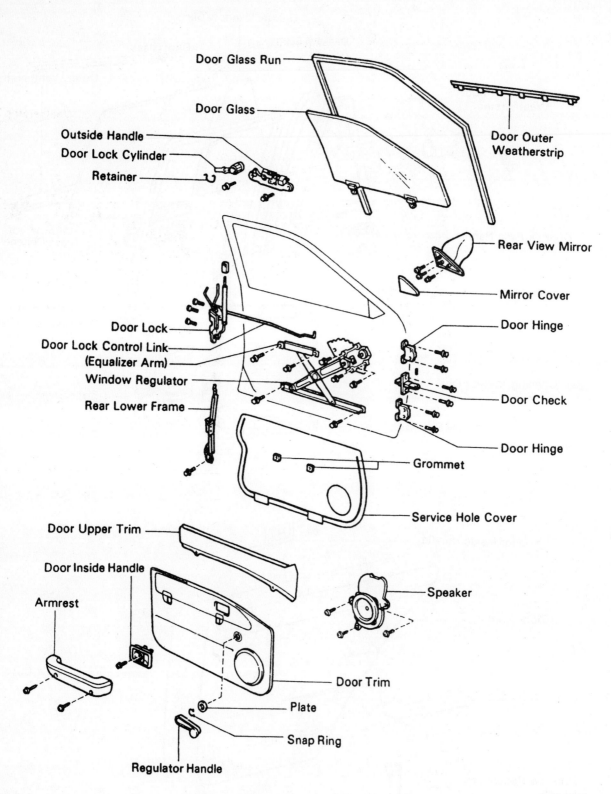

Door Glass Run

Door Glass

Outside Handle

Door Lock Cylinder

Retainer

Door Outer Weatherstrip

Rear View Mirror

Mirror Cover

Door Lock

Door Lock Control Link (Equalizer Arm)

Window Regulator

Rear Lower Frame

Door Hinge

Door Check

Door Hinge

Grommet

Service Hole Cover

Door Upper Trim

Door Inside Handle

Armrest

Speaker

Door Trim

Plate

Snap Ring

Regulator Handle

85990045

Fig. 43 Front door components on 1991-1994 4-door sedans

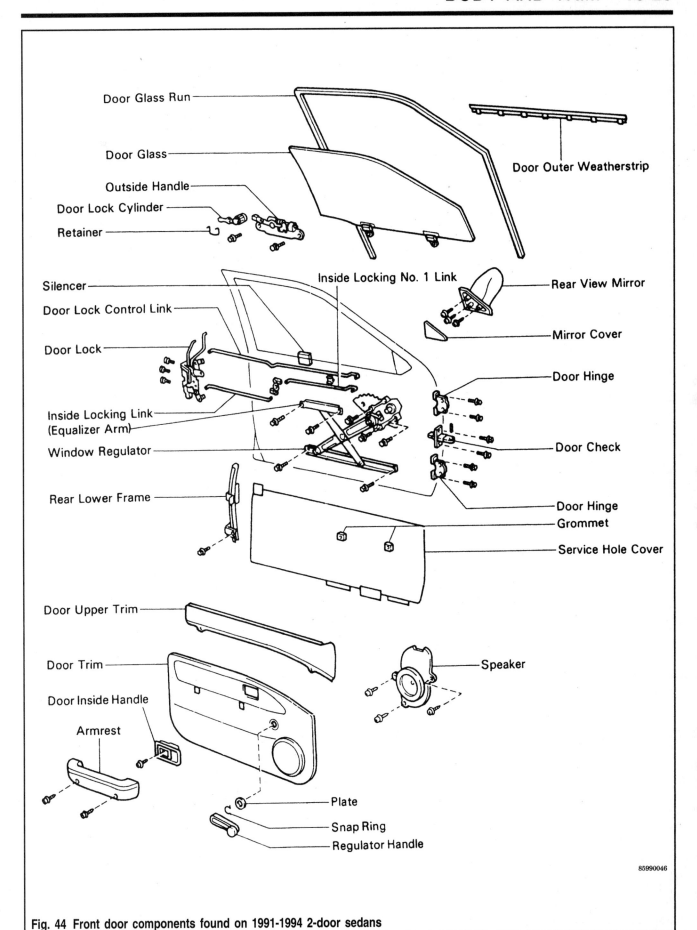

Fig. 44 Front door components found on 1991-1994 2-door sedans

Door Glass Run

Door Glass

Outside Handle

Door Lock Cylinder

Retainer

Door Outer Weatherstrip

Silencer

Door Lock Control Link

Door Lock

Inside Locking No. 1 Link

Rear View Mirror

Mirror Cover

Door Hinge

Inside Locking Link
(Equalizer Arm)

Window Regulator

Door Check

Rear Lower Frame

Door Hinge

Grommet

Service Hole Cover

Door Upper Trim

Door Trim

Speaker

Door Inside Handle

Armrest

Plate

Snap Ring

Regulator Handle

85990046

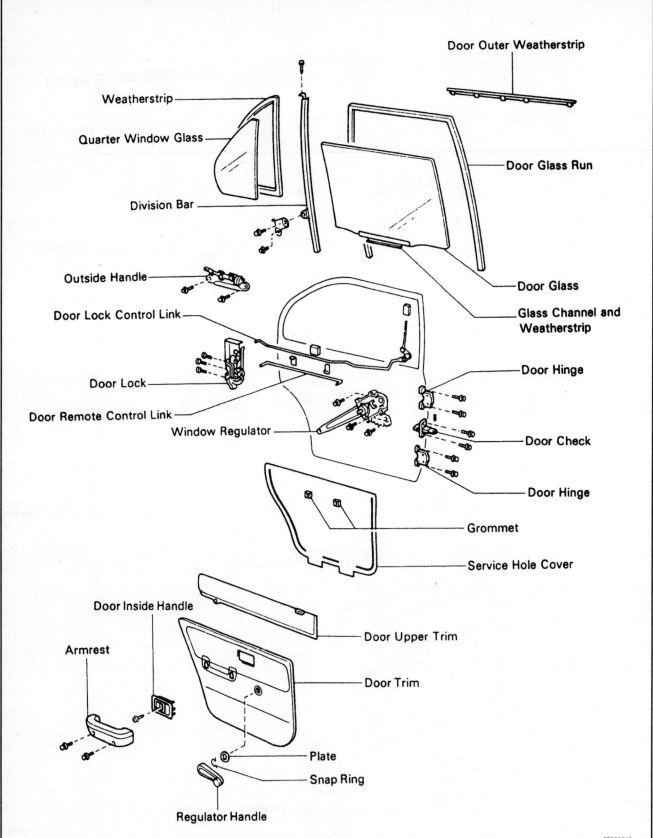

Door Outer Weatherstrip

Weatherstrip

Quarter Window Glass

Division Bar

Door Glass Run

Outside Handle

Door Lock Control Link

Door Lock

Door Remote Control Link

Window Regulator

Door Glass

Glass Channel and Weatherstrip

Door Hinge

Door Check

Door Hinge

Grommet

Service Hole Cover

Door Inside Handle

Armrest

Door Upper Trim

Door Trim

Plate

Snap Ring

Regulator Handle

85990049

Fig. 45 Rear door components on 1991-1994 sedans

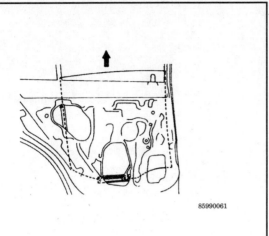

Fig. 48 Disconnect the window from the regulator arm, then carefully remove it from the rear door

Fig. 49 A series of small bolts secure the regulator to the rear door

To install:

8. If the window glass is to be replaced:
   a. Remove the sash channel from the glass.
   b. Apply a solution of soapy water to the sash channel.
   c. Install the channel to the new glass using a plastic hammer to tap the sash into place. Note that the sash channel must be exactly positioned on the glass or the bolt holes will not align at reinstallation.

9. Install the regulator and tighten the bolts evenly.
10. Install the window glass and connect it to the regulator arm.
11. If applicable, install the fixed glass and make certain it is correctly positioned.
12. Wind the window slowly up and down and observe its movement and alignment. The position of the glass can be adjusted by moving the equalizing arm bracket up or down.
13. Install the outer weatherstrip.
14. Install the water deflector, making sure it is intact and properly sealed.
15. Install the door trim panel.

Windshield Glass

REMOVAL & INSTALLATION

▶ See Figures 50, 51, 52, 53, 54, 55, 56, 57, 58, 59, 60 and 61

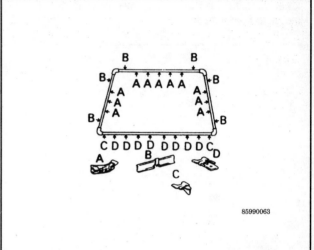

Fig. 50 Windshield moulding clip locations on wagons and 1984-1986 sedans

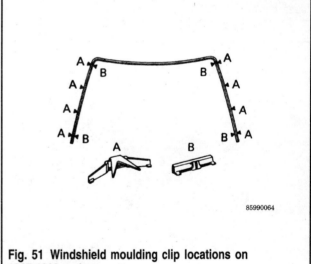

Fig. 51 Windshield moulding clip locations on 1987-1990 sedans

1. On 1987-1994 sedans, remove the hood.
2. Remove the wiper arms, cowl trim, inner rear view mirror and sun visors.
3. Remove the front pillar trim. Carefully pry the trim from the retaining clips, then pull the trim upwards to remove it.
4. Remove any other windshield trim inside the vehicle.
5. Remove the windshield moulding following these procedures:
   a. On wagons and 1984-1986 sedans, remove the lower windshield trim attaching screws, then carefully pry the moulding from the body.

b. On 1984-1990 models, apply tape to the body around the windshield to protect the paint finish. Using a small, thin prybar or scraper, pry the side mouldings from the retaining clips, then remove the mouldings.

c. On wagons and 1984-1986 sedans, remove the upper joint covers and upper moulding using the same process as the previous step.

d. On 1987-1990 sedans, cut off the upper moulding using a knife. Be careful not to damage the body. Remove the lower moulding attaching screws, then carefully pry the moulding from the body.

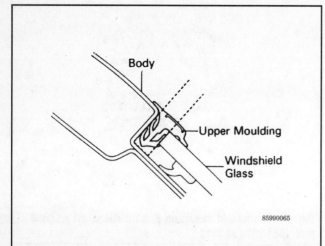

Fig. 52 The moulding should be cut with a knife in the area shown on 1987-1994 sedans

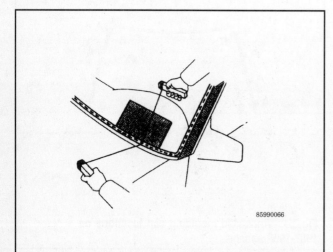

Fig. 53 Protect the dashboard and other finishes when cutting through the adhesive

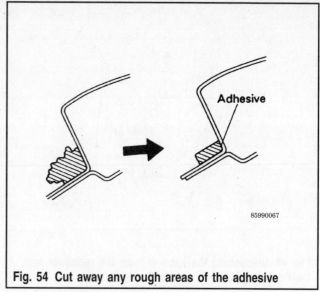

Fig. 54 Cut away any rough areas of the adhesive

e. On 1991-1994 sedans, cut off the windshield moulding using a knife. Be careful not to damage the body.

6. Push piano wire through from the interior. Tie both ends of the wire to wooden blocks.

➡When cutting, take care not to damage the paint and interior/exterior ornaments. To prevent scratching the dash panel when removing the windshield, place a plastic sheet between the piano wire and dash panel.

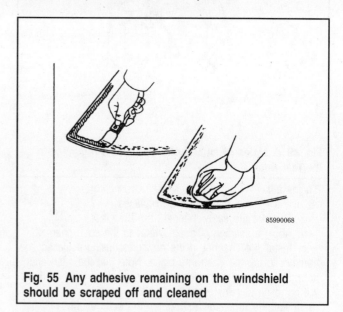

Fig. 55 Any adhesive remaining on the windshield should be scraped off and cleaned

7. Cut the adhesive by pulling the piano wire around it. Leave as much of the urethane layer on the body as possible when cutting.

8. With the help of an assistant, remove the glass.

To install:

9. Cut away any rough areas of the urethane layer with a knife. Clean the contact surface with alcohol.

10. Using a scraper, clean any gum remaining on the glass. Clean the surface with alcohol.

11. With the help of an assistant, carefully place the glass in position. Check that all contacting parts of the glass rim are perfectly even.

12. Place reference marks between the glass and body, then remove the glass.

13. Once again, clean the contact surface of the glass with alcohol. Do not touch the glass after cleaning it.

14. Install the windshield dam with double-stick tape. On 1984-1990 models, cut a V-wedge into the corner folds of the dam.

15. Apply the appropriate primers to the windshield and body. Mix the adhesive coating. Follow the instructions supplied by the manufacturer of the adhesive and primers.

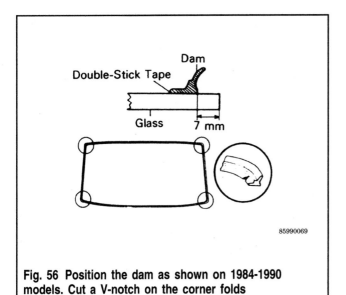

Fig. 56 Position the dam as shown on 1984-1990 models. Cut a V-notch on the corner folds

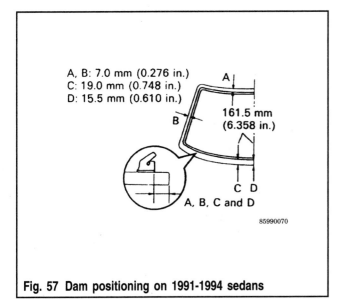

A, B: 7.0 mm (0.276 in.)
C: 19.0 mm (0.748 in.)
D: 15.5 mm (0.610 in.)
161.5 mm (6.358 in.)

Fig. 57 Dam positioning on 1991-1994 sedans

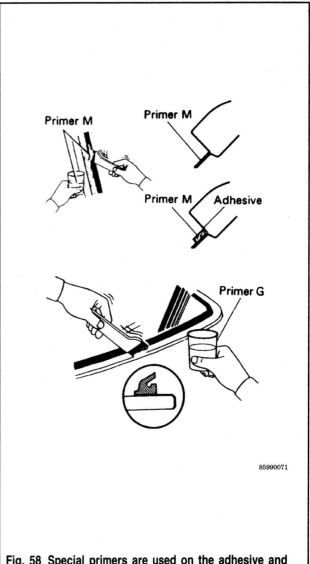

Fig. 58 Special primers are used on the adhesive and window glass

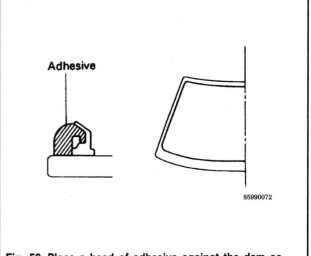

Fig. 59 Place a bead of adhesive against the dam as shown

16. Apply the adhesive along all the contact surfaces along the ridge of the dam.

17. With an assistant, position the glass so the reference marks are lined up, then press in around the rim of the contact areas to seat the glass. Using a spatula, apply adhesive around the glass rim.

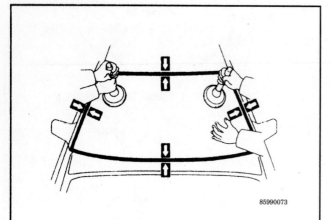

85990073

Fig. 60 With the aid of an assistant, position the glass on the vehicle. Strong suction cups makes this job easier

18. After the adhesive has hardened, water test the windshield for leaks. Seal any leaks with adhesive or auto glass sealer.

19. Replace any damaged moulding retaining clips.

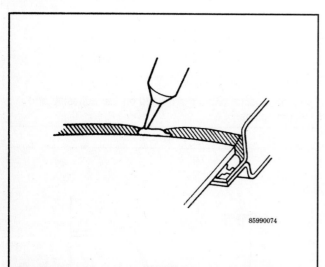

85990074

Fig. 61 Seal any leaks with adhesive or auto glass sealer

20. On wagons and 1984-1986 sedans, install the mouldings as follows:

   a. Install the clips into the moulding. Make sure the clips on the moulding and the fasteners on the body do not make contact.

   b. Fit the upper moulding and tap the fasteners on by hand. Install the upper joint covers.

   c. Fit on the side mouldings, then tap the fasteners in by hand. Install the lower joint covers and lower moulding.

21. On 1987-1990 sedans, install the mouldings as follows:

   a. Position the moulding onto the body.

   b. Tap the moulding with your hand to fasten the clips at the glass edge. At the same time, install the fasteners by tapping them by hand.

   c. Install the lower moulding with its screws.

22. On 1991-1994 sedans, install the moulding as follows:

   a. Using a knife, cut off any old adhesive around the moulding installation area.

   b. Apply adhesive at the moulding installation area.

   c. Position the new moulding onto the body, then tap it in by hand.

23. Install the interior trim and components removed earlier.

24. Install the cowl trim, wiper arms and hood.

Stationary Glass

REMOVAL & INSTALLATION

Wagons and 1984-1986 Sedans

▶ **See Figures 62, 63 and 64**

REAR DOOR GLASS

1. Lower the window and remove the door trim.

2. Remove the screw securing the division bar to the door under the weatherstrip. Remove the two lower attaching bolts.

3. Pull the glass run out from the division bar, then remove the bar from the window.

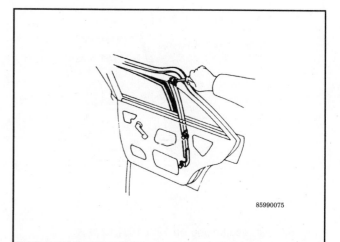

85990075

Fig. 62 The division bar attaching screw is usually hidden under the weatherstrip. It is also secured by bolts on the door panel

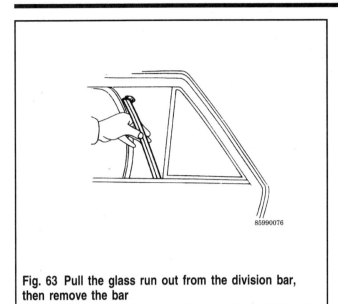

Fig. 63 Pull the glass run out from the division bar, then remove the bar

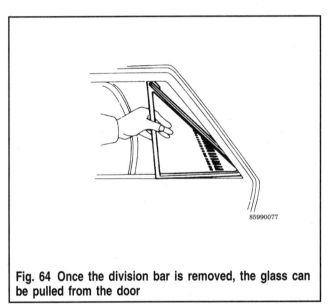

Fig. 64 Once the division bar is removed, the glass can be pulled from the door

4. Remove the glass from the door by pulling it forward.
5. Installation is the reverse of removal.

QUARTER WINDOW GLASS-SWING TYPE

1. Remove the screws securing the window lock and hinge plates.
2. Carefully remove the window from the vehicle.
3. Installation is the reverse of removal.

QUARTER WINDOW GLASS-FIXED TYPE

▶ **See Figures 65 and 66**

1. Remove the rear quarter trim panels surrounding the window.
2. If reusing the weatherstrip around the window:
   a. Using a small prybar, loosen the weatherstrip lip from the body. Tape the tip of the tool to prevent damage to the body finish.
   b. Force the weatherstrip lip from the interior to the body flange outside. Pull the glass outwards and remove it with the weatherstrip.

3. If not reusing the weatherstrip:
   a. From the outside, cut off the weatherstrip lip with a knife.
   b. Push the glass outwards and remove the glass.
   c. Remove the weatherstrip from the body.
   To install:
4. Attach the weatherstrip to the glass. Apply a cord along the weatherstrip groove.
5. Apply soapy water to the contact face of the weatherstrip lip and to the body flange.

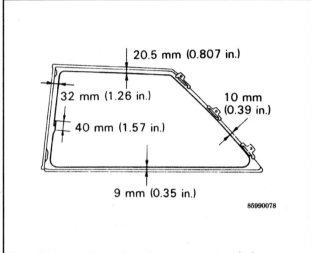

Fig. 65 Apply the seal to the rear quarter window as shown on 1987-1990 3-door sedans

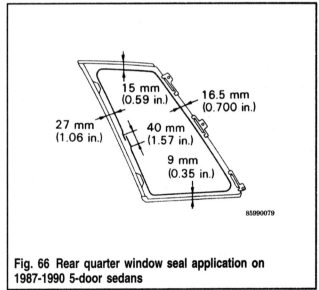

Fig. 66 Rear quarter window seal application on 1987-1990 5-door sedans

6. Have an assistant hold the glass in position on the body. Begin installation in the middle of the lower part of the window. Pull the cord from the interior while pushing the outside of the weatherstrip with your open hand.
7. To snug the glass in place, tap the outside of the window with your open hand.
8. Place masking tape around the weatherstrip to protect the paint and glass. Apply glass sealer between the weatherstrip and body. When the sealer is dry, remove the masking tape.

9. Install the interior trim panels removed earlier.

REAR WINDOW

▶ **See Figures 67, 68, 69, 70, 71, 72 and 73**

1. Remove the trim panels surrounding the window.
2. If applicable, remove the high-mount brake light and unplug the rear window defroster connector.
3. Remove the rear wiper arm, if equipped.

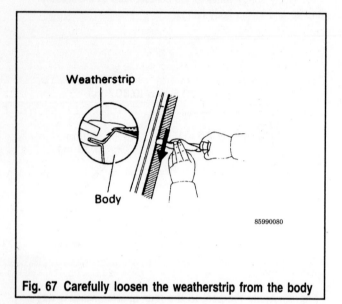

Fig. 67 Carefully loosen the weatherstrip from the body

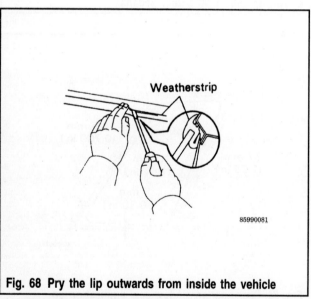

Fig. 68 Pry the lip outwards from inside the vehicle

4. If reusing the weatherstrip around the window:
   a. Using a small prybar, loosen the weatherstrip lip from the body. Tape the tip of the tool to prevent damage to the body finish.
   b. Force the weatherstrip lip from the interior to the body flange outside. Pull the glass outwards and remove it with the weatherstrip.

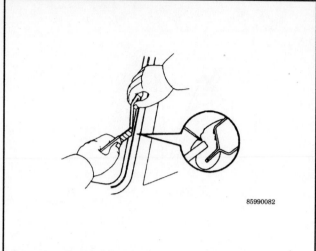

Fig. 69 If the weatherstrip is not to be reused, it can be cut with a knife

5. If not reusing the weatherstrip:
   a. From the outside, cut off the weatherstrip lip with a knife.
   b. Push the glass outwards and remove the glass.
   c. Remove the weatherstrip from the body.
To install:
6. Attach the weatherstrip to the glass. Apply a cord along the weatherstrip groove.

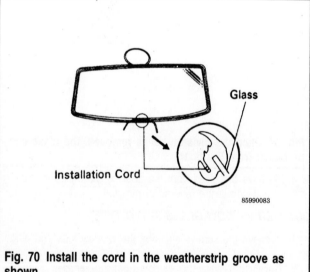

Fig. 70 Install the cord in the weatherstrip groove as shown

7. Apply soapy water to the contact face of the weatherstrip lip and to the body flange.
8. Have an assistant hold the glass in position on the body. Begin installation in the middle of the lower part of the window. Pull the cord from the interior while pushing the outside of the weatherstrip with your open hand.

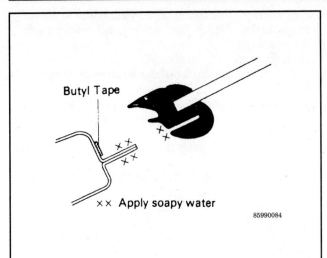

Fig. 71 Apply soapy water to the body and weatherstrip to aid in installation

Fig. 72 Have an assistant hold the window, then pull the cord to draw in the weatherstrip

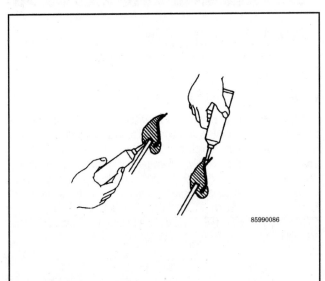

Fig. 73 Sealer should be applied to prevent leaks

9. To snug the glass in place, tap the outside of the window with your open hand.

10. Place masking tape around the weatherstrip to protect the paint and glass. Apply glass sealer between the weatherstrip and body. When the sealer is dry, remove the masking tape.

11. Install the interior trim panels, brake light and wiper arm removed earlier.

1987-1990 Sedans

REAR DOOR GLASS

1. Lower the window and remove the door trim.

2. Remove the screw securing the division bar to the door under the weatherstrip. Remove the two lower attaching bolts.

3. Pull the glass run out from the division bar, then remove the bar from the window.

4. Remove the glass from the door by pulling it forward.

5. Installation is the reverse of removal.

QUARTER WINDOW GLASS

1. Remove the trim panel surrounding the window.

2. From inside the vehicle, remove the nuts securing the ventilation louver, then pull the louver from its retaining clips.

3. Remove the nuts/screws securing the window. Using a knife, cut the adhesive from the window.

4. Carefully remove the glass from the body.

To install:

5. Clean the window and body contact areas with alcohol.

6. Coat the contact surface of the glass with an adhesive primer. Follow the manufacturer's instructions.

7. Apply the adhesive seal to the glass, slightly overlapping it at the bottom of the window.

8. Position the glass on the body, then install the retaining screws/nuts.

9. Install the ventilation louver with its retaining nuts.

10. Install the interior trim removed earlier.

REAR WINDOW

1. Remove the trim panels surrounding the window.

2. If applicable, remove the high-mount brake light and unplug the rear window defroster connector.

3. Remove the rear wiper arm, if equipped.

4. If reusing the weatherstrip around the window:

   a. Using a small prybar, loosen the weatherstrip lip from the body. Tape the tip of the tool to prevent damage to the body finish.

   b. Force the weatherstrip lip from the interior to the body flange outside. Pull the glass outwards and remove it with the weatherstrip.

5. If not reusing the weatherstrip:

   a. From the outside, cut off the weatherstrip lip with a knife.

   b. Push the glass outwards and remove the glass.

   c. Remove the weatherstrip from the body.

To install:

6. Attach the weatherstrip to the glass. Apply a cord along the weatherstrip groove.

7. Apply soapy water to the contact face of the weatherstrip lip and to the body flange.

8. Have an assistant hold the glass in position on the body. Begin installation in the middle of the lower part of the window.

Pull the cord from the interior while pushing the outside of the weatherstrip with your open hand.

9. To snug the glass in place, tap the outside of the window with your open hand.

10. Place masking tape around the weatherstrip to protect the paint and glass. Apply glass sealer between the weatherstrip and body. When the sealer is dry, remove the masking tape.

11. Install the interior trim panels, brake light and wiper arm removed earlier.

1991-1994 Sedans

REAR DOOR GLASS

1. Lower the window and remove the door trim.
2. Remove the screw securing the division bar to the door under the weatherstrip. Remove the two lower attaching bolts.
3. Pull the glass run out from the division bar, then remove the bar from the window.
4. Remove the glass from the door by pulling it forward.
5. Installation is the reverse of removal.

QUARTER WINDOW

1. If reusing the weatherstrip around the window:
   a. Using a small prybar, loosen the weatherstrip lip from the body. Tape the tip of the tool to prevent damage to the body finish.
   b. Force the weatherstrip lip from the interior to the body flange outside. Pull the glass outwards and remove it with the weatherstrip.
2. If not reusing the weatherstrip:
   a. From the outside, cut off the weatherstrip lip with a knife.
   b. Push the glass outwards and remove the glass.
   c. Remove the weatherstrip from the body.

To install:

3. Attach the weatherstrip to the glass. Apply a cord along the weatherstrip groove.
4. Apply soapy water to the contact face of the weatherstrip lip and to the body flange.
5. Have an assistant hold the glass in position on the body. Begin installation in the middle of the lower part of the window. Pull the cord from the interior while pushing the outside of the weatherstrip with your open hand.
6. To snug the glass in place, tap the outside of the window with your open hand.
7. Place masking tape around the weatherstrip to protect the paint and glass. Apply glass sealer between the weatherstrip and body. When the sealer is dry, remove the masking tape.

REAR WINDOW

1. If applicable, remove the high-mount brake light and unplug the rear window defroster connector.
2. If reusing the weatherstrip around the window:
   a. Using a small prybar, loosen the weatherstrip lip from the body. Tape the tip of the tool to prevent damage to the body finish.

b. Force the weatherstrip lip from the interior to the body flange outside. Pull the glass outwards and remove it with the weatherstrip.

3. If not reusing the weatherstrip:
   a. From the outside, cut off the weatherstrip lip with a knife.
   b. Push the glass outwards and remove the glass.
   c. Remove the weatherstrip from the body.

To install:

4. Attach the weatherstrip to the glass. Apply a cord along the weatherstrip groove.
5. Apply soapy water to the contact face of the weatherstrip lip and to the body flange.
6. Have an assistant hold the glass in position on the body. Begin installation in the middle of the lower part of the window. Pull the cord from the interior while pushing the outside of the weatherstrip with your open hand.
7. To snug the glass in place, tap the outside of the window with your open hand.
8. Place masking tape around the weatherstrip to protect the paint and glass. Apply glass sealer between the weatherstrip and body. When the sealer is dry, remove the masking tape.
9. Install the brake light removed earlier and engage the defroster electrical connection.

Inside Rear View Mirror

REMOVAL & INSTALLATION

The inside mirror is removed by carefully prying off the plastic cover and removing the retaining bolts. The inside mirror is designed to break loose from the roof mount if it receives moderate impact. If the mirror has come off due to impact, it can usually be remounted by installing a new mirror base rather than an entire new mirror. If the glass is cracked, the mirror must be replaced.

Seats

REMOVAL & INSTALLATION

Front Seats
▶ **See Figures 74 and 75**

The front seats are removed by disconnecting the mounting bolts holding the seat to the floor rails. The bolts may be under plastic covers which can be popped off with a small prybar. The seat assembly will come out of the car complete with the tracks and adjuster. When reinstalling the seat, make certain that the bolts are properly threaded and tightened to 27 ft. lbs. (37 Nm). SEAT MOUNTING AND RETENTION IS A CRITICAL SAFETY ITEM. NEVER ATTEMPT TO ALTER THE MOUNTS OR THE SEAT TRACKS.

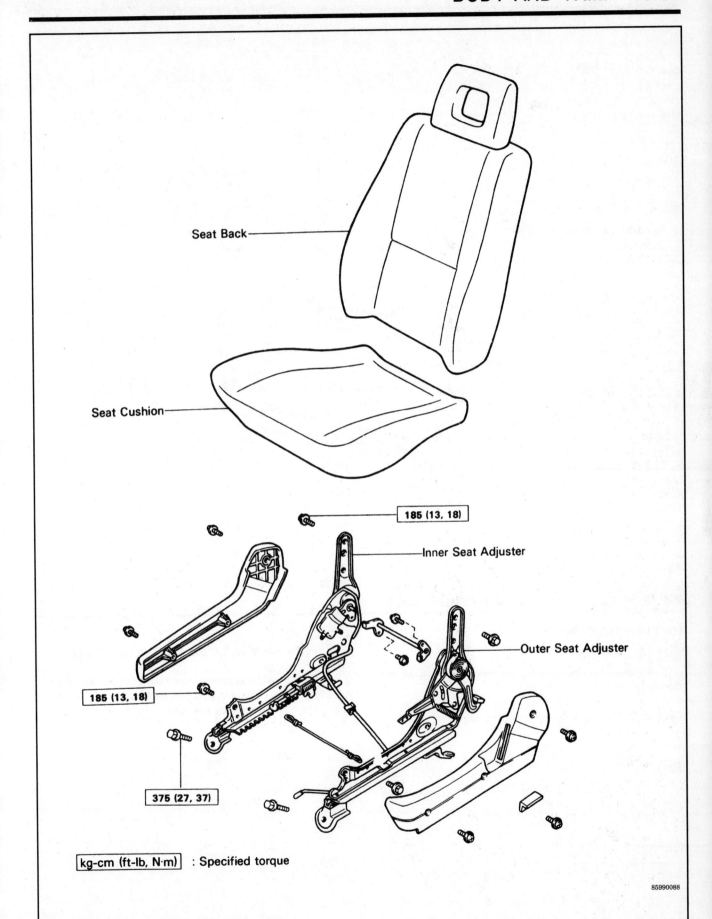

Seat Back

Seat Cushion

185 (13, 18)

Inner Seat Adjuster

Outer Seat Adjuster

185 (13, 18)

375 (27, 37)

kg-cm (ft-lb, N·m) : Specified torque

85990088

Fig. 74 Front seat found on 1987-1990 sedans

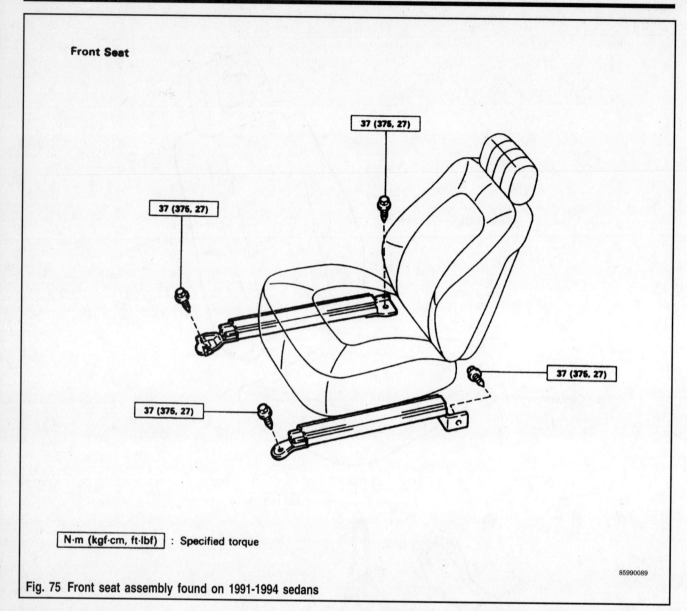

Front Seat

37 (375, 27)

37 (375, 27)

37 (375, 27)

37 (375, 27)

N·m (kgf·cm, ft·lbf) : Specified torque

85990089

Fig. 75 Front seat assembly found on 1991-1994 sedans

Rear Bench Seat Cushion

▶ See Figures 76 and 77

1. Pull forward on the seat cushion releases. These are small levers on the lower front of the cushion.
2. Pull upward on the front of the seat cushion and rotate it free. It is not retained or bolted under the seat back.

To install:

3. Fit the rear of the cushion into place under the seat back.
4. Push inward and downward on the front of the cushion until the releases lock into place. Make sure the seat is locked into place and the releases are secure.

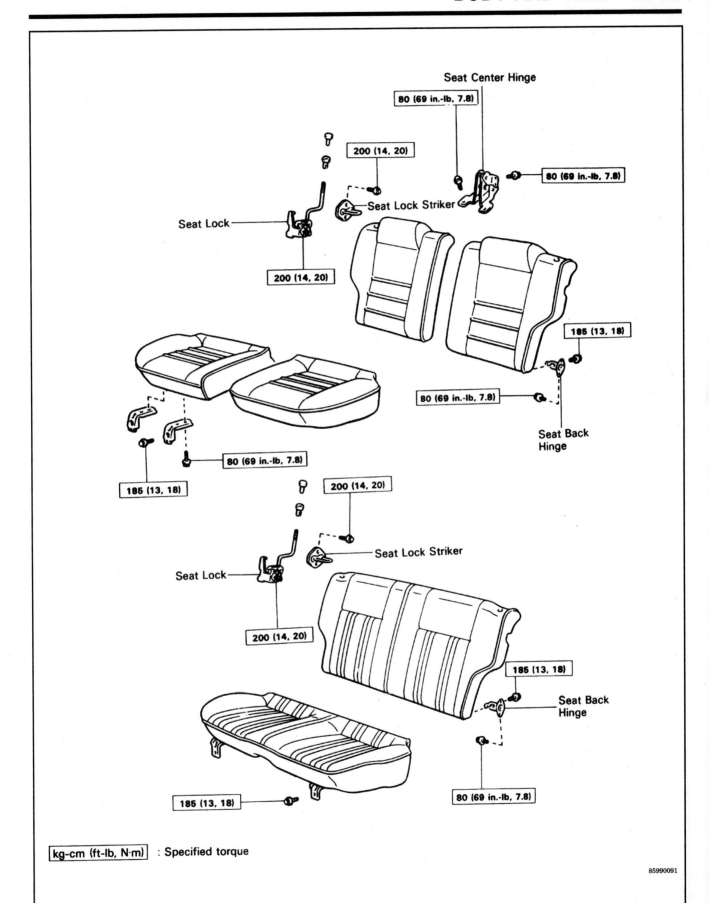

Seat Center Hinge

80 (69 in.-lb, 7.8)

200 (14, 20)

80 (69 in.-lb, 7.8)

Seat Lock

Seat Lock Striker

200 (14, 20)

185 (13, 18)

80 (69 in.-lb, 7.8)

Seat Back Hinge

80 (69 in.-lb, 7.8)

185 (13, 18)

200 (14, 20)

Seat Lock Striker

Seat Lock

200 (14, 20)

185 (13, 18)

Seat Back Hinge

185 (13, 18)

80 (69 in.-lb, 7.8)

kg-cm (ft-lb, N·m) : Specified torque

85990091

Fig. 76 Rear seats on 1987-1990 sedans

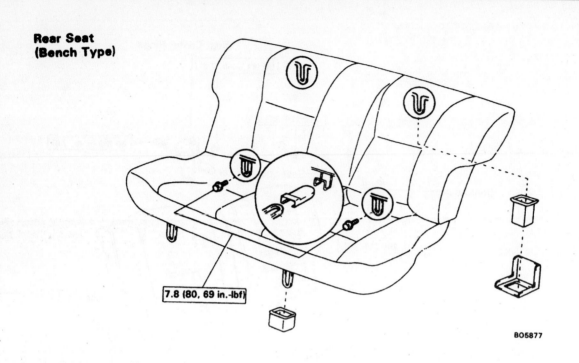

Rear Seat
(Bench Type)

7.8 (80, 69 in.-lbf)

BO5877

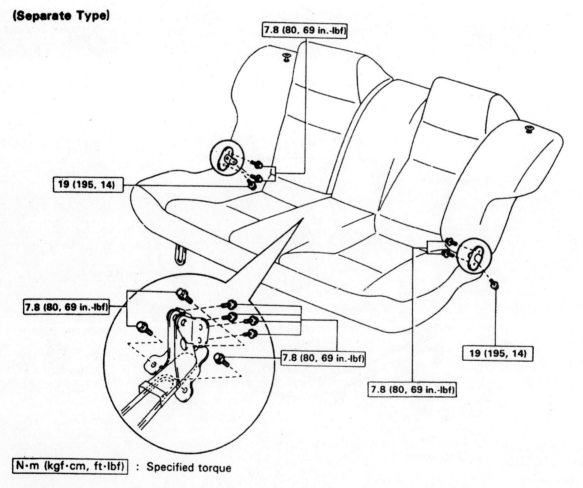

(Separate Type)

7.8 (80, 69 in.-lbf)

19 (195, 14)

7.8 (80, 69 in.-lbf)

7.8 (80, 69 in.-lbf)

7.8 (80, 69 in.-lbf)

19 (195, 14)

7.8 (80, 69 in.-lbf)

N·m (kgf·cm, ft·lbf) : Specified torque

85990092

Fig. 77 Rear seats found on 1991-1994 sedans

Rear Bench Seat Back

➡ **The seat bottom cushion need not be removed for this procedure, but access is improved with the cushion removed.**

1. Remove the lower bolts holding the seat back to the body.
2. Pull outward and push upward on the bottom edge of the seat back. This will release the seat back from the L-shaped hangers holding it.
3. Remove the seat back from the car.
To install:
4. Carefully fit the seat back onto the hangers.
5. Swing the back down and into place.
6. Install the lower retaining bolts and tighten them to 69 inch lbs. (7.8 Nm).

Split/Folding Rear Seat Cushion

1. At the front lower edge of the seat cushion, remove the bolts holding the seat cushion to the body. The bolts may be concealed under carpeting or trim pieces.
2. Pull upward on the front of the seat cushion and rotate it free. It is not usually retained or bolted under the seat back.
To install:
3. Fit the rear of the cushion into place under the seat back.
4. Push inward and downward on the front of the cushion until it is in place and the bolt holes align.
5. Install the retaining bolts and tighten them to 13 ft. lbs. (18 Nm).

Split/Folding Rear Seat Back

1. Push the seat back forward into a folded position.
2. Remove the carpeting from the rear of the seat back.
3. At the side hinge, remove the bolt holding the seat back to the hinge.
4. At the center hinge, remove the bolts holding the seat back to the hinge.
5. Remove the seat back from the car.
To install:
6. Install the seat back and install the bolts finger tight.
7. Tighten the side hinge bolt to 13 ft. lbs. (18 Nm).
8. Tighten the center hinge bolts to 69 inch lbs. (7.8 Nm).
9. Install the carpeting and trim on the rear of the seat back.

Seat Belts

REMOVAL & INSTALLATION

▶ **See Figures 78, 79, 80 and 81**

Seat belts are secured to the vehicle's body by a series bolts. These bolts are usually concealed by plastic covers which can be removed with a small prybar. For the rear seat belts, it is usually necessary to remove the seat cushion to access these bolts. Refer to the exploded views for proper bolt torque figures. These torque figures must be used when installing seat belts.

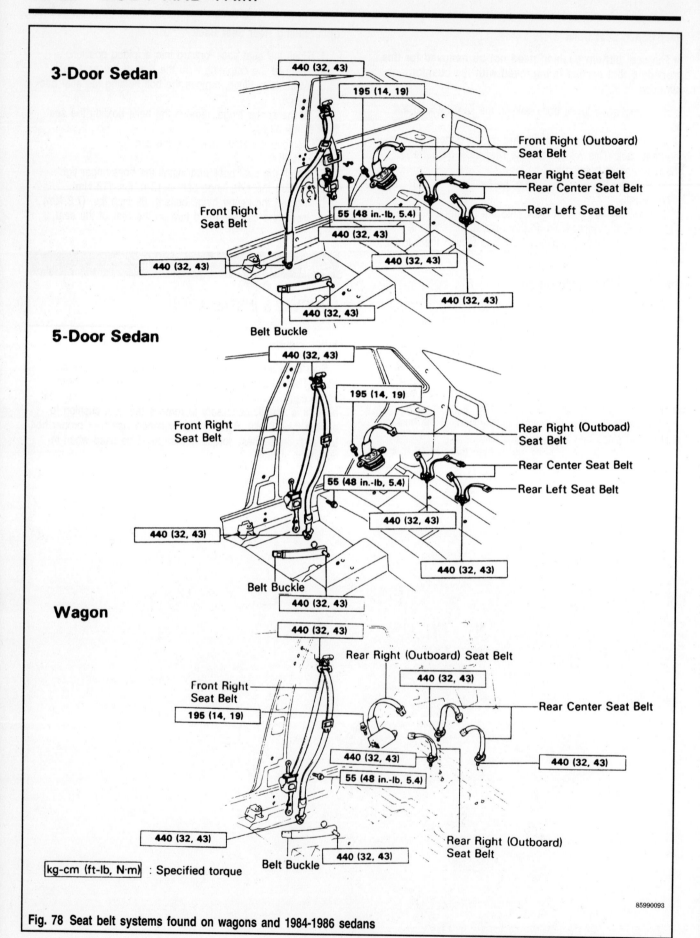

3-Door Sedan

440 (32, 43)

195 (14, 19)

Front Right (Outboard) Seat Belt

Rear Right Seat Belt

Rear Center Seat Belt

Rear Left Seat Belt

Front Right Seat Belt

55 (48 in.-lb, 5.4)

440 (32, 43)

440 (32, 43)

440 (32, 43)

440 (32, 43)

440 (32, 43)

440 (32, 43)

Belt Buckle

5-Door Sedan

440 (32, 43)

195 (14, 19)

Front Right Seat Belt

Rear Right (Outboad) Seat Belt

Rear Center Seat Belt

Rear Left Seat Belt

55 (48 in.-lb, 5.4)

440 (32, 43)

440 (32, 43)

440 (32, 43)

Belt Buckle

440 (32, 43)

Wagon

440 (32, 43)

Rear Right (Outboard) Seat Belt

Front Right Seat Belt

440 (32, 43)

195 (14, 19)

Rear Center Seat Belt

440 (32, 43)

55 (48 in.-lb, 5.4)

440 (32, 43)

440 (32, 43)

Rear Right (Outboard) Seat Belt

440 (32, 43)

Belt Buckle

kg-cm (ft-lb, N·m) : Specified torque

85990093

Fig. 78 Seat belt systems found on wagons and 1984-1986 sedans

3-Door

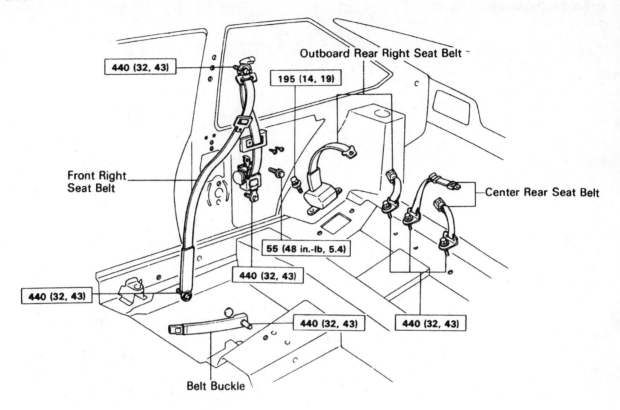

440 (32, 43)

Outboard Rear Right Seat Belt

195 (14, 19)

Front Right
Seat Belt

Center Rear Seat Belt

55 (48 in.-lb, 5.4)

440 (32, 43)

440 (32, 43)

440 (32, 43)

440 (32, 43)

Belt Buckle

5-Door

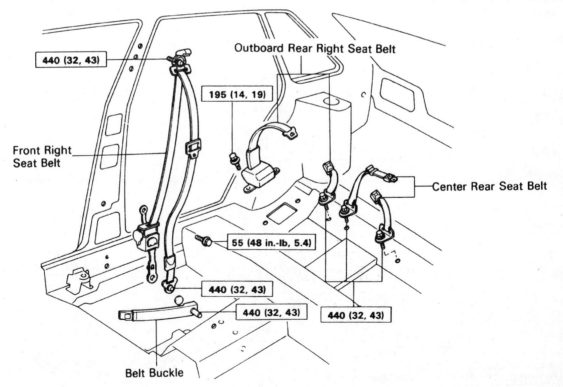

440 (32, 43)

Outboard Rear Right Seat Belt

195 (14, 19)

Front Right
Seat Belt

Center Rear Seat Belt

55 (48 in.-lb, 5.4)

440 (32, 43)

440 (32, 43)

440 (32, 43)

Belt Buckle

85990094

Fig. 79 Seat belts found on 1987-1990 sedans

**Front Seat Belts
(USA-for Passenger's Seat)**

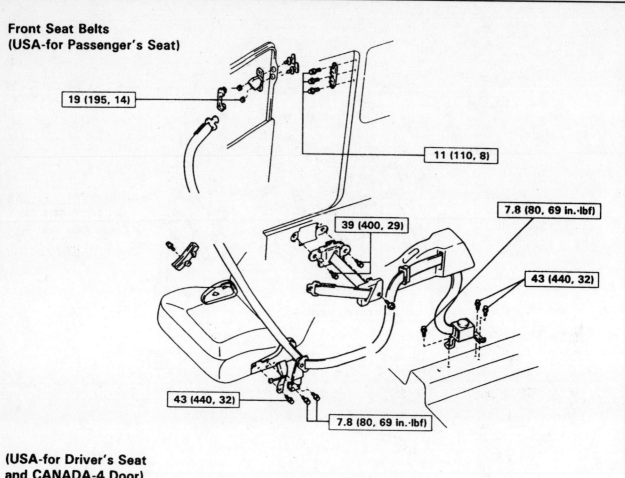

19 (195, 14)

11 (110, 8)

39 (400, 29)

7.8 (80, 69 in.·lbf)

43 (440, 32)

43 (440, 32)

7.8 (80, 69 in.·lbf)

**(USA-for Driver's Seat
and CANADA-4 Door)**

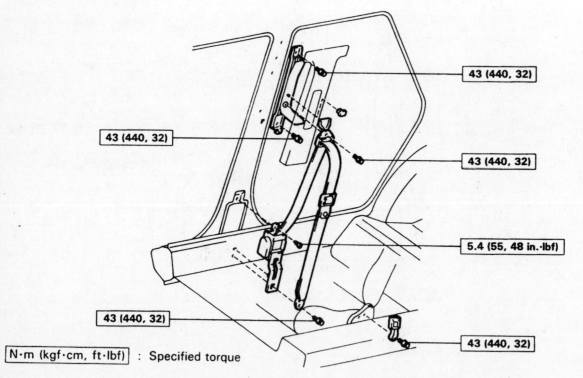

43 (440, 32)

43 (440, 32)

43 (440, 32)

5.4 (55, 48 in.·lbf)

43 (440, 32)

43 (440, 32)

N·m (kgf·cm, ft·lbf) : Specified torque

85990095

Fig. 80 Seat belts found on 1991-1994 4-door sedans

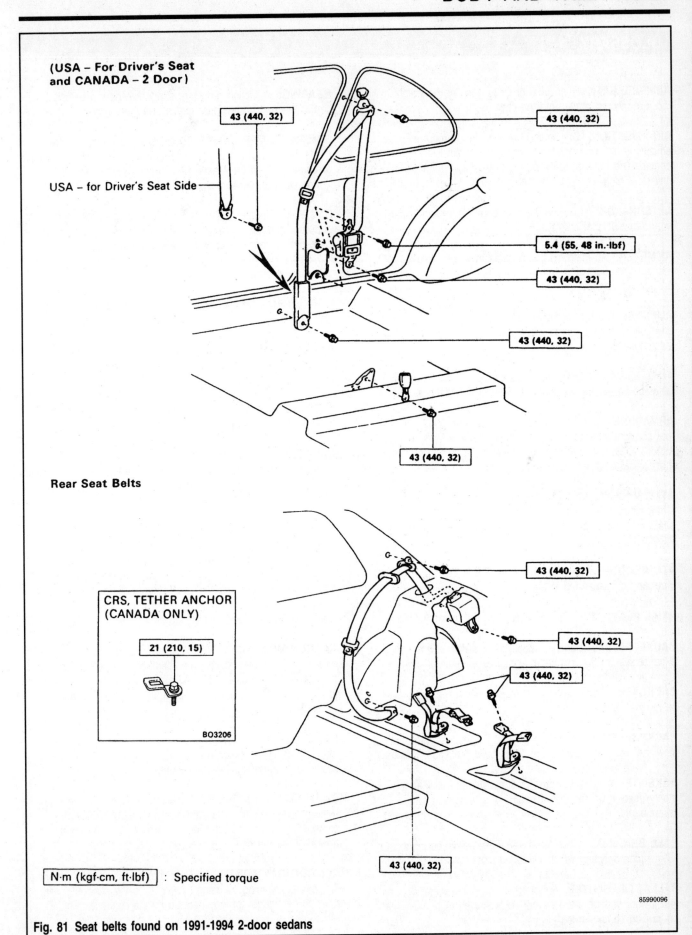

Fig. 81 Seat belts found on 1991-1994 2-door sedans

GLOSSARY

AIR/FUEL RATIO: The ratio of air to gasoline by weight in the fuel mixture drawn into the engine.

AIR INJECTION: One method of reducing harmful exhaust emissions by injecting air into each of the exhaust ports of an engine. The fresh air entering the hot exhaust manifold causes any remaining fuel to be burned before it can exit the tailpipe.

ALTERNATOR: A device used for converting mechanical energy into electrical energy.

AMMETER: An instrument, calibrated in amperes, used to measure the flow of an electrical current in a circuit. Ammeters are always connected in series with the circuit being tested.

AMPERE: The rate of flow of electrical current present when one volt of electrical pressure is applied against one ohm of electrical resistance.

ANALOG COMPUTER: Any microprocessor that uses similar (analogous) electrical signals to make its calculations.

ARMATURE: A laminated, soft iron core wrapped by a wire that converts electrical energy to mechanical energy as in a motor or relay. When rotated in a magnetic field, it changes mechanical energy into electrical energy as in a generator.

ATMOSPHERIC PRESSURE: The pressure on the Earth's surface caused by the weight of the air in the atmosphere. At sea level, this pressure is 14.7 psi at 32{248}F (101 kPa at 0{248}C).

ATOMIZATION: The breaking down of a liquid into a fine mist that can be suspended in air.

AXIAL PLAY: Movement parallel to a shaft or bearing bore.

BACKFIRE: The sudden combustion of gases in the intake or exhaust system that results in a loud explosion.

BACKLASH: The clearance or play between two parts, such as meshed gears.

BACKPRESSURE: Restrictions in the exhaust system that slow the exit of exhaust gases from the combustion chamber.

BAKELITE: A heat resistant, plastic insulator material commonly used in printed circuit boards and transistorized components.

BALL BEARING: A bearing made up of hardened inner and outer races between which hardened steel balls roll.

BALLAST RESISTOR: A resistor in the primary ignition circuit that lowers voltage after the engine is started to reduce wear on ignition components.

BEARING: A friction reducing, supportive device usually located between a stationary part and a moving part.

BIMETAL TEMPERATURE SENSOR: Any sensor or switch made of two dissimilar types of metal that bend when heated or cooled due to the different expansion rates of the alloys. These types of sensors usually function as an on/off switch.

BLOWBY: Combustion gases, composed of water vapor and unburned fuel, that leak past the piston rings into the crankcase during normal engine operation. These gases are removed by the PCV system to prevent the buildup of harmful acids in the crankcase.

BRAKE PAD: A brake shoe and lining assembly used with disc brakes.

BRAKE SHOE: The backing for the brake lining. The term is, however, usually applied to the assembly of the brake backing and lining.

BUSHING: A liner, usually removable, for a bearing; an anti-friction liner used in place of a bearing.

CALIPER: A hydraulically activated device in a disc brake system, which is mounted straddling the brake rotor (disc). The caliper contains at least one piston and two brake pads. Hydraulic pressure on the piston(s) forces the pads against the rotor.

CAMSHAFT: A shaft in the engine on which are the lobes (cams) which operate the valves. The camshaft is driven by the crankshaft, via a belt, chain or gears, at one half the crankshaft speed.

CAPACITOR: A device which stores an electrical charge.

CARBON MONOXIDE (CO): A colorless, odorless gas given off as a normal byproduct of combustion. It is poisonous and extremely dangerous in confined areas, building up slowly to toxic levels without warning if adequate ventilation is not available.

CARBURETOR: A device, usually mounted on the intake manifold of an engine, which mixes the air and fuel in the proper proportion to allow even combustion.

CATALYTIC CONVERTER: A device installed in the exhaust system, like a muffler, that converts harmful byproducts of combustion into carbon dioxide and water vapor by means of a heat-producing chemical reaction.

CENTRIFUGAL ADVANCE: A mechanical method of advancing the spark timing by using flyweights in the distributor that react to centrifugal force generated by the distributor shaft rotation.

CHECK VALVE: Any one-way valve installed to permit the flow of air, fuel or vacuum in one direction only.

CHOKE: A device, usually a moveable valve, placed in the intake path of a carburetor to restrict the flow of air.

CIRCUIT: Any unbroken path through which an electrical current can flow. Also used to describe fuel flow in some instances.

CIRCUIT BREAKER: A switch which protects an electrical circuit from overload by opening the circuit when the current flow exceeds a predetermined level. Some circuit breakers must be reset manually, while most reset automatically

COIL (IGNITION): A transformer in the ignition circuit which steps up the voltage provided to the spark plugs.

COMBINATION MANIFOLD: An assembly which includes both the intake and exhaust manifolds in one casting.

COMBINATION VALVE: A device used in some fuel systems that routes fuel vapors to a charcoal storage canister instead of venting them into the atmosphere. The valve relieves fuel tank pressure and allows fresh air into the tank as the fuel level drops to prevent a vapor lock situation.

COMPRESSION RATIO: The comparison of the total volume of the cylinder and combustion chamber with the piston at BDC and the piston at TDC.

CONDENSER: 1. An electrical device which acts to store an electrical charge, preventing voltage surges.
2. A radiator-like device in the air conditioning system in which refrigerant gas condenses into a liquid, giving off heat.

CONDUCTOR: Any material through which an electrical current can be transmitted easily.

CONTINUITY: Continuous or complete circuit. Can be checked with an ohmmeter.

COUNTERSHAFT: An intermediate shaft which is rotated by a mainshaft and transmits, in turn, that rotation to a working part.

CRANKCASE: The lower part of an engine in which the crankshaft and related parts operate.

CRANKSHAFT: The main driving shaft of an engine which receives reciprocating motion from the pistons and converts it to rotary motion.

CYLINDER: In an engine, the round hole in the engine block in which the piston(s) ride.

CYLINDER BLOCK: The main structural member of an engine in which is found the cylinders, crankshaft and other principal parts.

CYLINDER HEAD: The detachable portion of the engine, fastened, usually, to the top of the cylinder block, containing all or most of the combustion chambers. On overhead valve engines, it contains the valves and their operating parts. On overhead cam engines, it contains the camshaft as well.

DEAD CENTER: The extreme top or bottom of the piston stroke.

DETONATION: An unwanted explosion of the air/fuel mixture in the combustion chamber caused by excess heat and compression, advanced timing, or an overly lean mixture. Also referred to as "ping".

DIAPHRAGM: A thin, flexible wall separating two cavities, such as in a vacuum advance unit.

DIESELING: A condition in which hot spots in the combustion chamber cause the engine to run on after the key is turned off.

DIFFERENTIAL: A geared assembly which allows the transmission of motion between drive axles, giving one axle the ability to turn faster than the other.

DIODE: An electrical device that will allow current to flow in one direction only.

DISC BRAKE: A hydraulic braking assembly consisting of a brake disc, or rotor, mounted on an axle, and a caliper assembly containing, usually two brake pads which are activated by hydraulic pressure. The pads are forced against the sides of the disc, creating friction which slows the vehicle.

DISTRIBUTOR: A mechanically driven device on an engine which is responsible for electrically firing the spark plug at a predetermined point of the piston stroke.

DOWEL PIN: A pin, inserted in mating holes in two different parts allowing those parts to maintain a fixed relationship.

DRUM BRAKE: A braking system which consists of two brake shoes and one or two wheel cylinders, mounted on a fixed backing plate, and a brake drum, mounted on an axle, which revolves around the assembly.

DWELL: The rate, measured in degrees of shaft rotation, at which an electrical circuit cycles on and off.

ELECTRONIC CONTROL UNIT (ECU): Ignition module, module, amplifier or igniter. See Module for definition.

ELECTRONIC IGNITION: A system in which the timing and firing of the spark plugs is controlled by an electronic control unit, usually called a module. These systems have no points or condenser.

ENDPLAY: The measured amount of axial movement in a shaft.

ENGINE: A device that converts heat into mechanical energy.

EXHAUST MANIFOLD: A set of cast passages or pipes which conduct exhaust gases from the engine.

FEELER GAUGE: A blade, usually metal, of precisely predetermined thickness, used to measure the clearance between two parts.

FIRING ORDER: The order in which combustion occurs in the cylinders of an engine. Also the order in which spark is distributed to the plugs by the distributor.

FLOODING: The presence of too much fuel in the intake manifold and combustion chamber which prevents the air/fuel mixture from firing, thereby causing a no-start situation.

FLYWHEEL: A disc shaped part bolted to the rear end of the crankshaft. Around the outer perimeter is affixed the ring gear. The starter drive engages the ring gear, turning the flywheel, which rotates the crankshaft, imparting the initial starting motion to the engine.

FOOT POUND (ft.lb. or sometimes, ft. lbs.): The amount of energy or work needed to raise an item weighing one pound, a distance of one foot.

FUSE: A protective device in a circuit which prevents circuit overload by breaking the circuit when a specific amperage is present. The device is constructed around a strip or wire of a lower amperage rating than the circuit it is designed to protect. When an amperage higher than that stamped on the fuse is present in the circuit, the strip or wire melts, opening the circuit.

GEAR RATIO: The ratio between the number of teeth on meshing gears.

GENERATOR: A device which converts mechanical energy into electrical energy.

HEAT RANGE: The measure of a spark plug's ability to dissipate heat from its firing end. The higher the heat range, the hotter the plug fires.

HUB: The center part of a wheel or gear.

HYDROCARBON (HC): Any chemical compound made up of hydrogen and carbon. A major pollutant formed by the engine as a byproduct of combustion.

HYDROMETER: An instrument used to measure the specific gravity of a solution.

INCH POUND (in.lb. or sometimes, in. lbs.): One twelfth of a foot pound.

INDUCTION: A means of transferring electrical energy in the form of a magnetic field. Principle used in the ignition coil to increase voltage.

INJECTOR: A device which receives metered fuel under relatively low pressure and is activated to inject the fuel into the engine under relatively high pressure at a predetermined time.

INPUT SHAFT: The shaft to which torque is applied, usually carrying the driving gear or gears.

INTAKE MANIFOLD: A casting of passages or pipes used to conduct air or a fuel/air mixture to the cylinders.

JOURNAL: The bearing surface within which a shaft operates.

KEY: A small block usually fitted in a notch between a shaft and a hub to prevent slippage of the two parts.

MANIFOLD: A casting of passages or set of pipes which connect the cylinders to an inlet or outlet source.

MANIFOLD VACUUM: Low pressure in an engine intake manifold formed just below the throttle plates. Manifold vacuum is highest at idle and drops under acceleration.

MASTER CYLINDER: The primary fluid pressurizing device in a hydraulic system. In automotive use, it is found in brake and hydraulic clutch systems and is pedal activated, either directly or, in a power brake system, through the power booster.

MODULE: Electronic control unit, amplifier or igniter of solid state or integrated design which controls the current flow in the ignition primary circuit based on input from the pick-up coil. When the module opens the primary circuit, the high secondary voltage is induced in the coil.

NEEDLE BEARING: A bearing which consists of a number (usually a large number) of long, thin rollers.

OHM:(Ω) The unit used to measure the resistance of conductor to electrical flow. One ohm is the amount of resistance that limits current flow to one ampere in a circuit with one volt of pressure.

OHMMETER: An instrument used for measuring the resistance, in ohms, in an electrical circuit.

OUTPUT SHAFT: The shaft which transmits torque from a device, such as a transmission.

OVERDRIVE: A gear assembly which produces more shaft revolutions than that transmitted to it.

OVERHEAD CAMSHAFT (OHC): An engine configuration in which the camshaft is mounted on top of the cylinder head and operates the valve either directly or by means of rocker arms.

OVERHEAD VALVE (OHV): An engine configuration in which all of the valves are located in the cylinder head and the camshaft is located in the cylinder block. The camshaft operates the valves via lifters and pushrods.

OXIDES OF NITROGEN (NOx): Chemical compounds of nitrogen produced as a byproduct of combustion. They combine with hydrocarbons to produce smog.

OXYGEN SENSOR: Used with the feedback system to sense the presence of oxygen in the exhaust gas and signal the computer which can reference the voltage signal to an air/fuel ratio.

PINION: The smaller of two meshing gears.

PISTON RING: An open ended ring which fits into a groove on the outer diameter of the piston. Its chief function is to form a seal between the piston and cylinder wall. Most automotive pistons have three rings: two for compression sealing; one for oil sealing.

PRELOAD: A predetermined load placed on a bearing during assembly or by adjustment.

PRIMARY CIRCUIT: Is the low voltage side of the ignition system which consists of the ignition switch, ballast resistor or resistance wire, bypass, coil, electronic control unit and pick-up coil as well as the connecting wires and harnesses.

PRESS FIT: The mating of two parts under pressure, due to the inner diameter of one being smaller than the outer diameter of the other, or vice versa; an interference fit.

RACE: The surface on the inner or outer ring of a bearing on which the balls, needles or rollers move.

REGULATOR: A device which maintains the amperage and/or voltage levels of a circuit at predetermined values.

RELAY: A switch which automatically opens and/or closes a circuit.

RESISTANCE: The opposition to the flow of current through a circuit or electrical device, and is measured in ohms. Resistance is equal to the voltage divided by the amperage.

RESISTOR: A device, usually made of wire, which offers a preset amount of resistance in an electrical circuit.

RING GEAR: The name given to a ring-shaped gear attached to a differential case, or affixed to a flywheel or as part a planetary gear set.

ROLLER BEARING: A bearing made up of hardened inner and outer races between which hardened steel rollers move.

ROTOR: 1. The disc-shaped part of a disc brake assembly, upon which the brake pads bear; also called, brake disc.
2. The device mounted atop the distributor shaft, which passes current to the distributor cap tower contacts.

SECONDARY CIRCUIT: The high voltage side of the ignition system, usually above 20,000 volts. The secondary includes the ignition coil, coil wire, distributor cap and rotor, spark plug wires and spark plugs.

SENDING UNIT: A mechanical, electrical, hydraulic or electromagnetic device which transmits information to a gauge.

SENSOR: Any device designed to measure engine operating conditions or ambient pressures and temperatures. Usually electronic in nature and designed to send a voltage signal to an on-board computer, some sensors may operate as a simple on/off switch or they may provide a variable voltage signal (like a potentiometer) as conditions or measured parameters change.

SHIM: Spacers of precise, predetermined thickness used between parts to establish a proper working relationship.

SLAVE CYLINDER: In automotive use, a device in the hydraulic clutch system which is activated by hydraulic force, disengaging the clutch.

SOLENOID: A coil used to produce a magnetic field, the effect of which is produce work.

SPARK PLUG: A device screwed into the combustion chamber of a spark ignition engine. The basic construction is a conductive core inside of a ceramic insulator, mounted in an outer conductive base. An electrical charge from the spark plug wire travels along the conductive core and jumps a preset air gap to a grounding point or points at the end of the conductive base. The resultant spark ignites the fuel/air mixture in the combustion chamber.

SPLINES: Ridges machined or cast onto the outer diameter of a shaft or inner diameter of a bore to enable parts to mate without rotation.

TACHOMETER: A device used to measure the rotary speed of an engine, shaft, gear, etc., usually in rotations per minute.

THERMOSTAT: A valve, located in the cooling system of an engine, which is closed when cold and opens gradually in response to engine heating, controlling the temperature of the coolant and rate of coolant flow.

TOP DEAD CENTER (TDC): The point at which the piston reaches the top of its travel on the compression stroke.

TORQUE: The twisting force applied to an object.

TORQUE CONVERTER: A turbine used to transmit power from a driving member to a driven member via hydraulic action, providing changes in drive ratio and torque. In automotive use, it links the driveplate at the rear of the engine to the automatic transmission.

TRANSDUCER: A device used to change a force into an electrical signal.

TRANSISTOR: A semi-conductor component which can be actuated by a small voltage to perform an electrical switching function.

TUNE-UP: A regular maintenance function, usually associated with the replacement and adjustment of parts and components in the electrical and fuel systems of a vehicle for the purpose of attaining optimum performance.

TURBOCHARGER: An exhaust driven pump which compresses intake air and forces it into the combustion chambers at higher than atmospheric pressures. The increased air pressure allows more fuel to be burned and results in increased horsepower being produced.

VACUUM ADVANCE: A device which advances the ignition timing in response to increased engine vacuum.

VACUUM GAUGE: An instrument used to measure the presence of vacuum in a chamber.

VALVE: A device which control the pressure, direction of flow or rate of flow of a liquid or gas.

VALVE CLEARANCE: The measured gap between the end of the valve stem and the rocker arm, cam lobe or follower that activates the valve.

VISCOSITY: The rating of a liquid's internal resistance to flow.

VOLTMETER: An instrument used for measuring electrical force in units called volts. Voltmeters are always connected parallel with the circuit being tested.

WHEEL CYLINDER: Found in the automotive drum brake assembly, it is a device, actuated by hydraulic pressure, which, through internal pistons, pushes the brake shoes outward against the drums.

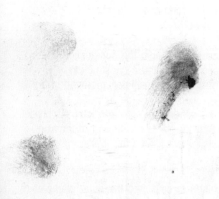

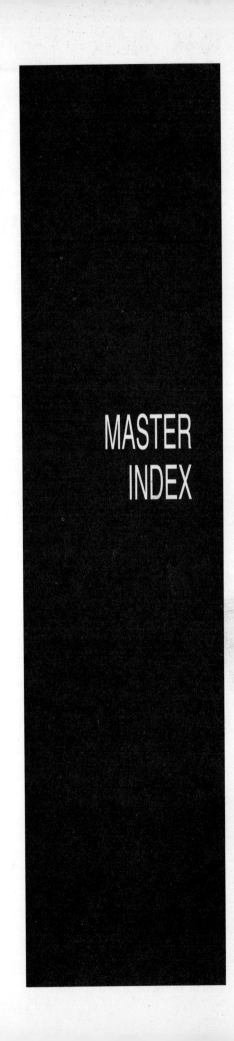

MASTER
INDEX